INTERACTIONS 9

Canadian Cataloguing in Publication Data

Main entry under title:
  Interactions 9

Includes index.
ISBN 0-13-258831-5

I. Mathematics – Juvenile literature.   I. Hope, Jack.

QA107.I59 1996   510   C96-930676-8

ISBN 0-13-258831-5

Prentice Hall, Inc., Englewood Cliffs, New Jersey
Prentice Hall International, Inc., London
Prentice Hall of Australia, Pty., Ltd., Sydney
Prentice Hall of India Pvt., Ltd., New Delhi
Prentice Hall of Japan, Inc., Tokyo
Prentice Hall of Southeast Asia (PTE) Ltd., Singapore
Editora Prentice Hall do Brasil Ltda., Rio de Janeiro
Prentice Hall Hispanoamericana, S.A., Mexico

CONTRIBUTING WRITERS/REVIEWERS
Prentice Hall Ginn Canada would like to gratefully acknowledge and thank the following educators who provided ideas and/or reviewed manuscript in the development of INTERACTIONS 9.

Attila Csisar	Carryl Koe
Marlene Lamb	Michelle Lawrence
Adriaan Mik	Jake Penner
Dr. Alan Taylor	James Wilson

PUBLISHER   MaryLynne Meschino

MANAGING EDITOR   Bonnie Di Malta

EDITORS   Shirley Barrett, Janice Nixon, Norma Kennedy, Jacqueline Williams

ART/DESIGN/PAGE MAKE-UP   ArtPlus Limited Design Consultants

Printed and bound in Canada

  B C D E F G – ML – 00 99 98 97 96

Jack Hope

Barry Scully

Jan Scully

Marian Small

Prentice Hall Ginn Canada

Using Interactions 9

The Interactions 9 text contains 10 developmental units and 2 investigation units.

Each developmental unit contains a number of lessons in which you will find these features:

1. The **Warm Up** gets you thinking about the new concept that you will explore in the lesson.

3. The **Understand and Apply** problems give you practice in using the math concepts.

2. The **Concept Development** section lets you explore and investigate new mathematical ideas.

4. The **Worked Example** logo identifies problems for which a similar problem and solution are modelled at the back of the book. There are usually two worked examples for each lesson.

5. The **Home Link** lets you apply math concepts to your life at home and in the community.

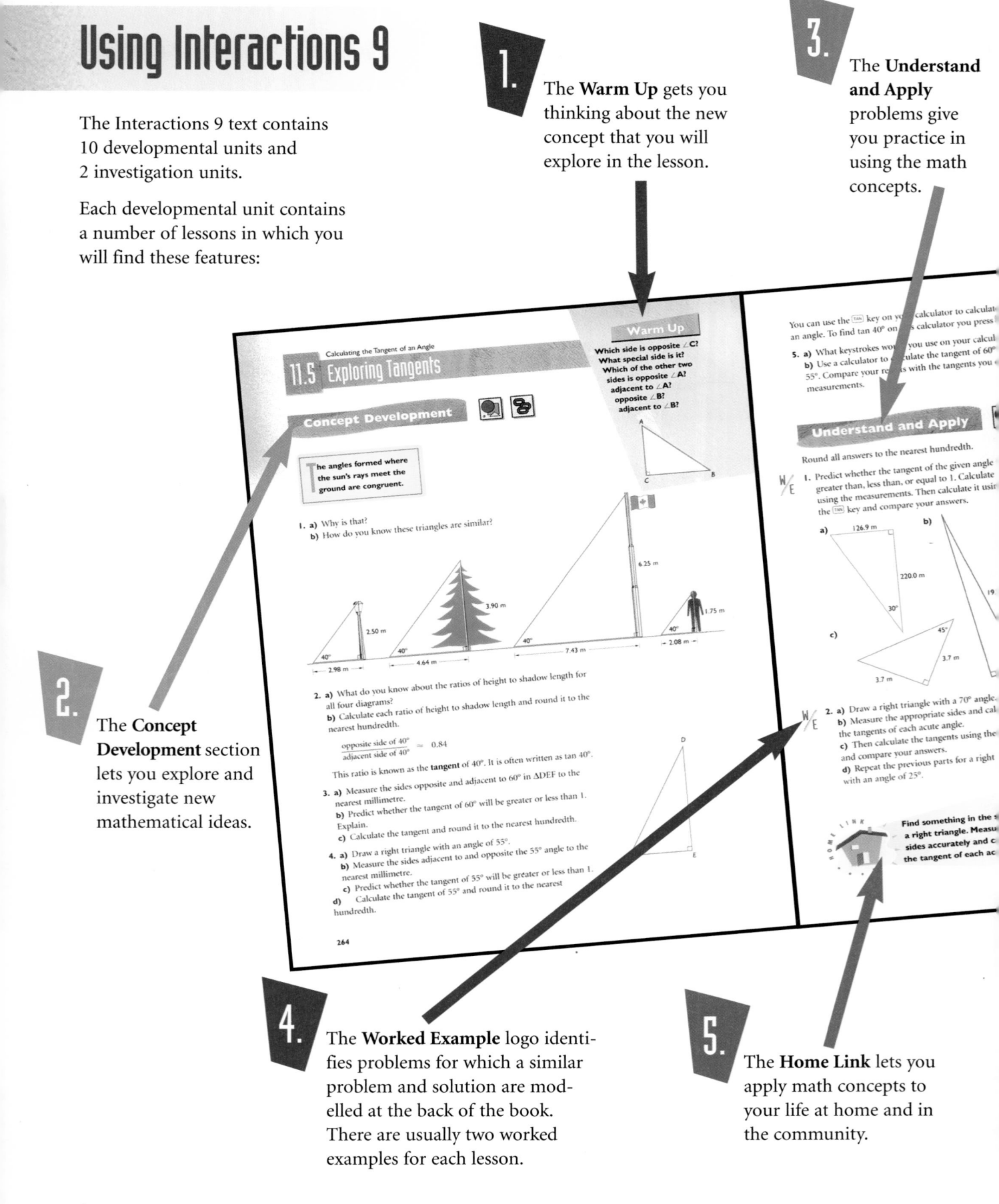

In each developmental unit, you will also find:

- A **PROBLEM SOLVING** page that provides opportunities to apply different problem solving strategies to the solution of problems.

- **PROBLEMS TO INVESTIGATE** pages on which you choose problems to explore and solve.

- **MORE THAN ONE STRATEGY** pages that show you that there is more than one way to solve a mathematical problem.

- A **MAKING SENSE OF DATA** page that lets you explore ways you can collect, display, and analyse data.

- A **PRACTISE WITH GAMES** page that allows you to practise skills and concepts through playing games.

- A **REVIEW AND PRACTISE** page with problems that review the concepts you have learned.

- A **TEST YOUR KNOWLEDGE** page with review problems that will ask you to reflect and think about what you have learned.

- A **COMMUNICATE YOUR KNOWLEDGE** page with problems that allow you to express your knowledge, thoughts, and feelings about the mathematics that you have learned in the unit.

In each investigation unit, you will find:

- Interesting, real-world topics in which you can apply the mathematics you have learned.

- **DID YOU KNOW** features in which you can apply math concepts to interesting situations from the real world.

At the end of the text, you will find:

- A unit-by-unit set of **WORKED EXAMPLES AND SOLUTIONS** beginning on page 302 to help you review and assess your understanding of the mathematical concepts.

- A **GLOSSARY** on pages 324–37 to help you review and understand the mathematical terms that are used in the lessons in the text.

- **ANSWERS** to all of the **UNDERSTAND AND APPLY**, **TAKE YOUR PICK**, **REVIEW AND PRACTISE**, and **TEST YOUR KNOWLEDGE** problems for each unit beginning on page 338.

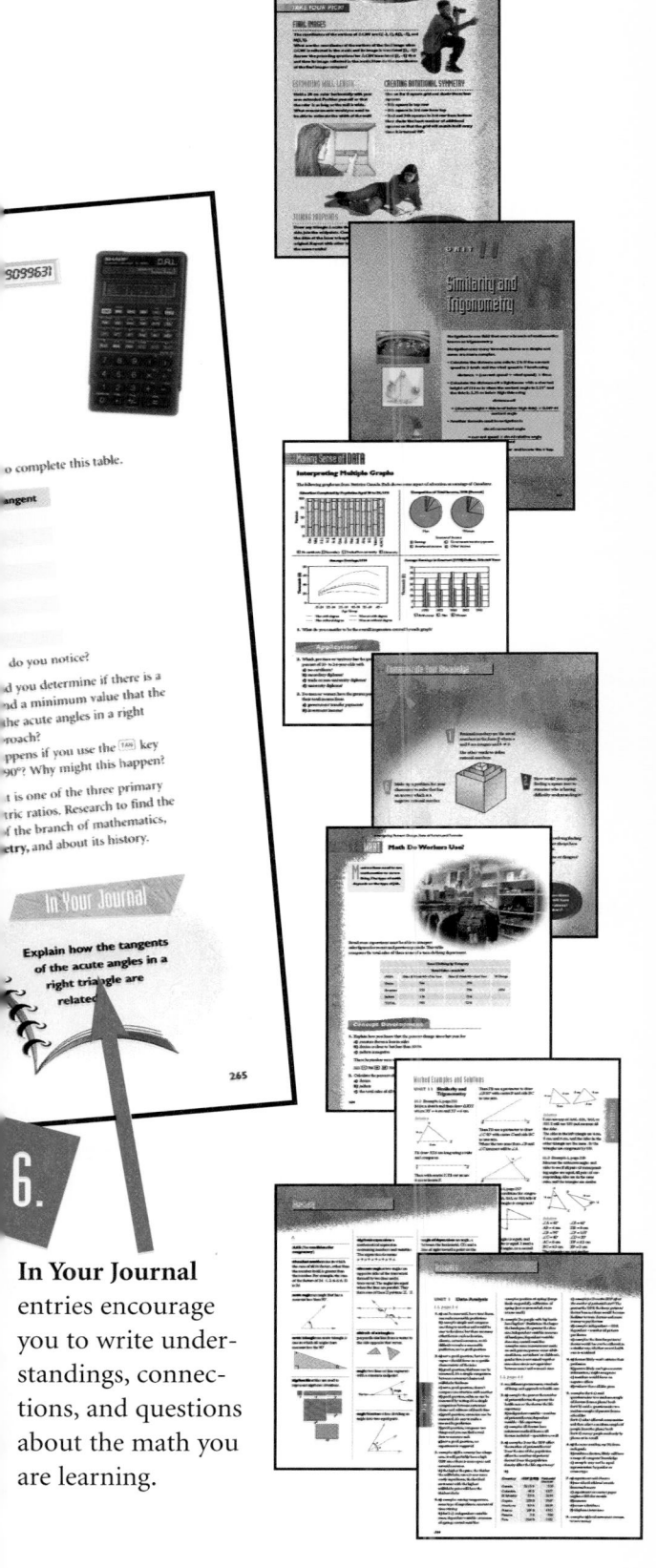

In Your Journal entries encourage you to write understandings, connections, and questions about the math you are learning.

Use of Computers

INTERACTIONS has numerous opportunities for you to use a computer. Computer software can help you support your math investigations and discovery by providing tools to help display, model, organize, graph, and present math data. Software programs allow you to experiment, create, and manipulate patterns, numbers, and drawings. Try to work with spreadsheets, databases, and math software to learn more about the capabilities of using a computer. The computer is a means to assist you with problem solving strategies.

As you use your Interactions 9 text you will see icons like these:

 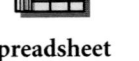       

| Text | Spreadsheet | Calculation | Geometry | Graphs | Manipulatives | Fraction Strips | Frames | Probability |

The icons will appear at the beginning of the Concept Development and/or Understand and Apply sections. They may also appear on the Problems to Investigate pages.
If you have access to the Math Tools software, you will be able to use it to help you to do some of the questions in these sections on the computer.

What the icons mean

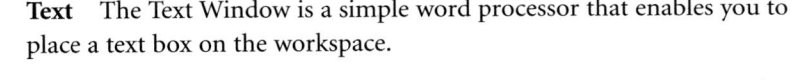

 **Text**   The Text Window is a simple word processor that enables you to place a text box on the workspace.

 **Spreadsheet**   The Spreadsheet Window is used for manipulating numbers. Like full-function spreadsheets, it is made up of cells, columns, and rows.

 Calculation   The Calculation Window can be used as one of four different kinds of calculators: a standard calculator, an algebraic calculator, a graphing calculator, and a fraction calculator.

 **Geometry**   The Geometry Window includes a set of tools that enables you to examine and experiment with different geometric concepts. It includes tools to create points, lines circles, angles, and polygons.

 Graphs   There are six different kinds of Graph Windows available. Included are coordinate graphs, line plots, bar graphs, line graphs, circle graphs, and pictographs.

 Manipulatives   A Manipulatives Window is an electronic workmat for computer versions of classroom manipulatives. Included are algebra tiles, base-ten blocks, connecting cubes, money, and decimal blocks.

 Fraction Strips   The Fraction Strips Window is an electronic version of a fraction strip or fraction bar.

Frames   A Frame consists of an array of squares that can be used for exploring such concepts as multiples, primes, composites, and square numbers, as well as some of the properties of addition, subtraction, multiplication, and division.

Probability   Probability comes alive with two tools that help explore the concept. Both a spinner and a set of number cubes are available for a variety of probability experiments.

Calculators

Within INTERACTIONS, you will find many opportunities to use the calculator for performing mathematical tasks. You provide the reasoning and strategies.

By using a calculator, you will begin to explore number patterns and relationships. A calculator can help you in developing number sense and estimation strategies. Calculators save you time and help you in the process of learning mathematics.

Try these questions to become familiar with the functions of your calculator. These examples will work with many calculators. Note that while the function keys on many calculators will produce these results, some calculators will function differently and you will need to refer to the instruction booklet that is supplied with your calculator.

BASIC CALCULATOR

EXAMPLE	FUNCTION KEYS	ANSWER
$273 + 572 =$	273 [+] 572 [=]	845.
$507 - 184 =$	507 [−] 184 [=]	323.
$295 \times 8 =$	295 [×] 8 [=]	2360.
$759 \div 23 =$	759 [÷] 23 [=]	33.
5^2 (squared)	5 [×] [=]	25.
5^3 (cubed)	5 [×] [=] [=]	125.
$\frac{1}{5}$ expressed as a decimal	1 [÷] 5 [=]	0.2
$\frac{125}{625}$ expressed as a percent	125 [÷] 625 [×] 100	20.
$\sqrt{5}$	5 [√]	2.2360679

SCIENTIFIC CALCULATOR

EXAMPLE	FUNCTION KEYS	ANSWER
$8^{-2} - 3^4 \times 5^2 =$	8 [yˣ] 2 [+/−] [=] [−] [(] 3 [yˣ] 4 [×] 5 [x²] [)] [=]	- 2024.98
$(5 \times 10^3) \times (3 \times 10^4) =$	5 [EXP] 3 [×] 3 [EXP] 4 [=]	150000000.
$42 \times (-5) + 120 =$	42 [×] 5 [+/−] [+] 120 [=]	- 90.
$\sqrt{6^2 + 9^2} =$	6 [x²] [+] 9 [x²] [=] [√]	10.82
$\frac{1}{6} + \frac{1}{7} =$	6 [x⁻¹] [+] 7 [x⁻¹] [=]	0.31
$2\pi \times 4^2 =$	2 [×] [π] [×] 4 [x²] [=]	100.53
$24 + (8 \times 2) =$	8 [×] 2 [=] [STO] 24 [+] [RCL] [=]	40.
$\frac{18 + 6}{15 - 8} =$	[(] 18 [+] 6 [)] [÷] [(] 15 [−] 8 [)] [=]	3.43

Contents

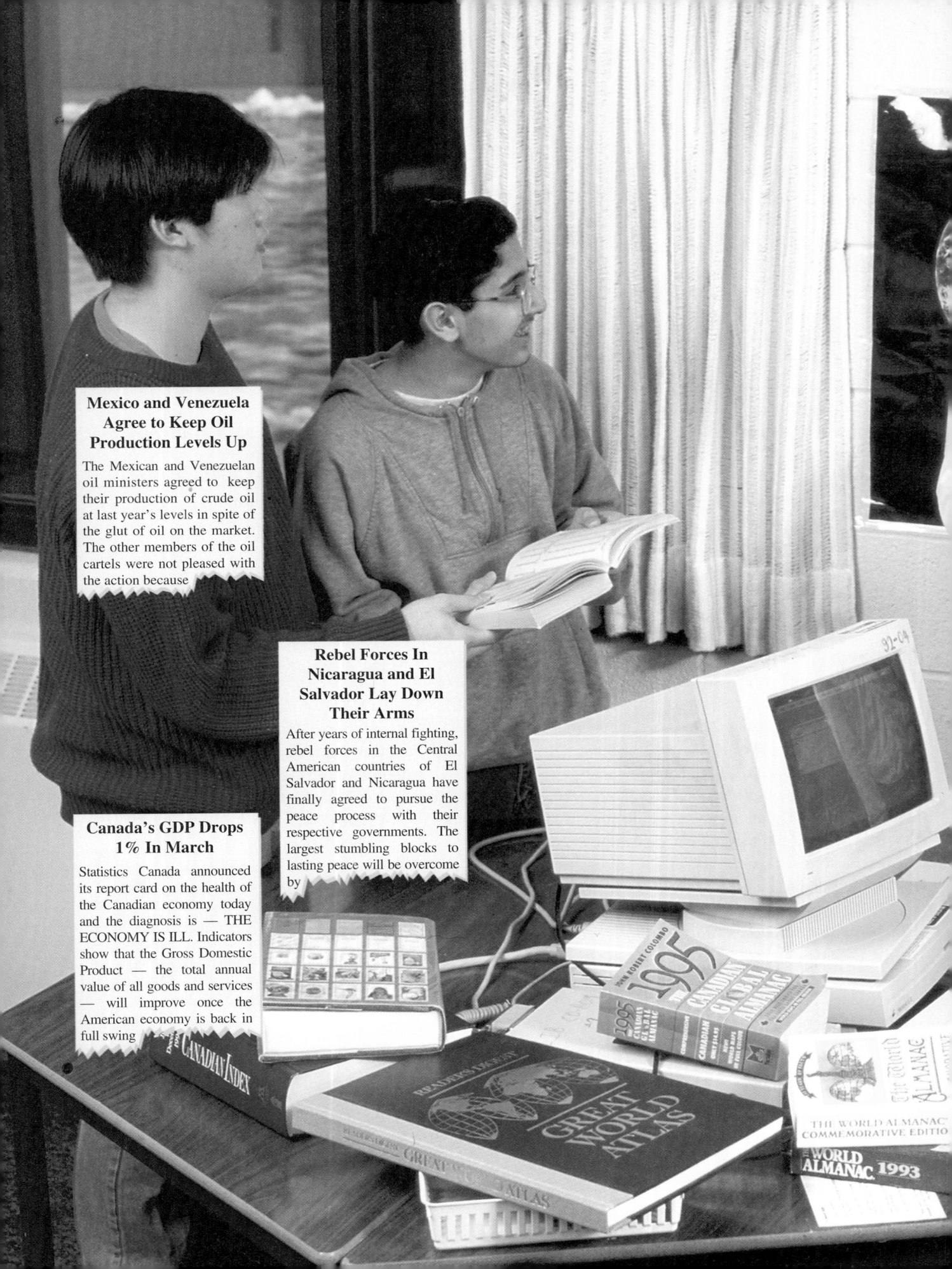

Mexico and Venezuela Agree to Keep Oil Production Levels Up

The Mexican and Venezuelan oil ministers agreed to keep their production of crude oil at last year's levels in spite of the glut of oil on the market. The other members of the oil cartels were not pleased with the action because

Rebel Forces In Nicaragua and El Salvador Lay Down Their Arms

After years of internal fighting, rebel forces in the Central American countries of El Salvador and Nicaragua have finally agreed to pursue the peace process with their respective governments. The largest stumbling blocks to lasting peace will be overcome by

Canada's GDP Drops 1% In March

Statistics Canada announced its report card on the health of the Canadian economy today and the diagnosis is — THE ECONOMY IS ILL. Indicators show that the Gross Domestic Product — the total annual value of all goods and services — will improve once the American economy is back in full swing

Data Analysis

- **What information about Canada and other countries can you obtain from the photo of Earth? from a computer database? from the newspaper articles?**

- **For a country, what might the relationship be between**

   a) **its land area and its population density (people/km^2)?**
   b) **its tourist business and its distance from the equator?**
   c) **its energy usage and its GDP?**
   d) **the amount of money it spends on arms and its economy?**

- **How would you test your predictions?**

- **Who might want to know what you found out?**

- **How might the results be useful?**

What are different ways to collect, display, and analyse data?

1.1 Creating Good Questions

Warm Up

A drawer contains all different pairs of socks but the socks aren't matched. Without looking in the drawer, how many socks do you have to take out before you get a matching pair? What other mathematical questions could you ask about the socks?

The students in **Mr. Barker's** class are researching information about countries in North America and South America. They found recent world data in a computer database, and compiled the following table using spreadsheet software.

Country	Population	Area (km^2)	GDP (U.S.$)	Literacy (%)
Argentina	32 901 234	2 766 890	101.2 B	95
Belize	229 143	22 960	373 M	91
Bolivia	7 323 048	1 098 580	4.6 B	78
Brazil	158 202 019	8 511 965	358 B	81
Canada	27 351 509	9 976 140	521.5 B	99
Chile	13 528 945	756 950	30.5 B	93
Colombia	34 296 941	1 138 910	45 B	87
Costa Rica	3 187 085	51 100	5.9 B	93
Ecuador	10 933 143	283 560	11.5 B	86
El Salvador	5 574 279	21 040	5.5 B	73
French Guiana	127 505	91 000	186 M	82
Guatemala	9 784 275	108 890	11.7 B	55
Guyana	739 431	214 970	250 M	95
Honduras	5 092 776	112 090	5.2 B	73
Mexico	92 380 721	1 972 550	289 B	87
Nicaragua	3 878 150	129 494	1.6 B	57
Panama	2 529 902	78 200	5 B	88
Paraguay	4 929 446	406 750	7 B	90
Peru	22 767 543	1 285 220	20.6 B	85
Suriname	410 016	2 505 810	1.4 B	95
United States	254 521 000	9 372 610	5673 B	98
Uruguay	3 141 533	176 220	9.1 B	96
Venezuela	20 675 970	912 050	52.3 B	88

(Note: Most information in the database is given for 1992. For literacy, most are 1990 estimates and refer to educated citizens age 15 and over.)

Concept Development

1. **a)** Which numerical figures do you think are exact? approximate? Explain.

   b) How would you calculate population density? Calculate the population density for the country you think has the least value.

   c) How would you calculate GDP per person? Calculate the GDP per person for the country you think has the greatest value.

After studying the information, the students posed a question that compares one set of data to another. "Is there a relationship between the area of a country and its population?"

2. What other, similar questions can you create from the table that you might investigate?

Understand and Apply

1. Maria and Huang listed features of a good question to investigate.

   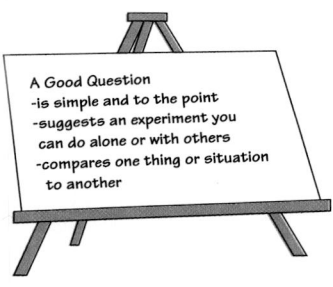

   A Good Question
   - is simple and to the point
   - suggests an experiment you can do alone or with others
   - compares one thing or situation to another

   a) What other feature(s) would you add to the list?

   b) Do you think the question about area and population created by Mr. Barker's class is a good question? Why or why not?

   c) Do you think the questions you created in Problem 2 in *Concept and Development* are good questions? Why or why not?

   d) Pass your questions to classmates for their opinions. Use the suggestions to make improvements to your questions.

2. Assess whether or not each question has the features of a good question. Defend your choice.

   a) Which brand of fruit juice is the best?

   b) Which fast-food restaurant chain makes the thickest milkshake?

   c) Why does the sky become cloudy in the afternoon of a hot, humid, summer day?

   d) Which fast-food restaurant chain has the saltiest french fries?

   e) What effect do different masses added to a spring have on the amount of extension of the spring?

   f) Does the number of patients per doctor affect the life expectancy of a population of a country?

   g) How do birds fly?

3. Before you investigate a question, you should make a prediction of how the two situations might be related to each other. Provide an explanation for your prediction.

a) Write two predictions for your good questions from Problem 1. d). Explain your predictions.

b) Write two predictions for the questions you identified as good in Problem 2. Provide explanations.

c) Pass your predictions to other classmates for their opinions. Use the suggestions to make improvements to your predictions.

4. Once you've made your prediction, you should identify and classify the variables in your investigation. There are three kinds of variables. For example:

   For an investigation of fast-food restaurants and thickest milkshakes, one variable is the name of the restaurant. This variable is the one you change and is called the **independent variable**. The second variable is the thickness of the shake. It changes as the restaurant changes. It is called the **dependent variable**.

   The third kind of variable controls the fairness of the investigation. They are called **control variables**. There can be many control variables in an investigation. For example, it's important to compare milkshakes which are the same flavor and size of serving. Flavor and serving size would be control variables.

   a) Identify three or more control variables for an investigation of milkshake thickness.

   b) Identify the independent variable, dependent variable, and at least two control variables for the good questions from Problems 1. d) and 2.

5. Create four different good questions to investigate and explain why each is good. Write a prediction for each and identify all of the variables. Share your results with the rest of the class.

If the area of a country is relatively small, the population will probably be small too — there's less land to live on.

The smaller the area, the greater the population density should be — there's less room to spread out!

In Your Journal

When you investigate a relationship between two situations, does it matter if you switch the independent variable with the dependent variable? Give examples.

1.2 Collecting the Facts

A local library is in danger of being closed down. The Parent-Teacher Association agrees to conduct a survey to determine how many people use or would use the library on a regular basis. Describe *what*, *where*, *who*, and *how* for conducting the survey.

The students found database information on the life expectancy of males and females in Central and South America, and the number of patients per doctor. They wondered, "Is there a connection between the number of patients per doctor and life expectancy?"

Concept Development

They organized a **sample** of their data in a table.

Country	Colombia	El Salvador	Guyana	Honduras	Mexico	Panama	Peru
Patients/ Doctor	1277	3244	3367	2238	1592	900	1102
Life Expectancy (in years) Male/Female	69/74	68/75	61/68	65/68	69/76	73/77	63/67

1. Research the same data for Canada. How does it compare? Provide possible reasons.

2. a) How do you think the original data for the countries might have been collected? Brainstorm different methods.
   b) Do you think each method would be an appropriate way to collect the data? Why or why not?
   c) Which method do you think is the best? Justify your choice.

1. The students collected data for only some of the countries in Central and South America. Can they make valid predictions about all the countries in these areas, based on the sample? Explain.

2. **a)** What prediction would you make about the relationship between the number of patients per doctor and life expectancy? Explain.
   b) Identify the independent and dependent variables.
   c) Provide 2 or 3 possible control variables.

3. **a)** Use the data from the tables on pages 2 and 4, to create two different questions to investigate.
   b) Organize your data in a table to help you see patterns.
   c) What prediction would you make? Explain.
   d) What are the independent and dependent variables?
   e) What are 1 or 2 possible control variables?
   f) Find out if your prediction holds for other countries that don't appear in the table.
   g) Share your results with the rest of the class.

4. Sometimes samples of data may not give an accurate picture of a population because the sample may favor or be biased toward one group or situation over another.
   How might each of these samples be biased?
   a) A group of doctors are asked about the quality of care that patients receive.
   b) A group of parents are asked about the reading ability of their children.
   c) The members of a stop-the-highway association are asked about the effects of building a new super-highway.
   d) A group of students at a pizza restaurant are surveyed about their favorite refreshment.

5. Who would you sample to obtain unbiased results for each of the questions in Problem 4? Justify your choice.

6. A questionnaire is prepared to be sent to a sample of the students in your school. The questionnaire focuses on the following question: Should the school use only one make of computers or several?

a) How many and which students should be included in the sample?
b) How would you distribute the questionnaire to avoid biased results? Explain.
c) Identify any possible biases.

In Your Journal

What are some concerns you should consider when you collect information from a sample of the population? How would you overcome each concern?

7. What different methods of collecting and organizing data would you use if you were to investigate each of these questions?
   a) Which brand of paper towel will absorb the most water?
   b) How does height affect a person's running speed?
   c) Does the wing span of a paper airplane affect the flying time?
   d) Is there a relationship between height and *armstretch*, which is the distance between fingertips with arms fully extended?
   e) How does the fitness level of a country affect its health costs?
   f) Which pizza restaurant has the quickest delivery service?
   g) Create your own question for investigation.

8. What if you performed a complete investigation of each question in Problem 7?
   • Who might want to know what you found out?
   • How might the results be useful?

Create and conduct an investigation for a question that interests your household. Share the results of your investigation with the rest of the class.

Organizing Data

There are many ways to organize this data. →

Active Volcanoes

Chile: Guallatiri – 6060 m	Chile: Lascar – 5641 m
Ecuador: Cotopaxi – 5897 m	Colombia: Purace – 4590 m
Mexico: Popocatepetl – 5451 m	Chile: Tupungatito – 5640 m
Guatemala: Tacana – 4078 m	Indonesia: Rindjani – 3726 m
Indonesia: Semeru – 3676 m	Ecuador: Sangay – 5230 m
Guatemala: Tajumulco – 4220 m	Indonesia: Slamat – 3428 m

Here are some. Can you think of more?

1. You can make a tally chart.

Country	Tally	Total
Chile	I/I	3
Ecuador	I/	2
Colombia	I	1
Mexico	I	1
Guatemala	I/	2
Indonesia	I/I	3

2. You can use a table.

Country	Name of Volcano	Height (m)
Chile	Guallatiri	6060
	Lascar	5641
	Tupungatito	5640
Ecuador	Cotopaxi	5897
	Sangay	5230
Colombia	Purace	4590
Mexico	Popocatepetl	5451
Guatemala	Tajumulco	4220
	Tacana	4078
Indonesia	Rindjani	3726
	Semeru	3676
	Slamat	3428

3. You can use a computer database to sort the data in different ways and for different purposes.

Name of Volcano	Height (m)	Country
Cotopaxi	5897	Ecuador
Guallatiri	6060	Chile
Lascar	5641	Chile
Popcatepetl	5451	Mexico
Purace	4590	Colombia
Rindjani	3726	Indonesia
Sangay	5230	Ecuador
Semeru	3676	Indonesia
Slamat	3428	Indonesia
Tacana	4078	Guatemala
Tajumulco	4220	Guatemala
Tupungatito	5640	Chile

Height (m)	Name of Volcano	Country
3428	Slamat	Indonesia
3676	Semeru	Indonesia
3726	Rindjani	Indonesia
4078	Tacana	Guatemala
4220	Tajumulco	Guatemala
4590	Purace	Colombia
5230	Sangay	Ecuador
5451	Popocatepeti	Mexico
5640	Tupungatito	Chile
5641	Lascar	Chile
5897	Cotopaxi	Ecuador
6060	Guallatiri	Chile

Understand and Apply

1. Use methods 1 to 3 to organize this data about islands:

   Arctic Ocean: Greenland – 2 175 600 km^2
   Indian Ocean: Borneo – 725 545 km^2
   Atlantic Ocean: Newfoundland – 112 300 km^2
   Arctic Ocean: Baffin – 476 065 km^2
   Indian Ocean: Madagascar – 590 000 km^2

   Pacific Ocean: Honshu – 228 000 km^2
   Arctic Ocean: Victoria – 212 197 km^2
   Pacific Ocean: New Guinea – 777 000 km^2
   Atlantic Ocean: Great Britain – 218 041 km^2

2. What are some advantages and disadvantages of each method?

Problems to Investigate

THE GREAT PREDICTOR

Choose a favorite magazine that contains advertisements but don't look through it yet. Determine the total number of pages and then predict and record the number of 2-page ads, full-page ads, half-page ads, quarter-page ads, and ads that are less than a quarter of a page. Open the magazine and count the actual number of each size of ad. How close was your estimate to the actual number of each size of ad? Which size of ad is the most common? the least common?

THE FLIP TEST

Choose any magazine that contains advertisements, but don't open it yet. Predict and record the percent of quarter-page or smaller ads in each location — left-page gutter, left-page edge, right-page gutter, or right-page edge.

left-page gutter

right-page edge

left-page edge   gutter   right-page gutter

Open the magazine and count the total number of quarter-page or smaller ads. Then find the percent in each of the four locations. Which location is most common? Use your results to predict for a similar-sized magazine. Check. Was your prediction close?

WHAT'S THE QUESTION?

The variables for an investigation are: number of stirs, size of the container, temperature of the liquid, and stirring speed. What question or questions might be investigated?

SEARCHING FOR DEPENDENTS

Gwen and Kwai are investigating questions that deal with snack foods. What dependent variables would you suggest for the given independent variable?
a) brand of cola
b) brand of pretzels
c) flavor of popping corn

COLLECTION METHODS

What different information about the people of Canada and other nations could you gather using each method?
a) survey or poll   b) questionnaire
c) census   d) observation
e) secondary source
(newspapers, magazines, journals)

Make up other problems about collecting and organizing data. Post them on the bulletin board for your classmates to solve.

7

1.3 Graphing Scattered Data

Terri created this table for polygor

Number of sides	3	4	5	6
Number of diagonals	0	2	5	9

a) Continue the pattern.
b) Draw the graph.
Is it reasonable to join the points? Explain.

Several students in Mr. Barker's class have relatives who live in Central America or in South America. Many of their relatives attend secondary school. They decided to investigate the following question.

"How does the number of secondary school students affect the literacy rate of a country?"

Concept Development

1. What might they have predicted about their question before collecting the data?

They used their computer database to find information on the percent of a country's population that reached secondary school. Then they organized their data in a spreadsheet and used graphing software to create a scatter plot.

2. a) Why do you think the data was displayed on a **scatter plot** and not on another type of graph?
   b) Why are the data points not joined with line segments?

Country	Reached Secondary School (%)	Literacy (%)
Argentina	74	95
Bolivia	37	78
Brazil	38	81
Canada	100	99
Chile	70	93
Colombia	56	87
Costa Rica	42	93
Ecuador	56	86
El Salvador	24	73
Guatemala	20	55
Guyana	56	95
Honduras	36	73
Mexico	55	87
Nicaragua	42	57
Panama	59	88
Paraguay	31	90
Peru	65	85
Suriname	51	95
Uruguay	73	96
Venezuela	54	88

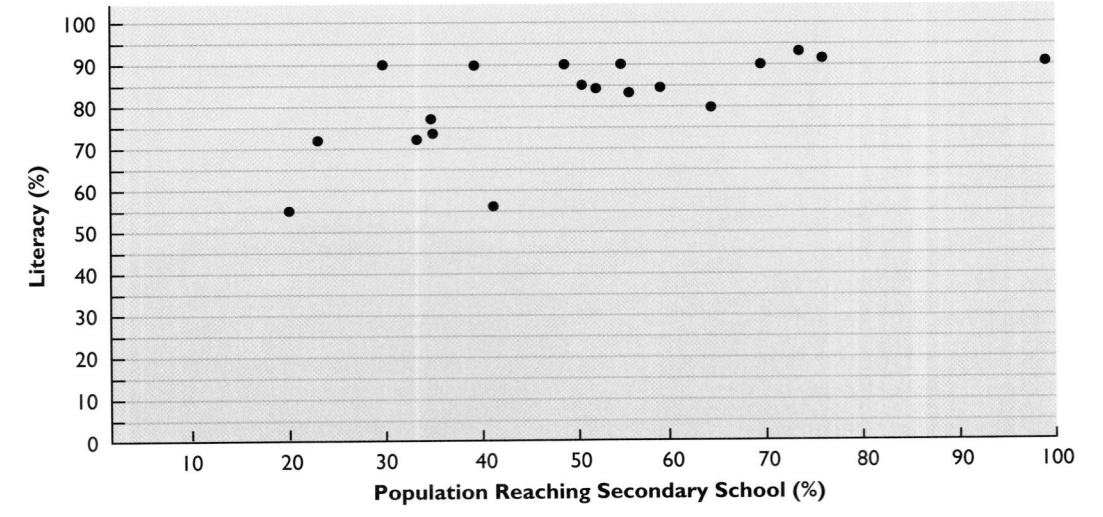

Secondary Students and Literacy in Canada and Central and South America

1. a) Where do you notice any clusters of points on the scatter plot?
b) Where does most of the clustering occur?
c) What does the clustering of points tell you about the data?

2. a) In which direction is the pattern of the points slanting – up to the right? down to the right?
b) Which country or countries do not fit the pattern shown? What factors may cause them not to fit the pattern?
c) Based on the direction of the slant, what relationship do you see between the two sets of data?
d) Is the relationship weak or strong? Justify your choice.

3. a) Which percent population reaching secondary school occured most often?
b) What countries do these percents correspond to?
c) Do countries with the same percent of the population reaching secondary school also have the same literacy percent? Provide examples to support your response.
d) What explanation would you provide for your response to part (c)?

4. a) What other patterns do you notice from the scatter plot? Share your patterns with the rest of the class.
b) Create 2 or 3 problems from the scatter plot. Pass your problems to classmates to solve.

5. Which form of displaying data do you find easier to interpret, the table of data or the scatter plot? Why?

6. The statistician for a basketball team recorded the number of personal fouls and points scored for each player in a table.

Sweater Number	Personal Fouls	Points Scored
2	69	471
5	52	244
9	11	17
29	91	301
31	6	18
38	60	575
47	69	325
58	38	62
59	85	230
63	19	22
75	45	122
76	17	51
82	10	10
84	130	643
89	5	12
90	108	362
99	41	164

a) What prediction would you make for this question:
How does the number of personal fouls a player makes affect the number of points scored by the player?
b) Make a scatter plot. Use the pattern shown on your plot to determine how well you predicted.
c) Does the scatter plot show a strong or weak relationship between the two sets of data? Justify your choice.
d) How well could you predict the number of points scored by a player who has 40 personal fouls?

7. Use data from the tables on pages 2 and 8 for the following questions. Write and explain a prediction about how the two sets of data might be related.

Then make a scatter plot. Use the pattern shown on your plot to determine how well you predicted. Compare your scatter plots with your classmates'.

a) How does population density affect the literacy rate?

b) How does the GDP per person of a country affect the percent of the population who reach secondary school?

8. a) Choose one of the following questions to investigate. What prediction would you make about a possible relationship between the two sets of data?

b) Identify the independent variable, the dependent variable, and 2 possible control variables.

c) Display your data in a scatter plot.

d) Write a report of your findings, then share it with the rest of the class.

• Is there a relationship between the price in Canadian dollars versus American dollars for magazines and books?

• Is there a relationship between the measurement around a person's head and the measurement around the waist?

• How does the distance that a student lives from school affect the time it takes to travel to school each morning?

• Is there a relationship between the number of cars in the school parking lot at 9:00 a.m. and the day of the week?

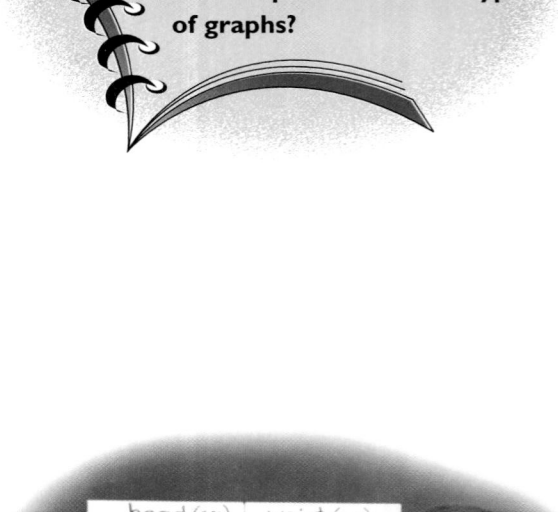

In Your Journal

For what types of data would a scatter plot be useful?

What are some benefits of using a scatter plot over other types of graphs?

Search through magazines and newspapers for data displayed in scatter plots. Bring examples to display on the bulletin board and discuss.

Finding the Line of Best Fit

1.4 Working the Line

Warm Up

Describe a situation that could be represented by this scatter plot.

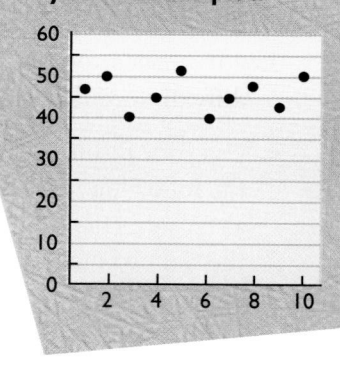

The students in Mr. Barker's class are analysing the graph, "Secondary Students and Literacy in Canada and Central and South America," found on page 8. They observed that the points in their scatter plot slant upwards to the right. The shape made by the majority of the points appears to be linear, or in the shape of a line.

Concept Development

1. Use a piece of thin string or a ruler to create a straight line through the points in the scatter plot found on page 8.
   a) Where does your line begin? end?
   b) Where did you place your line so it best represents all of the points?
   c) How many points are above your line? below your line? on your line?

2. Compare the placement of your line with your classmates'. What decisions did they make before they placed their line?

Finding a line to represent the points in a scatter plot that forms a linear pattern is called finding the **line of best fit**.

3. a) As a class, where was the most agreed-upon placement of the line of best fit?
   b) What are the different ways your classmates used to find this line?

Understand and Apply

1. Use a piece of thin string or a ruler to locate the line of best fit for each scatter plot. Use methods suggested by your classmates.
   Use a different method for each plot.
   Describe your method.

a)

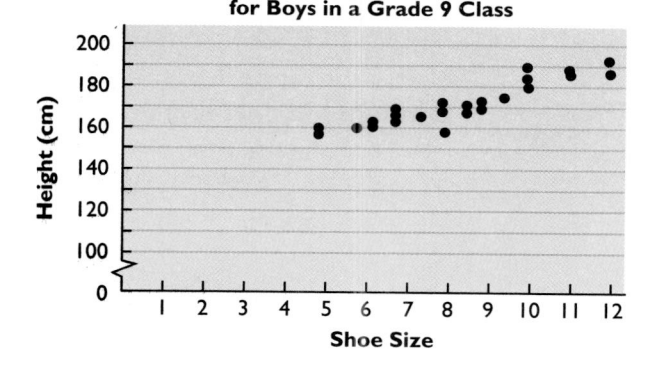

Shoe Size Versus Height for Boys in a Grade 9 Class

b)

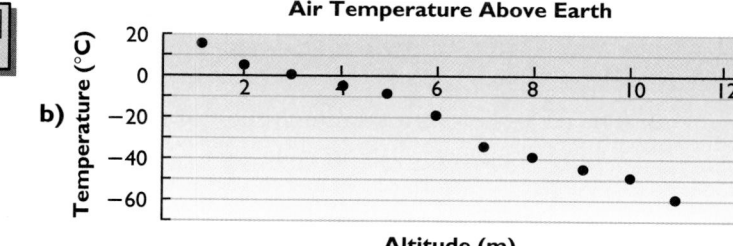

Air Temperature Above Earth

c)

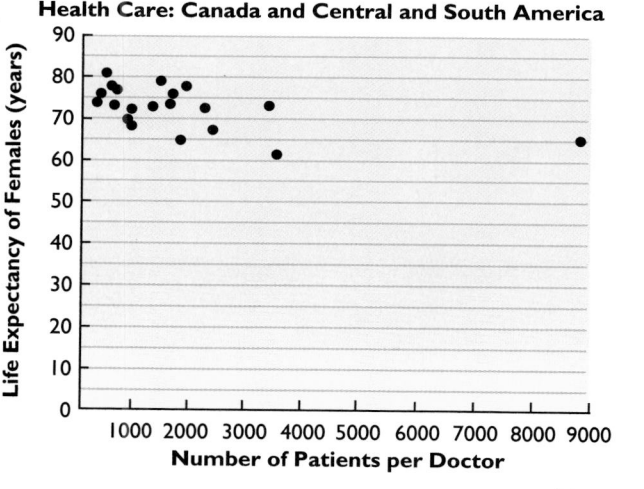

Health Care: Canada and Central and South America

11

2. Compare the placement of your line and the methods you used in Problem 1 with your classmates'. How are they the same? different?

3. For which scatter plot in Problem 1 was it most difficult to find the line of best fit? Explain.

4. Use your results from Problem 1 in to answer the following.
a) What is the significance of the direction of the slant of the line?
b) What control variables would you have used in the collection of data for each plot?
c) What do the data points above the line represent? What about the points below and on the line?

W/E
5. Is it possible to find a line of best fit for this scatter plot? Explain.

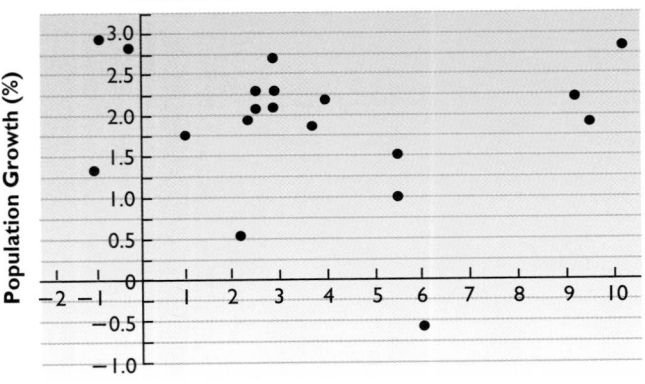

6. The table shows the winning times for the Women's Olympic 100-m run.

Year	Time (s)	Year	Time (s)
1928	12.20	1968	11.00
1932	11.90	1972	11.07
1936	11.50	1976	11.01
1948	11.90	1980	11.06
1952	11.50	1984	10.97
1956	11.50	1988	10.54
1960	11.00	1992	10.82
1964	11.40		

a) Display the data in a scatter plot. Find the line of best fit.
b) Use your line to predict the winning time for the next two Olympic Games.
c) What are some difficulties in using a line of best fit for predicting running times?
d) List other examples besides athletics where lines of best fit may have limitations.

7. Use your previously drawn scatter plots to identify those that would produce lines of best fit. Find the line of best fit for each plot.
If you have a Texas Instrument TI-81 graphing calculator, you can use the following procedure to find the line of best fit.

To enter your data:

> Select the **STAT** menu.
> Select the **DATA** submenu.
> Select **EDIT** and enter your data.

To draw the scatter plot:

> Select the **STAT** menu.
> Select the **DRAW** submenu.
> Select **SCATTER** and press **ENTER**.

To draw the line of best fit:

> Select the **STAT** menu.
> Select the **CALC** submenu.
> Select **LinReg**.
> Write the values shown for *a* and *b*.
> Select the **DRAW menu**.
> **Select DrawF.**
> Type the expression for your values of *a* and *b*, *bx* + *a*, and press **ENTER**.

In Your Journal

What is the purpose of the line of best fit? How does it relate to the data in a scatter plot? How is a scatter plot different from a line graph?

Creative Ways to Display Data

> **G**raphs are a useful way to represent information so we can see patterns and trends that may not be easily recognized in numerical forms. Graphic artists use their creativity to add interesting visual effects to familiar graphs such as the circle, bar, and stacked bar graphs.

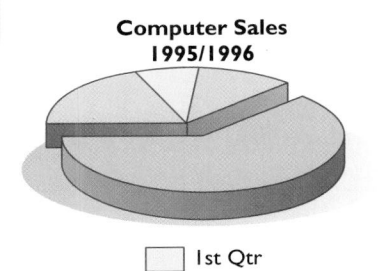

Computer Sales 1995/1996

☐ 1st Qtr
☐ 2nd Qtr
☐ 3rd Qtr
☐ 4th Qtr

3-D Circle Graphs

In a **circle graph** the whole is broken into several parts or sectors. Displaying the data in this way shows how the size of each sector compares to the whole and to the other sectors.

1. What effect is created in this graph? Why do you think the artist separated one sector from the others?

Multiple Bar Graphs

In a **multiple bar graph**, sets of bars are used to show comparisons between related data.

2. a) How is this display about water like a multiple bar graph?
   b) What effect is created by displaying the data as shown?

Stacked Bar Graphs

A **stacked bar graph** is used to compare data collected from particular groups. The stacking of the parts shows the size of each part related to the whole group and to the other parts.

3. a) How is this display about Fossil Fuels like a stacked bar graph?
   b) What effect is created by displaying the data as shown?

Applications

4. What other ways have you learned to display data?

5. What type of graph would you use to display the data for these situations? Explain your choice. What interesting and creative effects would you add to your graph?
   a) the populations of the countries in Central America and South America
   b) the areas of the countries in Central America
   c) how a boy or girl in Brazil would spend a typical day
   d) life expectancy for males and females in South American countries
   e) the growth of a plant over 3 or 4 months
   f) the number of goals, assists, and penalties for a hockey player over a month of the season

Problems to Investigate

A NAMELESS PLOT

This scatter plot is missing several important details. What are possible titles for the axes? What information might be displayed by the data points? Provide more than one answer.

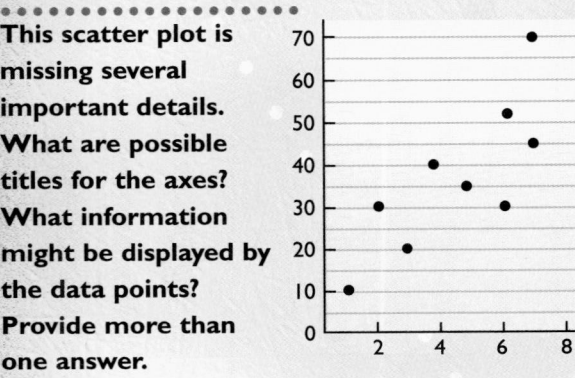

DECISIONS-DECISIONS

Adrian has difficulties deciding which set of data is the independent variable and which is the dependent variable. Adrian created 2 scatter plots using the same data, but he reversed the placement of the data along the axes. For both scatter plots the line of best fit was the same line. How is this possible? What might the plots look like?

A DIFFERENT SLANT

Frances collected data about her classmates' feelings towards their final grade in mathematics last year. She created a scatter plot and found the line of best fit as shown. What might the data have looked like? If she reversed the placement of her data between the axes, what would the line of best fit look like?

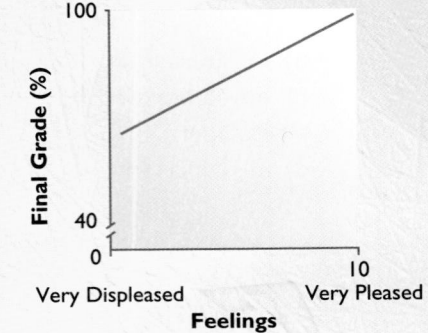

THE FINAL CHECK

Jay makes a scatter plot of the data and finds a line of best fit. He has 129 data points. How can he check that he has plotted them all without counting each one?

A SWISHER

Suppose your school radio station hires you to call the play-by-play action for their basketball games. Colleen Szabo is the top player and her record of attempted shots and distance from the basket are shown in the scatter plot. Use the information from the plot to describe Colleen's performance on the court for your listening audience.

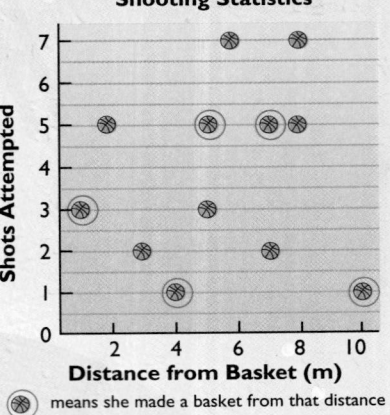

Colleen Szabo's Basketball Shooting Statistics

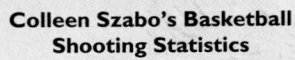

🏀 means she made a basket from that distance

Make up other problems about displaying data. Post them on the bulletin board for your classmates to solve.

1.5 Using Our Logic

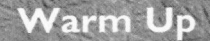

Everytime I forget my calculator at home I have a math test. So, forgetting my calculator causes math tests. Is this an appropriate conclusion to make? Why or why not? Make up a similar statement and explain if the conclusion is appropriate.

Vishal and Janet researched information to see if there is a relationship between the GDP per person and the average number of children born per woman for Canada and Central and South America. They displayed this data in a scatter plot.

Country	GDP per Person (U.S. $)	Average Number of Children Born per Woman
Argentina	3100	2.8
Belize	1653	3.8
Bolivia	630	4.5
Brazil	2300	3.0
Canada	19 400	1.8
Chile	2300	2.5
Colombia	1300	2.6
Costa Rica	1900	3.2
Ecuador	1070	3.5
El Salvador	1010	4.0
French Guiana	2240	3.6
Guatemala	1260	4.6
Guyana	300	2.4
Honduras	1050	4.8
Mexico	3200	3.3
Nicaragua	425	4.6
Panama	2040	3.0
Paraguay	1460	4.4
Peru	920	3.3
Suriname	3400	2.9
Uruguay	2935	2.4
Venezuela	2590	3.3

Fertility and GDP per Person in Canada and Central and South America

Concept Development

They used the scatter plot to make the following conclusion:

For the majority of these countries, as the GDP per person increases the average number of children born per woman decreases.

1. a) What feature(s) of the scatter plot would lead to this conclusion?
   b) Do you think this conclusion is a logical one to make based on the data? Why or why not?

2. What other conclusion(s) would the features of the scatter plot and data in the table lead you to make? Justify each of your conclusions.

1. a) Which countries do not fit the pattern shown by the scatter plot? What factors may cause these countries not to fit the pattern?
b) Could you confidently predict the average number of children per woman for a country based on the GDP? Explain. Does the scatter plot show a strong or a weak relationship? Justify your choice.

2. a) Do countries with the same GDP per person also have the same average number of children born per woman? Provide examples to support your response.
b) What explanation can you provide for your response to part (a)?

3. a) Do countries with the same average number of children born per woman also have the same GDP per person? Provide examples to support your response.
b) What explanation can you provide for your response to part (a)?

4. a) Use thin string or a ruler to determine the line of best fit of the above scatter plot. Compare your placement of the line with your classmates'.
b) Explain the meaning of the points above your line and below your line.
c) Use your line to predict the average number of children born per woman for a country with a GDP per person of U.S.$2800. How well can you predict with your line?
d) At what point does your line become ineffective for predicting? Explain.

5. The array below shows the population of Brazilian youth under the age of 15. The numerical figures represent the population every 5 years beginning with 1955.

26 646 000, 31 649 000, 36 933 000, 40 491 000,
43 325 000, 45 748 000, 49 366 000, 51 653 000,
51 886 000, 50 279 000, 49 065 000, 48 646 000,
48 699 000, 48 446 000, 47 678 000

a) How do you think the data was collected? How do you think the population beyond the present day's information was predicted?
b) Plot the data.
c) What patterns are shown in the data?
d) Who might be interested in this information? Why?

6. Use your scatter plot from Lesson 1.3 which relates personal fouls and points scored to answer the following.
a) Suppose you were the statistician for the team, what conclusion would you make from the scatter plot?
b) Based on your conclusion, what advice would you give the coach? Explain.

7. The table shows the home attendance for a baseball team and the outcome of the game – win (W) or loss (L).

July	10	11	12	14	16	17
Attendance	13 409	16 398	18 283	11 255	12 683	16 793
Outcome	L	W	W	L	L	W
July	20	22	26	29	30	31
Attendance	12 411	13 109	19 001	20 675	21 573	12 728
Outcome	L	L	W	W	W	W

a) What relationship exists between home attendance and the outcome of the game? What conclusions can you make from the data?
b) What advice would you give to the owner to improve the number of wins of the team?
c) Would a line of best fit be appropriate to represent the data? Why or why not?
d) How well can you predict the attendance for a given day?

8. Devise, conduct, and then write a thorough report on an experiment that investigates whether the time of day affects reaction time. You might consider the time taken to catch a ruler, pencil, or piece of paper about the size of a $5 bill. Share your report with the rest of the class. Be prepared to justify any conclusions you make.

What possible conclusions can you make about attendance at school and marks? What control variables might affect the validity of the conclusions?

1.6 Reading Between the Lines

One billboard claims that Carrie is the #1 Real Estate agent in Canada. The billboard across the street says Miko is the #1 agent. Explain how this is possible.

The students in Mr. Barker's class are discussing the validity of this information on acid rain and its effects on the environment.

* The Ontario Ministry of the Environment estimates that as many as 4000 lakes in that province alone are already unable to support life because of acid rain. Thousands more in other parts of Eastern Canada are dead or dying; and European lakes are also suffering the same fate. Within the next 20 years, the $620-million sport and commercial fishery of the pre-Cambrian Shield will suffer a loss of 20% to 50%.

* Trees covering 4 million hectares of Europe are now showing injury and dying from acid rain. Signs of injury are already appearing in Canada; the maple syrup industry of Central Canada is seriously threatened. The value of Canada's forests is estimated at $4 billion a year; even a 10% reduction in forest productivity over the next 25 years would be expensive, in resources and in jobs.

* Respiratory ailments related to sulphur and nitrogen oxides in the air are estimated to be costing Canada $160 million a year.

The Canadian Green Consumer Guide

Concept Development

1. What might be a good title for the article? Justify your choice.

2. a) What conclusions are made in the article?
   b) Who might have made these conclusions?
   c) Do you think the conclusions follow logically from the data? Why or why not?

1. Use the article on page 17 to answer the following questions.

   a) How many lakes are there in Ontario? What percent of all of the lakes do these 4000 make up?

   b) How might the Ministry of the Environment have estimated the number of lakes suffering from acid rain to be about 4000?

   c) What kind of "life" is the Ministry referring to? How would the Ministry know whether or not these lakes supported life before they made their statement?

   d) How would the Ministry know that acid rain is destroying the lakes? Besides acid rain, what other factors might prevent lakes from supporting life?

   e) What are the boundaries and size of the pre-Cambrian Shield Region? About how many lakes are found in this region?

2. The book the article appears in was published in 1988.

   a) Estimate the minimum and maximum amount of money that will be lost by the sport and commercial fishery in the pre-Cambrian Shield Region between 1988 and 2013.

   b) Calculate the average amount lost per year.

   c) Use the average amount lost per year to estimate the amount lost to date. Research the real amount lost. How close is your estimate?

3. Create several questions to ask about the other parts of the article to help you make sense of the information. Share your questions with the rest of the class.

4. In a television commercial, a toothpaste manufacturer claims 2 out of 3 dentists recommend Brand X over other brands of toothpaste. What does this statement mean? How might they have arrived at that claim?

5. Use this article to answer the questions that follow.

Teen TV viewing down sharply from '80s: StatsCan

OTTAWA – ... Last year, <Canadians> spent on average 22.7 hours a week in front of the boob tube, watching television and movie videos, a half hour less than in 1990 and 90 minutes less than in the mid-80's, Statistics Canada said yesterday.

And the steepest slide in viewing has been among children, teens and young adults, who watch least of all.

There's no single explanation but it may just be that young people are spending more time playing video games, an activity not included in the figures on TV viewing. ... maybe they're doing more homework.

... Teens spent 17.1 hours a week viewing TV last year, the least time of all the age groups, while younger children averaged 17.7 hours, 90 minutes less than 5 years earlier, the steepest slide.

The amount of television watched generally rose with age to more than 30 hours a week for those 60 and over — 36.4 hours for older women and 32.4 for older men.

And among older Canadians the time spent watching TV has remained relatively stable.

... the trend is bringing Canada in line with the rest of the world. Outside the U.S., North Americans watch more television than non-North Americans and Canadians watch less TV than Americans.

It could simply be ... that the stuff they're seeing on TV is not overly relevant. ... It could be related to something as distant as immigration patterns, ... television, with its focus on North American, particularly U.S., culture would have less attraction for immigrants.

... Canadians are spending more time at other screens. While TV was extremely successful at beating the book back, it appears it's not as good at beating back Internet, computers, and interactive systems where you negotiate your time and have a meeting with your screen.

The Toronto Star, August 24, 1995

---

a) What is the article about?

b) How do you think the information about hours spent watching television was collected?

c) Was the information collected from the entire population or a from a sample? Explain.

d) Does the article convince you that teen television viewing is down sharply from the 80s? Why or why not?

e) What conclusions are made in the article? Do you think the conclusions follow logically from the data? Why or why not?

f) What reasons are given for a drop in television viewing by all groups? What might be other possible reasons?

g) Survey your classmates to determine the average number of hours spent watching television in a week. How does this compare to the time reported for teens? Explain why there may be differences in the results.

h) Create 2 or 3 other questions to help you make sense of the article. Share them with the rest of your class.

6.

> ... The unemployment rate will rise to an average of 9.8 per cent in 1996 from 9.6 per cent this year, Informetrica Ltd. predicted. Further, it's forecasting that unemployment will remain near 10 per cent until the turn of the century.
>
> *The Toronto Star, September 6, 1995*

a) Unemployment rates are usually given as *seasonally adjusted* rates.
What does this mean and what does this indicate about our real unemployment rate?

b) Are these percents based on a sample or on the entire population? Explain your choice.

c) What percents would you identify as being near 10%?

d) How can they predict the unemployment rate for the end of 1995, 1996, and for the turn of the century?

e) Will there be a decrease in the number of jobs, or an increase in the number of people looking for work to cause such high unemployment? Explain your choice.

7. Collect other articles from newspapers and magazines, or quotes from radio and television that contain information that needs clarification to make the conclusions more understandable. Read each article and create several questions to help you understand the article. Share the articles and questions with another group or with the entire class.

HOME LINK

Read a consumer report about a product your family might be buying in the future. Make notes about what information was presented and how it was gathered. Did reading the report sway your decision on what brand you would buy? Why or why not? Share the report with your classmates.

In Your Journal

Make a list of questions to ask when a company makes what appears to be exaggerated claims about a new product or service.

Problems to Investigate

TALL TALES

Ms. Smith gives the same math test to students from Grades 3 to 9 and asks them to indicate their height on their test paper.

a) What conclusion(s) might you make for these two sets of data?

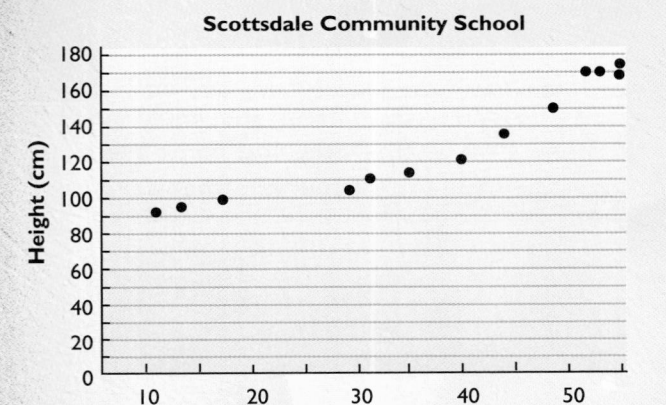

Scottsdale Community School

b) What factors should Ms. Smith take into account?
c) What other pairs of real-life data show a relationship where hidden factors exist that may affect making a logical conclusion?

ELLIPTICAL PLOT

Loop a 30-cm length of string around 2 tacks. Move a pencil around inside the loop to draw an ellipse. Mark 12 points anywhere on the boundary of the curve. Label the points A, B, C, ..., L and the tack holes W and Z.

Measure from W to each of the points and record the 12 lengths as the independent variable. Measure from Z to each of the 12 points and record these lengths as the dependent variable.

Make a scatter plot. What relationship exists between the distances measured from W and Z? Predict what would happen to the pattern of the dots as the tack holes are moved closer together. What conclusion can you make?

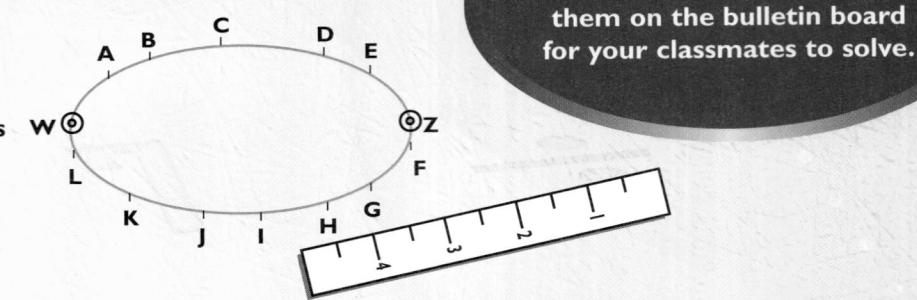

READ THE CLUES

Seven friends each played a video game several times and recorded their scores for each game on a computer program. Then the program crashed and they lost their data. However, they remembered enough to create a scatter plot. Use these clues to make the plot. What assumptions can you make based on these clues?

* Dan and Theo played the same number of times, but Theo had a greater score.
* Pradish and Trina had the same score even though Pradish played fewer games.
* Hafsa played the fewest games of all.
* Gina had the greatest score of all.
* Vince played the second greatest number of games but had the lowest score of everyone.

BRAND X OR Y?

A magazine ad states that 90% of the people surveyed thought that Brand **X** was better than or no different from Brand Y. What percent of those surveyed could have thought that Brand Y was better than or no different from Brand **X**?

Make up other problems about analysing data. Post them on the bulletin board for your classmates to solve.

Solve Problems by Thinking Logically

MISLABELLED LOOT

Three identical bags contain coins but are labelled incorrectly. Each label belongs on one of the other two bags. How can you place the labels correctly by removing only one coin from any one bag? No peeking is allowed.

▶ *Understand the Problem*

1. What are you asked to do?

2. What do you know?

3. Where will you begin?

▶ *Think of a Plan*

To solve the problem, Tyrone and Shirley used logic.

4. Explain Tyrone's logic.

▶ *Carry Out the Plan*

5. Assuming Tyrone pulls a penny from the "Pennies and Dimes" bag, describe the logical reasoning involved in solving the problem.

If I reach inside a bag marked "Pennies and Dimes" and I pull out a penny, I know the bag contains only pennies.

▶ *Look Back*

6. How would the solution be different if Tyrone had pulled a dime from the "Pennies and Dimes" bag?

Applications

JUST A SNACK

Five friends ordered 2 pizzas and 3 submarine sandwiches. Tammy and Rifka ordered different foods. Raffi and Tammy ordered the same foods. Rifka and Jenny didn't order the same thing. Grant was served first. What did each friend order?

WHO BROKE IT?

"Who broke my window?" snarled Mr. Scrooge at the 3 children. Kim said, "I didn"t." Buster said, "Kyle did." Kyle said, "Buster is lying." Only one child is telling the truth. Who did it?

THE RAFTERS

The bridge across a river is unsafe to use. The only means to cross the river is by using a raft that carries either 1 adult or 2 children. How many times must the raft cross the river if there are 5 adults and 2 children?

1. Assess whether each question has the features necessary to conduct a further investigation. Defend your choice.
   a) Which tennis ball lasts longer?
   b) How does a calculator know how to find the value for the square root of any number?
   c) Is there a relationship between the life expectancy of the people and the GDP of their country?
   d) Do students who do their homework all the time do well on quizzes and tests?

2. a) What prediction would you make for this investigation question: "Does the depth you place a tomato plant in the soil affect the size of tomatoes produced?"
   b) Identify the independent variable, dependent variable, and 2 control variables.

3. a) Create a question to investigate and explain why you consider it to be a good question.
   b) Write a prediction and identify the variables. Include 1 or 2 control variables.

4. The table shows the number of oil changes per year and the corresponding engine repair costs.
   a) Name several ways this data might have been collected. Which way might be the most efficient?
   b) Who might be interested in the data? Why?
   c) How would you organize the data to help you see patterns and make conclusions?
   d) Is there enough information to make a conclusion(s)? What conclusions can you make?

Oil Changes per year	Repair Costs ($)
3	278
5	285
2	475
3	381
1	689
4	390
6	96
4	250
3	425
2	645
0	600
10	0

5. A questionnaire is prepared to be sent to a sample of the population of a mid-sized town. The questionnaire focuses on this question: "Should a law be passed by government to force all tricycle and bike riders to wear helmets?"
   a) How large a sample should be included?
   b) Who should the questionnaires be sent to in order to avoid biased results? Why?
   c) Identify any possible biases.

6. Create a scatter plot that shows a weak relationship between two sets of data. What might your plot represent?

7. Create a scatter plot that shows an upward slant of the data points and a strong relationship. What might your plot represent?

8.

Losing Ground

The environmental group Friends of the Earth estimates that each kilometre of road or highway takes up about 6.5 hectares of land. In Ontario alone there are 155 000 km of highways, roads, and streets, adding up to a million hectares of land given over to motor vehicles. Our cities devote one-third of their area to roads and streets. Highways consume the largest amount of space per kilometre, but even relatively small roads can cause major controversy where they run through environmentally sensitive areas.

The Canadian Green Consumer Guide

a) What conclusions are made in the article? Do they follow logically from the data? Why or why not?
b) What type of roads or highways might have been used to arrive at 6.5 hectares?
c) Do you think they surveyed all cities or just a sample? Explain. What biases might have occurred?
d) The article claims: *highways consume the largest amount of space per kilometer.* What might they be comparing this against? List three other things made by humans that take up a large amount of area.

Play each game with a partner.

Best Fit Concentration

Shuffle the Line of Best Fit cards. Place them face down in an array.

Players take turns flipping over two cards in search of a match.

- If the cards match, the player takes them and continues to turn over cards as long as matching pairs are found.
- If the pairs don't match, the player turns them face down in the same position and the next player takes a turn.

The game ends when all the matching pairs of cards are found.

The player with the most pairs wins.

Spin It

Use a spinner and the set of Spin It cards.

The first player spins the spinner and draws a card. The number on the spinner tells how many control variables the player must provide for the investigation question on the card.

If the player is able to provide the correct number of suitable control variables within an agreed-upon time limit, the player takes the card. Play switches to the other player.

If the player is unable to complete the task within an agreed-upon time limit, the card is placed at the bottom of the deck. Play switches to the other player.

Each card taken counts as 1 point. Each correct and appropriate control variable named counts as 1 point.

The game ends when the deck is empty.

The player with the most points wins.

What effect does the kind of bird-seed used have on the number of birds coming to a feeder?

How does the size of container affect the length of time a candle will stay lit?

Which brand of paper towel absorbs the most water?

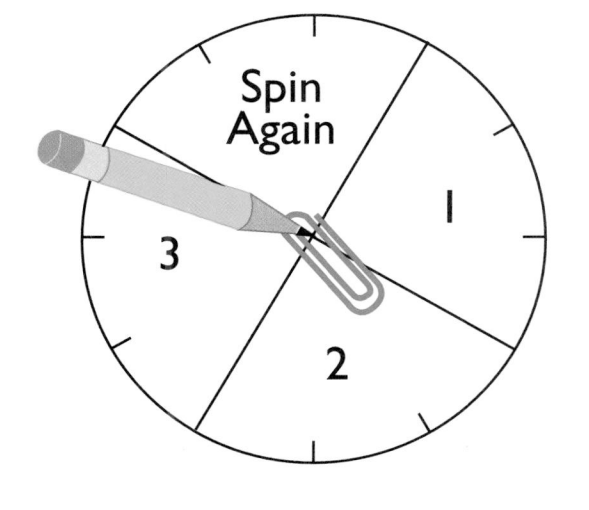

1. A classmate posed the following question to investigate.
   "Why are there always unpopped kernels when I pop corn?"
   What suggestions would you give to help a classmate write a question with the features of a good question?

2. Identify 2 or 3 control variables for an investigation on each of the following.
   a) the life span of different lightbulbs
   b) the effectiveness of different kinds of salt in melting winter ice
   c) the speed in which various seeds germinate
   d) mass versus volume for several samples of the same substance

3. Write a prediction for each question to investigate.
   a) How does the shape of the petals of a flower affect its ability to cause pollination?
   b) How does the depth of a lake or large pond affect the temperature of the water?
   c) How is temperature related to time of day over a two-day period?

4. Make a list of the different ways you would collect data for each investigation in Problem 3. Justify your choices.

5. a) What does clustering of points tell you about the two sets of data in a scatter plot?
   b) How can you tell if the relationship between the two sets of data is strong or weak?
   c) What does a downward slant of the data points tell you about the relationship between the two sets of data?
   d) What does an upward slant of the data points tell you?

6. Analyse the scatter plot to answer this question. Does the mass of a bike affect its jumping height?

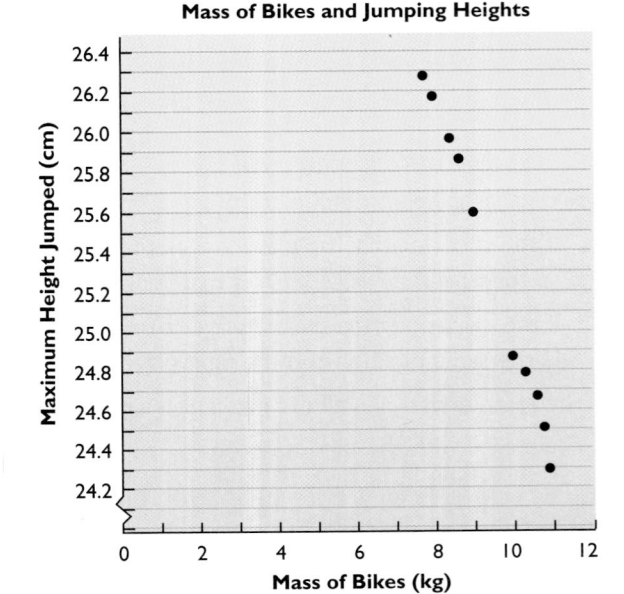

Mass of Bikes and Jumping Heights

a) What pattern is shown by the data points?
   b) Does the scatter plot show a weak or strong relationship between the two sets of data points? Explain your choice.
   c) How well can you predict the maximum height jumped for a bike with a mass of 9 kg? Explain.
   d) Use the scatter plot to create a line of best fit.
   e) What conclusion(s) can you make?

7. How can you tell when a scatter plot will not have a line of best fit? Create a scatter plot that would not have a line of best fit.

8. Describe the steps you use to find the line of best fit when the points are spread out.

9. Describe 2 real-life situations in which the line of best fit would be ineffective for predicting results. Justify your choices.

10. The crime rate in a large Canadian city is on the rise. The media claims that an increase in the number of police officers will cause a dramatic 20% decrease in crime.
    a) Do you think the conclusion is logical or illogical? Justify your choice.
    b) What factors might prevent a decrease in crime?

Communicate Your Knowledge

1. What was the most interesting information you found out about Canada and countries in Central and South America? Explain to a classmate why this might be valuable information.

7. Make an entry in your journal describing an interesting investigation you were involved in and why you found it interesting.

2. Make predictions about birth rates, overall fitness levels, literacy levels, life expectancy, ... for countries that are almost the same size as Canada. Why might they be similar? different?

6. Write about an article you read that presented a conclusion that followed logically from the given data, and one whose conclusion was not logical.

3. What information would be valuable to know if you were planning to spend a year or more in a country you'd like to visit? Why? How would you gather the data?

5. Identify the features of a scatter plot that may help others understand the information it is meant to communicate.

4. Describe to a classmate how you find the line of best fit for data on a scatter plot.

What else would you like to investigate about Canada and other countries, or about phenomena in our everyday lives?

UNIT 2

Powers and Roots

These students are displaying different sizes of cubes.

- How do the cubes compare in volume?

- The smallest cube has a volume of 1 cm^3. What's the length of each edge? How do you know? What's the area of each face?

- The mid-size cube has 10 cm edges. What's its volume? What's the area of each face? Explain why the volume could be expressed as 10^3 cm^3 and the area of each face as 10^2 cm^2.

- The box can hold 1 000 000 mL. What's its volume in cubic centimetres? How do you know? What's the area in square centimetres of each face of the box? Explain how you calculated. Express the area and the volume as a power of ten.

- The floor of the room is 10 m by 10 m. Express the floor area in square centimetres as a power of 10. Explain what you did.

- If the room had a 10 m ceiling, what would be the room's volume in cubic centimetres as a power of ten? Explain what you did.

Why are numbers such as 1, 4, 9, and 16 called *square* numbers? How would you describe numbers such as 1, 8, 27, and 64? Explain.

27

2.1 Amplifying Powers

Electronic equipment such as radios and televisions contain devices called amplifiers which change incoming weak signals into stronger signals. These stronger signals are eventually converted into audible sounds.

Warm Up

Complete the sequences.

10^1 10^2 10^3 10^4 10^5 10^6

10 100 ▨ ▨ ▨ ▨

$(-10)^1$ $(-10)^2$ $(-10)^3$ $(-10)^4$ $(-10)^5$ $(-10)^6$

-10 100 ▨ ▨ ▨ ▨

Explain why $(-10)^3 \neq 10^3$ but $(-10)^4 = 10^4$.

Often, the strength of the signal is increased in stages by using a series of amplifiers.

The first amplifier multiplies the incoming signal 1 000 000 times, or by a factor of 10^6.
The second amplifies the signal again, this time 1000 times, or by a factor of 10^3.
By the time the signal has passed through both amplifiers, it has increased by a factor of $10^6 \times 10^3$.

$10^6 \times 10^3$

10^6 10^3

Concept Development

1. Michael concludes that the signal was amplified altogether by a factor of 10^9. He uses the standard form for each of the powers to help him multiply.

   Describe the relationship between the exponents of the two factors, $10^6 \times 10^3$, and the number of zeroes in the product, 1 000 000 000.

2. Jana arrives at the same conclusion by thinking of each power as a product of equal factors.

   Describe the relationship between the exponents of the two factors, $10^6 \times 10^3$, and the exponent of the product, 10^9.

3. Which method do you prefer, Michael's or Jana's? Why?

4. Describe another series of amplifiers that would produce an amplification factor of 10^9. Explain.

$10^6 \times 10^3 = 1000\,000 \times 1000$
$= 1\,000\,000\,000$
$= 10^9$

10^6 is $10 \times 10 \times 10 \times 10 \times 10 \times 10$

10^3 is $10 \times 10 \times 10$

So,

$10^6 \times 10^3 = (10 \times 10 \times 10 \times 10 \times 10 \times 10) \times (10 \times 10 \times 10)$

$= 10^9$

1. Find each total amplification factor.

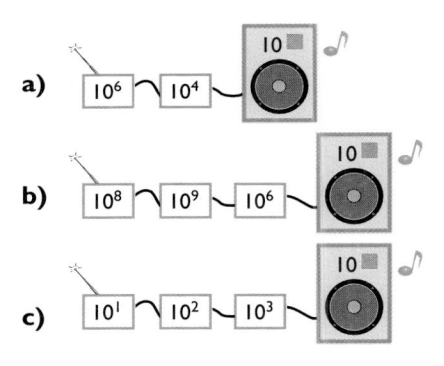

a)

b)

c)

2. Find the missing exponents.

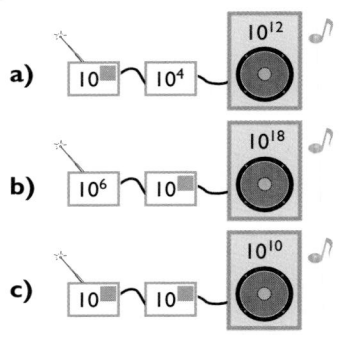

a)

b)

c)

3. a) Write 7^5 as a product of equal factors. Write 7^2 as a product of equal factors.
   b) Explain why $7^5 \times 7^2 = 7^7$.

4. Express each as a power with a single exponent.
   a) $3^7 \times 3^6$ **b)** $(-5)^8 \times (-5)^3$
   c) $6^5 \times 6^9$ **d)** $2^8 \times 2^7$

5. Which pairs of exponents make this statement true? $5^{\blacksquare} \times 5^{\blacksquare} = 5^{12}$
   a) ^{2} and ^{6}
   b) ^{10} and ^{2}
   c) ^{3} and ^{4}
   d) ^{6} and ^{6}
   e) ^{9} and ^{3}

6. Write a rule to describe how to calculate $a^m \times a^n$. Explain why the rule can't be used to calculate $2^5 \times 3^5$.

7. Express each product as a power with a single exponent.
   a) $3^5 \times 3^8$
   b) $5^8 \times 5^3 \times 5^7$
   c) $6^2 \times 6^5 \times 6^4$
   d) $(-9)^8 \times (-9)^7$
   e) $10^5 \times 10^7$
   f) $10^2 \times 10^9 \times 10^0$
   g) $(-10)^0 \times (-10)^9$
   h) $7^3 \times 7^6$
   i) 25×125
   j) 16×64
   k) $27 \times 27 \times 9$
   l) $1000 \times 1\,000\,000$

8. Complete the chart below.

10^5	10^4	10^3	10^2	10^1	10^0	10^{-1}	10^{-2}	10^{-3}	10^{-4}	10^{-5}
						$\dfrac{1}{10^1}$	■	■	■	$\dfrac{1}{10^5}$
100 000	■	■	■	■	■	$\dfrac{1}{10}$	■	■	■	$\dfrac{1}{100\,000}$
						0.1	■	■	■	■

9. a) Complete the chart. Use a calculator to complete the decimal pattern.

2^5	2^4	2^3	2^2	2^1	2^0	2^{-1}	2^{-2}	2^{-3}	2^{-4}	2^{-5}
						$\frac{1}{2^1}$	▨	▨	▨	$\frac{1}{2^5}$
32	▨	▨	▨	▨	▨	$\frac{1}{2}$	▨	▨	▨	$\frac{1}{32}$
						0.5	▨	▨	▨	▨

b) Explain the meaning of the negative exponent.
c) What's the calculator doing to get the decimal values?
d) The power 2^3 is 64 times as great as 2^{-3}. Explain how you know. How do 4^3 and 4^{-3} compare?

10. Write a rule for changing a power with a negative exponent, a^{-n}, to a power with a positive exponent. Why is it important to include $a \neq 0$?

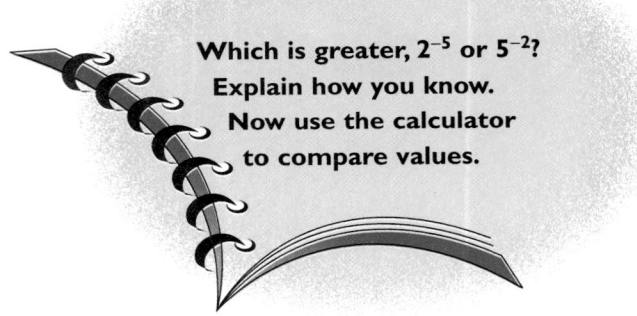
11. a) Explain why $2^0 = 1$.
b) A power that has an exponent of zero is equal to 1, $a^0 = 1$. Explain why a cannot be zero.

12. a) Complete the following to express $2^{-3} \times 2^5$ as a power with a single exponent.

$$2^{-3} \times 2^5 = \left(\frac{1}{2 \times 2 \times 2}\right) \times (2 \times 2 \times 2 \times 2 \times 2)$$

b) Repeat for $2^3 \times 2^{-5}$ and $2^{-3} \times 2^{-5}$.
c) Does the rule, $a^m \times a^n = a^{m+n}$, apply when m and/or n are negative?

13. Express each as a power with a single exponent.
a) $(-3)^{-4} \times (-3)^{-8}$
b) $4^7 \times 4^{-2} \times 4^{-2}$
c) $10^{-6} \times 10^{-3}$

14. Which pairs of exponents make this equation true? $5^{\blacksquare} \times 5^{\blacksquare} = 5^5$
a) ^{2} and $^{-3}$ **b)** $^{-8}$ and ^{3} **c)** $^{-3}$ and ^{8}
d) $^{-2}$ and $^{-3}$ **e)** ^{10} and $^{-5}$ **f)** ^{5} and ^{0}

15. Without finding the products, which are greater than 1? equal to 1? less than 1?
a) $2^3 \times 2^{-4}$ **b)** $10^5 \times 10^{-2}$
c) $5^{-7} \times 5^7$ **d)** $4^{-9} \times 4^{-7}$
e) $8^4 \times 8^{-4}$ **f)** $3^7 \times 3^5$
g) $5^0 \times 5^0$ **h)** $5^{-3} \times 5^{-5}$
i) $9^{-5} \times 9^8$ **j)** $10^{-6} \times 10^4$
k) $8^0 \times 5^0$ **l)** $\frac{1}{2^3} \times 2^3$
m) $\frac{1}{5^4} \times \frac{1}{5^3}$ **n)** $\frac{1}{10^6} \times 10^{-6}$
o) $8^2 \times \frac{1}{8^4}$

16. Guess and test to find values for n.
a) $n^4 \times n^2 = 64$
b) $n^3 \times n^2 = 243$
c) $n^2 \times n^1 = 125$
d) $n^3 \times n^0 = 64$
e) $n^3 \times n^2 \times n^0 = 32$
f) $n^0 \times n^0 = 1$

2.2 Comparing Exponential Fortunes

Warm Up

Write these amounts in standard form.

4.1×10^3 5.29×10^3
20×10^6 0.07×10^6
11.87×10^6 0.2×10^6
2×10^9 5.01×10^9
14.8×10^9 6.075×10^9
6.2 billion 3.07 million

This table shows the wealth, in U.S.$, of the ten richest people in the world as of 1994.

Name	Business	Country	$Billion
William H. Gates III	Computer Software	U.S.A.	12.9
Warren Edward Buffet	Stock Market	U.S.A.	10.7
Hans Rausing	Packaging	Sweden	9.0
Yoshiaki Tsutsumi	Real Estate	Japan	9.0
Paul Sacher	Pharmaceuticals	Switzerland	8.6
Tsai Wan-lin	Insurance & Finacial Services	Taiwan	8.5
Lee Shau Kee	Real Estate	Hong Kong	6.5
Kenneth Thomson	Media, retailing, real estate	Canada	6.5
Chung Ju-Yyung	Diversified	Korea	6.2
La Ka-shing	Real Estate, infrastructure	Hong Kong	5.9

Concept Development

1. Jesse is calculating how many years it would take to spend Bill Gates's fortune at the rate of $1 million per year. She writes each power as a product of equal factors. Complete her calculation. Write the answer in standard form.

$$\frac{12.9 \text{ billion}}{1 \text{ million}} = \frac{12.9 \times 10^9}{10^6}$$

$$= \frac{12.9 \times 10 \times 10 \times 10 \times \cancel{10 \times 10 \times 10 \times 10 \times 10 \times 10}}{\cancel{10 \times 10 \times 10 \times 10 \times 10 \times 10}}$$

2. David writes the division this way.

$$\frac{12.9 \text{ billion}}{1 \text{ million}} = \frac{12.9 \times 10^9}{10^6}$$

$$= \frac{12.9 \times 10^3 \times 10^6}{10^6}$$

a) Why did he write 10^9 as $10^3 \times 10^6$?
b) Complete his work.

3. Show how to find the missing exponent.

a) $\dfrac{10^9}{10^3} = 10^{\blacksquare}$ **b)** $\dfrac{10^{12}}{10^5} = 10^{\blacksquare}$

c) $(-7)^7 \div (-7)^4 = (-7)^{\blacksquare}$ **d)** $3^5 \div 3^4 = 3^{\blacksquare}$

4. For each equation above, describe the relationship among the exponents.

Kenneth Thomson

Understand and Apply

W/E **1.** How many years would it take to spend Ken Thomson's fortune at each annual rate?
- **a)** $1 000 000
- **b)** $100 000
- **c)** $10 000

2. Write a rule for dividing powers with the same base, $a^m \div a^n$ or $\frac{a^m}{a^n}$. Explain why the rule cannot be used to calculate $6^6 \div 3^2$ or $\frac{7^6}{9^4}$.

W/E **3.** Find the missing exponents.
- **a)** $7^5 \div 7^3 = 7^{\blacksquare}$
- **b)** $\frac{6^{\blacksquare}}{6^4} = 6^5$
- **c)** $10^5 \div 10^0 = 10^{\blacksquare}$
- **d)** $\frac{10^7}{10^0} = 10^{\blacksquare}$
- **e)** $(-4)^9 \div (-4)^{\blacksquare} = (-4)^{-2}$
- **f)** $12^{-6} \div 12^3 = 12^{\blacksquare}$
- **g)** $\frac{9^6}{9^4} = 9^{\blacksquare}$
- **h)** $10^4 \div 10^{-5} = 10^{\blacksquare}$
- **i)** $10^{-6} \div 10^{\blacksquare} = 10^{-14}$
- **j)** $\frac{4^{\blacksquare}}{4^{\blacksquare}} = 4^{-3}$
- **k)** $5^0 \div 5^4 = 5^{\blacksquare}$
- **l)** $(-2)^4 \div (-2)^{-5} = (-2)^{\blacksquare}$

4. Which pairs of exponents make this statement true if the first exponent in each pair goes in the numerator? $\frac{(-3)^{\blacksquare}}{(-3)^{\blacksquare}} = (-3)^4$
- **a)** 12 and 3
- **b)** 6 and 2
- **c)** 8 and 2
- **d)** 7 and 3
- **e)** 2 and –2

5. a) Write $10^3 \times 10^{-3} = 1$, substituting $\frac{1}{10^3}$ for 10^{-3}. Is the equation still true? Explain.
- **b)** Explain why $\frac{1}{10^{-3}}$ can be substituted for 10^3 in $10^3 \times 10^{-3} = 1$. What does this show about the relationship between $\frac{1}{10^{-3}}$ and 10^3?
- **c)** Use $2^5 \times 2^{-5} = 1$ to prove that $\frac{1}{2^{-5}} = 2^5$.

6. Use the relationship, $\frac{1}{a^{-m}} = a^m$, $a \neq 0$, to complete these.
- **a)** $\frac{1}{10^{-5}} = 10^{\blacksquare}$
- **b)** $\left(-\frac{1}{2}\right)^{-3} = (-2)^{\blacksquare}$
- **c)** $\frac{1}{5^{\blacksquare}} = 5^4$

7. a) Why is dividing by 10^3 the same as multiplying by 10^{-3}?
- **b)** Why is dividing by 10^{-3} the same as multiplying by 10^3?

8. Complete.
- **a)** $5^5 \div 5^2 = 5^{\blacksquare} \times 5^{\blacksquare}$
- **b)** $\frac{10^3}{10^{-6}} = 10^{\blacksquare} \times 10^{\blacksquare}$
- **c)** $(-6)^8 \div (-6)^5 = (-6)^{\blacksquare} \times (-6)^{\blacksquare}$
- **d)** $10^{\blacksquare} \div 10^{\blacksquare} = 10^7 \times 10^{-4}$

9. How can you use multiplication to divide powers? Explain using examples $5^{15} \div 5^8$ and $\frac{3^5}{3^{-8}}$.

10. Do you think Bill Gates's fortune could be spent in one lifetime at a rate of $1 million a month? Which calculation does <u>not</u> find the number of years it would take at this rate? Explain why.
- **a)** $\frac{12.9 \times 10^9}{12 \times 10^6}$
- **b)** $\frac{12.9}{12} \times 10^9 \times 10^6$
- **c)** $\frac{12\,900 \times 10^6}{12 \times 10^6}$
- **d)** $\frac{12\,900}{12} \times 10^6 \times 10^{-6}$

11. a) Calculate how many years it would take to spend $12.9 billion at a rate of $1 million a month.
- **b)** Which of the calculations in Problem 10 did you use to find the answer? Explain why.

12. Choose three other billionaires from the table. Estimate how many years it would take to spend each fortune at a rate of $1 million
- **a)** a month.
- **b)** a week.
- **c)** a day.

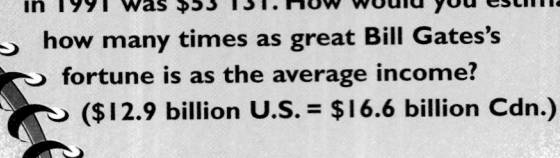

In Your Journal

The average annual family income in Canada in 1991 was $53 131. How would you estimate how many times as great Bill Gates's fortune is as the average income? ($12.9 billion U.S. = $16.6 billion Cdn.)

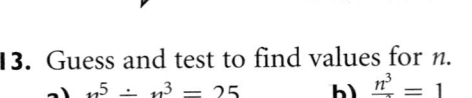

13. Guess and test to find values for n.
- **a)** $n^5 \div n^3 = 25$
- **b)** $\frac{n^3}{n^3} = 1$
- **c)** $n^8 \div n^3 = 243$
- **d)** $n^3 \div n^0 = 216$
- **e)** $n^{-5} = \frac{1}{32}$
- **f)** $\frac{1}{n^{-2}} = 36$

14. Evaluate. Express each answer in standard form.
- **a)** $\frac{5^5}{5^3} + 5^{-6} \times 5^8$
- **b)** $6^2 \div 6^3 \times \frac{6^2}{6^7} \times 6^7$
- **c)** $8^{-4} \div 8^{-5} - 2^6 \times 2^{-4}$
- **d)** $10^{-4} \times 10^4 \times \frac{10^5}{10^3} + 2^3$

2.3 Comparing Measurement Prefixes

Prefixes are used to indicate the relative sizes of measurements. This table shows some of the prefixes used with the litre. For example, one kilolitre (kL) is 10^3 or 1000 times as great as one litre.

Metric Prefix Table								
Prefix	– – –	kilo	mega	giga	tera	peta	exa	zetta	yotta
Symbol	L	kL	ML	GL	TL	PL	EL	ZL	YL
No. of Litres	10^0	10^3	10^6	10^9	10^{12}	10^{15}	10^{18}	10^{21}	10^{24}

Concept Development

1. a) How many litres is a megalitre? a gigalitre?
Express each answer as a power and in standard form.
b) A megalitre could be called the *square* of a kilolitre because $10^3 \times 10^3 = 10^6$ and $10^3 \times 10^3 = (10^3)^2$. What does this indicate about the relationship between 10^6 and $(10^3)^2$?
c) Explain why a gigalitre might be called the *cube* of a kilolitre. What does this indicate about the relationship between 10^9 and $(10^3)^3$?

2. Complete.
a) $(10^2)^3 = 10^2 \times 10^2 \times 10^2$
$\qquad = 10^{\blacksquare}$
b) $(10^3)^4 = 10^{\blacksquare} \times 10^{\blacksquare} \times 10^{\blacksquare} \times 10^{\blacksquare}$
$\qquad = 10^{\blacksquare}$
c) $(10^4)^3 = 10^{\blacksquare} \times 10^{\blacksquare} \times 10^{\blacksquare}$
$\qquad = 10^{\blacksquare}$
d) $(2^{\blacksquare})^3 = 2^6 \times 2^6 \times 2^6$
$\qquad = 2^{\blacksquare}$
e) $(3^3)^{\blacksquare} = 3^{\blacksquare} \times 3^{\blacksquare} \times 3^{\blacksquare} \times 3^{\blacksquare}$
$\qquad = 3^{\blacksquare}$
f) $[(-5)^4]^3 = (-5)^{\blacksquare} \times (-5)^{\blacksquare} \times (-5)^{\blacksquare}$
$\qquad = (-5)^{\blacksquare}$

Expressions such as $(10^3)^2$ and $(10^3)^3$ are called **powers of powers** because the base of the power is also a power.

W/E 1. Find the missing exponents.
   a) $10^{20} = (10^4)^{\blacksquare}$ b) $(-5)^{15} = [(-5)^{\blacksquare}]^3$
   c) $(10^7)^3 = 10^{\blacksquare}$ d) $3^{24} = (3^{\blacksquare})^{\blacksquare}$

2. Write a rule to change a **power of a power**, $(a^m)^n$, to a power with a single exponent.

3. Express each power of a power as a power with a single exponent and with a number name from the chart below.
   a) There are about $(10^3)^5$ ants on Earth.
   b) In one snowflake there are about $(10^9)^2$ molecules.
   c) In four months $(10^7)^3$ flies will have descended from a single pair of flies.

Number Names for Large Numbers	
10^9 I billion	10^{18} I quintillion
10^{12} I trillion	10^{21} I sextillion
10^{15} I quadrillion	

4. Explain why $(5^6)^3 = (5^3)^6$ by writing each as a product of equal factors.

5. How can knowing the rule $a^{mn} = (a^m)^n$ help find the square root of 2^{10}?

6. The prefixes in the table on page 33 are also used with other metric units. By examining the prefixes *kilo* and *giga*, you will notice that a *terametre* could be called the *square* of a *megametre* because $(10^6)^2 = 10^{12}$. Find relationships between prefixes to complete these statements.
   a) The *cube* of a megagram is a ▒▒▒ gram because $(10^{\blacksquare})^3 = 10^{\blacksquare}$.
   b) The *square* of a gigalitre is a ▒▒▒ litre because $(10^{\blacksquare})^2 = 10^{\blacksquare}$.
   c) The *square* of a terametre is a ▒▒▒ metre because $(10^{\blacksquare})^2 = 10^{\blacksquare}$.

7. The power of a power $(2^{-3})^2$ has the same value as the power 2^{-6}.
   a) Why doesn't $(2^{-3})^2$ have the same value as $(-2)^6$?
   b) Why do -2^6 and $(-2)^6$ have different values?

W/E 8. Write each as a fraction or in standard form. Use $(3^2)^4 = 6561$ to help you.
   a) $(3^2)^{-4}$ b) $(3^{-2})^4$ c) $(3^{-2})^{-4}$

9. How would you substitute the digits 1, 2, and 3 for *a*, *b*, and *c* in the expression $(a^b)^c$ to create the power with the greatest value? least value?

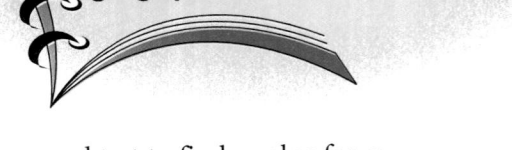

In Your Journal

The number *googol* is $(10^{10})^{10}$. How many zeroes are there in its standard form? A *googolplex* is 10^{googol}. How would you estimate how long it would take to write the standard form for a googolplex?

10. Guess and test to find a value for *n*.
   a) $(n^2)^3 = 729$ b) $(n^2)^4 = 256$
   c) $(n^0)^{-6} = 1$ d) $(n^3)^4 = 1$
   e) $(n^3)^2 = 64$ f) $(n^{-4})^2 = \dfrac{1}{256}$

11. Evaluate. Express each in standard form.
   a) $\dfrac{5^3}{5^2} \times 4^6 \times \dfrac{4^{-2}}{(4^2)^2}$
   b) $(3^{-2})^{-2} + 4^5 \times \dfrac{4^2}{4^6}$
   c) $5^{-2} \times 5^3 + \dfrac{(2^0)^5}{7^{-4}} \times 7^{-4}$
   d) $10^{-3} \times 10^5 + (6^3)^0 - \dfrac{4^8}{4^7}$

12. You can use the rule $a^{mn} = (a^m)^n$ and a calculator to order the powers $2^{500}, 3^{400}, 4^{300}$, and 5^{200}.
   a) Find the missing exponents and then order the powers from greatest to least. Explain your answer.
   2^{500} 3^{400} 4^{300} 5^{200}
   $(2^{\blacksquare})^{100}$ $(3^{\blacksquare})^{100}$ $(4^{\blacksquare})^{100}$ $(5^{\blacksquare})^{100}$
   b) Order these powers: $3^{666}, 4^{555}, 5^{444}, 6^{333}$.
   c) Create a similar ordering problem and give it to a classmate to solve.

2.4 Analysing Mental Calculations

Do the following calculation mentally. Explain what you did.

$2^4 \times 7^5 \times 5^2 \times 2^{-4} \times 7^{-4}$

Create another mental calculation.

Some people are able to perform what seem to be amazing feats of mental calculations.

Often, there's a simple explanation or what might be considered a trick.

What's $2^{10} \times 5^{10}$? That's easy. It's 10 billion.

Concept Development

Look at the calculation again. You can think of each factor, 2^{10} and 5^{10}, as a product of equal factors and then rearrange the factors.

$$2^{10} \times 5^{10}$$

$$(2 \times 2 \times 2 \times 2 \times 2 \times 2 \times 2 \times 2 \times 2 \times 2) \times (5 \times 5 \times 5 \times 5 \times 5 \times 5 \times 5 \times 5 \times 5 \times 5)$$

$$2 \times 5 \times 2 \times 5 \times 2 \times 5 \times 2 \times 5 \times 2 \times 5 \times 2 \times 5 \times 2 \times 5 \times 2 \times 5 \times 2 \times 5 \times 2 \times 5$$

1. a) Express the product as $(2 \times 5)^{\blacksquare}$ and as $10^{\blacksquare}$.
  b) Describe the relationship between the factors, 2^{10} and 5^{10}, and the product 10^{10}.

2. Predict the product, in standard form, for $2^5 \times 5^5$. Describe the steps you would follow to calculate it.

3. Complete each step to write each calculation as a single power.

a)	$3^3 \times 7^3 \rightarrow$	$(3 \times 3 \times 3) \times (7 \times 7 \times 7) \rightarrow$	$(3 \times 7) \times (3 \times 7) \times (3 \times 7) \rightarrow$	$(3 \times 7)^{\blacksquare} = 21^{\blacksquare}$
b)	$5^4 \times 3^4 \rightarrow$	$(5 \times 5 \times 5 \times 5) \times (3 \times 3 \times 3 \times 3) \rightarrow$	$\rightarrow$	$=$
c)	$2^{\blacksquare} \times 6^{\blacksquare} \rightarrow$	$\rightarrow$	$\rightarrow$	$(2 \times 6)^5 =$

4. Even though both calculations, $3^3 \times 7^3$ and $2^5 \times 5^5$, can be simplified to a single power, it is easier to mentally calculate $2^5 \times 5^5$. Why?

Understand and Apply

1. Complete.
  a) $5^5 \times 4^5 = (5 \times 4)^{\blacksquare} = 20^{\blacksquare}$
  b) $(-2 \times 7)^6 = (-2)^{\blacksquare} \times 7^{\blacksquare} = (-14)^{\blacksquare}$
  c) $\blacksquare^{-4} \times \blacksquare^{-4} = (3 \times 5)^{-4} = \blacksquare^{\blacksquare}$
  d) $(\blacksquare \times \blacksquare)^6 = 5^6 \times 4^6 = 20^{\blacksquare}$
  e) $2^6 \times 7^6 \times 5^6 = (2 \times 7 \times 5)^{\blacksquare} = \blacksquare^{\blacksquare}$
  f) $(5^3 \times 4^3)^2 = [(5 \times 4)^{\blacksquare}]^2 = (5 \times 4)^{\blacksquare} = 20^{\blacksquare}$

35

2. Write a rule for multiplying powers with different bases but the same exponents, $a^m \times b^m$.

W/E

3. Express each as a single power. Identify which you could calculate mentally. Explain.

a) $2^5 \times 5^5$
b) $(-5)^5 \times (-3)^5$
c) $2^{14} \times 5^{14}$
d) $(-4)^6 \times 6^6$
e) $3^3 \times 9^3 \times 2^3$
f) $2^{-7} \times 5^{-7}$
g) $(3^2 \times 5^2)^3$
h) $4^7 \times 7^7 \times 2^7$

4. Powers with bases such as 100, 1000, 10 000 can be written as powers of 10.

$$100^2 = (10^2)^2$$
$$= 10^4$$

Express each as a power of 10.

a) 100^3 **b)** 100^5 **c)** 1000^8 **d)** 1000^2

W/E

5. Express each as a power of 10.

a) $25^2 \times 4^2$
b) $2^7 \times 50^7$
c) $20^{-5} \times 5^{-5}$
d) $250^4 \times 4^4$
e) $2^3 \times 10^3 \times 5^3$
f) $20^3 \times 10^3 \times 50^3$

In Your Journal

Explain how you could estimate the value of $(2 \times 3)^3$. Estimate, then use your calculator to evaluate it. How do your answers compare?

6. Find two factors whose product is 1 million. Neither factor can end in zero. (Hint: Express 10^6 as a product of a power of 2 and a power of 5.)

7. To calculate $5^3 \times 4^3$ mentally, think

$$(5 \times 4)^3 = 20^3$$
$$= (2 \times 10)^3$$
$$= 2^3 \times 10^3$$
$$= 8 \times 1000$$
$$= 8000$$

Find each product mentally.

a) $5^2 \times 6^2$ **b)** $5^4 \times 4^4$
c) $5^3 \times 6^3$ **d)** $25^2 \times 8^2$

8. The following explains why $(5^3 \times 3^4)^2$ can be expressed as the product of two powers, $5^6 \times 3^8$.

$$(5^3 \times 3^4)^2 = (5^3 \times 3^4) \times (5^3 \times 3^4)$$
$$= (5^3 \times 5^3) \times (3^4 \times 3^4)$$
$$= 5^6 \times 3^8$$

Explain why $(3^4 \times 2^3)^2 = 3^8 \times 2^6$.

9. Express each as a product of two powers.

a) $(5^8 \times 3^4)^3$ **b)** $(3^7 \times 4^5)^4$ **c)** $(10^2 \times 4^7)^3$

10. The expression $\dfrac{3^3}{4^3}$ can be expressed as $\left(\dfrac{3}{4}\right)^3$ because

$$\frac{3^3}{4^3} = \frac{3 \times 3 \times 3}{4 \times 4 \times 4}$$
$$= \left(\frac{3}{4}\right)^3$$

a) Explain why $\dfrac{7^4}{8^4}$ can be written as $\left(\dfrac{7}{8}\right)^4$.

b) Write a rule for dividing powers with different bases but the same exponent, $\dfrac{a^m}{b^m}$ or $a^m \div b^m$ when $b \neq 0$.

11. Explain why $7^4 \div 8^4$ can also be expressed as $7^4 \times 8^{-4}$.

12. Complete.

a) $\left(\dfrac{2}{3}\right)^4 = \dfrac{2^\blacksquare}{3^\blacksquare}$
b) $\left(\dfrac{5}{6}\right)^{-7} = \dfrac{5^\blacksquare}{6^\blacksquare}$
c) $\left(\dfrac{\blacksquare}{\blacksquare}\right)^5 = \dfrac{10^\blacksquare}{11^\blacksquare}$
d) $\left(\dfrac{-5}{7}\right)^4 = \dfrac{(-5)^\blacksquare}{7^\blacksquare}$
e) $(3 \div 4)^\blacksquare = \dfrac{3^3}{4^3}$
f) $\left(\dfrac{4}{5}\right)^\blacksquare = 4^6 \div 5^6$
g) $\left(\dfrac{2}{3}\right)^4 = 2^\blacksquare \times 3^\blacksquare$
h) $[5 \div (-6)]^{-7} = 5^\blacksquare \times (-6)^\blacksquare$
i) $(-3 \div 7)^4 = (-3)^\blacksquare \times 7^\blacksquare$

13. a) Explain each step in this calculation. Express the answer in standard form.

$$\frac{10^7}{2^5} = \frac{10^2 \times 10^5}{2^5}$$
$$= \frac{10^2 \times (5 \times 2)^5}{2^5}$$
$$= \frac{10^2 \times 5^5 \times 2^5}{2^5}$$

b) Follow a similar procedure to solve $\dfrac{10^8}{2^3}$.

14. Evaluate. Express each answer in standard form.

a) $2^3 \times 5^3 \times 10^{-3} \times \dfrac{6^9}{(6^3)^3}$

b) $\dfrac{10}{10^{-4}} \times (3^2)^2 \times 2^{-4} \times 5^{-4}$

Problems to Investigate

WHAT WATT?

The power of an electrical signal can be measured in watts (W). Microwave towers send a signal with a power of 20 W. By the time the signal reaches the next tower 50 km away, the signal has been reduced to 0.000 000 1 W. What amplification factor is needed to boost the power of the signal back to 20 W?

TRICKY SUBSTITUTION

What value would you substitute for a so that the standard form for the expression $a \times 2^{50}$ ends in 0? ends in 00? (The value a cannot end in 0.)

APPROACHING ONE

Find the sum of each calculation to complete the pattern.

2^{-1} $2^{-1} + 2^{-2}$ $2^{-1} + 2^{-2} + 2^{-3}$ $2^{-1} + 2^{-2} + 2^{-3} + 2^{-4}$

$\dfrac{1}{2}$ ■   ■   ■

If the pattern continued indefinitely, would it reach 1? Explain.

BROKEN KEYS

How would you find 81^3 on your calculator without using the 8 or 1 keys?

AS GREAT AS

How many times as great as 3^{-4} is 3^4? Express your answer as a power and in standard form.

REDUCING EXPONENTIALLY

A photocopier is set to reduce by 67% or by a factor of about $\frac{2}{3}$. If a figure on the original picture is 20 cm long, it will be $20 \times \frac{2}{3}$ cm long when reduced. If the reduced copy is then reduced again, how long will the figure be? Each reduced copy is placed back on the copier to be reduced. Which of these calculations does <u>not</u> represent the length of the figure on the tenth reduced copy? Explain.

$20 \times \left(\frac{2}{3}\right)^{10}$ $20 \times \frac{2^{10}}{3^{10}}$

$20 \div \left(\frac{2}{3}\right)^{-10}$ $20 \div \left(\frac{2}{3}\right)^{10}$

How long will it be?

Make your own broken key puzzle and give it to a classmate to solve.

2.5 Simplifying Calculator Calculations

The surface area of Earth is about **509 700 000 km²** and its volume is about **1 083 208 840 000 km³**. The diameter at the equator is about **12 800 km**.

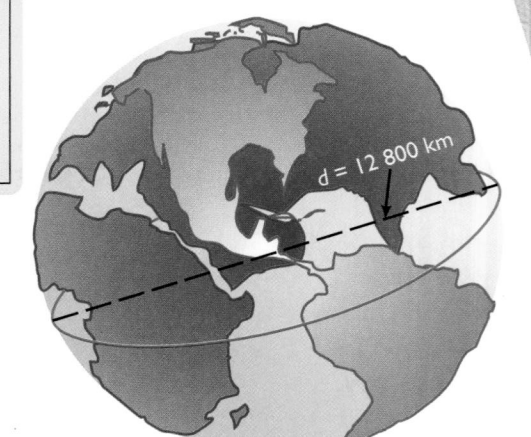

d = 12 800 km

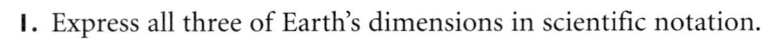

Concept Development

1. Express all three of Earth's dimensions in scientific notation.

2. Suppose Earth were a cube that measured 12 800 km across at its *equator*, would its surface area and volume be the same? Explain.

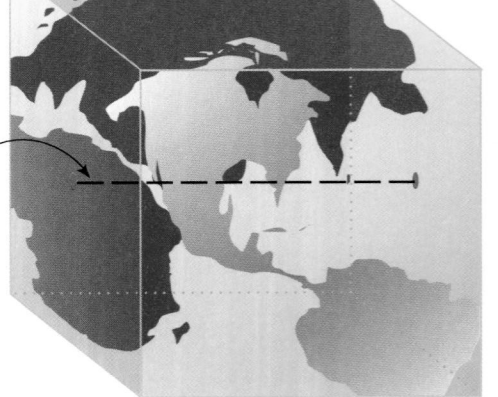

d = 12 800 km

3. **a)** What formula would you use to find the surface area of a cube?

   b) Explain each step of this calculation.

$$SA\ (km^2) = 6 \times (12\ 800 \times 12\ 800)$$
$$= 6 \times (1.28 \times 10^4) \times (1.28 \times 10^4)$$
$$= 6 \times (1.28 \times 1.28) \times (10^4 \times 10^4)$$

$$= 6\ \boxed{\times}\ 1.28\ \boxed{\times}\ 1.28\ \boxed{=} \quad \boxed{9.8304}$$
$$= 9.8304 \times 10^8$$
$$= 983\ 040\ 000\ km^2$$

4. Use a similar method to find the volume, in cubic kilometres, of the *cubic earth* in scientific notation and in standard form.

5. Why was it easier to find the surface area and volume by multiplying the diameter expressed in scientific notation rather than in standard form?

1. Use a calculator and rule, $a^m \times a^n = a^{m+n}$, to find each product in scientific notation.
   a) $(1.23 \times 10^9) \times (4.23 \times 10^8)$
   b) $(3.1 \times 10^7) \times (1.1 \times 10^9)$
   c) $(5.01 \times 10^{11}) \times (1.98 \times 10^{12})$
   d) $(7.12 \times 10^8) \times (1.39 \times 10^9)$

2. Explain why the missing exponent is 18 and not 17.
   $(6 \times 10^8) \times (5 \times 10^9) = 3 \times 10^{\blacksquare}$

3. Predict the exponent for the power of ten factor in each product when the product is in scientific notation.
   a) $(2 \times 10^9) \times (3.2 \times 10^7) = \blacksquare \times 10^{\blacksquare}$
   b) $(3.1 \times 10^{11}) \times (4.8 \times 10^8) = \blacksquare \times 10^{\blacksquare}$
   c) $(5 \times 10^9) \times (1.5 \times 10^8) = \blacksquare \times 10^{\blacksquare}$
   d) $(6.01 \times 10^5) \times (7.8 \times 10^9) = \blacksquare \times 10^{\blacksquare}$

4. Write each calculation in scientific notation. Then calculate the product and express it in scientific notation.
   a) $2\,170\,000\,000 \times 7\,120\,000$
   b) $542\,000\,000 \times 487\,000\,000\,000$
   c) $3\,470\,000\,000\,000 \times 50\,200\,000$
   d) $9\,900\,000 \times 98\,000\,000$

In Your Journal

You multiply $987\,654 \times 123\,456$ on a non-scientific 8-digit calculator and the display reads

| E 1219.3181 |

What does this mean? Show how you could use scientific notation to multiply the two numbers.

5. You can also use scientific notation to divide large numbers. Use a calculator and the exponent rule, $a^m \div a^n = a^{m-n}$, to express this quotient in scientific notation.
   $3\,450\,000\,000 \div 23\,000\,000$
   $= (3.45 \times 10^9) \div (2.3 \times 10^7)$
   $= (3.45 \div 2.3) \times (10^9 \div 10^7)$

6. a) Explain why the missing exponent is 3 and not 4.
   $(6 \times 10^{10}) \div (8 \times 10^6) = 7.5 \times 10^{\blacksquare}$
   b) Explain why the missing exponent is -5 and not -4.
   $(6 \times 10^6) \div (8 \times 10^{10}) = 7.5 \times 10^{\blacksquare}$

7. Predict the exponent in each quotient when the quotient is in scientific notation.
   a) $(8 \times 10^9) \div (4 \times 10^{12}) = \blacksquare \times 10^{\blacksquare}$
   b) $(3 \times 10^9) \div (4 \times 10^5) = \blacksquare \times 10^{\blacksquare}$
   c) $(9 \times 10^6) \div (3 \times 10^{13}) = \blacksquare \times 10^{\blacksquare}$
   d) $(6 \times 10^8) \div (9 \times 10^{12}) = \blacksquare \times 10^{\blacksquare}$

8. Find each missing number and then find the answer in scientific notation.
   a) $1\,350\,000\,000 \div 2\,400\,000$
   $= (1.35 \times 10^{\blacksquare}) \div (2.4 \times 10^{\blacksquare})$
   b) $2\,400\,000 \times 1200 = (\blacksquare \times 10^6) \times (1.2 \times 10^{\blacksquare})$
   c) $630 \text{ million} \div 30 \text{ billion} = \frac{6.3 \times 10^{\blacksquare}}{3 \times 10^{\blacksquare}}$
   d) $4\,980\,000\,000 \div 6\,573\,000\,000$
   $= (4.98 \times 10^{\blacksquare}) \div (6.573 \times 10^{\blacksquare})$

9. Find each quotient in scientific notation.
   a) $(1.35 \times 10^8) \div (2.4 \times 10^7)$
   b) $\dfrac{6.8 \times 10^{12}}{3.4 \times 10^9}$
   c) $(6.3 \times 10^8) \div (3.1 \times 10^{10})$
   d) $\dfrac{7.12 \times 10^{11}}{1.09 \times 10^{13}}$

10. If you multiply small numbers such as 0.000 17 and 0.000 003 2 on a non-scientific calculator, the display might indicate that an error has occurred or it might show "0". Why?

11. You can multiply very small numbers on a calculator using scientific notation.

$$0.000\ 17 \times 0.000\ 003\ 2$$
$$= (1.7 \times 10^{-4}) \times (3.2 \times 10^{-6})$$
$$= (1.7 \times 3.2) \times (10^{-4} \times 10^{-6})$$

a) Complete the calculation and express the product in scientific notation.
b) How many digits would a calculator display require to display the entire product in standard form?

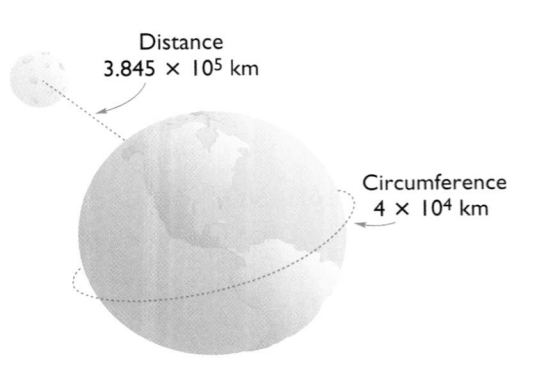

In Your Journal

Describe the steps you would take to change a decimal such as 0.000 000 010 2 to scientific notation. Describe the steps you would take to change $9.003\ 06 \times 10^{-12}$ to standard form.

12. Change each calculation to scientific notation. Then find the answer and express it in standard form.
a) $0.000\ 067 \times 0.004\ 51$
b) $0.000\ 076 \times 5\ 689\ 000$
c) $0.000\ 539 \times 0.0098 \times 12\ 000\ 000$
d) $0.000\ 000\ 45 \div 0.000\ 36$
e) $0.000\ 004 \div 0.000\ 000\ 2$
f) $6\ 000\ 000\ 000 \times 0.000\ 000\ 12$

13. $(3.05 \times 10^{-5}) \times (4.26 \times 10^4)$ is about 1 because
$$(3.05 \times 10^{-5}) \times (4.26 \times 10^4)$$
$$= (3.05 \times 4.26) \times (10^{-5} \times 10^4)$$
$$\cong 12 \times 10^{-1}$$
$$= 1.2$$
Explain why $(5.413 \times 10^{10}) \times (1.1 \times 10^{-9})$ is about 50.

14. Estimate the standard form for these calculations.
a) $(2.161 \times 10^{-7}) \times (5.923 \times 10^{10})$
b) $(8.131 \times 10^6) \div (4.091 \times 10^3)$
c) $(2.6901 \times 10^9) \div (5.0709 \times 10^3)$

15. About how many times as great is the surface area of the *cubic earth* as the surface area of Earth? How do the volumes compare? Explain how you estimated.

16. The distance from Earth to the moon is about 3.845×10^5 km. The circumference of Earth at the equator is about 4×10^4 km. About how many times as far is the distance from Earth to the moon as the distance around Earth?

Distance
3.845×10^5 km

Circumference
4×10^4 km

17. The mass of one of the smallest organisms on Earth is about 1×10^{-6} g. About how many of these organisms would have a combined mass equal to your mass?

2.6 Performing Calculator Calculations

When you multiply 11 111 111 and 55 555 555 on a non-scientific calculator, the display indicates that an error has occurred.
If you do the same calculation on a scientific calculator, the display will read:

$$6.172839383^{14}$$

The largest number that can be displayed on a 10-digit scientific calculator is 9.999 999 999 × 10^{99}. The smallest number is 1 × 10^{-99}. About how many times as great is the larger number as the smaller number? Explain how you estimated.

Concept Development

The number 14 in the display, called the **exponent**, indicates that the first number in the display, the **mantissa**, is multiplied by 10^{14}.

$$11\ 111\ 111 \times 55\ 555\ 555 = 6.172\ 839\ 383 \times 10^{14}$$

1. What does it mean when a non-scientific calculator indicates that an error has occurred?

2. a) Examine the two factors, 11 111 111 and 55 555 555. How could you have predicted the **exponent** 14?
b) Which of these calculations would also display the **exponent** 14? Explain.

20 000 000 × 30 000 000   55 555 555 555 × 11 111

20 000 000 × 50 000 000   20 000 × 200 000 × 500 000

c) Multiply 11 111 111 and 55 555 555 on your scientific calculator. Do you get the same result?
d) How could the product be estimated without using a calculator?

3. The [EXP] key can be used to enter numbers that are expressed in scientific notation.

These keystrokes would be used on some calculators to multiply (9.574×10^{12}) and (4.763×10^{13}).

9.574 [EXP] 12 [×] 4.763 [EXP] 13 [=]

a) What is the purpose of the [EXP] key?
b) Enter the appropriate keystrokes on your calculator to find the product using the [EXP] key. What answer do you get?
c) Explain why the **exponent** is 26 and not 25.

1. Write the keystrokes that you would use on your calculator, using the $\boxed{\text{EXP}}$ key, for each calculation. Predict the **exponent** and then find the answer for each.

   a) $8.362 \times 10^6 \times 5.497 \times 10^5$

   b) $\dfrac{4.12 \times 10^7}{2.21 \times 10^5}$

2. Locate the $\boxed{y^x}$ key on your scientific calculator. The following keystrokes would be used to multiply (9.5×10^6) and (4.1×10^9) on some calculators.

   9.5 $\boxed{\times}$ 10 $\boxed{y^x}$ 6 $\boxed{\times}$ 4.1 $\boxed{\times}$ 10 $\boxed{y^x}$ 9 $\boxed{=}$

   $$3.895^{16}$$

   a) What is the purpose of the $\boxed{y^x}$ key?

   b) Write the keystrokes for the same calculation in Problem 1 (a) using the $\boxed{y^x}$ key.

   c) Enter the keystrokes. Do you get the same answer?

   d) Compare the functions of the $\boxed{\text{EXP}}$ and $\boxed{y^x}$ keys. Consider disadvantages and advantages.

3. Write the keystrokes for your calculator, using the $\boxed{y^x}$ key, for each calculation. Predict the **exponent** for each. Enter the keystrokes to check. Explain why the bracket keys, $\boxed{(}$ and $\boxed{)}$, must be used in part (b).

   a) $5.3 \times 10^6 \times 3.3 \times 10^{12}$

   b) $2.13 \times 10^5 \div (1.2 \times 10^4)$

4. The $\boxed{+/-}$ key is used to enter negative exponents. These keystrokes could be entered to divide 4.8×10^6 by 3×10^{-26} on some calculators.

   4.8 $\boxed{\text{EXP}}$ 6 $\boxed{\div}$ 3 $\boxed{\text{EXP}}$ 26 $\boxed{+/-}$ $\boxed{=}$

   a) Describe what the $\boxed{+/-}$ key does.

   b) Predict the exponent. Enter the appropriate keystrokes to check. What answer did you get?

   c) Write the calculation for these keystrokes.

   2.76 $\boxed{\text{EXP}}$ 2 $\boxed{+/-}$ $\boxed{\times}$ 3.08 $\boxed{\text{EXP}}$ 4 $\boxed{=}$

5. Write the keystrokes you would use to calculate $(5.1 \times 10^6) \times (2.34 \times 10^{-2})$.

6. Calculate and express each answer in scientific notation.

   a) $3.09 \times 10^9 \times 6 \times 10^{-7}$

   b) $5.2 \times 10^9 \times 3.46 \times 10^6$

   c) $4.94 \times 10^9 \div 1.9 \times 10^{-3}$

   d) $1.09 \times 10^{-7} \times 4.6 \times 10^9$

   e) $\dfrac{1 \times 10^{10}}{4 \times 10^3}$

   f) $2.7 \times 10^{-5} \times 6.5 \times 10^{-3}$

   g) $3.9483 \times 10^7 \div 3.21 \times 10^6$

   h) $\dfrac{9.3225 \times 10^{-2}}{1.65 \times 10^{-7}}$

In Your Journal

Describe some different ways to estimate 99 999 999 × 88 888 888 without using a calculator and then check using a scientific calculator.

7. The $\boxed{\text{EXP}}$ and $\boxed{y^x}$ keys can also be used to find the values of powers and expressions. Explore the functions of these two keys by using your calculator to find the values of 10^4 and 2^3. Explain what you did.

8. Write the keystrokes and value for each.

   a) 10^{-5} b) 21^8 c) $4^8 \div 3^9$ d) $12^{-5} \times 2^{99}$

9. Enter these 3 sets of keystrokes. Compare the results of each. What do you notice? Explain why.

   5 $\boxed{\text{EXP}}$ 2 $\boxed{\times}$ 2 $\boxed{\text{EXP}}$ 2 $\boxed{=}$

   5 $\boxed{\text{EXP}}$ 8 $\boxed{\times}$ 6 $\boxed{\text{EXP}}$ 9 $\boxed{=}$

   1345675 $\boxed{\times}$ 1234987 $\boxed{=}$

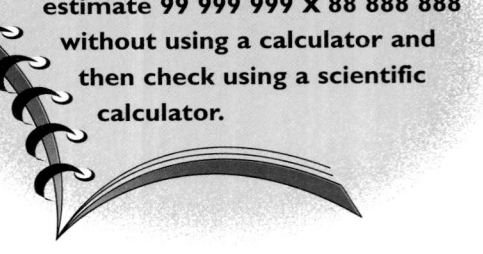

2.7 Finding Dimensions of Square Fields

This table shows the approximate area of the infield for several baseball leagues.

League	Ages	Infield (m²)
Little League	9 – 12	335
Bronco League	9 – 12	455
Pony League	13 – 14	595
Colt League	15 – 16	753

Warm Up

A number is entered into a calculator and then the square root key is pressed four times. The display shows $\boxed{2.}$. What was the number? Explain what you did.

Concept Development

1. The infield of a baseball field approximates the shape of a square.
a) What does this tell you about the lengths of the baselines?
b) What formula is used to find the area of a square?
c) Explain how you could use area of a square to find the length of its sides.

2. For a square that has an area that can be expressed as a power, you can use the exponent rule, $x^{mn} = (x^m)^n$, to find the length of its sides.

$$729 \text{ m}^2 = 3^6 \text{ m}^2$$
$$= (3^3)^2 \text{ m}^2$$
so $\sqrt{729}$ is 3^3 or 27 m

How would you use the exponent rule to find the length of each side of a square with an area of 1 million m²?

3. For very small square areas that can be expressed as a power, you can also use the exponent rule.

$$0.000\,001 \text{ mm}^2 = 10^{-6} \text{ mm}^2$$
$$= (10^{-3})^2 \text{ mm}^2$$
so $\sqrt{0.000\,001} = 10^{-3}$ or 0.001 mm

Use the exponent rule to find the length of each side of a square with an area of 0.000 000 01 mm².

Understand and Apply

1. Use the exponent rules to find the square roots of these numbers. Express each square root as a power.
a) 10 000 000 000
b) 1 000 000 000 000
c) 0.0001
d) 10^{-14}
e) 10^8
f) 10 thousand
g) 2^{10}
h) 5^{-4}
i) 3^6

2. Will the method used in Problem 1 work for powers with odd exponents? Explain.

3. Write a rule for finding the square root of a power with an even exponent, $\sqrt{a^m}$.

4. Recall the exponent law, $a^m \times b^m = (ab)^m$. A similar law can be developed for calculating square roots.

$\sqrt{4} \times \sqrt{9} = 2 \times 3$

$\sqrt{4 \times 9} = 2 \times 3$ because

$\sqrt{4 \times 9} = \sqrt{(2 \times 2) \times (3 \times 3)}$

So, $\sqrt{4} \times \sqrt{9} = \sqrt{4 \times 9}$

a) Use the same approach to explain why $\sqrt{100} \times \sqrt{25} = \sqrt{100 \times 25}$.

b) Write a rule for finding $\sqrt{a} \times \sqrt{b}$.

5. Complete. Express each product in standard form.

a) $\sqrt{12} \times \sqrt{3} = \sqrt{12 \times 3}$
   $= \sqrt{\blacksquare}$
   $= 6$

b) $\sqrt{20} \times \sqrt{5} = \sqrt{20 \times \blacksquare}$
   $= \sqrt{\blacksquare}$
   $= \blacksquare$

c) $\sqrt{\blacksquare} \times \sqrt{2} = \sqrt{64}$
   $= \blacksquare$

d) $\sqrt{2} \times \sqrt{8} = \sqrt{(\blacksquare \times \blacksquare)}$
   $= \sqrt{\blacksquare}$
   $= \blacksquare$

e) $\sqrt{10^5} \times \sqrt{10^7} = \blacksquare$

6. Explain why $\sqrt{2 \times 8}$ is easier to calculate than $\sqrt{2} \times \sqrt{8}$.

7. The following explains why $\sqrt{\frac{4}{9}} = \frac{\sqrt{4}}{\sqrt{9}}$.

$\sqrt{\frac{4}{9}} = \frac{2}{3}$ because $\sqrt{\frac{4}{9}} = \sqrt{\frac{2 \times 2}{3 \times 3}}$
   $= \sqrt{\frac{2}{3} \times \frac{2}{3}}$

$\frac{\sqrt{4}}{\sqrt{9}} = \frac{2}{3}$ because $\sqrt{4} = 2$ and $\sqrt{9} = 3$

So, $\sqrt{\frac{4}{9}} = \frac{\sqrt{4}}{\sqrt{9}}$

a) Explain why $\sqrt{\frac{9}{16}} = \frac{\sqrt{9}}{\sqrt{16}}$.

b) Write a rule for finding $\sqrt{\frac{a}{b}}$ and $\sqrt{a \div b}$.

8. Complete, expressing each in standard form or as a fraction.

a) $\sqrt{\frac{4}{25}} = \frac{\sqrt{4}}{\sqrt{25}}$
   $= \blacksquare$

b) $\sqrt{36 \div 81} = \sqrt{\blacksquare} \div \sqrt{\blacksquare}$
   $= \blacksquare$

c) $\frac{\sqrt{72}}{\sqrt{8}} = \sqrt{\frac{\blacksquare}{\blacksquare}}$
   $= \sqrt{\blacksquare}$
   $= \blacksquare$

d) $\sqrt{100 \div 144} = \blacksquare$

e) $\sqrt{\frac{25}{100}} = \blacksquare$

9. Calculate each and express the answer in standard form.

a) $\sqrt{\frac{10^{-10}}{10^{-12}}} - \sqrt{27} \div \sqrt{3}$

b) $\sqrt{10^{-8} \times 10^{12}} + \sqrt{10} \times \sqrt{10}$

c) $\sqrt{2} \times \sqrt{18} + \sqrt{75} \div \sqrt{3}$

d) $\sqrt{2} \times \sqrt{8} + \sqrt{\frac{48}{12}}$

10. Predict which number in each pair is greater and then use a square root rule to check. Were you correct?

a) 10^8 or $\sqrt{10^8}$ b) 10^{-8} or $\sqrt{10^{-8}}$

11. The square root of a power with a negative exponent is greater than the power itself, for example, $\sqrt{10^{-6}} > 10^{-6}$. Explain why.

12. Examine this method for estimating square roots of very large and small numbers.

$\sqrt{432\ 111\ 234\ 456\ 789\ 718} \cong \sqrt{43 \times 10^{16}}$
   $= \sqrt{43} \times \sqrt{10^{16}}$

$\sqrt{43}$ is between 6 and 7 or about 6.5

a) Complete the calculation. Express the estimated square root in standard form.

13. Estimate each square root. Express it in standard form.

a) $\sqrt{1\ 666\ 999\ 999}$ b) $\sqrt{400\ 567\ 321}$

c) $\sqrt{0.003\ 735\ 987}$ d) $\sqrt{0.000\ 000\ 000\ 001}$

In Your Journal

Find powers of 2 that when multiplied by 2^3 are perfect squares. What do you notice about the exponents of each power?

Estimating Products and Quotients

There are many ways to estimate 1 345 678 213 421 ÷ 0.035 21.
Here are some. Can you think of more?

1. **You can estimate each number to the nearest power of 10.**

$$\frac{1\ 345\ 678\ 213\ 421}{0.035\ 21} \cong \frac{1\ 000\ 000\ 000\ 000}{0.01}$$
$$\cong \frac{10^{12}}{10^{-2}}$$
$$= 10^{14}$$

2. **You might use scientific notation.**

$$\frac{1\ 345\ 678\ 213\ 421}{0.035\ 21} \cong \frac{1.35 \times 10^{12}}{3.52 \times 10^{-2}}$$
$$\cong 0.38 \times 10^{14}$$
$$= 3.8 \times 10^{13}$$

3. **You could write each number as the product of a number and a power.**

$$\frac{1\ 345\ 678\ 213\ 421}{0.035\ 21} \cong \frac{13.5 \times 10^{11}}{3.5 \times 10^{-2}}$$
$$= 3.8 \times 10^{13}$$

4. **You can use number sense.**

$$\frac{1\ 345\ 678\ 213\ 421}{0.035\ 21} \cong \frac{1.3 \text{ trillion}}{0.04}$$
$$= \frac{1.3 \text{ trillion}}{\frac{1}{25}}$$
$$= 1.3 \text{ trillion} \times 25$$
$$\cong 30 \times 10^{12}$$
$$= 3 \times 10^{13}$$

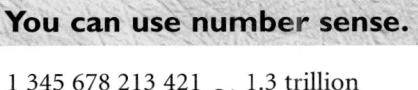
Understand and Apply

Estimate each two ways.

1. 987 654 321 012 345 ÷ 123 456 789 098 765

2. 222 222 222 222 222 × 0.555 555 555 555

3. 1 000 000 000 000 × 0.000 000 000 000 1

4. $\dfrac{1\ 243\ 546\ 576\ 879}{0.978\ 675\ 646\ 354\ 2}$

Problems to Investigate

MIGHTY SMALL

The diameter of the smallest virus is about 1.7×10^{-10} m. About how many would fit across the width of your desk or table? Explain what you did to estimate.

MENTAL SQUARES

Wim Klein calculated 87^{16} by successively squaring 87. Use an exponent rule to explain his method. How many times did he have to square 87?

CROWDED SQUARE

It is predicted that the population of Earth will be about 6.3 billion by the year 2000. Estimate the area and dimensions of a square in which 6.3 billion people could stand comfortably. (Hint: First estimate the number of people that can stand comfortably in a 1 m² square.)

JUST CHECKING

A mental math whiz was asked to find $\sqrt{999\ 998\ 000\ 001}$. His answer was 999 999. He said that he found it by squaring 999 999. He did this by calculating $27^2 \times 37\ 037^2$. Explain why his method works. Check his answer by estimating the square root of 999 998 000 001.

HOW FAR CAN YOU SEE?

To estimate the distance in kilometres, d, an observer can see an object on the horizon from a certain height in metres, h, the formula $d = 3.6\sqrt{h}$ can be used.
About how far could a person see from a height of 355 m? Explain why the formula $\sqrt{12.96\ h}$ could also be used.

THE PERFECT DISPLAY

What is the greatest perfect square that will fit, in standard form, on an 8-digit, non-scientific calculator display?

Investigate numbers written in scientific notation in science reference books. Make a list of situations where scientific notation is used.

Making Sense of DATA

Graphing to Represent Relationships

The data in the table below was entered into a spreadsheet program.

- The first row contains a value, b, which represents the base of a power from -5 to 5.
- The second row contains a value, b^2, which is the square of the base.
- The third row contains a value, $2b^2$, which is two times the square of the base.

1. a) Complete the table.

b	-5	-4	-3	-2	-1	0	1	2	3	4	5
b^2	25	16									
$2b^2$	50	32									

b) Why are the values for b^2 and $2b^2$ positive?

2. This is what a graph of the data looks like. Compare the graphs for (b, b^2) and $(b, 2b^2)$.

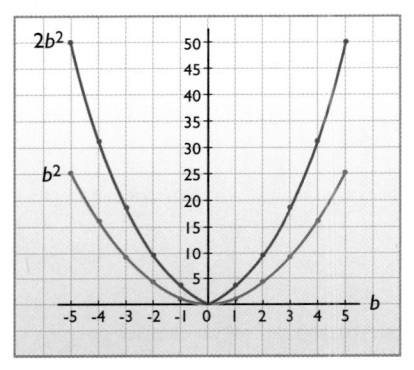

3. Predict what the graph for $(b, 3b^2)$ will look like. Use grid paper or a computer graphing program to check.

Applications

Use grid paper or graphing software.

4. a) Complete the table

b	-5	-4	-3	-2	-1	0	1	2	3	4	5
b^2	25	16									
b^3	-125										

b) Plot the coordinates (b, b^2) on a grid. Plot the coordinates (b, b^3) on the same grid.
c) Compare the two graphs.

5. a) Complete the table.

b	0	1	2	3	4	5	6	7	8	9	10
b^2	0	1									
$\sqrt{b}$	0	1									

b) Plot the coordinates (b, b^2) on a grid. Plot the coordinates $(b, \sqrt{b})$ on the same grid.
c) Compare the two graphs.
d) Add the values $2\sqrt{b}$ and $\sqrt{4b}$ to the table.
e) Plot the coordinates $(b, 2\sqrt{b})$ and $(b, \sqrt{4b})$ on the same grid. Compare the graphs.

Solve Problems by Making Tables

LAST TWO DIGITS

What are the last two digits of 6^{1000}?

6 $\boxed{y^x}$ 1000 $\boxed{=}$ $\boxed{E \qquad 0.}$

6 $\boxed{y^x}$ 10 $\boxed{=}$ $\boxed{60466176.}$

▶ Understand the Problem

1. What are you asked to find?
2. What do you know?
3. Where will you begin?

▶ Think of a Plan

Sean and Brandon started off by trying to find the value of 6^{1000} using a calculator. They discovered the value was greater than $9.999\ 999\ 999 \times 10^{99}$. They then thought that they would use the calculator to find the values of 10 consecutive powers of 6, record the values in a table, and then look for a pattern.

▶ Carry Out the Plan

Power	6^1	6^2	6^3	6^4	6^5	6^6	6^7	6^8	6^9	6^{10}
Last 2 Digits	6	36	16	96	76	56	36	16	96	76

4. Explain why the last digit is always even.

5. Describe the pattern.

6. Sean noticed that when the exponent was a multiple of 5, the last two digits were 76. How might this help predict the last two digits of 6^{1000}?

▶ Look Back

7. Does the answer make sense? How could you check?

Applications

CLOSER AND CLOSER

Find the square root of $\frac{1}{2}, \frac{2}{3}, \frac{3}{4}, \frac{5}{6}, \frac{7}{8}, \frac{8}{9}$, and $\frac{9}{10}$. What do you notice?

CONSECUTIVE SQUARES

Substitute the numbers from 0 to 10 in the expression $\sqrt{x^2 + 2x + 1}$. What do you notice? Predict the value of the expression when $x = 100$.

LAST DIGIT

Find the last digit of 7^{100}.

1. a) Draw a diagram to explain the difference between 2^3 and 3^2.
   b) Which is greater, 2^3 or 3^2? 2^{-3} or 3^{-2}? What do you notice?

2. There are about 10^{15} ants on Earth. If each ant has a mass of 10^{-5} g, what's the total mass of all the ants on Earth in
   a) grams? b) kilograms? c) tonnes?

3. The volume of a cube is 729 cm^2. What are its dimensions and surface area? Explain what you did.

4. In ancient Egypt the expression $\left(\frac{4}{3}\right)^4$ was used to approximate π. Write $\left(\frac{4}{3}\right)^4$ as a fraction and as a decimal.

5. Use the exponent rules and guess and test to find n. Explain what you did.
   a) $(n^5)^{-6} = 1$
   b) $n^2 \times n^{-1} = 5$
   c) $\frac{1}{n^{-2}} = 25$
   d) $n^3 \times n^{-2} = 10$
   e) $n^3 \div n^0 = 125$
   f) $(n^{-3})^2 = \frac{1}{729}$

6. Explain how you would calculate $(5 \times 4)^3$ in two different ways.

7. Explain why $(2^3)^2$ can be written as a power of 2 with a single exponent.

8. Explain why $25^7 \times 4^7$ is easy to calculate mentally.

9. Evaluate. Express the answer in standard form.
   a) $\frac{10^5}{10^4} \times 5^8 \times \frac{5^{-4}}{(5^2)^2}$
   b) $\frac{5^5}{5^7} \times 7^{-6} \times \frac{(7^2)^3}{8^0} \times \frac{1}{5^{-2}}$
   c) $6^9 \times (6^{-3})^3 + 10^0 + \frac{4^3}{4^{-3}} \times 4^{-6}$

10. Make up an expression similar to those in Problem 9 that has an answer of 1.

11. Explain why $(9.99 \times 10^{12}) \times (1.99 \times 10^{-10})$ is about 2000.

12. a) What keystrokes would you use on your scientific calculator to calculate $5 \times 10^6 \div (8 \times 10^{-6})$? Predict the exponent.
    b) When is it preferable to use the $\boxed{\text{EXP}}$ key rather than the $\boxed{y^x}$ key?

13. Use the digits 1, 2, 3, 4 and 5, each only once, to create a power with
    a) the greatest possible value that can be displayed on your scientific calculator.
    b) the least possible value that can be displayed on your scientific calculator.

14. Calculate each. Express answers in scientific notation.
    a) $15\,400\,000 \times 62\,000$
    b) $\frac{8 \times 10^5}{4 \times 10^{12}}$
    c) $(2.0 \times 10^4)^3$
    d) $\sqrt{75} \div \sqrt{3}$
    e) $\sqrt{10^3} \times \sqrt{10^5}$
    f) $\sqrt{800} \times \sqrt{800}$
    g) $\frac{7.36 \times 10^{-6}}{3.907 \times 10^{-12}}$
    h) $1.093\,02 \times 10^{23} \times 9.42 \times 10^{-6}$
    i) $3 \times 4^9 \times 10^7 \times 5^{-2}$

Practise With Games

Powers of Powers

Play this game in groups of 2, 3, or 4.

- Remove the Kings and Queens from a deck of cards.

- Let the Jack represent 0.

- Shuffle the cards and deal three cards to each player.

- Each player selects one card as the base and the other two as exponents, that is $(a^b)^c$.

- The player with the greatest power scores two points. In the case of a tie, each player scores one point.

- Continue playing until the cards are depleted.

- The player with the most points is the winner.

Example:

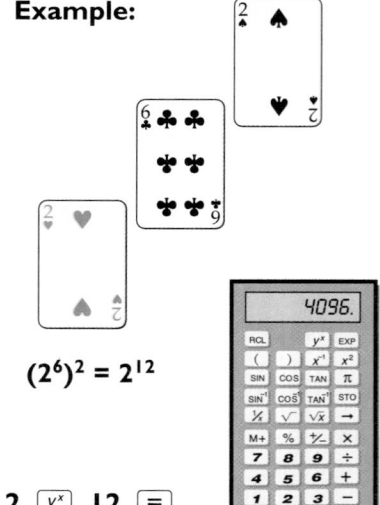

$(2^6)^2 = 2^{12}$

$2 \boxed{y^x} 12 \boxed{=}$

Rolling Roots

Play this game in groups of 2, 3, or 4.

- Each player rolls two dice and forms the product.

- Scoring:
    1 point if its square root is greater than 3
    2 points if its square root is ≤ 3
    3 points if it is a perfect square
    4 points if its square root is even
    5 points if its square root is odd

- Play until each player has had 10 rolls.

- The player with the greatest score wins.

Example:

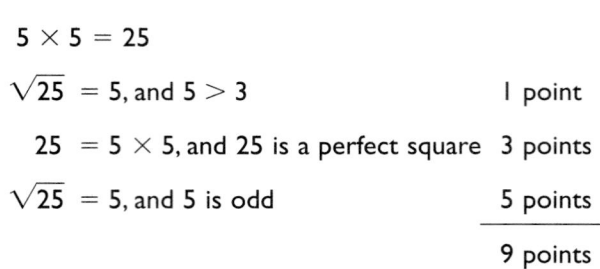

$5 \times 5 = 25$	
$\sqrt{25} = 5$, and $5 > 3$	1 point
$25 = 5 \times 5$, and 25 is a perfect square	3 points
$\sqrt{25} = 5$, and 5 is odd	5 points
	9 points

Problems to Investigate

DOUBLING PRICES

If the price of a hamburger doubles every 10 years, about how much would it cost in 100 years? Use $2^{10} \cong 1000$ to help you estimate.

MENTAL MULTIPLICATION TRICK

Copy and complete.

$12 \times 14 = 168$ $13^2 = 169$
$44 \times 46 = \blacksquare$ $45^2 = \blacksquare$
$32 \times 34 = \blacksquare$ $33^2 = \blacksquare$
$101 \times 103 = \blacksquare$ $102^2 = \blacksquare$

Compare each product in the left column to the perfect square in the right column. What do you notice? Predict the product for 49×51. Check to see if you are right.

SUM OF CUBES

Complete each sum and find the missing base. Predict and then check the next two sums in the pattern.

$1^3 = 1^2$
$1^3 + 2^3 = \blacksquare^2$
$1^3 + 2^3 + 3^3 = \blacksquare^2$

SAME NUMBER

The surface area of a cube and its volume have the same numerical value. What are the dimensions of the cube?

DIGITAL ROOTS

The digital root of a number is found by adding its digits until only 1 digit remains. The digital root of both 49 and 256 is 4 because $4 + 9 = 13$ and $3 + 1 = 4$ and $2 + 5 + 6 = 13$ and $1 + 3 = 4$.

What are the possible digital roots of a perfect square? Explain how you can check if 2 987 654 321 is a perfect square.

HOW MANY BLINKS?

A blink is roughly estimated to take about 10^{-5} of a day. How many seconds is this? How long in blinks is each school day? How old are you in blinks?

Create some powers and roots problems of your own. Give them to a classmate to solve.

1. Explain why $(-2)^6$ is positive but $(-2)^7$ is negative.

2. Substitute both positive and negative numbers for n in the expression $2n^2 + 1$. Why is the expression always positive? always an odd number?

3. Explain why
   a) $2^2 \times 2^3 = 2^5$
   b) $2^6 \div 2^3 = 2^3$
   c) $2^8 \div 2^5 = 2^8 \times 2^{-5}$

4. The Sultan of Brunei had a personal fortune of $37 billion in 1993.
   a) Write his fortune in scientific notation.
   b) How long would it take to spend his entire fortune at a rate of $1 million/day? $1 million/year?

5. How would knowing $2^6 = 64$ help you find the value of $(2^3)^4$?

6. Use the exponent rules to explain why $2^{100} = 4^{50}$.

7. How would you calculate $2^6 \times 5^5$ mentally?

8. Evaluate these expressions using the exponent rules.
   a) $\dfrac{6^3}{6^2} \times 5^6 \times \dfrac{5^{-2}}{(5^2)^2} \times 2^3 \div 2^2$
   b) $20^3 \times 5^3 \times \dfrac{10^3}{10^6} + (3^2)^0$
   c) $(2\times3)^4 \div 6^3 \times \dfrac{6^{-6}}{(6^2)^{-3}}$

9. Explain how you know that 2, 3, and 12 are all divisors of 6^{20}.

10. Use scientific notation to estimate these quotients.
    a) $8\ 424\ 684\ 926 \div 24\ 000\ 456.$
    b) $0.0467 \div 946\ 732\ 916$
    c) $6\ 397\ 217 \times 62\ 943\ 602$

11. Explain why $\boxed{0.000000001}$ becomes $\boxed{1^{-10}}$ after the keys $\boxed{\div}$ 10 $\boxed{=}$ are pressed.

12. What keystrokes would you use to enter
    a) $7 \times 10^{-3} \times 3 \times 10^{-8}$? Find the product. Explain why the exponent is -10 and not -11.
    b) $\dfrac{4 \times 10^{-7}}{8 \times 10^{-23}}$? Find the product. Explain why the exponent is 15 and not 16.

13. Calculate. Express answers in scientific notation.
    a) $6.2 \times 10^8 \times 8.09 \times 10^{17}$
    b) $9.002\ 09 \times 10^{-7} \div (6.094\ 27 \times 10^{-18})$

14. Write the calculations for these keystrokes. Find each answer.
    a) 6 $\boxed{\text{EXP}}$ 7 $\boxed{+/-}$ $\boxed{\div}$ 3.01 $\boxed{\text{EXP}}$ 9 $\boxed{=}$
    b) 3 $\boxed{y^x}$ 8 $\boxed{\times}$ 4 $\boxed{y^x}$ 6 $\boxed{+/-}$ $\boxed{=}$
    c) 5 $\boxed{\times}$ 10 $\boxed{y^x}$ 3 $\boxed{\div}$ $\boxed{(}$ 3 $\boxed{\times}$ 10 $\boxed{y^x}$ 4 $\boxed{)}$ $\boxed{=}$

15. Express each square root in standard form.
    a) $\sqrt{1\text{ million}}$
    b) $\sqrt{5^{-4}}$
    c) $\sqrt{0.000001}$

16. If $x = 3^{18}$ what is x^2? $\sqrt{x}$?

17. Explain how you would calculate $\sqrt{32} \times \sqrt{2}$ mentally.

18. Estimate.
    a) $\sqrt{25\ 673\ 928}$
    b) $\sqrt{0.000\ 001\ 01}$

1. Why is this expression easy to calculate mentally?

$$10^{-3} \times 2^8 \times 3^2 \times 10^3 \times 2^{-7} \times 5^9 \times 2^9$$

Make up another expression that's easy to calculate.

2. How can the exponent rules help you explain why 4^{15} is a perfect square?

6. Explain why the numbers 20 and 5 are not perfect squares but 20×5 is.

3. How would you help Jennifer estimate the product?

5. How does a scientific calculator operate differently from a non-scientific calculator?

When I multiplied 6 267 820 400 and 547 234, my calculator displayed "E."

What questions do you still have about powers and roots?

4. How would you find 6^6 on your calculator without using the 6 key?

Transformations

Many designs such as those found in paintings, logos, crafts, decorating, and architecture show transformations.

- How might the flooring pattern have been created using translations? reflections? rotations? Which of the other designs might have been created by all three transformations?

- Which designs show enlargements and reductions?

- Which transformations are related to symmetry? Tell how.

- Describe the symmetry you see in the designs.

- Which design do you like best? Why?

Why do you think transformations are used so often in designs?

3.1 Reflecting Shapes

Warm Up

Draw and identify the coordinat
of the vertices of a polygon tha
a) is completely in the 4th
quadrant
b) is partly in each of the fou
quadrants
c) has a vertex at the origin
d) has all of its vertices on
the axes

2nd	1st
3rd	4th

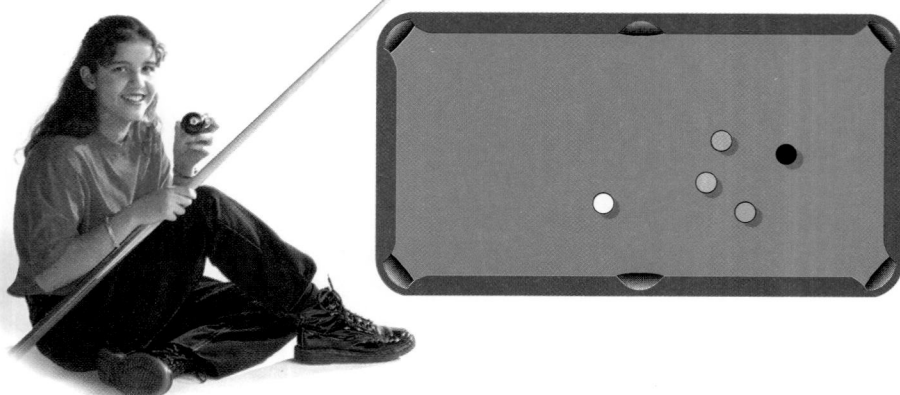

Deanna is practising her pool shots. She wants to hit the black ball with the white cue ball.

Concept Development

Deanna imagines the image of the black ball if it were reflected in the side of the table. Then she aims at the image.

1. Why do you think Deanna didn't try to hit the black ball with the white cue ball directly?

2. Imagine the image of the black ball if it were reflected in the right side of the table. Which of these three pool cues is best aimed to hit the black ball? Explain.

a)

b)

c)

1. a) Copy this diagram onto grid paper. Fold, use a Mira, or flip a tracing in line *m* to locate the image of quadrilateral *LUCY*. Label it *L'U'C'Y'*.

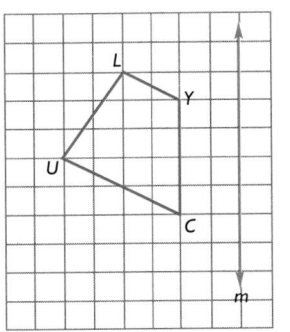

A label like *L'* is read *L prime*.

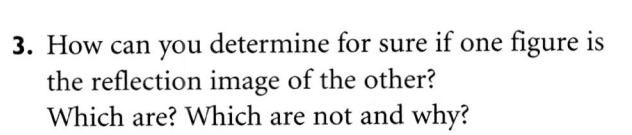

In Your Journal

Write about the positions of the original figure and its image relative to their reflection line.
Tell how the original figure and its reflection image are alike and how they are different.

b) Compare the size, shape, and orientation of *L'U'C'Y'* with *LUCY*.

c) At what angle does the line passing through *L'* and *L* intersect line *m*? Is this true for the lines passing through other pairs of corresponding vertices?

d) How does the distance measured in grid spaces from *L'* to line *m* compare to that from *L* to line *m*? Is this true for distances from other pairs of corresponding vertices?

2. Copy each diagram onto grid paper. Locate and label each reflection image.

a)

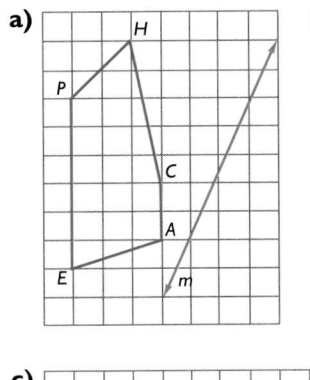

b)

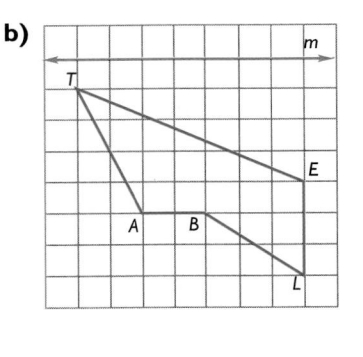

c)

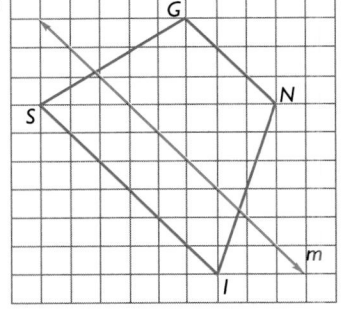

3. How can you determine for sure if one figure is the reflection image of the other? Which are? Which are not and why?

a) **b)**

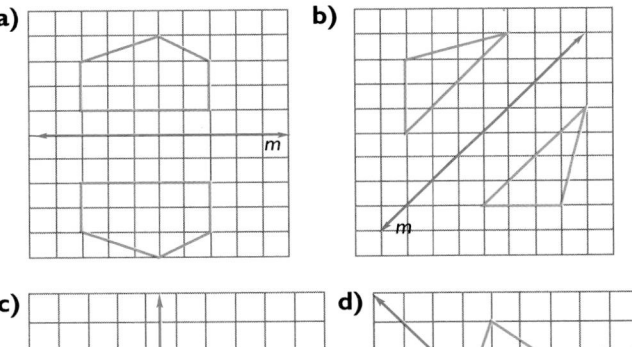

c) **d)**

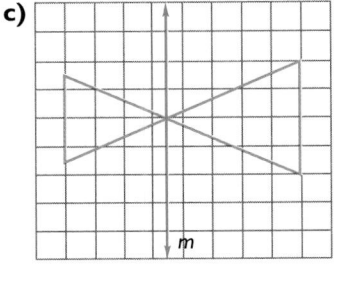

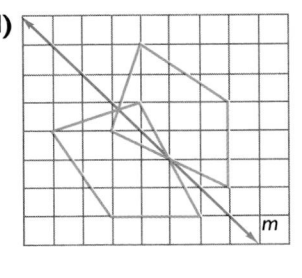

57

4. Copy each diagram onto grid paper. How can you locate the reflection line?
Locate it and label the vertices of the image.

a)

b)

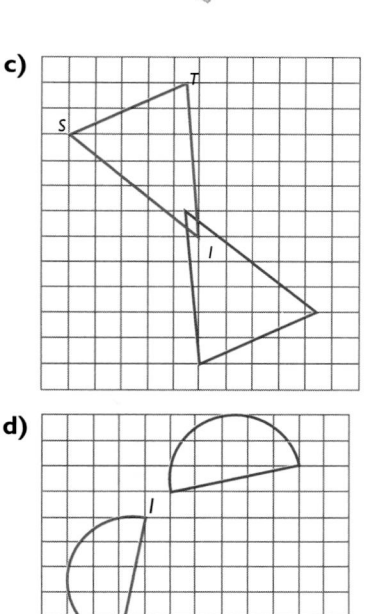

c)

d)

5. Jennifer thought △DEF must be the reflection image of △ABC because the figures appeared to be congruent.

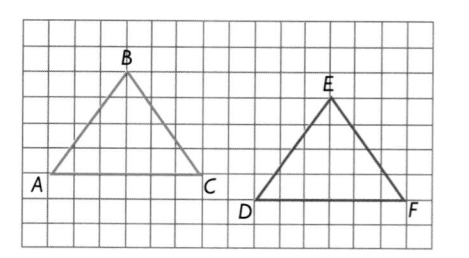

a) Describe several methods she could use to determine if the triangles are congruent.
Use one of the methods to check.
b) Is △DEF a reflection image of △ABC? Explain.

6. What property of reflections enables you to locate the reflection image of each figure without folding, using a Mira, or tracing? Copy each diagram onto grid paper. Locate and label each reflection image.

a)

b)

c)

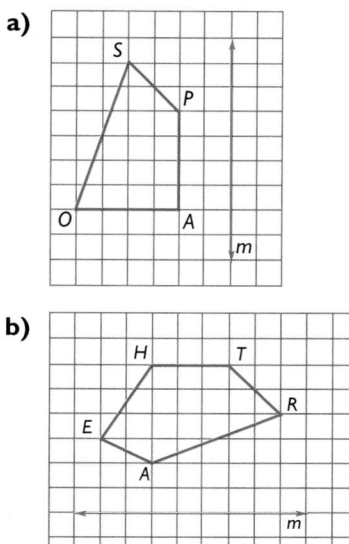

7. Copy each diagram onto grid paper. Locate a shot that will hit the black ball with the white cue ball.

a)

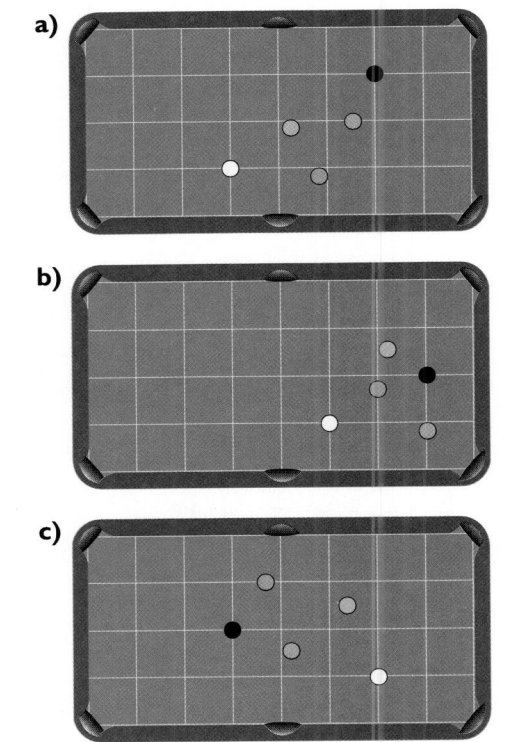

b)

c)

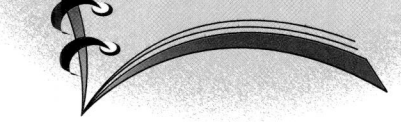

In Your Journal

Describe how the coordinates of a figure change when it is reflected
  • **in the x-axis**
  • **in the y-axis**

8. a) Draw quadrilateral *NEAT* on a coordinate grid, with $N(0, 3)$, $E(7, 4)$, $A(2, 6)$, and $T(-1, 5)$.
b) Reflect it in the x-axis and label the image.
c) Write the ordered pair for each vertex of the image.
d) Describe how the coordinates of the vertices change when the figure is reflected in the x-axis.
e) Repeat parts (a) to (d) for any quadrilateral that is in at least two quadrants.

9. a) Draw pentagon *HOMER* on a coordinate grid, with $H(2, 5)$, $O(0, 0)$, $M(3, -4)$, $E(7, -1)$, and $R(7, 2)$.
b) Reflect it in the y-axis and label the image.
c) Write the ordered pair for each vertex of the image.
d) Describe how the coordinates of the vertices change when the figure is reflected in the y-axis.
e) Repeat parts (a) to (d) for any triangle that is in all four quadrants.

10. In which axis was each point reflected?
a) $M(2, 5) \rightarrow M'(-2, 5)$
b) $V(-3, 6) \rightarrow V'(3, 6)$
c) $G(5, -1) \rightarrow G'(5, 1)$
d) $N(-1, -2) \rightarrow N'(1, -2)$
e) $K(-3, -5) \rightarrow K'(-3, 5)$
f) $W(3, -4) \rightarrow W'(-3, 4)$
Plot the pairs of points to check.

11. a) Draw any quadrilateral in the second quadrant of a coordinate grid. Identify its coordinates.
b) Perform three separate reflections so that the image is in each of the other quadrants. Identify the coordinates of each image.
c) For each reflection, identify the reflection line and describe how the coordinates of the quadrilateral change.

12. What are the coordinates of the vertices of the image of each reflection?
a) $\triangle BAT$ reflected in the x-axis, with $B(-2, 4)$, $A(-3, -1)$, and $T(2, 2)$.
b) parallelogram *FLIP* reflected in the y-axis, with $F(-2, 3)$, $L(-4, -2)$, $I(4, -2)$, and $P(5, 3)$
Draw each figure and locate its image to check.

13. You can reflect shapes using graphics software on a computer. Create some shapes that have line symmetry using a computer.

HOME LINK
What sports do you play or watch that use reflections? Explain how.

Warm Up

Plot any point on a coordinate gr
What are its coordinates when
is moved
a) left 4?
b) up 6?
c) right 3?
d) down 2?
e) left 1 and up 2?
f) right 4 and down 3?

To draw a prism with an equilateral triangle base, Sam traced around a triangular pattern block. Then he slid it and traced around it again. Then he joined corresponding vertices.

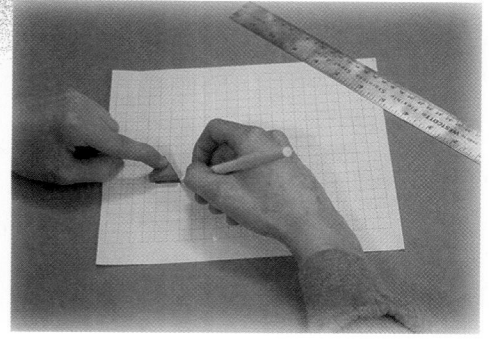

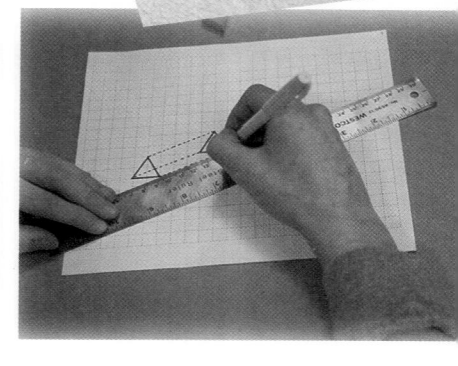

Concept Development

1. What do we call this sliding motion?

2. Which translation arrow applies to the translation Sam made sliding the triangle?

   a)   b)   c)
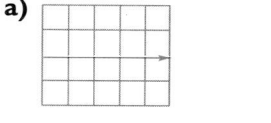
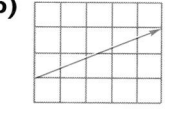

3. Which translation rule applies to Sam's translation?
   a) (R5, U2)   b) (R5, D2)   c) (L5, U2)

4. a) Draw a prism with a square base on a grid using a translation.
   b) What translation rule did you use?

Understand and Apply

1. a) What translation rule corresponds to this translation arrow?

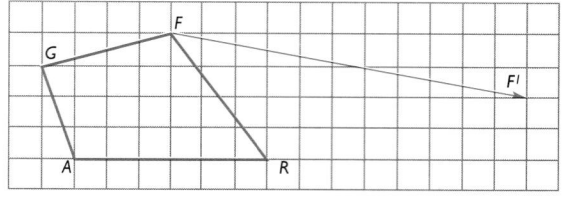

   b) Copy the diagram onto grid paper. Slide a tracing along the arrow or count grid spaces to locate the image, quadrilateral $G'A'R'F'$.

   c) Compare the size, shape, and orientation of $G'A'R'F'$ with $GARF$.
   d) Measure the length of the arrow from F to F'.
   e) Join the other pairs of corresponding vertices. In what two ways are these line segments like line segment FF'?

2. Integers can be used for translation rules. (L2, U1) is expressed $[-2, 1]$ and (R4, D7) is $[4, -7]$. How would these arrows and rules be expressed using integers?

a)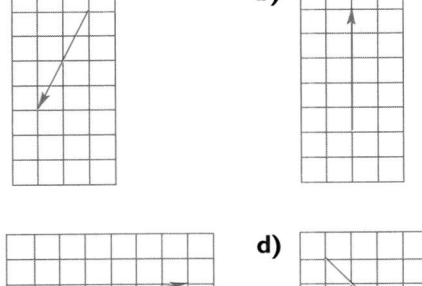

b)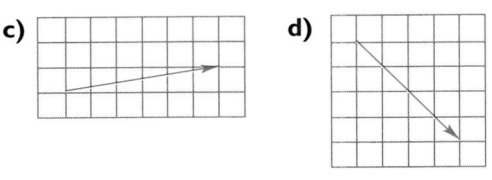

c)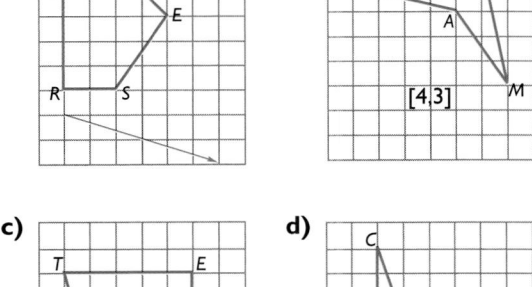

d)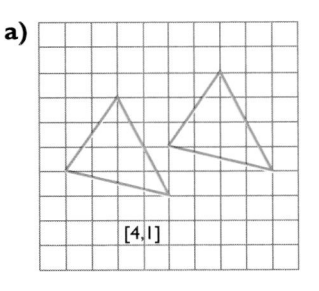

e) (R6, D1) **f)** (R0, U3)

g) (L3, D2) **h)** (L5, U7)

3. Draw a translation arrow on grid paper for each rule.
a) $[0, 4]$ **b)** $[5, 0]$ **c)** $[6, 6]$
d) $[-4, -4]$ **e)** $[4, -1]$ **f)** $[-2, 5]$
g) $[-1, -3]$ **h)** $[-2, 7]$ **i)** $[3, -2]$

4. Copy each diagram onto grid paper. Locate and label each translation image.

a)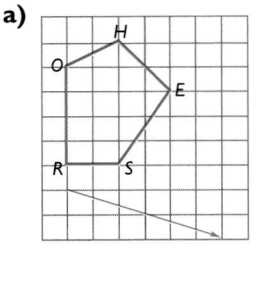

b)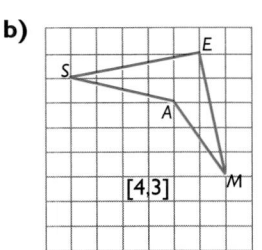

c)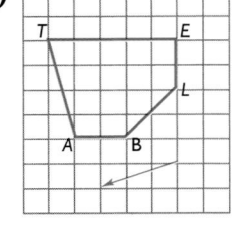

d)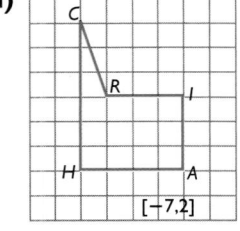

5. How can you determine for sure if one figure is the translation image of the other? Which are? Which are not and why?

a)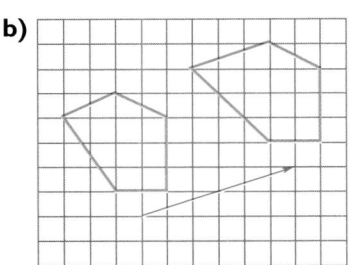

b)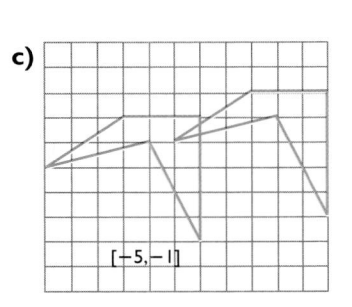

c) [−5,−1]

d)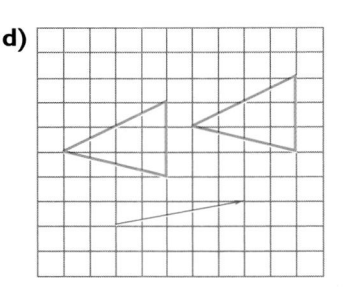

6. Copy each diagram onto grid paper. How can you find the translation arrow and rule? Find them and label the vertices of each image.

a)

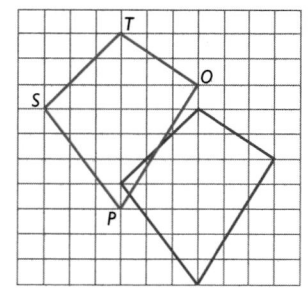

b)

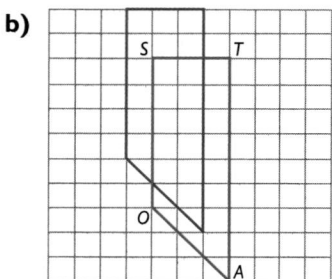

c)

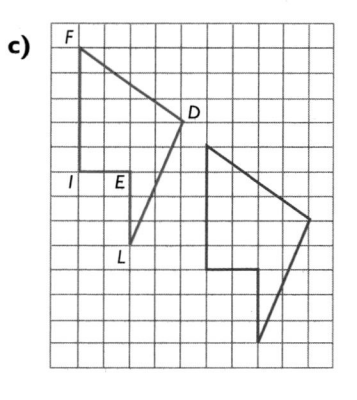

7. What translation rules would move the images in Problem 6 back to the originals?

8. a) Draw △*HAT* on a coordinate grid, with *H*(3, 8), *A*(1, 4), and *T*(4, 3).
b) Translate it [4, 0] and label the translation image.
c) Write the ordered pair for each vertex of the image.
d) Describe how the coordinates of the vertices change when the figure is translated.

9. Repeat Problem 8 for
a) pentagon *TIGER*, with *T*(−5, −1), *I*(−7, −3), *G*(−7, −5), *E*(−2, −5), and *R*(−2, −3), and translate it [0, 6]
b) quadrilateral *STOP*, with *S*(2, 6), *T*(−1, 4), *O*(0, 0), and *P*(5, 1), and translate it [−7, 5]

Describe how the coordinates of a figure change when it is translated.

10. What is the translation rule for each?
a) *D*(3, 11) → *D*′(6, 11)
b) *J*(0, 7) → *J*′(0, −3)
c) *M*(2, 2) → *M*′(−1, 3)
d) *Q*(3, 1) → *Q*′(4, −5)
Plot each pair of points to check.

11. a) Draw any triangle in the third quadrant of a coordinate grid. Identify its coordinates.
b) Perform three separate translations so that the image is in each of the other quadrants. Identify the coordinates of each image.
c) For each translation, identify the translation rule and describe how the coordinates of the triangle change.

12. What are the coordinates of the vertices of the image of each translation?
a) point *A*(−3, 4) translated [1, 8]
b) point *B*(−2, −1) translated [−1, 4]
c) line segment CD translated [6, −2], with *C*(3, −5) and *D*(−1, 1)
d) parallelogram *TUNA* translated [5, −3], with *T*(−4, 2), *U*(−6, −2), *N*(0, −2), and *A*(2, 2)
Draw each and locate its image to check.

13. Three-dimensional (3-D) drawings can be created with graphics software on a computer. You select, grab, and drag a figure a definite distance and direction. Then you join the vertices of the object and image. Create some 3-D drawings using a computer.

14. Polygon *W*′*A*′*T*′*E*′*R*′, with *W*′(−4, 3), *A*′(−5, 0), *T*′(1, −2), *E*′(0, 0), and *R*′(1, 2), was the result of subtracting 4 from each *x*-coordinate of the vertices of *WATER*.
a) What was the translation rule?
b) Draw the original figure and its image.

3.3 Rotating Shapes

A fan can be rotated to match its present position. Jordan and Jonah are finding the smallest angle of rotation for this match to occur.

Warm Up

Draw some regular polygons. Locate all the lines of symmetry in each. How many turns of equal size can be made to match each polygon to its original position? What do you notice?

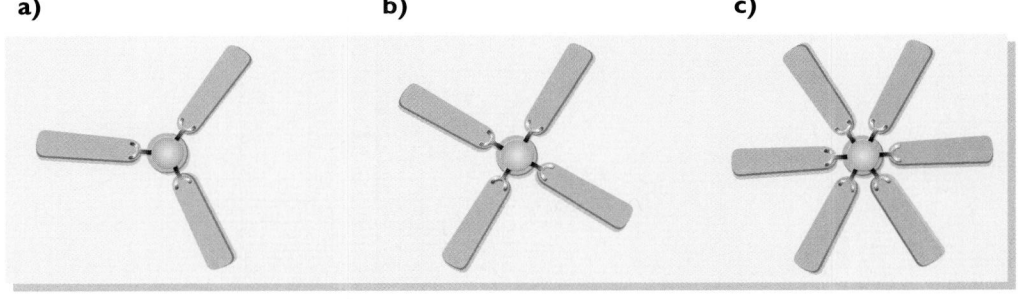

Jordan is measuring.　　　　　　　　　　　　　　　　Jonah is calculating.

Concept Development

1. Explain and finish each student's work.

2. What is the smallest angle of rotation that would turn each fan to match its present position?

   a)　　　　　　　　　　b)　　　　　　　　　　c)

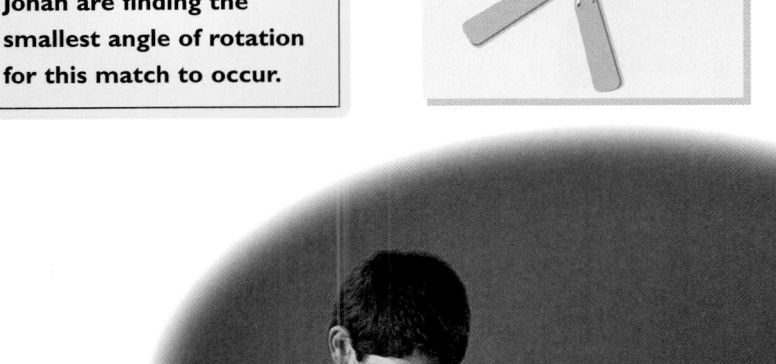

3. Does it matter which direction, clockwise or counterclockwise, it turns?

4. Describe each angle of rotation, giving the number of degrees, its direction, and its centre of rotation.

   a)　　　b)　　　c)　　　d)

1. **a)** Copy this entire diagram onto grid paper. Trace it and then place a pencil on the turn centre *O*. Turn the tracing according to the angle of rotation shown. Locate the image △*C′A′T′*.

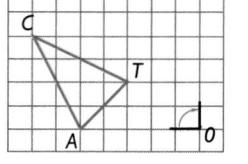

b) Compare the size, shape, and orientation of △*C′A′T′* with △*CAT*.

c) Join *T* to *O* and *T′* to *O′*. Measure △*TOT′*. Measure line segments *OT* and *OT′*.

d) Join the other pairs of corresponding vertices to *O*. Measure the angles and the line segments. What do you notice?

2. Copy each diagram onto grid paper. Locate and label the rotation image.

a)

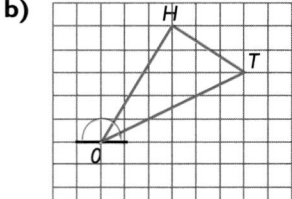

b)

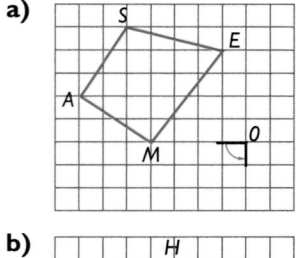

c)

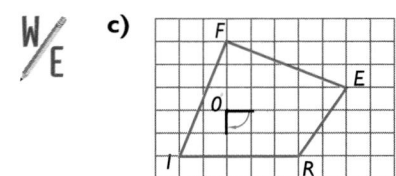

W/E

3. Find the rotation image of △*HOT* in Problem 2 (b) for a rotation of 180° counterclockwise about *O*. What do you notice?

4. How can you determine for sure if one figure is a rotation image of another about a given point? Which are? Which are not and why?

a)

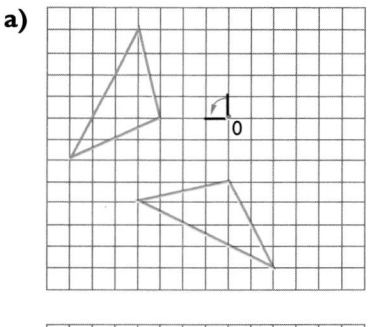

b)

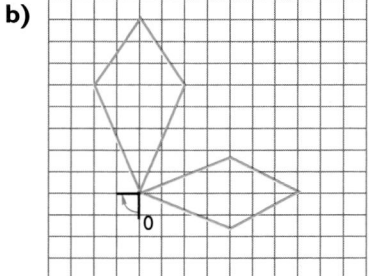

c)

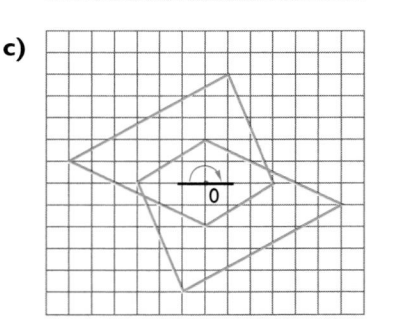

d)

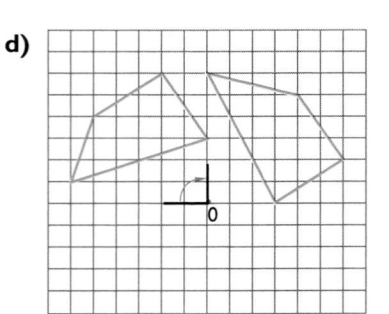

What relationship exists between the line segments formed by joining corresponding vertices to the centre of rotation?

What relationship exists among the angles formed by joining corresponding vertices to the centre of rotation?

Tell how the original figure and its image are alike and how they are different.

5. Copy each diagram onto grid paper. How can you find the angle of rotation (number of degrees, direction, and centre)? Find it and label the vertices of the image.

a)

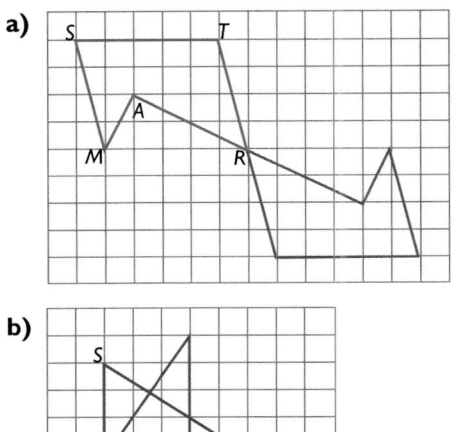

b)

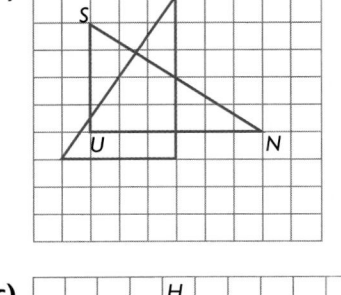

c)

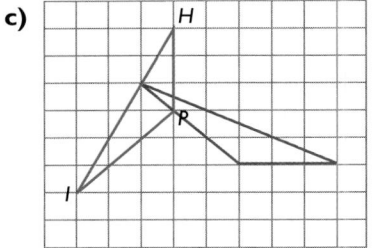

6. What angle of rotation would move each image in Problem 5 back to the original?

7. a) Draw △*HIT* on a coordinate grid, with *H*(5, 7), *I*(2, 2), and *T*(6, 1).
b) Rotate it 180° about the origin and label the image.
c) Write the ordered pair for each vertex of the image.
d) Describe how the coordinates of the vertices change when the figure is rotated 180° about the origin.
e) Repeat parts (a) to (d) for trapezoid *MATE*, with *M*(−2, 4), *A*(−4, 1), *T*(4, 1), and *E*(4, 4), and for △*BIT*, with *B*(1, 5), *I*(−4, 1), and *T*(1, −2).

8. a) Draw parallelogram *GAME* on a coordinate grid, with *G*(3, 4), *A*(2, 1), *M*(5, 1), and *E*(6, 4).
b) Rotate it 90° clockwise about the origin and label the image.
c) Write the ordered pair for each vertex of the image.
d) Describe how the coordinates of the vertices change when the figure is rotated 90° clockwise about the origin.
e) Repeat parts (a) to (d) for △*FAR*, with *F*(−2, 4), *A*(−2, 1), and *R*(2, 2), and for △*SIP*, with *S*(1, 3), *I*(−2, −1), and *P*(4, −2).

9. a) Draw △*SAD* on a coordinate grid, with *S*(−3, 1), *A*(−4, −5), and *D*(0, −3).
b) Rotate it 90° counterclockwise about the origin and label the image.
c) Write the ordered pairs for each vertex of the image.
d) Describe how the coordinates of the vertices change when the figure is rotated 90° counterclockwise about the origin.
e) Repeat parts (a) to (d) for △*BIN*, with *B*(5, 3), *I*(−1, 6), *N*(−4, −3), and for quadrilateral *SOLE*, with *S*(5, −3), *O*(0, 0), *L*(−2, 5), and *E*(−5, −4).

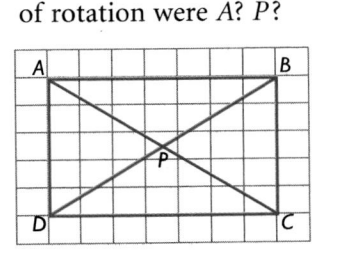

In Your Journal

Describe how the coordinates of a figure change when it is rotated about the origin
• 180°
• 90° clockwise
• 90° counterclockwise

W E

10. What is the angle of rotation for each rotation about the origin?
a) *H*(3, −6) → *H*′(6, 3)
b) *M*(−1, 2) → *M*′(1, −2)
c) *Y*(−3, 1) → *Y*′(1, 3)
Plot each pair of points to check.

11. Rectangle *ABCD* was transformed and the image lies on top of *ABCD*. What single rotation would this result from if the centre of rotation were *A*? *P*?

12. What are the coordinates of the vertices of the image of each rotation about the origin?
a) point *A*(−3, 4) 90° clockwise
b) point *B*(4, −5) 180°
c) line segment *CD* 180°, with *C*(3, −5) and *D*(−1, 1)
d) line segment EF 90° counterclockwise, with *E*(1, −6) and *F*(3, 2)
e) △*PAL* 90° clockwise, with *P*(−5, 4), *A*(−1, −3), and *L*(4, 3)
Draw each and locate its image to check.

13. a) Draw △*DOG* on a coordinate grid, with *D*(3, 1), *O*(6, 1), and *G*(5, 3).
b) Locate the centre of rotation at (3, 1).
c) Rotate △*DOG* 90° clockwise about the rotation centre and label the image.
d) How are the figures similar? different?
e) Repeat parts (a) to (d) for △*BAT*, with *B*(−1, 2), *A*(1, 0), and *T*(−1, −1), and rotation centre (−2, −2).

14. You can rotate figures using graphics software on a computer. Create some shapes with rotational symmetry on a computer.

What things around your home, both inside and outside, rotate about a fixed point like a fan? What is the smallest angle of rotation to turn each one to match its starting position?

HOME LINK

More Than One Strategy

Locating a Rotation Image

There are several ways to locate the image of a triangle rotated 180° about a point.
Here are some. Can you think of others?

1. You could use a double reflection.

Reflect the
triangle
in a line
by folding.
Then reflect
the image
in a line
perpendicular
to the first
reflection line.

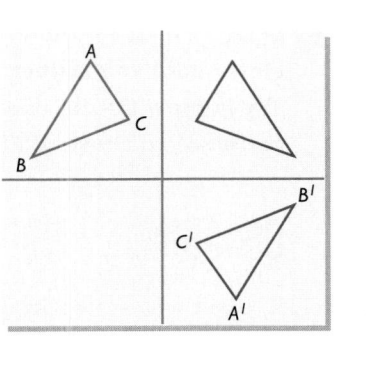

2. You could turn a tracing of the triangle 180° about the point.

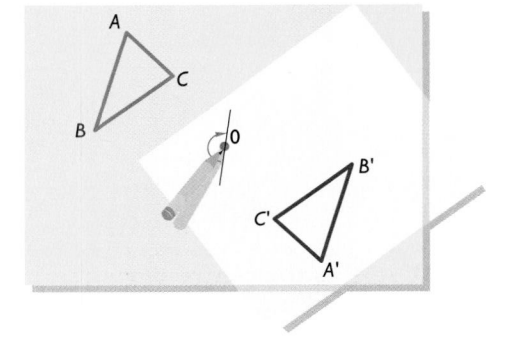

3. You can use a coordinate grid and the fact that the *x*- and *y*-coordinates of the image have signs opposite to the original for a 180° rotation about the origin.

$A(-4, 6) \rightarrow A'(4, -6)$
$B(-7, 1) \rightarrow B'(7, -1)$
$C(-2, 3) \rightarrow C'(2, -3)$

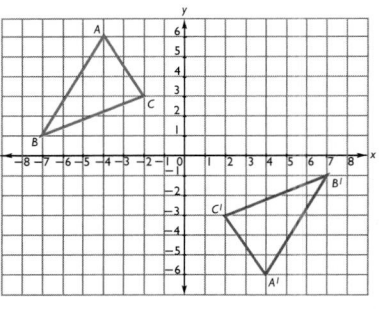

4. You might use a protractor and a ruler and the properties of a rotation.

$AO = A'O \qquad BO = B'O \qquad CO = C'O$
$\angle AOA' = \angle BOB' = \angle COC' = 180°$

5. You might use a computer with graphics software.

Understand and Apply

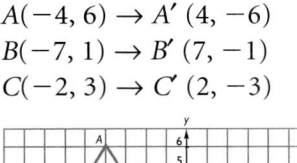

1. Use two ways to locate the rotation image of
   a) a parallelogram rotated 90° clockwise about one of its vertices

   b) a pentagon rotated 180° about an external point
   c) a triangle rotated 90° counterclockwise about an internal point

67

Problems to Investigate

OVERLAPPING

The outline of the overlap of a figure and its translation image is a triangle. Draw what the figure and its image might look like. Do they have to be triangles?

REFLECTING IN Y = X

Plot points $(-7, -7)$, $(-1, -1)$, and $(5, 5)$. Draw a line through them.
This is the line $y = x$.
Draw parallelogram *FLIP*, with $F(-5, 4)$, $L(-7, 1)$, $I(-3, 1)$, and $P(-1, 4)$.
How could you reflect *FLIP* in the line $y = x$?
Try it. How do the coordinates of the image compare to those of *FLIP*?

ROTATING RECTANGLE

Use *T* as the centre of rotation and rotate *TILE* so that its image is on top of it. Describe the rotation. What if *O* were the centre of rotation? Draw and label the images for your rotations.

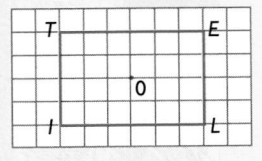

CONGRUENCY TRANSFORMATIONS

Explain why reflections, translations, and rotations are called **congruency transformations**.

ACTION MOVIE

Plan an action using translations, rotations, and/or reflections. Draw 10 consecutive stages of it on 10 congruent squares. Staple the squares together at the top and flip them to view your movie.

Make up some other problems about transformations. Post them on the bulletin board for your classmates to solve.

3.4 Enlarging and Reducing

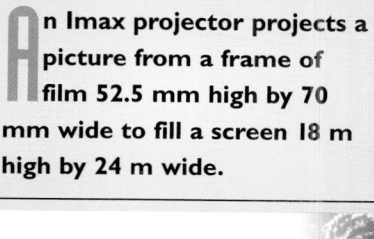

An Imax projector projects a picture from a frame of film 52.5 mm high by 70 mm wide to fill a screen 18 m high by 24 m wide.

Warm Up

Draw a block letter such as one of your initials on a 1-cm grid. How many squares does your letter cover? Use a larger and then a smaller grid to draw the same letter covering the same number of squares. How are all the letters alike? different?

Concept Development

1. Use your calculator and round to the nearest whole number to find
   a) how many times as high the picture is on the screen as on the frame of film.
   b) how many times as wide.

2. A **dilatation** is a transformation that multiplies or divides all the linear dimensions of an object by the same amount.
   a) Why might that amount be called a **scale factor**?
   b) Is the Imax projection a dilatation?

3. Dilatations are either **enlargements** or **reductions**.
   a) Which is an Imax projection?
   b) What is an example of the other?

Understand and Apply

1. Round the Imax scale factor to the nearest 50. Use it to estimate each size on the screen.
   a) a person 40 mm high on a frame
   b) a wave 30 mm high on a frame
   c) a snake 60 mm long on a frame
   d) a pool 50 mm wide on a frame

2. a) Copy this diagram onto grid paper. Include the centre of dilatation, O.

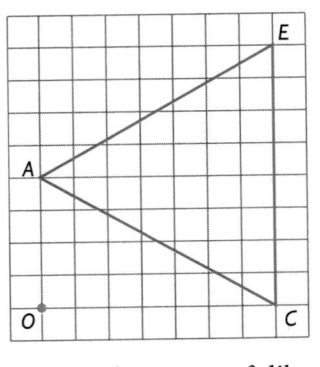

b) Join the centre of dilatation, O, to A.
c) Measure the length OA in millimetres.
d) Extend OA to double its length. Name the end point A′.
e) Repeat steps (b), (c), and (d) for the other vertices and draw the image.
f) Visually compare the size, shape, and orientation of the image with the original figure.
g) Measure and compare the lengths of corresponding sides in millimetres and the degree measures of corresponding angles. What do you notice?

3. Repeat Problem 2 for this diagram, except triple the lengths.

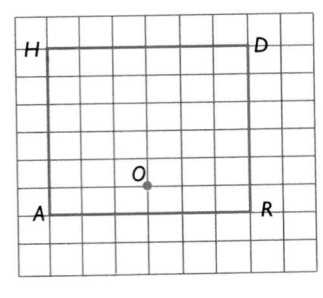

In Your Journal

A figure and its dilatation image are similar. What relationship exists between the corresponding sides of similar figures? between corresponding angles?

How are similar figures alike? different?

4. a) Copy this diagram onto grid paper.

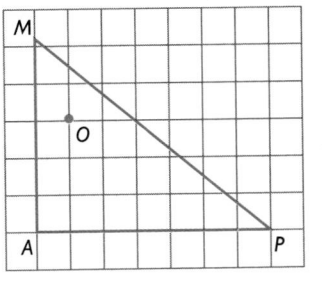

b) Join O to M.
c) Measure the length OM.
d) Halve the length OM and name the midpoint M′.
e) Repeat steps (b), (c), and (d) for the other vertices and draw the image.
f) Repeat steps (f) and (g) from Problem 2 for this image and the original figure.

5. a) How can you determine if the two figures in each of these pairs are similar?
b) Which pairs have similar figures? Which do not and why?
c) Which pairs show dilatations with centre O?

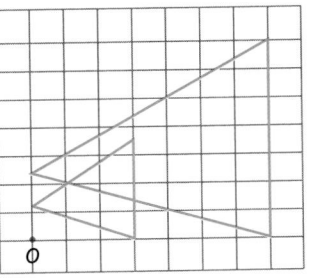

6. Copy each diagram onto grid paper. How can you find the centre of dilatation and the scale factor? Find them and label the vertices of the image.

a)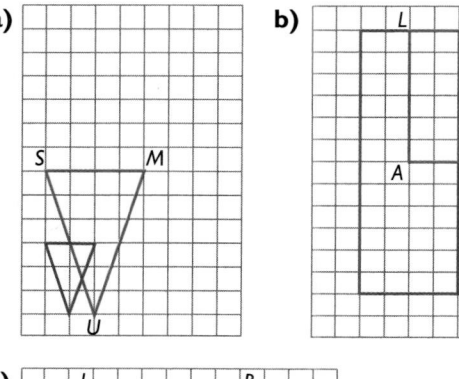

b)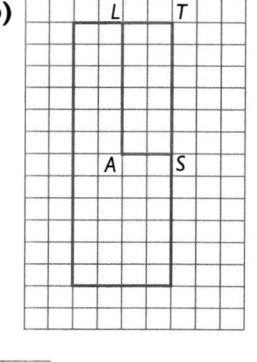

c)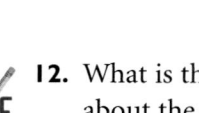

7. What scale factor and centre of dilatation would take each image in Problem 6 back to the original figure?

8. What is the scale factor of each?
   a) a 15 cm × 10 cm print enlarged to 45 cm × 30 cm
   b) a 480 cm × 200 cm drawing reduced to 48 cm × 20 cm
   c) a 35 mm × 35 mm slide enlarged to a 1.05 m × 1.05 m screen image
   d) a 3.9 m long car reduced to a model 78 mm long

9. a) Draw parallelogram *PEAR* on a coordinate grid, with $P(-1, 2)$, $E(0, -3)$, $A(5, 1)$, and $R(4, 6)$.
   b) Locate its dilatation image using a scale factor of 2 and the origin as the centre of dilatation.
   c) Write the ordered pair for each vertex of the image.
   d) Describe how the coordinates of the vertices change when the dilatation occurs.
   e) Explain how you know the original and its image are similar.

10. Repeat Problem 9 for hexagon *ORANGE*, with $O(0, 0)$, $R(0, -4)$, $A(4, -6)$, $N(8, -2)$, $G(8, 2)$, and $E(4, 4)$. Use a scale factor of $-\frac{1}{2}$.

11. Repeat Problem 9 for pentagon *GRAPE*, with $G(-3, 2)$, $R(-3, -1)$, $A(-2, -2)$, $P(-1, 0)$, and $E(-1, 2)$. Use a scale factor of 3.

In Your Journal

Describe how the coordinates of the vertices of a figure change for a dilatation about the origin with a given scale factor.

12. What is the scale factor for each dilatation about the origin?
   a) $H(3, -6) \rightarrow H'(6, -12)$
   b) $M(8, 4) \rightarrow M'(2, 1)$
   c) $Y(-3, 1) \rightarrow Y'(-9, 3)$

Plot each pair of points to check.

13. What are the coordinates of the vertices of the image of each dilatation about the origin?
   a) $\triangle PEA$ with $P(0, 6)$, $E(-3, -3)$, and $A(3, -6)$ and a scale factor of $\frac{1}{3}$
   b) rectangle *BEAN* with $B(-1, 2)$, $E(-1, -1)$, $A(4, -1)$, and $N(4, 2)$ and a scale factor of 4
   c) hexagon *RADISH* with $R(-2, 4)$, $A(-6, 0)$, $D(-4, -2)$, $I(2, -4)$, $S(4, 0)$, and $H(2, 4)$ and a scale factor of $\frac{1}{2}$
   d) $\triangle CAT$ with $C(2, 3)$, $A(4, 6)$, and $T(5, 4)$ and a scale factor of 2
   Draw each figure and locate its image to check.

Find examples of enlargements and reductions at home. Determine the scale factor of each.

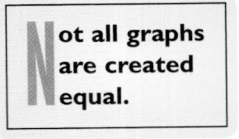

Interpreting Misleading Graphs

> **N**ot all graphs are created equal.

1. How are these graphs alike?

2. How are they different?

3. Tell whether you think each graph accurately displays that "Our" sales are four times "Theirs" or whether it misleads. Explain why.

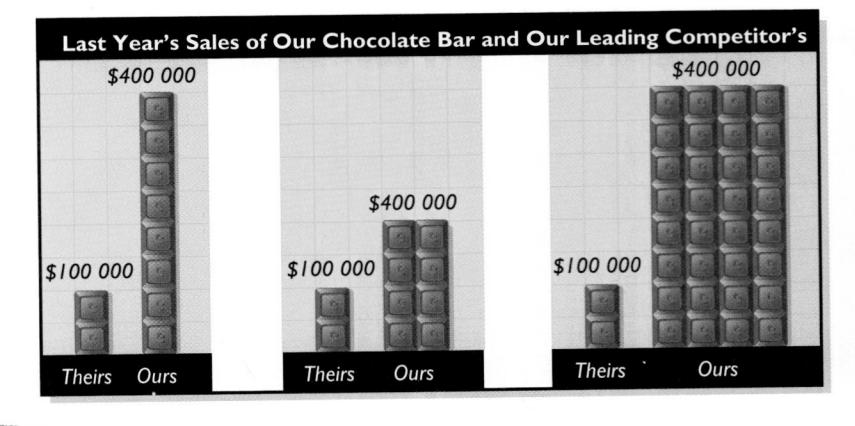

Last Year's Sales of Our Chocolate Bar and Our Leading Competitor's

$400 000

$100 000

Theirs   Ours

$400 000

$100 000

Theirs   Ours

$400 000

$100 000

Theirs   Ours

Applications

4. Is each graph accurate or misleading? Explain. How could you make the misleading ones accurate?

a)

Daily Servings of Grain Products

up to 12

up to 5

Old   New

Canada's Food Guide

b)

Daily Servings of Vegetables & Fruit

up to 10

up to 5

Old   New

Canada's Food Guide

c)

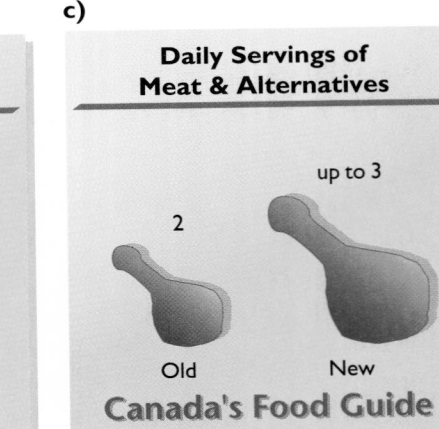

Daily Servings of Meat & Alternatives

up to 3

2

Old   New

Canada's Food Guide

5. **a)** Why might misleading graphs be used?
   b) How might you attempt to justify the misleading graphs on this page?

6. The increase in the maximum number of daily servings for grain products is seven times the increase for meat and alternatives. Draw a graph that might be used by
   a) manufacturers of breads or cereals
   b) beef or poultry farmers
   Tell why you drew each graph as you did.

7. Find data in newspapers or magazines. Display it in
   a) an accurate graph
   b) a misleading, but justifiable, graph
   Exchange your misleading graph with 2 or 3 classmates.
   Ask them to explain how you justified it.

TAKE YOUR PICK!

SIMILAR COINS

Trace around a dime and a quarter. Show how you could find the dilatation centre.

What happens to the centre as the coins move away from each other? move toward each other? overlap?

MOVING THE CENTRE

Draw $\triangle BIG$ on a coordinate grid, with $B(2, 3)$, $I(-3, 0)$, and $G(-1, -4)$. Locate its dilatation image with a scale factor of 2 and centre at (1, 1). Write the ordered pair of each vertex of the image. Repeat with centre (2, 2) and again with centre (1, 2). Describe how the coordinates of the vertices change when the dilatation centre is not the origin.

NEGATIVE SCALE FACTOR

To locate the vertices of an image enlarged about the origin, you multiply the coordinates of the vertices by the scale factor.
The vertices of $\triangle HAT$ are $H(1, 1)$, $A(4, -2)$, and $T(4, 2)$.
$\triangle H'A'T'$ is an enlargement about the origin with a scale factor of -2. What are its vertices? Locate both $\triangle HAT$ and $\triangle H'A'T'$ on a coordinate grid.
Describe the effects of a negative scale factor.

AREA DOUBLED

Two figures are similar.
Estimate the scale factor when the area of the enlarged image is double the area of the other. Use these squares to see how accurate you were.

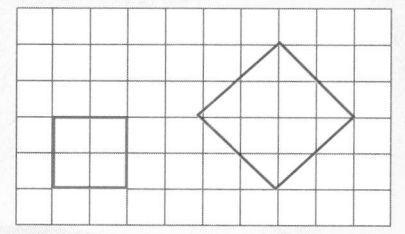

Make up some other problems about dilatations and similar figures. Post them on the bulletin board for your classmates to solve.

Solve Problems by Working Backwards

Try this problem before going on.

THE KITE

This kite is the result of a reflection in the x-axis, followed by a rotation of 90° counterclockwise about the origin, followed by a translation of $[-8, -1]$. Where was it originally?

▶ ## *Understand the Problem*

1. What are you asked to find?
2. What do you know?
3. Where will you begin?

▶ ## *Think of a Plan*

To solve this problem, Monica and Mila worked backwards.

> We should perform the opposite transformations in the opposite order. First translate (8,1), then rotate 90° clockwise about the orgin, and finally reflect in the x-axis.

▶ ## *Carry Out the Plan*

4. Perform Monica's and Mila's suggested transformations to locate *KITE*.

▶ ## *Look Back*

5. How could you check to see if you're right?

Applications

THE COOKIES

Roy baked a batch of cookies. He served $\frac{1}{4}$ of them to some friends. He gave $\frac{1}{3}$ of the remaining cookies to one friend to take home to his sisters. He has $2\frac{1}{2}$ dozen cookies left. How many were in the batch?

ROTATING BOX

$\triangle B''O''X''$ is the result of a 90° clockwise rotation about the origin and then a 180° rotation about X'. Where was $\triangle BOX$ originally?

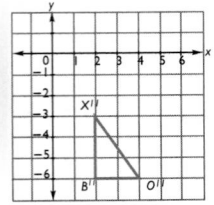

DAILY SERVINGS

The mean number of daily servings of fruit and vegetables that Audrey ate one week was 8. On each of five of the days, she ate 10, 7, 8, 9, and 9 servings. How many servings did she eat each of the other two days?

GROWING BACTERIA

A bacteria culture doubles in number every hour. There are 65 536 bacteria at midnight. What was the count 12 h earlier?

Review and Practise

1. Draw each figure on a grid and locate its image.
   a) $\triangle ABC$, with $A(1, -7)$, $B(4, 0)$, and $C(2, 3)$, translated $[-5, 2]$

   b) parallelogram $DEFG$, with $D(-1, 2)$, $E(-3, -1)$, $F(4, -1)$, and $G(6, 2)$, reflected in the y-axis

   c) $\triangle HIJ$, with $H(1, 7)$, $I(1, 3)$, and $J(6, 6)$, rotated $90°$ clockwise about the origin

   d) $\triangle KLM$, with $K(-2, 2)$, $L(-4, -2)$, and $M(-1, -2)$, for a dilatation about the origin with a scale factor of 2

   e) quadrilateral $NPQR$, with $N(-2, 3)$, $P(-3, -1)$, $Q(1, -3)$, and $R(3, 4)$, rotated $180°$ about the origin

   f) $\triangle STU$, with $S(0, 5)$, $T(-3, -2)$, and $U(2, 0)$, reflected in the x-axis and then the image translated $[5, -2]$

2. What are the coordinates of the image of each line segment?

   a) AB, with $A(-6, -1)$ and $B(2, 3)$, translated $[0, -6]$

   b) CD, with $C(-2, -2)$ and $D(7, -1)$, reflected in the x-axis

   c) EF, with $E(0, 3)$ and $F(6, -2)$, rotated $180°$ about the origin

   d) GH, with $G(-8, 0)$ and $H(2, -4)$, for a dilatation about the origin with a scale factor of $\frac{1}{2}$

   e) IJ, with $I(-3, 1)$ and $J(1, 4)$, rotated $90°$ clockwise about the origin

   f) KL, with $K(-1, 4)$ and $L(2, 1)$, reflected in the y-axis and then a dilatation of the image about the origin with a scale factor of 3

   g) MN, with $M(-3, 2)$ and $N(5, 1)$, rotated $90°$ counterclockwise about the origin

3. Copy each diagram onto grid paper. Identify the transformation and explain how you know the figures are congruent. Identify the reflection line, or the translation rule, or the angle, direction and centre of rotation.

   a)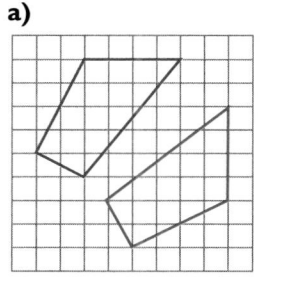

   b)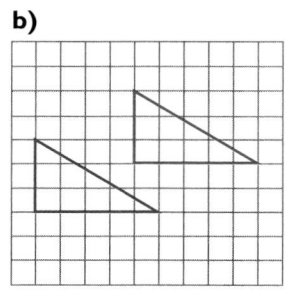

4. Which pairs of triangles are similar? Explain. Which pairs show a dilatation with centre O? Explain. Are your answers the same? Why or why not?

   a) **b)**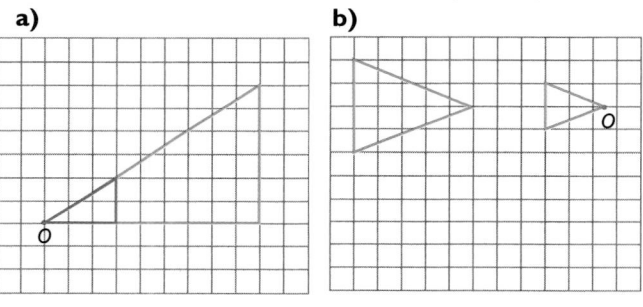

   c)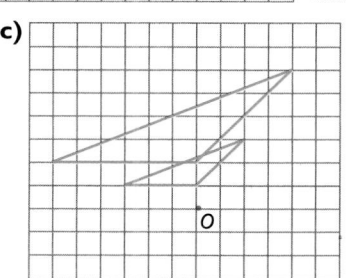

5. Complete these statements to express the transformations algebraically.
   a) $P(x, y)$ reflected in the x-axis $\rightarrow P'(x, \blacksquare)$
   b) $P(x, y)$ reflected in the y-axis $\rightarrow P'(-x, \blacksquare)$
   c) $P(x, y)$ translated $[a, b] \rightarrow P'(x + a, \blacksquare)$
   d) $P(x, y)$ rotated $180°$ about the origin $\rightarrow P'(-x, \blacksquare)$
   e) $P(x, y)$ rotated $90°$ clockwise about the origin $\rightarrow P'(\blacksquare, \blacksquare)$
   f) $P(x, y)$ rotated $90°$ counterclockwise about the origin $\rightarrow P'(\blacksquare, \blacksquare)$
   g) $P(x, y)$ under a dilatation with scale factor k and centre of origin $\rightarrow P'(\blacksquare, \blacksquare)$

Practise With Games

Scale Factor of Three

Play in groups of 2, 3, or 4.

Each player

*   makes a set of 12 pentominoes using grid paper.

*   enlarges his or her cross-shaped pentomino by a scale factor of three. Each enlargement becomes each player's puzzle base.

*   uses as many of the other 11 pentominoes as necessary to tile his or her enlargement.

The first player to completely tile his or her enlargement wins.

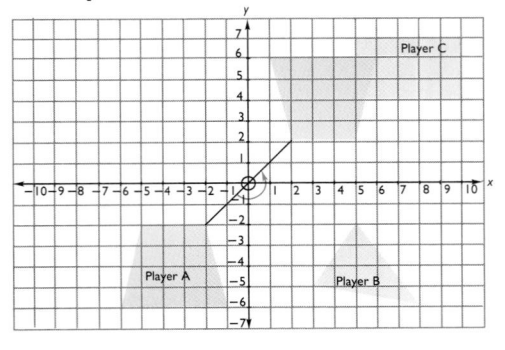

Example:

Player A: 1 point for passing over triangle;
2 points for overlapping rectangle.
Total — 3 points

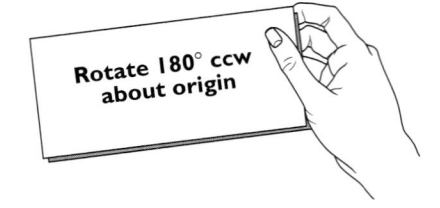

Rotate 180° ccw about origin

Overlap or Pass Over

Play in a group of 3.

Shuffle the 12 transformation cards.
Place them face down in a pile.
Each player

*   traces and cuts out one of the three figures shown to the left.

*   places his or her figure on a 0.5-cm coordinate grid. (The three figures should be in three different quadrants on the same coordinate grid.)

Players take turns drawing cards and performing the transformations on their figures. Points are awarded as follows:

*   If a player's figure passes over another player's figure during the transformation, he or she scores 1 point.

*   If a player's figure overlaps or touches another player's figure as a result of the transformation, he or she scores 2 points and takes another turn.

If the cards are used up, reshuffle and use again.
The first player to reach 15 points wins.

TAKE YOUR PICK!

FINAL IMAGES

The coordinates of the vertices of △CAN are C(−3, 3), A(3, −1), and N(1, 5).

What are the coordinates of the vertices of the final image when △CAN is reflected in the x-axis and its image is translated [3, −1]? Answer the preceding questions for △CAN translated [3, −1] first and then its image reflected in the x-axis. How do the coordinates of the final images compare?

ESTIMATING WALL LENGTH

Hold a 30 cm ruler horizontally with your arm extended. Position yourself so that the ruler is as long as the wall is wide. What measurements would you need to be able to estimate the width of the wall?

CREATING ROTATIONAL SYMMETRY

Use an 8 x 8 square grid and shade these four squares.
• 5th square in top row
• 6th square in 3rd row from top
• 2nd and 5th squares in 3rd row from bottom
Now shade the least number of additional squares so that the grid will match itself every time it is turned 90°.

JOINING MIDPOINTS

Draw any triangle. Locate the midpoint of each side. Join the midpoints. Compare the lengths of the sides of the inner triangle with those of the original. Repeat with other triangles. Do you get the same results?

Make up some other problems about transformations. Post them on the bulletin board for your classmates to solve.

1. What type of transformation is suggested by each?
   a) looking through binoculars
   b) walking through a revolving door
   c) opening a combination lock
   d) moving along a conveyor belt
   e) riding a Ferris wheel

2. Describe what happens to the coordinates of a point for each transformation.
   a) a translation
   b) a reflection in the x-axis
   c) a reflection in the y-axis
   d) a rotation 180° about the origin
   e) a rotation 90° clockwise about the origin
   f) a rotation 90° counterclockwise about the origin
   g) a dilatation about the origin with a given scale factor

3. Use your answers to Problem 2 to help you determine which transformation was performed.
   a) $M(4, -7) \rightarrow M'(16, -28)$
   b) $V(3, -5) \rightarrow V'(-5, -3)$
   c) $K(2, -5) \rightarrow K'(11, -6)$
   d) $B(-3, -7) \rightarrow B'(-3, 7)$
   e) $F(12, -9) \rightarrow F'(4, -3)$
   f) $Y(-5, 2) \rightarrow Y'(5, 2)$
   g) $G(-4, -2) \rightarrow G'(4, 2)$
   h) $N(-5, 1) \rightarrow N'(-1, -5)$

4. a) What types of transformations are referred to as congruency transformations? Explain why.
   b) Which types might be called similarity transformations? Explain why.

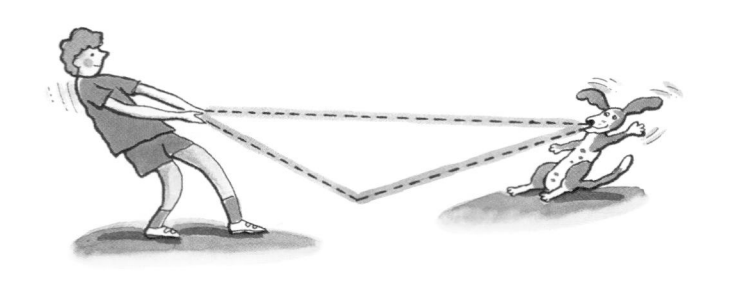

5. What single transformation gives the same result as reflecting $\triangle GHI$, with $G(2, 4)$, $H(1, 1)$, and $I(5, 2)$, in the x-axis and then rotating the image 180° about the origin?

6. What single transformation gives the same result as reflecting $\triangle PQR$, with $P(-3, 4)$, $Q(-5, 1)$, and $R(0, 1)$, in the y-axis and then translating the image $[6, 0]$?

7. $\triangle MAP$ was translated $[4, -1]$ and then rotated 90° counterclockwise. What was its original position?

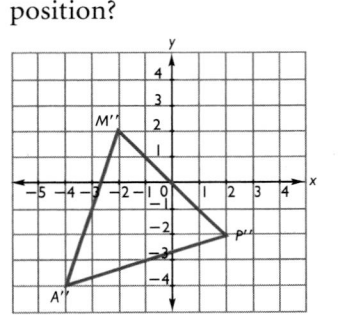

8. Draw any triangle in the third quadrant of a coordinate grid. Identify two single transformations of different types that would result in the image being completely in each quadrant.
   a) first   b) second
   c) third   d) fourth

9. Describe where the dilatation centre is and what the scale factor could be.

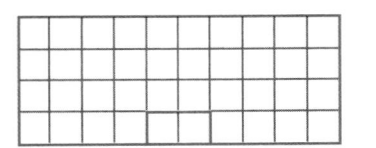

10. The area of a dilatation image is 3 cm² and the area of the original figure is 27 cm². What is the scale factor?

11. What scale factor would result in a congruent image?

12. Can a dilatation image of a square ever be a non-square rectangle? Explain.

Communicate Your Knowledge

1. Explain how to locate the image of a figure rotated 180° about the origin.

2. How can both these students be right?

The reduction is $\frac{1}{16}$ of the original.

The reduction is $\frac{1}{4}$ of the original.

5. Create a collage of pictures from newspapers and magazines that show transformations in sports.

4. Tell how each image — translation, rotation, reflection, dilatation — is different from each of the others.

3. Which properties do translations and dilatations have in common? Which are different?

What questions do you still have about transformations?

Rational Numbers

Vancouver Canucks 1994 Playoffs

NO.	PLAYER	GP	G	A	P	+/−	S
10	P. Bure	24	16	14	30	7	101
16	T. Linden	24	12	13	25	3	67
14	G. Courtnall	24	9	10	19	10	77
22	J. Brown	24	6	9	15	7	76
7	C. Ronning	24	5	10	15	−2	69
8	G. Adams	23	6	8	14	1	46
32	M. Craven	22	4	9	13	10	38
21	J. Lumme	24	2	11	13	8	53
23	M. Gelinas	24	5	4	9	−1	35
25	N. Lafayette	20	2	7	9	13	24
44	D. Babych	24	3	5	8	4	26
4	J. Diduck	24	1	7	8	1	32
27	S. Momesso	24	3	4	7	7	38
3	B. Hedican	24	1	6	7	13	22
28	B. Glynn	17	0	3	3	5	11
20	J. Charbonneau	3	1	0	1	1	4
17	J. Carson	2	0	1	1	1	2
18	S. Antoski	16	0	1	1	−3	4
19	T. Hunter	24	0	1	1	−2	8
15	J. Mcintyre	24	0	1	1	−3	12
1	K. McLean	24	0	1	1	0	0
5	D. Murzyn	7	0	0	0	−4	7
29	G. Odjick	10	0	0	0	0	3

P - Games Played; G - Goals; A - Assists; P - Points; S - Shots

In 1994 the Vancouver Canucks lost the Stanley Cup to the New York Rangers in the 7th game.

Use the 1994 Canucks Playoffs Statistics.

- How many goals did the team score in the playoffs?

- How are the points calculated?

- How many points did the team have in the playoffs?

- Find the shooting percent (the ratio of goals to shots as a percent) for each player, rounded to the nearest whole percent.

What do the numbers in the +/− column mean? What do the players with a positive number have in common? What do the players with a negative number have in common?

4.1 Exploring Sets of Numbers

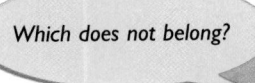

Which does not belong?

Describe at least six different ways to group these numbers into two sets.

2, 3, 4, 5, 6, 7, 8

Try to use a way that no one else will.

−2, because it is negative and the others are positive

Concept Development

1. a) Do you agree with Chris's answer?

b) To which sets of numbers do 6, 4, 3, and 5 belong that −2 does not belong?

2. Match each set of numbers with its description.

   a) integers

   b) whole numbers

   c) rational numbers

   d) natural numbers

   i. set of counting numbers

   ii. set of numbers, $\frac{a}{b}$, where a and b are integers and $b \neq 0$

   iii. set of counting numbers and 0

   iv. set of whole numbers and their opposites

3. Draw four nesting boxes and label each one with one of the four sets of numbers above to show how the sets of numbers are related.

Understand and Apply

1. Give three examples of each.

   a) a natural number

   b) a whole number

   c) an integer

   d) a rational number

2. Give two examples of each.

   a) a whole number that is also a natural number

   b) an integer that is also a whole number

   c) a rational number that is also an integer

   d) a rational number that is also a whole number

3. Give one example of each if possible.

   a) a whole number but not a natural number

   b) an integer but not a whole number

   c) a rational number but not a whole number

   d) a rational number but not an integer

4. a) Explain why 7 belongs to all four sets of numbers.

   b) Explain why −7 is a rational number but not a whole number.

5. To which sets does each number belong?

   a) 15   **b)** −2   **c)** 0

   d) $\frac{3}{4}$ **e)** $-\frac{1}{3}$ **f)** −0.75

4.2 Rationalizing Numbers

When $-\dfrac{7}{12}$ is expressed in decimal form, you can write either

$$-0.583\ 333\ 333... \text{ or } -0.58\overline{3}.$$

$$7 \div 12 \boxed{+/-} \boxed{=}$$

Concept Development

1. When expressed in decimal form, is $-\dfrac{7}{12}$
   - terminating?
   - repeating?
   - non-terminating, non-repeating?

2. **a)** Which type of decimal is each group of rational numbers?

   Group A $\quad -\dfrac{3}{8} \quad \dfrac{7}{25} \quad -\dfrac{9}{20} \quad \dfrac{3}{50}$

   Group B $\quad \dfrac{7}{15} \quad -\dfrac{1}{22} \quad \dfrac{5}{12} \quad -\dfrac{13}{27}$

   b) Express each denominator as a product of prime factors.
   c) What do you notice about the prime factors in each group?
   d) Predict the type of decimal that each of these rational numbers is.

   $$\dfrac{13}{40} \quad -\dfrac{11}{200} \quad -\dfrac{1}{24} \quad \dfrac{5}{32} \quad -\dfrac{7}{18} \quad -\dfrac{9}{44}$$

   Check your predictions.

> Rational numbers are either terminating or repeating when expressed in decimal form.
>
> Non-terminating, non-repeating decimals cannot be expressed in fractional form so they are not rational numbers. They are **irrational numbers**.
>
> **Real numbers** are the set of rational numbers and irrational numbers.

Understand and Apply

1. Which of the following decimals are rational numbers?
   a) $-0.616\ 116\ 111\ 611\ ...$
   b) $2.5\overline{1}$
   c) $-0.233\ 333\ ...$
   d) $-3.276\ 286\ 786\ ...$
   e) $8.\ 245\ 454\ 454\ ...$
   f) 3.788
   g) $-11.232\ 442\ 555\ ...$

2. $\sqrt{2}$ is an irrational number.
   a) What is its value on your calculator?
   b) Which square roots of numbers from 3 to 24 do not appear to terminate or repeat?

3. The ratio of diameter to circumference of circles is a constant, π. Is π a rational or irrational number? Explain.

In Your Journal

Where would a box for irrational numbers fit in the set of nesting boxes that you drew in the previous lesson? Explain why.

4.3 Finding Principal and Negative Square Roots

Warm Up

What are the dimensions of the largest rectangular garden you could enclose with 24 m of fencing?

The area of this square piece of fabric is 25 cm².

Concept Development

1. What is the length of one side of the fabric square? Explain.

$5 \times 5 = 25$ so $\sqrt{25} = 5$. $\sqrt{25}$ is the **principal** or positive square root of 25.

2. Is there another square root of 25? Explain your thinking.

3. Even though $-5 \times (-5) = 25$ and $-\sqrt{25}$ (the negative square root of 25) $= -5$, 5 cm is the only answer for the length of the side of the fabric square. Explain why.

The area of the square face of this wooden cube is 50 cm².

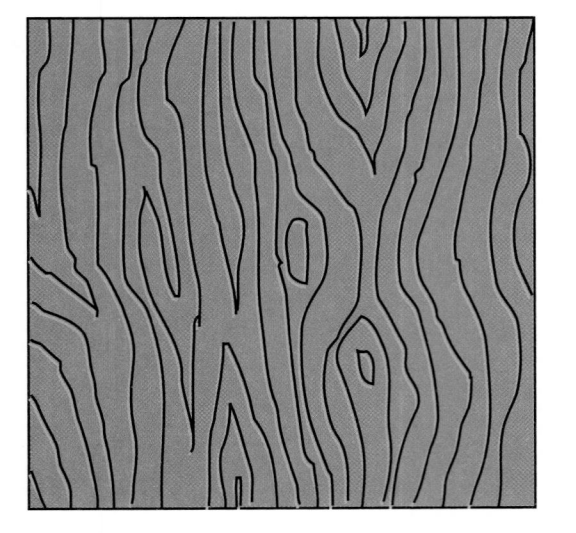

W/E

4. Estimate and then use a calculator to calculate the length of one side of the square face.

Explain what you did. Did you find $\sqrt{50}$ or $-\sqrt{50}$?

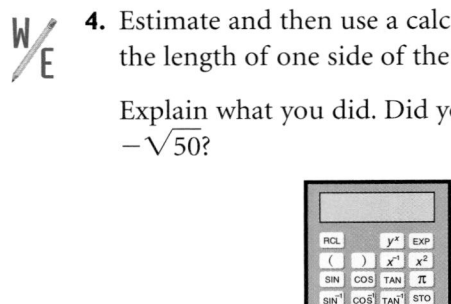

1. Evaluate.

a) $\sqrt{81}$ **b)** $\sqrt{30.25}$ **c)** $\sqrt{121}$

d) $\sqrt{6.76}$ **e)** $-\sqrt{4}$ **f)** $-\sqrt{70.56}$

g) $-\sqrt{4.41}$ **h)** $\sqrt{3600}$ **i)** $-\sqrt{4900}$

2. Describe each and evaluate if possible.

a) $\sqrt{64}$ **b)** $-\sqrt{64}$ **c)** $\sqrt{-64}$

3. Estimate and calculate.

a) $\sqrt{10}$ **b)** $-\sqrt{45}$ **c)** $-\sqrt{24}$

d) $-\sqrt{32}$ **e)** $\sqrt{18}$ **f)** $-\sqrt{60}$

4. Which parts of Problem 3 are rational numbers?

5. What are two values that satisfy each equation?
a) $x^2 = 16$ **b)** $m^2 = 6.25$
c) $h^2 = 169$ **d)** $y^2 = 29.16$
e) $n^2 = 39.69$ **f)** $w^2 = 3.24$

6. A square garden has an area of 36 m². How many possible values are there for the length of one side? Explain.

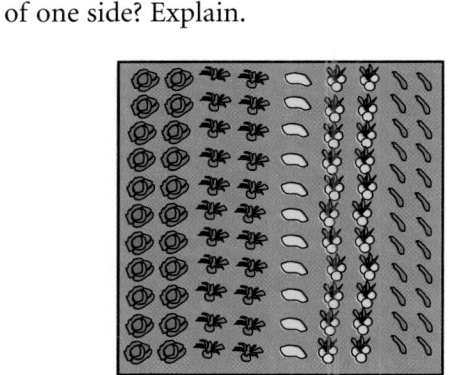

7. A circle has an area of 221.6 cm². How many possible values are there for the radius? What are they? Explain what you did.

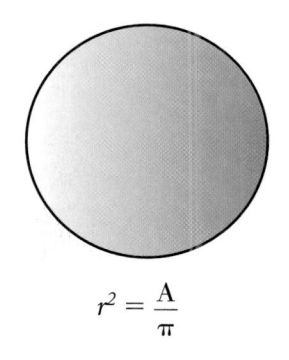

$$r^2 = \frac{A}{\pi}$$

8. A can has a volume of 1592 cm³ and a height of 12 cm. How many possible values are there for the radius? What are they? Explain what you did.

$$r^2 = \frac{V}{\pi h}$$

9. When you know two sides of a right triangle and are finding the third,
a) what relationship do you use?
b) why do you use only the positive square root?

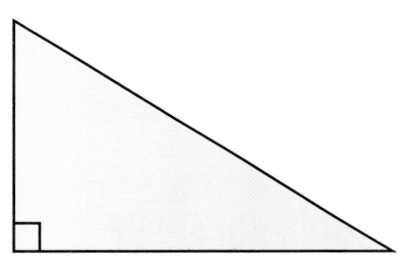

10. A square has one vertex at (0,0) on a coordinate grid. If its area is 16 square units, what are the possible integer coordinates of the other three vertices?

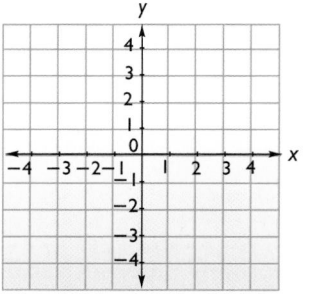

In Your Journal

Describe situations where you use both the positive and the negative square roots and situations where you use only the positive square root.

Problems to Investigate

BETWEEN

Find a rational number and an irrational number between $0.\overline{63}$ and $0.\overline{64}$. Find a second example of each.

GREATER OR LESS

When is the square root of a number less than the number and when is it greater?

TRUE OR FALSE

Is each statement true or false? Explain.

- All rational numbers can be expressed in decimal form.
- All numbers in decimal form are rational numbers.

HOW MANY?

How many different rational numbers can you create using each of 2, 3, 4, a decimal point, and a negative sign once. List the numbers from greatest to least.

ROOT OF A ROOT OF A ROOT

Find the square root of 123 456 789 on your calculator. Keep finding the square root of the result. What do you notice? Repeat with 987 654 321.

THE VERTICES ARE . . .

A square with an area of 8 square units has one vertex at (0, 0) on a coordinate grid. What are the possible integer coordinates of the other three vertices?

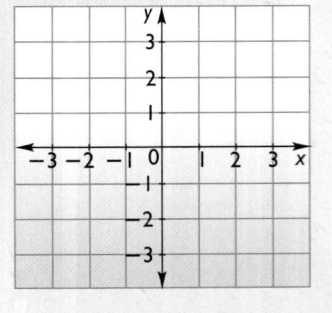

Make up other problems about the structure or interrelationships of rational numbers. Post them on the bulletin board for your classmates to solve.

4.4 Estimating Amounts

Warm Up

Estimate and then calculate mentally to decide if 150 pamphlets are enough for 5 classes with 28, 32, 26, 31, and 29 students.

Neil has $20 ready to pay for these groceries.

1 box of cereal	$4.29/box
2 packages of pasta	$1.29/package
1 bag of apples	$2.99/bag
1 bunch of broccoli	$1.49/bunch
1 can of orange juice	$1.09/can
2 cans of soup	$0.89/can
1 loaf of bread	$1.69/loaf
1 carton of eggs	$1.79/carton

Concept Development

1. a) How would you estimate the cost of all the items on Neil's list?
 b) Is $20 enough to pay for them?

Neil estimated.

> 4.25, 5.50, 6.75, 9.75, 11.25, 12.25, 13.25, 14.25, 16.00, 17.75

2. Explain how Neil estimated. Compare to how you estimated.

Understand and Apply

1. Estimate the perimeter of each shape.

a)

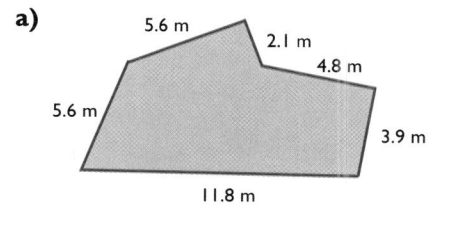

5.6 m
2.1 m
4.8 m
5.6 m
3.9 m
11.8 m

b)

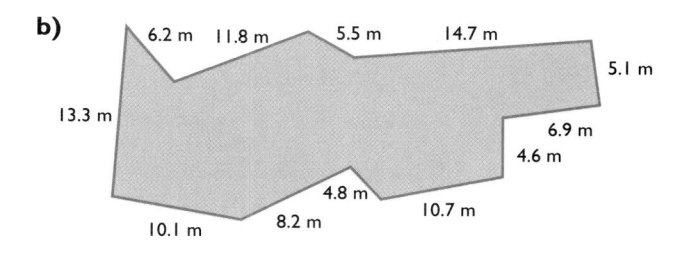

6.2 m 11.8 m 5.5 m 14.7 m
5.1 m
13.3 m
6.9 m
4.6 m
4.8 m
10.1 m 8.2 m 10.7 m

2. Estimate the area or volume of each.

a) Area $= lw$

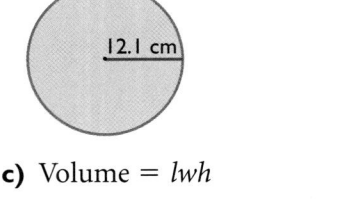

9.7 m

28.6 m

b) Area $= \pi r^2$

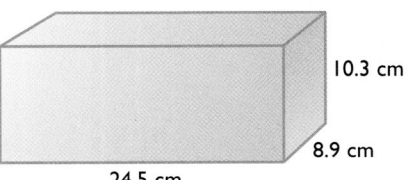

12.1 cm

c) Volume $= lwh$

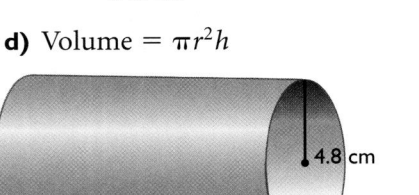

10.3 cm

8.9 cm

24.5 cm

d) Volume $= \pi r^2 h$

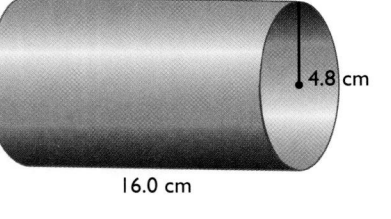

4.8 cm

16.0 cm

e) Surface area $=$ Combined area of all faces

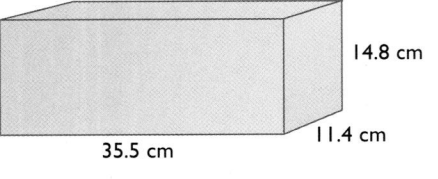

14.8 cm

11.4 cm

35.5 cm

f) Area $= \pi(R^2 - r^2)$

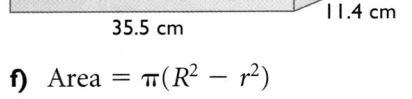

R=8.6 cm

r=3.9 cm

3. Estimate the total cost before taxes.
   a) 3 CDs @ \$16.77 each
   b) 1 shirt @ \$36.79 each
       1 pair of jeans @ \$49.98/pair
       2 pairs of socks @ \$3.79/pair
   c) 3 tubes of toothpaste @ \$1.19/tube
       4 toothbrushes @ \$1.85 each
   d) 2 grapefruits @ \$1.99 for 5
   e) 6 boxes of tissues @ \$1.85 for 2
   f) 1.74 kg of pears @ \$3.79/kg

4. The following calculations were done with a calculator. Estimate to see if each answer is reasonable.
   a) $4.57 + 9.25 - 12.3 = 26.12$
   b) $-56.3 + 9.77 - 31.25 = 34.82$
   c) $-3.96 \times (-47.3) = 187.308$
   d) $97.8 \div (-0.5) = -19.56$
   e) $(-16.3 - 7.88)5 = 42.1$
   f) $\dfrac{-3.2(4.8 + 9.3)}{2} = -156.48$
   g) $\dfrac{-4.5 \times (-36.2)}{5} = 32.58$

5. Estimate.
   a) $3.4 + (-11.6) - 12.8$
   b) $-87.5 + 124.7 \times 4$
   c) $37.9 \div 7.2 \times 4.4$
   d) $3.4^2 - \dfrac{21}{18}$
   e) $(4.1 - 7.8)3 + 53$
   f) $7.21^2 \div (-9.83)$
   g) $\dfrac{3.2(15.9 - 34.6)}{0.5}$
   h) $\dfrac{4.5^2 + 52.1 - 72.35}{16}$

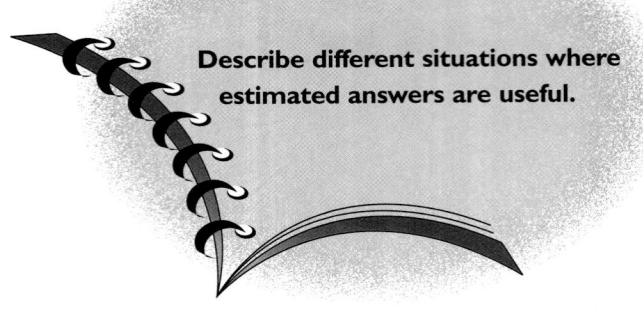

In Your Journal

Describe different situations where estimated answers are useful.

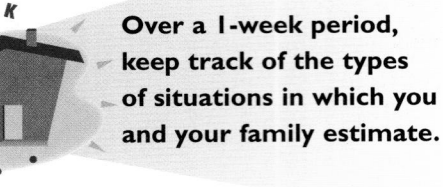

HOME LINK

Over a 1-week period, keep track of the types of situations in which you and your family estimate.

4.5 Practising Efficient Keystrokes

Warm Up

Describe how you would calculate $\dfrac{4^2 - 3^5 + 2}{5^2}$ on your calculator.

Hilary and Andrew are calculating the area of this trapezoid using $A = \dfrac{(a + b)h}{2}$.

They calculate $\dfrac{(6.5 + 8.7)4.8}{2}$.

6.5 cm

4.8 cm

8.7 cm

Concept Development

1. What keystrokes would you use to find the area?

Hilary presses 6.5 ⊞ 8.7 ⊟ ⊠ 4.8 ÷ 2 ⊟   *36.48*

Andrew presses ⦅ 6.5 ⊞ 8.7 ⦆ ⊠ 4.8 ÷ 2 ⊟   *36.48*

2. a) Why did Hilary press ⊟ after the addition but not after the multiplication?
 b) Explain and compare their methods.
 c) Compare their methods with yours.

To evaluate $\dfrac{41.7 + 28.5}{9.6 + 6.8 - 11.4}$, Andrew uses the

⦅ and ⦆ keys again.

⦅ 41.7 ⊞ 28.5 ⦆ ÷ ⦅ 9.6 ⊞ 6.8 ⊟ 11.4 ⦆ ⊟   *14.04*

Hilary uses the memory keys instead, STO and RCL.

9.6 ⊞ 6.8 ⊟ 11.4 ⊟ STO 41.7 ⊞ 28.5 ⊟ ÷ RCL ⊟   *14.04*

3. a) What does each key STO and RCL do? What keys on your calculator perform these memory functions?
 b) Explain and compare Hilary's and Andrew's methods.
 c) How would you evaluate the expression?
 d) Which uses the fewest keystrokes?

To evaluate $\dfrac{3.8^2}{9.5 - 14.6}$, you can use the reciprocal function, ⅟ₓ or x^{-1}.

9.5 ⊟ 14.6 ⊟ ⅟ₓ ⊠ 3.8 x^2 ⊟   *-2.831372549*

4. a) How would you use the reciprocal key on your calculator to evaluate the expression above? Record your keystrokes.
 b) Evaluate the expression using the ⦅ and ⦆ keys. Repeat, using the memory keys. Record your keystrokes for each.
 c) Which method do you prefer? Which uses the fewest keystrokes?

1. Darren won a contest and must answer this skill-testing question correctly.

$$2.6 - 4.3 \times 3.5$$

Estimate the answer to determine what a reasonable answer would be when calculating.

2. Darren tried each of these sets of keystrokes on his calculator to find an exact answer. Keystrokes (a) and (b) gave him the wrong answer. Why?

   a) 4.3 ⊠ 3.5 ⊟ 2.6 ⊜

   b) 2.6 ⊟ 4.3 ⊜ ⊠ 3.5 ⊜

   c) 4.3 ⊠ 3.5 [STO] 2.6 ⊟ [RCL] ⊜

   d) 2.6 ⊟ 4.3 ⊠ 3.5 ⊜

   e) 4.3 ⊠ 3.5 ⊬ ⊞ 2.6 ⊜

3. Keystrokes (c), (d), and (e) all resulted in the correct answer, but Darren decided (d) was most efficient. Why?

4. Estimate and then calculate the height of this cylinder using each method. Record your keystrokes.

   $$h = \frac{V}{\pi r^2}$$

   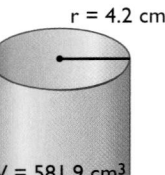

   a) using the reciprocal key
   b) using the brackets keys
   c) using the memory keys

   r = 4.2 cm

   V = 581.9 cm³

5. Which method in Problem 4 do you prefer? Which is the most efficient?

6. a) Find the average of these times using and recording two different sets of keystrokes you consider efficient.

   11.5 s   10.5 s   12.2 s

   b) Which is more efficient?

7. A set of keystrokes using the memory keys for $(23.1 - 17.3) \times (18.2 + 4.6)$ on some calculators is

   23.1 ⊟ 17.3 [STO] 18.2 ⊞ 4.6 ⊜ ⊠ [RCL] ⊜.

   Use and record other sets of keystrokes to determine the one with the fewest keystrokes.

8. a) Estimate and then calculate

   $$\frac{61.2}{12.6 \times (17.4 - 7.8)}$$

   by using and recording several different sets of keystrokes.
   b) Explain each set.
   c) Which set uses the fewest keystrokes?

9. Estimate and then calculate using an efficient set of keystrokes. Justify why you used the set of keystrokes you did.

   a) $(11.8 + 15.3) \times 5.75$
   b) $-4.5 \times (2.8 + 6.7)$
   c) $\dfrac{7.8 + 8.2}{2.5^2}$
   d) $\dfrac{1}{10.7 - 8.9}$
   e) $\dfrac{3^2}{9.75 + 4.1 + 2.5}$
   f) $\dfrac{14.12 - 58.6}{4.45}$
   g) $(2.6 + 3.9) \times (4.3 - 8.5)$
   h) $\dfrac{45.9}{7.5 \times (6.4 - 8.5)}$

10. a) Find the radius of this sphere by using and recording two different sets of keystrokes you consider efficient.

   $$r = \sqrt{\frac{\text{Surface Area}}{4\pi}}$$

   Surface Area = 706.8 cm²

   b) Which is more efficient?

In Your Journal

Describe how you use
• the equals key to complete subparts
• the memory keys
• the reciprocal key
• the brackets keys
to be efficient.

4.6 Deciding How to Solve

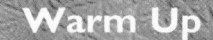

Warm Up

If the average of these high temperatures is −1°C, what was the temperature on Thursday? Explain how you solved the problem.

M	T	W	T	F	S	S
−5	−3	0		−2	1	0

The bank rate, the rate that the Bank of Canada charges for loans to banks, rose to 7.02%.

Bank rate rises

Canada's bank rate rose yesterday by 15 basis points

8

7.02

7

0

| 24 | 31 | 7 | 14 | 21 | 28 | 5 | 12 | 18 | 25 | 1 |

May   June   July   Aug.

Source: Bank of Canada

7.00 − 0.15 is 6.85 so 7.02 − 0.15 is 6.87.

Concept Development

To find what the bank rate was before it rose 15 basis points, Nina calculates 7.02 − 0.15 because she knows 15 basis points means 0.15.

Exchange Rates in Canadian Dollars	
Austria shilling	0.1451
Brazil real	1.5702
Finland mark	0.3367
Hong Kong dollar	0.1822
Iraq dinar	2.3553
Netherlands guilder	0.9089
Singapore dollar	1.0139
UK pound	2.2257

1. a) Which of the countries listed have a basic currency unit worth more than our dollar?
   b) How much would you receive in each of those currencies for $500 Canadian?

1. Use the *Exchange Rates* table.

a) How much would you receive for $500 Canadian in each of the currencies whose basic unit is worth less than our dollar?

b) Which country's unit of currency is closest in value to our dollar? How did you decide?

c) If you had 5000 Brazilian real, how many Canadian dollars would you receive?

d) If you had 5000 Finnish marks, how many Canadian dollars would you receive?

2.

1993 World Series Champions Toronto Blue Jays		
	hits	**at bats**
Alamar, Roberto	192	580
Carter, Joe	153	603
Molitor, Paul	211	636
Olerud, John	200	551
White, Devon	163	598

a) Joe Carter's batting average is 0.254. How is batting average calculated?
b) Calculate the batting average for each of the other players.
c) List the players from best to worst batting average.
d) Find the average of the five players' batting averages.
e) If Paul Molitor had been at bat two more times but didn't make any more hits, would his batting average increase or decrease? Explain.

3. Three workers take 4 h, 4 h, and 5 h respectively to unload a truck alone. How long would it take all three workers working together to unload the truck? Hint: What fraction of the truck can each worker unload in an hour?

4. How much more would it cost to take a 1500 km trip in a car with a fuel consumption rate of 12.7 L/100 km than in a car with a fuel consumption rate of 6.3 L/100 km if the cost of fuel is $0.55/L?

5. Use this weekly pay statement.

Employee	Earnings		Deductions				Net
	Regular	Other	Tax	CPP	UIC	Hosp Ins.	
Ken Tom	$214.89		$19.00	$2.50	$2.15	$11.25	$179

a) How is net pay calculated?
b) What percent of Ken's earnings are his deductions?
c) Ken works 20 h each week. What are his earnings per hour and his net pay per hour?

6. a) How do you find unit price?
b) Find the unit prices of these peanut butters.

Super Brand	475 mL	$4.89
Value Brand	450 mL	$4.95
Star Brand	518 mL	$5.44

c) Assuming the quality is comparable, which is the best buy?

7. Find the length of each line segment.

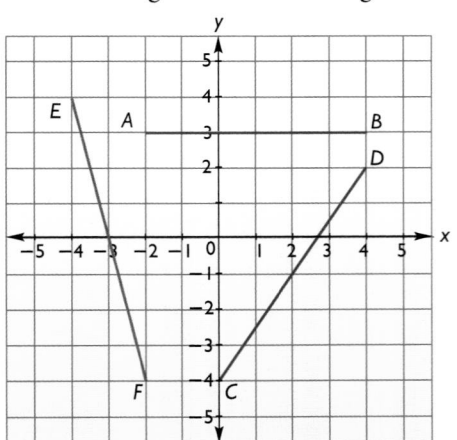

8. Some countries use the Fahrenheit temperature scale. This formula converts Fahrenheit temperature to Celsius, $C = \frac{5}{9}(F - 32)$.

Convert each Fahrenheit temperature to Celsius.
a) 212°F   **b)** 32°F   **c)** 99.8°F
d) 68°F   **e)** 0°F   **d)** −40°F

9. A swimming pool is filled using three hoses of different sizes. One hose can fill the pool in 8 h by itself. Another hose can fill it in 12 h by itself. The third hose can fill it in 24 h by itself. If all three hoses are used at the same time, how long does it take to fill the pool?

More Than One Strategy

Using a Scientific Calculator

There are several ways to use a scientific calculator to evaluate
$\dfrac{154.56}{2.3 \times (14.5 + 7.9)}$ on this calculator.

Here are some. Can you think of any others?

1. You might use the brackets keys and memory keys to evaluate the denominator first.

2.3 $\boxed{\times}$ $\boxed{(}$ 14.5 $\boxed{+}$ 7.9 $\boxed{)}$ $\boxed{\text{STO}}$ 154.56 $\boxed{\div}$ $\boxed{\text{RCL}}$ $\boxed{=}$ $\quad\fbox{3.}$

2. You can use the equals key to complete subparts and the memory keys to evaluate the denominator first.

14.5 $\boxed{+}$ 7.9 $\boxed{=}$ $\boxed{\times}$ 2.3 $\boxed{\text{STO}}$ 154.56 $\boxed{\div}$ $\boxed{\text{RCL}}$ $\boxed{=}$ $\quad\fbox{3.}$

3. You could use the brackets keys and the reciprocal key to evaluate the denominator first.

2.3 $\boxed{\times}$ $\boxed{(}$ 14.5 $\boxed{+}$ 7.9 $\boxed{)}$ $\boxed{\div}$ 154.56 $\boxed{=}$ $\boxed{1/x}$ $\quad\fbox{3.}$

4. You might use the equals key to complete subparts and multiply by the denominator using the reciprocal key.

14.5 $\boxed{+}$ 7.9 $\boxed{=}$ $\boxed{\times}$ 2.3 $\boxed{=}$ $\boxed{1/x}$ $\boxed{\times}$ 154.56 $\boxed{=}$ $\quad\fbox{3.}$

5. You can enter in order by using the brackets keys.

$154.56 \div [2.3 \times (14.5 + 7.9)]$

154.56 $\boxed{\div}$ $\boxed{(}$ 2.3 $\boxed{\times}$ $\boxed{(}$ 14.5 $\boxed{+}$ 7.9 $\boxed{)}$ $\boxed{)}$ $\boxed{=}$ $\quad\fbox{3.}$

Understand and Apply

Evaluate each two ways.

1. $2.7 - 3.5^3 \times 4.4$
2. $\sqrt{200} - 4.4^2$
3. $\dfrac{8.61 \times 3.01^2}{-15.82 + 9.35}$
4. $\left[\dfrac{4(3.2) - 6(8.5)}{2(5.7)}\right]^2$

Problems to Investigate

ESTIMATE

Tell how you would estimate the value of this expression quickly and in your head.

$$\frac{4.61\,(3.75 + 6.28)}{13.62 \div 2.11}$$

CONTINUOUS RATIONAL

Evaluate the following expression with a calculator.

$$\cfrac{1}{2 + \cfrac{1}{2 + \cfrac{1}{2 + \cfrac{1}{2 + \cfrac{1}{2}}}}}$$

GREATEST VOLUME

Estimate and calculate to determine which solid has the greatest volume.

$$V = s^3 \qquad V = \frac{4}{3}\pi r^3 \qquad V = \pi r^2 h$$

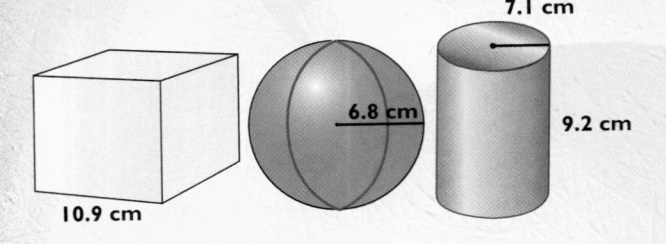

10.9 cm   6.8 cm   7.1 cm   9.2 cm

DIAPHANTUS

Diaphantus was a Greek mathematician. When he died, his epitaph read as follows: Diaphantus passed $\frac{1}{6}$ of his life in childhood, $\frac{1}{12}$ in youth, and $\frac{1}{7}$ as a bachelor young man. His son was born 5 years after his marriage but 4 years before he reached $\frac{1}{2}$ his father's age at death.
How old was Diaphantus when he died?

EFFICIENT KEYSTROKES

Estimate and then calculate this expression using an efficient set of keystrokes. Justify why you did it the way you did.

$$\frac{7.1[14.5 - (8.6 + 2.3^2)]}{2.5 \times 7.8 - 3.8^2 - 0.729}$$

CALCULATING π

Many mathematicians have studied π. Gottfried Leibniz showed that the value of π could be found using

$$4 - \frac{4}{3} + \frac{4}{5} - \frac{4}{7} + \frac{4}{9} - \blacksquare + \blacksquare - \ldots$$

What are the next two rational numbers? Calculate the value of π using this expression as far as the rational numbers you included.

Make up some other problems involving calculating with rational numbers. Post them on the bulletin board for your classmates to solve.

Interpreting Multiple Graphs

The following graphs are from Statistics Canada. Each shows some aspect of education or earnings of Canadians.

Education Completed by Population Aged 20 to 24, 1991

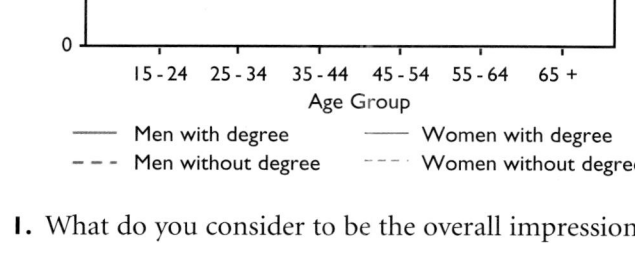

☐ No certificate ☐ Secondary ☐ Trades/Non-university ☐ University

Composition of Total Income, 1990 (Percent)

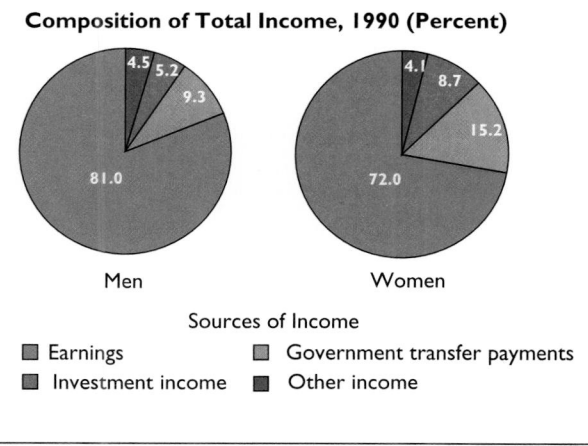

Sources of Income

☐ Earnings ☐ Government transfer payments
☐ Investment income ☐ Other income

Average Earnings, 1990

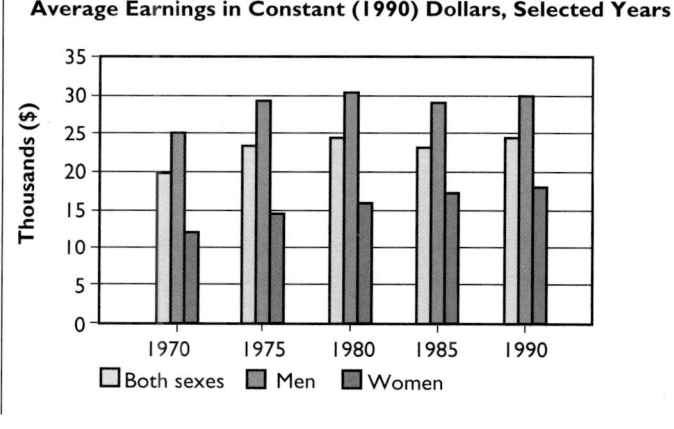

— Men with degree   — Women with degree
– – – Men without degree   – – – Women without degree

Average Earnings in Constant (1990) Dollars, Selected Years

☐ Both sexes ☐ Men ☐ Women

1. What do you consider to be the overall impression created by each graph?

Applications

2. Which province or territory has the greatest percent of 20- to 24-year-olds with
  a) no certificate?
  b) secondary diploma?
  c) trade or non-university diploma?
  d) university diploma?

3. Do men or women have the greater percent of their total income from
  a) government transfer payments?
  b) investment income?

4. a) Which group (gender and education) has the greatest fluctuation in their earnings? the least?
  b) At which age group is the greatest difference in the earnings of those with and without a university degree for men? women?

5. a) Between which two years shown did the average earnings increase the most for men?
  b) Between which two years did the average earnings decrease for both sexes and for men, but marginally increase for women?

Solve Problems by Looking for Patterns

LET THE GAMES BEGIN

Each of 16 badminton teams are to play each of the other teams once. How many games will be played?

▶ **Understand the Problem**

1. What are you asked to find?
2. What do you know?
3. Where will you begin?

▶ **Think of a Plan**

Dana solved this problem by drawing diagrams and then looking for a pattern.

▶ **Carry Out the Plan**

▶ **Look Back**

4. Is there an expression or formula you could use to solve the problem another way?

Number of Teams	2	3	4	5
Number of Games	1	3	6	10
Pattern	$\frac{1 \times 2}{2}$	$\frac{2 \times 3}{2}$	$\frac{3 \times 4}{2}$	$\frac{4 \times 5}{2}$

So 16 teams would play $\frac{15 \times 16}{2}$ or 120 games.

Applications

Solve each by first using a strategy such as drawing diagrams, working backwards, or making a table, and then looking for a pattern.

PLAY BALL

How many games would 8 softball teams play if each team played each other team twice?

TAKE A NUMBER

The bake shop has number cards from 1 to 99 for customers to take to ensure that they are served in order. How many of each digit from 0 to 9 are on the 99 number cards?

REPEATING DECIMALS

• Express these rationals in decimal form. Look for a pattern.

$$\frac{1}{9}, -\frac{4}{9}, \frac{6}{9}, \text{ and } 1\frac{7}{9}$$

Now use the pattern to change these rationals to fractional form. $0.\overline{2}, -0.\overline{3}, -0.\overline{8}, \text{ and } 1.\overline{5}$

• Express these rationals in decimal form. Look for a pattern.

$$\frac{23}{99}, -\frac{47}{99}, \text{ and } -\frac{76}{99}$$

Now use the pattern to change these rationals to fractional form. $0.\overline{31}, -0.\overline{57}, \text{ and } 1.\overline{83}$

• What are $0.\overline{123}, -0.\overline{457}, -0.2\overline{546}, \text{ and } 0.4\overline{007}$ in fractional form?

1. Give two examples of each.
   a) an integer that is not a whole number
   b) a rational number that is not an integer
   c) an irrational number

2. a) Which types of decimals are rational numbers?
   b) Give two examples of each type of decimal from part (a).

3. What are the values for each unknown?
   a) $m^2 = 361$
   b) $h^2 = 37.21$
   c) $k^2 = 3844$
   d) $w^2 = 96.04$

4. What is the length of each side of the square table top?

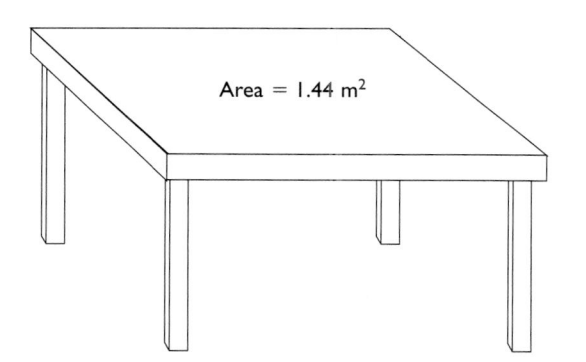

Area = 1.44 m²

5. What is the length of side p rounded to 1 decimal place?

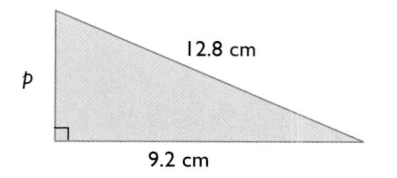

12.8 cm

p

9.2 cm

6. Estimate each answer.
   a) $4.6 + 5.2 + 8.3 + 10.7$
   b) $4.21(7.36 + 8.79)$
   c) $\dfrac{18.32 - 4.65}{7.96 - 5.21}$

7. Estimate the perimeter and the area of this backyard.

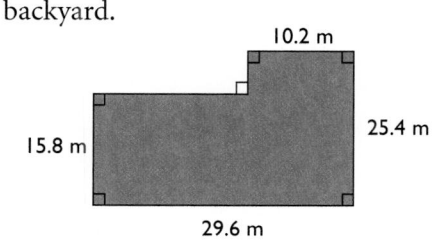

10.2 m

15.8 m

25.4 m

29.6 m

8. Estimate and then calculate each using an efficient set of keystrokes.
   a) $6.8 + 7.9 \times 3.5$
   b) $\dfrac{17.1}{13.5 - 2.1}$

9. Sylvia is paid $10.35/h. Calculate how much she earns working these hours.

Fri.	Sat.	Sun.
$4\frac{1}{2}$ h	$8\frac{3}{4}$ h	$3\frac{1}{4}$ h

10. The costs to taxpayers to house one inmate in jail overnight are as shown.

Newfoundland	$134
Prince Edward Island	$121
Nova Scotia	$120
New Brunswick	$ 83
Quebec	$ 91
Ontario	$116
Manitoba	$ 86
Saskatchewan	$ 74
Alberta	$ 83
British Columbia	$106
Yukon	$101
Northwest Territories	$ 96

a) What is the difference between the greatest cost and the least cost?
b) Find each average cost.

mean   median   mode

Practise With Games

Play each game in a group of 2, 3, or 4 players.

Square Root Concentration

- Use the 30 Square Root Cards (one card in each pair shows a whole number in the square root symbol and the other card shows the square root of the number or its decimal approximation).

- Shuffle the cards and place them face down in an array.

- Turn up two cards.

- If the cards represent the same number, take the cards.

- If the cards do not represent the same number, turn the cards face down again.

- Take turns until no cards are left.

- The player with the most cards wins.

Example:

$\sqrt{2} \approx 1.41$ so take the cards.

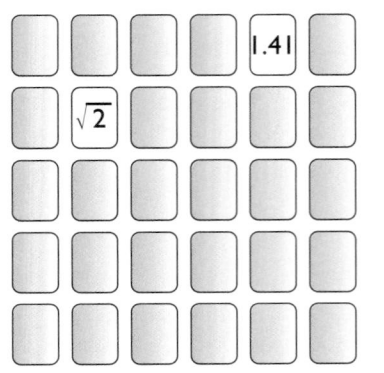

Rational Number 21

- Use the 24 Rational Number Cards.

- Shuffle the cards and deal each player 3 cards.

- Use the numbers on your 3 cards and any of addition, subtraction, multiplication, division, squaring, finding the square root, and brackets to create an expression close to 21.

- The player closest to 21 scores 1 point.

- Continue playing.

- The first player to score 5 points wins.

Example:

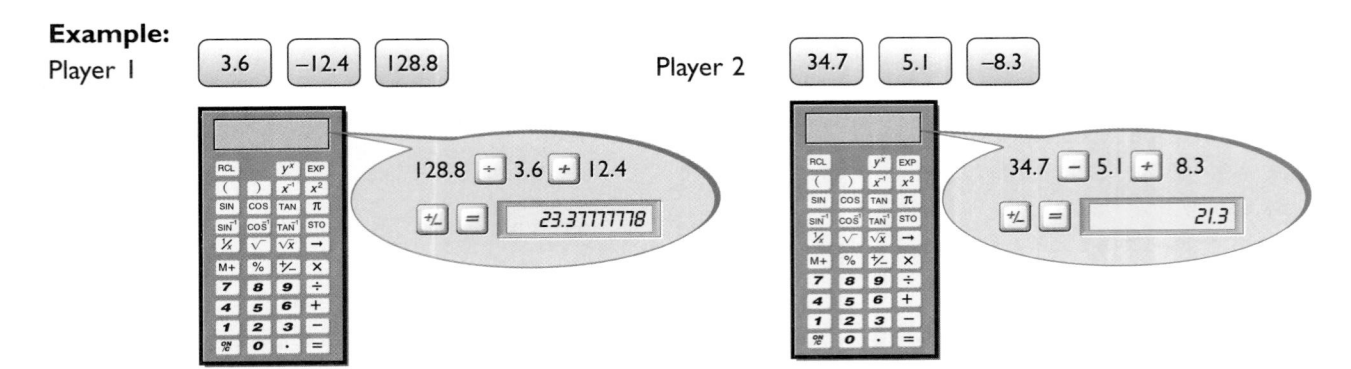

Player 2 scores 1 point because 21.3 is closer than 23.38 to 21.

Problems to Investigate

RATIONAL? INTEGER? WHOLE?

Explain why −4 is both a rational number and an integer but not both an integer and a whole number.

SQUARES

The largest square has an area of 144 cm². Each square is twice the area of the next smallest square. Find the length of the sides of each square.

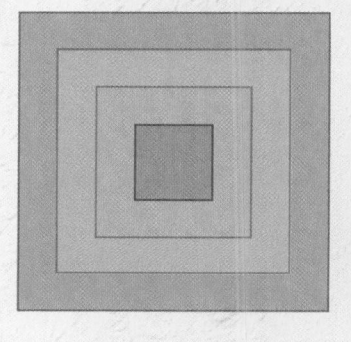

MAGIC SQUARE

Find the magic number and complete the magic square.

	168.2		53.0	103.4
161.0	31.4	45.8	96.2	110.6
24.2		89.0		153.8
67.4	81.8		146.6	
	126.0			

AREAS OF CIRCLES

The area of a circle is quadrupled. What will happen to its radius?

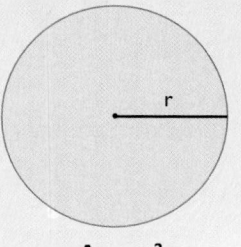

$A = \pi r^2$

CALCULATOR ORDER

How would you rate each set of keystrokes to evaluate 2.3 + 4.5 × 7.2?

- 4.5 [×] 7.2 [+] 2.3 [=]
- 2.3 [STO] 4.5 [×] 7.2 [+] [RCL] [=]
- [(( ] 4.5 [×] 7.2 [ )] [+] 2.3 [=]
- 4.5 [×] 7.2 [=] [+] 2.3 [=]
- 2.3 [+] 4.5 [×] 7.2 [=]

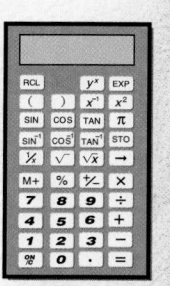

HANDSHAKES

If 21 people attend a meeting and each person shakes hands with each of the other people, how many handshakes will occur?

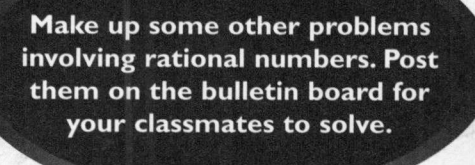

Make up some other problems involving rational numbers. Post them on the bulletin board for your classmates to solve.

1. **a)** To which sets of numbers does 10 belong?
   b) How can a number belong to more than one set of numbers?

2. **a)** What are the three types of decimals?
   b) Give an example of each type.
   c) Which types of decimals are rational numbers? Why?

3. Why is the square root of 5 an irrational number?

4. Evaluate if possible.
   a) $\sqrt{169}$ **b)** $-\sqrt{225}$ **c)** $\sqrt{-196}$

5. What are the values for x in $x^2 = 77.44$? Explain your answer.

6. A can has a volume of 2760 cm^3 and a height of 19 cm. How many possible values are there for the radius? What are they?

$$V = \pi r^2 h$$

7. Estimate the total cost.
   0.6 kg of raisins @ $3.90/kg
   0.25 kg of almonds @ $11.85/kg
   1.1 kg of flour @ $1.39/kg
   0.45 kg of sugar @ $2.19/kg

8. Estimate to see if these calculated answers are reasonable.
   a) $(48.3 - 19.6)^2 \div 25.2 = -13.3$
   b) $\dfrac{21.5 - 13.2 \times 8.6}{9.5} = 7.5$
   c) $197.5 \div (-15.8) + 12.5 = 0$

9. Record and justify an efficient set of keystrokes that can be used to evaluate $3.2 \times 4.6 - 1.5 \times 2.7$.

10. Estimate and then calculate using an efficient set of keystrokes. Justify why you used the set of keystrokes you did.
    $$\frac{10.9 + 8.6}{15.2 - 9.5 \times 2.1}$$

11. A rectangular pool is surrounded by a patio of a uniform width. What is the area of the patio?

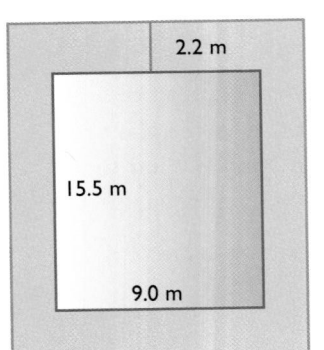

2.2 m

15.5 m

9.0 m

12. This graph shows the speed of particles.

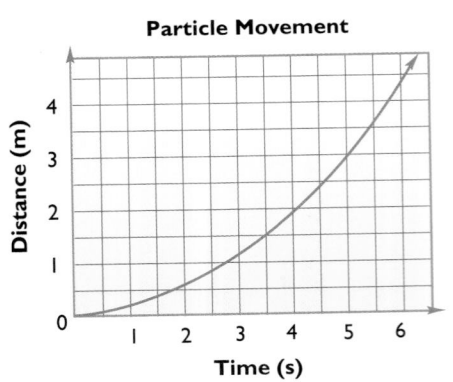

Particle Movement

Distance (m)

Time (s)

   a) How far does the particle move in
   4 s?   2 s?   3 s?   5 s?
   b) How long does it take the particle to move 4.5 m?
   c) Use the formula $d = 0.125t^2$ where d is the distance in metres and t is the time in seconds to find the answers to parts (a) and (b).
   d) Compare your answers from part (c) with those from parts (a) and (b).

1. Rational numbers are the set of numbers in the form $\frac{a}{b}$ where a and b are integers and $b \neq 0$.

Use other words to define rational numbers.

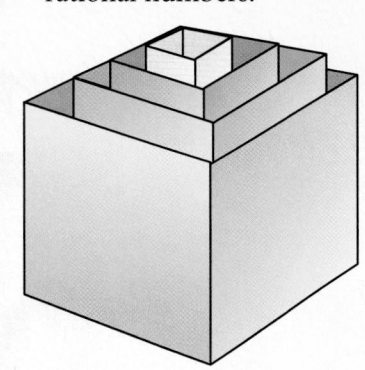

6. Make up a problem for your classmates to solve that has an answer which is a negative rational number.

2. How would you explain finding a square root to someone who is having difficulty understanding it?

5. To evaluate this expression

$$\frac{4.2}{7.9 + 18.3}$$ Pat used these keystrokes.

4.2 $\boxed{\div}$ 7.9 $\boxed{+}$ 18.3 $\boxed{=}$

Will Pat get the correct answer? If not, how would you change the keystrokes?

3. Problems involving finding a square root always have two answers.

Do you agree or disagree? Explain why.

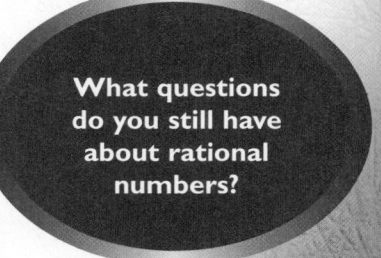

What questions do you still have about rational numbers?

4. Why is it important to be good at estimating the results of calculations involving rational numbers?

PIZZA

Ingredients

Pepperoni		Salami
Fresh Hot Pepper	Ham	Sun Dried Tomato
Fresh Mushrooms	Hot Peppers	Sliced Tomato
Green Peppers	Double Cheese	Anchovies
Bacon	Green Olives	Pineapple
Onion	Black Olives	Ground Beef
Italian Sausage	Capicollo	Fresh Garlic
Capers	Artichoke	Roasted Red Peppers

*Thin or Thick Crust, Extra Pizza Sauce, Chili Pepper, Fresh Garlic
Available upon request at no extra charge.*

SMALL 11"	MEDIUM 13"	LARGE 15"	PARTY SIZE 15" x 21"
Basic	Basic	Basic	Basic
$6.50	$8.75	$10.25	$14.00

Additional Ingredients: (Per Item)

$0.75	$1.00	$1.25	$1.75

Delivery — $1.00

Polynomials (I)

These students are investigating the cost of pizza for a class party.

- Write and evaluate an expression to show the number to order for a party for your class.
    a) party-size pizzas
    b) additional toppings

    For a different class, what numbers might change? remain the same? Explain.

- Suppose 2 other classes ordered the same as your class. What is the expression for the cost for all 3 classes? Write the expression without, then with delivery charges.

- Suppose the prices of pizza doubled and the prices of additional toppings tripled. What is the expression for the new cost without delivery charges for your class? all 3 classes?

- Use algebra to represent your expressions for pizza.

Describe another situation in which algebra might be used to represent expressions. Identify the quantities that might change and those that would likely remain the same.

5.1 Staying the Same or Changing

Warm Up

All vowels are worth a certain amount, and consonants are worth a different amount. Determine the value for Saskatoon if Regina is worth $54, Winnipeg $90, Victoria $96, and Calgary $60.

When Duncan and Lee studied these advertisements, they realized that each situation has factors that are fixed or **constant** and factors that are **variable**. They started a list of each.

YANKEES
vs
BLUE JAYS

at
The SKYDOME
Saturday, June 5
Game starts at 1:30
Ticket Prices: $8, $15, $20

Listen To
103.5
CMUS-FM

Every Morning
Monday to Friday
6:30 to 9:00 a.m.

Dave and Monica
They'll Make You Laugh
And Play All Your Favorites

Concept Development

1. Do you agree with their examples of constants and variables? Why or why not?

2. What other examples can you add to their list? Justify your choices.

3. How would you explain to a classmate how to identify a constant? a variable?

Constants and variables are also used in algebra to create algebraic expressions and equations.

4. The expression $4a^2 - 19 - 12b + 11cd$ contains four **terms**. One of the terms is $-12b$.
   a) Identify the other terms.
   b) Which is the constant term? Explain why it's constant.

5. The term $-12b$ contains the variable b. Name the other variables in the expression.

6. The integer -12 in the term $-12b$ is called the **numerical coefficient**.
   a) What does the numerical coefficient mean?
   b) Name the other numerical coefficients in the expression.
   c) How would you explain to a classmate how to identify a numerical coefficient?

7. Is there a constant in an expression such as $3a^3b^2$? Explain.

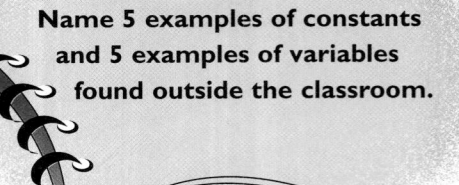

In Your Journal

Name 5 examples of constants and 5 examples of variables found outside the classroom.

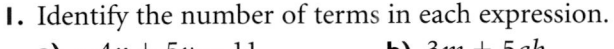

1. Identify the number of terms in each expression.
   a) $-4x + 5y - 11$ b) $3m + 5ab$
   c) $m^2 + 3m - 9d + 2$ d) $-2abc$

2. Examine the expressions in Problem 1. The + and − signs are part of the terms. Why don't $3m$ in part (b) and m^2 in part (c) have signs?

3. Identify the variables, constants, and numerical coefficients.
   a) $2h + 4t - 18m + 19$
   b) $-6a^4b$ c) $3ab - 12a^2 - 1$
   d) $-5bc^3 - 4c + r - 11$
   e) $-x^4$ f) $-bd + h$
   g) $\dfrac{x^2}{5}$ h) $A = \dfrac{bh}{\pi}$
   i) $4x - 3 = 2y$ j) $C = 2\pi r$

4. a) Use all seven cards to create four different algebraic expressions.

   b) List the number of terms, numerical coefficients, and constant term(s) for each expression.
   c) What is the least number of terms that can be in the expression? the greatest number?

5. Create an expression that contains:
   a) one term   b) two terms
   c) three terms   d) more than 4 terms

6. A term does not have to contain a variable. Create an expression with two terms and no variables. Why is this called a numerical expression?

7. $2n^2 + 5$ is an expression and $2n^2 + 5 = 55$ is an equation. How does an equation differ from an expression?

8. Create an equation that contains:
   a) two terms   b) three terms

9. Create an equation that has
   a) two variables, one constant, and two terms
   b) two variables, one constant, and three terms

10. Create an expression with
   a) two variables, one constant, and three terms
   b) two variables, one constant, and two terms
   c) two constants, two variables, and three terms
   d) no constants, one variable, and two terms

11. a) Create 12 different-looking expressions with all of the cards.

   b) What is the greatest number of terms that can be in the expression? the least number? What is the greatest number of constants that can be in the expression? the least number?
   c) Look for expressions that appear to be different but are really the same. Explain why they are the same.
   d) Which expressions are not the same? Explain why they aren't.

12. Duncan and Lee also looked at a poster advertising an upcoming rock concert in a park. List as many variable and constant factors that you can think of about the concert.

13. What everyday events contain variables and constants? Compare your list with that of a classmate or group. How many different events were listed in all?

HOME LINK
Find 4 or 5 situations from news and advertising for which constants and variables are presented. Identify the constant and variable factors.

Evaluating Polynomial Expressions

5.2 Valuing Expressions

Geometric patterns can often be represented by algebraic expressions.

Concept Development

1. What pattern do you see in this series of diagrams?

Diagram   **1**   **2**   **3**

Jacob found a relationship between the diagram number and the number of hexagons in the diagram.

He described the relationship in words.

The number of small hexagons in any diagram is found by squaring the diagram number and multiplying by 3, then subtracting three times the diagram number and adding one.

He wrote the relationship as an algebraic expression:

$$3d^2 - 3d + 1$$

2. How would you verify that his expression works for diagrams 1, 2, and 3? Explain your method to a classmate. How are your methods similar? different?

3. a) Explain to a classmate how you would determine the number of hexagons in diagram 10 and in diagram 25.

b) What calculation does this set of keystrokes represent?

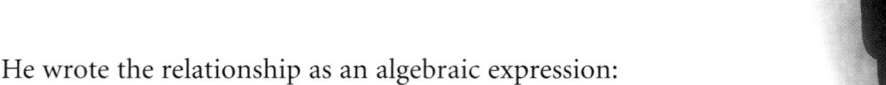

Use a calculator to find the number of hexagons in diagram 10 and diagram 25.

Understand and Apply

1. Find the value of each expression when
$m = 1, 2, 3, 4, 6, 8, 9$.
   a) $5m$ b) $m + 5$ c) $m - 5$
   d) $5 - m$ e) $\dfrac{m}{5}$ f) $\dfrac{5}{m}$

2. a) For which expression(s) in Problem 1 does the value of the expression increase as the value for m increases?
   b) Which expression increases in value the fastest? slowest? Explain why.
   c) What happens to the value of each expression as m doubles in value ($m = 1, 2, 4, 8$)? triples in value ($m = 1, 3, 9$ and $2, 6$)? quadruples in value ($m = 1, 4$ and $2, 8$)?

3. Find the value of each when $n = 1, 2, 3, 4, 6, 8, 9$.
   a) $5n^2$ b) $n^2 + 5$ c) $n^2 - 5$
   d) $5 - n^2$ e) $\dfrac{n^2}{5}$ f) $\dfrac{5}{n^2}$

4. a) For which expression(s) in Problem 3 does the value increase as the value for n increases?
   b) Which expression increases in value the fastest? slowest? Explain why.

5. Find the value of each when $b = 1, 2, 3, 4, 6, 8, 9$.
   a) $5b^3$ b) $b^3 + 5$ c) $b^3 - 5$
   d) $5 - b^3$ e) $\dfrac{b^3}{5}$ f) $\dfrac{5}{b^3}$

6. a) For which expression(s) in Problem 5 does the value increase as the value for b increases?
   b) Which expression increases in value the fastest? slowest? Explain why.

7. Substitute the values $-1, -2, -3, -4, -6, -8, -9$ for the variables in Problems 1, 3, and 5. Which expressions have a value that is the opposite? Explain why.

8. Create an expression for each property:
   a) doubling the value of the variable doubles the value of the expression
   b) adding one to the value of the variable increases the value of the expression by one
   c) subtracting one from the value of the variable increases the value of the expression by one
   d) changing the value of the variable to its opposite changes the value of the expression to its opposite

9. a) Find the value of $n^2 - n + 41$ for
   $n = 2, 4, 7, 10, 20, 25, 31$.
   b) How are the values similar?
   c) Find the value when $n = 41$. Does its value have the same properties as those in part (a)? Why or why not?

10. Find the value when $x = -3, -2, -1, 0, 1, 2, 3$.
    a) $x^2 + 2x - 4$ b) $x^2 + 2x - 2$
    c) $x^2 + 2x$ d) $x^2 + 2x + 2$

11. Describe the change in the value of the expressions in Problem 10 as the value of the constant increases from -4 to $+2$.

12. The expression for the greatest area of a rectangular garden enclosed by 20 m of fencing is $(20\ell - 2\ell^2)$ square metres, where ℓ represents the length of the rectangle. What whole number value for ℓ gives the greatest area? How do you know?

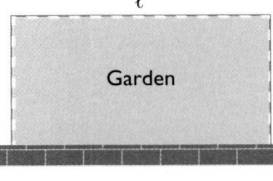

13. The cost, in dollars, to rent a van is given by the expression $33d + 0.2k$, where d is the number of days rented and k is the number of kilometres driven. Find the rental cost.
    a) $d = 3$ and $k = 1500$ km
    b) $d = 6$ and $k = 3215$ km
    c) $d = 2$ and $k = 1276$ km, but the first 500 km are free

14. Find three values for x and three values for y which make $-3x^2 - y^3$ positive.

15. Find three values for a and three values for b which make $4a^2 + b^3$ negative.

Choose 3 or 4 items from take-out menus and create an algebraic expression to represent the cost of a meal made up of these items.

Making Sense of DATA

Spreadsheet Formulas

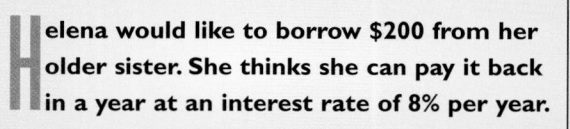

Helena would like to borrow $200 from her older sister. She thinks she can pay it back in a year at an interest rate of 8% per year.

1. How much interest will she have to pay on the loan? Explain what you did to find the interest.

Helena uses the simple interest formula, $I = PRT$, to determine the interest owing (P represents the principal, R represents the rate, and T represents the time period).

She uses a spreadsheet to keep track of the data.

She creates headings to organize the information.

She formats columns A and D for currency to two decimal places and column B for percent to two decimal places.

	A	B	C	D	E	F
1	Principal ($)	Rate (%)	Time (yrs)	Interest ($)		
2	$200.00	8.00%	1	= A2*B2*C2		
3						
4						

She enters 200 in cell A2, .08 in cell B2, 1 in cell C2, and the formula to calculate the interest, =A2*B2*C2, in cell D2.

2. Explain what the formula A2*B2*C2 represents.

3. What amount will appear in cell D2 when the program evaluates the formula?

4. The formula in cell D2 will automatically recalculate the interest for any changes to cells A2, B2, and C2. What interest will Helena pay if
   a) the principal is doubled? tripled? halved? (R and T remain constant.)
   b) the rate is halved? doubled? (T and P remain constant.)
   c) the time is over 3 years? 1.5 years? 0.5 years? (P and R remain constant.)

Applications

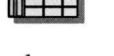

5. Helena wonders how the interest will be affected if she pays off the loan in less time. Redesign cells C1 and D2 so the spreadsheet will calculate the interest owing when the time is given in

   a) months
   b) days   (P and R remain constant.)

6. What interest will Helena pay if the time is
   a) 4 months? 5 months? 9 months?
   b) 120 days? 300 days? 90 days?

7. Write a heading for cell E1 and a formula for cell E2 so that the total amount to be paid back, interest and principal, is given in cell E2.

Problems to Investigate

POSTER PONDERING

How would you complete the poster so all missing information represents variable situations?

> ### The Computer Club Surfing On
>
> Date: _____
>
> Time: _____
>
> Location: _____
>
> Cost: _____

FOUR IN A ROW

The variables a, b, c, and d represent consecutive whole numbers but are not in order. Find values for a, b, c, and d so that the equation $a^2 - c^2 = b + d$ is true. How many groups of four can you find? Describe the pattern shown by their placement in the equation.

A TRYING PROBLEM

Find integer values for x and y for which the value of $8x + 1 - y^2$ is 0. What patterns do you notice for the values of x and y?

EVALUATION QUEST

Evaluate $2x + 6x^2 - 7$ when $x = -1$. For what values of x is the expression positive? negative?

EXPRESSIONS GALORE

Use all of these cards to make 12 different three-term expressions. (Assume no exponents.)

$$\boxed{4} \quad \boxed{+} \quad \boxed{5} \quad \boxed{m} \quad \boxed{n} \quad \boxed{-6}$$

If 2 is substituted for m, -2 for n, and 3 for p, which expression has the greatest value? least value? value closest to 0?
What if you allow exponents greater than 1?

> Make up other problems about terms and algebraic expressions. Post them on the bulletin board for classmates to solve.

5.3 Understanding Number Tricks

Each perimeter is 12x. Find
the missing lengths.

a)

4x

3x

2x

b)

2x

2x

c) an equilateral triangle
d) a regular hexagon
e) a regular decagon
f) a polygon of your
   choice

Duncan and Kim found
this number trick in a
puzzle book.

> **Think of a whole number.**
>
> **Multiply it by 4.**
>
> **Add 3.**
>
> **Double it.**
>
> **Subtract 6.**
>
> **What's your answer?**

Kim tried the trick, keeping her original number secret. Her final answer was 88.
Duncan was able to tell what Kim's original number was without going through the steps backwards.

Concept Development

1. **a)** Try the number trick. How is your final answer related
   to your original number?
   b) Try the trick again with another number. What do you notice
   when you compare your original number and final answer?
   c) What was Kim's original number?
   d) Do you think the trick will work for any whole number? integer?

		Duncan used algebra tiles to model the first four steps in the trick.	Kim wrote an expression to represent each step.
Step 1	Think of a whole number.		x
Step 2	Multiply it by 4.		$4x$
Step 3	Add 3.		$4x + 3$
Step 4	Double it.		$4x + 3 + 4x + 3$

2. What does each green rod represent? What variable did Kim use to represent the original number?

3. In Step 4, which tiles can be combined? cannot be combined? Explain.

4. Kim used the expression $8x + 6$ to describe the group of tiles in Step 4.
   a) How do you think Kim obtained the 8 in $8x$?
   b) Why can't $8x$ and 6 be combined?

5. How can Duncan use the tiles to show Step 5, which is to subtract 6? What expression should Kim write?

6. How does Kim's expression relate to your discovery in Problem 1 b)?

7. Terms such as x, $4x$, and $8x$ are called **like terms**. What is meant by *like terms*? Terms such as x and $4b$ are **unlike terms**. What is meant by *unlike terms*? List other like and unlike terms.

Understand and Apply

1. a) Use algebra tiles to model each step of this age trick. Use a green rod to represent the age, *a*.

Step 1   Write the age of a parent or guardian.
Step 2   Add 5 to that age.
Step 3   Double the result.
Step 4   Subtract 8.
Step 5   Divide by 2.
Step 6   Subtract 1.
Step 7   Read your result.

b) Write the expression for each step.

c) How would you determine the age, or find *a*, after Step 3?

2. A number trick has six steps. Step 1 is to write a number. At the end of Step 4 there are three green rods and three red squares. Step 6 gives the original number.

a) What might Steps 5 and 6 be? Model them with tiles.

b) What might Steps 2, 3, and 4 be? Model them with tiles and write the expression for each step.

3. Examine a green rod and a red square.

a) Explain the differences between the two tiles.

b) How do you know that *x* and 1 are not like terms?

c) How do you know that *x* and −*x* are like terms?

4. Examine a green rod and a green square.

a) Explain the differences between the two tiles.

b) How do you know that x and x^2 are not like terms?

c) How do you know that x^2 and $-x^2$ are like terms?

5. Identify the like terms in each row.

a) $2x, 2, -3x, 2x^2, -3$

b) $7a, -7a, a^2, a, 7$

c) $-4, -4b, -4b^2, 3b^2, b^3, 3b$

d) $a^3, 2a^2, 2a^3, a, -3a^2, -4a$

6. a) The orange rod represents the variable *y*. What does the orange square represent? What if the orange rod is flipped over? What if the orange square is flipped over?

b) Write the expression to describe what happens when an orange square and a flipped orange square are combined. Why do you think this is called the "zero model"?

7. a) Use quantity, color, and shape to describe each group.

b) Write an expression for each group.

Group I   Group II   Group III

8. Write an expression for the following combined groups from Problem 7.

a) Group I + Group II   **b)** Group III + Group I

c) all 3 groups

9. Simplify the expressions by combining like terms. Model with algebra tiles.

a) $4x + 5 - 2x$ **b)** $x^2 - 3x + 2x^2$

c) $-x - 3 + x^2 + x$ **d)** $3y + 5 - 6x - 4y$

e) $x^2 + y + x + y^2 + x^2 + y$

10. How can you solve Problem 9 without using algebra tiles?

11. a) The term $6y$ can be written as the sum of two terms. What might the terms be?

b) In what different ways can $6y$ be written as the sum of three terms?

12. a) Explain why $4x + 1$ and $1 + 4x$ always have the same value.

b) Explain why $4x + 1$ and $1 - 4x$ do not always have the same value.

Write another pair of expressions that don't always have the same value.

13. a) Create three like terms for $-5xy$. Now, create two unlike terms.

b) Repeat part (a) for $3a^2b^2$ and $-xy^2$.

Estimate the dimensions of a room at home in relation to one of your paces, *p*. What is the perimeter of the room in terms of *p*?

111

5.4 Modelling with Algebra Tiles

> Algebra tiles can be used to model expressions.

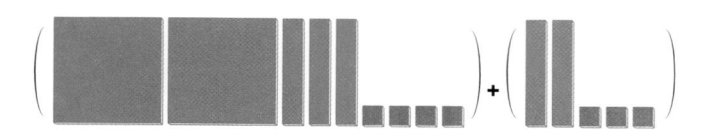

Prina uses algebra tiles to represent this addition:

$$(2x^2 + 3x + 4) + (2x + 3)$$

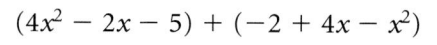

Concept Development

1. Which tiles can be combined? Why?

2. How many tiles of each size and color will be in the sum?
   Write an expression to represent the sum.

3. a) Which size and color of tiles would you use to model this addition?

   $$(4x^2 - 2x - 5) + (-2 + 4x - x^2)$$

   b) Which tiles would you combine to find the sum of the expressions?
   Write a new expression.

Understand and Apply

1. For each of these additions modelled with algebra tiles
   • write the algebraic expression.
   • display the sum using tiles.
   • show your display in more than one way.
   • compare your displays with a classmate.
     How do they differ?

   a)

   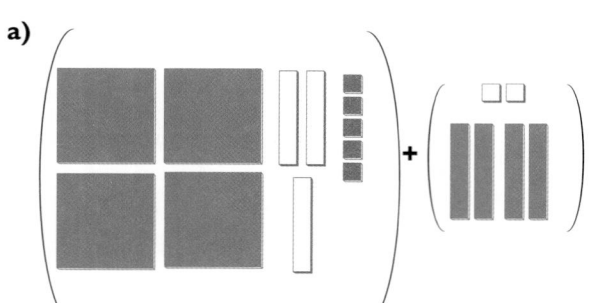

   b)

   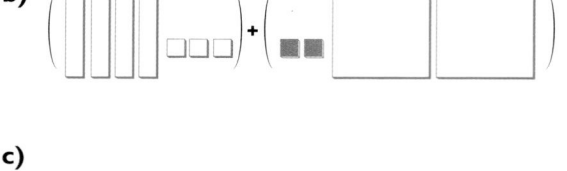

   c)

   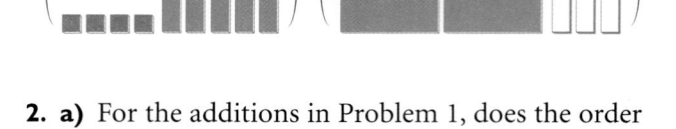

2. a) For the additions in Problem 1, does the order in which the tiles are displayed in the sum matter? Why or why not?
   b) Write the new expression for each part in Problem 1.

Prina challenged her group with this addition problem.

$(x^2 - 3x + 2) + (4x^2 - x - 4)$

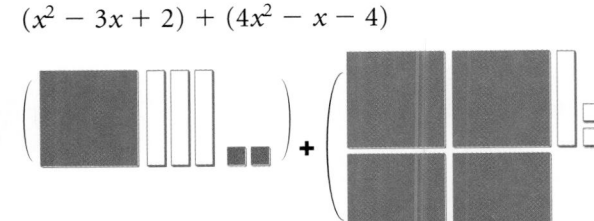

Each student wrote the algebraic expression for the sum a different way:

Luane wrote $5x^2 - 2 - 4x$.

Guy wrote $-2 - 4x + 5x^2$.

Michelle wrote $5x^2 - 4x - 2$.

3. Explain why each is correct. What does this tell you about the order of terms in an algebraic expression?

4. The following display represents the sum of two groups of tiles.

a) What two groups of tiles might have been combined? Find two possible solutions.
Write the algebraic equations for each addition.
b) Compare your equations with a classmate's. How many different ones did you find?

5. Paul and Peter each showed one expression and covered the other expression to be added. They also showed the tiles for each sum. In each case, what tiles would represent the missing expression? Write the expression that represents the missing tiles.

a)

$(-4x + 2x^2) + (\rule{3cm}{0.4cm}) = $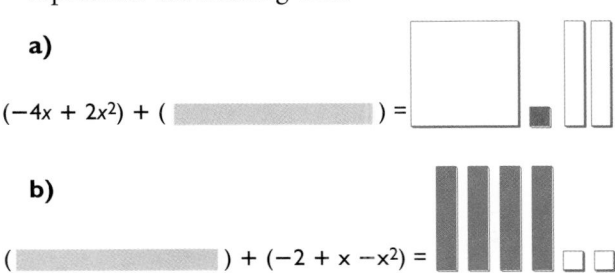

b)

$(\rule{3cm}{0.4cm}) + (-2 + x - x^2) = $

6. Sherry wants to subtract two expressions.
$(2x^2 + x - 2) - (x^2 - 2x + 1) = \rule{2cm}{0.4cm}$
She uses a related addition problem to find the difference.

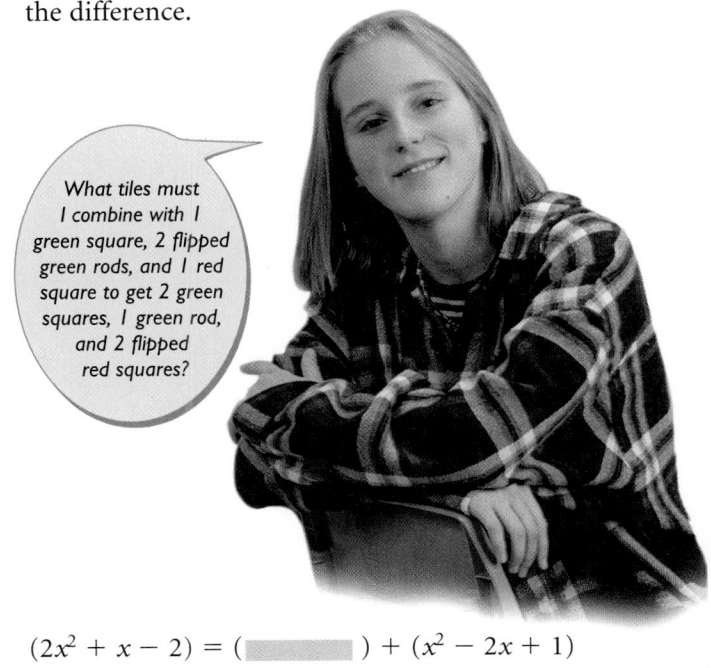

What tiles must I combine with 1 green square, 2 flipped green rods, and 1 red square to get 2 green squares, 1 green rod, and 2 flipped red squares?

$(2x^2 + x - 2) = (\rule{2cm}{0.4cm}) + (x^2 - 2x + 1)$

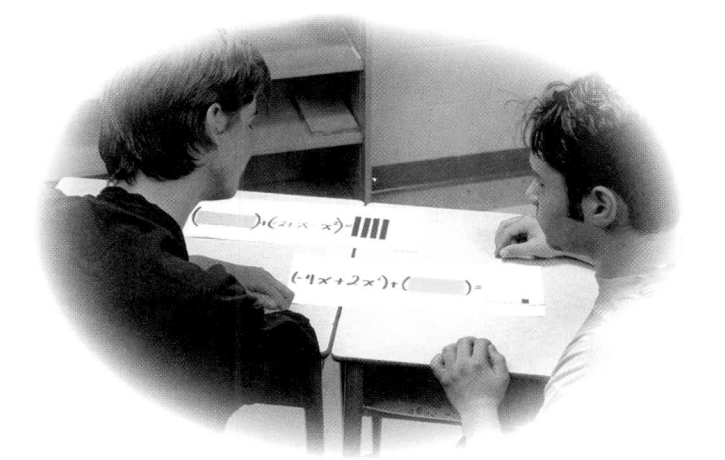

a) Which tiles make the related addition sentence true?
b) Write the expression.

7. The related addition problem is shown for each subtraction problem. What set of tiles makes both sentences true? Write the expression.

a) $(3 - 2x + x^2) - (2x^2 + x) = ($ _____ $)$

$(3 - 2x + x^2) = ($ _____ $) + (2x^2 + x)$

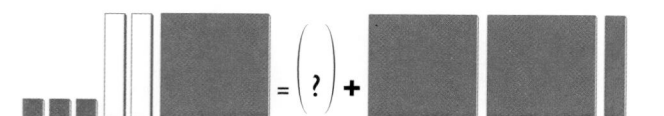

b) $(-x - x^2) - (-3x^2 - 2x + 1) = ($ _____ $)$

$(-x - x^2) = ($ _____ $) + (-3x^2 - 2x + 1)$

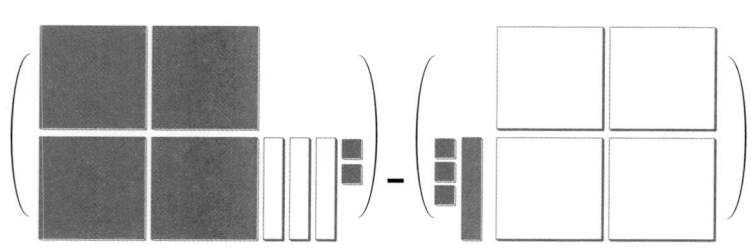

8. Find the missing expression. Explain what you did.

$(5x - 3x^2 - 2) - (-3 + 4x^2) = ($ _____ $)$

$(5x - 3x^2 - 2) = ($ _____ $) + (-3 + 4x^2)$

9. a) Use algebra tiles to show the difference. Explain your choice.

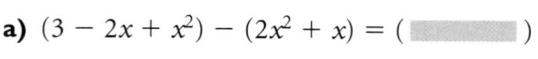

b) Write the algebraic equation for the subtraction.

10. a) Use algebra tiles to show the difference. Explain your choice.

$(6x - x^2) - (x^2 + 3) = $ _____

b) Write the algebraic expression for the difference.

11. Use algebra tiles to make each sentence true. Explain your choice. Write the missing expressions.

a) $($ _____ $) - (4 - 2x + x^2) = -6 + 3x + x^2$

b) $(-5 - 7x) - ($ _____ $) = -4x + 3x^2$

12. Paula uses a number line to find the difference between like terms, one at a time.

$(4x^2 + 3x - 1) - (5x^2 - 4x + 3) = $ _____

For the x^2 terms, $4x^2$ and $5x^2$, she thinks, "What number added to 5 gives 4?"

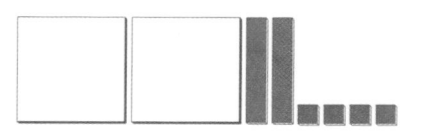

a) What's the difference between $4x^2$ and $5x^2$?
b) Use the number line to find the difference between the x terms. Explain what you did.
c) What's the difference between the constant terms?
d) What expression represents the entire difference?

13. Use a number line to find each difference.

a) $(x^2 + 4x + 5) - (3x^2 - 3x - 2)$
b) $(-4 - 5x + 4x^2) - (2x^2 - 4x)$

14. Two expressions are subtracted, and the tile display for the difference is

a) If this represents double the number of each tile in the first expression, what are the tiles in the first expression? in the second expression?
b) If this represents half the number of each tile in the second expression, what are the tiles in the second expression? in the first expression?

In Your Journal

Explain how you would use algebra tiles to calculate $(3x^2 - 2x - 1) - (x^2 + 3x - 2)$.

5.5 Finding Totals and Differences

a) Evaluate $\frac{a}{2} + \frac{a}{2}$ for three different values of a. What do you notice about each sum? Explain why this happens.

b) Predict the sum of $\frac{a}{3} + \frac{a}{3} + \frac{a}{3}$, when a is 10. Substitute to check.

The prices for the brunch and the matinee performance which follows it are posted separately.

Concept Development

Lee created an expression for the income from the sale of brunch tickets: $25a + 15t + 10c$

1. What do each of the variables and numerical coefficients represent? Could Lee have written the expression differently? Explain.

2. Create an algebraic expression for the income from the performance tickets.

3. **a)** Assuming the same people attended both, create an expression for the total income from the brunch and the performance. How can you make this expression the simplest it can be?
   b) What benefit is there in creating one expression for the total income for both?

4. **a)** Create an expression to represent the difference in income between the brunch and the performance. How can you simplify the expression?
   b) What benefit is there in creating one expression to represent the difference in income between the two events?

Understand and Apply

1. Explain how you would add the two expressions for each. Use algebra tiles if necessary. Then write the new expression.

   a) $3x^2 + 5x + 7$ **b)** $4x^2 + 6x - 11$
   $+(7x^2 + \ x + 6)$ $+(3x + 5 + 2x^2)$

   c) $(-2x + 4x^2) + (3 + 4x - 5x^2)$
   d) $(3 + 6x) + (3x^2 - 4x)$

2. Use the ticket prices to create each expression. Simplify if necessary.
   a) income from teens and children for the performance
   b) income from teens and children for the brunch
   c) income from teens and children for both the brunch and the performance

3. **a)** Evaluate the expression in each part of Problem 2 for 375 teens and 135 children.

   b) What are the benefits of evaluating the expression in part (c) over adding the results from parts (a) and (b)?

4. Which of the following will not contain an x^2 term in the sum? Justify your choice.

   a) $(-4x + 2x^2 + 6) + (2x^2 - 2x - 4)$
   b) $(-7 + 5x - x^2) + (8x + x^2 + 11)$
   c) $(-12x^2 + 3) + (4 + 11x^2)$
   d) $(-1 - 4x + 6x^2) + (-6x^2 + 4x - 3)$

5. **a)** Which expressions in Problem 4 will not contain an x term in the sum? Justify your choice.
   b) How can you predict if a type of term will appear in the sum by looking at the expressions?

6. Two expressions have been combined and simplified. What might the expressions be if
   a) the sum is $-2x^2 + x + 2$?
   b) the sum is $3x^2 - 4$?
   c) the sum is 0?

7. a) Write and simplify an expression for the perimeter of the shape.

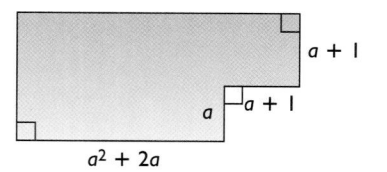

   b) What is the perimeter when $a = 2$ cm?
   c) Without evaluating, predict how the value for the perimeter changes if $a = 4$ cm?
   $a = 6$ cm? $a = 1$ cm? Justify your predictions.
   d) Evaluate to check your predictions in part (c).

8. a) To evaluate the perimeter of a square with sides measuring $(2x + 3)$ units, which of these expressions would you use? Explain.

$$(2x + 3) + (2x + 3) + (2x + 3) + (2x + 3)$$
$$4(2x + 3)$$
$$8x + 12$$

   b) Write an expression for the perimeter of an equilateral triangle with sides measuring $(x^2 + x)$ units.
   c) Write an expression for the perimeter of a regular hexagon with sides measuring $(3x + 5)$ units.

9. The perimeter of an isosceles triangle is $(5x + 4)$ units. What are three possible expressions for the lengths of each side?

10. Write a related addition sentence for each subtraction. Then, use the like terms from each expression and a number line to find the difference.
   a) $3x^2 + 5x + 6$
      $-(2x^2 + x + 2)$
   b) $5x^2 - 7x - 2$
      $-(6x^2 - 5x - 1)$

   c) $(6x^2 - 4x - 5) - (-2x^2 - x + 4)$
   d) $(5a - 2a^2) - (-4a^2 + a)$
   e) $(3 + 4b - 5b^2) - (-3b - 2 + 3b^2)$
   f) $(-11 - c^2 + 3c) - (-6c^2 + 1)$

11. In Problem 10, how else can you find the difference? Compare your method with a classmate's.

12. Which of the following will not contain an x^2 term in the difference? Justify your choice.
   a) $(-4x + 2x^2 + 6) - (2x^2 - 2x - 4)$
   b) $(-7 + 5x - x^2) - (8x + x^2 + 11)$
   c) $(-12x^2 + 3) - (4 + 11x^2)$
   d) $(-1 - 4x - 6x^2) - (-6x^2 + 4x - 3)$

13. a) In Problem 12, which difference will not contain an x term? Justify your choice.
   b) How can you predict if a type of term will appear in the difference by examining the expressions?

14. Two expressions have been subtracted. What might the expressions be if:
   a) the difference is $5x^2 + x + 3$?
   b) the difference is $-3x^2 - 4$
   c) the difference is 0?

15. Meredith is subtracting two expressions.

$$(3x - 2x^2 - 6) - (\text{*****}) = (\#\#\#\#\#\#)$$

   Create an expression for (******) so that the numerical coefficients in the difference,(######), will be
   a) greater than the corresponding numerical coefficients in the first expression
   b) less than the corresponding numerical coefficients in the first expression

16. a) Write an expression for the perimeter of each shape.
   b) Write an expression to show how much greater shape A's perimeter is compared to B's.

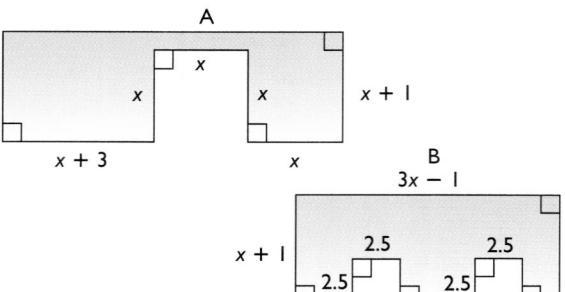

   c) What is the actual difference in the perimeters when $x = 5$ cm? $x = 2.5$ cm? $x = 20$ cm?

Problems to Investigate

WHAT TO DO?

The terms $6xy$ and $-6xy$ are like terms. What single change could you make to one of the terms so that they would be unlike terms? Give as many answers as possible.

MAGIC ALGEBRAIC SQUARE

In a magic square the sum of the rows, columns, and diagonals are equal. Use two-term and/or three-term expressions to complete this magic square. The magic sum is $3x^2 + 6x - 9$.

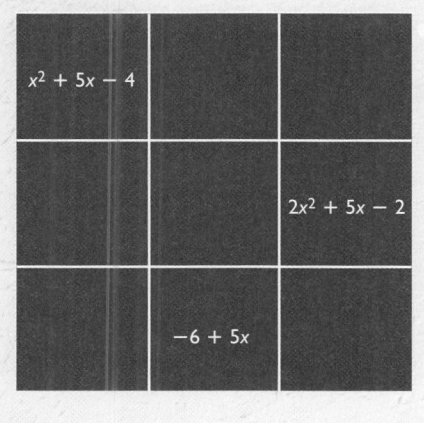

$x^2 + 5x - 4$		
		$2x^2 + 5x - 2$
	$-6 + 5x$	

THAT MAKES SENSE

Pauline evaluated $x^2 + 6x + 1$ and $3x^2 + x - 1$ for $x = 2$. What value would she get if she added the results? subtracted the results?
Try adding the expressions, then subtracting the expressions. Now evaluate the two resulting expressions for $x = 2$.
How do your and Pauline's results compare? What conclusions can you make? If the value for x were different, would your results differ? Explain.

CLASS PIZZA PARTY

Company A and company B are competing for your class pizza business. The expressions for the price of pizzas (p), toppings (t), and drinks (d) are
$6.50p + 0.75t + 0.90d$ for company A and
$7.00p + 0.50t + 0.65d$ for company B.
a) What is the difference in the 2 companies' prices for an order of pizza with toppings and drinks for your class?
b) How could the companies make their prices equal?

TWO-DIGIT MYSTERY

Joan wrote her age as $10x + y$. Her age with the tens and ones digits switched is $10y + x$. What do you observe about the sum of these two expressions? the difference between the two expressions? What conclusions can you make?

ARRANGING TILES

Arrange these tiles to form a rectangle with
a) the least possible perimeter. Write the algebraic expression.
b) the greatest possible perimeter. Write the algebraic expression. If the tiles touch only at the corners, what is the expression for the greatest possible perimeter?

Make up other problems about adding and subtracting algebraic expressions. Post them on the bulletin board for your classmates to solve.

5.6 Modelling Decks with Tiles

Warm Up

Find six 2- and 3-digit palindromic numbers, such as 66 and 131, that give a palindromic product when each is multiplied by 106. For example, 106 x 22 = 2332

Suppose a summer lodge is undergoing renovations. Gillian and Meghan use algebra tiles to model their plans for an extension to the existing deck.

Concept Development

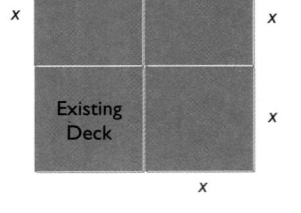

Gillian adds the lengths, $x + x + x + x + x + x$, to find the outside perimeter of the extension. Meghan finds the perimeter by multiplying $3(2x)$.

1. Examine the plan for the deck. What do the factors 3 and $2x$ represent in Meghan's expression?

2. **a)** Gillian's and Meghan's expressions are both correct. Explain.
   b) Simplify Gillian's expression. What does this tell you about Meghan's expression?

3. The girls plan two new flower beds — one with three green squares in a row, the other with four green squares in a row. Model both flower beds with tiles.
   a) Explain why $4(2x)$ and $5(2x)$ can be used to represent the perimeters of the two flower beds.
   b) Simplify both expressions to determine the perimeters for each flower bed. Explain what you did.

1. Arrange six green square tiles into a 1 × 6 rectangle.

a) What is the perimeter? Explain why the perimeter can be written as the product of 7 and $(2x)$.

b) Arrange the six square tiles into another rectangle. What is the perimeter? Write the perimeter as a product of two factors.

c) Explain how to simplify an expression such as $7(2x)$ which is made up of the product of two factors.

Gillian and Meghan use the grey rectangular tiles to model plans for a new dock.

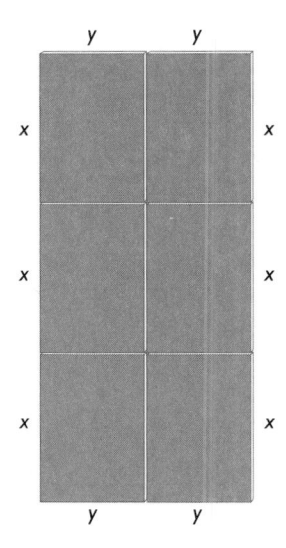

Gillian adds the individual areas,
$xy + xy + xy + xy + xy + xy$, to find the area.
Meghan finds the area by multiplying the length and the width, $3x(2y)$.

2. Simplify Gillian's expression to find an expression for the area. How does this compare to Meghan's expression?

3. Suppose each girl designs a larger new dock.

Gillian's Dock

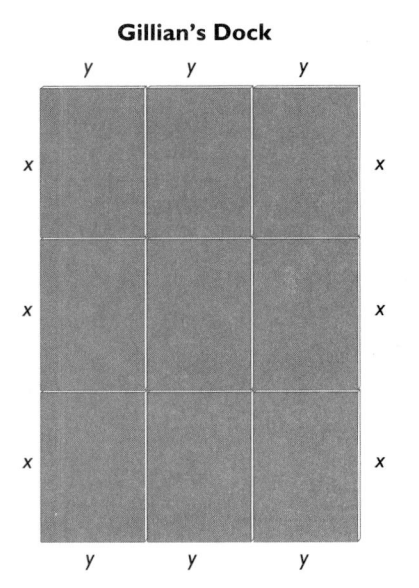

a) Explain why the expression $3x(3y)$ can be used to represent the area of Gillian's dock.

Meghan's Dock

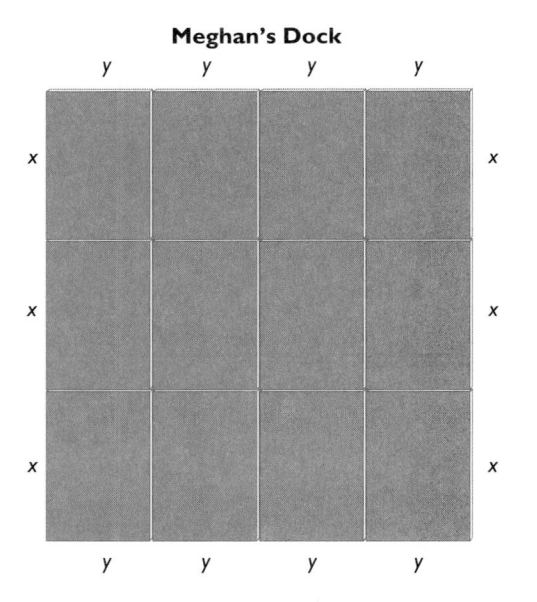

b) Explain why the expression $3x(4y)$ can be used to represent the area of Meghan's dock.

c) Write an expression to represent the area of each dock by simplifying the expressions in parts (a) and (b).

d) Explain how to simplify an expression which is made up of two factors such as $3x(4y)$.

4. Justin used algebra tiles to model the multiplication $2x(3y)$. How should he fill in the model? What is the product?

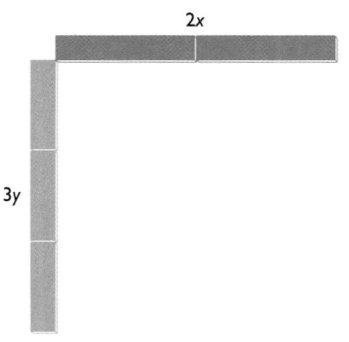

2x

3y

5. Model each with the tiles to find the product.
a) $2(4y)$ **b)** $5y(2x)$ **c)** $x(3y)$ **d)** $5(5x)$

6. Find the product.
a) $(4x)(5y)$ **b)** $(-3x)(-2y)$
c) $2(3x)(4y)$ **d)** $-3(6x)(-2y)$
e) $(-4y)(-4x)$ **f)** $(5xy)(-3)$
g) $(-5x)(-5y)(-5)$ **h)** $(-xy)(-2)(0)$

7. Gillian and Meghan use tiles to model plans for a new patio.

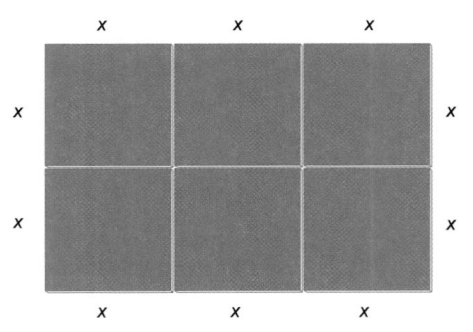

a) Gillian finds the area by adding the areas of each square, $x^2 + x^2 + x^2 + x^2 + x^2 + x^2$. Meghan multiplies the length and the width, $3x(2x)$. What is the area of the patio?

In Your Journal

a) Explain why 12xy and 12yx are equivalent, but 12x²y and 12xy² aren't.
b) Why is $(mn)^4$ not equivalent to mn^4?

b) What is an expression for the area if the patio is $3x$ by $3x$? $4x$ by $3x$?
c) Explain how you simplified $3x(3x)$ and $4x(3x)$ to find an expression for each area.

8. a) Explain how finding the product of $x^2 \times x^3$ is like finding the product of $3^2 \times 3^3$.
b) Explain how finding the product of $x^2 \times y^3$ is like finding the product of $3^2 \times 5^3$.

9. Model with tiles to find each product.
a) $2y(4y)$ **b)** $(2y)(2y)$
c) $x(3x)$ **d)** $5x(2x)$

10. Find the product.
a) $(-3y^3)(2y)$ **b)** $(5x^3)(-2y^2)$
c) $(3xy^2)(2x^2)$ **d)** $3(x^2y)(xy^2)$
e) $-4(x^2y^2)(2x^2y)$ **f)** $(ab^3)(5a^3b)$
g) $-2(-3abc)(-4a^2b^3c)$

11. a) Does $(a^3)^2 = a^6$? Check by evaluation.
b) Does $(5mn)^2 = 5^2 \times m^2 \times n^2$? Check by evaluation.
c) Explain how these keystrokes evaluate the equation, $(xy^2)^3 = x^3y^6$.

(1 ✕ 2 x^2) y^x 3 =
1 y^x 3 ✕ 2 y^x 6 =

Does $(xy^2)^3 = x^3y^6$? Explain.

12. Explain the error in each statement. Correct it.
a) $a^3 \times a^5 = a^{15}$ **b)** $(a^6)^4 = a^{10}$
c) $a^5 + a^2 = a^7$ **d)** $a^3 \times b^4 = (ab)^7$

5.7 Modelling Walkways with Tiles

Chad and Jeremy are planning a rectangular walkway from the lodge to the dock. They use algebra tiles to model their plan.

Warm Up

A queen-size patchwork quilt has 440 squares, each with an area of 121 cm². The length to width ratio is 10:11.
a) What's the length? width? area?
b) How many squares are in a twin-size quilt if it is the same length as the queen, but length to width is 4:3?

Concept Development

1. The width of the walkway is 2 units.
The area is $8x$ square units.
a) What is the length? How did you find it?
b) How can you use the area and width to find the length?

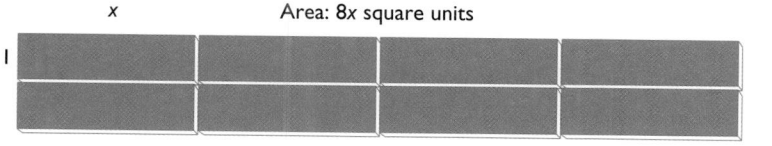

x   Area: 8x square units

2. Suppose they rearrange the same tiles in two different ways.

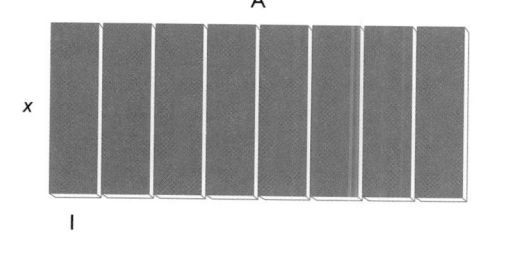

A

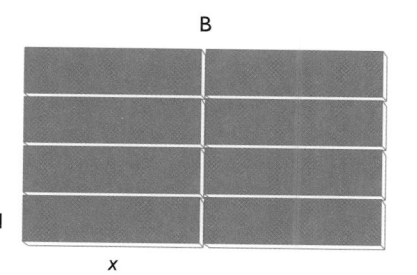

B

a) How has the area changed? Explain.
b) What is the width of walkway A?
c) What is the width of walkway B?
d) Explain how you could use division to find the width of both walkways.

3. a) Use eight green rods to make another rectangular walkway. What is the length and width?
b) Explain how the area and one dimension can be used to determine the other dimension.

1. Twelve orange rods can be arranged into a rectangular walkway.
   a) How do you know the area is $12y$ square units?
   b) How many different-looking walkways can you create? What are the dimensions of each?
   c) For which walkway in part (b) could you use the expression $\frac{12y}{6}$ to find the length? Explain.
   d) For which walkway in part (b) could you use the expression $\frac{12y}{4}$ to find the length? Explain.
   e) Explain how to simplify the expressions in parts (c) and (d) to find an expression for each missing dimension.

2. Chad and Jeremy use grey rectangular tiles to model a walkway.

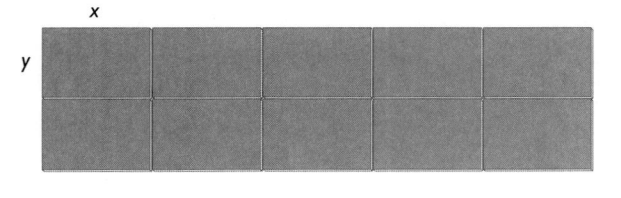

   a) What is the area of the walkway?
   b) Chad adds the length of each tile to find the length, $x + x + x + x + x$. Jeremy finds the length by dividing the area by the width, $\frac{10xy}{2y}$. What is the length of the walkway?

3. Suppose each boy designs a larger walkway.

Chad's walkway

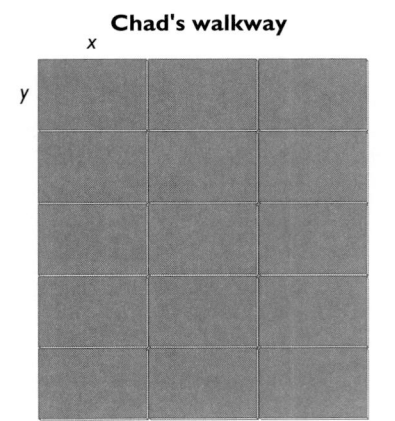

   a) Explain why the expression $\frac{15xy}{3y}$ can be used to represent the width of Chad's walkway.

Jeremy's walkway

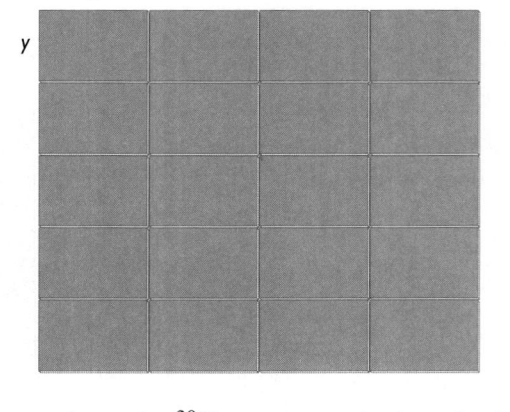

   b) Explain why $\frac{20xy}{5x}$ represents the length of Jeremy's walkway.
   c) What steps would you follow to simplify the expressions in parts (a) and (b) to find the other dimensions?

4. Model these with tiles. Find each quotient.
   a) $\frac{9x}{3}$
   b) $\frac{8y}{4}$
   c) $\frac{7x}{x}$
   d) $\frac{6xy}{2x}$
   e) $14xy \div 7y$

W/E 5. Find each quotient.
   a) $15x \div 5x$
   b) $18y \div (-3)$
   c) $(-24xy) \div (2x)$
   d) $\frac{-24ab}{-8ab}$
   e) $12abc \div 3ac$
   f) $(-18hk) \div (-k)$
   g) $(-27mnp) \div (-3n)$
   h) $\frac{18nm}{2np}$

6. Chad and Jeremy use green squares to model a walkway.

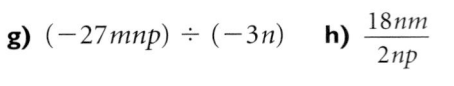

   a) What is the area?
   b) Chad adds the lengths of four tiles to find the length. Jeremy finds the length by dividing the area by the width. Write an expression to represent Jeremy's solution. What is the length of the walkway?

7. Use the area and length given in an expression to represent the width of each walkway.
a) area of $24x^2$ square units and a length of $6x$ units
b) an area of $30y^2$ square units and a length of $2y$ units

8. Explain how to simplify both expressions in Problem 7.

9. a) Explain how finding the quotient of $y^5 \div y^2$ is like finding the quotient of $3^5 \div 3^2$.
b) Explain how finding the quotient of $(x^4y^5) \div (x^3y^4)$ is like finding the quotient of $(2^4 \times 3^5) \div (2^3 \times 3^4)$.

10. Find each quotient.
a) $x^8 \div x^5$ **b)** $m^9 \div m^2$
c) $p^7 \div p$ **d)** $12m^6 \div 2m^4$
e) $(-15h^7) \div (3h^2)$ **f)** $(h^4m^5) \div (h^2m^2)$
g) $(w^8p^9) \div (p^4w^3)$
h) $(-12c^6b^5) \div (-3c^4b^2)$
i) $(15h^9g^7) \div (-5g^4h^3)$

In Your Journal

Explain how to verify that the quotient is correct.

$(-9x^2y)(6x) \div 3x = -18x^2y$

11. a) Use $\frac{x^3}{x^3}$ to explain why $x^0 = 1$.
b) Use $\frac{y^5}{y^5}$ to explain why $y^0 = 1$.
c) What statement can you make about powers with zero exponents? Why does the base have to be non-zero?

12. Which have the same value? Explain.
a) m^0 **b)** $(-m)^0$ **c)** $-(m)^0$ **d)** $-m^0$

13. a) Use $\frac{x^3}{x^4}$ to explain why $x^{-1} = \frac{1}{x}$.
b) Use $\frac{y^4}{y^5}$ to explain why $y^{-1} = \frac{1}{y}$.
c) What statement can you make about powers with negative exponents? Why does the base have to be non-zero?

14. Express each as a power with a positive exponent.
a) m^{-1} **b)** m^{-2} **c)** $(mn)^{-4}$ **d)** $3y^{-1}$
e) $(3y)^{-1}$ **f)** $-3y^{-1}$ **g)** $(-3y)^{-1}$ **h)** $(3y)^{-2}$

15. Divide.
a) $\dfrac{12mn^{-2}}{6mn^2}$ **b)** $\dfrac{24a^2b^3}{8a^5b^4}$ **c)** $\dfrac{51x^{-4}y^6}{17x^2y^{-2}}$

16. Model $3x^2 + 6x - 9$ with tiles.
a) Explain how you would use the tiles to solve $\dfrac{3x^2 + 6x - 9}{3}$.
b) What tiles represent the quotient? Write the expression that represents the quotient.

17. Model and solve each with tiles. What tiles and expression represent each quotient?
a) $\dfrac{3x^2}{3}$ **b)** $\dfrac{6x}{3}$ **c)** $\dfrac{9}{3}$

18. a) How does the quotient from Problem 16 compare with the quotients of the individual terms in Problem 17?
b) How do the three expressions in Problem 17 relate to the expression in Problem 16 (a)?

19. Use what you discovered in Problems 16 – 18 to find each quotient. Explain what you did. Use algebra tiles if necessary.
a) $\dfrac{5y^2 + 10y + 10}{5}$ **b)** $\dfrac{6xy + 12y}{3}$ **c)** $\dfrac{6x^2 - 6x - 12}{-2}$

20. Find each quotient.
a) $\dfrac{8xy + 12x^2}{4x}$ **b)** $\dfrac{10y^2 + 4xy + 2y}{2y}$
c) $\dfrac{12x^3 - 16x^2 + 8x}{4x}$ **d)** $\dfrac{9mn + 6m^2 + 3m}{3m}$
e) $\dfrac{10a^2b^2 + 5a^3}{-5a}$ **f)** $\dfrac{-a^2b^3 + a^3b^2 - a^2b^2}{-a^2b^2}$

21. Divide.
a) $\dfrac{8mn + 7m^2 + 4m}{2m}$ **b)** $\dfrac{2mh + 3hn + 5mn}{mnh}$
c) $\dfrac{10a^2b^2 + 5b^3 + 5a}{5a}$ **d)** $\dfrac{16x - 12x^2y^2 + 4xy^2}{4xy}$
e) $\dfrac{8wz - 16wz^2 - 16w^2z}{8w^2z^2}$
f) $\dfrac{4pq - 9p^2q^2 - 7p^3q^3}{2p^4q^4}$

More Than One Strategy

Dividing by a Monomial

There are many ways to find the quotient of $\dfrac{6x^2 + 4x}{2x}$.
Here are some. Can you think of others?

1. You can divide each term in the numerator by the divisor and then add the results.

$$\frac{6x^2 + 4x}{2x} = \frac{6x^2}{2x} + \frac{4x}{2x}$$

$$= \frac{\cancel{(2)}\,(3)\,\cancel{(x)}\,(x)}{\cancel{(2)}\,\cancel{(x)}} + \frac{\cancel{(2)}\,(2)\,\cancel{(x)}}{\cancel{(2)}\,\cancel{(x)}}$$

$$= 3x + 2$$

2. You can use the meaning of division.

How many groups of $2x$ are there in $6x^2$ and in $4x$?
$6x^2$ can be written as $(2x) \times (3x)$. There are $3x$ groups of $2x$ in $6x^2$.
$4x$ can be written as $(2x) \times (2)$. There are 2 groups of $2x$ in $4x$.

$$\frac{6x^2 + 4x}{2x} = 3x + 2$$

3. You can use algebra tiles to make a rectangle.

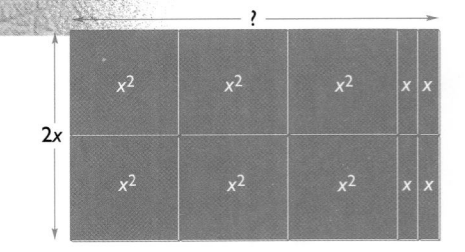

The area of the rectangle is $6x^2 + 4x$ and the width is $2x$.
The quotient is the length of the rectangle: $3x + 2$

$$\frac{6x^2 + 4x}{2x} = 3x + 2$$

4. You can use inverse operations.

$$\frac{6x^2 + 4x}{2x} = \frac{6x^2}{2x} + \frac{4x}{2x}$$

$\dfrac{6x^2}{2x}$ means $2x \times \blacksquare = 6x^2$, so $\blacksquare = 3x$

$\dfrac{4x}{2x}$ means $2x \times \bullet = 4x$, so $\bullet = 2$

The quotient is $3x + 2$. $\dfrac{6x^2 + 4x}{2x} = 3x + 2$

Understand and Apply

Show two different ways to find each quotient.

1. $\dfrac{8x^2 + 6x}{2}$

2. $\dfrac{-6x - 12x^2}{3x}$

3. $\dfrac{8ab + 4ac}{-2a}$

4. $\dfrac{3xy + 5xyz}{xy}$

5. $\dfrac{8x^3 + 2x^4 - 4x^2}{2x^2}$

6. $\dfrac{-9c^2d^3 + 3c^3d^2}{-3c^2d^2}$

Problems to Investigate

AN ARRANGEMENT OF TILES

A group of algebra tiles makes a rectangle with an area of 24xy square units. What are the dimensions of the rectangle if the perimeter is $16x + 6y$ units?

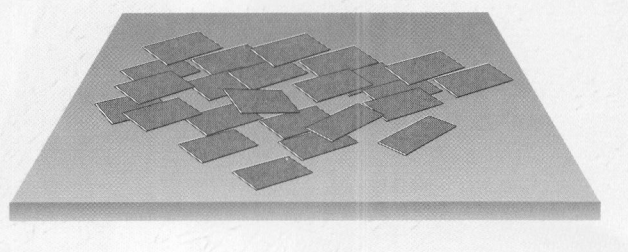

MAGIC MULTIPLICATION SQUARE

The products of the rows and columns in this magic square are equal.
Use single-term algebraic expressions to complete the magic square if the magic product is $24x^4y^4$.

	$3xy$	
$3x^2y$		
		$3y$

SHARING TILES

Altogether, Davis, Sandi, and Ahmed have 24 tiles in their container. The container has green square x^2-tiles, green rod x-tiles, and red unit tiles. The number of each type of tile can be divided equally among the three of them. How many of each type of tile could there be in the container? How many answers can you find?

GREAT EXPLANATIONS

Why don't $6xy \div 3$ and $3 \div 6xy$ have the same quotient? Write an explanation.

FOOD STAINS

What integers, exponents, operation signs, and variables are hidden?

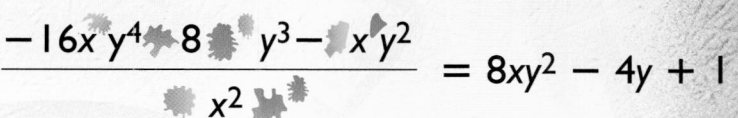

$$\frac{-16x^{\blacksquare}y^4 \blacksquare 8 \blacksquare y^3 - \blacksquare x^{\blacksquare}y^2}{\blacksquare x^2 \blacksquare^{\blacksquare}} = 8xy^2 - 4y + 1$$

EVALUATION QUEST

Evaluate $x^{-3} + y^3$ for $x = 2$ and $y = -2$, and then for $x = -2$ and $y = 2$. How are the results different? alike?

Make up other problems about multiplying and dividing algebraic expressions. Post them on the bulletin board for your classmates to solve.

Solve Problems by Using More Than One Way

Try this problem before going on.

What is the greatest perimeter possible when you use all of these tiles to form a rectangle?

▶ Think of a Plan

To solve the problem, Mavis decided to form different rectangles with the tiles. She planned to find the perimeter of each by measuring and then using the perimeter formula, $P = 2l + 2w$.

Aaron decided to find the perimeters another way – by writing an algebraic expression for the perimeter of each rectangle.

▶ Carry Out the Plan

4. Which tile arrangement has the greater perimeter? Explain.

5. Is there another arrangement with a greater perimeter?

▶ Look Back

6. What if the rectangle does not have to be completely filled?

▶ *Understand the Problem*

1. What are you asked to do?

2. What do you know?

3. Where will you begin?

> Your perimeter can be represented by $6x + 8$. Mine is $6x + 10$.

> My rectangle's perimeter is $2(15.5 \text{ cm}) + 2(9 \text{ cm}) = 49 \text{ cm}$. Yours is $2(18 \text{ cm}) \times 2(7.5 \text{ cm}) = 51 \text{ cm}$

Applications

THE SHADY AREA

How many different ways can you find each shaded area? Find the areas.

A   B

TALL VERSUS SQUATTY

Use two identical pieces of looseleaf paper. Take one piece and form a cylinder by joining the widths together. With the other piece, form a cylinder by joining the lengths together. How many different ways can you determine which cylinder has the greater volume? Which cylinder has the greater volume?

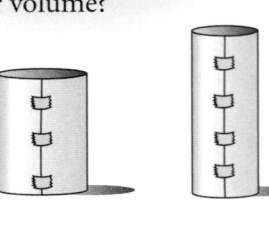

A SHINING SUM

How many different ways can you find the sum of the interior angles A, B, C, D, and E of the star? What is the sum?

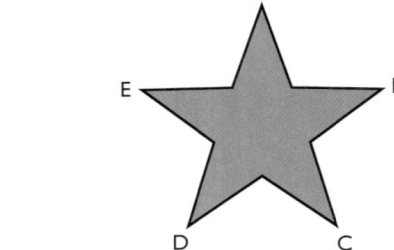

126

1. Name the constant, variable(s), and numerical coefficients for each expression.

   a) $24 + 3x$
   b) $-3bc - 12x - 5$
   c) $a^2 - 12 - a$

2. Create an expression containing these number of terms.

   a) 5   b) 4   c) 6

3. Evaluate each when $b = -3$.

   a) $3b - 12$
   b) $2b^2 + 3b - 12$
   c) $-12 - 3b^2 + 3b$

4. Create an expression with three terms that has a value of -1 when $m = 2$.

5. Create an expression with three terms that has a value of 2 when $b = -1$.

6. Which are like terms in each group? Explain.

   a) $mn, nm, 2m, m^n, -5m$
   b) $-d^2, -2d, cd^2, 3d^2, c^2d$
   c) $ab, ac, abc, bac, 2cba$
   d) $m^2n^2, mn^2, m^2n, n^2m^3, n^2m^2, mn$

7. Write an expression for each perimeter.

   a)
   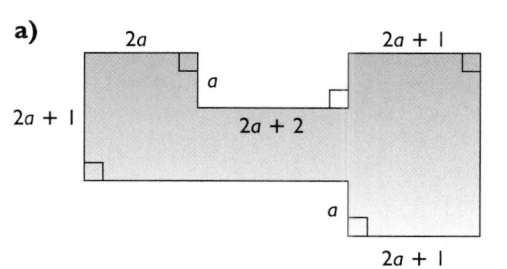

   b)
   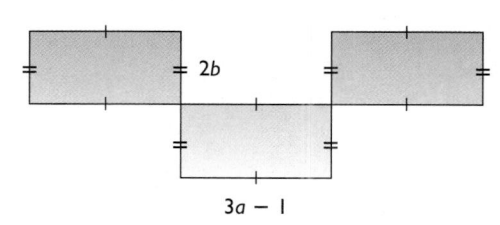

8. Write an expression for the sum of the tiles.

   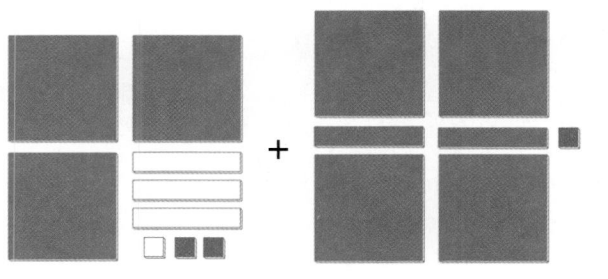

9. Write an expression for the difference between the two groups of tiles in Problem 8.

10. Find the sum or difference.

    a) $(2x^2 + 8x + 5) + (x^2 - 6x - 3)$
    b) $(10y^3 - 6y + 3) - (4y^3 - y + 2)$
    c) $(-5p - 3r) - (2p + 4 - 5r)$
    d) $-7xy - (6x - 3xy + 4x - 5yx)$

11. One side of a square sheet of metal is $5mn$ units. What's the area?

12. The area of a rectangular rug is $48a^2b^2$ square units. The length is $16a^2$ units. What's the width?

13. Find the product or the quotient.

    a) $3ab \times 7dk$ b) $(-2ac)(-4ac)$

    c) $(6r)(-r)$ d) $\dfrac{6abc}{2b}$

    e) $(-4gh) \div (-2hk)$ f) $\dfrac{16d^3}{8d}$

    g) $-15a^4b^3 \div 5a^2b$

14. Use algebra tiles to find the quotient. Write an expression to represent it.

    $$\dfrac{4x^2 + 6x - 4}{2}$$

15. Find the quotient.

    a) $\dfrac{6ab + 2bc}{2b}$ b) $\dfrac{9a^3 + 12a^4 - 15a^2}{-3a^2}$

Practise with Games

Play each game with a partner.

Like Term Concentration

- Use the set of Like Term cards. Shuffle them and place them face down in an array.

- Take turns turning over two cards. If the cards show like terms the player takes them. That player continues until no match occurs.

- The game ends when all cards are matched. The player with the most pairs wins.

16xy and −8yx are like terms.

Spin, Roll, and Create

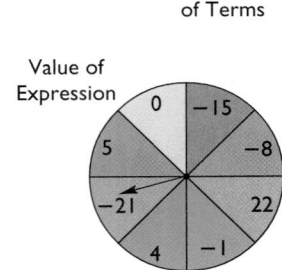

- Use a pair of dice and two spinners like the ones shown.
- Take turns rolling the dice and spinning the spinners to create an expression.
  In order to create an expression, each player:
  - spins the Number of Terms spinner to determine the number of terms.
  - spins the Value of Expression spinner to determine the value of the expression when evaluated.
  - rolls the dice and uses the sum of the numbers to determine the value to be substituted for the variable in the expression (player decides if it will be negative or positive)
- The player then tries to create an expression and then evaluate it.
  Note: All expressions must have at least one squared term.

- Score 3 points if the expression has two terms, and when evaluated, gives the value spun. Score 4 points if it has three terms, and when evaluated, gives the value spun.

- If a player can't create an expression that works, the opponent may try to create one.

- The first player to reach 21 points is the winner.

Example:

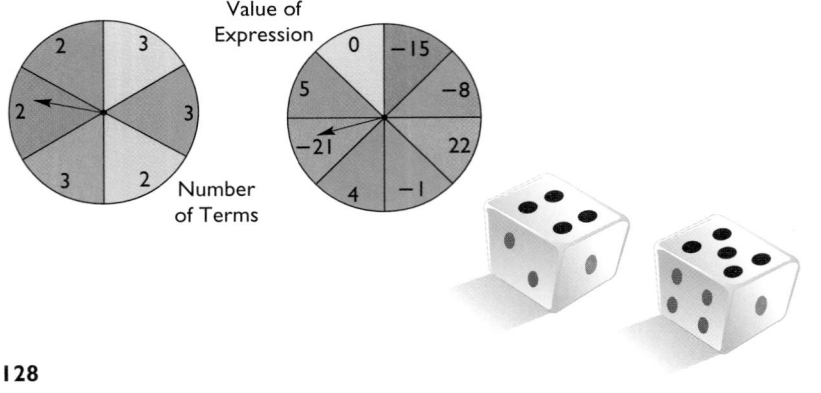

Your expression must have two terms and a value of −21 when 9 or −9 is substituted for the variable.

$$-x^2 + 60$$
$$= -(9^2) + 60$$
$$= -21$$

You score 3 points.

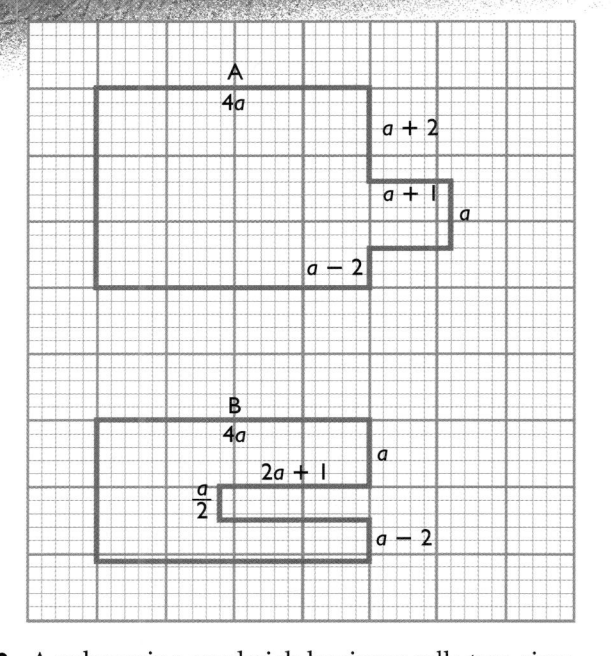

1. Create two different expressions so that each has one constant, two variables, and three numerical coefficients.

2. What information would you include in a poster to advertise a dance at your school? Include two or three constants and two or more variables.

3. Find three values for x for which the value of $-2x^2 + 3x - 2$ will be greater than -5.

4. Find two values for m for which the value of $5 - 2m + m^2$ will be between 14 and 25.

5. Miron combined two groups of tiles to get the following result.

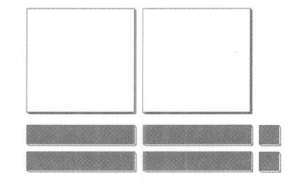

   What tiles might have been in each group? Provide two different solutions.

6. Write an equation for each solution in Problem 5.

7. Hafsa subtracted two groups of tiles to get the following result.

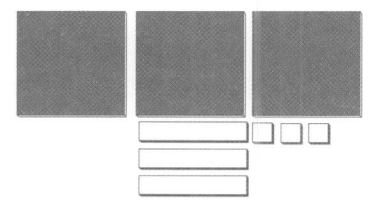

   What tiles might have been in each group? Provide two different solutions.

8. Write an equation for each solution in Problem 7.

9. Use the diagrams that follow.
   a) Predict which perimeter is greater. Check by substituting $a = 5$.
   b) Write an expression which represents the difference between the two perimeter expressions.
   c) For what value of a would perimeter A be equivalent to perimeter B?

10. A submarine sandwich business sells two sizes of sandwiches: small basic assorted for $2.99, and large basic assorted for $4.55. Each additional filling for a small sandwich is $0.50, and $0.75 for a large sandwich.
    a) Create an expression to represent the income from the sale of small and large sandwiches with additional fillings.
    b) The income from Saturday's sandwich lunch sales is about $250. How many of each size sandwich and additional fillings might have been sold?

11. The area of a deck is $18x^2$ square units. What are possible lengths and widths of the deck? Model the deck with tiles. How many different lengths and widths are possible to model?

12. The area of a dock is $24y^2$ square units. The length is six times its width. What are the dimensions?

13. a) The area of a rectangular board is $4x^2 + 10x$ square units. The length is $4x$ units. What is the width?
    b) What is the width if $x = 8$ cm? 16 cm? 4 cm?
    c) Does doubling the value for x also double the width? Does halving the value for x also halve the width? Why or why not?

14. Jason recalls that the quotient had an 8, an x, and a y^2 in it. He remembers seeing a 2 in the divisor and maybe more, but he's not sure. What are three possible expressions he might have divided?

1. Explain to a partner how to determine the number of terms in the expression $-3ab + 5b - 6abc - a$.

2. The expression $-4x^3 - 3x + 2$ is evaluated for $x = -5$. Write a note in your journal explaining how you know the result will be positive.

6. How would you use tiles to show the meaning of this expression?
$$\frac{4x^2 + 6x + 2}{2}$$

3. Explain how you would use algebra tiles to find the difference.
$$(3x + 4 + 2x^2) - (-2 - 3x^2 + 3x)$$

5. The area of a rectangular pizza is $24x^2$ square units. The width is $0.5x$ units. How would you find the length of the pizza?

4. How would you explain to a friend how to correct this error?
$$(3x^3)(4x^2) = 12x^6 \quad \times$$

What questions do you still have about algebraic expressions?

Investigating Earning and Spending

Alan Pain owns a farm in Aneroid, Saskatchewan. He has kept records of wheat prices, diesel fuel prices, and new tractor prices over the years.

- Why might the price of wheat vary so much from year to year?

- Calculate the change in prices for each year compared to 1947.

- How do you know fuel prices in 1994 had increased more than 700% since 1947?

- Calculate the percent increase or decrease in the price of wheat, fuel, and tractors for each year compared to those in 1947. Tell what you notice.

- Calculate the ratio of wheat to fuel prices for each year. Tell what you notice.

- In 1995, the price of wheat was about $112/t. The cost of a new pickup truck was about $24 000.

  In 1995 how many tonnes of wheat had to be sold to buy a new truck?

- In 1947, how many tonnes of wheat had to be sold to buy a new truck worth about $1400?

Year	wheat prices $ per tonne	fuel prices $ per litre	Tractor ($)
1947	$56.22	$0.04	$1 296.00
1956	$58.79	$0.05	$7 800.00
1976	$238.83	$0.11	$15 300.00
1994	$73.49	$0.35	$100 000.00

 # Do Teens Earn Money?

This table contains information about the number of carriers and the rate of pay for delivering newspapers in three cities in Western Canada in November, 1995.

Carrier Information and Rate of Pay for Three Canadian Newspapers, November, 1995

	number of carriers	rate of pay $/paper	average number of delivered papers/carrier	number of days delivered in a week	monthly subscription rate
Calgary Herald	880	0.1274	75	7	$13.50
Saskatoon Star Phoenix	902	0.1146	100	6	$11.25
Winnipeg Free Press	1500	0.1065		7	$13.00

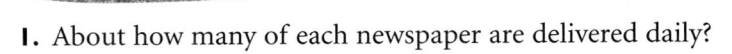
Concept Development

1. The *Winnipeg Free Press* has 600 adults and 900 youths delivering papers. Adults deliver an average of 150 papers and youths deliver an average of 100 papers each day.
   a) What percent of the total number of carriers is each age group?
   b) About how many Winnipeg Free Press papers are delivered each day?

2. About how much money does an average carrier earn each
   a) day?   **b)** week?   **c)** month?   **d)** year?

Applications

1. About how many of each newspaper are delivered daily?

2. About what does it cost each newspaper to have its papers delivered each day?

3. **a)** About what percent of the monthly subscription rate is the cost of delivery for each newspaper?
   b) What other expenses besides deliveries might a newspaper have?

4. One adult carrier for the *Calgary Herald* delivers about 650 papers a day.
   a) About how much can she earn in one year assuming she delivers everyday?
   b) Why might most carriers deliver fewer papers than she does?

5. Investigate and report on the rate of pay and average number of papers delivered for a newspaper in your area. Find out what percent of the total circulation is delivered by carriers.

DID YOU KNOW

Each weekday in 1994, an average of 499 683 *Toronto Star* papers were circulated. On Saturday, an average of 737 513 were circulated, and on Sunday, 507 282. What percent of the weekly circulation is Saturday's? the weekend's? each weekday's? How do these percents compare to the *Edmonton Journal* with 161 376 papers circulating daily (Mondays to Thursdays and Saturdays), 195 988 on Fridays, and 153 716 on Sundays?

Students in the Junior Achievement Program form companies to sell products and services. A group of high school students in Prince Albert, Saskatchewan, formed a company called Games 'n' Roses to make, market, and sell a horserace game they created.

This income statement shows the company's revenue and expenses.

INCOME STATEMENT FOR GAMES 'N' ROSES		
REVENUE		
Sales Income	$1628.47	
Other Income	$5.00	
		$1633.47
EXPENSES		
Materials	$696.87	
Wages & Salaries	$216.75	
Commissions	$160.53	
Bonuses & Incentives	$50.94	
Equipment Rental	$30.00	
Other Expenses	$9.99	
Jr. Achievement Payment	$45.00	$1210.08
Net Income Before Tax		$423.39
Profits Tax (50%)		$211.70
Net Income After Tax		$211.69
Pre-Tax Share Value		
After-Tax Share Value		

6. a) Discuss with a classmate what each item listed in the first column means.
b) How was each amount in the third column calculated?

7. What percent of the expenses was the cost of
a) materials?
b) wages and salaries?
c) commissions?

8. Games 'n' Roses sold 20 shares to investors at a cost of $5 per share. They used these funds to start the production of their game. Each investor shares in any profits or losses according to the number of shares purchased.
a) The net income before tax was $423.39. Explain why each share value before tax was $21.17
b) Calculate the after-tax value of each share.
c) What is the increase in share value from the original value?
d) What is the percent increase in share value?

9. The company sold over 70 games.
a) What data in the table can be used to calculate the approximate sale price of each game? Calculate the approximate price.
b) What data in the table can be used to calculate the average commission paid for selling each game? Calculate the average commission.
c) Calculate the average commission as a percent of the cost of a game.

In Your Journal

About 34% of full-time high school students have a part-time job during the school year. What fraction is this? Did more or less than $\frac{2}{3}$ of students not have a part-time job? Describe how you would conduct a survey in your class or school to determine the fraction and percent of students that have part-time jobs.

  # Math Do Workers Use?

> **M**ost workers need to use mathematics to earn a living. The type of math depends on the type of job.

Retail store supervisors must be able to interpret sales figures for recent and previous periods. This table compares the total sales of three areas of a teen clothing department.

Teen Clothing by Category			
Total Sales—week 40			
AREA	Sales $ Week 40—This Year	Sales $ Week 40—Last Year	% Change
Denim	566	294	
Sweaters	222	706	-68.6
Jackets	114	216	
TOTAL	902	1216	

Concept Development

1. Explain how you know that the percent change since last year for
   a) sweaters shows a loss in sales
   b) denim is close to but less than 100%
   c) jackets is negative

These keystrokes were used to calculate the percent change for sweaters —

222 ⊟ 706 ⊜ ⊡÷ 706 ⊜ | -0.685552407 |

2. Calculate the percent change for
   a) denim
   b) jackets
   c) the total sales of all three areas

Applications

Financial planners use spreadsheets to estimate the earnings of investments over several years. This table shows how an investment of $1000 might increase over several years at different interest rates.

Investment Earnings at Three Rates			
Number of years	1981 rate 15.42 %	1991 rate 4.48 %	1993 rate 0.77 %
5	$2 048.36	$1 244.99	$1 039.10
10	$4 195.76	$1 550.00	$1 079.72
15	$8 594.41	$1 929.73	$1 121.94
20	$17 604.41	$2 402.50	$1 165.80

1. To find the total value of $1000 for the first 4 years at 15.42% on her calculator, Charlene repeatedly multiplied each annual amount by 1.1542 using the constant function of her scientific calculator.

1000 ☒ 1.1542 🟰 🟰 🟰 🟰

a) Does your calculator perform the constant function? If so, write the keystrokes for your calculator for Charlene's calculation. Are they the same?

b) Explain why she multiplied 1000 by 1.1542 four times.

c) How many times would she press the 🟰 key to find the value after 20 years?

d) How else might she have calculated the total amount after four years?

e) Calculate the total value after 4 years for each rate.

2. Examine the table.
a) What is the increase in value after 20 years for each interest rate?
b) Estimate the percent increase after 20 years for each rate.

3. Investigate the current interest rate for money kept in a savings account at a local bank. How long would it take for $1000 to double itself? triple itself? Explain how you calculated.

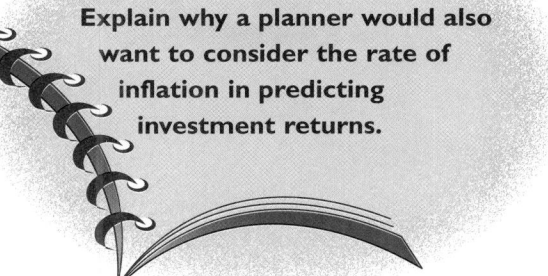

In Your Journal

Explain why a planner would also want to consider the rate of inflation in predicting investment returns.

This formula is one of many that can be used by health care workers to determine medicine dosage for children when the adult dosage is known.

$$c = \frac{(a + 1)}{24} \times d$$

(c is the dosage for a child in millilitres, d is the adult dosage in millilitres, and a is the age of the child in years)

For example, if the adult dosage is 12 mL, the dosage for a 3-year-old would be

$$C = \frac{(3 + 1)}{24} \times 12$$
$$= \frac{1}{6} \times 12$$
$$= 2 \text{ mL}$$

4. Explain why $c = \dfrac{ad + d}{24}$ could also be used.

5. a) How can you tell that the dosage for an 11-year-old will be about half the adult dosage by examining the formula?
b) At what age is the child's dosage about 25% of the adult dose?

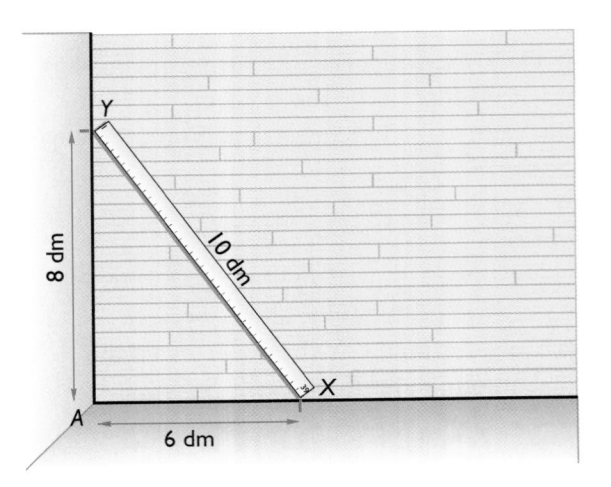

6. Examine the dosage information on several packages of non-prescription liquid medicines. How do the dosages recommended for adults compare to the dosages for 11-year-olds? 13-year-olds? Does the formula apply?

Health care workers often have to interpret the results of blood tests. An adult in good health will have a red cell count of about 5.0×10^{12}/L and a white blood cell count of about 5.0×10^{9}/L.

7. a) What is the ratio of red to white cell counts in a healthy adult?
b) What is the ratio of white to red cell counts as a fraction? decimal?
c) What would each blood cell count be per millilitre instead of per litre?
d) A sample of about 10 mL to 20 mL of blood is usually needed for a test. About how many of each type of cell can be found in a sample?
e) The average adult has about 5 L of blood. About how many red and white blood cells are in a healthy adult?
f) In leukemia patients, the white cell count can be as high as 1.0×10^{11}/L. How many times as great is this count as the normal count?

To ensure that, when a building is constructed, the adjacent walls will be perpendicular, carpenters sometimes do the following. A point X is located along one wall 6 units from corner A. A point Y is located 8 units from corner A along the adjacent wall. If the distance XY is 10 units then the walls will form a right angle at corner A.

8. Explain how you know AY is perpendicular to AX.

9. For each of these measurements from corner A, what is the length of XY if the walls are at right angles?
a) $AX = 30$ cm, $AY = 40$ cm
b) $AX = 9$ dm, $AY = 12$ dm

10. Find a corner in a room and use a metre stick to represent XY. Adjust the metre stick so that it starts at 0.8 m from the corner. Is the other end 0.6 m from the corner? Explain your findings.

Automotive machinists use the formula for the volume of a cylinder to calculate the volume or displacement of each cylinder in an automobile engine.

$$\text{volume} = \text{height} \times \text{area of base} = h\,\pi r^2$$

11. Find the volume or displacement of this cylinder in
   a) cubic centimetres
   b) millilitres
   c) litres

Cylinder Specifications for a 1955 Chev V8 Engine

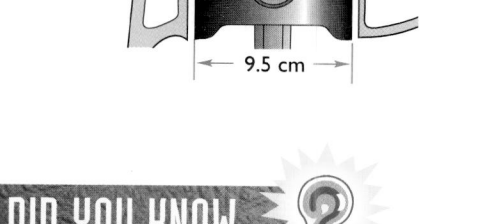

7.6 cm

9.5 cm

12. What is the displacement in litres for an engine with eight 1955 Chev V8 cylinders?

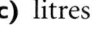

HOME LINK

Investigate and report on examples of mathematics used recently in a work environment by someone you know.

DID YOU KNOW

Fishing limits expressed as kilograms per hectare (kg/ha) of lake surface are used by biologists to protect lakes from overfishing by commercial fishermen. The following table shows the total allowable catch for four species of fish in Reindeer Lake in northern Saskatchewan and Manitoba.

Species	kg/ha
Whitefish	1.5
Walleye	0.5
Pike	0.3
Lake Trout	1.0

NORTHWEST TERRITORIES

Reindeer Lake

MANITOBA

SASKATCHEWAN

ONTARIO

The surface area of Reindeer Lake is 665 000 ha.

• Calculate the allowable catch for each species in kilograms and in tonnes.

• What is the total allowable catch in tonnes for all species?

 **Can We Learn About the Canadian Labor Force?**

Statistics Canada publishes data annually about employment. This table shows annual labor force estimates.

Year	Population aged 15 and over (000s)	Labor Force		
		Employed (000s)	Unemployed (000s)	Total (000s)
1950	9 615	4 976	186	5 163
1960	11 831	5 965	446	6 411
1970	14 528	7 919	476	8 395
1980	18 053	10 708	865	11 573
1990	20 430	12 572	1109	13 681

Canadian Labor Force 1950–1990

Concept Development

1. **a)** What does "(000s)" represent?
   b) Discuss how the data in each of the columns are related for 1950.

2. Why did Statistics Canada report data only for ages 15 and over?

3. **a)** Explain how you know that there were about twice as many people aged 15 and over in 1990 as in 1950.
   b) Investigate the populations of Canada in 1950 and in 1990. How do they compare?

4. The **participation rate** is the fraction of the population aged 15 and over that are working or actively seeking work. It is usually reported as a percent. For example, the participation rate for 1950 is calculated below. Change the decimal to a percent to one decimal place.

$$\frac{5163}{9615} = 5163 \div 9615 = \boxed{0.5369735}$$

5. Before calculating the participation rate for each of the other years, estimate whether the rate will be higher, lower, or about the same as for 1950. Calculate to check.

6. The **employment rate** is the percent of the total labor force that is employed. To find the employment rate for 1950, 4976 is divided by 5163.
   a) Estimate and then calculate the employment rate for 1950.
   b) Estimate and then calculate the employment rate for the other years.
   c) What do you notice?

The media are more likely to report the unemployment rate rather than the employment rate.

1. Use each percent found in Problem 6 of *Concept Development* to find the unemployment rate for each year.

2. The unemployment rate in 1994 was 10.3%. How many times as great as the 1950 rate is this rate?

3. The number of employed women in Canada increased to 5.6 million in 1993 from 3.4 million in 1975.
a) What was the average annual increase in number of employed women from 1975 to 1993?
b) What was the percent increase in employment for women between 1975 and 1993?

In Your Journal

List at least two reasons for the increase in employed women from 1975 to 1993.

DID YOU KNOW

Examine and discuss this graph which compares the percent of employment in 1991 of people with and without disabilities. Summarize your findings about how employment rates for those with and without disabilities compared. Consider differences among the age groups and between genders.

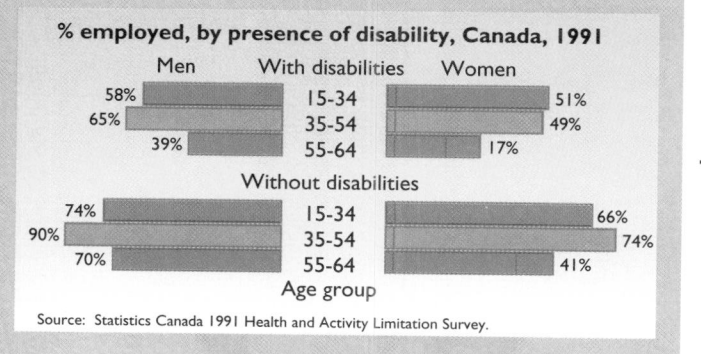

% employed, by presence of disability, Canada, 1991

With disabilities — Men / Women
- 15-34: 58% / 51%
- 35-54: 65% / 49%
- 55-64: 39% / 17%

Without disabilities — Men / Women
- 15-34: 74% / 66%
- 35-54: 90% / 74%
- 55-64: 70% / 41%

Age group

Source: Statistics Canada 1991 Health and Activity Limitation Survey.

4. The table shows the average 1993 earnings of women working full-time as a percent of the earnings of men with the same level of education and in the same age category. Examine and discuss the data in the table. Summarize your findings about how women's and men's earnings compared in 1993.

Average Earnings of Women and Percent of Men's Earnings—Canada, 1993

Level of Education	Age Group					
	25–34		35–44		45–54	
	Earnings $	% of men's	Earnings $	% of men's	Earnings $	% of men's
High school graduate	23 860	74	25 270	68	27 100	67
University graduate	36 450	84	43 910	77	43 950	72

5. a) Jack estimates that male high school graduates aged 45-54 earn about 50% more than female high school graduates in the same age group. Explain Jack's reasoning.
b) Use similar reasoning to estimate how much more men earn than women for the category of high school graduates, aged 25-34.

> Women earn 67% or about $\frac{2}{3}$ of what men earn, so men earn $\frac{3}{2}$ or $1\frac{1}{2}$ as much as women.

6. a) Explain why solving for m in the equation below calculates the average annual earnings for a 25- to 30-year-old male with a high school education. Find m.

$$\frac{74}{100} = \frac{23\,860}{m}$$

23860 ☒ 100 ÷ 74 ═

b) Calculate the men's earnings for each of the other women's earnings in the high school graduate category.

7. Use the data in the table to calculate the total amount in 1993 dollars a woman might expect to earn, from age 25 to 55, for each level of education. Compare the results. What do you notice?

WHAT Do Canadians Spend Money On?

> **Each day in 1994, Canadians spent**
>
> - a total of $4 416 712 in 16 161 beauty parlors and barber shops
> - an average of $22.73 on a house mortgage
> - an average of $18.89 on rent
> - a total of $958 904 on ice cream
> - a total of $41 369 863 on potato chips

Concept Development

1. Estimate and calculate
   a) the average amount spent each day at each beauty parlor and barber shop
   b) the annual cost of a house mortgage
   c) the annual cost of rent
   d) the annual sales of ice cream
   e) the annual sales of potato chips

2. The population of Canada on July 1, 1994, was 29 248 100. Estimate and then calculate the *per capita* daily spending on ice cream and potato chips.

> *Per capita* is a Latin phrase meaning "per person."

3. Each day in Canada during 1994, men spent $931 507 and women spent $2 465 753 on health and beauty products.
   a) Calculate the ratio of women's spending to men's spending as a decimal.
   b) Calculate the percent of total spending on health and beauty products spent by men and by women.

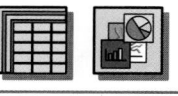

In 1992, on average each Canadian household spent these amounts on clothing:

women's wear	$1065
girls' wear	103
men's wear	717
boys' wear	91

1. Would you say these are weekly, monthly, or annual estimates?

2. What percent of household spending on clothes is for
   a) males?   **b)** females?

3. Each day in 1994, Canadians ate 273 973 kg of pasta worth about $191 780. Find the amount eaten per capita and the amount spent per capita.

4. Each day in 1994, Canadians spent an average of $40 921 917 on the GST. The GST in 1994 was 7%. Estimate and then use this proportion to find the total amount spent on goods and services that are subject to the GST.

$$\frac{\text{amount of GST \$}}{\text{total amount spent \$}} = \frac{7}{100}$$

5. The average Canadian family of four in 1994 had an income of $57 696 and paid total taxes of $27 203. Estimate and then calculate the percent of income that is used to pay taxes.

6. As of March 31, 1995, the total amount of Canadian federal and provincial government debt was about $750 billion. Estimate and then calculate the per capita debt.

It has been estimated that it costs about $160 741 in 1994 dollars to raise a child from birth to age 18.

Estimate then calculate the
a) annual cost   **b)** daily cost
c) cost of raising you to your present age

Team Marketing Report, a sports business newsletter, calculates a **fan cost index** that measures the cost for a family to attend an NHL game. It includes tickets, drinks, hot dogs, programs, caps, and parking.

NHL Game Attendance Costs, 1995		
TEAM	Average Single Ticket Price	Fan Cost Index for a family of 4
Vancouver Canucks	$49.50	$281.26
Calgary Flames	$38.00	$219.40
Winnipeg Jets	$32.39	$193.37
Edmonton Oilers	$29.65	$184.08
Toronto Maple Leafs	$51.15	$291.60
Ottawa Senators	$43.81	$249.26
Montreal Canadiens	$40.00	$226.50

7. For each team, what was the cost to attend all 42 home games for a family of four?

8. For each team what percent of the fan cost index is the cost of tickets?

The table lists the per capita annual expenses of selected items for Canadians from 1966 to 1993.

Canadian Expenses per capita, 1966–1993 in dollars ($)					
EXPENSE	1966	1975	1980	1990	1993
Rent & fuel	337	773	1 452	3 371	3 659
Food	331	641	970	2 344	1 582
Clothing	157	307	485	806	773
New & used cars	118	241	348	808	685
Restaurants & hotels	110	294	500	951	929
Other	843	2 043	3 416	6 708	7 609
Total	1 896	4 299	7 171	14 988	15 237

9. Calculate the percent of each total for each year of
   a) rent and fuel   **b)** food

10. Compare the percents in Problem 9. What do you notice?

11. a) Choose a year. Construct a circle graph to show the proportion of each expense to the total.
   b) Before starting, explain how you know that close to half of the graph will be "Other."

WHAT Do Canadians Own?

The table shows the percent of Canadian households owning selected home electronic devices and appliances.

Appliance/Electronic Device Ownership (%), Canada, 1960–1990				
ITEM	1960	1970	1980	1990
Electric stoves	56.2	78.6	89.4	93.9
Freezers	11.5	33.2	51.0	56.8
Telephones	83.3	93.9	97.6	98.5
Televisions	80.6	96.0	97.7	99.0
Households (000s)	4 404	5 784	7 787	10 203

Concept Development

1. What do you notice about the data?

2. Explain how you know that
   a) in 1960, over 2 200 000 households owned an electric stove
   b) in 1970, about 1 900 000 households owned a freezer
   c) in 1990, about 10 000 000 households owned a telephone or television
   d) the number of households increased by about 75% from 1960 to 1980

3. a) Explain how you know that ownership of a freezer shows the greatest percent increase of all household items from 1960 to 1990.
   b) These keystrokes calculate the percent increase for the electric stove from 1960 to 1990.

   93.9 ⊟ 56.2 ⊜ ⊡ 56.2 ⊜
   Calculate the percent increase between 1960 and 1990 for each item.

4. Why would you predict that ownership of a telephone or television would not show a great percent increase after 1990?

Applications

 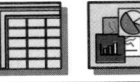

The table shows the percent of households with selected equipment and services across Canada.

% Ownership of Selected Services/Equipment, Canada, 1995					
		Service/Equipment (%)			
Province	Households (000s)	Cable TV	VCRs	CD Players	Computers
Newfoundland	194	82.0	83.5	41.2	19.6
Prince Edward Island	50	68.0	80.0	38.0	16.0
Nova Scotia	357	75.6	81.2	41.2	22.4
New Brunswick	286	69.2	81.1	38.1	19.9
Quebec	2937	64.2	77.7	44.3	23.5
Ontario	4143	78.2	84.3	49.0	32.5
Manitoba	419	66.8	79.7	44.4	24.8
Saskatchewan	385	59.0	77.9	39.7	23.4
Alberta	1009	70.7	86.1	52.4	34.2
British Columbia	1463	85.4	84.3	52.8	32.7

1. What do you notice about the data?

2. Explain how you know that
   a) there are twice the number of households in Quebec compared to British Columbia.
   b) about 500 000 Alberta households have a CD player
   c) about 3 000 000 households in Ontario have cable
   d) about 100 000 households in Manitoba have computers

3. Choose one province. Calculate the number of households that have each item.

The table shows total households and the number of households owning at least one motor vehicle (automobiles, vans, and trucks) in 1995 across Canada.

Motor Vehicle Ownership, Canada, 1995			
	Total Households (000s)	Households with at least 1 motor vehicle (000s)	no motor vehicles (000s)
Canada	11 243	9 430	1 814
Newfoundland	194	158	36
Prince Edward Island	50	43	6
Nova Scotia	357	295	63
New Brunswick	286	242	43
Quebec	2 937	2 356	581
Ontario	4 143	3 459	684
Manitoba	419	358	60
Saskatchewan	385	339	46
Alberta	1 009	916	93
British Columbia	1 463	1 263	201

4. a) Calculate the percent of households in each province that own at least one motor vehicle.
   b) In which provinces is vehicle ownership greater than the national average?
   c) Which province has the greatest proportion of households owning automobiles?

5. Construct two circle graphs—one to show the proportion of households with at least 1 vehicle and no vehicle in your province and another for Canada.

6. In 1993, a total of 13 477 896 vehicles were registered in Canada. If the population was 28 940 600, determine the number of vehicles per capita.

7. In 1989, a total of 348 000 motorcycles and 30 000 mopeds were registered in Canada. In 1993, a total of 309 000 motorcycles and 26 000 mopeds were registered.
   a) Calculate the actual decrease and then the percent decrease for each vehicle.
   b) List some possible reasons for the decrease.

DID YOU KNOW

Explain what calculations you would perform to determine how American and Canadian passenger car ownership compared to worldwide ownership in 1990.

Passenger Car Ownership, Canada, U.S.A., and Worldwide, 1990		
	Population (000s)	Passenger Cars (000s)
World	5 292 000	438 525
Canada	26 522	12 622
USA	249 975	143 550

HOME LINK

Conduct a survey in your class and school about ownership of telephones and radios. How does the result of your survey compare to the national results?

Telephone/Radio Ownership by Number of Items (%), Canada, 1995		
Number	Telephones (%)	Radios (%)
One	24.2	17.9
Two	36.9	25.6
Three or more	37.5	55.4

143

 **HOW** # Have Prices and Costs Changed?

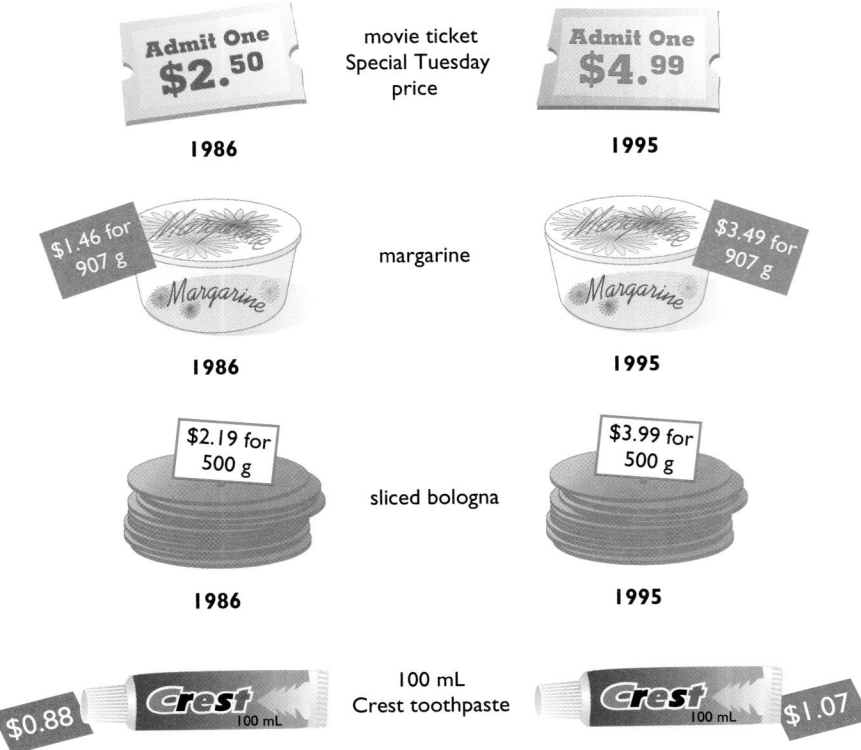

movie ticket
Special Tuesday
price

Admit One **$2.50**
1986

Admit One **$4.99**
1995

margarine

$1.46 for 907 g
1986

$3.49 for 907 g
1995

sliced bologna

$2.19 for 500 g
1986

$3.99 for 500 g
1995

100 mL
Crest toothpaste

$0.88 **Crest** 100 mL
1986

Crest 100 mL $1.07
1995

Concept Development

1. Which of the items above show the greatest and least
   a) actual increase from 1986 to 1995?
   b) percent increase from 1986 to 1995?

Statistics Canada investigates the average price of certain goods and services. If the goods and services cost $100 in 1986 and $120 in 1995, the *Consumer Price Index* (CPI) would be 120.

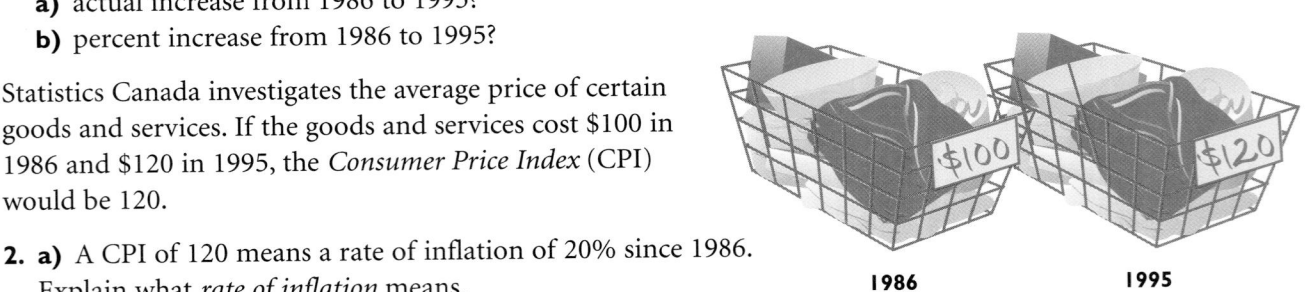

$100
1986

$120
1995

2. a) A CPI of 120 means a rate of inflation of 20% since 1986. Explain what *rate of inflation* means.
   b) What is the rate of inflation for a CPI of 105? a CPI of 137.3?

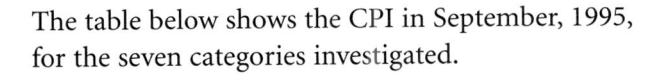
The table below shows the CPI in September, 1995, for the seven categories investigated.

Consumer Price Index, Canada, 1995

CATEGORY	CPI (Consumer Price Index)
Food	125.5
Shelter	134.1
Household Operations & Furnishings	122.2
Clothing & Footwear	132.7
Transportation	138.7
Health & Personal Care	135.4
Recreation, Education & Reading	146.2

1. Which statements are true? Explain.
   a) Transportation costs have increased the most since 1986.
   b) Food costs have increased about $\frac{1}{4}$ since 1986.
   c) Clothing and footwear costs are about $\frac{1}{3}$ higher than in 1986.

2. Use the appropriate CPI for each 1986 item to estimate and then calculate the 1995 cost.
   a) musical tape cassette $8.97
   b) chicken breast $6.37/kg
   c) men's dress shoes $69.99
   d) 10 kg flour $4.69
   e) downhill ski package (skis, boots, poles, bindings) $189.95
   f) new Mazda RX7 sports car $18 995.00

3. Solve this proportion to give the 1986 price for a $45 men's sweater bought in 1995.
$$\frac{132.7}{100} = \frac{\$45.00}{x}$$

4. Find the 1986 price for each 1995 item.
   a) color TV $389.99
   b) women's jacket $69.93
   c) air/hotel to Orlando, FL from Saskatoon, SK, $679.00
   d) wallet $8.99
   e) 1 kg of boneless chicken breasts $8.49 kg

This line graph shows the average annual CPI in Canada over selected years.

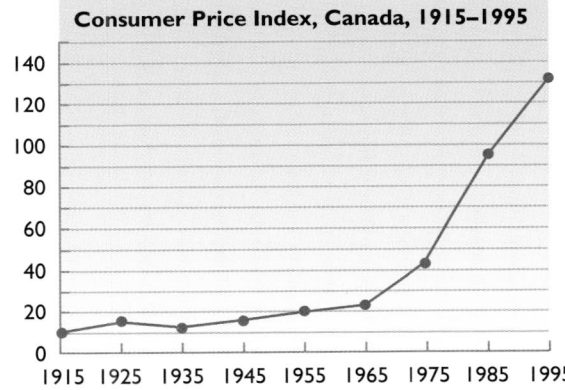

5. **a)** Between which years did costs decrease?
   b) Why might prices have decreased during that period?

6. Explain why you can say that prices in 1985 were about 10 times greater than in 1915.

7. **a)** Between which years was the greatest increase? How do you know?
   b) Express the increase as a percent.

DID YOU KNOW ?

The highest annual inflation rate in the world in 1994 was that of Brazil at 1120.4. Canada's inflation rate in 1994 was 130.2.

If an item cost $10 in 1986, how much would you expect to pay in 1994 in Brazil? in Canada?

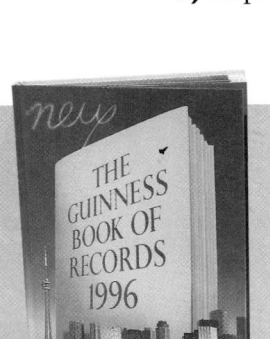

Making Sense of DATA

Using and Interpreting Formulas

Traffic accident investigators use formulas in their jobs. They might substitute the length of a tire skid and an estimate of the *drag* or *friction factor* to estimate the speed of a vehicle involved in a traffic accident.

$S = \sqrt{256\, \ell\, f}$
ℓ = skid length in metres
f = drag or friction factor, which can range from 0 to about 1.5
S = speed in km/h

If $f = 1$ and $\ell = 4$ m

$S = \sqrt{256\,(4)\,(1)}$ $\quad$ 256 [×] 4 [=] [√] [=] $\quad$  *32.*
$\ = 32$ km/h

1. What is meant by *drag*? Why might it vary?

2. **a)** Explain why the formula shows that a longer skid mark means a greater speed.
   b) Explain why greater friction or drag means a greater speed.

3. Describe an accident situation for which the formula might underestimate the speed of a vehicle.

Applications

4. Use the formula to estimate the speed for each skid mark. Assume $f = 1$, which indicates good tire, road, and brake conditions.
   a) 36 m
   b) 72 m

5. Compare each estimated speed in Problem 4. Is it true that a skid mark that is twice as long as another skid mark indicates twice the speed? Explain.

6. Estimate the speed for each:
   a) $f = 0.5$ or fair conditions, $\ell = 200$ m
   b) $f = 1.0$ or good conditions, $\ell = 100$ m
   Compare each estimated speed. What do you notice? Why did you get these results?

7. Some investigators might use the formula $S = 16\sqrt{\ell f}$ while others might use $S^2 = 256\,\ell f$. Explain.

8. Sometimes formulas are used to create tables for quick reference.
   a) Complete the table.

| Skid Length, ℓ (m) | Speed (km/h) | | |
| | Friction Factor, f | | |
	0.5	1.0	1.5
1	11.3		
2	16.0		
3	19.6		
4			
5			

   b) Use the table to estimate the speed for a friction factor of 0.5 and a 3.5 m skid. Use the formula to check.
   c) Repeat part (b) for a friction factor of 1.25 and a 2 m skid.

Communicate Your Knowledge

1. What other information would you need to know before agreeing with the headline?

Canadian Families Better Off in 1994 Than in 1971

	1971	1994
Average Family Income	$10 113	$54 153

2. Women in Tanzania, East Africa, earn about 92% of what men earn. In Canada, women earn about 63% of men's wages. What other information would you need to know to determine whether Tanzanian women are better off than Canadian women?

3. Who is correct? Explain.

Prices have stopped rising.

No, they're still rising but not as fast as before.

6. The graph shows the percent of total federal income tax collected from individual Canadians and corporations. Tell what you notice.

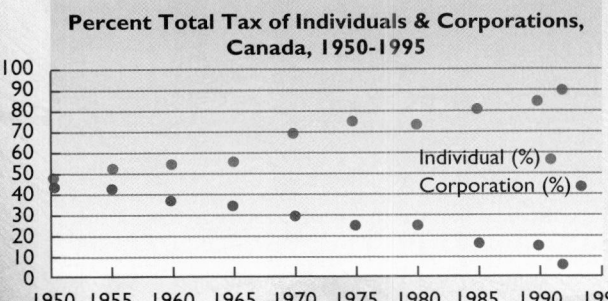

Percent Total Tax of Individuals & Corporations, Canada, 1950-1995

Individual (%)
Corporation (%)

1950 1955 1960 1965 1970 1975 1980 1985 1990 1995

4. Suppose you invested $100 in a savings account in 1995. The annual interest is 10% for each of the next 5 years. Explain why you can be certain to have more than $150 after 5 years.

5. Suppose workers in a company get a 10% raise in 1995 but take a 10% cut in 1996. Will they be earning the same salary as they did before receiving the raise? Explain.

What else would you like to know about earning and spending? How could you find out?

Polynomials [II]

Algebra is used by the engineers who operate "The Bungee Zone" at Nanaimo on Vancouver Island.

- What variables do you think the engineers have to consider each day to maintain the safety of the jumps?

- How do you think each of these variables would affect a jump?

- What other variables should "The Bungee Zone" consider that might affect its business?

Look through catalogs, magazines, or cookbooks for examples of situations that can be represented by algebraic expressions. Write a possible expression for each and tell what the variables represent.

7.1 Multiplying a Polynomial by a Monomial

Algebra tiles can be used to multiply expressions such as $3(x + 1)$ or $3x(x + 1)$.

a) Complete the Magic Square so that the sums of the rows, columns, and diagonals are the same.
b) Is the square still "magic" if you multiply every cell by a positive number? a negative number?

8	4
-2	6
0	

Concept Development

1. Multiplication often represents sets. Use algebra tiles to display $3(x + 1)$ as 3 sets of $(x + 1)$.

2. **a)** How did you arrange the tiles for Problem 1?

Alexa displays the tiles this way:	Tennille displays the tiles another way:
	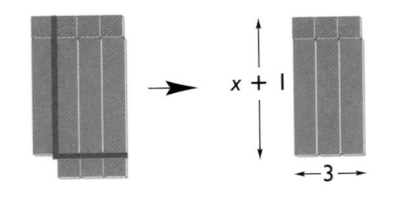

   b) What is the result of $3(x + 1)$?

3. Multiplication also represents the area of a rectangle. Use algebra tiles to display $3(x + 1)$ as the area of a rectangle with dimensions 3 and $(x + 1)$.

4. **a)** How did you arrange the tiles for Problem 3?

Alexa uses guiding tiles this way:	Tennille uses guiding tiles another way:
Alexa models the area using the most suitable tiles.	Then she removes the guiding tiles.	Tennille models the area using the most suitable tiles.	Then she removes the guiding tiles.

   b) What is the result of $3(x + 1)$?

150

5. **a)** Do both area methods in Problem 4 give the same result?
   b) Are the guiding tiles included in the result? Explain.
   c) Do both area methods shown in Problem 4 and set methods shown in Problem 2 give the same result?

6. **a)** Why can't you display $3x(x + 1)$ as sets? Explain why.
   b) Use algebra tiles to model the area $3x(x + 1)$.

7. **a)** How did you arrange the tiles for Problem 6?

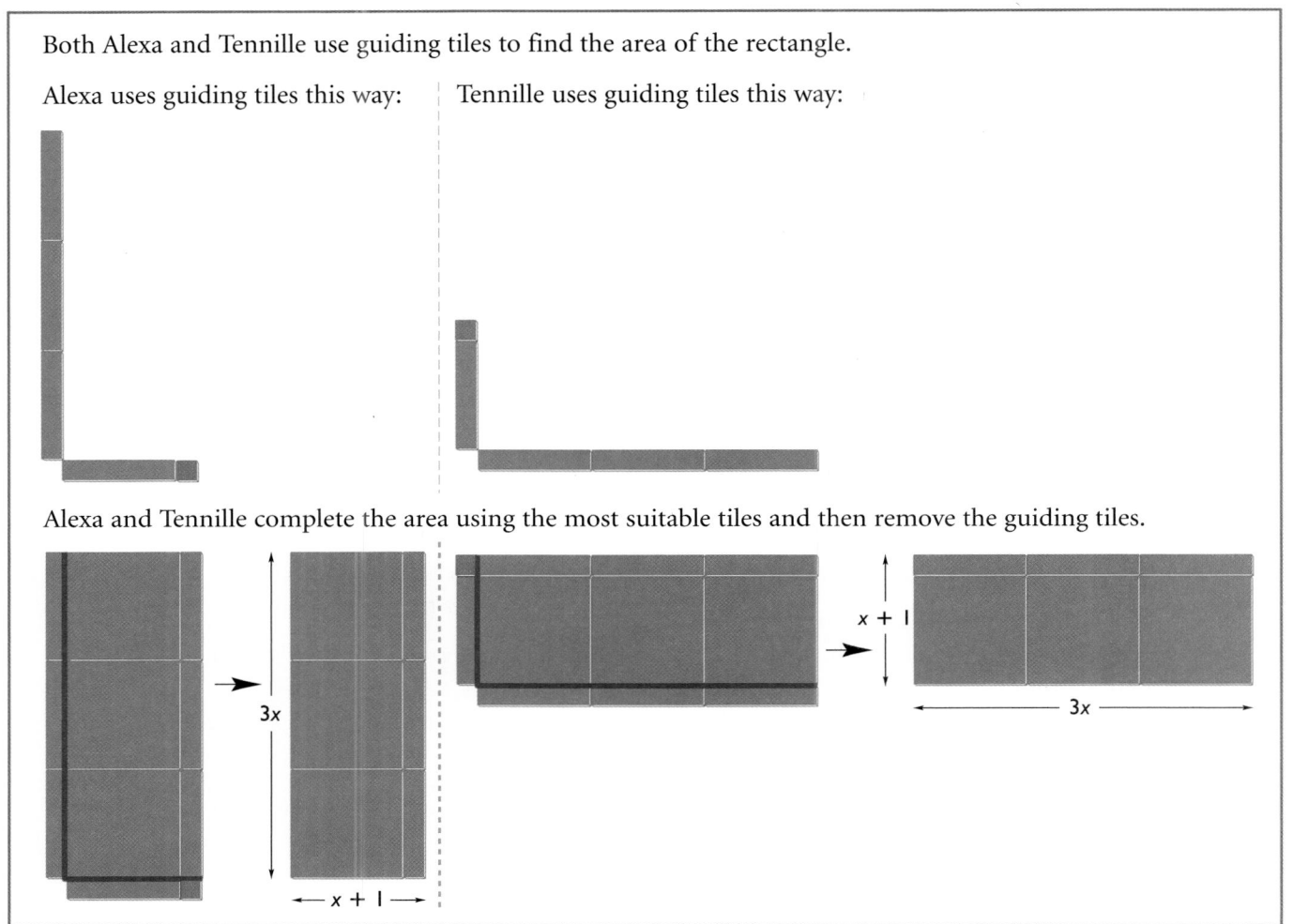

Both Alexa and Tennille use guiding tiles to find the area of the rectangle.

Alexa uses guiding tiles this way: | Tennille uses guiding tiles this way:

Alexa and Tennille complete the area using the most suitable tiles and then remove the guiding tiles.

$3x$

$\longleftarrow x + 1 \longrightarrow$

$x + 1$

$3x$

b) What is the result of $3x(x + 1)$?
c) Do both area methods give the same result?

8. Use algebra tiles to find the area for the rectangle with the following dimensions.
   a) $2(x + 1)$ **b)** $2x(x + 1)$ **c)** $3(2y + 1)$
   d) $3y(2y + 1)$ **e)** $2x(x + y + 2)$

9. If algebra tiles were not available, what pattern can you use to find each product? Show and use this pattern to find the following products.
   a) $2(x + 1)$ **b)** $2x(x + 1)$ **c)** $3(2y + 1)$
   d) $3y(2y + 1)$ **e)** $2x(x + y + 2)$

In Your Journal

Explain what polynomials and monomials are. Give several examples for each. Describe the pattern you can use to multiply any monomial by any polynomial such as $a(a + b + c)$.

Understand and Apply

1. State the dimensions and product for each area model.

   a)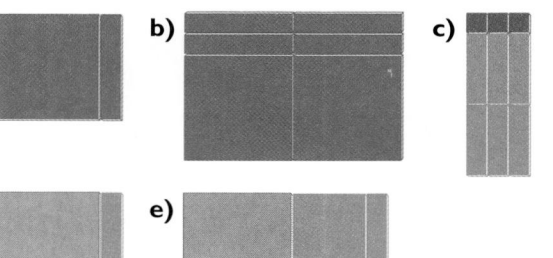

   b)

   c)

   d)

   e)

2. Which of the following can be modelled with tiles using the set method? Which ones must be modelled using the area method? Explain. Use tiles to find the product.
   a) $x(3x + 1)$
   b) $4(3y + 1)$
   c) $y(2x + y + 1)$
   d) $3(2x + y + 3)$

3. Use tiles to find each product.
   a) $3(2x + 3)$
   b) $x(2x + 3)$
   c) $4(x + 1)$
   d) $y(3y + 2)$
   e) $2x(x + 2)$
   f) $3y(y + 3)$
   g) $x(2x + 2y + 3)$
   h) $3y(x + y + 1)$

4. Use the pattern you described in Problem 9 of *Concept Development* to find the following products without using tiles.
   a) $2x(3x + 5)$
   b) $3y(2y + 3)$
   c) $4(3x + 2y + 1)$
   d) $2y(2y + 4)$
   e) $3x(y + 2)$
   f) $4y(x + 2y + 3)$

5. Use algebra tiles to check your products in Problem 4.

6. Explain why this area model represents the product of $2x(x - 2)$.

   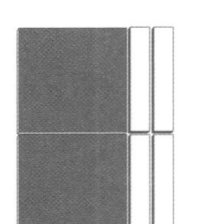

7. a) Without using tiles, find the product of $-3(-2x + 3)$.
   b) Use algebra tiles to show the product. How do you determine when the tiles should be flipped?

8. Find the product.
   a) $2(5x^2 - 6)$
   b) $x(x + 3y + 1)$
   c) $a^2(3a + 1)$
   d) $3p(2 - 3p + p^2)$
   e) $-3t(2t^2 - t - 2)$
   f) $4x^2y(-2x + y^2)$

W/E 9. Find the perimeter and area.

   a)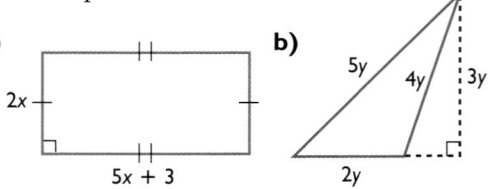
   b)

10. Your regular salary is w dollars per hour and your overtime salary is $10 more per hour. Write an expression to represent how much you would earn if you work 52 h in a regular 40 h week?

11. Sketch the rectangle, then find the area.
    a) The width of the rectangle is x. The length is three units more than the width.
    b) The width of the rectangle is x. The length is four units more than three times the width.
    c) The length of the rectangle is x. The width is two units more than half the length.

12. Find the products, then simplify.
    a) $4(2x + 3) - 2(x + 4)$
    b) $3p(2p + q - 1) - 4p(p - q + 1)$
    c) $-3d^2(d + e - 4) - d(d^2 - de + 2)$

13. Check your results in Problem 12 by substituting values, then evaluating.

14. Apply the pattern for multiplying polynomials by monomials to mentally calculate the following products. For example,

    $25 \times 32 = 25(30 + 2) = 750 + 50 = 800$
    a) 15×21
    b) 21×43
    c) $6 \times 2\frac{1}{2}$

HOME LINK

Estimate the dimensions of a bathroom at home in relation to the length of the bathtub, b. What is the area of the bathroom floor in terms of b?

Making Sense of DATA

Lines of Best Fit

Researchers will often create a question to investigate to help us expand our understanding of the world around us. The researchers make a prediction about how one piece of information may be related to another. Then they check to see if their prediction is true by collecting and organizing appropriate data and making observations on the data.

For example: Is the length of the bone from the edge of the shoulder to the elbow, *b*, related to the height of a female, *h*?

1. Make a prediction about the relationship between height and upper arm bone length.

2. Collect data for the length of the particular bone and the height for each female in two or three grade 9 classes.

Females	
b (cm)	*h* (cm)
23.0	134.0
24.0	137.5

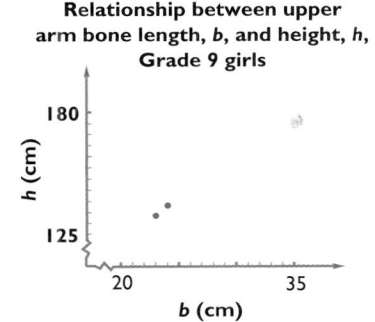

Relationship between upper arm bone length, *b*, and height, *h*, Grade 9 girls

3. Construct a scatter plot to display your information, then find the line of best fit for your displayed data.

4. How well does your line of best fit help in estimating the height of a female from her upper arm bone length? Explain.

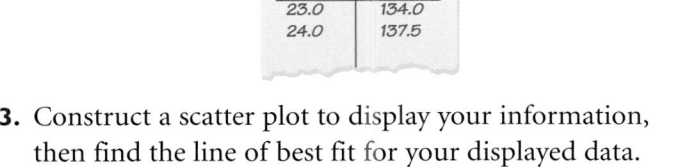

Applications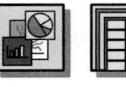

5. Construct a scatter plot of the same information for an equal number of grade 9 males and determine a line of best fit. How do the lines of best fit compare for females and males?

6. Researchers found that an estimate of the height of a female can be determined from the relation: $h = 2.75\,b + 71.48$. A similar relation for male height is: $h = 2.89\,b + 70.64$.
   a) Make a table of values for males. Create a graph.

Males	
$h = 2.89b + 70.64$	
b (cm)	*h* (cm)
20.0	128.44
22.0	
24.0	

b) How does your graph compare to the line of best fit for your scatter plots?
   c) Repeat parts (a) and (b) for females.

7. An anthropological dig uncovered a skeleton with these measurements:
   height – 138 cm
   length of upper arm bone – 23 cm
   Are the skeletal remains those of a male or a female? Explain.

7.2 Working Backwards to Find Common Factors (I)

What digits are represented by the letters?
a) HO × HO = HAW
b) (AS)² = WAS

All numbers have factors. These factors can be determined by working backwards to find either the sets, or the dimensions for the area of a rectangle.

12 has 1 set of 12 and a 1 × 12 area, 2 sets of 6 and a 2 × 6 area, or 3 sets of 4 and a 3 × 4 area.

I see 3 different sets and dimensions.

Concept Development

1. Monomials can be written as factors. Work backwards with algebra tiles, showing sets or area to find the factors of the following monomials.
   a) $2x$ b) $3y$ c) $6x$

2. a) How did you arrange your tiles for Problem 1?

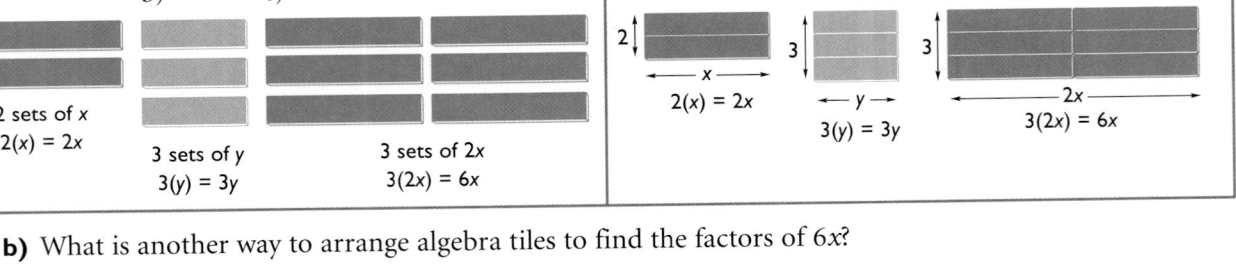

Adir works backwards using sets.

a) 2 sets of x
$2(x) = 2x$

b) 3 sets of y
$3(y) = 3y$

c) 3 sets of 2x
$3(2x) = 6x$

Anish works backwards by finding the dimensions for the given area of a rectangle.

a) $2(x) = 2x$

b) $3(y) = 3y$

c) $3(2x) = 6x$

   b) What is another way to arrange algebra tiles to find the factors of $6x$?

3. Polynomials can be written as factors. Work backwards with algebra tiles, showing sets or area to find the factors of the following polynomials.
   a) $2x + 2$ b) $3y + 6$ c) $2x + 4y$

4. How did you arrange your tiles for Problem 3?

Adir works backwards using sets.

a) 2 sets of (x + 1)
$2(x + 1) = 2x + 2$

b) 3 sets of (y + 2)
$3(y + 2) = 3y + 6$

c) 2 sets of (x + 2y)
$2(x + 2y) = 2x + 4y$

Anish works backwards by finding the dimensions for the given area of a rectangle.

a) $2(x + 1) = 2x + 2$

b) $3(y + 2) = 3y + 6$

c) $2(x + 2y) = 2x + 4y$

5. Work backwards using algebra tiles to find the dimensions for the given area of each rectangle. Write the dimensions as factors of the following polynomials.

   a) $4x + 4$ **b)** $3x + 6$ **c)** $5y + 5$ **d)** $3y^2 + 6x$

Understand and Apply

1. Write the monomial as a product of its factors. Use algebra tiles if necessary.

   a) $5x$ **b)** $2y$ **c)** $8x$ **d)** $10y$

2. Find the missing factors.

   a) $6w^2 = (2w)(\blacksquare)$ **b)** $12mn = (3m)(\blacksquare)$
   c) $10pq = (5)(\blacksquare)$ **d)** $8m^2p = (2m)(\blacksquare)$
   e) $-4ef = (-2f)(\blacksquare)$ **f)** $-20d^2 = (-4d)(\blacksquare)$

3. Use algebra tiles to find the missing factors.

   a) $6x + 6y = (\blacksquare)(x + y)$
   b) $5x + 10 = (\blacksquare)(x + 2)$
   c) $6y + 3 = (3)(\blacksquare + \blacktriangle)$
   d) $8x + 4y = (4)(\blacksquare + \blacktriangle)$
   e) $4y + 2x = (\blacksquare)(2y + x)$
   f) $12y + 3x + 6 = (3)(\blacksquare + \blacktriangle + \bullet)$

In Your Journal

If you were to find the factors of a polynomial without using algebra tiles, how would you determine the first factor? Once you know the first factor, how would you determine the second factor? Use your pattern to factor.

   a) $3x - 9$ **b)** $6a + 12$
   c) $4n - 2m$ **d)** $12d + 8e$

4. Find the factors. Use algebra tiles if necessary. Check your factors by multiplying.

   a) $3x + 6$ **b)** $6y + 9$ **c)** $6x + 3$
   d) $3x + 6y$ **e)** $10x + 5y$ **f)** $6y + 8x$
   g) $2x + 2y + 2$ **h)** $3x + 3y - 3$

5. Find the factors.

   a) $4a + 2b$ **b)** $3mn - 6p$
   c) $12x + 18z$ **d)** $8a - 4b + 12c$
   e) $5m^2 + 10n^2$ **f)** $10ef + 15f - 20e$

6. The area of a rectangle is given. Sketch the diagram and label the dimensions. Then find the perimeter.

   a) $4x^2 + 8$ **b)** $6y + 3$ **c)** $8y + 6x$

7. Evaluate mentally by factoring.

   a) $9 \times 8 + 9 \times 3$
   b) $14 \times 12 - 14 \times 10$
   c) $98 \times 99 + 98 \times 1$

8. Create your own mental calculation questions similar to Problem 7. Pass them to a partner to calculate.

9. Jerrod decided to give identical sets of marbles to each of his grandchildren. He bought 12 small bags of red marbles, 9 medium-size bags of blue marbles, and 6 large bags of yellow marbles.
   a) Write an algebraic expression to represent the total number of marbles.
   b) Factor the expression to find out how many grandchildren Jerrod had, and how many bags of marbles were in each set.

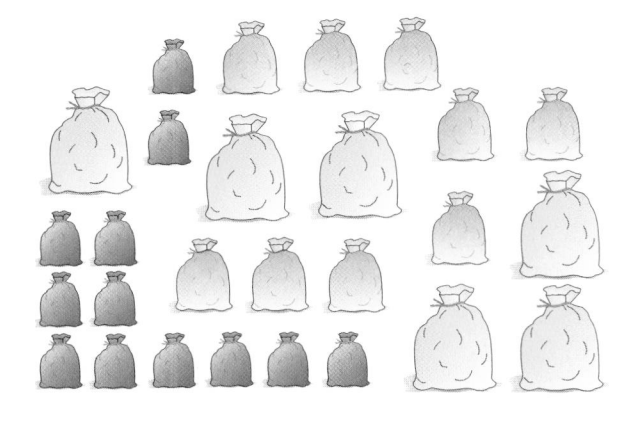

7.3 Working Backwards to Find Common Factors (II)

Warm Up

Choose any two 2-digit numbers. Find the greatest common factor (GCF) and the least common multiple (LCM) of the numbers. Compare the product of the two numbers with the product of their GCF and LCM. What do you notice?

Many polynomial expressions have numerical and variable common factors. These factors can be determined by working backwards to find dimensions for the area of a rectangle.

Concept Development

1. a) Arrange algebra tiles to display $3x^2 + 6xy$ as a rectangle.
   b) What are the dimensions of the rectangle?

2. a) How did you arrange the tiles for Problem 1?

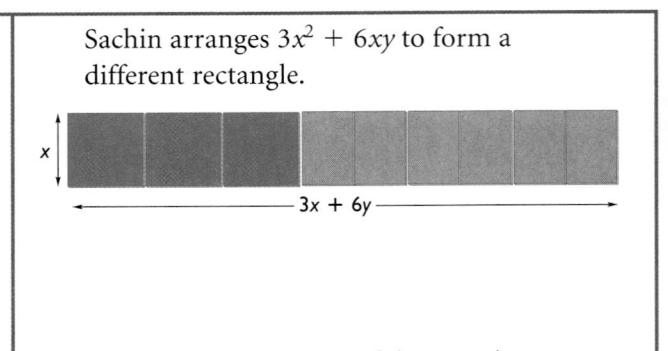

Grant arranges $3x^2 + 6xy$ to form a rectangle.

The dimensions of his rectangle are $3x$ and $(x + 2y)$.

Sachin arranges $3x^2 + 6xy$ to form a different rectangle.

His dimensions are x and $(3x + 6y)$.

b) Both Grant and Sachin are correct although $3x$ by $(x + 2y)$ is preferred since all common factors – both numerical and variable – have been found. Restate this convention in your own words.

3. Use algebra tiles to find the dimensions formed by the rectangle for the following expressions.

   a) $x^2 + 2x$ **b)** $y^2 + 4y$
   c) $x^2 + xy$ **d)** $2x^2 + 2xy$
   e) $2y^2 + 6y$ **f)** $4xy + 2y$

1. Use algebra tiles to find the missing factors.

a) $x^2 + 5x = (\blacksquare)(x + 5)$
b) $2y^2 + y = y(\blacksquare + \blacktriangle)$
c) $2x^2 + 3xy = (\blacksquare)(2x + 3y)$
d) $4x^2 + 6x = 2x(\blacksquare + \blacktriangle)$
e) $3xy + 3y^2 = (3y)(\blacksquare + \blacktriangle)$
f) $6y^2 - 3xy = (\blacksquare)(2y - x)$
g) $2y^2 + y + xy = (\blacksquare)(2y + 1 + x)$
h) $4y^2 + 4y - 2xy = 2y(\blacksquare + \blacktriangle - \bullet)$

In Your Journal

If you were to find the factors of a polynomial without using algebra tiles, how would you determine the first factor? Once you know the first factor, how would you determine the second factor? Use your pattern to factor
a) $4xy + 2x$ **b)** $3xy + 3y$
c) $6x^2 + 4xy$ **d)** $2y^2 - 4y$

2. Find the factors. Use algebra tiles if necessary. Check your factors by multiplying.

a) $3xy + 6x$
b) $2xy + 4y$
c) $6y^2 + 4y$
d) $8x + 6x^2$
e) $7xy + 7y$
f) $10x + 2x^2$
g) $2x^2 + 4x + 2xy$
h) $6x^2 + 3x + 6xy$
i) $4x^2 + 2x + 6xy$

3. Find the factors. Check by multiplying.

a) $4a^2b + 8ab$
b) $6m^2n^2 - 12mn$
c) $6de - 8d^2$
d) $4f - 8f^2 + 12ef$
e) $6c^2d + 4cd - 8d^2$
f) $6gh - 12g^2h^2$

4. The area of a rectangle is given. Find the dimensions, then the perimeter.

a) $24a^2b + 18ab^2$
b) $48m^2n^2 + 36m^2n$
c) $15pq - 10p + 20p^2q$

5. Factor the following formulas for surface area. Then substitute the given values to find each surface area.

a)   S.A. = $2bh + 2hH + 2bH$

$b = 3$ cm
$h = 4$ cm
$H = 6$ cm

b)   S.A. = $bh + 3bH$

$b = 5$ cm
$h = 4$ cm
$H = 10$ cm

c)   S.A. = $2\pi r^2 + 2\pi rH$

$r = 4$ cm
$H = 10$ cm

6. The volume of a rectangular solid is $60p^3 + 120p^2$. The length is $5p$ and the width is $4p$. Write an expression to represent the height.

In Your Journal

How are factoring and multiplication related?

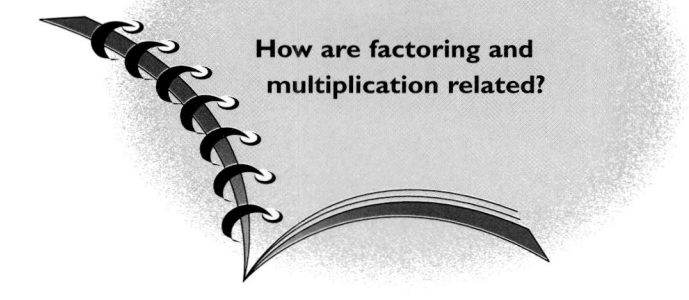

TAKE YOUR PICK!

USING DIVISION

Find the greatest common factor, ■,
for $3x^2 - 6x$.

Calculate $\dfrac{3x^2 - 6x}{■} = ▲ - ●$.

Then find $3x^2 - 6x = ■(▲ - ●)$.

Use division to help you factor the following.

a) $18a - 21a^2$ b) $30m^2 + 12m$
c) $8e + 4e^2 + 12ef$ d) $14p^2 - 28pq + 35pq^2$

MANY POSSIBILITIES

Use algebra tiles to find all the possible
dimensions formed by the rectangle
with area $6x^2 + 12x$. Which dimensions
represent the expression after it has
been factored completely?

COMPLEX FIGURES

a) Use algebra tiles to form the
connected rectangles represented by
$(x^2 + x) + (xy + y)$. Write the dimensions
of each rectangle.

■ (▬▬) + ▲ (▬▬)

b) Create one rectangle using all the
algebra tiles for $x^2 + x + xy + y$. Write
the dimensions. How are the dimensions
related to the connected rectangle
represented by $(x^2 + x) + (xy + y)$?
Repeat for $y^2 + y + xy + x$
and $2xy + 4y + 2x^2 + 4x$

NEGATIVE TILES

Use algebra tiles
a) to find the product of $3x(x + y - 1)$
b) to factor $2x^2 - 4x$

SURFACE AREA

a) Write an expression for the surface area
of the following shapes.

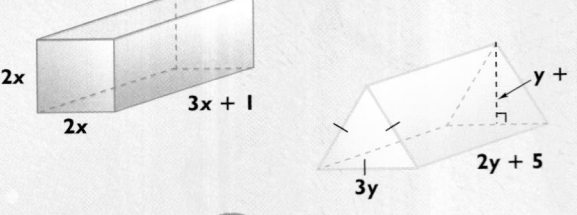

b) If the variable is 10 cm, what surface
area do these keystrokes calculate?

3 ⊠ 10 Ⓒ 7 ⊠ 10 ⊞ 16 ⦆ 🟰

c) Evaluate if the value of each variable is
10 cm.

Make up similar questions and
post them on the bulletin board
for classmates to solve.

7.4 Multiplying a Polynomial by a Binomial

Warm Up

Draw the next figure.
a) Write an expression to describe your rule.
b) Predict the number of dots in the ninth figure.

The width of a rectangle is $x + 1$. The length is two units more than the width. You can use algebra tiles to find the area of the rectangle.

Concept Development

1. Use algebra tiles to display $(x + 1)(x + 1 + 2)$ or $(x + 1)(x + 3)$ as the area of a rectangle.

2. a) How did you arrange the tiles for Problem 1?

Seema uses guiding tiles this way:

Alim uses guiding tiles this way:

Seema and Alim complete the area and then remove the guiding tiles.

$x + 3$

$x + 1$

$x + 1$

$x + 3$

b) What is the result of $(x + 1)(x + 3)$?

3. Do both of these expressions for Problem 2 have the same result? What is the final result?

| Seema wrote: $(x + 1)(x + 3) = x^2 + 3x + 1x + 3$ | Alim wrote: $(x + 1)(x + 3) = x^2 + 1x + 3x + 3$ |

4. Is it possible to use sets to display $(x + 1)(x + 3)$? Explain.

5. Use algebra tiles to find the areas.
   a) $(x + 1)(x + 2)$
   b) $(x + 4)(x + 1)$
   c) $(y + 2)(y + 2)$
   d) $(4x + 1)(x + 2)$
   e) $(2y + 1)(y + 2)$
   f) $(3y + 1)(2y + x + 1)$

6. If algebra tiles were not available, what pattern can you use to find each product? Show and use the pattern to find the products. Check your products using algebra tiles.
   a) $(y + 2)(y + 1)$
   b) $(3x + 1)(x + 1)$
   c) $(2y + 3)(y + 2)$
   d) $(3x + 1)(x + 2)$
   e) $(4y + 1)(y + 2)$
   f) $(x + y)(x + y + 1)$

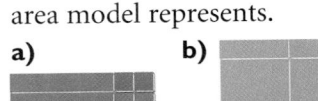
1. State the dimensions and the product that each area model represents.

   a) 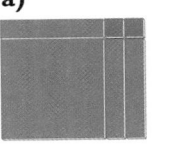 **b)** 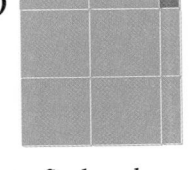 **c)**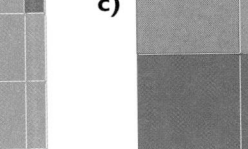

 W/E 2. Use algebra tiles to find each product.
   a) $(y + 1)(y + 3)$ **b)** $(2x + 3)(x + 1)$
   c) $(x + y)(2x + y)$ **d)** $(3x + y)(x + y)$
   e) $(x + 1)(x + y + 1)$ **f)** $(x + y)(3x + y + 1)$

3. How is the number of unit tiles in the upper right corner related to the unit tiles in the dimensions?

4. Use the pattern to find the products without using tiles.
   a) $(y + 6)(y + 2)$ **b)** $(2y + 1)(y + 3)$
   c) $(3x + 1)(x + 1)$ **d)** $(x + y)(2x + y)$
   e) $(x + 1)(x + 2y + 1)$ **f)** $(x + y)(x + 2y + 1)$

5. Use tiles to check your products in Problem 4.

In Your Journal

Explain what a binomial is. Give several examples. Describe the pattern you can use to multiply a binomial by any polynomial, such as $(a + b)(a + b + c)$.

6. Use the pattern to find the products.
   a) $(2a + 1)(a + 3)$ **b)** $(2b + 3)(3b + 1)$
   c) $(4c + 3)(c + 1)$ **d)** $(3d - 1)(d + 2)$
   e) $(4e - 5)(2e + 1)$ **f)** $(m - 3)(2m - 5)$
   g) $(5f + 1)(2e + f - 1)$
   h) $(4n - 3)(m + 2n - 3)$

7. Check your multiplication sentences in Problem 6 by substituting values, then evaluating.

W/E 8. **a)** Use the pattern to find the product of $-2x - 3$ and $3x + 4$.
   b) Use algebra tiles to show the product. How do you determine which tiles should be flipped?

9. Find the products. What pattern do you notice?
   a) $(y + 2)(y + 2)$ **b)** $(2x + 3)(2x + 3)$
   c) $(2x - 5)(2x - 5)$ **d)** $(3y + 1)^2$
   e) $(4x + 3)^2$ **f)** $(2x + y)^2$

10. Find the products. What pattern do you notice?
   a) $(y + 2)(y - 2)$ **b)** $(x + 3)(x - 3)$
   c) $(2x - 1)(2x + 1)$ **d)** $(3y - 4)(3y + 4)$
   e) $(3x - 2)(3x + 2)$ **f)** $(2x + 3y)(2x - 3y)$
   g) $(-y - 2)(-y + 2)$ **h)** $(2 + x)(2 - x)$

11. Why do you think each product in Problem 10 is called a "difference of squares"?

12. Find the perimeter and area.

   a) 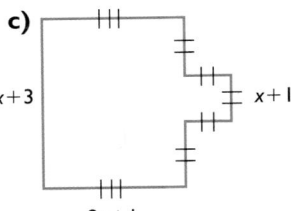 **b)**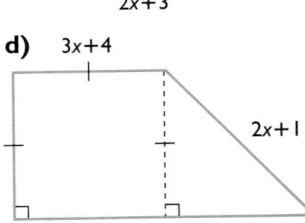

   c) 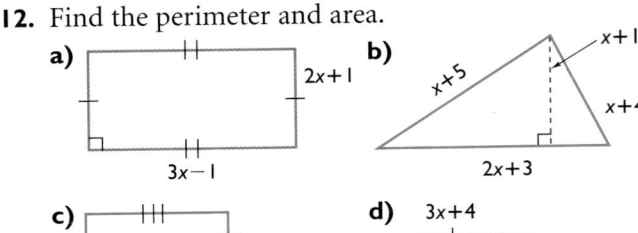 **d)**

13. Apply the pattern for multiplying two binomials to mentally calculate the products. For example,

$$21(19) = (20 + 1)(20 - 1)$$
$$= 400 - 20 + 20 - 1$$
$$= 399$$

   a) 29×31 **b)** 92×88 **c)** 57×63

14. Find the products, then simplify.
   a) $(x - 1)(x + 2) + (2x + 3)(x - 1)$
   b) $(x + y)(x - y) - 4x(x + y)$
   c) $(2y + 1)(y - 3) + (y + 1)^2$
   d) $(3y + 2)^2 + (y - 1)^2$
   e) $(3m - 2)(3m + 2) + (m - 4)^2$
   f) $(x + 2y)^2 + (x - y)^2$
   g) $(3d - 1)(d + 2) - (d - 3)(d - 1)$

15. **a)** Write an expression that can be used to find the area of the matting around the picture.
   b) Simplify the expression.
   c) Evaluate if $n = 3$.

More Than One Strategy

Multiplying Binomials by Polynomials

There are several ways to multiply $x + 3$ and $x - 1$.
Here are some. Can you think of others?

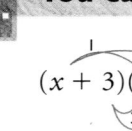

You can use algebra tiles.

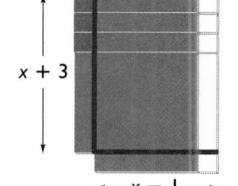

$$(x + 3)(x - 1) = x^2 - 1x + 3x - 3$$
$$= x^2 + 2x - 3$$

You can draw a diagram.

$$(x - 1)(x + 3) = x^2 - 1x + 3x - 3$$
$$= x^2 + 2x - 3$$

You can use a pattern.

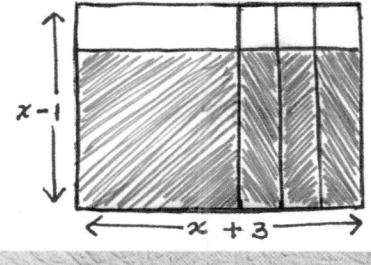

$$(x + 3)(x - 1) = x^2 - 1x + 3x - 3$$
$$= x^2 + 2x - 3$$

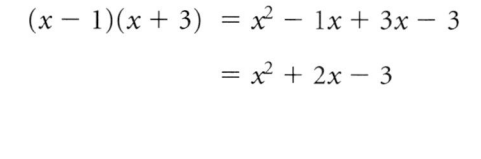

You can use a different pattern.

$$(x + 3)(x - 1) = x^2 - 3 - x + 3x$$
$$= x^2 + 2x - 3$$

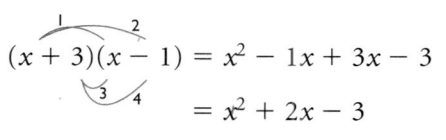

Understand and Apply

1. Use two of the methods to find each product. Try to use each of the four methods at least once.

a) $(x + 5)(x + 2)$ **b)** $(x + 5)(x - 4)$

c) $(x - 5)(x - 4)$ **d)** $(x - 4)(x + 4)$

e) $(x - 4)(x - y - 1)$

2. Which method do you prefer? Why?

3. Explain how you would calculate $(x + y + 1)(x + 2y + 2)$.

7.5 Working Backwards to Find Factors of Trinomials

An expression representing the area of a rectangle is $x^2 + 6x + 8$. The dimensions of this rectangle are represented by the factors of $x^2 + 6x + 8$.

Warm Up

What are the dimensions of the rectangular box? Create a similar problem for a partner to solve.

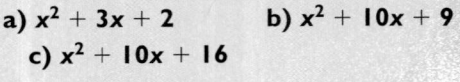

120 cm²   96 cm²   80 cm²

Concept Development

1. **a)** How can you arrange the algebra tiles to display $x^2 + 6x + 8$ as a rectangle?
   b) What are the dimensions of the rectangle?

2. **a)** Explain why Ambareen's display is *not* correct, and Ginette's display *is* correct.

Ambareen arranges $x^2 + 6x + 8$ like this:	Ginette arranges $x^2 + 6x + 8$ like this:
	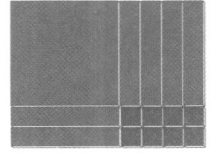

   b) Write the area as a product of the length and the width.

W/E **3.** Use tiles to find the dimensions of each rectangle. Write the area as a product of length and width.
   a) $x^2 + 4x + 4$
   b) $x^2 + 7x + 6$
   c) $x^2 + 7x + 12$
   d) $y^2 + 6y + 9$
   e) $x^2 + 11x + 18$
   f) $y^2 + 4y + 4$
   g) $y^2 + 8y + 12$
   h) $y^2 + 9y + 8$
   i) $x^2 + 3xy + 2y^2$

In Your Journal

If you were to find the factors of a trinomial without using algebra tiles, how would you determine the fir term in each factor? What appears to be the pattern between the last terms in the factors ar the last term of the trinomial? What appears be the pattern between the last terms in the factors and the middle term of the trinomial? Use your pattern to factor
   a) $x^2 + 3x + 2$ b) $x^2 + 10x + 9$
   c) $x^2 + 10x + 16$

1. Use tiles to find the dimensions formed by the rectangle for the following trinomial expressions. Find the missing factor(s).
   a) $x^2 + 5x + 6 = (x + 3)()$
   b) $y^2 + 4y + 3 = (y + 1)()$
   c) $x^2 + 6x + 5 = (x + 1)()$
   d) $y^2 + 11y + 30 = (y + \blacksquare)(y + \blacktriangle)$
   e) $x^2 + 2x + 1 = (x + \blacksquare)(x + \blacktriangle)$
   f) $x^2 + 9x + 20 = (x + \blacksquare)(x + \blacktriangle)$

2. Write the trinomial expression as a product of factors. Use algebra tiles if necessary.
   a) $x^2 + 5x + 4$ b) $y^2 + 5y + 6$
   c) $x^2 + 8x + 12$ d) $y^2 + 8y + 16$
   e) $y^2 + 9y + 18$ f) $x^2 + 9x + 14$

3. Check your factors in Problem 2 by multiplying.

4. Use your pattern to factor.
   a) $x^2 + 2x - 8$ b) $x^2 + 4x - 5$
   c) $y^2 + 3y - 10$ d) $x^2 - x - 2$
   e) $y^2 - 2y - 3$ f) $x^2 - 5x - 6$
   g) $a^2 + 5a + 6$ h) $b^2 - 7b + 10$
   i) $c^2 + 11c + 10$ j) $d^2 - 5d + 6$
   k) $f^2 - 10f - 11$ l) $z^2 + 6z - 16$

5. For Problem 4g) to 4l), check your factors by multiplying.

6. Examine this procedure for factoring a polynomial for which the tiles do not form a rectangle. $x^2 + 2x - 8$

   Step 1
   Start to form a rectangle with tiles that represent the polynomial.

   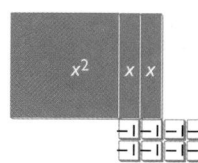

   Step 2
   Fill in the rectangle with rods that do not add value – the zero model. $-2x + 2x = 0$

   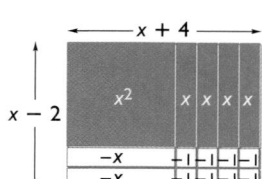

   Step 3
   Multiply the dimensions of the rectangle to check. $(x + 4)(x - 2) = x^2 + 2x - 8$

   Use the procedure to check Problem 4b) to 4f).

7. The formula for the area of a rectangular pool built by the Luxury Pool Company is $x^2 + 9x + 18$, and for Popular Pool Company it is $x^2 + 10x + 24$.
   a) Find the expression for the side length that is the same for both companies.
   b) Find the expressions for the unequal sides.
   c) Which pool would fit in a rectangular yard with area $x^2 + 10x + 21$? Explain.

8. Find the common factor. Then factor.
   a) $2a^2 + 8a + 6$ b) $3b^2 + 6b + 3$
   c) $5y^2 - 25y + 20$ d) $10y^2 - 30y + 20$

9. Express each **difference of squares** as a trinomial. Use the pattern to find the factors. Use tiles to check parts (a) and (b).
   a) $x^2 - 1 = x^2 \blacksquare x - 1$
   $ = (?)(?)$
   b) $y^2 - 9 = y^2 \blacksquare y - 9$
   $ = (?)(?)$
   c) $x^2 - y^2 = x^2 \blacksquare xy - y^2$
   $ = (?)(?)$
   d) $x^2 - 4y^2 = x^2 \blacksquare xy - 4y^2$
   $ = (?)(?)$

10. Factor each difference of squares.
    a) $x^2 - 25$ b) $x^2 - 49$ c) $x^2 - 9y^2$

11. Use tiles to display each rectangle. Express the area as a product of the dimensions. Check your answers by substitution.
    a) $2x^2 + 3x + 1$ b) $2y^2 + 5y + 3$
    c) $3y^2 + 5y + 2$ d) $4x^2 + 4x + 1$

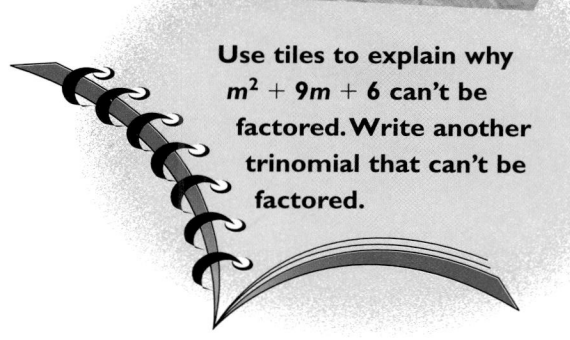

In Your Journal

Use tiles to explain why $m^2 + 9m + 6$ can't be factored. Write another trinomial that can't be factored.

7.6 Simplifying Expressions

Calculate mentally.
a) $(70 \times 36) + (30 \times 36)$
b) $(53 \times 76) + (47 \times 76)$
c) $(68 \times 49) + (32 \times 49)$
Create two other numerical expressions like those above. Write the pattern as an algebraic expression.

Aaron's class is playing a game called "Sprinter." They have to use all their skills in multiplying and factoring to expand, then simplify expressions.

Each group agrees on an answer then holds up their slate. If the answer is correct, their sprinter moves ahead one lap. The first team to finish all the laps in the race wins.

Concept Development

1. Write your solution if the game question is

> Expand
> $2x(x+3)(x+1)$

2. a) Are both methods below correct for the card in Problem 1?

Aaron's group expands then simplifies the question this way:	Another group expands then simplifies the question another way:
$2x(x + 3)(x + 1)$	$2x(x + 3)(x + 1)$
$= (2x^2 + 6x)(x + 1)$	$= 2x(x^2 + 1x + 3x + 3)$
$= 2x^3 + 2x^2 + 6x^2 + 6x$	$= 2x^3 + 2x^2 + 6x^2 + 6x$
$= 2x^3 + 8x^2 + 6x$	$= 2x^3 + 8x^2 + 6x$

b) Describe the difference between the two methods.

3. Write your solution if the game question is

> Expand
> $-x(x-1)^2$

4. a) Is the method below correct for the card in Problem 3?

Aaron's group expands then simplifies this way:

$$-x(x - 1)^2 = -x(x - 1)(x - 1)$$
$$= (-x^2 + x)(x - 1)$$
$$= -x^3 + x^2 + x^2 - x$$
$$= -x^3 + 2x^2 - x$$

b) How might the other group have expanded then simplified the question?

c) Describe the difference between the two methods.

5. Write your solution if the game question is [Simplify, then factor $-2x(x-2)+6x(x-1)$]

6. a) Describe the difference between the two methods below for the card in Problem 5.

Aaron's group expands, simplifies, then factors:	Another group also expands, simplifies, and factors:
$-2x(x-2)+6x(x-1)$	$-2x(x-2)+6x(x-1)$
$= -2x^2 + 4x + 6x^2 - 6x$	$= -2x^2 + 4x + 6x^2 - 6x$
$= 4x^2 - 2x$	$= 4x^2 - 2x$
$= x(4x - 2)$	$= 2x(2x - 1)$

b) Which method is considered more correct? Explain.

Understand and Apply

1. Expand, then simplify, each of the following.
   a) $3y(y + 2)(y - 3)$
   b) $-4e(2e + 5)(e - 1)$
   c) $-x(2x - 3)(2x + 3)$
   d) $-5(2m - 5)^2$
   e) $6d - 2d(3d - 1)^2$
   f) $3(x - 2)^2 + (x - 1)(x + 3)$
   g) $4(y + 2)(y - 1) - (y - 3)^2$

2. Identify and explain the error. Show the correct method of simplification.
   a) $4x(x - 1)(x - 4)$
   $= 4x^2 - 4x(x - 4)$
   $= 4x^2 - 4x^2 + 16x$
   $= 16x$
   b) $3x - 2x(x - 1)^2$
   $= x(x - 1)(x - 1)$
   $= x^2 - x(x - 1)$
   $= x^2 - x^2 + x$
   $= x$
   c) $4x(2x - 1)(x + 3)$
   $= 4x + 2x^2 + 6x - x - 3$
   $= 2x^2 + 9x - 3$

3. Check your results in Problem 2 by substituting values, then evaluating.

In Your Journal

Write an explanation that would prevent a student from making any of the errors shown in Problem 2.

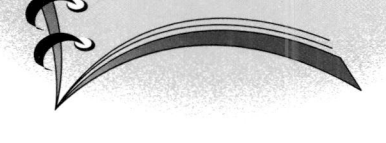

4. Describe the error a student might make in each. Now simplify.
   a) $3(x - 1) - 2x - x(x + 3)$
   b) $5y + 3y(y - 1)(y + 4)$

W/E **5.** Write all the factors.
   a) $3x^2 + 6x + 3$ **b)** $6x^2y - 12xy - 18y$
   c) $-3m^3 - 15m^2 + 18m$

6. Simplify the following expressions by combining like terms, identifying any common factors, and then factoring.
   a) $x^2 + 7x + 10$ **b)** $3x^2 + 15x + 18$
   c) $6x^2 - 3x + x^2 - 18x + 7$
   d) $5x^2 - 11x + 3x^2 + 32 - 29x$

7. Simplify, then factor if possible.
   a) $-4x^2 - 7x - 1 + 10x^2 + 4x + 1$
   b) $3y^2 - y + 4 + 6y^2 + 4y - 4$
   c) $4x^2 + 8x - 4 - 3x^2 - 5x + 6$
   d) $-3y^2 + 5y - 10 + 4y^2 - 3y - 5$
   e) $-3x(x - 2) + 4x(x + 1) + 9$
   f) $-y(y + 2) + 2y(y + 2) - 1$
   g) $5x^2 + 7x - 10 - 2x^2 - 10x + 4$
   h) $-5x^3 + 10x - x^2 + 3x^3 - x^2 + 2x$
   i) $-4(2x - 1) - 2(x - 3) - x(x + 1)$
   j) $-3x(x - 1)(x + 4) + 7x(x - 1)(x + 2)$

W/E **8. a)** Find the quotient of $\dfrac{12x^3 - 16x^2 + 8x}{4x}$ by dividing each term in the numerator by the term in the denominator.
   b) Find the quotient by factoring the numerator first. What do you notice?

9. Factor the numerator, then divide.
   a) $\dfrac{6x^3 + 4x^2 + 2x}{2x}$ **b)** $\dfrac{4y^5 + 8y^3 - 2y^2}{2y^2}$
   c) $\dfrac{y^2 - 9y - 22}{3y + 6}$ **d)** $\dfrac{8e^2f^3 - 16e^4f^4 + 4e^5f^3}{4e^2f^3}$

165

Problems to Investigate

WHAT'S MISSING?

The trinomial x^2 ▪$x + 18$ has six different pairs of binomial factors. What are the possible values for the numerical coefficient ▪?

MENTAL MATH

Find the product of each.

$(x - 1)^2$ $(y + 2)^2$ $(2f + 1)^2$ $(3e + 2)^2$

What's the pattern?

Use the pattern to calculate the following square products.

a) $42^2 = (40 + 2)^2$ b) 65^2
c) 99^2 d) 78^2

QUOTIENT QUANDARY

Factor the numerator and denominator, if possible. What is the resulting quotient?

a) $\dfrac{4x^2y + 8xy}{4xy}$

b) $\dfrac{x^2 + 8x - 20}{x - 2}$

c) $\dfrac{5x^2 + 6x + 3}{3x + 3}$

VERSATILE TILES

Use algebra tiles to model the following products.

a) $2x(x - 3)$
b) $(x + 2)(x - 1)$

Explain your reasoning for using $+x, -x, +1, -1$ tiles as you completed the area.

ROOT MAGIC

Use algebra tiles to find the factors of the following products.

a) $4x^2 + 4x + 1$
b) $9x^2 + 6x + 1$
c) $4y^2 + 12y + 9$

Do you see a pattern that could help you factor each trinomial without using the tiles? Explain.

DIFFERENCE OF SQUARES

Janet factored $n^2 - 1$ as $(n + 1)(n - 1)$. Use the pattern for difference of squares to calculate these mentally.

a) $74^2 - 26^2$ b) $601^2 - 399^2$

Make up similar problems and post them on the bulletin board for classmates to solve.

Solve Problems by Guessing and Testing

Try this problem before going on.

Alim was given this mystery to solve before he could join a club called The Mysterious Minds.

The number is a multiple of 7.
The number is between 1 and 100.
The number when divided by 3 or 5 has a remainder of 1.
What's the number?

▶ Understand the Problem

1. What are you asked to find?

2. What do you know?

3. Where will you begin?

▶ Make a Plan

Alim uses algebra. He lets n represent the number. Then he guesses and tests.

▶ Carry Out the Plan

4. **a)** Why isn't 4 listed for $\frac{n}{3}$?

   Why aren't 6, 11, and 16 listed for $\frac{n}{5}$?

   b) Which number(s) in the chart satisfies all the clues?

$\frac{n}{7}$ divides evenly into	7, 14, 21, 28, 28, 35, 42, 49, 56, 63, 70, 77, 84, 91, 98
$\frac{n}{3}$ has a remainder of 1	7, 28, 49, 70, 91
$\frac{n}{5}$ has a remainder of 1	21, 56, 91

▶ Look Back

5. Read the mystery clues again. Does the mysterious number work?

Applications

Use algebra and guess and test to help you solve these problems.

ANIMAL CRACKERS

In a barn there are 15 animals, only chickens and cows. The total number of legs is 50. How many of each animal are there?

CENTS FOR SENSE

Sachin received $0.05 for each quiz he passed and was fined $0.10 for each quiz he failed. Altogether he passed 7 times as many quizzes as he failed, and he earned $1.00. How many quizzes did he write?

GOT ANY CHANGE?

Change for one dollar consists of 12 coins that are either nickels or dimes. How many nickels and how many dimes are there?

JUST MOTORING

Anish rode his motorcycle at 60 km/h to Rishi's house. He returned home on the same road at 90 km/h. If his total time on the road was 2 h, how far do Anish and Rishi live from each other?

1. Use algebra tiles to represent the area model for each product. Write an expression to represent the product.

a) $2x(x + 3)$

b) $(x + 3)(x + 4)$

c) $(2x + y)^2$

d) $(x - 3y)(x + 3y)$

2. Find the perimeter and area of the following shapes.

a)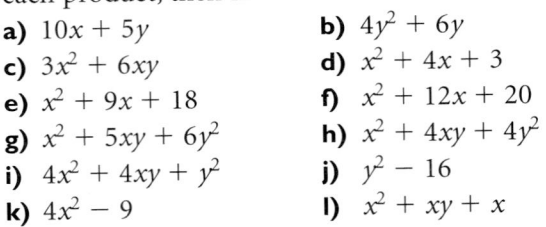

b)

c)

3. Simplify.

a) $4x(2x + 1) + x(x - 1)$

b) $-3y + 2y(y - 3) - (y + 2)$

c) $2y(2x - y - 1) - (x + y + 3)$

d) $-3x(x - 2y - 4) - x(x + 2y + 1)$

e) $(d + 4)(d + 6)$

f) $(3f - 1)(f + 2)$

g) $(4m - 3)(m + 1)$

h) $(3p + 2)^2$

i) $(5p - 3)(5p + 3)$

j) $(2x - 3)^2 + (3x - 1)(3x + 1)$

k) $(2d - 5)(2d + 5) + (d - 2)^2$

l) $(4e + 5)^2 + (2e - 1)(e - 3)$

4. Use algebra tiles to represent the area model for each product, then find the dimensions.

a) $10x + 5y$

b) $4y^2 + 6y$

c) $3x^2 + 6xy$

d) $x^2 + 4x + 3$

e) $x^2 + 9x + 18$

f) $x^2 + 12x + 20$

g) $x^2 + 5xy + 6y^2$

h) $x^2 + 4xy + 4y^2$

i) $4x^2 + 4xy + y^2$

j) $y^2 - 16$

k) $4x^2 - 9$

l) $x^2 + xy + x$

5. Factor.

a) $8y - 12$

b) $12xy - 18x$

c) $42p^2q - 48pq$

d) $14mn + 49n$

e) $32ef^2 + 16e^2f - 24ef$

6. Factor, if possible.

a) $x^2 + 11x + 30$

b) $y^2 + 7x + 12$

c) $x^2 - 10x - 24$

d) $x^2 - 10x + 16$

e) $x^2 + 10x - 24$

f) $y^2 + 5y - 24$

g) $c^2 - 3c - 18$

h) $d^2 + 6d - 12$

i) $m^2 - m - 12$

7. Factor.

a) $x^2 - 16$

b) $4y^2 - 4$

c) $d^2 - 9$

d) $16f^2 - 25$

8. Factor fully.

a) $3x^2 + 9x + 6$

b) $4y^2 + 24y + 20$

c) $2m^2 - 6m - 8$

d) $5ef^2 + 5ef - 30e$

9. Express the volume of each shape as a polynomial.

a)

$2x+1$

b)

$2x$

$3x+1$

$4x+5$

10. Simplify.

a) $4x(2x - 1)(x + 3)$

b) $(3y - 1)^2 + (2y - 3)(y + 1)$

c) $5m(4m - 5)^2$

d) $3e - 2e(e - 1)(e + 3)$

e) $(4p - 2)^2 - (2p - 3)(2p + 3)$

f) $7x - 3x(2x + y - 5)$

11. Simplify, then factor.

a) $5a^2 - 6a - 10 - 4a^2 + 10a - 2$

b) $7d^2 + 4de - 4d^2 - de$

c) $-3m(m - 4) + 7m(m - 2) - 5(2m - 1) + 4$

d) $(e - 4)(e + 4) + 12$

Practise With Games

Binomial Bingo

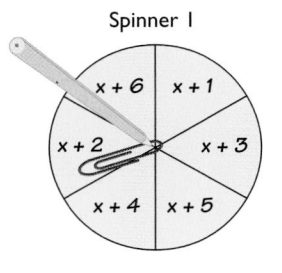

Spinner 1

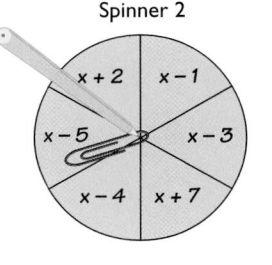

Spinner 2

Play in groups of six.

- Each player chooses any binomial from Spinner 1 and another from Spinner 2 and writes their product in one space of a 5 X 5 Bingo card. Players continue until all 25 squares on each player's card have been filled in with products. (Each binomial on both spinners should be used at least once. Binomials may be used more than once.)

- Players take turns spinning Spinner 1 then Spinner 2. If a player's card shows the product of the two binomials spun, s/he marks the square.

- The first player to have 5 marked squares in a row, column, or diagonal wins.

Old Poly

Example:

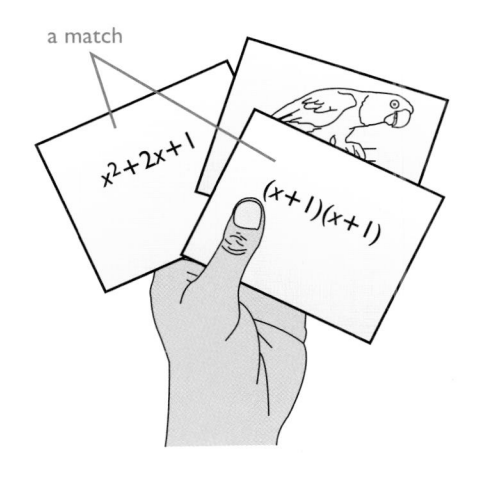

a match

$x^2 + 2x + 1$

$(x + 1)(x + 1)$

Play in groups of three or four.

- The dealer shuffles all the cards – 19 Trinomial Cards, 19 Factors Cards, and one Old Poly card – and deals them out.

- The players match Polynomial Cards with Factors Cards in their hands. The matched pairs are placed face up on the table.

- Players pass unused cards to the player on their right. Players can add to their matched pairs, if possible.

- Now the player to the left of the dealer draws a card from anyone in the group. If the drawn card matches a card in his/her hand, it is added to his/her matched pairs; otherwise the player keeps the card.

- Players, in clockwise order, take turns drawing cards from any player's hand.

- Play continues until all matches are made, leaving one player with the "Old Poly" card. Players are eliminated from the game as their cards are depleted.

- The person left with Old Poly is the winner! (or loser)

1. Find the factors.
   a) $8xy - 6z$ b) $3y^2 + 9y$
   c) $15x^2 + 5y^2$ d) $-4x^2 + 20x - 12xy$

2. Express the volume of each shape as a polynomial.
   a)
   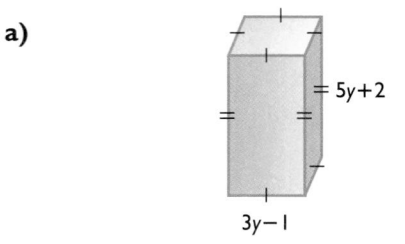
   5y+2
   3y−1

   b)
   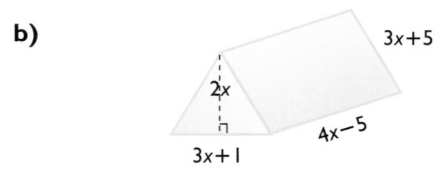
   3x+5
   2x
   4x−5
   3x+1

   c)
   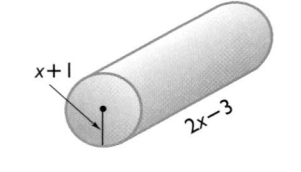
   x+1
   2x−3

3. Write the surface area of each shape in Problem 2 as a polynomial.

4. Use algebra tiles to find each product. Explain why the area model is a correct model for finding these products.
   a) $3x(x - 1)$
   b) $(x + 1)(x - 2)$
   c) $(x + y)(x + y - 1)$

5. a) The trinomial $y^2 \blacksquare y - 24$ has eight different pairs of binomial factors. What are possible values for $\blacksquare$?
   b) The trinomial $x^2 \blacksquare xy - 9y^2$ has two different pairs of binomial factors. What are the values for $\blacksquare$? What is special about one of the pairs of binomial factors?

6. Find the area of each circle as a polynomial with the given radius.
   a) $x + 8$ b) $8 - x$ c) $r + 10$

7. Explain why $x^2 - 25$ can be factored but $x^2 + 25$ cannot.

8. Use algebra tiles to find the factors of the following difference of squares.
   a) $x^2 - 4$
   b) $x^2 - 36$
   c) $4x^2 - y^2$
   Explain your reasoning for using $(+x)$ and $(-x)$ tiles as you completed the area.

9. Show two ways to factor $4y^2 - 16$.

10. Calculate mentally using the factors of a difference of squares.
    a) $35^2 - 25^2$
    b) $18^2 - 15^2$
    c) $31^2 - 26^2$

11. Rational numbers are numbers that can be written as the quotient of two integers. The denominator cannot equal zero. Some rational numbers can be simplified;
    for example, $\frac{4}{20} = \frac{4}{4 \times 5}$ or $\frac{1}{5}$.
    The rational number is simplified by dividing by the greatest common factor.

    Simplify the following rational expressions by factoring the numerator and/or denominator, then dividing by the greatest common factor.
    a) $\dfrac{12x^3 + 15x^2 - 9x}{3x}$
    b) $\dfrac{4x^2y + 2x}{2xy}$
    c) $\dfrac{x^2 + 6x + 8}{2x^2 + 8x}$

12. The distance in kilometres that a marathon runner travelled can be expressed as $3x^2 + 30x + 27$, and the time spent travelling was $x + 1$ hours.
    a) What was the runner's speed?
    b) What might be a reasonable value for x?

Communicate Your Knowledge

1. How is multiplying a monomial by a polynomial different from multiplying two monomials?

2. Explain the difference between expanding or multiplying, and factoring.

7. When you factor, what do you first look for? How can you check that you have factored an expression correctly?

6. Write an example of how variables and operations with variables can help you communicate an idea.

3. How do concrete materials help you understand how to multiply? how to factor?

5. Create a magic trick similar to the one below. Explain algebraically how this trick and your trick work.

Write your age.
Add 10.
Double the result.
Add your age plus one.
Divide by 3.
Tell your result.

4. How do algebra tiles help you do the following questions?

Expand $2a^3(-3a + 2b + 1)$.

Factor completely $7m^3 - 14m^2 + 21m$.

What questions do you still have about multiplying and factoring polynomials?

Probability

One of the fundraising events run by a local service group is a raffle. This year, the raffle tickets are being sold for $5 each or three for $10. The winner receives an all-expense trip for two to Disneyworld which includes airfare, five-day passes, and accommodation.

- What would you need to know to estimate your chances of winning?

- Suppose tickets were sold only to students in your school and each student bought one ticket. What would be each student's chance of winning? Why wouldn't the chance of winning increase if each student bought three tickets?

- Suppose only 1000 tickets were made available and all of them were sold. What is the probability of winning if you bought one ticket? three tickets?

- Why might two friends decide to buy two tickets together and split the prize if either wins?

VOLLEYBALL TEAM
RAFFLE
Win $2500 and help your school volleyball teams raise money to go to the regionals!
TICKETS ARE $5 each
Better hurry, only 1000 tickets available!

SCHOOL POOL RENOVATION RAFFLE
WIN $5000 AND HELP CONTRIBUTE TO THE SCHOOL POOL FUND
Tickets are $10 each
Buy now before all 500 tickets are gone!

Which of the two raffles advertised is the better bet? Explain.

8.1 Making Predictions About Shared Events

Jane and Bella sit next to each other in class. They were surprised to discover that they were both born in the same season.

Warm Up

Which do you think is most likely — that two students selected randomly from your school will be the same gender, have the same hair color, or share a birthday? Which do you think is least likely? Explain.

Concept Development

1. What do you think the probability is of two people having the same birth season? Is it 0? $\frac{1}{4}$? $\frac{1}{2}$? $\frac{3}{4}$? 1? Explain.

2. Estimate the probability by conducting a class survey. Compare your birth season with that of a student sitting near you. Make a class record of pairs that are the same and different.

---

16 pairs of students were surveyed. (?) pairs shared birth seasons
(?) pairs had different birth seasons

---

3. **a)** What fraction of the pairs shared birth seasons?
   b) Estimate the probability of two people sharing the same birth season.

4. Copy and complete this tree diagram to find the probability another way. Explain what you did.

Person A	Person B	Season Combinations	Same/Different
Sp	Sp	Sp - Sp	S
	Su	Sp - Su	D
	F	Sp - Fall	D
	W	Sp - Win	D
Su			
Fall			
Win			

5. Why might the probabilities found in a class survey differ from those found using a tree diagram?

6. Bryndon found the probability by calculating. How does Bryndon's calculated answer compare to the results of the tree diagram? survey? Explain.

> *You could pick any of the 4 seasons for Person A so the probability for A is $\frac{4}{4}$ or 1. Person B must have been born in the same season as B so there's only 1 out of 4 seasons to consider so the probability for B is $\frac{1}{4}$.*
>
> *Probability (Same Seasons) = P(A) x P(B) = 1 x $\frac{1}{4}$ = $\frac{1}{4}$*

7. a) Do you think the probability of two people sharing birth months will be greater or less than the probability of sharing birth seasons? Explain.
   b) Draw a tree diagram to find out.
   c) Calculate to find the probability. $P(\text{Same Months}) = P(A) \times P(B)$

8. Do you think it's surprising that two students sitting next to each other have the same birth season? birth month? Explain.

Understand and Apply

> *If the probability of two people having the same birth season is $\frac{1}{4}$ then the probability of different birth seasons must be $\frac{3}{4}$.*

3. Suppose two people have different birth months.
   a) In what months could Person A have been born?
   b) How many birth months are left for Person B?
   c) Complete this calculation to find the probability of two people having different birth months.

   $P(\text{Different Months}) = P(A) \times P(B)$

   d) Check your calculation using the tree diagram from Problem 7 in *Concept Development*.

1. Is Tara right? Explain.

2. Check Tara's reasoning by
   a) using the tree diagram in Problem 4 of *Concept Development*
   b) using Bryndon's thoughts to complete his calculation.

> *Person A could have been born in any season so the probability for A is 1. For Person B, you have 3 out of 4 seasons to choose from if his birth season is different, so the probability for B is $\frac{3}{4}$.*
>
> *Probability (Different Seasons) = P(A) x P(B) = [?]*

4. Find the probability of two people having Spring birthdays by
a) using the tree diagram in Problem 4 of *Concept Development*
b) completing Bryndon's calculation

The probability that Person A was born in the Spring is $\frac{1}{4}$ because there's only 1 out of 4 seasons to consider. The probability that Person B was born in the Spring is also $\frac{1}{4}$.

P (Spring - Spring) = $P(A) \times P(B)$ = ?

5. What calculation would you use to find the probability that two people were born in the Summer? Fall? Winter?

6. What is the probability that two people were born in January? June? Explain.

In Your Journal

Why would the probability of having a birthday in May be slightly different from the probability of having a birthday in February? Explain why it's reasonable to ignore these differences when calculating probabilities.

Find out on which day of the week you were born. Calculate the probability that any three people will have been born on the same day of the week as you.

7. To find the probability that three people were born in the Spring, a tree diagram could be used.

Person A	Person B	Person C	Season Combinations	Same/Different
Sp	Sp	Sp	Sp - Sp	S
		Su	Sp - Su	D
		F	Sp - Fall	D
		W	Sp - Win	D
	Su			
	F			
	W			
Su				
Fall				
Win				

a) Without completing the tree diagram, you can tell that there are 64 possible season combinations. Explain.
b) Why don't you need to complete the tree diagram to know the number of Spring-Spring-Spring combinations?
c) What's the probability of three people being born in the Spring?
d) Complete this calculation to find the probability another way.

$P(\text{Spring-Spring-Spring}) = P(A) \times P(B) \times P(C)$

8. Calculate the probability that, in a group of three friends — John, Ashraft, and Janice
a) all will have different birth months
b) all will have January birth months
c) John will have a January birth month, Ashraft will have a February birth month, and Janice will have a March birth month
d) John will have a January birth month and the other two will have June birth months

9. What is the probability that
a) two people share the same birthday?
b) two people have different birthdays?
c) two people were born on April 1st?

10. Make up and solve a probability problem about students sharing birthdays.

8.2 Drawing Diagrams to Predict Results

Fold a square piece of paper as shown. What fraction of the square is shaded? How does the calculation $\frac{1}{2} \times \frac{1}{2} \times \frac{1}{3}$ relate to the way you folded the paper?

Jenkins High is a grade 9 to 12 school with a population of about 1200 students. There are about the same number of students in every grade. The ratio of boys to girls is about 1:1. One student is to be chosen randomly to represent the school at a regional youth conference.

Concept Development

1. What is each student's probability of being chosen? Explain.

2. What is the probability that the student will be in grade 9? a girl? Explain.

3. Work in groups to conduct a simulation to find the probability that the student will be both a girl and a grade 9 student. Use two spinners as shown in the photo.
   a) What is the probability of choosing a grade 9 girl?
   b) Compare your results with other groups. Discuss any significant differences.

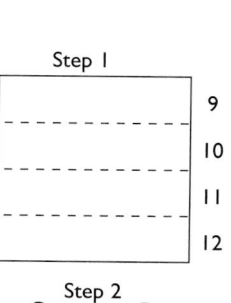

Let's do 32 sets of spins and then find the fraction of the time we spun "girl - grade 9".

4. Aaron found the probability by drawing a diagram.
   a) Why did Aaron divide the square into fourths in Step 1?
   b) Why did he divide the diagram down the middle in Step 2?
   c) Why did he shade a section of the diagram?
   d) What's the probability that the student is both a girl and in grade 9?

5. Why might the probabilities found by conducting a simulation and drawing a diagram differ?

6. What other probabilities can you find using Aaron's diagram?

1. Suppose there were equal numbers of students in each grade but there were 800 girls and 400 boys at Jenkins High.

   a) Is the probability that the student is a grade 9 girl greater or less than $\frac{1}{8}$? Explain.

   b) Explain why the diagram would look like this.

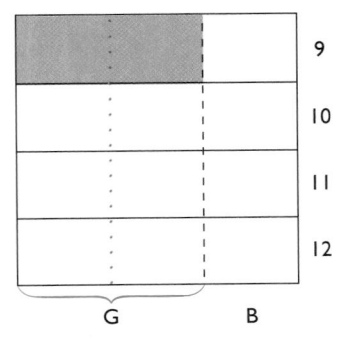

   c) What's the probability that the student would be a grade 9 girl? a grade 12 boy?

2. Draw a diagram to show the probability of choosing a grade 11 boy if there were 900 boys and 300 girls at Jenkins and equal numbers in each grade.

3. Draw a diagram to show the probability of choosing a grade 9 boy if the ratio of boys to girls was 1:1 but there were 600 grade 9s and 200 in each of grades 10, 11, and 12.

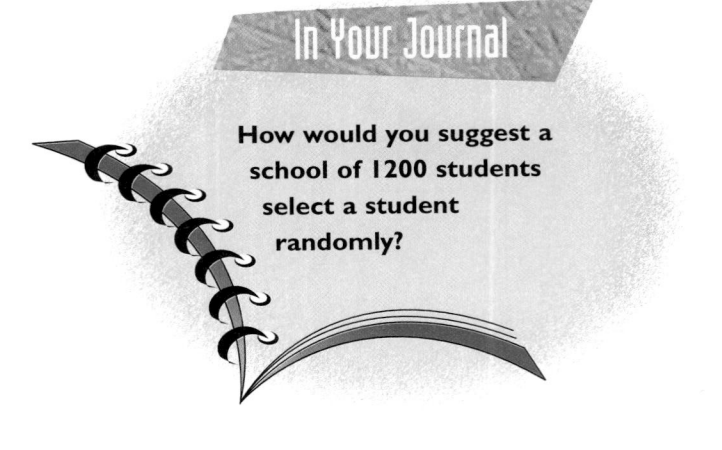

In Your Journal

How would you suggest a school of 1200 students select a student randomly?

4. Courses at Jenkins are taught in semesters. During the first semester, $\frac{1}{2}$ the students in each grade are taking English. Examine this series of diagrams.

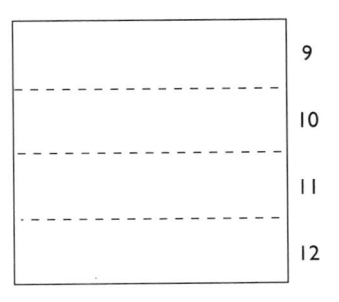

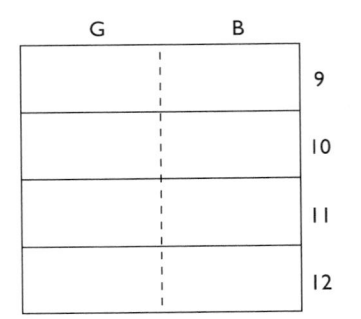

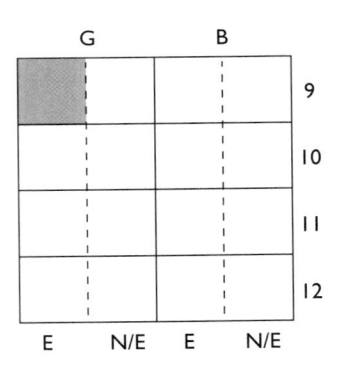

   a) What fraction of the student population is in each grade?

   b) What is the ratio of girls to boys?

   c) Explain how this series of diagrams shows the probability of choosing a grade 11 girl taking English.

5. Suppose there were 200 grade 9s, 200 grade 10s, 400 grade 11s, and 400 grade 12s at Jenkins. The ratio of girls to boys is still 1:1 and half the students are taking English. Draw a diagram to find the probability of choosing a grade 10 boy who is not taking English.

6. In Mrs. Curten's class of 31 students, 21 are taking Physics, 14 take the bus, and 16 are on a school team.

a) Copy and complete this diagram to estimate the probability of choosing a student from the class who takes the bus, is on a team, and is not taking Physics.

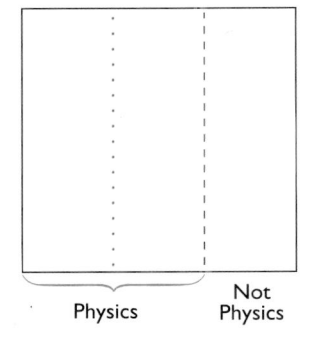

b) What other probabilities does your diagram show?

What fraction of your family is male? female? under 18 years of age? 18 years or over? Draw a diagram to find the probability of randomly choosing a family member that is male and under 18.

7. This series of diagrams shows the probability of choosing a boy taking French from a class of 24 students.

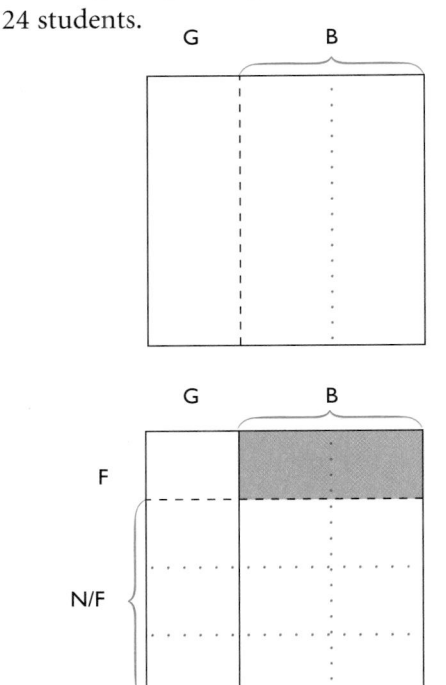

Use the diagrams to answer these questions.
a) What is the ratio of girls to boys in the class?
b) How many students in the class take French?
c) What is the probability of choosing a girl who is not taking French?

8. Create a probability problem for this series of diagrams.

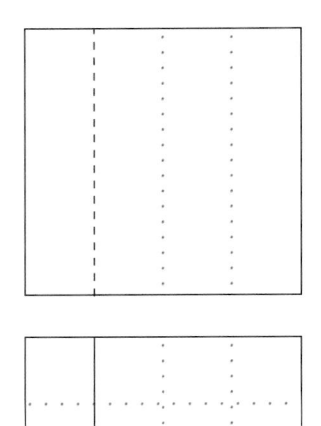

9. Create a probability diagram problem about your school or class.

179

More Than One Strategy

Finding Probabilities

What is the probability that three people, given the choice of numbers 1, 2, or 3, would all choose the same number?

There are many ways to find the probability. Here are some. Can you think of more?

1. You can draw a tree diagram to find the expected probability.

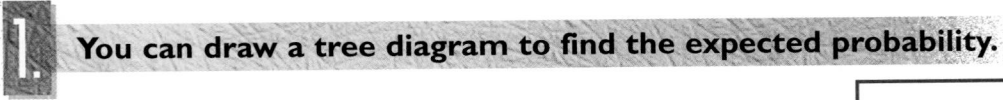

> Of the 3 × 3 × 3 or 27 possible number combinations, there are 3 same-number combinations (1, 1, 1 and 2, 2, 2 and 3, 3, 3). The probability is $\frac{3}{27}$ or $\frac{1}{9}$.

2. You can calculate to find the expected probability.

Person A can pick any of the 3 numbers so the probability is $\frac{3}{3}$ or 1. Person B and Person C each have to pick the same number as Person A, so the probability for each is $\frac{1}{3}$.

$$P(\text{Same 3 Numbers}) = P(A) \times P(B) \times P(C) = 1 \times \frac{1}{3} \times \frac{1}{3} = \frac{1}{9}$$

3. You can do a simulation to find the experimental probability.

Use a die. If you roll a 1 or a 6 call it *choosing 1*, a 2 or a 5 is *choosing 2*, and a 3 or a 4 is *choosing 3*. Roll the die three times to simulate three people choosing numbers. Repeat many times. What fraction of the time did you roll the same number?

4. You can do an experiment to find the experimental probability.

Ask each of 3 people to write a number from 1 to 3. Record their choices. Repeat many times. What fraction of the time do all 3 choose the same number?

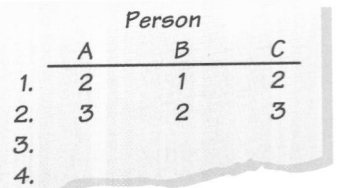

	Person		
	A	B	C
1.	2	1	2
2.	3	2	3
3.			
4.			

Understand and Apply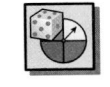

Solve two of these problems, each in two different ways.

1. You roll 2 dice. What's the probability that one number will be a factor of the other?

2. You toss 4 coins. What's the probability that they will all land heads?

3. You have a bag of 2 red, 2 green, and 2 black candies. What's the probability of drawing first a red one, then a green one, and finally a black one in 3 different draws?

4. You write down a secret 2-digit number. What's the probability that someone will guess it?

Problems to Investigate

CALCULATING COMBINATIONS

Debbie always forgets the combination to her lock. She remembers the first number but rarely the second and third. The numbers can be from 0 – 49. What is the probability of Debbie guessing her combination? How much less likely is she to guess her combination if she forgets all three numbers? Is it possible for Debbie to open her lock in ten tries, if she remembers the first number? Explain.

WORKING BACKWARDS

A box has 12 cubes in 4 colors — green, yellow, blue, and red — and two sizes, small and large. The probability of choosing a large, green, cube is $\frac{1}{8}$. What's the probability of choosing a green cube? a large cube? Use a diagram to explain.

LEFTIES

The chance that someone is left-handed is about $\frac{1}{10}$. Calculate the expected probability that, among three friends
• no one will be left-handed
• all three will be left-handed
Describe how you could use a spinner to find the experimental probabilities by conducting a simulation.

GUESS AND TEST

Suppose you guessed true or false to ten test questions. How do you think you'd score? Conduct a simulation to find out. Flip a coin to simulate guessing each question — heads means your guess was true and tails means your guess was false. Now use the coin again to determine the correct answer for each question. Repeat several times. Find the average score.

1. T
2. T
3. F
4.
5.

DIFFERENT DICE

Suppose you were playing a game with two of these three tetrahedral dice. Which two dice would you choose to roll to get a sum of 8? Explain. What's the probability of rolling the sum of 12 using all three dice?

Create a probability problem for which you could find the probability experimentally and by calculating.

8.3 Playing Lotteries

Jane and Brad's class is conducting a lottery. They call it Lottery 2/6 because you select 2 different numbers from 1 to 6. To win, your 2 numbers must match both numbers drawn, in the order they are drawn.

Warm Up

What is the chance of guessing each phone number correctly? Explain how you arrived at your answers.

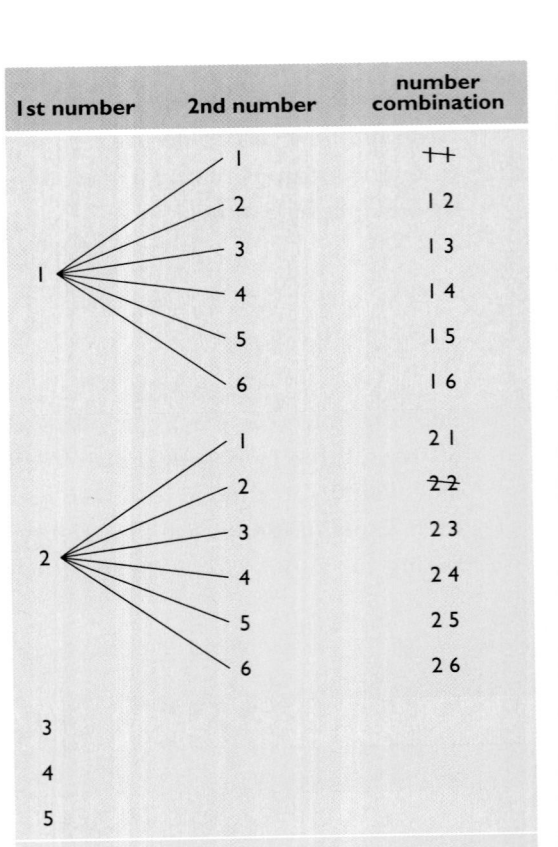

Concept Development

Janet feels she has a good chance of winning because her selected numbers, 4 and 2, are her lucky numbers. Brad feels his chances are better because he chose his two numbers randomly by rolling dice.

1. Who do you think has a better chance of winning, Brad or Janet? Explain.

2. Janet started a tree diagram to find her probability of winning.
   a) Why did she delete the number combinations 11 and 22?
   b) Copy and complete the tree diagram to find Janet's and Brad's chances of winning. What do you notice?
   c) Is there any number combination which is any luckier than another? Explain.

3. Suppose there are 30 students in a class. Why is it possible for there to be more than one winner? no winner?

4. Would the chances of winning increase or decrease if the order of the numbers didn't matter? For example, both combinations 12 and 21 would win if the numbers 1 and 2 were drawn. Use your tree diagram from Problem 2 to explain.

1st number	2nd number	number combination
1	1	~~1 1~~
	2	1 2
	3	1 3
	4	1 4
	5	1 5
	6	1 6
2	1	2 1
	2	~~2 2~~
	3	2 3
	4	2 4
	5	2 5
	6	2 6
3		
4		
5		
6		

Understand and Apply

To play Lotto 6/49, you choose six different numbers from 1 to 49. If all six numbers match the six numbers drawn in any order, you win the jackpot prize. You can choose the numbers or let the machine choose for you.

1. There are 13 983 816 different number combinations. What's the probability that the six-number combination you choose will win the jackpot?

2. The probability of being injured by lightning in any given year has been estimated at $\frac{1}{685\,000}$. Which is more likely, winning the jackpot in Lotto 6/49 or getting injured by lightning? How much more likely?

3. How do you think the lottery machine chooses the numbers?

4. a) If you bought 13 983 816 tickets, all with different six-number combinations, what would be the probability of winning the jackpot? Explain.
   b) David figures that if he buys 6 991 908 tickets, all with his favorite number combination: 5, 10, 15, 20, 25, 30, he will have a 50% chance of winning the jackpot prize. He's only partly right. Explain.
   c) Even if every Canadian played Lotto 6/49, it's quite possible that no one would win the jackpot prize. Explain.

5. Many people choose number combinations for personal reasons — reasons which are not based on expected or experimental probabilities. Explain why each of the people below might think his or her method would select a winning combination.

6. People sometimes team up to buy lottery tickets as a group. How might this increase the chance of winning for each player?

7. Investigate several different lottery games. Find the probability of winning the jackpot prize for each one. Compare the probabilities of winning with the value of the jackpot prize for each lottery. Would you say that the lottery with the greatest value jackpot is the one that you are least likely to win? Explain.

8. Why do people play lotteries even though they know that the chances of winning are small?

9. a) Why might this lottery ad be considered misleading?

> With almost
> 14 million ways
> to win,
>
> how can you lose?

   b) Look for lottery ads in the media. Do you think the ads accurately reflect the probability of winning?

Survey a group of people including family members and friends. What fraction play lotteries regularly? occasionally? don't play at all? For those that do play, find out what systems they use to select numbers.

I choose 3 numbers less than 25 and 3 greater than 25.

I'd never play a number like 8, 16, 24, 32, 40, 48. A number like 2, 11, 23, 39, 45, 48 would be luckier.

I never use the same numbers twice.

I let the machine choose my numbers.

I don't use the numbers drawn last time.

8.4 Calculating Baseball Odds

Warm Up

What do people mean when they say the chances are 50-50? 60-40? List several situations where probability might be expressed this way.

These statistics were reported about Toronto Blue Jay players for the 1995 season as of August 15.

Batters	Avg	AB	H	2B	3B	HR	BB	SO	E
Perez	.308	26	8	2	0	1	1	4	1
Alomar	.305	370	113	17	7	11	40	37	3
White	.291	364	106	21	5	9	26	82	2
Olerud	.274	350	96	22	0	6	54	38	2
Sprague	.265	355	94	22	1	16	35	58	11
Carter	.262	386	101	17	0	15	27	50	6
Parrish	.195	154	30	7	0	4	13	48	0

Concept Development

Answer Problems 1 to 5 to familiarize yourself with the baseball statistics.

1. To find a *batting average* (Avg), you divide the number of hits (H) by the number of times at bat (AB). How can Perez and Alomar have similar batting averages when Alomar has been up to bat 370 times and Perez only 26?

2. A *hit* (H) can be a *single*, a *double* (2B), a *triple* (3B), or a *home run* (HR). Use the table to find the number of singles that White hit.

3. The *strikeout* (SO) column shows the number of times each batter has struck out. Perez has struck out four times. Carter has struck out 50 times. Does this mean Carter's more likely to strike out?

4. When a batter *walks* to first base without a hit, it's a *base on balls* (BB). Olerud has had 54 bases on balls. Sprague has 35 bases on balls in about the same number of times at bat. What does that tell you about Olerud's batting abilities compared to Sprague?

5. The *error* (E) column shows the number of times a player makes a fielding mistake which allows the other team an unearned advantage. What do you need to know about each player before comparing errors?

6. a) Explain what Perez's average of .308 means.
   b) How was Perez's average calculated?
   c) What is the probability of Perez not getting a hit?

7. Another way to express probabilities is in the form of *odds for and against*. The odds for and against Perez getting a hit is the ratio

308 : 692

odds for getting a hit ← → **odds against getting a hit**

a) How do the numbers in this ratio relate to Perez's batting average?

b) Why might someone say that the odds are about 3:7?

Peter figures that the probability of getting dessert with supper at home is about $\frac{3}{7}$ or 3:4. What does this mean? Estimate the probability that every time you eat supper, you will have dessert.

Understand and Apply

1. Choose three other players. For each, describe the probability of getting a hit as a decimal (Avg), a fraction, and as an odds ratio.

2. Examine the table for Perez's performance.
a) The probability of Perez getting a hit each time he bats can be expressed as a decimal, .308, a fraction, $\frac{8}{26}$, or as an odds ratio, 8:18. Express the probability, in these three ways, of Perez hitting

a home run   a triple   a double   a single

b) If you consider only the eight times Perez has hit this season, the probability of Perez getting a home run each time he hits is $\frac{1}{8}$ or 1:7. Express the probability as a fraction and as an odds ratio for Perez hitting

a triple   a double   a single

In Your Journal

A batter might have a lifetime average of .265 but his average against a particular pitcher might be .750. What does this mean? Express each of these two probabilities as a fraction and as an odds ratio.

3. Why is the probability of Perez hitting a home run each time he hits greater than the probability of hitting a home run each time he bats?

4. The probability that Alomar will hit a home run each time he hits is $\frac{11}{113}$ or 11:102. The probability for White is $\frac{9}{106}$ or 9:97.
a) Why is it difficult to compare probabilities in these forms?
b) How would you compare the probabilities?

5. Which of the seven players is most likely to hit a home run each time he hits? What are his odds?

6. Which player is least likely to strike out each time he bats? What are his odds?

7. A player's odds of getting a hit last season were about 2:8. This season, the odds are about 4:6. What does this tell you about the player's performance? Explain.

8. Why might the odds of getting a hit based on a player's lifetime statistics differ from the odds based on the season's statistics?

9. Explain how sports statistics might be used.

10. Find statistics on your favorite players. Express probabilities as odds for and against.

Making Sense of DATA

Alternative Ways to Express Odds

> **F**orrest Gump was the 2:1 favorite to win the Oscar for best picture in March 1995.

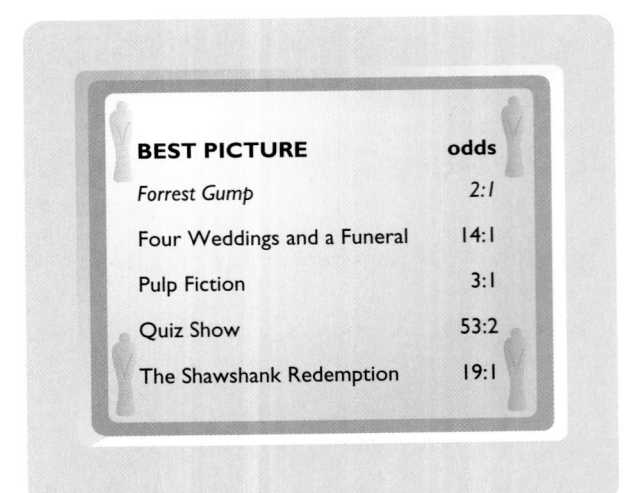

BEST PICTURE	odds
Forrest Gump	2:1
Four Weddings and a Funeral	14:1
Pulp Fiction	3:1
Quiz Show	53:2
The Shawshank Redemption	19:1

This data is available on the Oscarnet web site.

1. Examine the listed odds for the five movies in the Best Picture category. Order the movies from best to least favorite. Explain how you used the data to order the movies.

2. Sometimes odds are used to compare the probability that an event will occur with the probability that the event will not occur. For example, odds of 2:1 would mean that the chance of the event occurring is $\frac{2}{3}$ and the chance of it not occurring is $\frac{1}{3}$. What do these odds mean?
   3:2   4:1   5:7

3. Odds used to express Oscar predictions are interpreted differently. Odds of 2:1 mean that, of all the people surveyed who voted on Best Picture, half of them thought that *Forrest Gump* would win the Oscar. What would higher odds like 14:1 mean for the movie *Four Weddings and a Funeral*?

Applications

4. What fraction of those voting thought that *Quiz Show* would win? *Pulp Fiction* would win? *The Shawshank Redemption* would win?

5. Suppose these are the results of an opinion survey about the Oscar winner.

	Number of votes
Forrest Gump	50
Four Weddings and a Funeral	10
Pulp Fiction	20
Quiz Show	5
The Shawshank Redemption	10
Various Other Movies	5

a) What fraction of the people thought *Forrest Gump* would win? What are *Forrest Gump's* odds of winning an Oscar?

b) Find the odds of winning for the remaining movies.

c) How do these odds compare to the actual odds reported on the Oscarnet shown above?

6. Horse racing also posts probabilities this way. A horse with odds of 2:1 has a greater chance of winning than a horse with odds 10:1. How are odds used in horse racing?

7. Compare the two different types of odds. How are they alike? different?

Problems to Investigate

TAKE YOUR PICK!

REPORTED RESULTS

The results of a random opinion poll of the club membership gave Keri the lead for the position of president in the club elections. She was considered the 3:2 favorite. Explain why Keri should consider each of the following factors before estimating her chances of winning.

• how the odds were calculated
• only 60% of club members are eligible to vote
• past turnouts for elections have averaged 50% of eligible voters

WHETHER WEATHER

On Saturday, the forecast for rain was 70% and John decided to go biking. On Sunday, the chance of rain decreased to 30% but he decided not to go biking. List several factors which might have affected John's decision about whether to go biking or not.

DICEY DECISIONS

If you roll two dice, the odds of a certain event occurring are 1:2. List several events that these odds could describe.

EYES AND ODDS

How would you conduct a survey to determine the odds of a person having blue eyes?

BETTER BET

Which lottery is the better bet? Explain.

lottery 4/29 with a jackpot prize of $2 million
lottery 4/19 with a jackpot prize of $4 million

Investigate other forms of contests such as draws. Find out the number of tickets sold, the value of the prizes, and how they choose winners. Calculate the odds of winning.

Solve Problems by Conducting Experiments

Try this problem before going on.

RUNNING ROWS

If you toss a coin ten times, what is the probability that you will have four or more heads or four or more tails in a row?

▶ Make a Plan

To solve the problem, both Tara and Randi conducted experiments. Tara decided to actually toss ten coins, twenty times. Randi decided to conduct a simulation.

▶ Carry Out the Plan

Tara flipped four or more heads or four or more tails seven times.

Randi used the computer to randomly generate 10 rows of 10 digits, 1 or 2. She typed ⬜= RAND ⬜(2 ⬜) ⬜return in the cell of a spreadsheet and then copied and pasted the contents until 100 cells had numbers.
Each row of the spreadsheet simulates the flipping of 10 coins. The 1s represent heads and the 2s tails. Randi had 5 rows with four or more heads or four or more tails.

4. **a)** Tara estimates the probability at 35%. Explain her estimate.
   b) Randi's results were 50%. Explain why Randi's results might be different.

5. How do your results compare to Tara's and Randi's? Explain any differences.

▶ Understand the Problem

1. What are you asked to find?
2. What do you know?
3. Where do you begin?

▶ Look Back

6. What other probabilities can be estimated using your results?

Applications

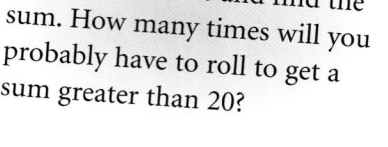

PRIME PROBABILITY

You pick six random whole numbers less than 10. What is the probability that at least half will be prime? You can use the random key on your calculator to generate random numbers. ⬜RANDOM

MAGIC MULTIPLES

Three people each choose a number from 1 to 10. What is the probability that at least one of the numbers is a multiple of one of the others?

TWENTISOMETHING

You roll four dice and find the sum. How many times will you probably have to roll to get a sum greater than 20?

Review and Practise

1. You roll two dice. Use a tree diagram to find the probability that
   a) the sum of the numbers will be even
   b) the product will be even
   c) the difference will be even

2. In three different draws, you pick three number cards from 1 to 10. Calculate to find the probability that
   a) all three numbers will be 6 or greater
   b) you will draw all fives

3. Calculate to find which is most likely.
   a) that three friends are all right-handed (the probability of being left-handed is $\frac{1}{10}$)
   b) you pick a Queen from each of three different decks of cards

4. Design a simulation or experiment to find the probability of three students having blue eyes.

5. In a club of 24 members, 8 are girls. Of the 24, 6 are in grade 10 and 18 are in grade 9. Copy and complete this diagram to show the probability of choosing a club member that is a grade 10 boy.

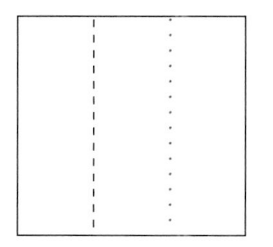

6. a) Copy and complete this diagram to find the probability that, if you chose three students randomly on three separate occasions, they will all be girls.
   b) What's the probability of choosing two boys and then one girl?

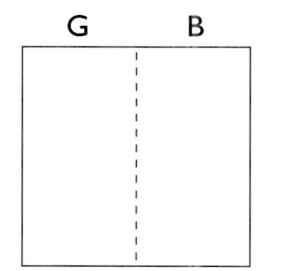

7. Which of these lotteries do you have the greater chance of winning? Explain.

   Lottery 5/10   You select five different numbers from 1 to 10.

   Lottery 5/10-R   You select five numbers from 1 to 10. You may repeat numbers.

8. Which of these lotteries do you have the greater chance of winning? Explain.

   Lottery 6/10-O   You select six different numbers from 1 to 10. They must match the order of the lottery draw.

   Lottery 6/10   You select six different numbers from 1 to 10. The order doesn't matter.

9. What is the odds-for-and-against ratio for each of these probabilities?
   a) $\frac{3}{8}$ b) $\frac{5}{9}$ c) $\frac{1}{100}$

10. The odds for and against winning are given. What's the probability of winning, as a fraction, for each?
    a) 3:8   b) 4:5   c) 34:13

11. Put these probabilities in order from most to least likely. (Odds are expressed as odds for and against.)
    a) 1:2   b) $\frac{3}{8}$ c) 9:10   d) 183:67

12. The results of a pre-referendum opinion survey estimated the odds of a yes vote at 2:1. Would you predict a yes vote in the referendum? Explain.

Dicey Differences

Play with a partner and two dice.

• Determine who will be Player A and Player B.

• Take turns rolling two dice.

• Find the difference between the 2 numbers rolled.

• If the difference is 2 or less, Player A scores a point. If it's 3 or greater, Player B scores.

• Play until a player reaches 5 points.

Play the game five times. Do you think it's a fair game?

Copy and complete this tree diagram to find the expected probability of each possible difference. Use the expected probabilities to explain why the game is fair or not fair.

If the game is not fair, change the differences assigned to each player and/or the number of points scored by each player to make it fair.

Player A scores.

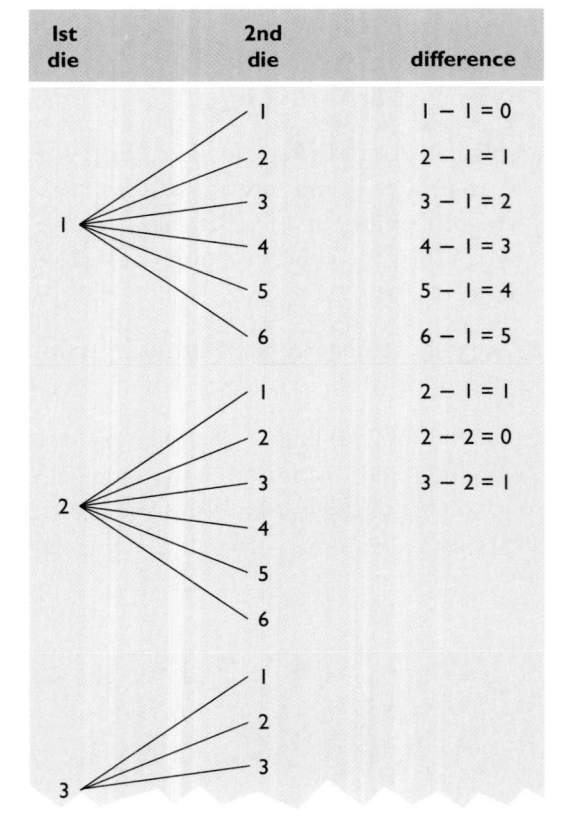

1st die	2nd die	difference
1	1	1 − 1 = 0
	2	2 − 1 = 1
	3	3 − 1 = 2
	4	4 − 1 = 3
	5	5 − 1 = 4
	6	6 − 1 = 5
2	1	2 − 1 = 1
	2	2 − 2 = 0
	3	3 − 2 = 1
	4	
	5	
	6	
3	1	
	2	
	3	

Create a Fair Game

• Make up a game which uses two or three different colored dice.

• The game must involve fractions and it must be fair.

• Play the game several times and then write up the rules.

• Include an explanation which uses expected probabilities to explain why the game is fair.

Problems to Investigate

CANADIAN CONTENT

Three Canadians are chosen randomly to represent Canada at a world conference. What is the approximate probability that all three chosen will be from Ontario? Alberta? Nova Scotia?

Population Across Canada			
(in thousands)			
CANADA	27 297	ONT	10 085
NFLD	568	MAN	1092
NS	900	ALTA	2 546
NB	724	BC	3 282
PEI	130	YT	28
QUE	6 897	NWT	58

MULTIPLYING TO AD

What are the odds of losing the jackpot in a lottery where you choose five numbers from 1 to 100? The numbers may be repeated and the order in which they are drawn is important. Write an ad for the lottery which would reflect the chances honestly yet still persuade people to play.

LESS THAN TEN

Find the experimental probability of getting a sum less than 10 when you add three random numbers from 0 to 9. You might use a spinner or the random function on your calculator to generate random numbers. How does your experimental probability compare to the expected probability found using a tree diagram?

SLIM PICKINGS

A person picks a card from a deck and then returns it. He picks again. He wins if both cards are the same suit. How does this diagram shows his probability of winning? Draw a diagram to show the probability of
• getting two cards of the same color
• getting two cards with the same number.

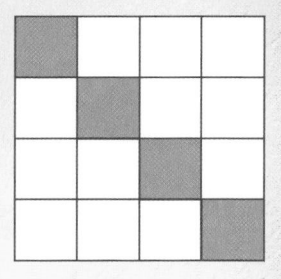

DRAWING MARBLES

You have a bag of six marbles — two red, two blue, and two black.
• What are the odds of drawing two red ones in two draws? a red, then a blue, and finally a black in three draws? two red ones and then a blue?
• How many marbles would you have to draw before you could be certain of drawing a red one? Explain.
• Describe an experiment for finding the number of marbles that you would likely have to draw before drawing a red one.

Make up a similar probability problem. Solve it before challenging a classmate to solve it.

1. You are rolling three dice. Use a tree diagram to find the most likely product.

2. About 1 in 4 teachers in Toronto is a man. Calculate the probability that, if three Toronto teachers are chosen randomly, they all will be women.

3. a) Catherine is rolling three standard dice. Calculate the probability of rolling three fives.
b) Assuming Brenda has already rolled a five for her first roll, calculate the probability of Brenda rolling three fives in three rolls.
c) Why is the probability of rolling three fives different for Catherine and Brenda?

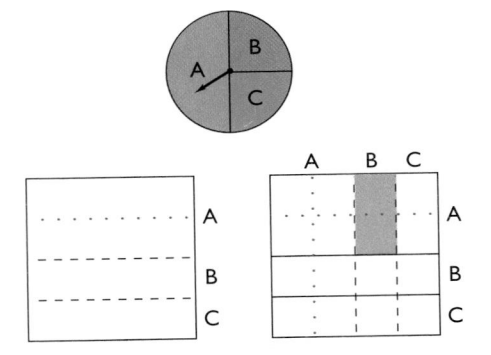

4. a) You spin this spinner twice. What sequence of letters does this series of diagrams show the probability of spinning?

b) Which letter sequence is most likely? least likely? Explain.
c) Calculate the probability of spinning the spinner three times and getting three As. three Bs.
d) What is the probability of the letter sequence A, B, and then C?

5. Suppose the ratio of boys to girls in a school is 1:2 and, of the 1200 students, 400 are in grade 9, 200 in grade 10, 200 in grade 11, and 400 in grade 12.
a) Design a simulation using two different colored dice to find the probability of randomly choosing a grade 9 girl.
b) Copy and complete this diagram to find the expected probability of choosing a grade 9 girl.

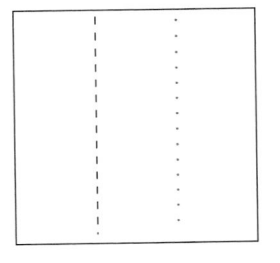

6. The odds of winning the Lotto BC jackpot are 1:3 838 379.
a) What is the probability of winning? losing?
b) How many tickets would you have to buy to have a $\frac{1}{3}$ chance of winning? Why would each ticket have to have a different number combination?

7. The probability is less than $\frac{1}{2}$. What do you know about the numbers, a and b, in the odds ratio, $a{:}b$?

8. The odds of losing are given. What's the probability of winning for each?
a) 56:23   **b)** 3:7   **c)** 865:349
d) 9:10   **e)** 6:5   **f)** 1:7

9. Order the odds in Problem 8 from most likely to lose to least likely to lose.

10. You are playing a game with two dice. Player A scores if the sum is a prime number and Player B scores if it's composite. Find the odds of winning for each player. Is it a fair game? If not, what could you do to make it fair?

Communicate Your Knowledge

1. Explain why many calculated probabilities involving dice have denominators which are powers of 6.

2. Describe several different ways you could find the probability of tossing a coin and getting five heads in a row. Which method do you prefer and why?

6. Think about games that you play. What makes games fair for all players?

3. It is more likely that the day of the month will be odd than even. Why? How would you find the probability?

5. What questions should you ask before deciding to play a lottery?

4. Describe several situations where people might ignore expected or experimental probabilities and make decisions based on personal reasons.

Describe some situations where an understanding of probabilities might help someone in real life.

UNIT 9

Measurement and Geometry

While many containers are rectangular prisms and cylinders, some are other types of prisms.

- Which type of prism is the Toblerone box?

- Which type of prism is the Droste Pastilles box?

- Which type of prism is the Grünland cheese box?

- Which type of prism will the Pizza Delight box be when it is made from its net? Sketch the prism.

- How can you use a net to find surface area?

- How can you use a net to find volume?

- Which measurement of the pizza box is most indicative of the size of pizza it will hold?

When viewed from the front, which containers will appear rectangular? Sketch their front views.

9.1 Exploring Pyramids

Warm Up

What are the dimensions of two different prisms that would have the same volume as this prism?

10

3 cm

5 cm

In 2580 B. C., Egyptian laborers completed the Great Pyramid of Cheops.

The original height of the Great Pyramid of Cheops was 146.5 m. Its base is a square with each side 230 m long. Its volume is about 2.5 million m³.

Concept Development

Suppose a prism with the same base and height as the Great Pyramid was built.

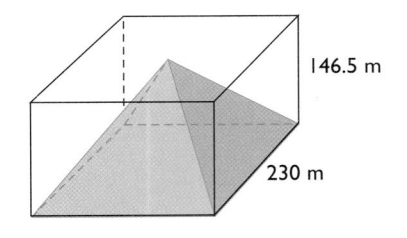

146.5 m

230 m

1. **a)** What would the volume of the prism be?
   b) About what fraction of the volume of the prism is the volume of the Great Pyramid?

2. a) Make a pyramid and a prism with the same base and height.

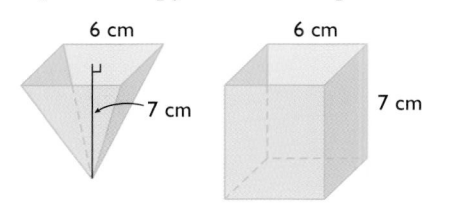

6 cm   6 cm

7 cm   7 cm

b) Predict how many times you could fill
the pyramid and empty it into the prism.
c) Check your prediction.

3. a) What is the formula for the volume of any prism?
b) Based on your findings in Problem 2, what is the
formula for the volume of any pyramid?

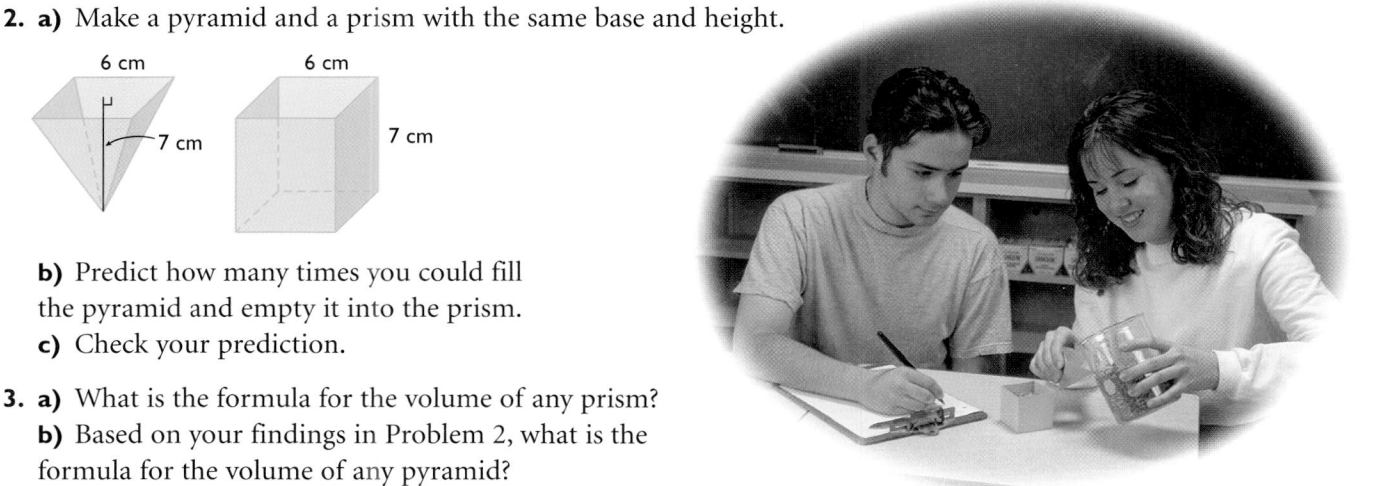

Understand and Apply

Round final answers to 1 decimal place when
appropriate.

I. Find the volume of each pyramid.

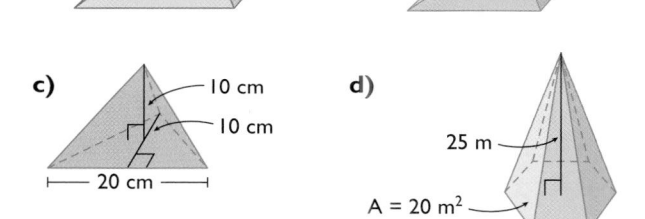

a) 10 cm   30 cm   **b)** 50 cm   2 m

c) 10 cm   10 cm   20 cm   **d)** 25 m   A = 20 m²

2. When the volume of a pyramid is known, what is
the formula for
a) its height?   **b)** the area of its base?

3. Find the height of each pyramid.

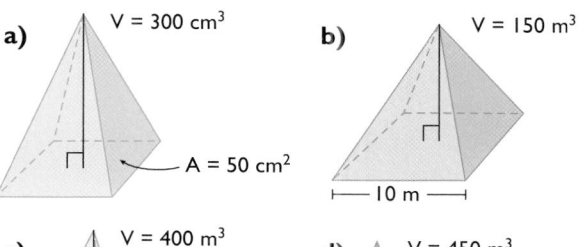

a) V = 300 cm³   A = 50 cm²   **b)** V = 150 m³   10 m

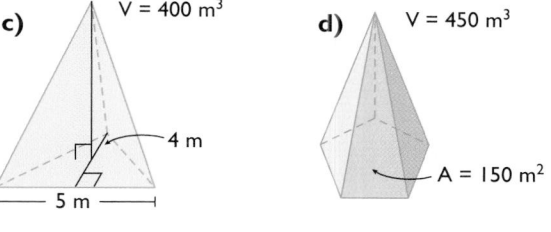

c) V = 400 m³   4 m   5 m   **d)** V = 450 m³   A = 150 m²

4. The largest pyramid ever built is in Mexico.
While it is only 54 m tall, its volume is about
3.3 million m³.
a) What is the area of its square base?
b) What is the side length of its base?

5. The oldest pyramid in Mexico has a volume of
63 840 m³ and a height of 30 m. What is the
side length of its square base?

6. The Muttart Conservatory in Edmonton has
four display pyramids. Each of the two smaller
pyramids has a volume of 2286 m³ and a height
of 18 m. Each of the other two has a volume of
5280 m³ and is 6 m taller. What are the areas of
the bases?

7. If the volume of a pyramid is 30 000 m³, what are two possible sets of dimensions?

8. What is the height of a pyramid with the same volume and same base area as each prism?

a)
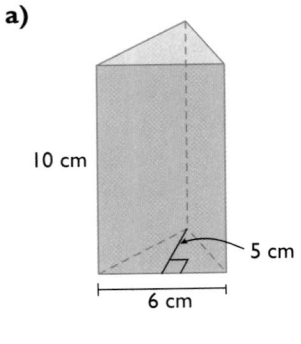
10 cm
5 cm
6 cm

b)
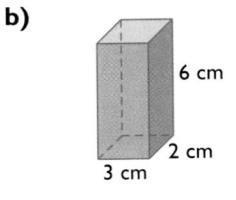
6 cm
2 cm
3 cm

9. What is the height of a prism with the same volume and same base area as each pyramid?

a)
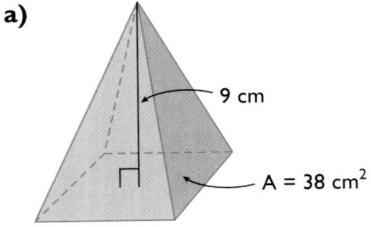
9 cm
A = 38 cm²

b)
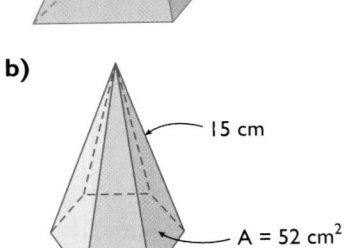
15 cm
A = 52 cm²

10. Predict which pyramid has the greater volume. Check your prediction.

a)
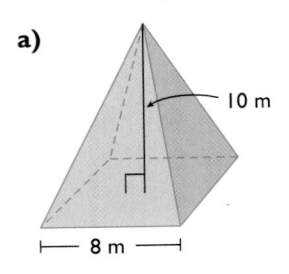
10 m
8 m

b)
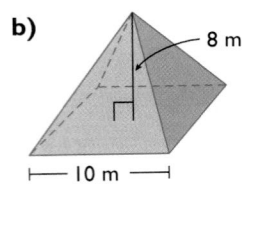
8 m
10 m

11. Repeat Problem 10 for these pyramids.
a) square pyramid with length of side of base 8 m and height 5 m
b) square pyramid with length of side of base 5 m and height 8 m

12. Repeat Problem 10 for these pyramids.
a) square pyramid with length of side of base 10 m and height 5 m
b) square pyramid with length of side of base 5 m and height 10 m

13. What conclusion can you draw from Problems 10-12?

14. The volume of a typical two-story house is about 1000 m³. About how many houses together would equal the volume of
a) the Great Pyramid of Cheops?
b) the largest pyramid ever built?
c) the oldest pyramid in Mexico?

15. About how many classrooms the size of yours together would equal the volume of
a) The Great Pyramid of Cheops?
b) the largest pyramid ever built?
c) the oldest pyramid in Mexico?

16. If your classroom were a pyramid with the same volume and the same base as it has now, what would its height be?

17. Create and solve a pyramid volume problem of your own. Challenge a classmate to solve it.

In Your Journal

Correct this statement and tell why it needs correction.

Pyramids have $\frac{1}{3}$ the volume of prisms.

9.2 Exploring Cones

This drinking cup is cone shaped.

Warm Up

About what fraction of the volume of the prism is the volume of the cylinder? Explain.

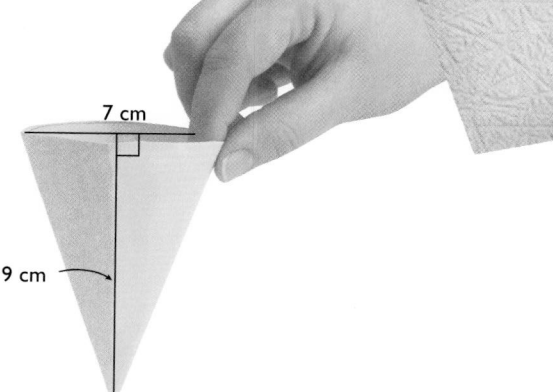

Concept Development

1. Is the drinking cup more likely to hold 100 mL or 350 mL of water? Explain.

2. **a)** What is the volume of this square pyramid?
   b) The square pyramid's side length is the same as the cone's diameter. Their heights are also the same. How do you know that the volume of the cone is less than the volume of the pyramid?
   c) Would the volume of the pyramid be a good estimate for the volume of the cone? Explain.

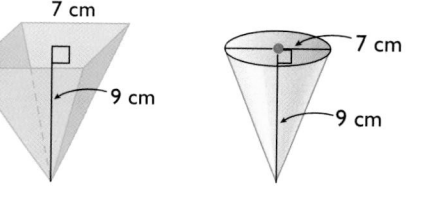

3. **a)** What is the formula for the volume of a cylinder?
   b) What is the volume of this cylinder with the same diameter and the same height as the cone?
   c) About what fraction of the volume of the cylinder do you think the volume of the cone is? Explain your thinking.

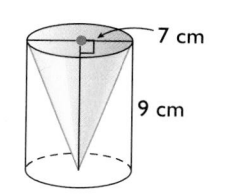

4. **a)** Make a cylinder and a cone with the same base and height.
   b) Predict how many times you could fill the cylinder and empty it into the cone.
   c) Check your prediction.

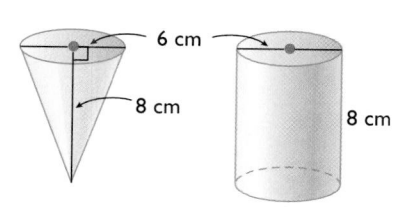

5. Based on your findings in Problem 4, what is the formula for the volume of a cone?

Understand and Apply

Use the π key on your calculator. Round final answers to 1 decimal place.

1. Find the volume of each cone.

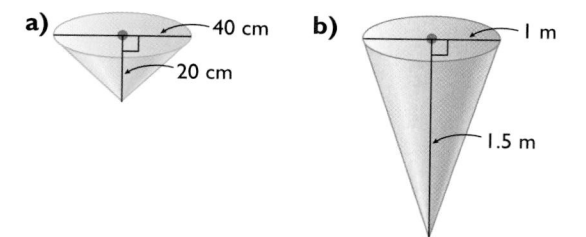

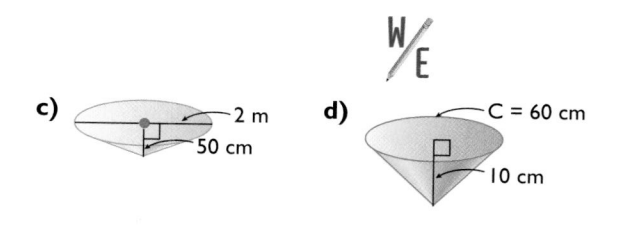

2. When the volume of a cone is known, what is the formula for
   a) its height?   b) its radius?

3. Find the height of each cone.

a) V = 300 m³
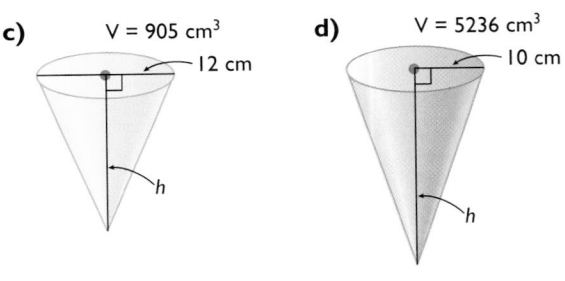
   10 m
   h

b) V = 1250 m³
   8 m
   h

c) V = 905 cm³
   12 cm
   h

d) V = 5236 cm³
   10 cm
   h

4. Find the radius of each cone.

a) V = 785 cm³
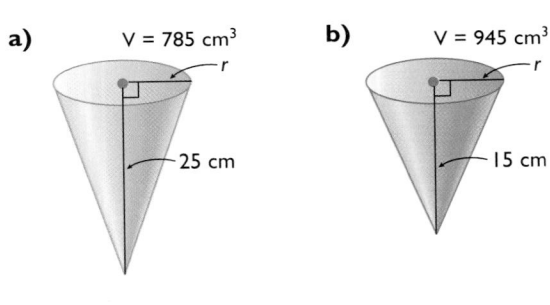
   r
   25 cm

b) V = 945 cm³
   r
   15 cm

c) V = 1510 cm³
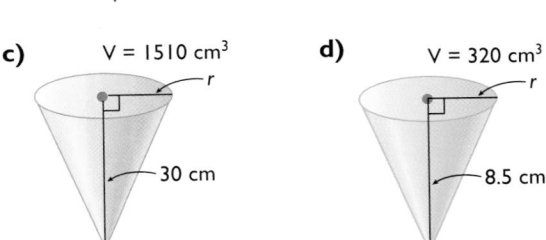
   r
   30 cm

d) V = 320 cm³
   r
   8.5 cm

W/E 5. If the volume of a cone is 150 m³, what are two possible sets of dimensions?

6. If you wanted a cone-shaped drinking cup to hold about 200 mL, what diameter and height could it be?

7. What is the height of a cone with the same volume and same base area as each cylinder?

a) 12 cm
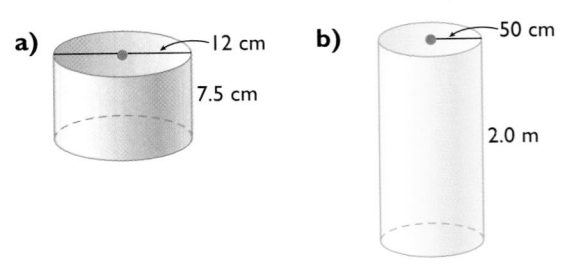
   7.5 cm

b) 50 cm
   2.0 m

8. What is the height of a cylinder with the same volume and same base area as each cone?

a) 6.5 cm
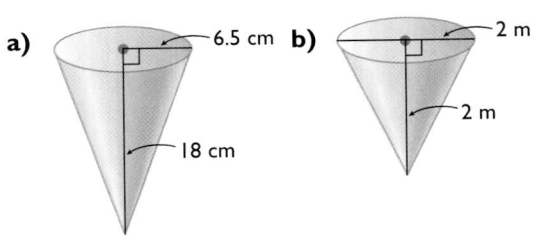
   18 cm

b) 2 m
   2 m

9. What happens to the volume of a cone when each measurement is doubled?
   a) height   b) diameter   c) area of base

10. What are the dimensions (height and radius), of two different cones with the same volume as this one?

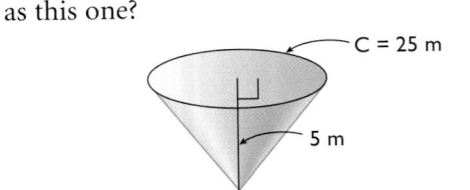
   C = 25 m
   5 m

HOME LINK

Measure and find the volume of some cones such as drinking cups, ice cream cones, and party hats.

9.3 Designing Packages

Which container has the greater surface area? What percent greater is it?

Manufacturers choose the shape of their packages to help sell their products.

3.3 cm

25 cm

9.5 cm

5 cm

18 cm

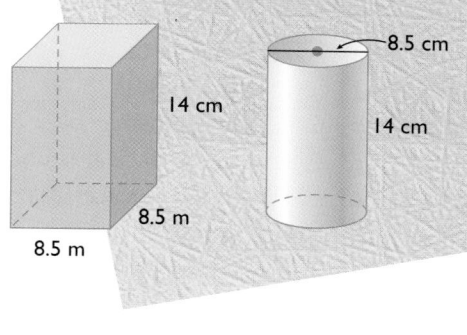

8.5 cm

14 cm

14 cm

8.5 m

8.5 m

Concept Development

1. This box will hold as much cereal as the Oatmeal Crisp box.
   a) Find the volumes of both boxes to verify this.
   b) Do you think both boxes would require the same amount of cardboard to make them?
   c) Find the surface area of both boxes to verify your answer to part (b).

12 cm

Cereal

12 cm

15.625 cm

2. This can will hold as much soup as the Campbell's Soup can.
   a) Find the volumes of both cans to the nearest whole number to verify this.
   b) Do you think both cans would require the same amount of metal?
   c) Find the surface area of both cans to verify your answer to part (b).

4 cm

6.46 cm

3. Why might a manufacturer choose to use a package that requires more material?

Understand and Apply

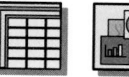

Use the π key on your calculator. Round final answers to 1 decimal place.

1. a) Use 12 connecting cubes. Design three different rectangular prism boxes that would just hold the cubes.
   b) Which box would use the least material? Explain what you did.

2. a) Use 24 connecting cubes. Design a box to just hold the cubes arranged each way.

| 1 by 1 by 24 | 1 by 2 by 12 |
| 2 by 2 by 6 | 2 by 3 by 4 |

   b) What is the volume and surface area of each prism?
   c) What do you notice?

3. a) Use 27 connecting cubes. Design three different boxes that will just hold the cubes.
b) Which box would use the least material? How do you know?

4. a) What is the surface area of a cube made from 27 connecting cubes?
b) Build a prism using cubes arranged 1 by 3 by 6.
c) What is its surface area and volume?
d) Compare the surface area and volume of the prism in part (b) with the cube in part (a).
e) Could you make a prism with the same surface area but a greater volume than the cube? Explain.

5. Rice is packaged in 1000 cm³ boxes. What dimensions of a rectangular prism box would use the least material? How do you know?

In Your Journal

The prism with the least surface area for a given volume is a cube. The prism with the greatest volume for a given surface area is a cube. Do you agree? Give examples to justify your thinking.

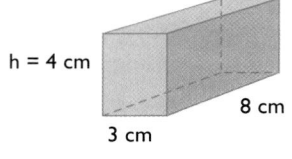

6. a) Find the volume and surface area of this box.

h = 4 cm
8 cm
3 cm

b) If the height is doubled, what would be the new volume and surface area?
c) Which has the greater percent increase, the surface area or the volume?

7. a) Find the volume and surface area of this can.

5 cm
20 cm

b) If the radius is tripled, what would be the new volume and surface area?
c) Which has the greater percent increase, the surface area or volume?

8. Each of these cans has a radius of 3 cm.

a) Complete both tables for $r = 3$.

h (cm)	$SA = 2\pi r^2 + 2\pi rh$ (cm²)	h (cm)	$V = \pi r^2 h$ (cm³)
4		4	
5		5	
6		6	
7		7	
8		8	
9		9	
10		10	

b) Graph both relations.
c) Which graph changes more quickly?

9. a) Cut out two pieces of paper 12 cm by 6 cm.
b) Make a cylindrical tube by rolling one piece of paper.
c) Make another tube by rolling the other piece the other way.
d) Why are their surface areas the same?
e) What is the volume of each?

10. a) Imagine circles for both ends of both cylinders in Problem 9.
b) Calculate the surface area for both cylinders.
c) Which is the more cost effective to make? Explain.

11. Boxes with dimensions 6 cm by 3 cm by 2 cm are to be packed in a carton which is 24 cm by 8 cm by 11 cm.
a) What is the best arrangement to get the most boxes in a carton? How many boxes will fit?
b) If all the carton's dimensions are doubled, how many boxes would fit?

HOME LINK

Two houses have the same volume and insulation. Which would lose more heat in the winter — a cube-shaped house or a long rectangular prism-shaped house? Explain.

9.4 Designing Shapes with Greatest Area or Least Perimeter

Warm Up

The area of a circle
is 78.5 cm².
What is its radius?
its circumference?

Saskatchewan is shaped almost like a trapezoid.

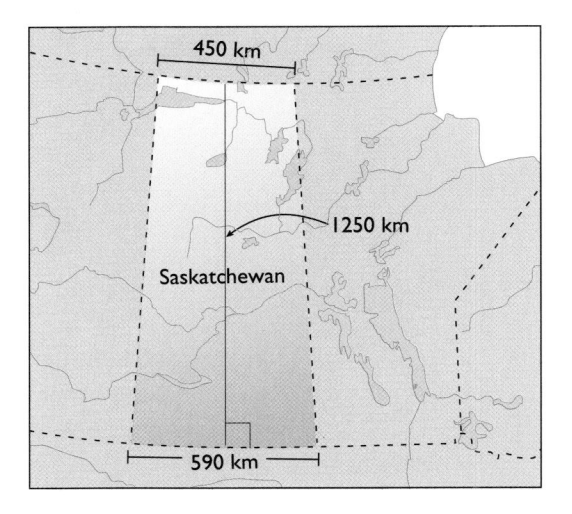

450 km

1250 km

Saskatchewan

590 km

Concept Development

1. What is the area of Saskatchewan?

2. a) What are the dimensions of a rectangle with the same area and height as Saskatchewan?
b) What is the perimeter of this rectangle?

3. a) What is the side length of a square with the same area as Saskatchewan?
b) What is the perimeter of this square?

4. a) What is the radius of a circle with the same area as Saskatchewan?
b) What is the perimeter, or circumference, of this circle?

5. Which of the three shapes in Problems 2, 3, and 4 has the least perimeter?

Understand and Apply

Use the π key on your calculator. Round final answers to 1 decimal place.

1. a) Use 36 square tiles. Design all the different rectangles possible.
b) Suppose a frame was made to enclose each of the rectangles in part (a). Which shape would require a frame with the least material?

2. Repeat Problem 1 with 16 square tiles.

In Your Journal

Describe the shape with the least perimeter for a given area. Describe the shape if it must be rectangular.

3. Use centimetre grid paper and draw rectangles with these dimensions. Then find the perimeter and area of each.

   a) 11 cm by 1 cm
   b) 10 cm by 2 cm
   c) 9 cm by 3 cm
   d) 8 cm by 4 cm
   e) 7 cm by 5 cm
   f) 6 cm by 6 cm

4. Repeat Problem 3 with these dimensions.

   a) 7 cm by 1 cm
   b) 6 cm by 2 cm
   c) 5 cm by 3 cm
   d) 4 cm by 4 cm

5. The perimeter of Prince Edward Island is about 1107 km.

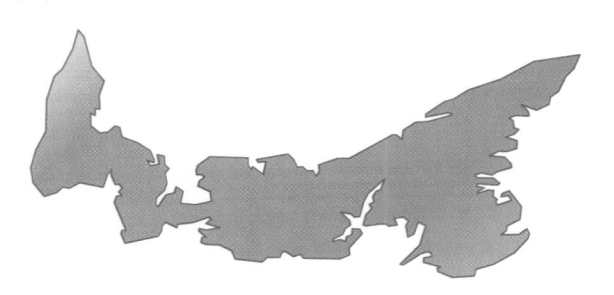

   a) What are the dimensions of a non-square rectangle with the same perimeter as Prince Edward Island? What is its area?
   b) What is the side length of a square with the same perimeter as Prince Edward Island? What is its area?
   c) What is the radius of a circle with the same perimeter as Prince Edward Island? What is its area?
   d) Which of the three shapes has the greatest area?
   e) The area of Prince Edward Island is about 5660 km^2. Why is its area so much less than any of the shapes with the same perimeter?

6. Many rectangles, a square, and a circle all have perimeters of 30 cm.

   a) Find the dimensions of at least three rectangles, the square, and the circle.
   b) Find the area of each.
   c) Which shape has the greatest perimeter?

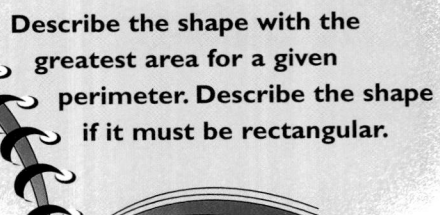

In Your Journal

Describe the shape with the greatest area for a given perimeter. Describe the shape if it must be rectangular.

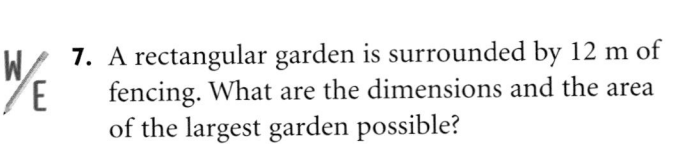

7. A rectangular garden is surrounded by 12 m of fencing. What are the dimensions and the area of the largest garden possible?

8. Fencing comes in 1 m long units that cannot be cut or bent. A rectangular garden is to be fenced on all four sides by 14 m of fencing. What are the dimensions and the area of the largest garden possible?

9. A square display area in one corner of a store is being set up. What are the dimensions and the area of the largest area that can be roped off on two sides with 10 m of rope?

10. Chicken wire fencing can be bent anywhere. What shape of fence would you choose to enclose the largest area possible? If the length of fencing is 18.5 m, what is the shape's area?

11. a) A rectangle has an area of 32 m^2. What is the least perimeter it could have? What type of rectangle is it?
   b) A shape has an area of 32 m^2. What is the least perimeter it could have? What shape is it?

Measure to find the perimeter of a floor of any room in your home.
• **What are the dimensions of a rectangular floor with the same perimeter but the greatest possible area?**
• **What are the dimensions of a rectangular floor with the same area and the least possible perimeter?**

Making Sense of DATA

The Most Useful Measurement

> **M**ost things can be measured in several different ways. Some measurements are used to find other measurements. In certain situations, some measurements are more useful than others.

A swimming pool is described in terms of its
- length
- width
- depth
- perimeter
- area
- volume
- capacity

The length would be the useful measurement to someone interested in swimming laps.

1. In what situation would each of the other measurements be useful?

Applications

2. For a lawn, when would each measurement be most useful?
   a) perimeter
   b) area

3. For a bag of lawn fertilizer, when would each measurement be most useful?
   a) mass
   b) coverage

4. For a lake, when would each measurement be most useful?
   a) length
   b) depth
   c) surface area
   d) perimeter

5. For a carton, when would each measurement be most useful?
   a) length, width, and height
   b) mass
   c) capacity
   d) volume
   e) surface area

6. A notebook computer is described as
   a) 486 microprocessor
   b) 4 MB RAM
   c) 30 cm wide, 21 cm deep, 5 cm high
   d) 2.2 kg mass
   When might each measurement be most useful?

7. Tell when any five of these car measurements might be most useful.
   - 2.2 L engine
   - 130 horsepower engine
   - 16 valve engine
   - 4-speed automatic transmission
   - 4.7 m long, 1.8 m wide, 1.4 m high
   - 1300 kg mass
   - 1.0 m head room in front
   - 1.1 m leg room in front
   - 370 L cargo capacity
   - 7.3 L/100 km highway fuel consumption

More Than One Strategy

Calculating with Perimeters and Areas

There are several ways to calculate how much less the perimeter of this circle is compared to the perimeter of this rectangle with the same area.

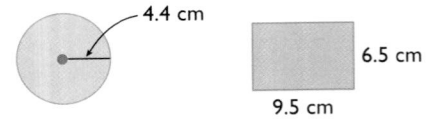

4.4 cm

6.5 cm

9.5 cm

Here are some using a calculator. Can you think of any others?

1. You could perform the calculations in three steps.

Step 1: P (of rectangle) $= 2(l + w)$
$= 2(9.5 + 6.5)$ 2 ⊠ (9.5 ⊞ 6.5) ⊜ | 32. |
$= 32.0$

Step 2: $C = 2\pi r$
$= 2\pi(4.4)$ 2 ⊠ π ⊠ 4.4 ⊜ | 27.64601535 |
$= 27.6$

Step 3: $P - C = 32.0 - 27.6$
$= 4.4$ The difference is 4.4 cm.

2. You can create a formula for the difference between the perimeters and then perform the calculations in one step.

$P - C = 2(l + w) - 2\pi r$
$= 2(9.5 + 6.5) - 2\pi (4.4)$ 2 ⊠ (9.5 ⊞ 6.5) ⊟ 2 ⊠ π ⊠ 4.4 ⊜ | 4.353984648 |
$= 4.4$

The difference is 4.4 cm.

3. You might expand and factor a formula for the difference and then perform the calculations.

$P - C = 2 (l + w) - 2\pi r$
$= 2l + 2w - 2\pi r$
$= 2(l + w - \pi r)$
$= 2(9.5 + 6.5 - \pi\, 4.4)$ 2 ⊠ (9.5 ⊞ 6.5 ⊟ π ⊠ 4.4) ⊜ | 4.353984648 |
$= 4.4$

The difference is 4.4 cm.

Understand and Apply

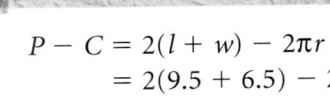

Perform each calculation in two ways.

1. A square and a rectangle have the same area. The rectangle is 13.8 cm by 5.2 cm and the square has 8.47 cm sides. How much less is the perimeter of the square than the rectangle?

2. A circle and a square have the same area. The radius of the circle is 8.8 cm. The square's sides are 15.6 cm. How much less is the perimeter of the circle than the square?

3. A square and a rectangle have the same perimeter. The rectangle is 12.2 cm by 8.2 cm. How much greater is the area of the square than the rectangle?

Problems to Investigate

TAKE YOUR PICK!

20 CUBES

Use connecting cubes to build prisms. What is the greatest surface area you can create with a volume of 20 cubic units? the least?

CIRCLES TO CONES

Draw and cut out a large circle. Divide it into eighths and then cut out one eighth. Form an open cone with the remaining seven-eighths. Find its volume. Cut out another eighth, form the cone, and find its volume. Repeat until you have determined how many eighths have to be removed to get the greatest volume.

BUMPING OUT

Each shape is made by bumping out a square on each side of the previous shape. Find the perimeter and area of each shape. What do you notice?

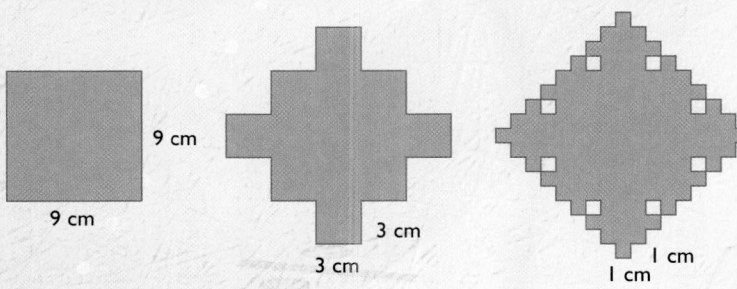

9 cm

9 cm

3 cm

3 cm

1 cm

1 cm

PANCAKES

A recipe makes 12 pancakes with diameters of 10 cm. If the batter was used to make one large circular pancake of the same thickness, why wouldn't it have a diameter of 120 cm? What would the diameter be?

RECTANGLES

A 4 cm by 6 cm rectangle has the same area as a 12 cm by 2 cm rectangle but its perimeter is less. Is there a rectangle with the same area that has even less perimeter? Explain.

TRUNCATED CONE

This yogurt container is a truncated cone. Explain how you could find its volume using the dimensions given. What is its volume?

7.5 cm

6.9 cm

5.6 cm

22.4 cm

Make up some other problems about measurement relationships. Post them on the bulletin board for your classmates to solve.

207

9.5 Base Plans and Elevations

What 3-dimensional object standing on its base looks like a circle from the top and a rectangle from the front? Describe the shapes of other objects when viewed from different vantage points.

T he brochure about Janine's new house showed this sketch, front elevation, and plan for the foundation. Plans for the first and second floor were also included.

The Newman Model

Front Elevation

Plan for the Foundation

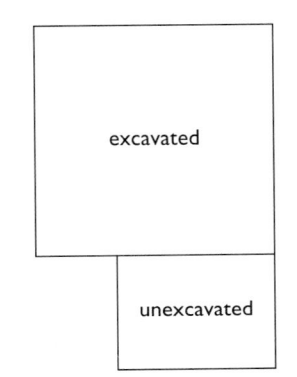

excavated

unexcavated

Concept Development

When the house was built, Janine drew the back and a side **elevation.**

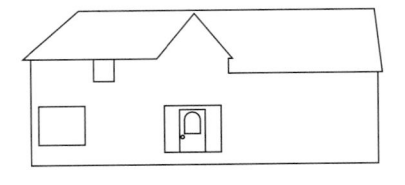

1. Which is which? How can you use measurement to find out?

The **base plan** for this model made of cubes is shown here. The base plan is also called the top elevation.

Base Plan/Top Elevation

(top)

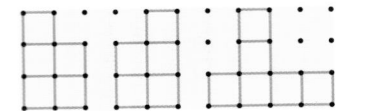

(right)

(left)   (front)

2. a) Which of these three drawings shows the model's front elevation? left elevation? right elevation?
b) Are any of the drawings the same as the back elevation? Explain.

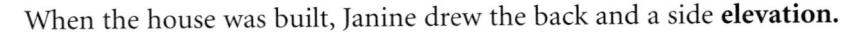

Understand and Apply

Use square dot paper.

1. Draw and label the base plan, front elevation, left elevation, and right elevation for each model. Make the model with cubes first.

a)

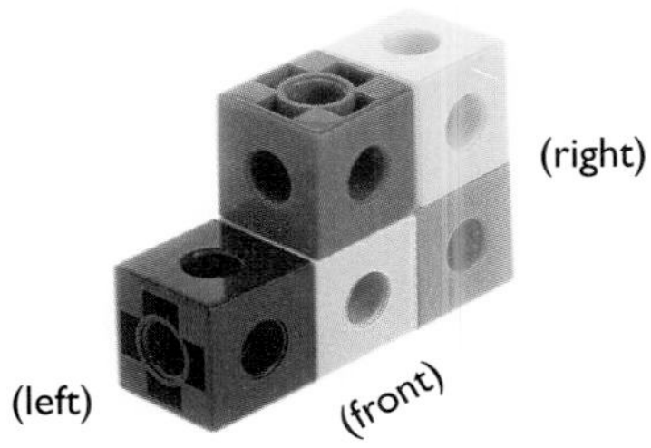
(right)
(left)
(front)

b)

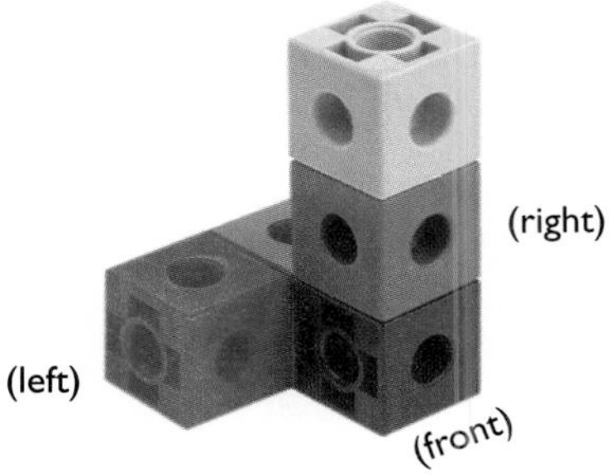
(right)
(left)
(front)

c)

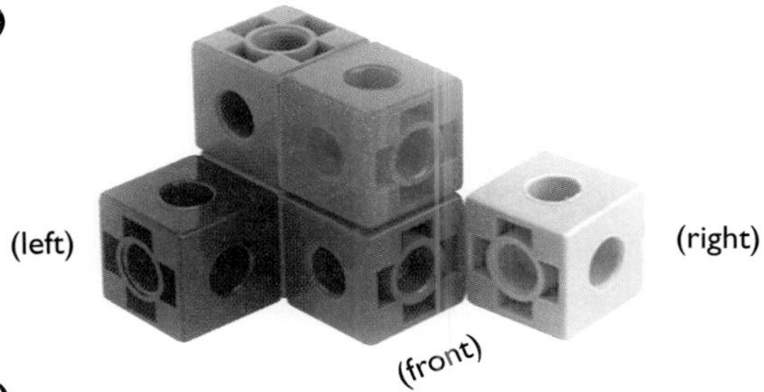
(left)
(right)
(front)

d)

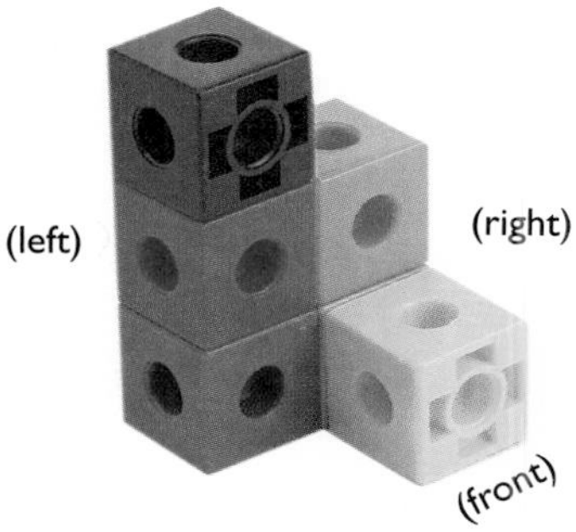
(left)
(right)
(front)

e)

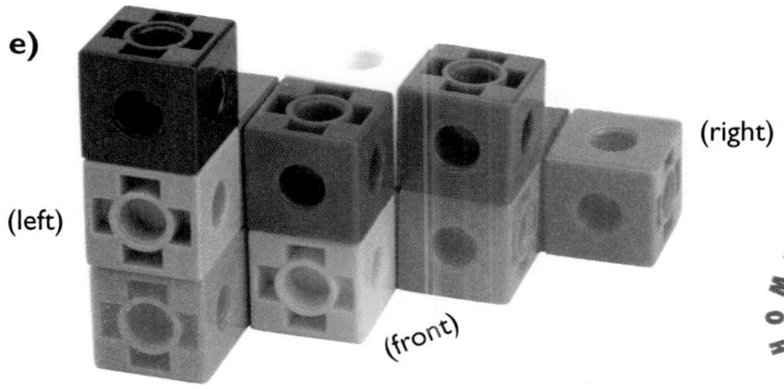
(right)
(left)
(front)

2. Draw and label the base plan, front elevation, left elevation, and right elevation for each.

a)

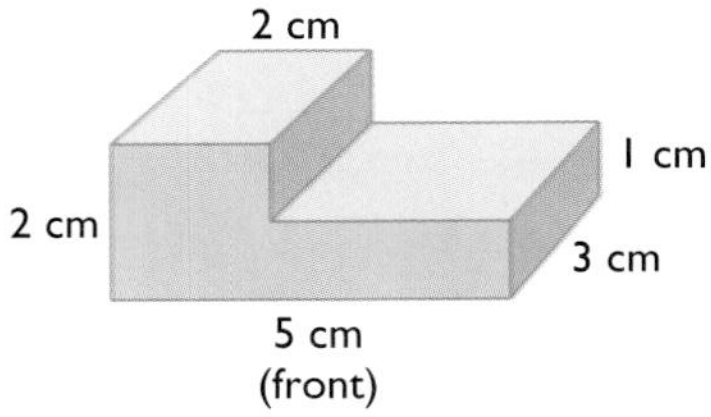
2 cm
1 cm
2 cm
3 cm
5 cm
(front)

b)

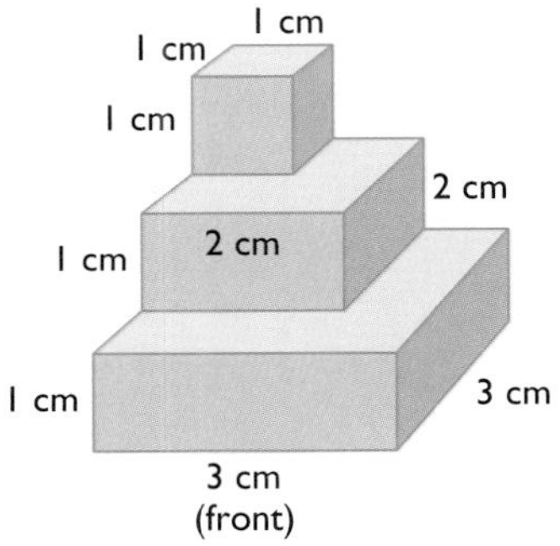
1 cm
1 cm
1 cm
2 cm
1 cm
2 cm
1 cm
3 cm
3 cm
(front)

c)

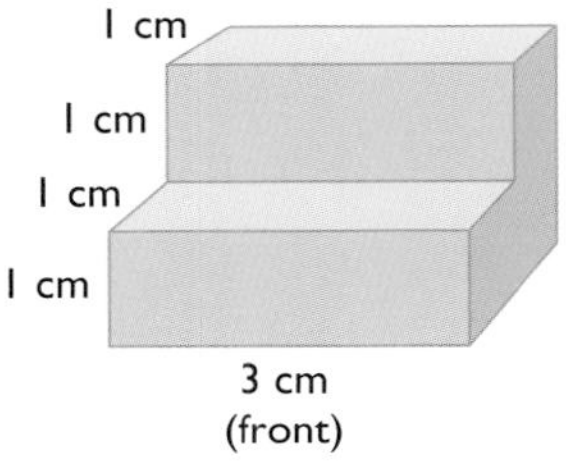
1 cm
1 cm
1 cm
1 cm
3 cm
(front)

d)

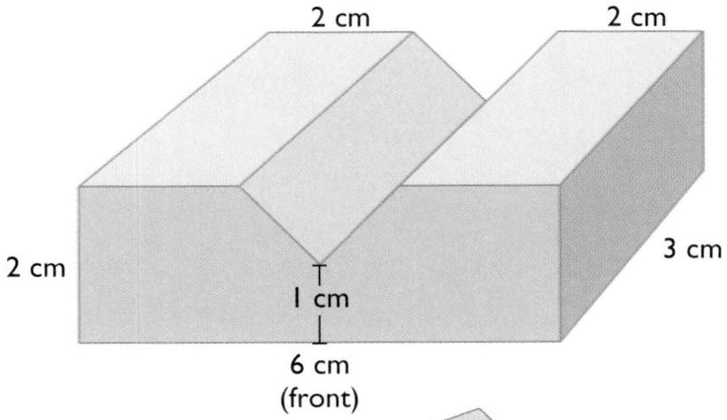
2 cm
2 cm
2 cm
3 cm
1 cm
6 cm
(front)

e)

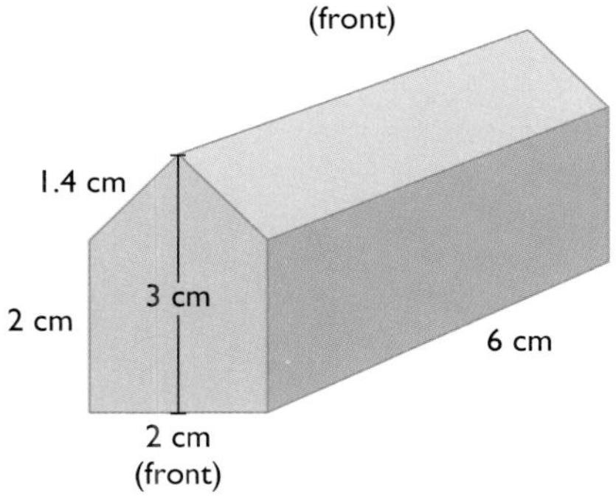
1.4 cm
3 cm
2 cm
6 cm
2 cm
(front)

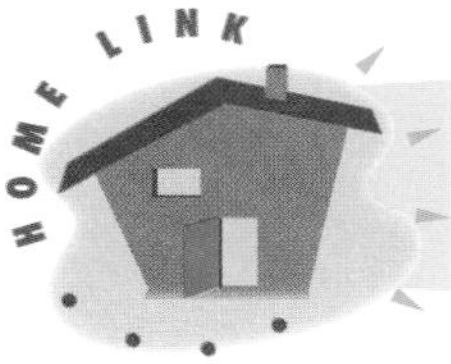
HOME LINK

Draw the plan for the foundation and two elevations of the building you live in.

9.6 Building and Sketching

Warm Up

How many 3-dimensional objects can you think of that look the same no matter what face you are looking at? What are they? When *do* they look different?

To build the model with the base plan and elevations shown, Laura and Scott use the base plan to make the same bottom layer.

| Base Plan | Front Elevation | Right Elevation |

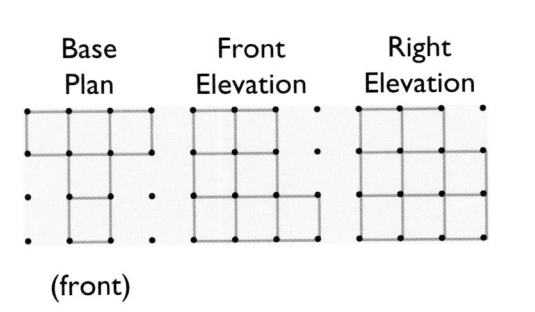

(front)

(front)

Concept Development

Using the front elevation, they both add two cubes to the model's right cube and none to the model's left cube.

1. Do you agree with Laura and Scott? Explain your thinking.

(front)

To add cubes to the model's middle cubes, they use the front and right elevations. They both add two cubes to the middle cube and one to the front cube. Laura adds two cubes to the back cube. Scott doesn't add any.

Laura's

(front)

Scott's

(front)

2. Could they both be right? Explain.

Laura and Scott use isometric dot paper to sketch their models. Both views are slightly from the top with the model's left front edges facing front.

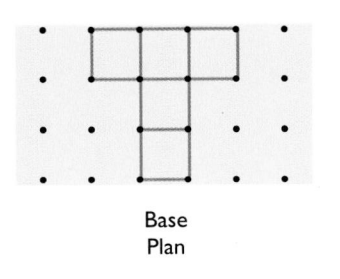

Laura's

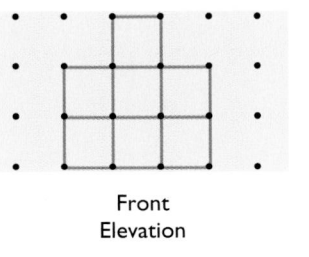

Scott's

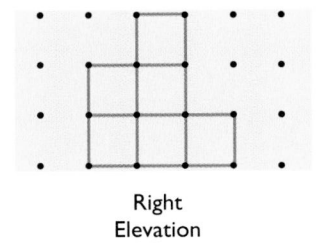

Laura's or Scott's?

3. Whose model is represented by the third sketch? How do you know? Describe the view.

4. Build a model with cubes and then sketch it on isometric dot paper. Compare yours with your classmates'.

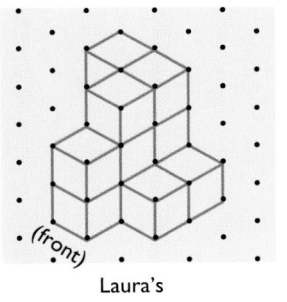

Base
Plan

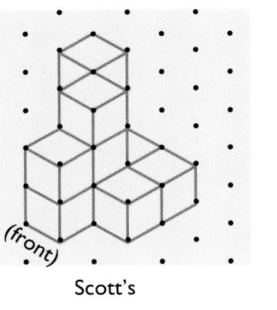

Front
Elevation

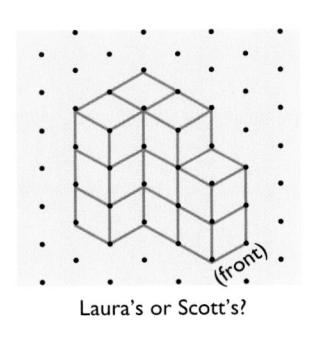

Right
Elevation

Understand and Apply

Use cubes and isometric dot paper.

1. Build a model for each.

a)

Base Plan	Front Elevation	Right Elevation

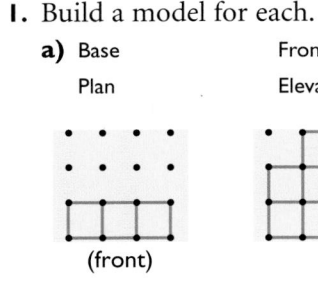

(front)

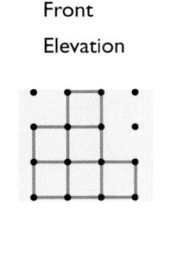

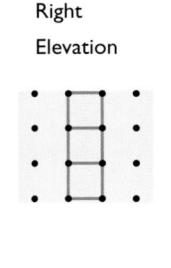

c)

Base Plan	Front Elevation	Right Elevation

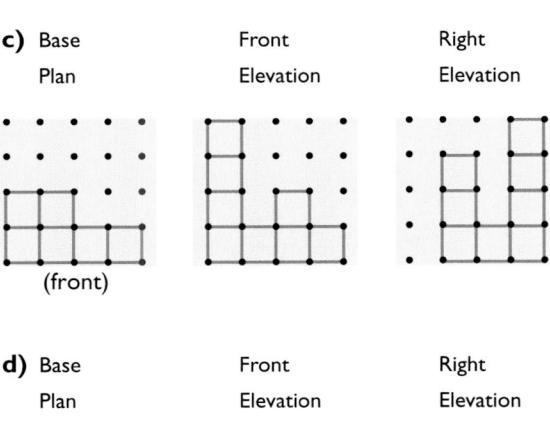

(front)

b)

Base Plan	Front Elevation	Right Elevation

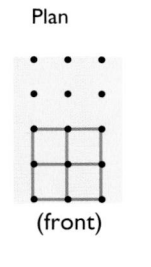

(front)

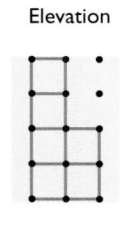

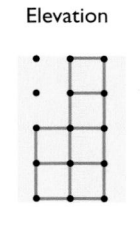

d)

Base Plan	Front Elevation	Right Elevation

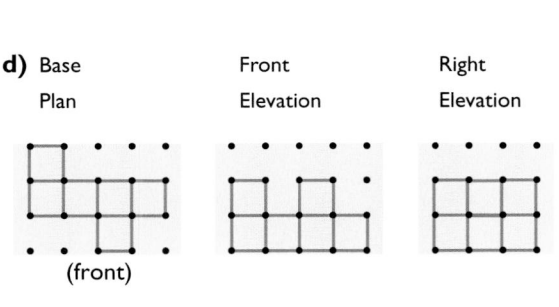

(front)

2. Sketch a model for each. Build the model first, if you wish.

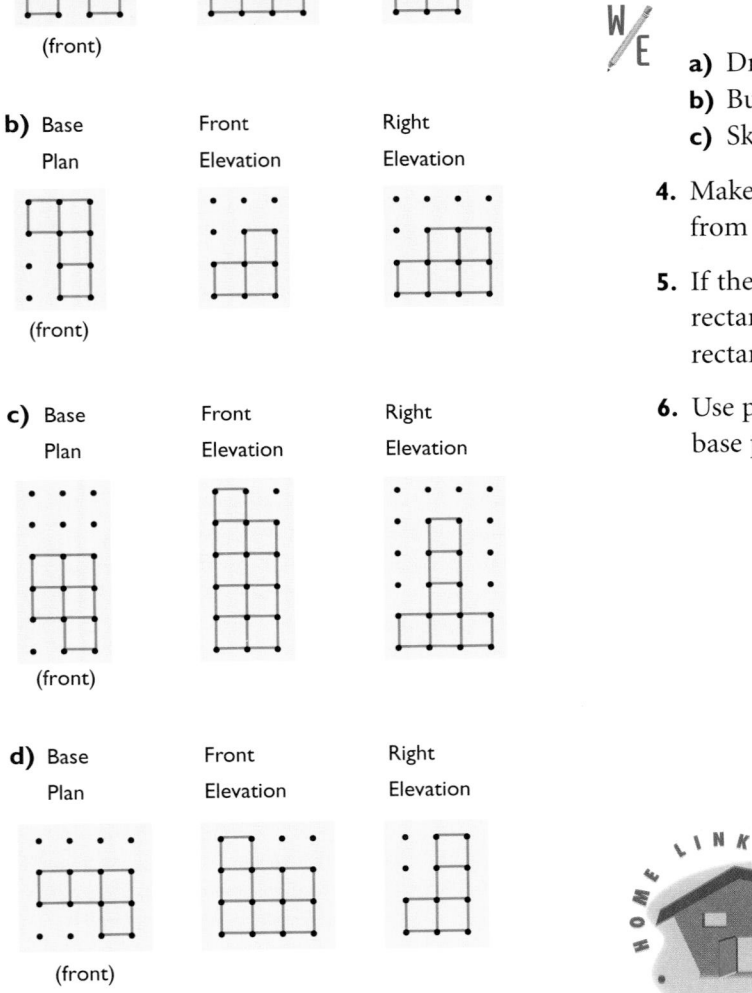

a) Base Plan   Front Elevation   Right Elevation

(front)

b) Base Plan   Front Elevation   Right Elevation

(front)

c) Base Plan   Front Elevation   Right Elevation

(front)

d) Base Plan   Front Elevation   Right Elevation

(front)

3. Base Plans can be drawn with numbers to tell how many cubes there are in each column.

Base Plan

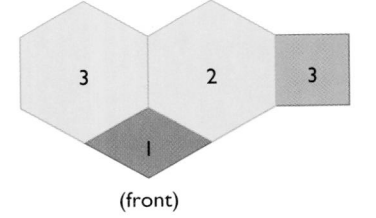

(front)

a) Draw the front and right elevations.
b) Build a model.
c) Sketch a model.

4. Make a base plan with numbers for each model from Problem 2.

5. If the base plan and all elevations of a model are rectangular, does the model have to be a rectangular prism? Explain.

6. Use pattern blocks to build a model from this base plan.

3   2   3

1

(front)

9.7 Solving Problems of Location

Draw a circle with a radius of 3 cm. How would you define a circle?

Draw a line segment parallel to another. How would you define parallel?

A dog is on a 6 m leash attached to a peg in the ground.

Concept Development

1. **a)** Make a scale diagram and locate some points that are 6m from the peg, *P*.

   b) Locate all the points that are 6 m from the peg. What shape is made?

   c) Shade the area that is within the dog's reach.

2. A fence is built around a 12 m by 6 m rectangular pool. The fence is exactly 3 m out from the sides and corners of the pool. Draw a scale diagram to show that the fence is not rectangular.

The dog above is to be leashed to a peg in this 20 m by 15 m fenced yard. The yard has vegetable and flower gardens as shown.

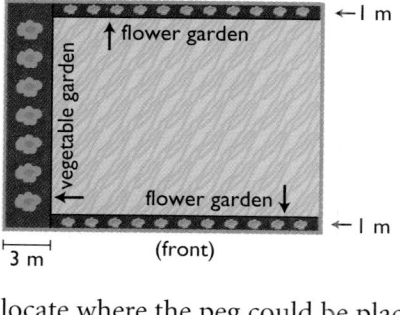

←1 m

↑ flower garden

vegetable garden

flower garden ↓

←1 m

3 m

(front)

To locate where the peg could be placed to provide the dog with the greatest area but to keep it out of the gardens, Pamela draws this scale diagram.

3. **a)** Which line segment is 6 m from the vegetable garden? back flower garden? front flower garden?

   b) Why did Pamela draw line segment GH?

   c) Where could the peg be placed?

Scale: 1 cm represents 2 m.   (front)

Understand and Apply

Draw a scale diagram or copy the given diagram, and use compasses when necessary.

1. Radio transmitter *T* can transmit a distance of 120 km. Show the area that can receive its transmissions.

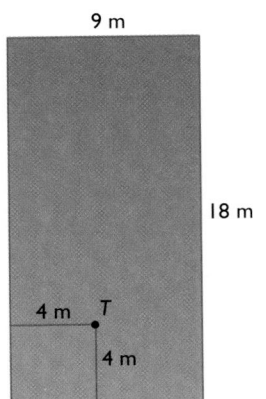

2. Radio transmitter *A* can transmit a distance of 150 km. Radio transmitter *B* is located 180 km due east of it, it can transmit a distance of 120 km. Transmitter *B* is located 200 km due north of radio transmitter *C* which transmits 150 km. Show the area that receives from
   a) just transmitter *A*   b) just transmitter *B*
   c) just transmitter *C*   d) all three transmitters
   e) any two of the three transmitters

3. This yard is to be sodded. The sod is to be 2 m away from the perimeter and 1 m from a new tree, *T*. Show the area to be sodded.

9 m

18 m

4 m   *T*

4 m

4. A monkey can reach out 60 cm from the sides of its travel cage. The cage has a rectangular base 150 cm by 120 cm. Show the area outside the cage that is within the monkey's reach.

5. A washroom at a campground is to be located the same distance from sleeping cabins *A* and *B*. Cabins *A* and *B* are 40 m apart.
   a) Show where the washroom could be located.
   b) Describe how you found the locations.

6. An eating cabin is to be located the same distance from sleeping cabins *A*, *B*, and *C* which are located as shown.
   a) Show where the eating cabin should be located.
   b) Describe how you found the location.

A •

• C

B •

7. A weeping willow tree is to be planted between two buildings. It must be planted at least 10 m from each building so that its roots will not damage the foundations. Show where it could be planted.

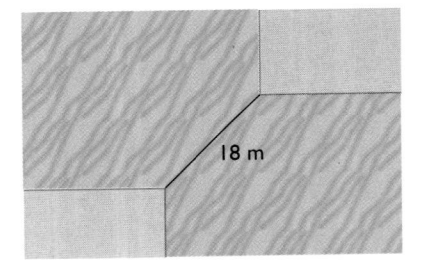

18 m

8. Statue *M* and statue *N* are located on one side of a high wall, *PQ*. Show from where
   a) both statues can be seen
   b) neither statue can be seen
   c) statue *M* but not statue *N* can be seen
   d) statue *N* but not statue *M* can be seen

P ⊤

• M

• N

Q ⊥

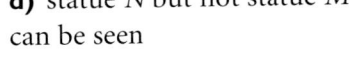

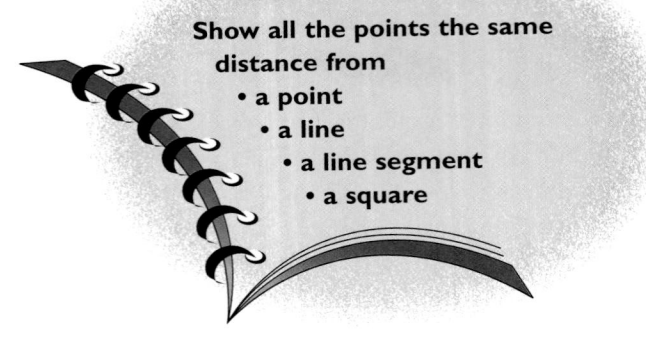

Show all the points the same distance from
• a point
• a line
• a line segment
• a square

Problems to Investigate

ROLLING CIRCLE

Show the path that would be made by
a) the centre, **C**, of the small circle as the small circle rolls around the large circle
b) a point, **P**, on the small circle as the small circle rolls around the large circle.

SAME VOLUME

Use connecting cubes to build three different models all with the same base plan and a volume of 20 cubic units. Sketch each on isometric dot paper. Draw a base plan with numbers for each.

TWO TACKS

- Place a loose loop of string around two tacks.
- Put a pencil inside the loop, pull the string taut.
- Move the pencil, drawing the path it makes.
  What does the path look like?

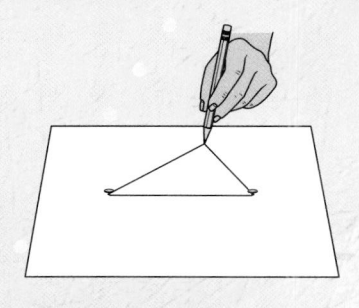

SQUARES

Copy the diagram.
- Locate the parts of the outer square that are 2 cm from the inner square.
- Locate all the points 2 cm from the inner square.
- Locate the parts of the outer square that are 2.8 cm from the inner square.
- Locate all the points that are 2.8 cm from the inner square.

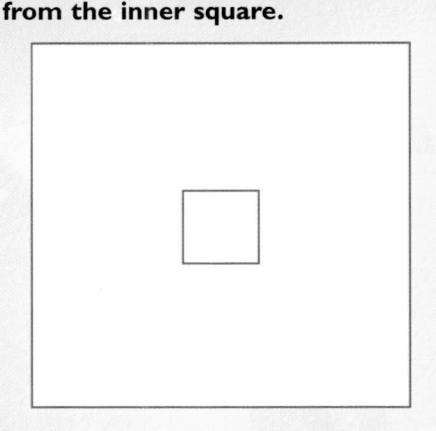

UP FRONT

Build three different models that have this front elevation. Sketch each on isometric dot paper.

Explain why a base plan with numbers would not be suitable for any of your models.

Research a famous structure. Draw and label its plan, front elevation, left elevation, and right elevation.

Solve Problems by Using Models

Try this problem before going on.

OPEN CONE

What is the height of an open cone made from $\frac{3}{4}$ of a circle that has a radius of 10 cm?

▶ Make a Plan

Dave's group solved this problem by making and measuring a model.

▶ Carry Out the Plan

▶ Look Back

4. Would cutting a cone made from $\frac{3}{8}$ of the circle be twice as tall?

▶ Understand the Problem

1. What are you asked to find?
2. What do you know?
3. Where will you begin?

The height is 6.6 cm.

Applications

CYLINDER VERSUS SPHERE SURFACE AREA

A cylinder and and a sphere have the same diameter and height. Do they have the same surface area?

HALF CONE?

The top of a cone is cut off at exactly half its height. Would the remaining cone have more than, less than, or exactly half of the volume of the original cone?

VOLUME OF A SPHERE

A sphere and a cylinder have the same diameter. The cylinder's height is the same as its diameter. Which would have the greater surface area — the sphere or the cylinder?

WRAPPING PACKAGES

This rectangular prism-shaped package has double the surface area of another. Will it require less than double, more than double, or exactly double the amount of ribbon to decorate it as shown?

Use the π key on your calculator. Round final answers to 1 decimal place, if appropriate.

1. a) What is the height of this pyramid?

Volume = 4000 cm³

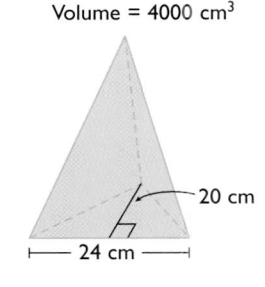

20 cm

24 cm

b) What is the height of a triangular prism with the same volume and same base?

2. A pyramid has a volume of 2700 cm³ and a height of 30 cm.
  a) What is the area of its square base?
  b) What is the side length of its base?
  c) What is the area of the base of a rectangular prism with the same volume and same height?

3. Find each unknown dimension.

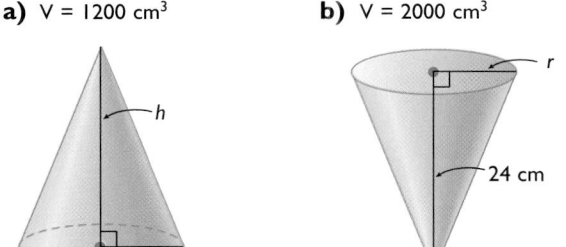

a) V = 1200 cm³

h

8 cm

b) V = 2000 cm³

r

24 cm

4. What are possible dimensions of a cone with the same volume as each cylinder?

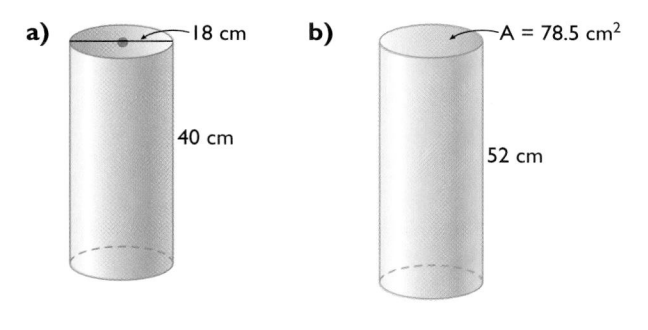

a) 18 cm

40 cm

b) A = 78.5 cm²

52 cm

5. Is there a box that would hold the same amount as this box but have less surface area? If so, what are possible dimensions?

17 cm

12 cm

3 cm

6. What are the dimensions and area of the largest field that can be surrounded by 50 m of fencing that
  a) can be cut or bent anywhere?
  b) comes in 1 m lengths and cannot be cut or bent?

7. Draw and label the base plan, front elevation, left elevation, and right elevation of each.

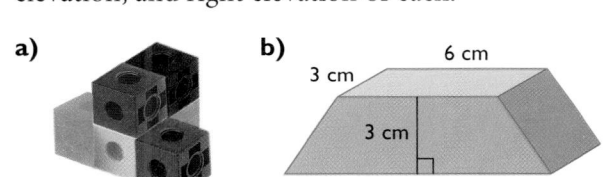

a)

(front)

b)

6 cm

3 cm

3 cm

10 cm

(front)

8. Sketch a model for this plan and elevations on isometric dot paper. Build the model first, if you wish.

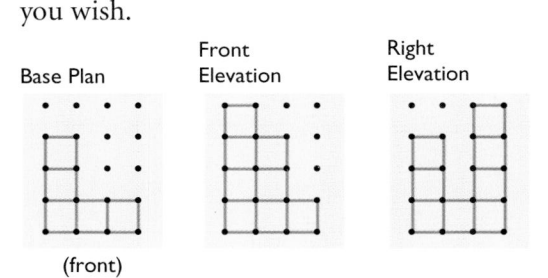

Base Plan

Front Elevation

Right Elevation

(front)

9. Show each area.
  a) within 2 m of A
  b) within 3 m of B
  c) within 2 m of A and 3 m of B

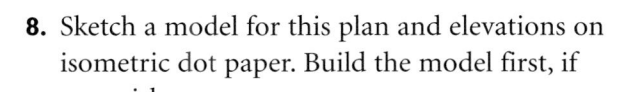

A

4 m

B

Practise With Games

Play each game in a group of 2, 3, or 4 players.

Rolling Volumes

- Use two different colored dice. Assign one color to be height and the other to be radius.

- Take turns rolling the dice.

- Use the numbers rolled as the height of a cone and the radius of its base.

- Calculate the volume. Round to the nearest whole number.

- Score as many points as your volume.

The first player with 500 points wins.

Example:

Let red be height and blue be radius.

$h = 3$ and $r = 4$

$V = \dfrac{1}{3}\pi r^2 h$

$= \dfrac{1}{3}\pi(4)^2(3)$ $\boxed{\pi}\ \boxed{\times}\ 4\ \boxed{x^2}\ \boxed{\times}\ 3\ \boxed{\div}\ 3\ \boxed{=}$ $\boxed{50.26548246}$

$\cong 50$

Score 50 points.

Building Models

Each player

- rolls a pair of dice.

- finds the sum of the numbers rolled.

- builds a model using that number of connecting cubes, trying to create the model with the least surface area possible.

The player with the least surface area scores two points.

If more than one player creates the least surface area, each scores one point.

Play ten rounds.

The player with the most points wins.

Example:

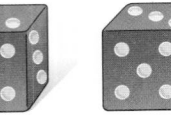

V = 5 cubic units

SA = 20 square units

Problems to Investigate

TAKE YOUR PICK!

MELTING ICE

Cut a 1L milk carton in half and half fill it with water. Place it in a freezer. When the water is frozen, remove the carton from the ice block and place the block of ice on a tray.

Fill another half carton with ice cubes. Then spread them out on another tray. Time how long it takes each tray of ice to melt.

How do you know both trays hold approximately the same volume of ice?

Which has the greater surface area— the block or the cubes?

Which melted faster?

What might you conclude about the relationship between melting and surface area?

STELLATED CUBES

An object is stellated if it has a pyramid which covers each of its faces.

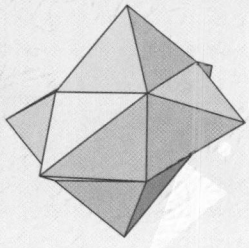

What is the volume of a stellated cube if its side length is 10 cm and the height of each pyramid is also 10 cm?

GREATEST SURFACE AREA

Use connecting cubes to build models. What is the greatest surface area you can create with a volume of 15 cubic units? Describe its shape.

8 CUBES

How many different models can you make with 8 connecting cubes and this base plan?

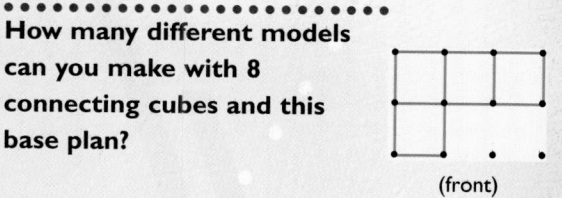

(front)

FOLLOW THE GRID

Copy this diagram. Find all the intersection points that are twice as many grid lines from point A as from point B.

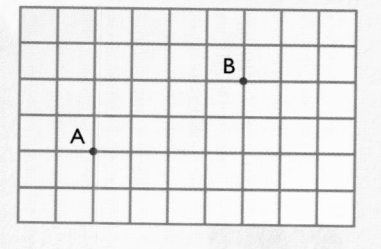

PENTOMINOES

Shapes made from five congruent squares joined along full sides are called pentominoes.

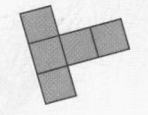

There are 12 pentominoes. Which has the least perimeter? Why?

Make up some other problems about measurement and geometry. Post them on the bulletin board for your classmates to solve.

219

Use the π key on your calculator. Round final answers to 1 decimal place, if appropriate.

1. What are possible dimensions of a square pyramid that has a volume that is 1000 cm³ greater than this pyramid?

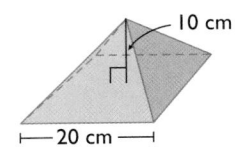

2. What are possible dimensions
   • length of the base of the triangular base
   • height of the triangular base
   • height of the pyramid
   of a triangular pyramid with the same volume as this square pyramid?

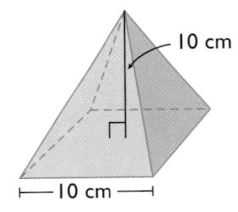

3. What are possible dimensions if each has a volume of 800 cm³?

   a) 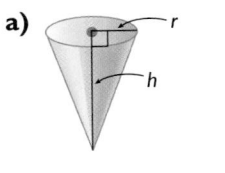   b)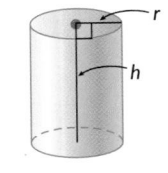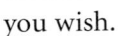

4. a) Use 18 connecting cubes. Design three different boxes that would just hold the cubes.
   b) Which box would use the least material?

5. What are the dimensions and surface area of the box with the least surface area that would hold 6 of these cans?

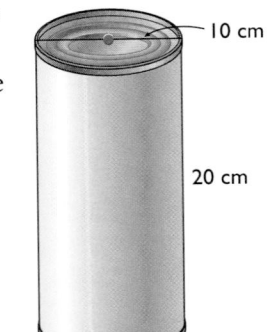

6. This can and square-based box have the same height. They each have a base with an area of 400 cm². Would the same amount of material be used to place labels around both containers? Explain.

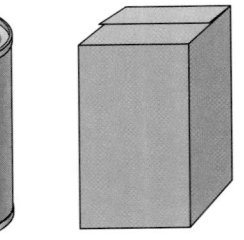

7. Draw and label the base plan, front elevation, left elevation, and right elevation of each.

   a)   b)

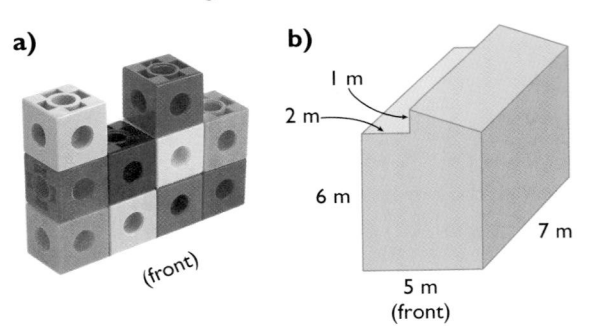

8. Sketch a model for this base plan and elevations on isometric dot paper. Build the model first, if you wish.

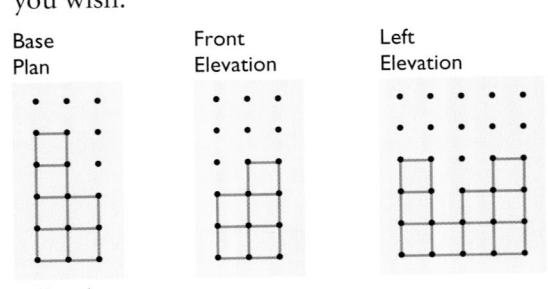

9. What is incorrect about this statement and why? The outside of this rectangular frame is exactly 6 cm out from the sides and corners of the rectangular picture.

Communicate Your Knowledge

1. How would you describe to a friend how to find the volume of a cone if you know its height and the circumference of its base?

2. Describe an experiment that you could perform to find the shape with the greatest area for a given perimeter.

3. Why might a cube be described as an economical shape for a box?

4. When is it more useful to draw the plan and the elevations of an object than to draw the object?

5. How would you tell a friend to locate the area that is within 2 cm of the outside of a rectangle?

6. A numbered base plan is given, and you know the numbers tell the height in cubes as well as the number of cubes in each column. If the front of the plan is not identified, could different models be made by different people? Explain.

3	4	2
1		2

What questions do you still have about measurement and geometry?

UNIT 10

Equations

In real-life situations people use algebraic expressions and equations to describe relationships.

• A parachutist's fall is calculated using the equation $d = 4.9t^2$. (t represents the time in seconds, and d the distance fallen in metres)
  Find the distance fallen after
  a) 5 s   b) 7.5 s   c) 12 s

• A theatre owner determines the theatre's minimum daily income using $I = \$8.50a + \$4.75s + \$3.50c$.
  (a represents the number of adults, s the number of seniors or students, and c the number of children)
  The daily income must be at least \$850. List several different combinations of numbers of adults, seniors/students, and children that must attend.

• A business owner calculates her profit using $P = I - C$. (I represents her income, C her cost, and P her profit)
  Substitute numbers for P, I, and C to see if she has a profit or loss when
  a) $I = C$ b) $I < C$ c) $I > C$

What other professions use expressions and equations? Describe the situations.

10.1 Varying Values

Mary said 4. I said 9.
Tom said 7. I said 15.
Jan said 11. I said 23.
Barry said 20. I said 41.
a) What's my rule?
b) What should I say
   if Farrah says 37?
c) What would
   Shamim say if I
   said 99?

A lli kept a chart of different trips that she took when she first got her driver's licence. She recorded her distance, speed, and time.

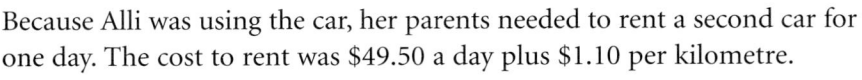

	Trip 1	Trip 2	Trip 3	Trip 4
Speed (km/h)	70	80	100	90
Time (h)	2	3	3.5	1.5
Distance (km)	140	240	350	135

Concept Development

1. Alli wrote several equations to show the relationship among distance (d), speed (s), and time (t). Which equations are correct? Explain.

$$st = d \qquad d = st \qquad d = ts \qquad s = \frac{d}{t} \qquad t = \frac{d}{s}$$

2. Calculate
   a) d if $s = 90$ km/h and $t = 4.5$ h
   b) t if $s = 50$ km/h and $d = 162.5$ km
   c) s if $t = 1.75$ h and $d = 150.5$ km

Because Alli was using the car, her parents needed to rent a second car for one day. The cost to rent was $49.50 a day plus $1.10 per kilometre.

3. a) Does Alli's expression, $49.50 + $1.10 d, represent the situation? What does d represent?
   b) How much will it cost if her parents want to travel 300 km? 550 km?
   c) Use Alli's expression to write an equation that represents the situation if the total cost was $324.50.
   d) Estimate the distance travelled if the total cost was $324.50.

Car Rental
$49.50 + $1.10d

4. a) Describe the difference between an algebraic expression and an equation.
   b) Where above did you use an equation?
   c) Write an equation for the rental cost using two variables, C for cost and d for distance.

Understand and Apply

1. Write an expression to represent each situation. Evaluate the expression if possible.
   a) The cost to rent a VCR is $10 per day plus a $25 deposit. How much will it cost to rent a VCR for 4 days? 10 days? d days?
   b) Licorice costs $3.75 for the first kilogram and $3.25 for each additional kilogram. How much would you pay for 3 kg? 10 kg? m kg?

2. Write an expression to represent each situation. Tell what each variable represents.
   a) the cost to rent a video game machine is $20 for the weekend and $4.50 for each game
   b) the cost to lease a car is $5000 down and $229 per month
   c) the taxi fare is a flat rate of $1.50 and $0.90 per kilometre
   d) the cost to buy fruit

Amount of Fruit	1	2	3	4
Cost ($)	2.50	5	7.50	10

3. Write an expression to represent each pattern.
   a) 2, 4, 6, 8, ...   **b)** 1, 3, 5, 7, ...
   c) 7, 10, 13, 16, ...   **d)** 2, 7, 12, 17, ...

4. Describe these expressions in words.
   a) $n - 4$ **b)** $2n + 10$
   c) $\$3.50f + \$0.25$ **d)** $50d$
   e) $\$0.25q + \$5.00$ **f)** $\$55 + \$10p$

5. Write an equation that represents each situation.
   a) the sum of these angles

   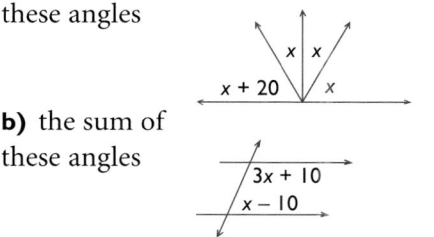

   b) the sum of these angles

   $3x + 10$
   $x - 10$

   c) the relationship between cost and the number of donuts

Donuts (dozen)	4	5	6
Cost ($)	18.40	23	27.60

d) the relationship between distance travelled and the speed of a commuter train

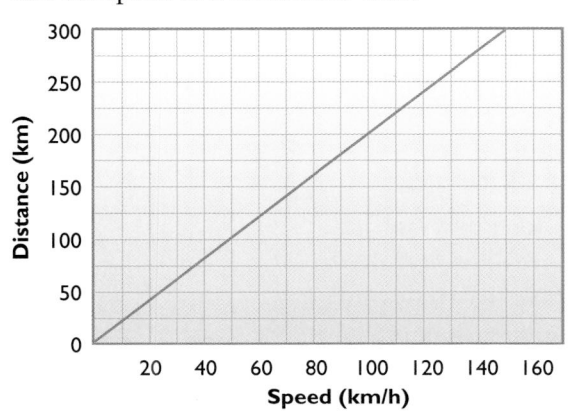

e) the relationship between volume and the number of test tubes

Number of test tubes	2	4	8	24
Volume (cm³)	6	12	24	72

f) the relationship between the number of nickels and a dollar coin
g) five more than four times a number is twenty-four
h) the sum of three consecutive numbers is 21

6. Create an equation for each expression in Problem 4. What is the value of the variable for your equation?

7. **a)** What number pattern will the computer print?
```
FOR N = 1 TO 10
  X = 2N − 1
  PRINT X
NEXT N
END
```
   b) Rewrite the second line in the program so that the computer will print 4, 7, 10, ...

8. **a)** Write an equation for this sentence. The product of the fourth power of a number, n, and the square of the same number is 64.
   b) Use the exponent rules and guess and test to find values for n.

HOME LINK

Write an expression and an equation to represent algebraic relationships at home, for example, the cost of purchasing a new appliance or book.

225

10.2 Matching Expressions and Equations

Explain why these equations are equivalent.

a) $C = 2\pi r$ and $C = \pi d$
b) $P = l + w + l + w$ and $P = 2(l + w)$
c) $3x - 7 = 2$ and $3x + 2 - 9 = 2$
d) $5x + 4 = 1$ and $-2x + 4 + 7x = -1 + 2$
e) $12 - 5n = -7$ and $-5n + 12 = -7$

For a math project, Mani made up a math game which is played like Concentration. It provides practice in finding equivalent expressions.

$\dfrac{x+3}{2}$

$x+3 \div 2$

Concept Development

1. a) Suppose you turned over these cards $\boxed{\dfrac{x+3}{2}}$ $\boxed{x+3 \div 2}$. Do they match? Explain.

b) Do these cards $\boxed{\dfrac{x}{2} + \dfrac{3}{2}}$ and $\boxed{2(x+3)}$ match either card in part (a)? Explain.

c) How can you check if two expressions are equivalent?

2. Create another card that matches $\boxed{\dfrac{x+3}{2}}$.

3. Create several pairs of cards, each with equivalent expressions.

4. Work in a group. Create a deck of cards using everyone's pairs of equivalent expressions. Play the game.

5. A similar game can be played with equivalent equations.
Mani creates these pairs of equation cards. Do they match? Explain.

a) $\boxed{x=6}$ and $\boxed{x+2=8}$ **b)** $\boxed{2x=6}$ and $\boxed{\dfrac{x}{3}=1}$ **c)** $\boxed{x+1=4}$ and $\boxed{2x+2=8}$

6. a) Create another equation card that matches $\boxed{x=6}$.

b) Create an equivalent equation to match each of these cards.

$\boxed{2x=4}$ $\boxed{x+2=7}$ $\boxed{2x+2=7}$ $\boxed{\dfrac{x}{2}+\dfrac{1}{2}=1}$

$\boxed{3x+2=10}$ $\boxed{\dfrac{x}{3}=1}$ $\boxed{\dfrac{x}{3}-1=\dfrac{x}{2}}$ $\boxed{x-3=5}$

c) Explain how you created each equivalent equation.

7. Copy and complete each of these equations to create

an equation equivalent to $\boxed{3x=9}$. **a)** $\boxed{3x+1=}$ **b)** $\boxed{x-1=}$ **c)** $\boxed{6x+2=}$ **d)** $\boxed{\dfrac{x}{3}=}$ **e)** $\boxed{\dfrac{x}{2}+\dfrac{1}{2}=}$

1. Mani creates the following equations. Which ones in each group are equivalent? Explain.

a) $x + 1 = 6$

$2x + 2 = 12$

$2x + 1 = 12$

b) $x - 4 = 10$

$\frac{x}{2} - 2 = 10$

$\frac{x}{2} - 2 = 5$

c) $\frac{x}{3} - \frac{5}{3} = \frac{1}{3}$

$\frac{x - 5}{3} = \frac{1}{3}$

$x - 5 = 1$

d) $2x + 1 = 4$

$6x + 3 = 12$

$3(2x + 1) = 12$

e) $6x - 4 = 8$

$-6x + 4 = -8$

$\frac{3x}{2} - 1 = 2$

f) $\frac{x}{2} + 1 = 4$

$x + 2 = 8$

$\frac{x}{4} + \frac{1}{2} = 1$

g) $\frac{x + 3}{2} = 2$

$x + 5 = 6$

$x + 3 = 4$

h) $\frac{x + 3}{4} = 2$

$x + 3 = 8$

$x + 1 = 6$

In Your Journal

Describe two different methods to determine if equations are equivalent.

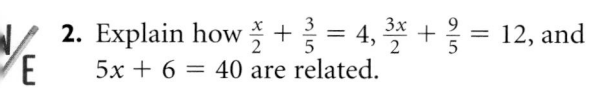

2. Explain how $\frac{x}{2} + \frac{3}{5} = 4$, $\frac{3x}{2} + \frac{9}{5} = 12$, and $5x + 6 = 40$ are related.

3. Work in a group.
- Each person creates an equation.
- Pass it to another group member to create 2 equivalent equations.
- Check each other's equations.
- Combine the cards into a deck and play Concentration involving a 3-card match.

4. a) Complete the table. Then write an equation to show the relationship between the amount of rain, r, and snow, s.

Snow (cm)	1.0	2.0	5.0	10.0	15.0	20.0
Rain (cm)	0.1	0.2	0.5	☐	☐	☐

b) Write two equivalent equations to show the relationship between rain and snow.

5. a) Complete the table. Then write an equation that relates the number of automobile carriers, c, with the number of automobiles that can be transported, a.

Number of carriers, c	Number of automobiles, a
7	56
12	96
20	160
25	☐
30	☐

b) Write two equivalent equations to show the relationship between automobiles and carriers.

6. The cost, C, in dollars for a large pizza from two different pizzerias is given by the equations $C_1 = \$7.85 + \$0.70t$ and $C_2 = \$6.95 + \$0.88t$, where t represents the number of toppings.

a) Are these equations equivalent?
b) Create two equivalent equations for each pizzeria.
c) Use guess and test to determine the number of toppings for which the costs of the pizzas are equal.

Equations From Data

A series of equilateral triangles
is made from toothpicks.

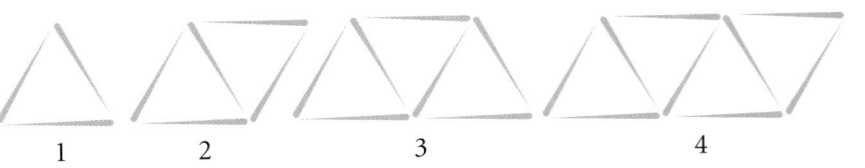

Number of triangles: 1   2   3   4

Knowing the number of triangles in a diagram can help you find the
number of toothpicks used.

The number of toothpicks can be determined from the number of
triangles by multiplying the number of triangles by 2, then adding 1.

An equation can be written to relate the number of triangles, n, and the
number of toothpicks, T. This equation can be used to determine the
number of toothpicks for any number of triangles in a diagram, as well
as the number of triangles for any number of toothpicks.

1. a) What equation can you write that connects the number of
toothpicks, T, and the number of triangles, n?
  b) Use your equation to find the number of toothpicks used to make
  100 triangles; 225 triangles.
  c) Use your equation to determine the number of triangles if 199
  toothpicks are used.

2. In the table, what is the constant difference between consecutive
values of T? How does this difference relate to the numerical
coefficient of n in the equation?

3. Graph the data. Is the relationship linear? Explain.

Number of triangles n	Number of toothpicks T
1	3
2	5
3	7
4	9

Applications

4. Write an equation for the data. Then draw the
graph. Tell which are linear.

a)

m	n
5	7
6	8
7	9
8	10

b)

x	y
0	−4
1	−1
2	2
3	5

c)

x	y
0	1
1	−1
2	−3
3	−5

5. Organize the coordinates from this graph in a
table. Write the equation.

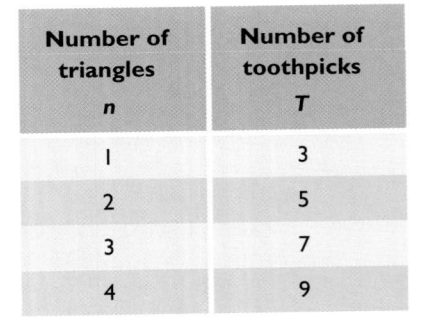

Problems to Investigate

THREE IN A ROW

Write an expression that represents the sum of three consecutive integers. Is the sum always divisible by 3? Explain.

CHANGING APPEARANCES

Write an expression without simplifying to describe each problem. Then write an equivalent expression. Choose a value for the variable and solve each problem.
a) There were twice as many women as men and ten more children than men. How many people were in the crowd?
b) Derek drove 3 h more than Erica and Josie drove three times as long as Erica. How many hours of driving was the trip?

GRAPHING EQUIVALENCE

Car rental company A charges $22 plus $0.90/km. Car rental company B charges $20 plus $1.00/km.
a) Represent each company's charges with an equation using two variables, d for distance and C for cost.
b) Make a table of values for each equation by substituting five values for the distance.
c) Create a graph for each table of values.
d) For what distance do the companies have an equivalent cost?

INVARIANT RATES

An invariant rate means the multiplier is always the same.
Complete the table. Create an equation to express the invariant rate in each table.

Mass (kg), m	0.5	1.0	2.5	5.0
Number of carrots, n	6	□	□	□

Number of slices, n	1	3	5	6
Mass of cheese (g), m	□	□	75	□

HOW CAN YOU TELL?

Write $=$ or $\neq$ to make each statement true. Explain.
a) $a + b + c$ ● $b + c + a$
b) $a - b$ ● $b - a$
c) $a \times b \div c$ ● $a \times (b \div c)$
d) $a + b \times c$ ● $b \times c + a$
e) $a + b \times c$ ● $a \times c + b$
f) $a \times (b + c)$ ● $(b + c) \times a$
g) $a \times (b - c)$ ● $a \times b - c$
h) $(a \times b) + c$ ● $(a + b) \times c$

Make up similar problems. Post them on the bulletin board for your classmates to solve.

10.3 Rearranging Formulas

The area of a circle is calculated using the formula $A = \pi r^2$ or $\pi r^2 = A$. Write the area formula in two ways for each shape.
a) a parallelogram
b) a triangle
Find the value for the variable h when b is 8 cm and A is 72 cm². Sketch each shape.

I n Canada and the United States the temperature is given in different units of measure. For example, 26°C is about 78°F (degrees Fahrenheit).

Concept Development

To find the temperature in degrees Fahrenheit, F, when you know the temperature in degrees Celsius, C, you multiply C by 9, divide by 5, and then add 32.

1. a) Write an algebraic equation which represents the formula for F.
   b) Check that it works by substituting known values. For example, when C is 0, F should be 32; and when C is 100, F should be 212.
   c) What is the Fahrenheit temperature when it is 20 degrees Celsius? -10 degrees Celsius?

If a Fahrenheit temperature is given, you can rearrange the formula to create an equivalent equation to find C in terms of F.
That is, $C =$ _____ or _____ $= C$.

To isolate C you must undo the operations in the formula for F.

2. a) What operations are used in the formula for F?
   b) $F - 32 = \frac{9C}{5}$ is equivalent to $F = \frac{9C}{5} + 32$. What was done to the second equation to get the first? What operation was undone?
   c) What must you do next to isolate the variable C? What operations are being undone?
   d) Change the formula for F to the equivalent formula for C by following the steps in parts (b) and (c). Check by substitution.

3. What is the Celsius temperature when it is
   a) 14 degrees Fahrenheit?
   b) 59 degrees Fahrenheit?

In Your Journal

Tell why $F = \frac{9C}{5} + 32$ and $F = \frac{9}{5} \times C + 32$ are equivalent. To isolate the variable C in both equations, do you follow the same steps? Explain. Why is it a good idea to check by substitution?

Solving an equation means writing an equivalent equation where one variable is alone on one side.

4. What operation(s) is used in each equation?
   What is the order to undo the operation(s) to isolate the variable?
   a) $r + 2 = 4$ **b)** $r - 2 = 4$ **c)** $2r = 4$ **d)** $\frac{r}{2} = 4$

   e) $2r + 2 = 4$ **f)** $2r - 2 = 4$ **g)** $\frac{r}{2} + 2 = 4$

5. Solve each equation in Problem 4. Write the equivalent equation, $r =$ _____.

6. An approximate relationship between Fahrenheit and Celsius, used to estimate mentally, is represented by F equals C plus 15, doubled.
   a) Write the equation.
   b) What is the approximate Fahrenheit temperature when it is 8°C? −8°C?
   c) What operation(s) exists in the formula?
   d) What is the order to undo the operation(s) to isolate C?
   e) Write the equivalent equation $C =$ _____.
   f) Express the formula in part (e) in words.
   g) What is the approximate Celsius temperature when it is 80°F? −20°F?

Understand and Apply

1. What is the inverse operation of each?
   a) $+5$ **b)** -5 **c)** $\times 5$
   d) $\div 5$ **e)** $\times (-5)$ **f)** $\div \frac{1}{5}$

2. What operations exist in each equation? What is the order of inverse operations to isolate the variable?
   a) $x + 4 = 10$ **b)** $x - 1 = 3$
   c) $2x = 6$ **d)** $-3x = 9$
   e) $\frac{x}{4} = 2$ **f)** $2x + 3 = 5$
   g) $-7 = 3x - 1$ **h)** $\frac{3x}{2} = 4$

3. Solve each equation in Problem 2. Why is it a good idea to check by substitution?

4. Use inverse operations to solve for x. Explain your steps.
   a) $\frac{2}{x} = 1$ **b)** $\frac{6}{x} = 2$ **c)** $\frac{4}{x} = 5$

5. Use inverse operations to isolate the underlined variable in each formula.
   a) $F = \underline{m}a$ **b)** $I = P\underline{R}T$
   c) $P = 2l + 2\underline{w}$ **d)** $A = p + pr\underline{t}$

6. Are the equations equivalent? Explain.

   a) $D = \frac{m}{V}$ and $V = \frac{m}{D}$

   b) $C = 2\pi r$ and $r = \frac{C}{2}$

   c) $v = u + at$ and $a = \frac{v - u}{t}$

7. The formula for the area of a trapezoid is $A = \frac{h(a + b)}{2}$. Write the formula to solve for
   a) h **b)** a **c)** b

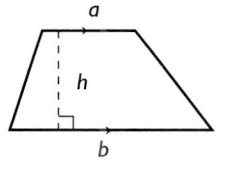

8. Complete the table using the formula in Problem 7.

A (cm²)	a (cm)	b (cm)	h (cm)
76	5	3	☐
30	2.5	☐	12
70	☐	5	20

Write an equation to find the total points earned by a hockey team, where w is the number of games won and t is the number of games tied. Display it in several equivalent forms. Use local information or the newspaper to determine the values of the variables for a local or professional hockey team.

10.4 Modelling Multi-Step Equations

Warm Up

What are the digits represented by the letters?

a)
```
      S O N G
  +   B I R D
  -----------
    S I N G S
```

b)
```
    T W E N T Y
    T W E N T Y
  + T H I R T Y
  -------------
  S E V E N T Y
```

> **O**ne bike rental store charges $3 an hour plus a $5 deposit. Another bike rental store charges $4 an hour with a $2 deposit.

Concept Development

Pablo wonders "For what number of hours will the charges for both rental stores be equal?"

To solve the problem, Pablo writes an equation and then models the equation using algebra tiles.

$$3x + 5 = 4x + 2$$

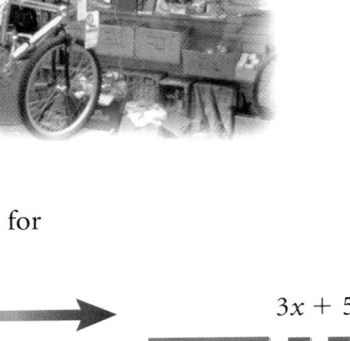

1. To place the terms with the variable x on one side, he uses the zero model.

  a) How many ($-x$) tiles did he use altogether? on each side?

  b) On which side did Pablo use the zero model?

$$3x - 3x + 5 = 4x - 3x + 2$$

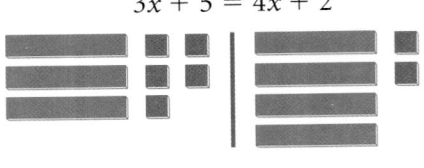

$$5 = x + 2$$

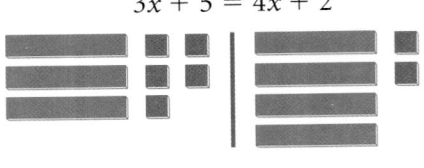

2. To place the numbers on one side, he uses the zero model again.

  a) How many (-1) tiles did he use on each side?

  b) On which side did Pablo use the zero model?

$$5 - 2 = x + 2 - 2$$

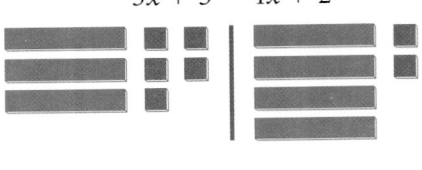

Pablo checks his result.

L.S. $3x + 5$	R.S. $4x + 2$
$= 3(3) + 5$	$= 4(3) + 2$
$= 9 + 5$	$= 12 + 2$
$= 14$	$= 14$

$$3 = x$$

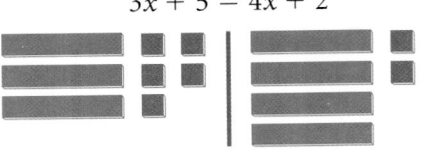

Pablo concludes that for 3 h, the rental charges are equal.

3. Algebra tiles are used to model, then solve $3x - 7 = -2x + 8$.
Explain what is happening in each step.

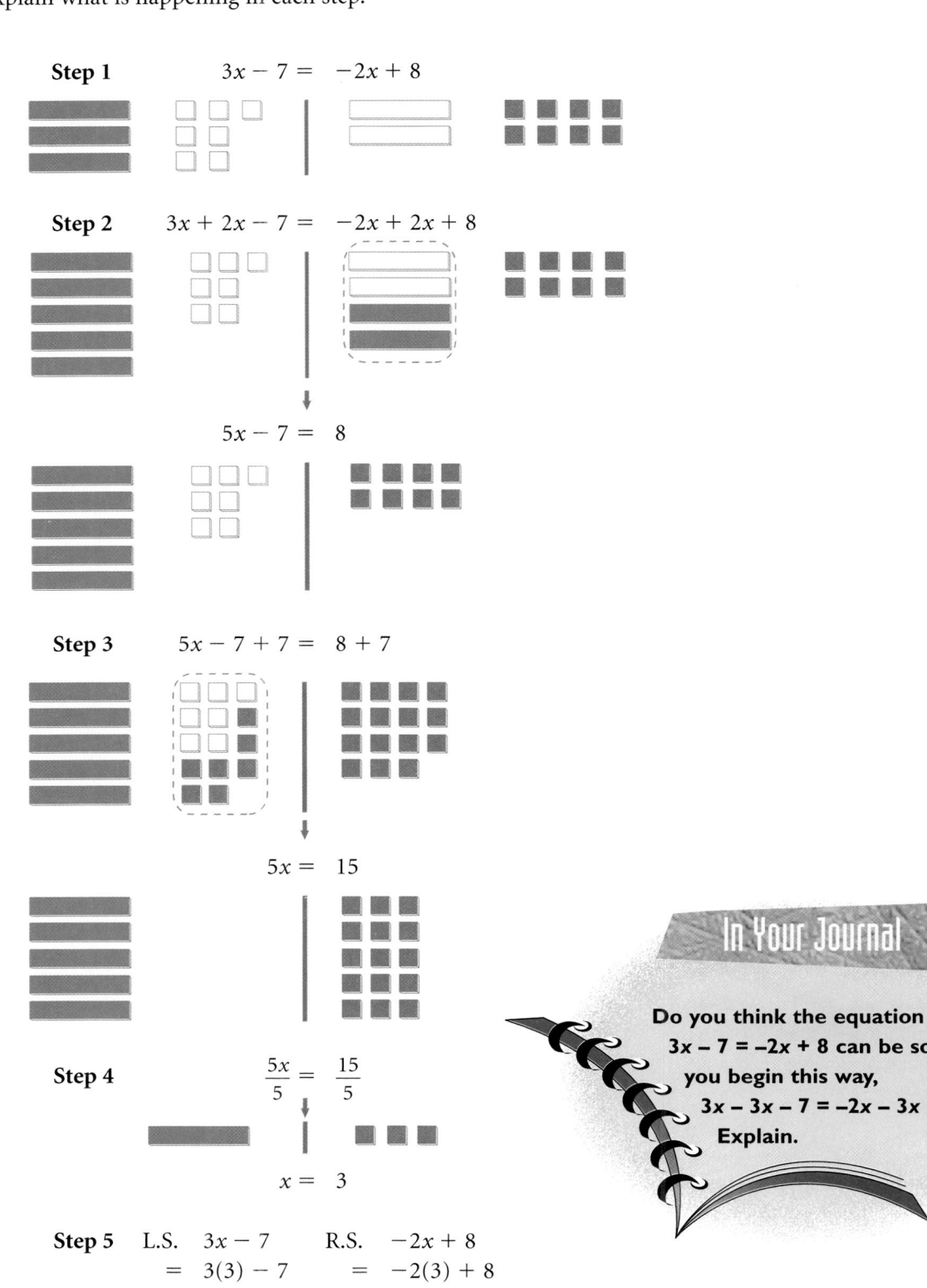

Step 1 $\quad\quad 3x - 7 = -2x + 8$

Step 2 $\quad 3x + 2x - 7 = -2x + 2x + 8$

$5x - 7 = 8$

Step 3 $\quad 5x - 7 + 7 = 8 + 7$

$5x = 15$

Step 4 $\quad\quad \dfrac{5x}{5} = \dfrac{15}{5}$

$x = 3$

Step 5 L.S. $\quad 3x - 7$ $\quad\quad$ R.S. $\quad -2x + 8$
$\quad\quad\quad = \quad 3(3) - 7$ $\quad\quad\quad\quad = \quad -2(3) + 8$
$\quad\quad\quad = \quad 9 - 7$ $\quad\quad\quad\quad\quad = \quad -6 + 8$
$\quad\quad\quad = \quad 2$ $\quad\quad\quad\quad\quad\quad = \quad 2$

In Your Journal

Do you think the equation
$3x - 7 = -2x + 8$ can be solved if
you begin this way,
$3x - 3x - 7 = -2x - 3x + 8$?
Explain.

233

Understand and Apply

1. Use the diagrams to solve the equation algebraically.

Step 1

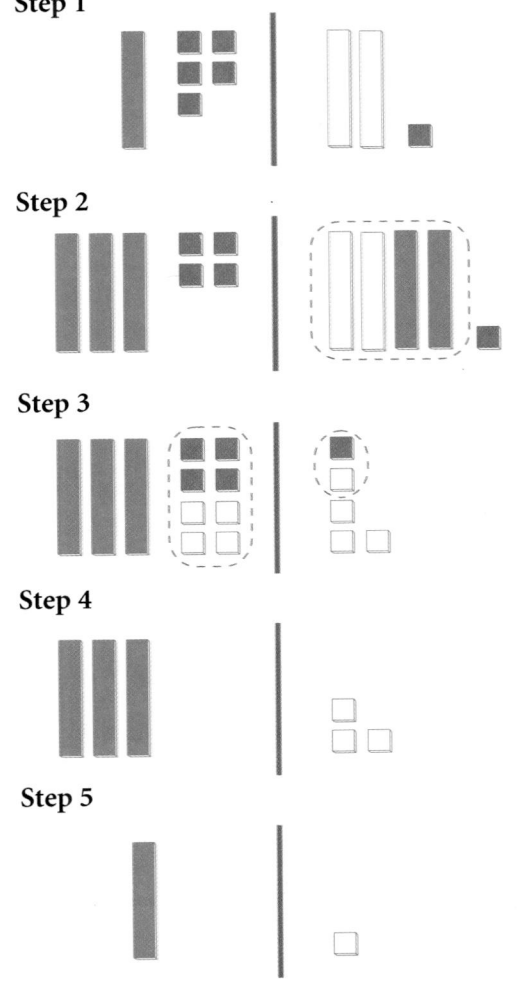

Step 2

Step 3

Step 4

Step 5

2. The equation $5x = 4 + 3x$ has been modelled with algebra tiles. Explain how you can use the tiles to explain a process for solving the equation algebraically.

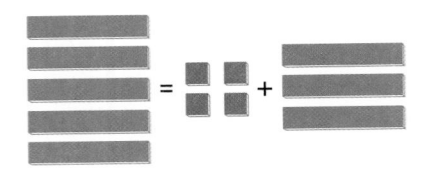

W/E 3. Solve using algebra tiles. Write your steps. Then check.
  a) $2x + 7 = 5$
  b) $10 = 3x + 1$
  c) $3x + 1 = x - 7$
  d) $5x - 3 = 2x + 6$
  e) $x - 4 = 3x + 2$
  f) $2x + 3 = 7x - 2$
  g) $-2x - 1 = x + 5$
  h) $3x - 4 = -x + 8$
  i) $-x + 3 = 5x - 9$
  j) $2x - 5 = -x + 7$

W/E 4. Use inverse operations to solve each equation by
  • placing the variable on one side of the equation
  • isolating the variable by placing the numbers on the other side of the equation
  • checking your result
  a) $3x - 1 = x + 2$
  b) $4x + 5 = 2x - 3$
  c) $-x + 1 = 3x - 3$
  d) $-2x - 1 = x + 5$
  e) $4x - 3 = x + 2$

5. Find the length of each side.
  a) Perimeter is 21 cm.

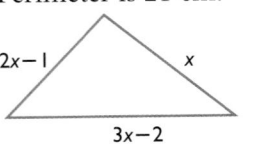

  b) Perimeter is 6 cm.

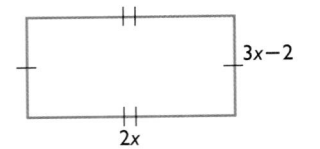

In Your Journal

Explain how algebra tiles demonstrate how inverse operations are used to solve equations.

234

10.5 Simplifying Equations

For a rectangular garden, Joel wants the length to be 3 m longer than twice the width. He plans to use 12 m of fencing, and needs to know what the garden's dimensions will be.

Concept Development

Joel follows these steps to solve the problem.

Step 1 – He draws a diagram and labels the width x and the length $2x + 3$.

Step 2 – He uses a formula for perimeter to create an equation.

$$P = 2\ell + 2w$$
$$12 = 2(2x + 3) + 2(x)$$

Step 3 – He models the equation using algebra tiles.

Step 4 – He simplifies the equation.

$$12 = 4x + 6 + 2x$$
$$12 = 6x + 6$$

Step 5 – He uses the zero model and inverse operations to solve the equation.

$$12 - 6 = 6x + 6 - 6$$
$$6 = 6x$$
$$\frac{6}{6} = \frac{6x}{6}$$
$$1 = x$$

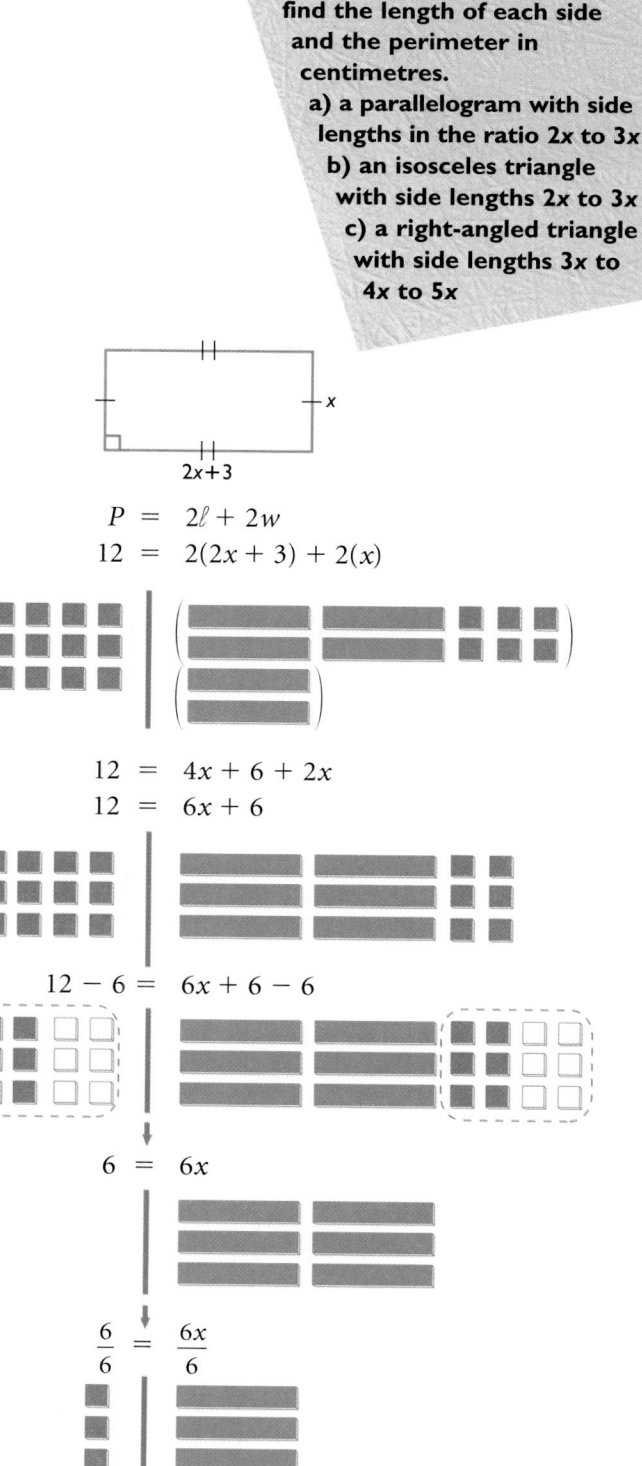

Step 6 –   He substitutes the value for x into his
                expressions for width and length.

> The width is x.
> The width is 1 m.
> The length is $2x + 3$.
> The length is $2(1) + 3$ or 5 m.

Step 7 –   He checks his dimensions.

$$P = 2\ell + 2w$$
$$= 2(5) + 2(1)$$
$$= 10 + 2$$
$$= 12$$

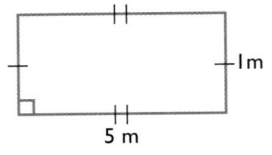

Marcia is also building a rectangular garden. She wants
the width to be one third of 2 m less than the length.
She plans to use all 12 m of fencing.

Marcia draws a diagram and labels the length x and the
width $\frac{1}{3}(x - 2)$ or $\frac{x-2}{3}$.

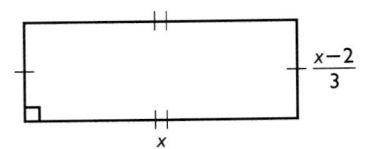

Marcia uses a formula for perimeter to write her equation.

$$P = 2(\ell + w)$$

$$12 = 2(x + \frac{x - 2}{3})$$

$$12 = 2x + 2\frac{(x - 2)}{3}$$

She simplifies the equation. $12 = 2x + \dfrac{2x - 4}{3}$

$$12 = 2x + \frac{2x}{3} - \frac{4}{3}$$

To clear the denominator, she multiplies each term by
the same number, the common denominator.

$$12 \times 3 = 2x \times 3 + \frac{2x}{3} \times 3 - \frac{4}{3} \times 3$$

$$36 = 6x + 2x - 4$$

She combines like terms. $36 = 8x - 4$

1. Solve Marcia's equation using inverse operations,
   then check the dimensions.

2. Why can't you model an equation such as

   $12 = 2(x + \frac{x - 2}{3})$ with algebra tiles?

236

1. Use algebra tiles to solve.
   a) $2(x + 1) = 3(x + 2)$
   b) $2(2x + 1) = 3(x + 1)$
   c) $2(4x - 5) = 3(-2x + 6)$

2. Solve, then check.
   a) $4(2x - 1) = 2(x + 4)$
   b) $2(3x - 1) = 5(x + 6)$
   c) $3(3y - 1) = 4(4y + 1)$
   d) $-3(4x - 1) = 5(-2x + 3)$
   e) $3(x - 4) + 5x = 2(3x - 1)$
   f) $2(-2y - 3) = 3(y - 2) - 7$

3. Determine the number to multiply by to clear the denominator.
   a) $\frac{1}{2} = \frac{3m}{4} - 1$
   b) $\frac{2n}{3} + \frac{1}{2} = \frac{3}{4}$
   c) $\frac{c}{4} = \frac{5c}{6} + \frac{1}{2}$
   d) $\frac{y + 1}{2} = \frac{2y - 3}{3}$

4. Solve.
   a) $\frac{1}{2} + \frac{3m}{4} = -1$
   b) $\frac{2y}{5} + \frac{1}{2} = \frac{3}{4}$
   c) $\frac{5}{6} = \frac{3d}{4} + \frac{1}{2}$
   d) $\frac{n}{2} - \frac{1}{3} = \frac{3}{4}$
   e) $\frac{x - 1}{5} = \frac{2x + 3}{4}$
   f) $\frac{3x - 1}{2} = \frac{x + 1}{3}$

5. a) Solve $\frac{m}{2} + \frac{1}{3} = \frac{3m}{4}$ using inverse operations. Do not clear the denominator first.
   b) Solve the equation again, this time clearing the denominator first.
   Which method do you prefer? Why?

6. Find the length of each side.
   a) Perimeter is 7 m.

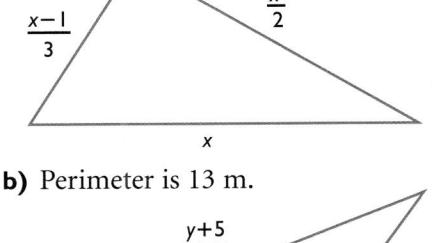

   b) Perimeter is 13 m.

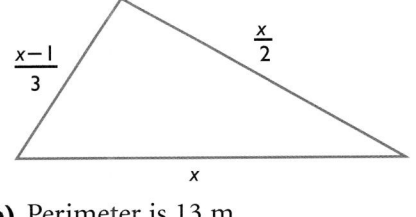

7. Why is there no solution for the equation $2(x - 1) = 2x + 5$?

8. Field crickets chirp faster as the air temperature rises. The approximate temperature in degrees Celsius can be determined using the equation $C = \frac{5(n + 8)}{9}$, where n represents the number of chirps made in 14 seconds. Find the number of chirps for each of the following temperatures.

   a) 10°C
   b) 15°C
   c) What is the lowest possible temperature that can be approximated using this equation? Explain.

9. Explain the steps you would use to solve each equation algebraically.
   a) $\frac{12}{x} = 6$
   b) $-\frac{12}{x} = 3$
   c) $-\frac{4}{x} = -8$

10. Simplify, then solve. Check your result.
    a) $(a - 1)^2 + 4^2 = (a + 1)^2$
    b) $(x + 3)(x - 3) = 16$

10.6 Creating Equations to Solve Problems

8.5 Million Dollar Jackpot Won By Students!!

Brittany, Jennifer, and Brad had invested weekly in LOTTO 6/49 tickets. Last Saturday they won the Jackpot! After a brief Mediterranean cruise, the students plan to complete their university education and make wise investments with their new wealth.

Concept Development

Brittany contributed $3, Jennifer $2, and Brad $5 to buy the winning ticket. To find out how much money each will receive, Brad lets x represent the value of one share of the money.

Brad creates this equation. $3x + 2x + 5x = 8\ 500\ 000$

The equation simplifies to $10x = 8\ 500\ 000$

Solve for x. $$\frac{10x}{10} = \frac{8\ 500\ 000}{10}$$
$$x = 850\ 000$$

Each share is $850 000.

Brittany receives 3 shares or 3($850 000) or $2 550 000.

1. Find Jennifer's and Brad's winnings.

2. At a record store, compact disks cost $14.00 for the first one and $13.00 for each additional one. Yolanda bought c compact disks and spent n dollars. Write an equation which represents the relationship between the number of compact disks and the total cost. Solve for c if she spent $53.00 altogether.

Understand and Apply

Create an equation for each problem, then solve. Check to make sure your solution is reasonable.

1. The band for a school dance charges $150 plus $90 per hour, not including set up and take down time. If the school has budgeted $555, how long can the band play?

2. A class is going to a theatrical performance. It costs $8.50 per person and $150 for the bus. If the class has earned $388 through fundraising to cover the trip, how many are in the class?

3. Melissa has $45 saved and earns $19.00 per week. Rebecca has $28 saved and earns $20.50 per week. Who will be the first to afford a school ski trip that costs $520?

4. Darren's Mathematics mark is 12% higher than his French mark. If the average of the two marks is 88%, what is each mark?

5. Bronwen received 80% on an English test. She got 45 marks. What was the total number of marks for the test?

6. If you are y years old now, how would you represent your age
   a) in 2 years?
   b) 2 years ago?
   c) 3 years from now?
   d) 5 years before now?

7. Archie's teacher refused to reveal her age. After being begged for a hint she finally admitted that in 12 years she would be three times as old as she was 30 years ago. How old is she?

8. Three brothers have ages that are three consecutive numbers. If the sum of their ages is 57, what are their ages?

9. A string 50 cm long is cut into three pieces. One piece is twice as long as the shortest piece, and the third piece is 10 cm longer than the shortest piece. What is the length of each piece?

10. Mr. Dean would like to build a deck with the length 4 m longer than twice the width. He has 56 m of railing. What are the dimensions of his deck?

11. Write an expression to determine the total amount of money in cents for
    a) x dimes
    b) $(y + 1)$ nickels
    c) $3w$ quarters
    d) $(2w + 1)$ dollar coins

12. Alex has four times as many quarters as nickels and five more dimes than nickels in his coin bank. If he has $12.00 in change in the coin bank, how many of each coin does he have?

13. Mark wanted to get a photograph enlarged so that the length and the width would be twice those of the original. Since the original cost $1.40, Mark assumed that the enlargement would cost $2.80. Does this seem reasonable? Explain.

14. At the opposite ends of a pool 480 m long, two swimmers jump in at the same time. One swims at 70 m/min, and the other swims at 80 m/min.
    a) What distance will each swim in x minutes?
    b) Draw a diagram to help you write an equation to represent where they meet.
    c) How many minutes will it take the swimmers to meet?
    d) How far will each have gone?

15. In a horse race, Brown Eyes is 10 m ahead of Dynamite. Brown Eyes is running at 15 m/s and Dynamite quickens the pace at 17 m/s. How long will it take Dynamite to catch up to Brown Eyes?

16. Create a similar age, money, or measurement problem. Give it to a partner to solve.

17. Suppose c represents the number of compact disks and $c + c + 4 + 2c = 56$. Write a problem using this information.

HOME LINK

Use newspapers or magazines to find puzzles that can be solved using a single variable equation.

Solving Equations

There are many ways to solve $2(2x + 1) = 3(x + 1)$.
Here are some. Can you think of others?

1. You can solve by guessing and testing after simplifying.

$2(2x + 1) = 3(x + 1)$ $\longrightarrow$ $4x + 2 = 3x + 3$

Guess for x	L.S. $4x + 2$	R.S. $3x + 3$	Is x High/Low?
-1	$4(-1) + 2 = -2$	$3(-1) + 3 = 0$	Low
0	$4(0) + 2 = 2$	$3(0) + 3 = 3$	Low
1	$4(1) + 2 = 6$	$3(1) + 3 = 6$	$\sqrt{}$ $\qquad x = 1$

2. You can use balance scales.

Each bag represents x and each dot represents one marble.

To isolate 1 bag, remove 3 bags from each side.

Then remove 2 marbles from each side.

One bag is equal to 1 marble.

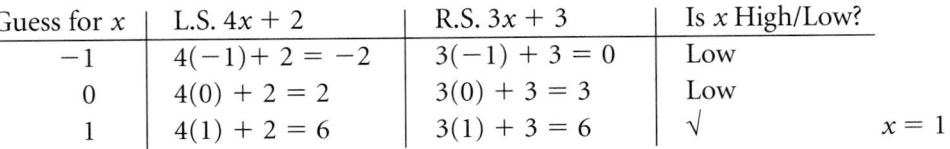

$2(2x + 1) = 3(x + 1)$ $\qquad\qquad$ $x + 2 = 3$ $\qquad\qquad$ $x = 1$

3. You can use algebra tiles.

Model the equation.

$2(2x + 1) = 3(x + 1)$

Isolate the x tiles – use the zero model.

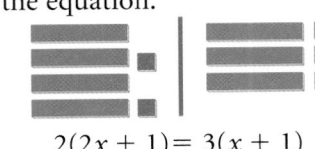

$x + 2 = 3$

Isolate the numbers – use the zero model.

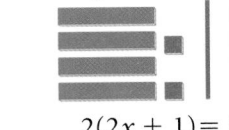

$x = 1$

4. You can use inverse operations to isolate the variable after simplifying.

$$\overbrace{2(2x + 1)} = \overbrace{3(x + 1)}$$
$$4x + 2 = 3x + 3$$
$$4x - 3x + 2 = 3x - 3x + 3$$
$$x + 2 = 3$$
$$x + 2 - 2 = 3 - 2$$
$$x = 1$$

Understand and Apply

Solve each equation using two methods. Check.

1. $2x + 5 = x - 1$ $\qquad$ **2.** $3(2x + 4) = 4(x - 1)$ $\qquad$ **3.** $\dfrac{x - 1}{3} = \dfrac{x}{2}$ $\qquad$ **4.** $\dfrac{x + 3}{5} = \dfrac{2x + 3}{9}$

Problems to Investigate

VERSATILE TILES

Use algebra tiles to
a) demonstrate the equivalency
of $3x - 4 = 5$ and $6x - 8 = 10$
b) solve $2(-x + 3) = -4$

SECTIONING OFF

A log measuring 2 m in length is cut
into three sections. One section is
twice as long as the shortest section,
and the other section is 20 cm longer
that the shortest section. Find the
length of each section.

WHAT'S IN THE BAG?

Each bag contains an equal
number of marbles. How many
marbles are in one bag?

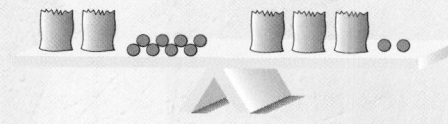

EQUATING PERIMETER AND AREA

a) Find expressions for the perimeter
and area of a rectangle whose length
is 4 m less than twice the width.
b) What value for the variable results
in the perimeter and area being equal?

CONSECUTIVE NUMBERS

Write an expression for each.
a) The sum of two consecutive numbers
is $2n + 7$. What is the greater number?
b) The sum of three consecutive numbers
is $6n + 9$. What is the least number?
c) The sum of four consecutive numbers
is $4n - 10$. What is the least number?

PROBLEM GENERATOR

Create a problem that would be
represented by each equation.
a) $2(c - 1) = c$
b) $\dfrac{(x - 1)}{2} = 5$

Make up similar problems.
Post them on the bulletin board
for your classmates to solve.

10.7 Testing Inequalities

Warm Up

Arrange the digits from I to 8 in the squares to make true statements.

■ + ■ < ■ + ■

■ − ■ > ■ + ■

> **W**rite your age. Write the age of a parent or guardian. Show the relationship between the two ages by writing an inequality using < or >.

Concept Development

1. Apply each operation to your inequality.
   - Add 2 to each side.
   - Subtract 2 from each side.
   - Multiply each side by 2.
   - Multiply each side by (-2).
   - Divide each side by 2.
   - Divide each side by (-2).
   a) Which operation(s) kept the inequality true?
   b) Which operation(s) resulted in the inequality being false?
   c) How can the false inequalities be rewritten to make them true?

2. **a)** Copy and complete this chart for an inequality that involves a negative number.
   b) Which operation(s) made the inequality false?
   c) How can the false inequalities be rewritten to make the statement true?
   d) Do the same rules apply when the inequality includes negative numbers?

Inequality	Operation to both sides	New inequality	True or false
$-5 < 10$	$+ 5$	$0 < 15$	True
$-5 < 10$	$- 5$		
$-5 < 10$	multiply by 5		
$-5 < 10$	multiply by (-5)		
$-5 < 10$	divide by 5		
$-5 < 10$	divide by (-5)		

3. Twice Marvin's age is less than his age increased by 10 years.
   a) Write the inequality using the variable a to represent Marvin's age.
   b) What operation to both sides of the inequality will isolate a in order to solve the inequality?
   c) How do you know that the inequality will still be true? (Hint: What did you discover in Problem 1?)
   d) Solve the inequality to find what ages Marvin might be.
   e) Check your solution by substituting appropriate values for a, from part (d), in your original inequality from part (a).

4. Explain what is happening in each step of this solution.

$$\frac{d}{-3} > 5$$

$$(-3)\frac{d}{-3} < 5(-3)$$

$$d < -15$$

1. Does the value for d make a true statement?
   a) $d - 1 \leq 7, d = 5$

   b) $3d + 2 > 8, d = 2$

   c) $\frac{d}{-3} > 5, d = 18$

   d) $\frac{d}{-2} - 1 \leq -3, d = 4$

   e) $-4d \geq 10, d = -2$

   f) $-2d + 3 < 11, d = -4$

2. Are $-3, 4, -7,$ and 7 all solutions to $2x - 3 > 5$? Explain.

3. When the inequality is solved, will the inequality sign reverse direction? Explain why or why not.
   a) $3x \leq -6$

   b) $3x - 1 > 5$

   c) $\frac{x}{-2} \leq 7$

   d) $-4x > 8$

   e) $-5x - 1 \geq 9$

   f) $\frac{x}{-3} + 1 < 7$

4. List in order the operations to undo to solve the inequality. Which inequality signs will reverse direction?
   a) $2y + 1 > 5$

   b) $-3y - 6 \leq 12$

   c) $\frac{y}{2} - 3 \leq 1$

   d) $\frac{y}{-5} + 1 > 2$

5. Solve, then check.
   a) $3x + 1 \leq 7$

   b) $4y - 1 > 2y + 3$

   c) $-2x + 1 > -3$

   d) $-5y + 2 \leq 2y - 5$

   e) $\frac{x}{2} - \frac{1}{3} \leq 2$

   f) $\frac{x}{-3} + 1 > 5$

   g) $-3(x + 4) \leq 6$

   h) $-2(2x - 1) \geq -5(x + 1)$

6. Student council charges $5.50 for each dance ticket. What is the least number of dance tickets to be sold to earn at least $1200?

7. Marvin is four years older than his sister. At least how old must each be if the sum of their ages is greater than 12?

8. Based on Marvin's age range in Problem 3 of *Concept Development* and his age range in Problem 7, what is his probable age?

9. If Tania received 68%, 73%, 84%, and 85% on her first four tests, what must her fifth mark be to get an average of at least 80%?

10. On a shopping trip Marcia had $250 to spend which must include tax. She purchased 3 sweaters at $29.98 each, 2 pairs of jeans at $34.95 each, and shoes at $24.95. What is the value of the last item she can purchase, including tax?

HOME LINK

Ask a family member or friend who is in business to help you list examples from business where inequality statements play a role in success.

In Your Journal

Explain why the inequality sign must sometimes be reversed when solving inequations.

10.8 Graphing Inequalities

Universities Have Minimum
Acceptance Standard of 85%

New Speeds on
Highways

MAXIMUM
100
km/h

MINIMUM
70
km/h

Fire Breaks Out In
Overcrowded Meeting Room
Room capacity of 30 was exceeded.

Warm Up

Label the graphs so that
each graph is an accurate
description of an inequality
relationship that exists in
your class or school. Write
a brief interpretation of
each graph using "fewer
than", "more than", …

a)   b)

Concept Development

1. Create an inequality for each of the above news releases.

The solution to an inequality contains more than one number.
These numbers can be graphed on

a whole number line,

$$0 \quad 1 \quad 2 \quad 3 \quad 4$$

an integer number line,

$$-2 \quad -1 \quad 0 \quad 1 \quad 2 \quad 3$$

or a real number line.

$$-2 \quad -1 \quad \frac{-1}{2} \quad 0 \quad \frac{1}{2} \quad 1 \quad 2 \quad 3$$

2. a) Why does a real number line suit the university
standards and speed situations best?

$$0 \quad 10\% \quad 20\% \quad 30\% \qquad\qquad x \geq 85\%$$

$$0 \quad 10 \quad 20 \quad 30 \qquad\qquad 70 \qquad\qquad 100$$
$$s \geq 70 \text{ and } s \leq 100$$

b) Why does a whole number line suit the room capacity?

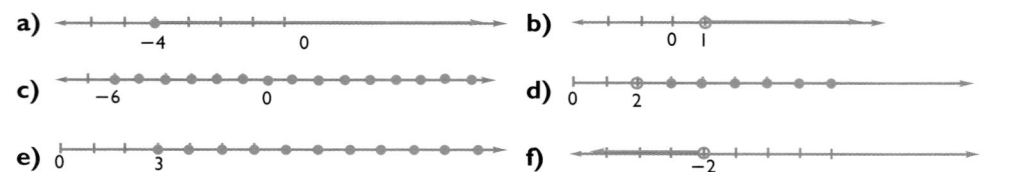

$$0 \qquad\qquad 10 \qquad\qquad 20 \qquad\qquad 30 \quad c \geq 30$$

In Your Journal

Describe the difference between
a) a whole number line and an
integer number line
b) a whole or integer number
line and a real number line

3. a) Use the variable x to create an inequality to
represent this situation: Riders must be 120 cm or
under to ride on certain rides at the amusement park.
b) Represent your inequality on a number line.
Explain why you chose the number line you used.

x belongs to the set of
integers (I), whole
numbers (N_o), or real
numbers (R).

4. Use the variable x to create an inequality for each graph.
State the number line to be used as $x \in$ I, $x \in N_o$, or $x \in$ R.

a)
$$-4 \qquad 0$$

b)
$$0 \quad 1$$

c)
$$-6 \qquad 0$$

d)
$$0 \quad 2$$

e) $0 \qquad 3$

f)
$$-2$$

1. Graph the solution set using an integer number line, then a real number line.

   a) $x \geq -4$ **b)** $y < 6$

   c) $w > -5$ **d)** $V \leq 2$

   e) $x - 5 < 12$ **f)** $y + 5 \geq -3$

2. Solve and graph when $x \in I$.

   a) $2x - 3 \geq -9$

   b) $2(x - 5) < 2$

   c) $3(x - 1) \leq -2(x + 1) + 4$

   d) $-4x + 1 \geq 9$

   e) $\frac{x}{2} - 1 \geq 3$

   f) $\frac{x}{-3} - 1 < 2$

   g) $-2x + 3 > 10$

   h) $-4(x-1) < 3x$

3. Solve and graph when $y \in R$.

   a) $y + 2 < 5$

   b) $3y - 8 \leq 7$

   c) $-2y - 1 \geq -3$

   d) $\frac{y}{-4} + 1 > 3$

   e) $-2y + 4 < -y + 7$

   f) $-4(y - 1) < 3y$

   g) $\frac{(y - 2)}{2} \leq 1$

   h) $\frac{(y - 1)}{2} > \frac{(2y + 1)}{3}$

4. Write an inequality that represents each graph.

   a)

   b)

   c)

   d)

   e)

   f)

5. State the set of numbers that each solution set in Problem 4 belongs to.

6. Write an inequality which would represent each situation. Graph the solution set.

   a)

MAXIMUM
90 km/h
MINIMUM
40 km/h

   b)

**Room Capacity
250 people**

   c)

MAXIMUM MASS
15 TONNES

7. The Matthews family has $1200 extra per month to spend on entertainment. To keep to their budget, how much can each of the six family members spend per week if they share the amount equally? Create an inequality. Graph the solution set.

Look for situations that involve inequalities, such as the height of an overpass on a highway, or the maximum capacity on a bus. Write the inequations and graph them on a number line.

H O M E   L I N K

TRUCKS
OVER 6.5 m

Problems to Investigate

TWO VARIABLE INEQUATIONS

$x + 2y < 10$ is an inequation with 2 variables, where $x, y \in I$. Copy and complete the charts to keep the statement true. Plot these 30 ordered pairs on coordinate axes. What do you notice?

x	−2	−2	−2	−2	−2	−1	−1	−1	−1	−1	0	0	0	0	0
y															

x	1	1	1	1	1	2	2	2	2	2	3	3	3	3	3
y															

TOOTHPICK TRIANGLES

Create triangles with the following numbers of toothpicks. Sketch as many different triangles as you can for each given number of toothpicks. What inequality relationship do you notice about the sides of a triangle?

What do you notice about the relationship between the lengths of the sides and the measure of the angles in a triangle?

Number of toothpicks	Sketches of possible triangles	Classification of each triangle
2		
3		
4		
5		
6		
7		
8		
9		

DIFFERENT GRAPHS

Draw a graph for $-11 \leq 2x + 5 \leq 11, x \in I$.
Draw a graph for $-11 \leq 2x + 5 \leq 11, x \in R$.
How are your graphs alike? different? Explain.

MAXIMUM PERIMETER

The perimeter of the hexagon is less than 48 cm. Express this as an inequation. Solve the inequation. List 3 possible lengths of the sides.

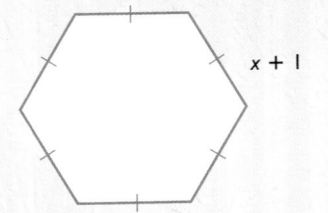

$x + 1$

Make up a similar perimeter problem. Give it to a partner to solve.

Solve Problems by Using Algebra

DRIVING DILEMMA

Traci kept a journal of a ski trip. She took 5.1 h to drive 402 km to the mountains. On the icy roads she drove 60 km/h. On the dry roads she drove 90 km/h. How many hours did Traci drive on icy roads?

▶ Understand the Problem

1. What are you asked to find?
2. What do you know?
3. Where will you begin?

Traci began by drawing a diagram and making a chart to help understand the problem and organize the information. ➡

402 km in 5.1h

	d (km)	s (km/h)	t (h)
icy roads		60	
dry roads		90	
totals	402		5.1

▶ Make a Plan

Traci uses algebra. She uses x to represent what is unknown – the time spent in hours on icy roads.

▶ Carry Out the Plan

She records x in the appropriate places in her chart, then uses the total to fill in the last column. ➡

	d (km)	s (km/h)	t (h)
icy roads		60	x
dry roads		90	$5.1 - x$
totals	402		5.1

4. Explain how $5.1 - x$ represents the time on dry roads.

Next, Traci uses the formula $d = st$ to complete the first column and then uses the first column to create an equation. ➡

	d (km)	s (km/h)	t (h)
icy roads	$60x$	60	x
dry roads	$90(5.1 - x)$	90	$5.1 - x$
totals	402		5.1

5. a) What equation would you write using the information involving distance?
   b) Does your equation agree with Traci's diagram? Explain.
   c) Solve the equation.

▶ Look Back

6. Is the answer reasonable?

Applications

PASSING THE LEADER

Two drivers leave Boonville on the same road 1 h apart. The first driver travels at 80 km/h. What speed must the second driver maintain in order to overtake the first driver in 4 h?

HOME IMPROVEMENT

The pane of glass in a square window is broken. A replacement pane is cut but it is 8 cm longer and 4 cm shorter than it should be. The area of the incorrect replacement pane is 88 cm² more than the area of the original pane. What should be the dimensions of a correctly cut replacement pane?

POPULATION CONTROL

In a northern lake, 150 fish were captured by nets, tagged, and then released. A month later, 100 fish were captured by nets. Of these, 30 had tags. How many fish would you estimate to be in the lake?

1. Create an equivalent equation for each.
   a) $2x + 3 = 5$
   b) $\frac{x}{2} - \frac{1}{3} = 2$
   c) $\frac{x-1}{3} = \frac{x+3}{3}$

2. Explain how you would determine if these equations are equivalent.
   $C = \pi d$ and $d = \frac{C}{\pi}$ and $\pi = \frac{C}{d}$

3. Solve for each underlined variable.
   a) $E = \underline{m}c^2$
   b) $y = \underline{m}x + b$
   c) $I = \frac{E}{R + r}$
   d) $V = \frac{2}{3}\pi r^2\underline{h}$

4. Solve by using inverse operations.
   a) $7x - 3 = 4x + 9$
   b) $\frac{y}{2} - 1 = 5$
   c) $\frac{y}{2} + \frac{2}{3} = \frac{5}{6}$
   d) $\frac{x+2}{4} = \frac{x-1}{3}$
   e) $-5x + 3 = -x - 9$
   f) $2(4x - 3) = 3(2x + 1)$
   g) $-3(x - 1) = 2(x + 9)$

5. Use algebra tiles to solve. Write your steps.
   a) $5x - 7 = 2x + 2$
   b) $2y - 4 = 4y + 6$
   c) $3x - 4 = x + 8$
   d) $-y + 1 = 4y - 4$
   e) $3(x + 1) = 2(x - 2)$

6. Create an equation to represent each situation.

   a)

Time (h)	1	2	3	...	10
Distance (km)	3.1	6.2	9.3	...	

   b) Quick Stitch company charged $70.00, based on a $10 flat fee plus $15 an hour for repairs.

   c)
   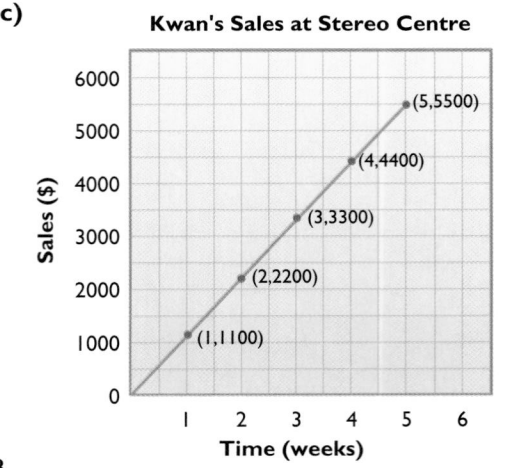

7. Two gardens have a difference in area of 48 m². In one garden the length is 2 m more than three times the width. In the smaller garden the width is the same but the length is 4 m less than three times the width. Create an equation, then solve it to find the dimensions.

8. A score of 15 on a test gives a mark of about 62%. What total is the test out of?

9. Two planes took off from the same airport at the same time and flew in opposite directions. Plane A flew 240 km/h and Plane B flew 320 km/h. Create an equation, then solve it to determine how long the planes had been flying when they were 1680 km apart? How far had each plane flown?

10. To print business cards, a company charges $12 as a set up fee and an additional $4 per box of 100 cards. What is the greatest number of boxes of cards you can have printed for under $100?

11. Create a problem using the formula $d = 0.32t$ (d is distance in kilometres and t is amount of time in seconds between seeing lightning and hearing thunder) to predict your distance from the centre of a thunder and lightning storm. Give it to a partner to solve.

12. Solve each inequality.
    a) $4x - 5 > 2x + 9$
    b) $5 - 2y < 3y + 10$
    c) $2(e + 3) \geq e - 8$
    d) $5(h - 2) - h < 2(3h + 2)$
    e) $\frac{x + 6}{-3} > 2$
    f) $\frac{x + 2}{4} \leq \frac{x - 1}{6}$

13. Graph the solutions to Problem 12 on a real number line.

Practise With Games

Play both games in pairs.

Tic Tac Toe

- Copy the Tic Tac Toe board onto a piece of paper.

- Deal six Equation Cards face down in a pile to each player.

- Flip a coin to determine which player begins.

- The first player turns over his/her top card, then solves the equation.

- The other player checks the solution by substitution. If the solution is correct, the first player records an X or O on the Tic Tac Toe board.

- Now the second player follows the same procedure.

- The first player to get a row of X's or O's wins the game.

$$2(x + 1) = 3x - 4$$

$$-3(2x - 1) = 4(x + 2)$$

$$\frac{x - 1}{2} + \frac{x}{3} = \frac{7}{6}$$

$$\frac{x}{4} = \frac{x - 1}{3}$$

Winner's Circle

$$3x - 1 = 5x + 7$$

$$\frac{x}{2} + \frac{1}{3} = \frac{x}{6}$$

- Place the deck of Equation Cards face down between players.

- Flip a coin to determine which player goes first.

- The first player rolls the die, turns over the top card, and has 60 s to solve the equation. The correct solution (to be checked by the other player) allows the first player to move a marker on the gameboard the number of spaces showing on the die. An incorrect solution allows the other player to move half the number rolled.

- If the number on the die matches the number on the gameboard where the marker lands, that player moves the marker again an equal number of spaces.

- Players alternate turns.

- The first player to reach the finish wins.

THE WINNER'S CIRCLE

1. A square garden is surrounded by square patio stones. What is the relationship between the length of a side of the garden and the number of patio stones?

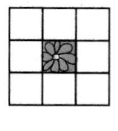 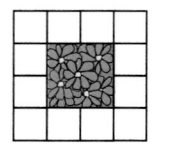 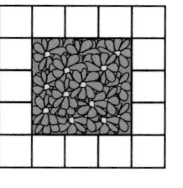

Length, *s*			
Number of stones, *n*			

2. Cab fare is $3.00 plus $1.10 for each kilometre.
a) Create an equation to show the relationship between the fare and distance travelled.
b) Rearrange the equation to show the relationship between distance travelled and the fares collected.

3. Use inverse operations to solve the following equations. Check each solution using tiles.
a) $3x - 2 = x + 8$ **b)** $2(y - 3) = 5y + 3$

4. Use algebra tiles to solve the following equations. Write your steps.
a) $5x + 2 = 3x - 6$ **b)** $4y - 3 = 6y - 5$
c) $3(y + 1) = 2(y - 1)$ **d)** $4(x - 1) = 2(x + 2)$

5. a) Check if $x = 1$, -2, or 5 is a solution to the
equation $\dfrac{x - 1}{2} + \dfrac{x}{3} = \dfrac{2x - 1}{3} + \dfrac{x - 1}{6}$.
b) Choose another number and check if it is also a solution.
c) Solve the equation. Use your result to explain what happened in parts (a) and (b).
d) Create your own equation that will have similar results.

6. Create an equation that has no solution.

7. A special round-trip fare from Toronto to Calgary is 35% off the regular fare. This special saves you $192.50. Create an equation for the situation. Find the regular price of the round-trip fare.

8. A scientist measured and recorded the following data for these substances. How do you think the volume was measured?

Substance	Density (g/cm³)	Mass (g)	Volume (cm³)
Gold	19.32	966	50
Water	1.00	250	250
Iron	7.87	787	100
Quartz	2.66	200	75
Paraffin Wax	0.87	435	500

a) Write an equation that shows the relationship between D, m, and V.
b) Determine two other values for mass and volume for each substance.
c) The density of aluminum is 2.70 g/cm³. What is the volume of a piece of aluminum foil if its mass is 75 g?

9. The second angle in a triangle is 10 degrees greater than the first angle. The third angle is three times as large as the first. What is the size of each angle?

10. Create an equation to determine the current cost of gasoline for different amounts.

11. Use $>$ or $<$ to make each statement true.
a) $x + 5 > 8$
     $x + 5 - 5$ ⬤ $8 - 5$
b) $x > 3$
     $2x$ ⬤ $2(3)$
c) $x < 3$
     $-2x$ ⬤ $-2(3)$
d) $4n > -8$
     $\dfrac{4n}{-4}$ ⬤ $\dfrac{-8}{-4}$

12. Jason has to keep his phone bill below $60. The basic charge is $18 and it costs $2/minute to call a friend in Europe.
a) Create the inequation.
b) Solve the inequation to determine how many minutes John can talk to his friend in a month.

Communicate Your Knowledge

1. Describe the types of equations that can be solved with algebra tiles. Give some examples. Also give some examples of equations that would be impossible to solve with algebra tiles. Explain why.

6. What do you have to watch for when solving and graphing inequations?

2. Demonstrate as many different ways as possible to create equations that are equivalent to $\frac{x+3}{2} = 4$.

5. Why are equations used to solve many types of problems? What other methods can be used?

3. Explain to a partner different ways to solve

$$2(x + 3) + 1 = 3x + 2(x - 1).$$

4. Explain why substitution is a better way to check a solution than solving the equation a second time.

What questions do you still have about equations and inequations?

Similarity and Trigonometry

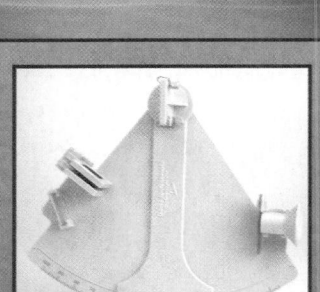

Navigation is one field that uses a branch of mathematics known as trigonometry.

Navigation uses many formulas. Some are simple and some are more complex.

• Calculate the distance one sails in 2 h if the current speed is 3 km/h and the wind speed is 7 km/h using

distance = (current speed + wind speed) × time

• Calculate the distance-off a lighthouse with a charted height of 114 m is when the sextant angle is 2.25° and the tide is 3.35 m below high tide using

distance-off =

$$\frac{\text{(charted height + tide level below high tide)} \times 0.049\,44}{\text{sextant angle}}$$

• Another formula used in navigation is

sine of corrected angle =

$$\frac{\text{current speed} \times \text{sine of relative angle}}{\text{boat speed}}$$

Examine your scientific calculator and locate the SIN key.

What other keys on your calculator
might be related to the SIN key?

11.1 Finding Congruent Triangles

Warm Up

Sketch △KEY where ∠*E* = 50°, *KE* = 8 cm, and *EY* = 5 cm. Then use a centimetre ruler, compasses, and a protractor to draw it.

This illustration is an optical illusion.

Concept Development

1. a) Do you think the two characters are congruent?
   b) How can you tell for sure?

2. Which of the following are always true about congruent shapes?
   a) same shape
   b) same size
   c) same orientation
   d) corresponding angles equal
   e) corresponding sides equal

3. a) Draw two congruent triangles which show that one of the above characteristics is not always true for congruence.
   b) How did you draw your triangles?
   c) Mark the sides that are equal and the angles that are equal.
   d) These are Gina's triangles. What method did she use?

254

4. If you could not
  • cut out a triangle to try to fit it on top of another
  • trace one triangle and try to fit the tracing on top of another
  • fold the page to try to fit one triangle on top of another
to test for congruency, what might you do?

5. Do you think it would be necessary to measure all three pairs of sides and all three pairs of angles to determine congruency?

Understand and Apply

Use a millimetre ruler, compasses, and a protractor to construct these triangles.

1. a) Make a sketch and then draw $\triangle ABC$ where $AB = 5$ cm and $BC = 8$ cm.
b) Compare your triangle with five other students'. Are they all congruent?

2. Repeat Problem 1 for $\triangle DEF$ where $\angle D = 60°$ and $DE = 6$ cm.

3. Repeat Problem 1 for $\triangle GHI$ where $\angle G = 50°$ and $\angle H = 75°$.

In Your Journal

To determine if two triangles are congruent, is it sufficient to measure any two corresponding parts? Explain.

4. a) Make a sketch and then draw $\triangle JKL$ where $\angle J = 40°$, $\angle K = 80°$, and $\angle L = 60°$.
b) Compare your triangle with five other students'. How are they alike? different? Are they all congruent?

5. Repeat Problem 4 for $\triangle MNO$ where $\angle M = 40°$, $\angle N = 50°$, and $NO = 6$ cm.

6. Repeat Problem 4 for $\triangle PQR$ where $\angle P = 25°$, $PQ = 6$ cm, and $\angle Q = 60°$.

7. Repeat Problem 4 for $\triangle STU$ where $ST = 4$ cm, $\angle T = 45°$, and $TU = 6$ cm.

8. Repeat Problem 4 for $\triangle VWX$ where $VW = 5$ cm, $WX = 7$ cm, and $\angle X = 40°$.

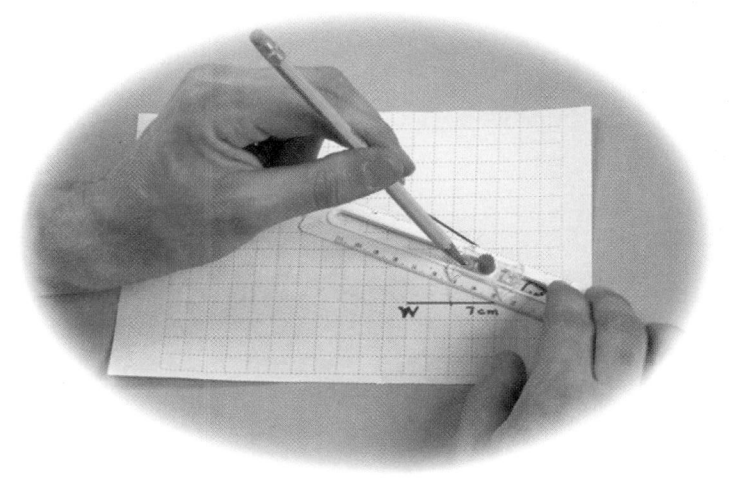

9. Repeat Problem 4 for $\triangle YZA$ where $YZ = 6$ cm, $ZA = 5$ cm, and $YA = 4$ cm.

10. To determine if two triangles are congruent, which of the following pairs of corresponding parts are sufficient to measure?
  • **AAA** (three angles)
  • **AAS** (two angles and a non-contained side)
  • **ASA** (two angles and a contained side)
  • **SAS** (two sides and a contained angle)
  • **SSA** (two sides and a non-contained angle)
  • **SSS** (three sides)
Describe all the ways you know to determine if two triangles are congruent.

11.2 Using Congruent Triangles

Which angles in each diagram are equal? Tell why.

To find the length of the pond, Alex and Trevor decided they could use congruent triangles.

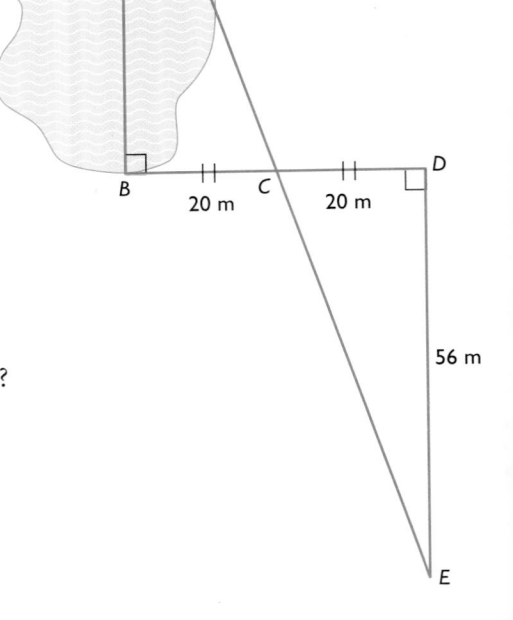

Concept Development

Trevor and Alex followed these steps.
- They noted a tree, *A*, on the bank at one end of the pond. They placed a stake, *B*, at the other end.
- They walked with a trundle wheel a distance of 20 m at right angles to the length of the pond and placed a stake, *C*.
- Then they continued walking another 20 m and placed a third stake, *D*.
- Next they walked at right angles to the previous walk until the tree was directly in line behind stake *C*. They placed a stake, *E*.
- Then they measured the length of their last walk from *D* to *E* to be 56 m.

1. a) Which pairs of corresponding sides in the triangles are equal? Why?
  b) Which pairs of corresponding angles are equal? Why?
  c) Why are $\triangle ABC$ and $\triangle EDC$ congruent?
  d) What is the length of the pond, *AB*? Why?

I. Which set of conditions for congruence AAS, ASA, SAS, or SSS tells why each pair of triangles is congruent?

a)

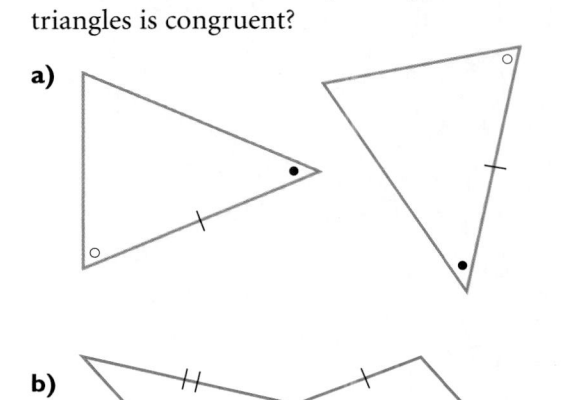

b)

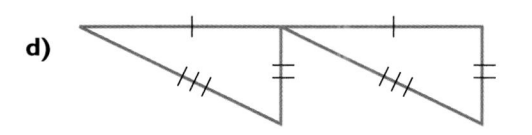

c)

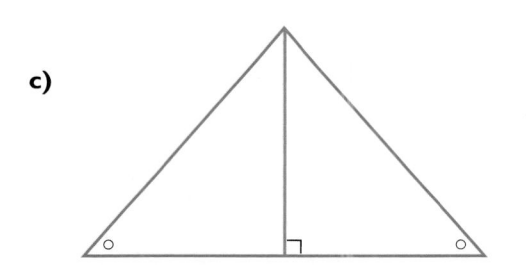

d)

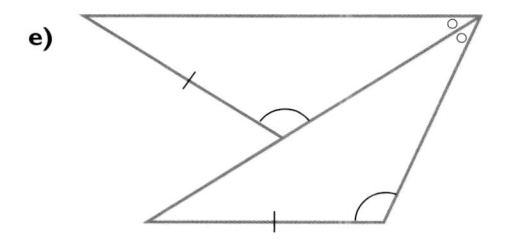

e)

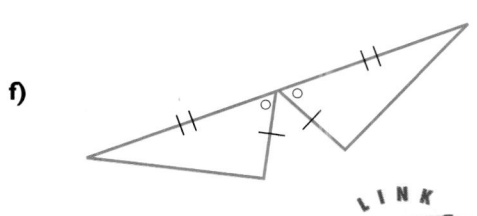

f)

2. Measure and use a set of conditions for congruence to determine if each pair of triangles is congruent.

a)

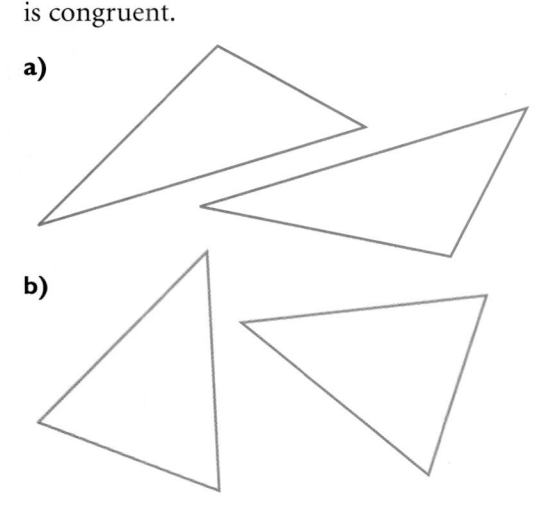

b)

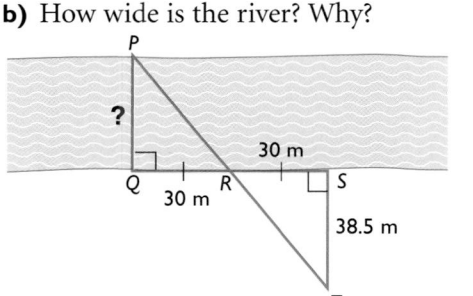

3. To find the width of a river, Gloria and Rhonda use congruent triangles.
   a) Why are the triangles congruent?
   b) How wide is the river? Why?

4. To find the length of a swamp, Corey and Pat use congruent triangles. Because there is a hill between D and E, they measure the distance from E to C.
   a) How can they calculate the length of the swamp?
   b) What is its length?

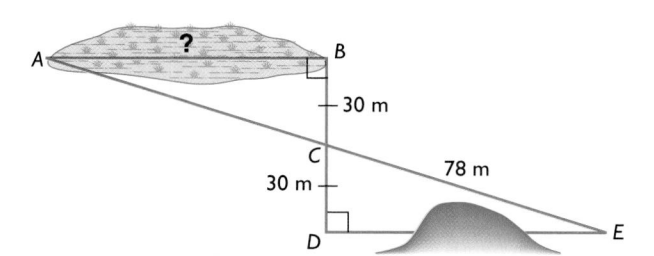

Measure a length or width indirectly using congruent triangles.

257

11.3 Finding Similar Triangles

These are similar.

Those are congruent. These are similar.

Concept Development

 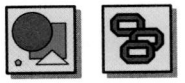

1. Which student do you agree with? Why?

2. Which of the following are always true for similar shapes?
   a) same shape
   b) same size
   c) same orientation
   d) corresponding angles equal
   e) corresponding sides equal

3. a) Are all congruent shapes similar? Explain.
   b) Are all similar shapes congruent? Explain.

4. a) Draw $\triangle ABC$ where $AB = 3$ cm, $BC = 4$ cm, and $AC = 2$ cm.
   b) Draw $\triangle DEF$ similar to ABC.
   c) What scale factor did you use?
   d) Measure the angles in both triangles. Which are equal?
   e) Measure the sides in $\triangle DEF$. Find the ratio of each pair of corresponding sides. What do you notice?
   f) Use what you discovered in part (e) to describe another characteristic of similar shapes.

5. These are Kyle's triangles.

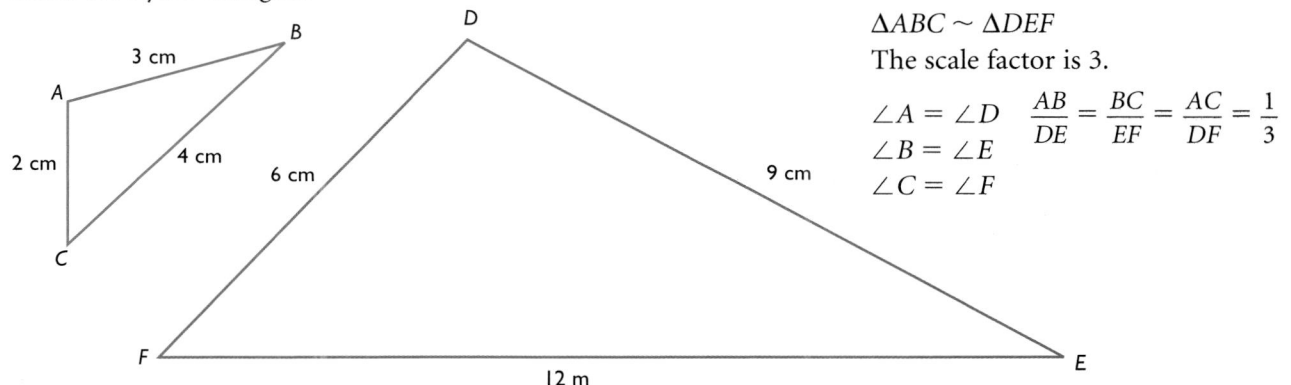

$\Delta ABC \sim \Delta DEF$
The scale factor is 3.

$\angle A = \angle D$ $\dfrac{AB}{DE} = \dfrac{BC}{EF} = \dfrac{AC}{DF} = \dfrac{1}{3}$
$\angle B = \angle E$
$\angle C = \angle F$

Use the measurements for each side in ΔABC and ΔDEF to find these ratios. What do you notice?
- $AB : BC : AC$
- $DE : EF : DF$

Understand and Apply

1. Measure the unknown angles and sides to see if all pairs of corresponding angles are equal and all pairs of corresponding sides are in the same ratio. Then the triangles are said to be similar.

a)

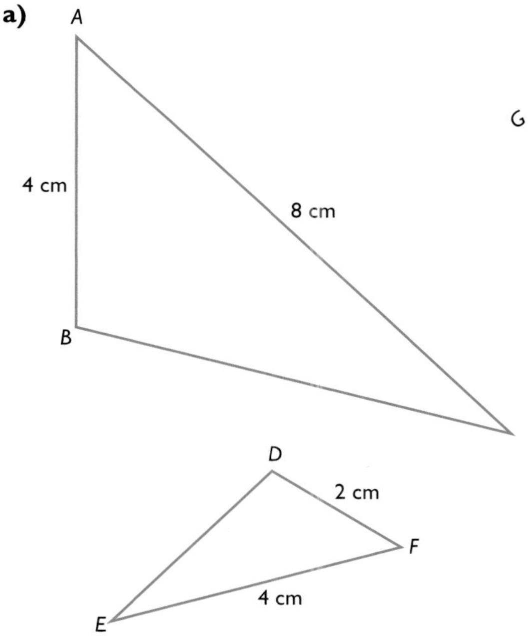

A

4 cm

8 cm

B

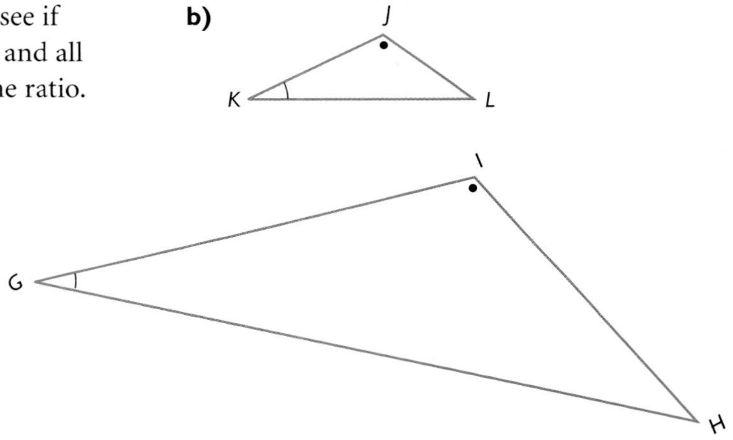

D   2 cm

E   4 cm   F

b)

J

K   L

\

G

H

c)

O

5 cm

M   N

P

10 cm

R

Q

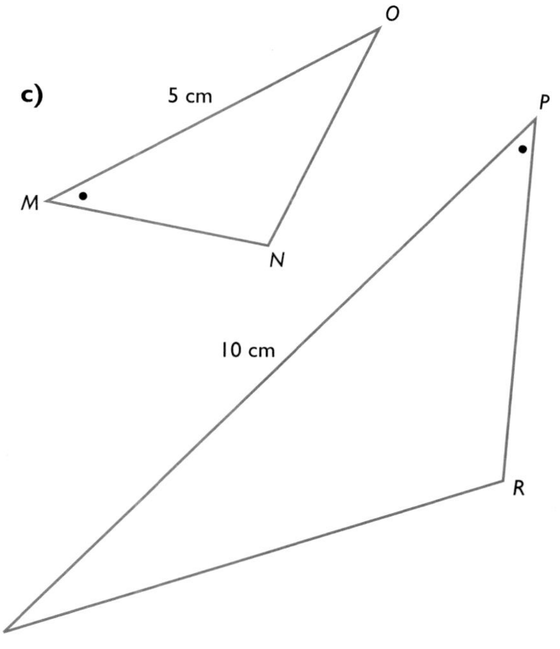

c)

2. Tell why each of the following would be more than necessary to determine if two triangles are similar.
   a) knowing or measuring all three pairs of angles
   b) knowing or measuring two pairs of corresponding angles and a pair of corresponding sides

3. Measure the unknown angles and sides to see if
   - all pairs of corresponding angles are equal
   - all pairs of corresponding sides are in the same ratio
   - the triangles are similar

a)

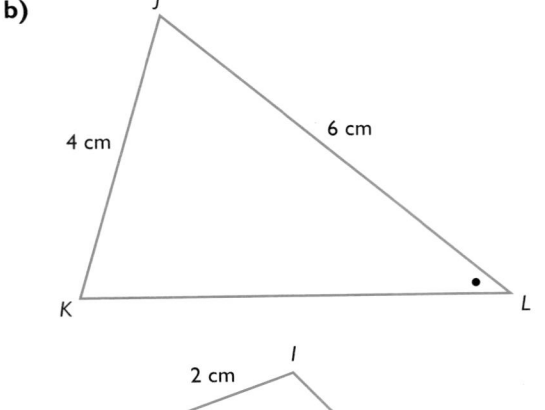

4. Explain why the triangles in Problem 3 b) were not similar but the ones in Problem 3 c) were.

b)

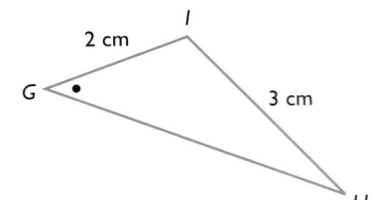

260

11.4 Using Similar Triangles

To find the height of a tree, Theresa uses similar triangles.

Concept Development

Theresa measures the tree's shadow. Then she stands a metre stick at right angles to the ground and measures its shadow.

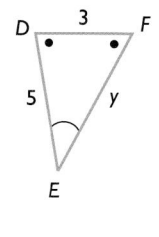
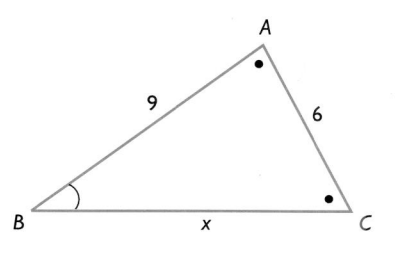
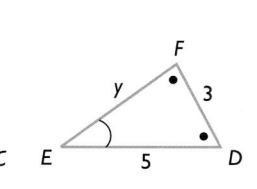

1. Because the sun is so far away, the angles $\angle A$ and $\angle D$ — where the sun's rays, represented by AB and DE, meet the ground — are equal. Explain why.

2. a) Why are the triangles similar?
   b) Which pairs of sides correspond?
   c) What proportion could you solve to find the height of the tree, h?
   d) What is the height of the tree?

To find the unknown sides in these similar triangles, Ian and Sandra sketch each triangle so that both are oriented the same way.

Ian reasons
6 is double 3, so
x is double 5, or 10.
3 is half of 6, so y is ▨

Sandra wrote this proportion.
$\frac{9}{y} = \frac{x}{5} = \frac{6}{3}$
Solve for x.
Solve for y.

3. Finish each student's work.

1. Find the unknown angles and sides in each pair of similar triangles.

a)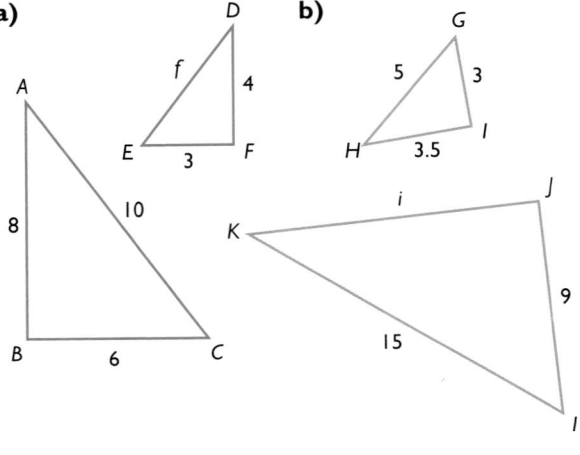

b)

d)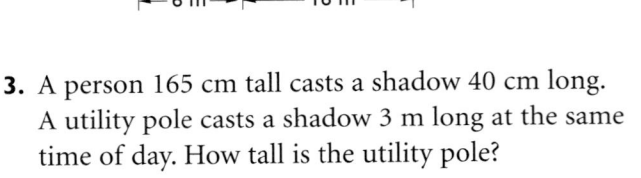

e)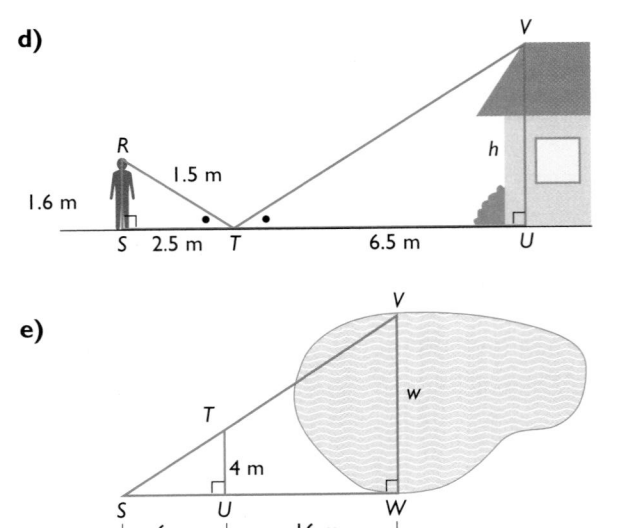

2. Identify corresponding sides in each pair of similar triangles. Then find the unknown length.

a)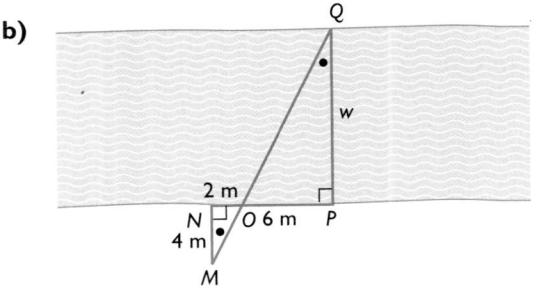

b)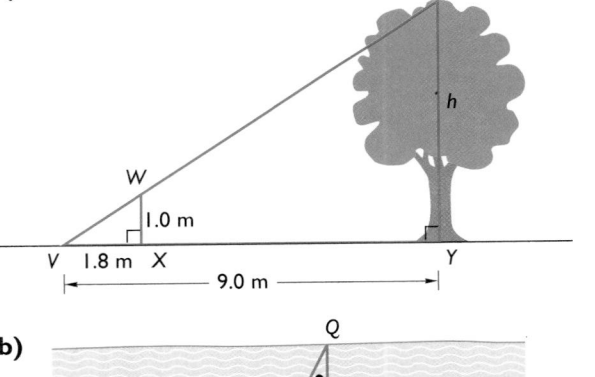

c)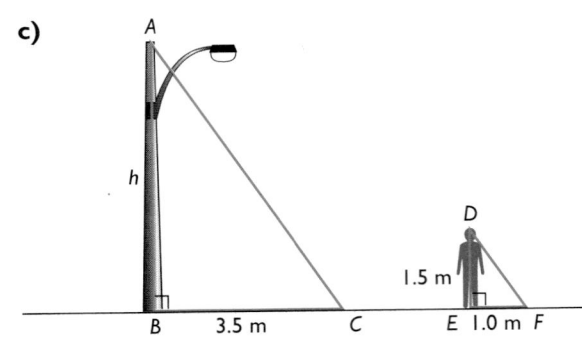

3. A person 165 cm tall casts a shadow 40 cm long. A utility pole casts a shadow 3 m long at the same time of day. How tall is the utility pole?

4. Doreen's backyard is triangular in shape. Two sides are 16 m and 12 m, and they form a 60° angle. She plans to plant some trees and shrubs and she makes a scale drawing of it. She draws a 60° angle and makes sides 8 cm and 6 cm on either side of it. Then she joins them and the third side is 7.3 cm. How long is the third side of her backyard?

5. Andrew places a mirror flat on the ground 30 m from a building. When he stands 0.6 m beyond the mirror, he can see the top of the building in the mirror. If his eyes are 1.5 m above the ground, how tall is the building? Hint: Which diagram in Problem 2 shows a situation like this?

6. A flagpole casts a shadow 4.2 m long at the same time that a metre stick casts a 0.7 m long shadow. How tall is the flagpole?

Decide how you could use similar triangles to find the height of a tree, pole, or building. Ask someone to help you take measurements. Prepare a solution that explains what you did, as well as shows the calculations.

Problems to Investigate

AREAS OF SIMILAR TRIANGLES

Draw a triangle on grid paper. Enlarge each side by 3. Find the area of each triangle. How are the areas related? Predict how the areas of a triangle and an enlargement with a scale factor of 4 are related. Check your prediction.

SHADOW LENGTHS

Investigate the lengths of shadows created in sunlight at different times of day. When are they the shortest?

SIMILAR OR CONGRUENT

Find or create an optical illusion that makes congruent shapes appear to be similar but non-congruent.

CONDITIONS FOR CONGRUENCE

Explain why **AAS** (two angles and a non-contained side) and **ASA** (two angles and a contained side) are actually the same conditions.

PAPER SIZES

Paper sizes A_1 to A_7 are similar to A_0.

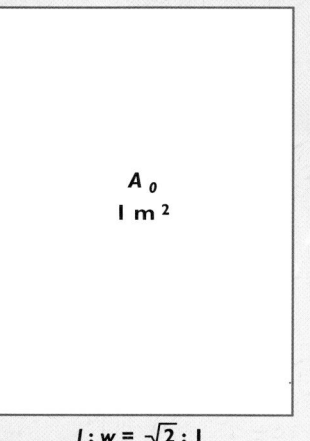

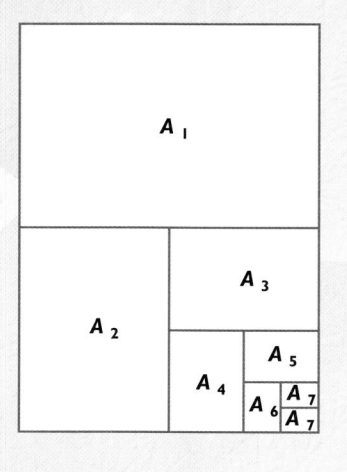

$l : w = \sqrt{2} : 1$

Show that A_1, A_2, and A_3 are similar to A_0 by showing that their ratios of length to width are equal to $\sqrt{2} : 1$.

HOW TALL?

A flag pole casts a shadow 1.9 m long at the same time a person 170 cm tall casts a shadow 0.3 m long. How tall is the flagpole rounded to the nearest tenth of a metre?

Make up some other problems about similarity or congruence. Post them on the bulletin board for your classmates to solve.

263

11.5 Exploring Tangents

Concept Development

Warm Up

Which side is opposite ∠C?
What special side is it?
Which of the other two
sides is opposite ∠A?
adjacent to ∠A?
opposite ∠B?
adjacent to ∠B?

The angles formed where the sun's rays meet the ground are congruent.

1. a) Why is that?
b) How do you know these triangles are similar?

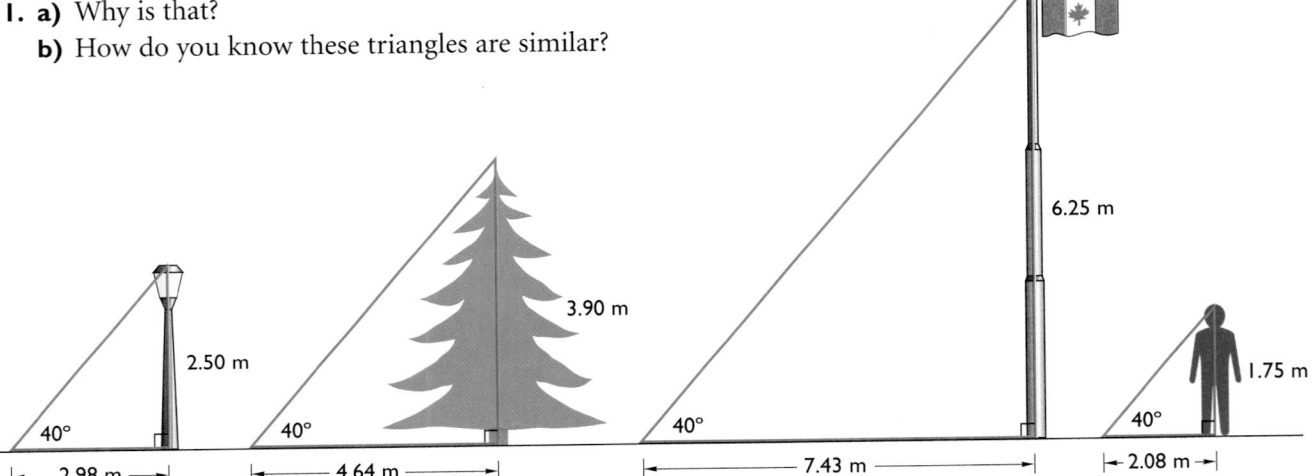

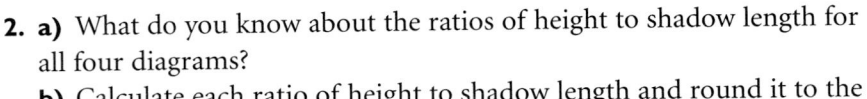

2.50 m — 2.98 m

3.90 m — 4.64 m

6.25 m — 7.43 m

1.75 m — 2.08 m

2. a) What do you know about the ratios of height to shadow length for all four diagrams?
b) Calculate each ratio of height to shadow length and round it to the nearest hundredth.

$$\frac{\text{opposite side of } 40°}{\text{adjacent side of } 40°} \approx 0.84$$

This ratio is known as the **tangent** of 40°. It is often written as tan 40°.

3. a) Measure the sides opposite and adjacent to 60° in ΔDEF to the nearest millimetre.
b) Predict whether the tangent of 60° will be greater or less than 1. Explain.
c) Calculate the tangent and round it to the nearest hundredth.

4. a) Draw a right triangle with an angle of 55°.
b) Measure the sides adjacent to and opposite the 55° angle to the nearest millimetre.
c) Predict whether the tangent of 55° will be greater or less than 1.
d) Calculate the tangent of 55° and round it to the nearest hundredth.

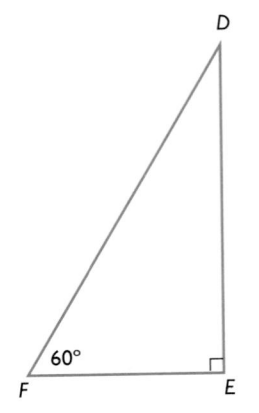

You can use the [TAN] key on your calculator to calculate the tangent of an angle. To find tan 40° on this calculator you press [TAN] 40 [=] to get

`0.839099631`

5. a) What keystrokes would you use on your calculator to find tan 40°?
b) Use a calculator to calculate the tangent of 60° and the tangent of 55°. Compare your results with the tangents you calculated using measurements.

Understand and Apply

Round all answers to the nearest hundredth.

1. Predict whether the tangent of the given angle is greater than, less than, or equal to 1. Calculate it using the measurements. Then calculate it using the [TAN] key and compare your answers.

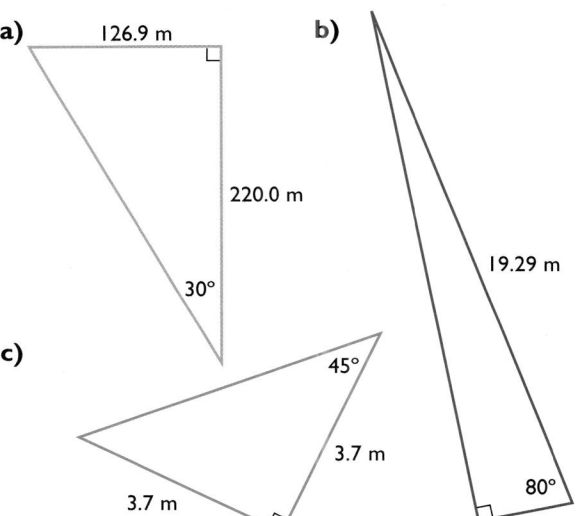

a) 126.9 m
220.0 m
30°

b) 19.29 m
80°
3.4 m

c) 45°
3.7 m
3.7 m

2. a) Draw a right triangle with a 70° angle.
b) Measure the appropriate sides and calculate the tangents of each acute angle.
c) Then calculate the tangents using the [TAN] key and compare your answers.
d) Repeat the previous parts for a right triangle with an angle of 25°.

3. Use the [TAN] key to complete this table.

Angle	Tangent
10°	
20°	
30°	
40°	
50°	
60°	
70°	
80°	

What pattern do you notice?

4. a) How could you determine if there is a maximum and a minimum value that the tangents of the acute angles in a right triangle approach?
b) What happens if you use the [TAN] key to find tan 90°? Why might this happen?

5. The tangent is one of the three primary trigonometric ratios. Research to find the meaning of the branch of mathematics, **trigonometry,** and about its history.

HOME LINK

Find something in the shape of a right triangle. Measure its sides accurately and calculate the tangent of each acute angle.

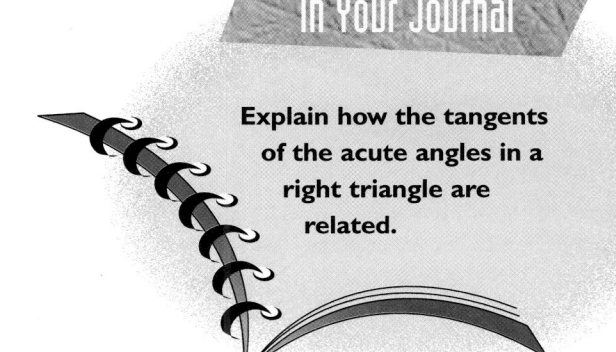

In Your Journal

Explain how the tangents of the acute angles in a right triangle are related.

11.6 Using the Tangent of an Angle to Solve Problems

Warm Up

Evaluate $\dfrac{5}{1.7^2}$ and then $\dfrac{6}{\tan 30°}$ on your calculator. Write the keystrokes you used.

The height of a kite can be found using the tangent of an angle. The angle of elevation to the kite is 58° from a point on the ground which is a horizontal distance of 15.8 m from the kite.

Concept Development

Lucas sketches a diagram and solves an equation to find the height.

1. What keystrokes would you use on your calculator to find h?

2. To find side g in $\triangle GHI$,   Stan uses the tangent of 32°.   Lois uses the tangent of 58° to find g.

$$\tan 32° = \frac{25}{g}$$
$$\tan 32° \times g = 25$$
$$g = \frac{25}{\tan 32°}$$
$$g = \blacksquare$$

$$\angle G = 90° - 32°$$
$$= 58°$$
$$\tan 58° = \blacksquare$$

Diagram: right triangle with vertices G (top right), H (bottom right, right angle), I (bottom left, 32°). Side $GH = 25$ m, side $IH = g$.

Finish each student's work. Record your keystrokes.

Understand and Apply

Round all answers to 1 decimal place.

1. The **angle of elevation** to the top of an apartment building is 30° from a point which is a horizontal distance of 140.5 m from the base of the building. How tall is the building?

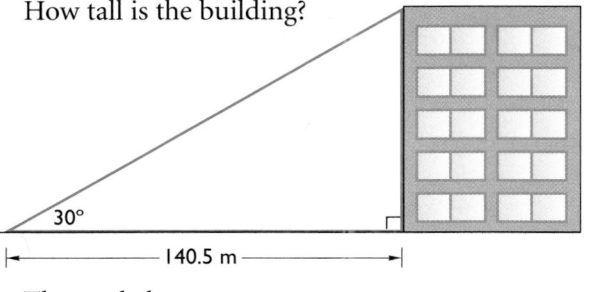

2. The angle between the left bank and a tree on the right bank is 48° from a point 30 m north. What is the width of the river?

3. A ramp to a building entrance which is 0.9 m above the ground makes an angle of 10° with the ground. How far is the bottom of the ramp from the building?

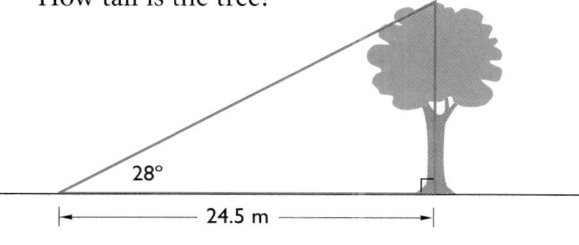

4. The length of a tree's shadow is 24.5 m and the sun's rays make an angle of 28° with the ground. How tall is the tree?

5. The following measurements were made to calculate the length of a lake. How long is the lake?

984 m 76°

6. The **angle of depression** from a cliff 158 m above sea level to one ship is 10° and to another ship directly in line behind the first ship is 24°. What is the distance between the ships?

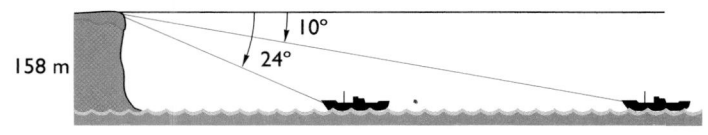

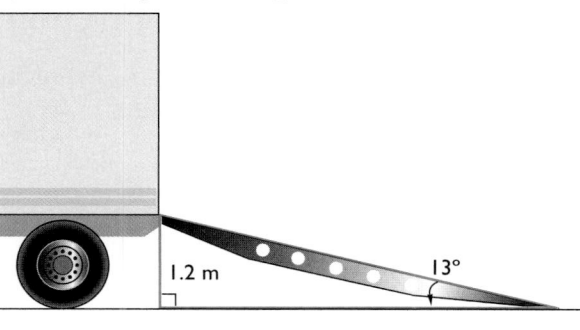

7. The floor of a truck is 1.2 m above the ground. A ramp makes a 13° angle with the ground.
a) How far is the bottom of the ramp from the truck?
b) How long is the ramp?

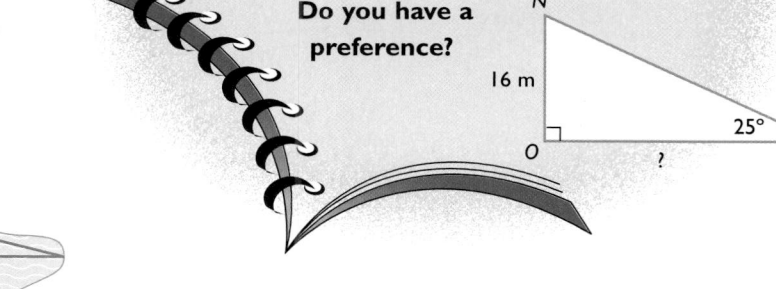

8. The angle of depression from a hot air balloon to a cyclist on the ground is 27°. The height of the balloon is 500 m. What is the horizontal distance between the balloon and the cyclist?

9. The horizontal distance between a ship and a satellite is 1542 km. The angle of elevation from the ship to the satellite is 88°. What is the height of the satellite?

W/E

In Your Journal

Explain why you can use either the tangent of ∠**M** or ∠**N** to find the unknown side.

Do you have a preference?

N
16 m
25°
O   ?   M

11.7 Exploring Sines and Cosines

Warm Up

What is special about each pair?

a) 6 and −6

b) $\frac{1}{15}$ and 15

c) $\dfrac{\text{side opposite } \angle A}{\text{side adjacent } \angle A}$

and

$\dfrac{\text{side opposite } \angle B}{\text{side adjacent } \angle B}$

d) $\dfrac{\text{side opposite } \angle A}{\text{side adjacent } \angle A}$

and

$\dfrac{\text{side adjacent } \angle B}{\text{side opposite } \angle B}$

Concept Development

1. A kite is flying over water. How might you find the height of the kite?

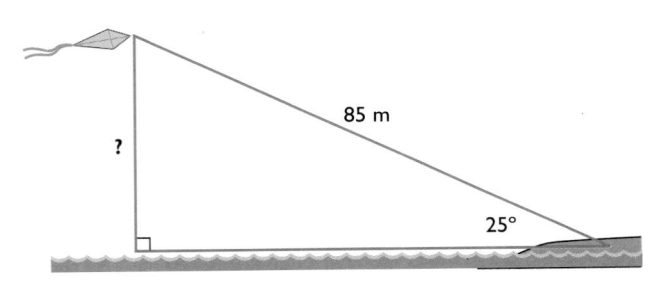

Since the length of the kite string, the hypotenuse, is the only side known, the tangent is not useful.

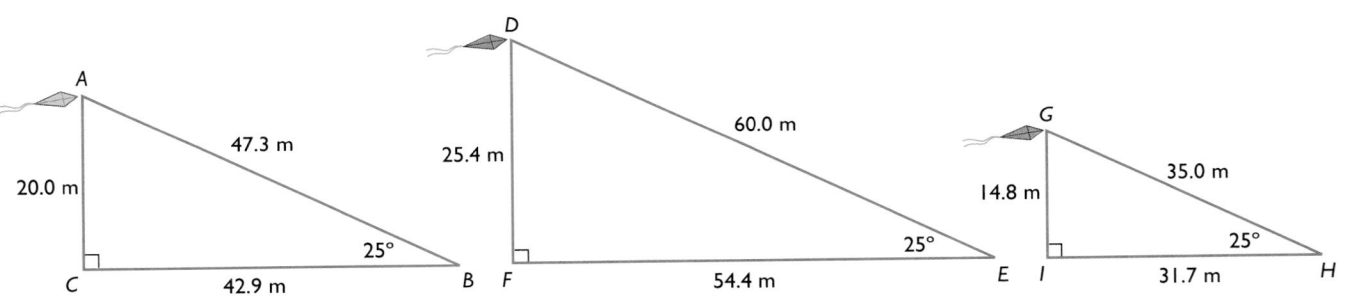

2. a) What do you know about the ratios of height to kite string length in the three similar triangles above?
b) Calculate each height to kite string length ratio and round it to the nearest hundredth.

$$\frac{\text{opposite side of } 25^\circ}{\text{hypotenuse}} \approx 0.42$$

This ratio is the **sine** of 25°, often written as sin 25°.

3. a) What do you know about the ratios of horizontal distance to kite string length in the similar triangles above?
b) Calculate each horizontal distance to kite string length ratio and round it to the nearest hundredth.

$$\frac{\text{adjacent side of } 25^\circ}{\text{hypotenuse}} \approx 0.91$$

This ratio is **cosine** of 25°, often written as cos 25°.

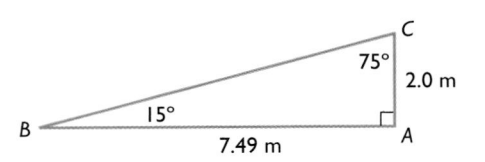

4. Calculate and round to the nearest hundredth these trigonometric ratios for $\triangle ABC$. What do you notice?
a) sin 15° **b)** sin 75° **c)** cos 15° **d)** cos 75°

You can use the [SIN] key and the [COS] key on your calculator like the [TAN] key. To find sin 15° on a calculator, you might press [SIN] 1 5 [=] to get

`0.258819045` .

5. a) What keystrokes would you use on your calculator to find sin 15°?
b) Calculate the four ratios above using your calculator. How do your answers compare?

6. Why are both the sine and cosine of any acute angle in a right triangle less than 1?

Understand and Apply

Round all answers to the nearest hundredth.

1. a) Predict whether the sine or cosine of the given angle in each triangle will be greater.
b) Calculate both the sine and cosine using the measurements.
c) Calculate both ratios using your calculator and compare you answers.

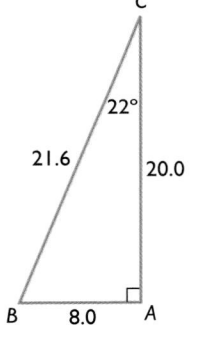

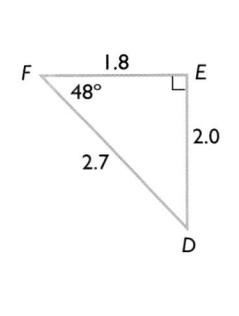

2. For each triangle calculate the sine and cosine for both acute angles by doing only two calculations.

a)   **b)**

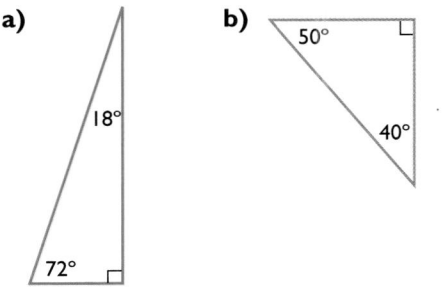

3. Complete.
a) Since sin 30° = 0.5, cos ▪ = 0.5.
b) Since sin 45° ≈ 0.707, cos ▪ ≈ 0.707.
c) Since sin 20° ≈ $\frac{11}{32}$, cos 70° ≈ ▪.

4. Find the length of the unknown side. Then calculate the sine, cosine, and tangent for both acute angles .
a)

G, 5 cm, P, 12 cm, I

b)

O, W, 7 cm, 25 cm, C

In Your Journal

Explain why knowing any two sides in a right triangle is sufficient information to calculate all three trigonometric ratios for the acute angles in the triangle.

5. Calculate sin 38°, then explain and complete.
a) If $AC = 0.62$, then $AB = $ ▪.
b) If $AC = 62$, then $AB = $ ▪.
c) The length of AC is 0.62 of ▪.
d) The length of AB is 1.61 times the length of ▪.

A, 38°, C, B

11.8 Using Trigonometric Ratios to Solve Problems

Warm Up

Find everything you can about this triangle using the given information.

A

70°

C

6 m

B

The gang plank joining a ship and pier is 25.5 m long and forms an angle of 62° with the ship.

62°

25.5 m

d

Concept Development

1. What ratio would you use to find the horizontal distance between the pier and the ship?

Roberta sketches a diagram and uses the sine of 62°.

Let d be the horizontal distance between the ship and the pier.

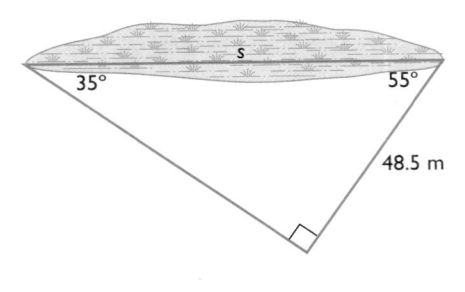

62°

25.5m

ship

pier

d

$$\sin 62° = \frac{\text{opposite side}}{\text{hypotenuse}}$$

$$\sin 62° = \frac{d}{25.5}$$

$$25.5 \times \sin 62° = d$$

$$22.5 = d$$

25.5 ⊠ ⌈SIN⌉ 62 ⌈=⌉

$$22.51516362$$

The horizontal distance is 22.5 m.

2. What keystrokes would you use on your calculator?

3. To find the length of this swamp,

Marlene uses the cosine of 55°.

Balki uses the sine of 35°.

35°

s

55°

48.5 m

$$\cos 55° = \frac{48.5}{s}$$

$$\cos 55° \times s = 48.5$$

$$s = \frac{48.5}{\cos 55°}$$

$$s = \blacksquare$$

$$\sin 35° = \frac{48.5}{s}$$

$$s = \blacksquare$$

Finish each student's work. Show your keystrokes.

4. Find d in Roberta's diagram of the gang plank using cosine.

Use sine, cosine, or tangent. Round all answers to 1 decimal place.

1. Decide if side *k* will be longer or shorter than the given side. Then find side *k*.

a)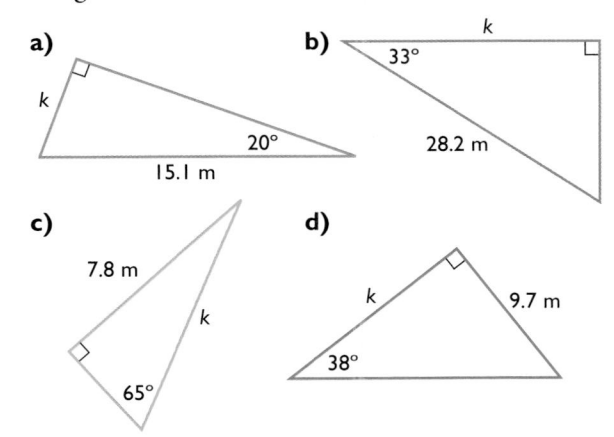

k

k

20°

15.1 m

b)

k

33°

28.2 m

c)

7.8 m

k

65°

d)

k

9.7 m

38°

2. A 6.8 m long ramp makes an 81° angle with the building. How high is the ramp where it meets the building?

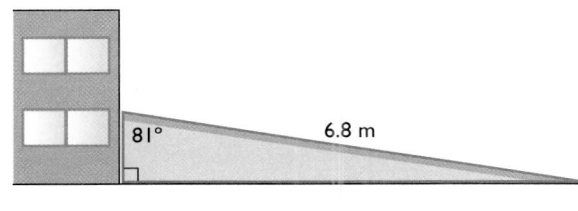

81°   6.8 m

3. The angle of depression from a plane to the top of a tower is 25°. The altitude of the plane is 1650 m higher than the top of the tower. What is the horizontal distance from the plane to the tower?

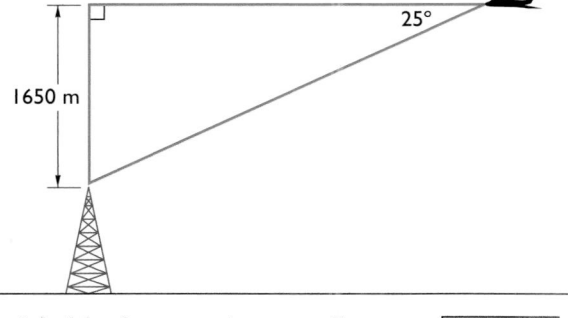

25°

1650 m

4. A ladder leans against a wall making a 24° angle. The base of it is 1.75 m from the wall. How long is the ladder?

24°

1.75 m

5. Shelf braces are 25 cm long and meet the shelf at a 35° angle. How far below the shelf do they meet the wall?

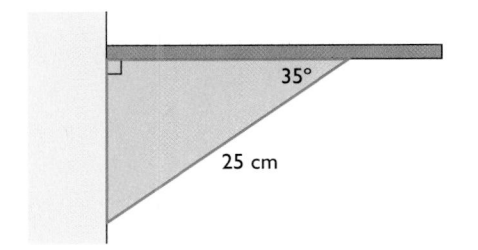

35°

25 cm

6. The angle to a tree on the north side of a gorge from a point that is a horizontal distance of 30 m east on the south side is 60°. What is the width of the gorge?

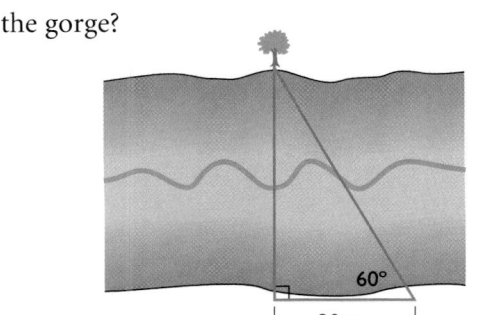

60°

30 m

7. Three islands are situated as shown. What is the distance between Pine Island and Balsam Island?

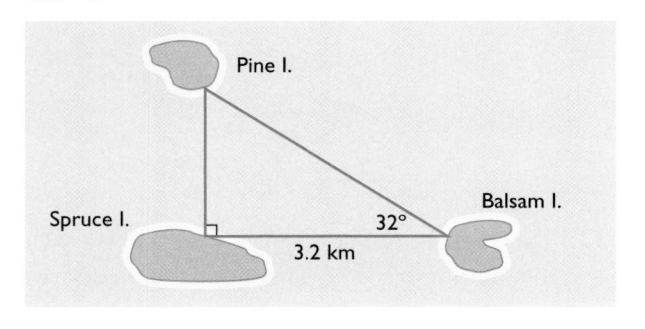

Pine I.

Spruce I.

Balsam I.

32°

3.2 km

8. A ramp reaches a height of 1.3 m above the ground and forms an angle of 10° with the ground at the other end. How long is the ramp?

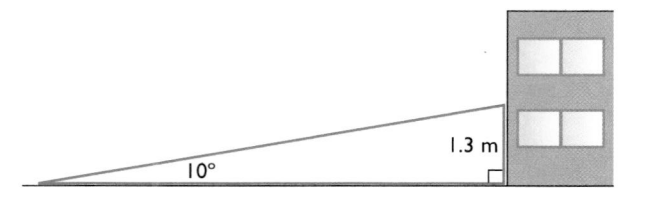

10°

1.3 m

9. A parachutist drops from a plane which is flying an altitude of 1220 m. The angle of drift is 12°. What is the horizontal distance between the drop location and the landing location?

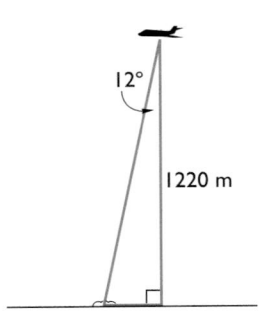

10. A 4.5 m ladder makes an angle of 70° with the ground. How far up the wall does it reach?

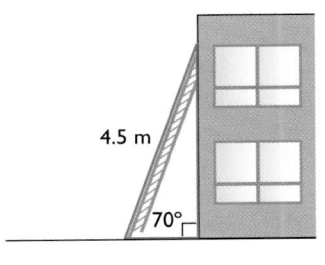

11. A kite string attached to a kite flying at an height of 18.4 m makes an angle of 32° with the ground. What is the length of the kite string?

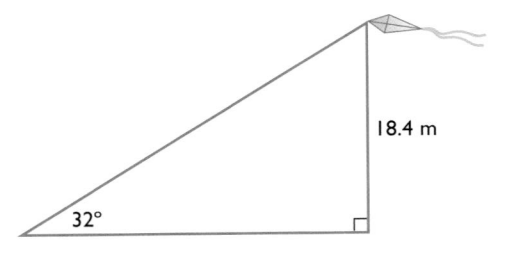

12. The angle of elevation from a ship to the light in a lighthouse is 7°. The light is 95 m above sea level. What is the horizontal distance between the ship and the lighthouse?

13. A guy wire is attached to a pole at a height of 3.9 m forming a 40° angle with the pole.
  a) How long is the guy wire?
  b) How far from the base of the pole is it attached to the ground?

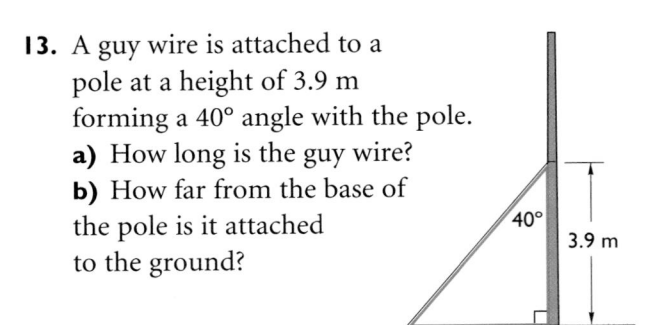

14. A kite string is extended 32.2 m and is held by a person at a height of 1.6 m above the ground. The angle the kite string makes with the height of the kite is 62°. What is the height of the kite?

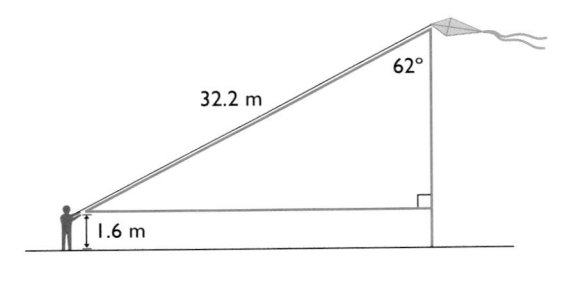

15. Four islands are situated as shown. What is the distance between
  a) Beaver Island and Deer Island?
  b) Mink Island and Elk Island?
  c) Mink Island and Deer Island?

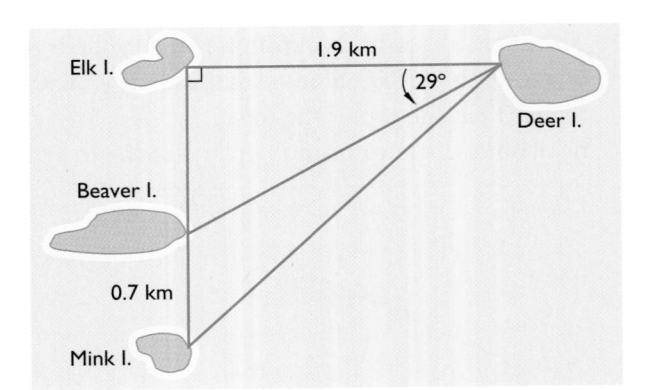

16. A ladder reaches 3.5 m up a wall making an angle of 25° where it touches the wall. How long is the ladder?

17. A kite string that is 30.5 m long makes an angle of 60° with the ground. How high is the kite?

11.9 Using Trigonometric Ratios to Solve Right Triangles

The landing location of a parachutist is never directly below the drop location. The air currents cause the parachutist to drift.

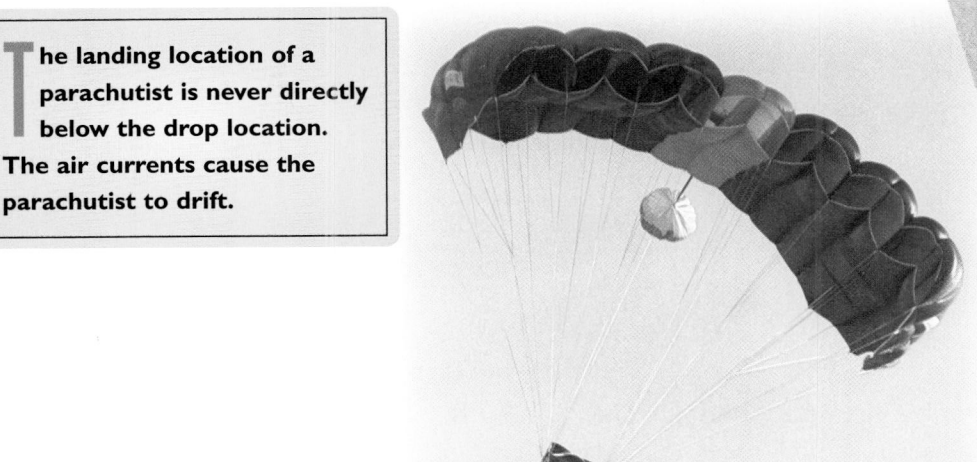

Concept Development

1. How could you calculate the angle of drift if you know the height, 1.2 km, at the time of the drop and the horizontal distance, 0.6 km, covered before landing?

Carol sketches a diagram, and then finds the angle with a tangent of $\frac{0.6}{1.2}$ or 0.5.

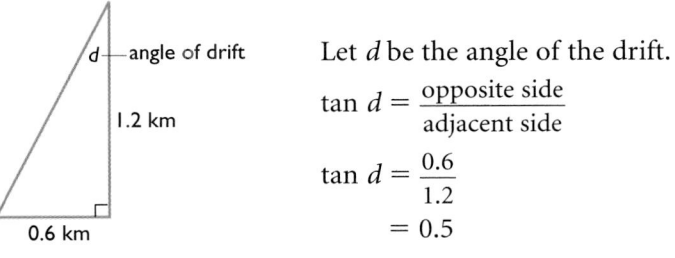

Let d be the angle of the drift.

$$\tan d = \frac{\text{opposite side}}{\text{adjacent side}}$$

$$\tan d = \frac{0.6}{1.2}$$

$$= 0.5$$

The tangent of the angle of drift is known. You can use the tangent to find the angle, d, by finding the **inverse of the tangent** on a calculator.

The second function of the TAN key is $\tan^{-1}$, the inverse of tangent.

For some calculators, the keystrokes are .5 TAN⁻¹.

For others, the keystrokes are TAN⁻¹ .5 =.

2. What keystrokes would you use on your calculator to find the inverse of the tangent?

3. What is the angle of drift rounded to the nearest tenth of a degree?

To solve a right triangle means to find all three angles and all three sides.

To solve $\triangle ABC$, Roger and Brent agree that three parts are already known: $b = 10.5$, $a = 14.0$, and $\angle C = 90°$. And, three parts need to be found: c, $\angle A$, and $\angle B$.

Roger uses the Pythagorean relationship to find side c. Then he uses the sine of $\angle A$ to find $\angle A$ and $\angle B$.

$$c^2 = 10.5^2 + 14.0^2 \qquad \sin \angle A = \frac{14.0}{17.5}$$
$$c = 17.5 \qquad\qquad \sin \angle A = 0.8$$
$$\angle A = 53.1°$$
$$\text{so } \angle B = 90° - 53.1°$$
$$= 36.9°$$

Brent uses the tangent of $\angle A$ to find $\angle A$ and $\angle B$. Then he uses the sine of $\angle A$, once $\angle A$ is known, to find side c.

$$\tan \angle A = \frac{14.0}{10.5} \qquad \sin 53.1° = \frac{14.0}{c}$$
$$\tan \angle A = 1.\overline{3} \qquad\qquad c = \frac{14.0}{\sin 53.1°}$$
$$\angle A = 53.1° \qquad\qquad c = 17.5$$
$$\text{so } \angle B = 90° - 53.1°$$
$$= 36.9°$$

4. Show another way to solve $\triangle ABC$.

5. Find $\angle D$ rounded to the nearest tenth of a degree.

Understand and Apply

Round all answers to 1 decimal place.

W/E **1.** Solve each triangle.

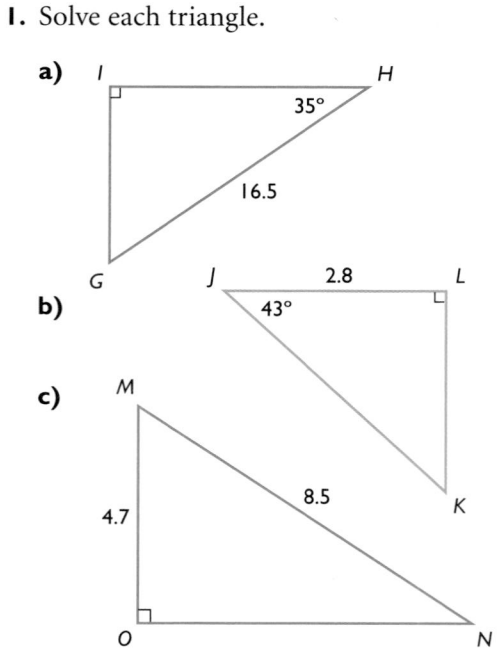

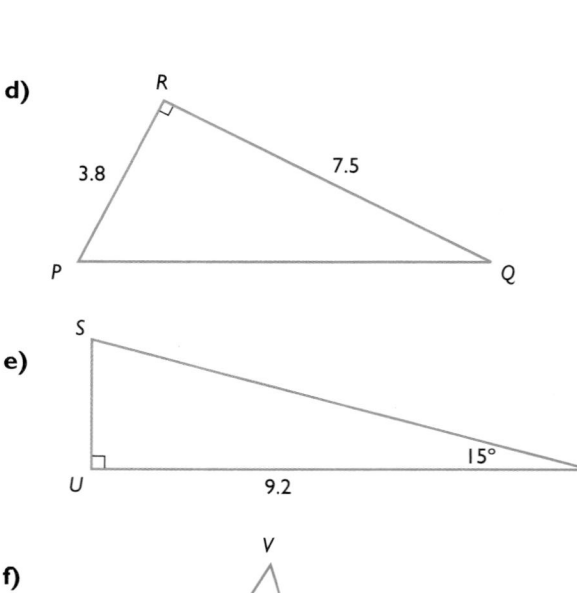

a)

b)

c)

d)

e)

f)

274

2. A straight slide is 2.2 m long. Its ladder is 1.56 m high. At what angle does the slide meet the ladder?

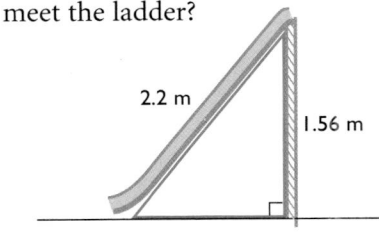

3. A ramp is 8.5 m long and covers a horizontal distance 8.4 m.
a) At what angle does it meet the ground?
b) What height does it reach?

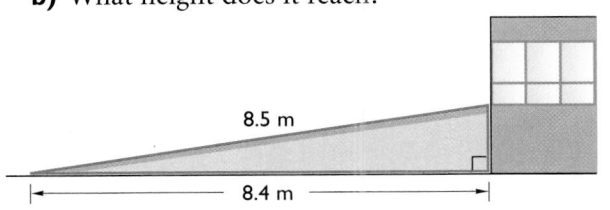

4. A kite string is 32.4 m long and the height the kite is flying at is 18.3 m. At what angle does the kite string meet the ground?

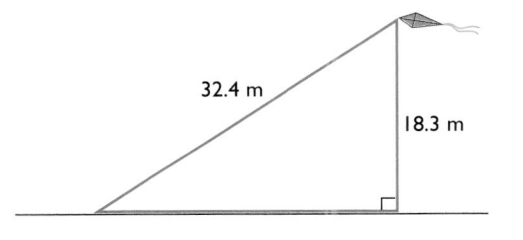

5. The diagonal distance from a ship to the light of a lighthouse is 5.42 km. The horizontal distance to the lighthouse is 5.41 km.
a) What is the angle of elevation from the ship to the light of the lighthouse?
b) What is the height of the lighthouse light above sea level?

6. A guy wire 4.7 m long reaches a pole 3.5 m above the ground. At what angle does the wire meet the
a) ground?
b) pole?

7. A plane flying at a height of 4.2 km is a horizontal distance of 80 km from a landmark. What is the angle of depression from the plane to the landmark?

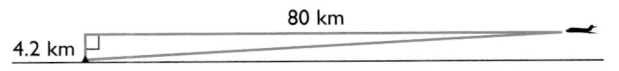

8. A rectangular field has dimensions 100 m by 60 m. Some cows walk diagonally from one corner to the opposite one. What angle does their path make with the longer side?

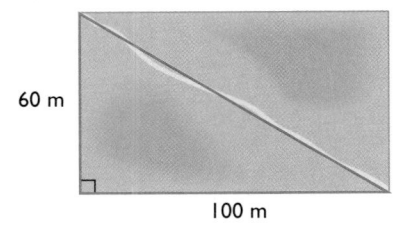

9. A storm blows a 8.5 m long pole onto a building. The top of the pole touches the building 6.9 m above the ground. What angle does the pole make with the ground?

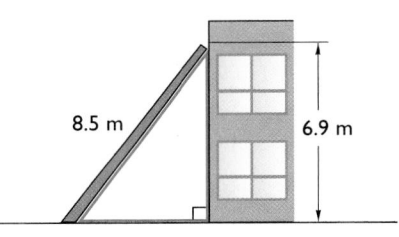

10. The ratio of the vertical height of a ladder to the distance its base is from the wall should be no greater than 3.73. What is the greatest angle that a ladder should make with the ground?

11. The ratio of the width to the length of a rectangle is 0.466 3. What angle does the diagonal make with each side?

12. Create a problem about each triangle and give your problems to others to solve.

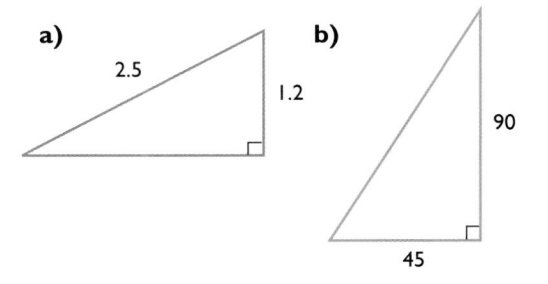

Problems to Investigate

USING COORDINATES

What is the measure of the acute angle at the origin in each triangle? Tell what you did.

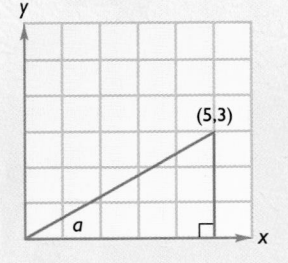

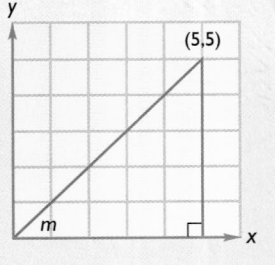

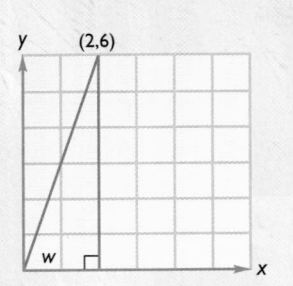

RELATING SIDES

Calculate the sine of each acute angle rounded to the nearest hundredth.

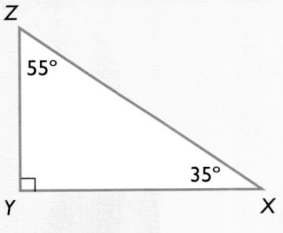

Complete these statements.
- The length of *XY* is ▓ of *XZ*.
- The length of *YZ* is ▓ of *XZ*.

What are possible lengths of the three sides?

SOLVING TRIANGLES

Solve each triangle.

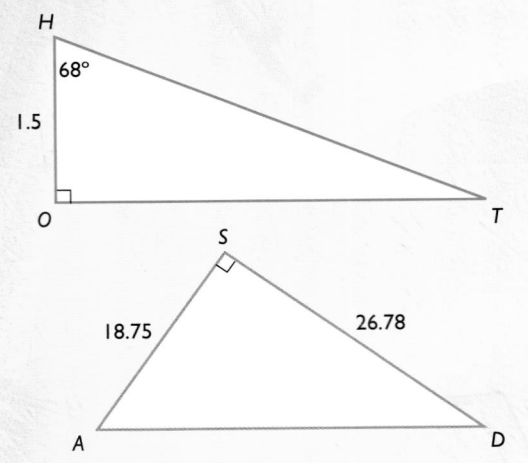

MEASURING ANGLES

You measure angles in diagrams using a protractor to the nearest degree. How do you think angles are measured in navigation and surveying? Research the units and the instruments used in navigation or surveying.

COTANGENT

Sine, cosine, and tangent are the three primary trigonometric ratios.

$$\frac{\text{adjacent side of } \angle A}{\text{opposite side of } \angle A} = \text{cotangent } \angle A \text{ or cot } \angle A$$

Find the cotangent of $\angle A$.

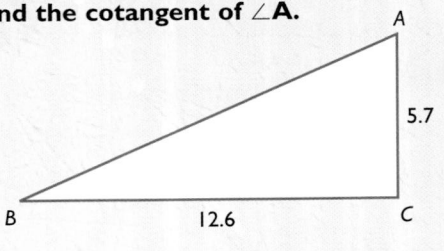

How is the cotangent of $\angle A$ related to the tangent of $\angle A$?

Calculate $\angle A$ and $\angle B$.

Make up some other problems about trigonometry. Post them on the bulletin board for your classmates to solve.

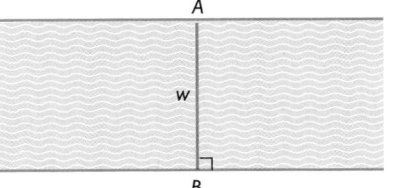

More Than One Strategy

Calculating Distance Indirectly

There are several ways to calculate the width of a river indirectly.
Here are some. Can you think of any others?

1. You might use congruent triangles.

Locate *C* and *D* so that *BC* = *CD*.
At right angles to the river, walk from *D* until *A* is in line behind *C*
and then measure the distance rounded to the nearest tenth of a
metre, *DE* = 373.7 m.
$\triangle ABC \cong \triangle EDC$, so *w* = 373.7.   The river is 373.7 m wide.

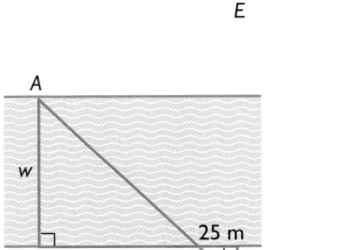

2. You can use similar triangles.

Locate *C* 100 m from *B* and then locate *D* 25 m from *C*.
At right angles to the river, walk from *D* until *A* is in line behind *C*
and then measure the distance, *DE* = 93.42 m.
$\triangle ABC \sim \triangle EDC$

$$\frac{w}{93.42} = \frac{100}{25}$$
$$w = 373.7$$ The river is 373.7 m wide.

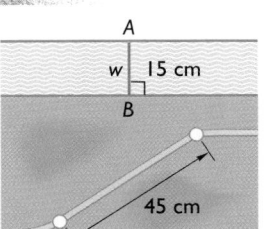

3. You might examine an aerial photograph and use proportion.

Measure *AB* on the map, 15 cm.
Measure another length such as a stretch of road on the map,
1121.1 m, and its length on the map, 45 cm.

$$\frac{w}{0.15} = \frac{1121.1}{0.45} \text{ (using metres)}$$
$$w = 373.7$$ The river is 373.7 m wide.

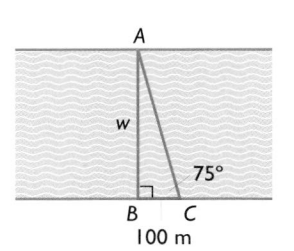

4. You could use a trigonometric ratio.

Locate *C* 100 m from *B* and measure $\angle C$, 75°.
$$\tan 75° = \frac{w}{100}$$
$$\tan 75° \times 100 = w$$
$$373.7 = w$$ The river is 373.7 m wide.

Understand and Apply

I. Explain how you could find each distance indirectly.
  a) the height of a tree   **b)** the length of a lake   **c)** the height of a plane   **d)** the width of a swamp

Interpreting Graphs

This graph shows the water levels relative to low tide for one day.

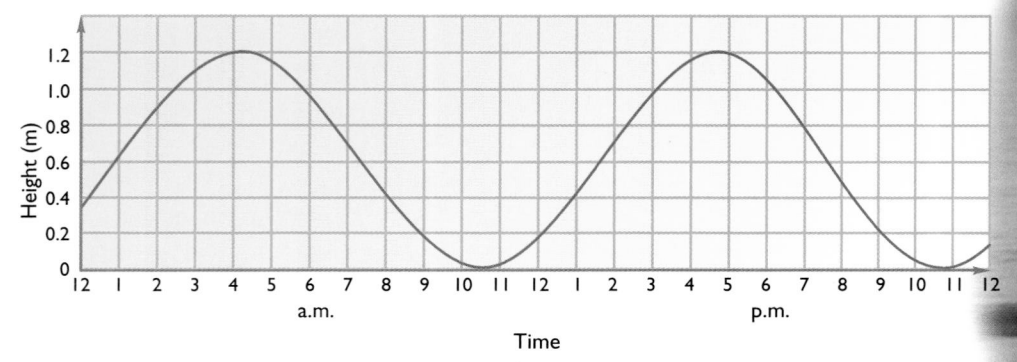

1. **a)** In one day, how many times is the tide high? low?
    b) How much does the water height vary between low and high tide?
    c) At what times was low tide? high tide?

Applications

2. This graph shows that the height of one seat on a Ferris wheel at the end of the arm through its centre is 9 m above the ground.
    a) How many revolutions are shown? Explain.
    b) How long is one revolution?
    c) What is the diameter of the Ferris wheel?

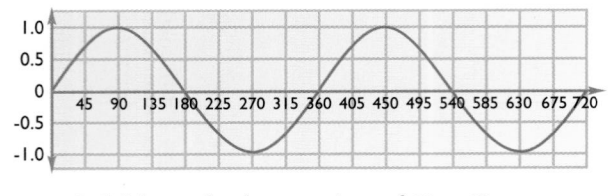

3. This graph shows the sines of angles from 0° to 720°. The maximum and minimum values for sine are 1 and −1.

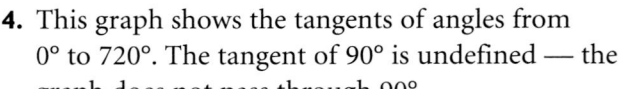

    a) Which angles have a sine of 1? −1?
    b) Which angles have a sine of −0.7?
    c) What is the sine of 135°?

4. This graph shows the tangents of angles from 0° to 720°. The tangent of 90° is undefined — the graph does not pass through 90°.
    a) Which other angles do not have a defined tangent?
    b) Which angles have a tangent of 0?

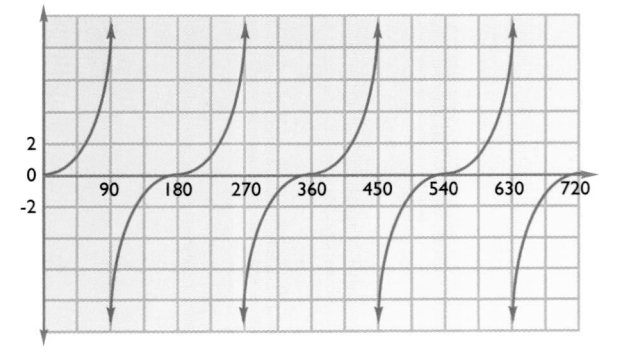

5. The cosine graph resembles one of the other trigonometric ratio's graph.
    a) Do you think it is the sine or the tangent graph? Why?
    b) Use your calculator to find the cosine for key angle values from 0° to 720° and plot them in a smooth curve.
    c) Make up some questions about your graph for others to solve.

Solve Problems by Drawing Diagrams

Try this problem before going on.

HOW TALL?

From the roof of one building, the angle of elevation to the top of another building is 39° and the angle of depression to the base of the other building is 55°. The buildings are 75 m apart. What is the height of the taller building?

▶ Understand the Problem

1. What are you asked to find?
2. What do you know?
3. Where will you begin?

▶ Make a Plan

Corrine decides to draw a diagram to help her solve the problem.

▶ Carry Out the Plan

Let $a + b$ be the height of the taller building where a is the **height** above the shorter building and b is the height of the shorter building.

$$\sin 39° = \frac{a}{75}$$
$$\sin 39° \times 75 = a$$
$$47.2 = a$$
$$\sin 55° = \frac{b}{75}$$
$$\sin 55° \times 75 = b$$
$$61.4 = b$$

4. Complete Corrine's solution.

▶ Look Back

5. Could Corrine have used a different trigonomic ratio to solve the problem? Explain.

Applications

LARGEST SQUARE

What are the dimensions of the largest square that will fit in a circle with a radius of 8 cm?

FLIGHT ALTITUDE

The angle of elevation from the top of a 20.0 m tower to a hot air balloon is 12°. The balloon is a horizontal distance of 2.0 km away. At what altitude is the balloon flying?

DISTANCE FROM CAMP

Rodney left his campsite and walked 1.5 km north, 2.3 km east, and 0.5 km south. At what angle south of west should he head to return directly to his campsite? How far must he walk?

BACKSLIDING

Curtis does not have the proper wax on his cross country skis. For every glide forward of 2.0 m, he slips back 0.5 m. How many glides forward will he have to make to cover 100 m?

Round answers to 1 decimal place when appropriate.

1. Sketch and then draw ΔMAT where $\angle M = 50°$, $MA = 5$ cm, and $\angle A = 40°$. Is it possible to draw a different triangle with these measurements? Explain.

2. Are ΔMAE and ΔAKE congruent? Explain why or why not.

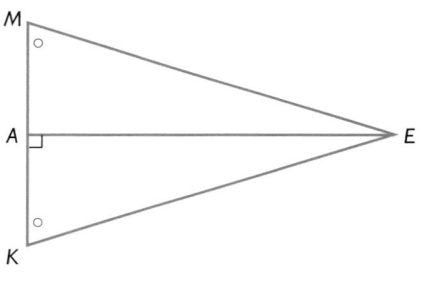

3. Are ΔBAG and ΔHOT similar? Explain why or why not.

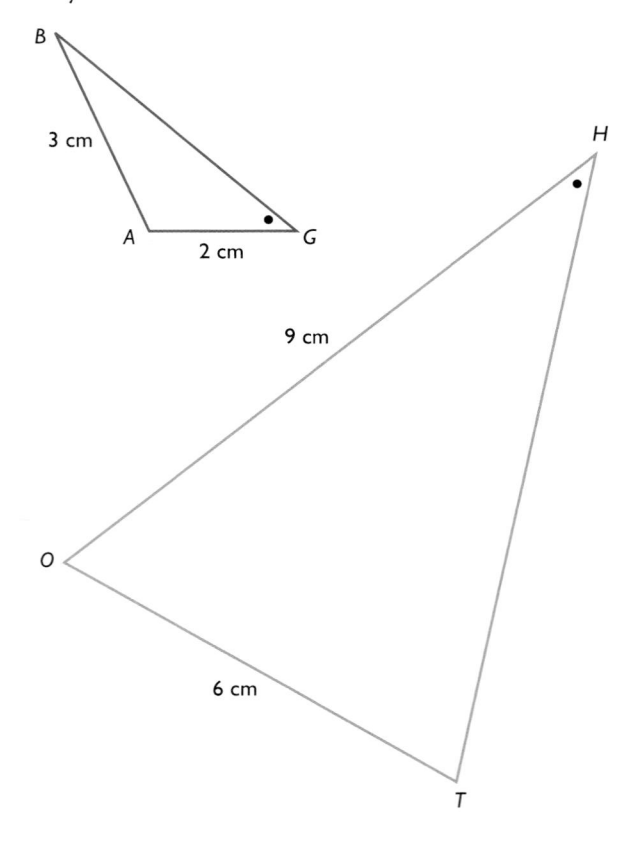

4. Find each unknown length.

a)

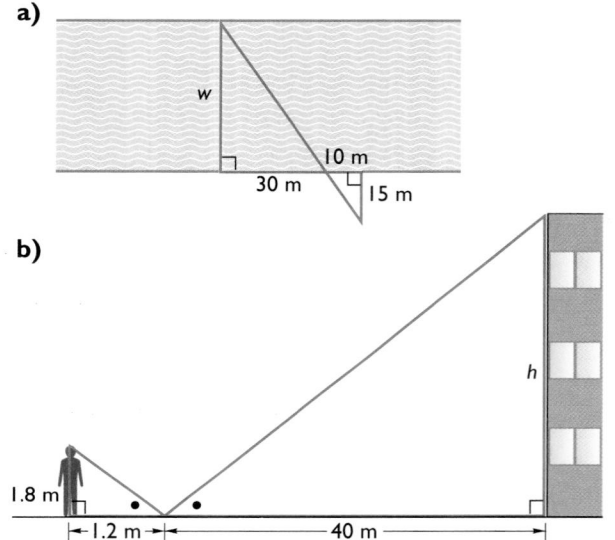

b)

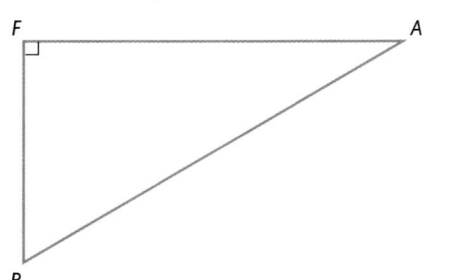

5. Without measuring ΔFAR or calculating,
a) is tan $\angle A$ greater than or less than 1?
b) which is greater — sin $\angle A$ or cos $\angle A$?

6. The length of a tree's shadow is 9.5 m and the sun's rays make an angle of 48° with the ground. How tall is the tree?

7. A ramp makes an 11° angle with the ground. It is 0.9 m above the ground at the other end. How long is the ramp?

8. A kite string is 38.5 m long and the kite is flying at a height of 16.2 m. What angle does the kite string make with the ground?

Practise With Games

Play these games in groups of 2, 3, or 4 players.

Greater, Less, or Equal

- Shuffle a deck of playing cards and place them face down in a pile.
- Draw a card but before you turn it over, predict whether the number of congruent small symbols (hearts, diamonds, spades, or clubs) will be greater than, less than, or equal to the number of congruent large symbols.
- If your prediction is correct, score 1 point.
- If your prediction is incorrect, score −1 point.
- Take turns drawing cards and predicting.
- Continue to play until all the cards have been turned over.
- The player with the highest score wins.

Variation:
Predict whether the number of similar symbols is greater than 4 OR 4 or less.

Example:

Player 1

Prediction: number of congruent small symbols > number of congruent large symbols

Score: −1 point since 2 < 5

Player 2

Prediction: number of congruent small symbols = number of congruent large symbols

Score: 1 point since 2 = 2

Trigonometric Race

- Use two different colored dice and a spinner.
- Let one color be adjacent and the other color be opposite.
- Toss the dice and spin the spinner.
- Calculate the angle with that sine, cosine, or tangent, finding the hypotenuse first if necessary.
- Take turns.
- The player with the greatest angle in each round scores 1 point.
- The first player with 10 points wins.

Example:

$$\text{hypotenuse}^2 = 2^2 + 6^2$$
$$\text{hypotenuse} = 6.324\,555\,32$$

$$\cos x° = \frac{\text{adjacent}}{\text{hypotenuse}}$$

$$\cos x° = \frac{2}{6.324\,555\,32}$$

$$\cos x° = 0.316\,227\,766$$
$$x° \approx 72$$

sine tangent cosine

adjacent

opposite

| 2 | x^2 | $+$ | 6 | x^2 | $=$ | $\sqrt{}$ | $=$ | | 6.32455532 |

| | 6.32455532 | | x^{-1} | $\times$ | 2 | $=$ | | 0.316227766 |

| | 0.316227766 | | $\cos^{-1}$ | $=$ | | 71.56505 |

Problems to Investigate

TAKE YOUR PICK!

TAN 0° AND TAN 90°

When the *x*-coordinate is 1, what is the tangent of the acute angle at the origin in the triangle?
What does this suggest that tan 0° and tan 90° are?

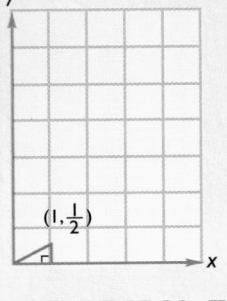
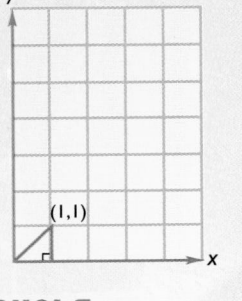
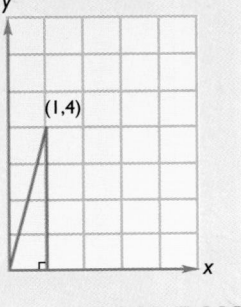
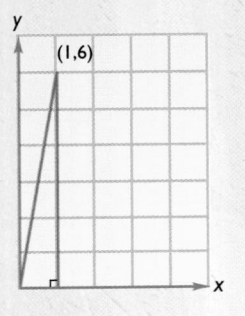

EQUILATERAL TRIANGLE

△*XYZ* is equilateral with all sides 2 units long. *XP* is perpendicular to *YZ*. What do you know about △*XYP* and △*XZP*? about *YP* and *ZP*? Explain. Use this to find cos 60°, sin 60°, and tan 60°. Check your results using the `COS`, `SIN`, and `TAN` keys.

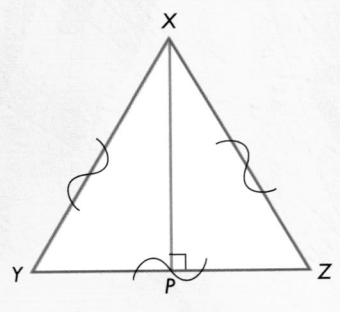

HEIGHT???

From the top of a viewing tower, the angle of depression to a cyclist is 8° and the angle of elevation to a taller tower is 12°. The cyclist is a horizontal distance of 900 m from the viewing tower. The second tower is a horizontal distance of 500 m from the viewing tower in the opposite direction. Is it possible to find the height of the second tower? Explain.

SCALE MODEL

A scale model of a building has a window 0.5 cm tall and 0.6 cm wide, and a door 0.75 cm tall and 0.3 cm wide. If the door is actually 2.1 m tall, find the window height and width, and the door width. What is the scale factor of the model?

CONGRUENT RIGHT TRIANGLES

If several students are given the length of the hypotenuse and one side to draw a right triangle, all the triangles drawn should be congruent. This is sometimes called the **HS** (hypotenuse side) condition for congruence. Try it.
Which of the conditions for congruence is HS a special case? Explain.

Make up some other problems about similarity or trigonometry. Post them on the bulletin board for your classmates to solve.

Round answers to 1 decimal place when appropriate.

1. Sketch and then draw ΔHIP where ∠H = 55°, HI = 5 cm, and IP = 4 cm. Is it possible to draw a different triangle with these measurements? Explain.

2. Draw a triangle congruent to this one by measuring ∠P and any two other parts.

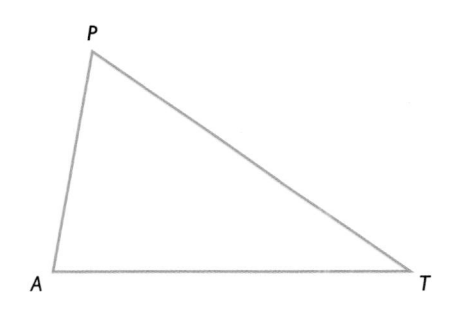

3. How can you be certain if two triangles are similar?

4. A tree casts a shadow 7.2 m long at the same time that a person 175 cm tall casts a shadow 140 cm long. How tall is the tree?

5. Why are similar triangles used more often than congruent triangles to find hard-to-measure distances?

6. a) Without calculating, what is the tangent of ∠O?

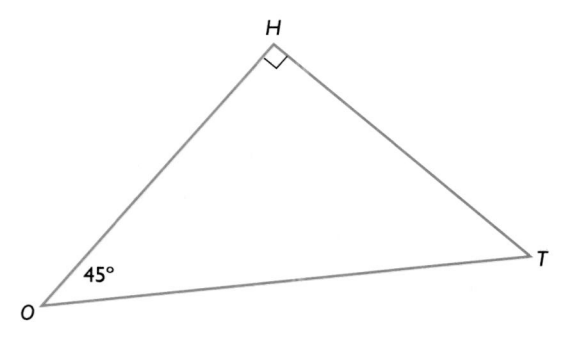

b) Use a square root to describe the sine and cosine of ∠O.

7. Solve each triangle.

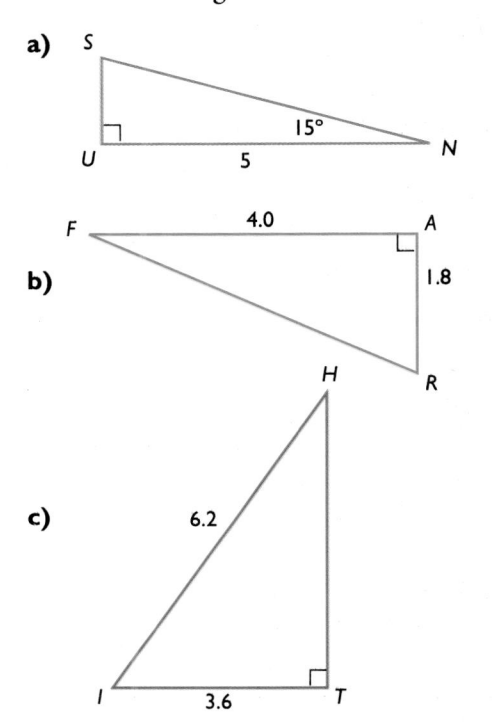

8. A ladder makes an angle of 70° with the ground. Its base is 1.8 m from the base of the building. How far up the building does the ladder go?

9. The angle of depression from the top of a 75 m tower to the closest edge of a forest fire is 4°. How close is the fire to the tower?

10. A guy wire 3.9 m long reaches a pole 3.1 m above the ground. What angles does the wire make with
a) the ground?
b) the pole?

11. Two buildings are 40 m apart. The angle of elevation from the top of the shorter building to the top of the taller building is 30°. The angle of depression from the top of the shorter building to the base of the taller building is 50°. What is the height of each building?

1. Are all congruent triangles similar? Are all similar triangles congruent? Explain.

6. Describe two different ways you can find measurements indirectly.

2. Explain how to predict by examining the side lengths of a triangle whether the tangent of an angle will be greater or less than 1.

3. How are trigonometric ratios related to similar right triangles?

5. Show and explain why two sides and one angle are sufficient conditions for congruence only if the angle is contained between those sides.

4. Explain why sine and cosine are always less than 1. How can you tell whether the sine or cosine of an angle will have the greater ratio?

What questions do you still have about similarity and trigonometry?

Investigating the Unusual

In 1994, a group of ten people built a record-breaking square pyramid of 4900 cans in 25 min 54 s.

- Explain why $1^2 + 2^2 + 3^2 + 4^2 + 5^2$ represents the number of cans in the top 5 layers. How many cans are there?

- This expression represents the number of cans in n layers. Use it to find how many cans are in the top 10 layers. $1^2 + 2^2 + 3^2 + 4^2 + 5^2 + ... + n^2$

- How could you use your result for the top 10 layers to find the number of cans in the top 9 layers? 11 layers?

- Another expression for the number of cans in n layers is
$$\frac{2n^3 + 3n^2 + n}{6}.$$
Do you get the same answer for the top 10 layers using it?

- Estimate the number of layers in the record-breaking pyramid. Substitute your estimate into the expression above to see if you are correct. Guess and test until you find the number of layers.

- How many cans were in the bottom layer? Explain.

 **HOW** # Can We Examine Unusual Manufactured Objects?

47.36 m

25.2 m

> n 1994, the Saskatchewan
> Seniors' Association made
> the world's largest quilt.

Concept Development

1. Use the world's largest quilt, and round all answers to 1 decimal place.
   a) Calculate its area and perimeter.
   b) How do the area and perimeter compare as a unit rate (m²/m)?
   c) How many times as great as the area of your classroom floor is its area?
   d) What would the dimensions and perimeter be for a square with the same area?
   e) For the square, what is area to perimeter as a unit rate?
   f) What do you notice about the rates in parts (b) and (e)? Explain.

Applications

Round all answers to 1 decimal place. Repeat parts (a) to (f) above for each of these unusual articles.

1.

457.81 m

Tablecloth
Made in Illinois, USA, 1990

1.37 m

2.

BUILT BY
ENGINEERING
STUDENTS IN 1993

3.17 m

Yo-yo built by engineering students

100 m

3.

70 m

ORDEM E PROGRESSO

Flag of Brazil

4. The world's largest popcorn box was filled by students in Florida in 1994. They spent several days popping corn to fill the box.

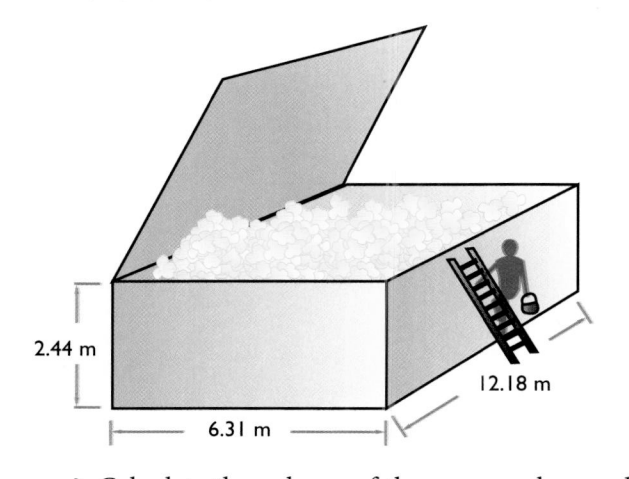

2.44 m
12.18 m
6.31 m

a) Calculate the volume of the popcorn box and the amount of cardboard used.
b) How do the volume and surface area compare as a unit rate (m³/m²)?
c) How many times as great as the volume of your classroom is the volume of the box?
d) Explain why you can use the $\boxed{\sqrt{}}$ key on your calculator to find the dimensions of a cube with the same volume.

187.5 $\boxed{\text{2nd}}$ $\boxed{\sqrt{}}$

e) For the cube, what is volume to surface area as a unit rate?
f) What do you notice about the rates in parts (b) and (e)? Explain.

5. If each 100 mL of popcorn kernels yields about 2 L of popped corn, how many litres of popcorn kernels were used to fill the box?

6. If each container holds the same amount of popcorn as the box in Problem 4, what would its height be?

a)

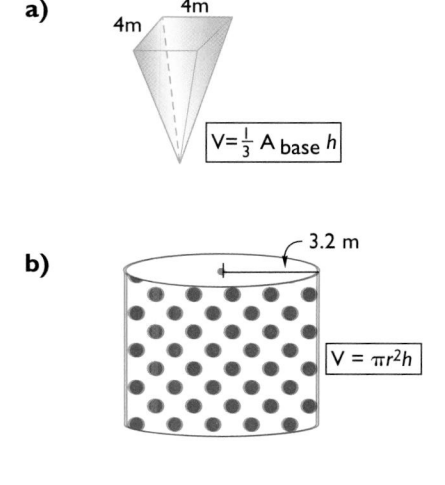

4m
4m

$V = \frac{1}{3} A_{\text{base}} h$

b)

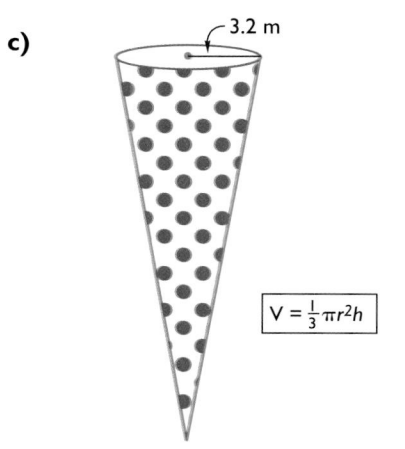

3.2 m

$V = \pi r^2 h$

c)

3.2 m

$V = \frac{1}{3}\pi r^2 h$

7. The Pentagon in Washington, D.C. is the world's largest office building. It is a regular pentagon. (Each inside angle of any regular pentagon is 108°.)

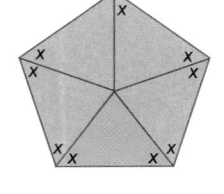

108°

281 m

a) To find the area of a regular pentagon, you can divide the pentagon into 5 triangles by drawing a bisector through each angle to the centre. How do you know the triangles are congruent? What is the measure of each angle *x*?

b) To find the area of a triangle, you need to know base and height. Which do you know for each of the 5 triangles? What is it?

x
x *x* *x* *x*
x *x* *x* *x*

c) To find the other dimension, you can use trigonometry. What ratio would you use? What is the other dimension?

h
x $\frac{1}{2}$ *b* *x*

$$sine = \frac{opposite}{hypotenuse}$$

$$cosine = \frac{adjacent}{hypotenuse}$$

$$tangent = \frac{opposite}{adjacent}$$

d) What is the area covered by the Pentagon?

8. Predict and then find the area of a regular pentagon with sides that are twice the length of the Pentagon's. Was your prediction close? Explain.

9. The English Channel tunnel, the world's longest underwater tunnel, was opened in 1994. It cost about $20 billion to build. A volume of about 1.45×10^6 m³ of earth was removed.
a) Estimate the cost to remove each cubic metre of earth. Explain how you calculated.
b) Calculate the dimensions of a cube with the same volume.

HOME LINK

Investigate and report on a manufactured wonder in your community, province, or anywhere in Canada. Create and solve a mathematical problem using the data.

The giant egg of Vegreville, Alberta.

WHAT **Unusual Facts Can We Find About Nature?**

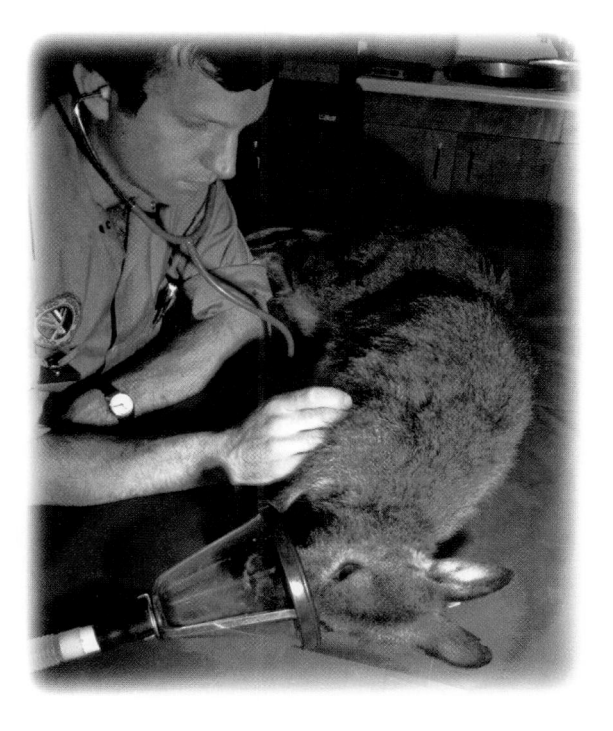

> **B**iologists have determined that most mammals have a natural life span of about 1 billion heartbeats despite differences in size.

Concept Development

1. Most species of shrew have an average heart rate of about 800 beats/min.

  a) How many times will a shrew's heart beat in 1 h? 1 d? 1 year?

  b) How many times will a shrew's heart beat in 2 years? 2.5 years? 3 years?

  c) Estimate the life span of a shrew in years.

2. This formula can be used to estimate the life span of a mammal in years, *a*, for a given heart rate in beats per minute, *h*.

$$a = \frac{1902.6}{h}$$

  a) Use the formula to estimate a shrew's life span.

  b) How does your answer compare to your estimate in Problem 1c)?

Applications

1. Most elephants have a heart rate of about 25 beats/min.

  a) How many times as long as a shrew's life span is an elephant's?

  b) Estimate an elephant's life span using

    • your answer to part (a)

    • the formula in Problem 2 above

2. a) Find your heart rate.

b) Use the formula and your heart rate to estimate a human's lifespan. Does the estimate seem reasonable? Explain.

What sorts of things affect heart rate? Explain how you would go about finding your average heart rate.

3. Most mammals take about 1 breath for every 4 heartbeats.

a) Predict your breath rate in breaths per minute.

b) Now measure your breath rate. How does it compare to your heart rate?

c) This formula is used to estimate lifespan in years, a, if you know breath rate, b.

$$a = \frac{1902.6}{4b}$$

How does this formula relate to the formula for estimating age based on heart rate? Explain.

d) Estimate a human's life span using your breath rate and this formula. Compare it to the life span you found in Problem 2b) above.

e) Write a formula for estimating the breath rate, b, if you know the life span in years, a. Explain what you did. $b = ?$

4. The greediest animal must be the larva of the polyphemus moth. It consumes an amount equal to 86 000 times its mass in its first few months. If a human baby ate at this rate, how many kilograms of food would it consume?

5. A gnat can flap its wings at a rate of 1000 flaps per second.

a) Express the rate in flaps per minute and in flaps per hour.

b) At what rate can you flap your arms in flaps per minute? flaps per hour?

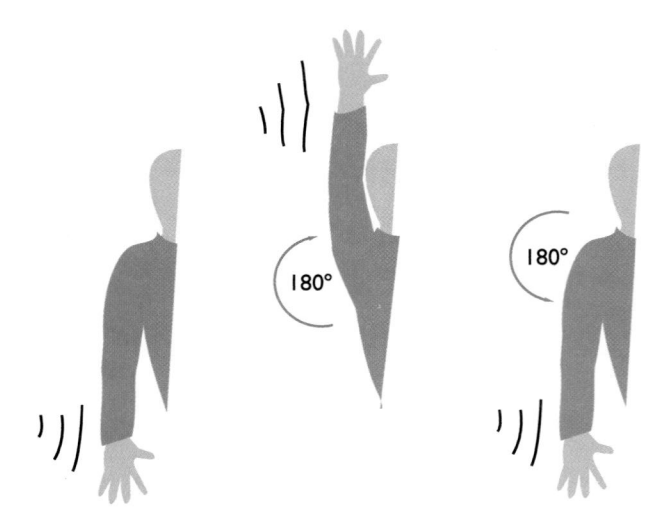

In one flap, the arm moves up 180° and down 180°.

6. To find the speed at which he can flap his arm in kilometres per hour, John found the circumference of a circle, 3.9 m, using his arm length, 0.62 m, as the radius. Then he changed the circumference to kilometres, 0.0039 km, and multiplied it by his flap per hour rate, 5040, to get 19.7 km/h.

a) Why did he find the circumference that he did?

b) Find your flap rate in kilometres per hour. Explain what you did.

c) What would your flap rate be in kilometres per hour if you could flap your arms at the same rate as the gnat?

7. Many shells and plants grow in spirals.

A spiral can be created by constructing an isosceles right triangle, and then constructing consecutive right triangles on the hypotenuse of the previous one.

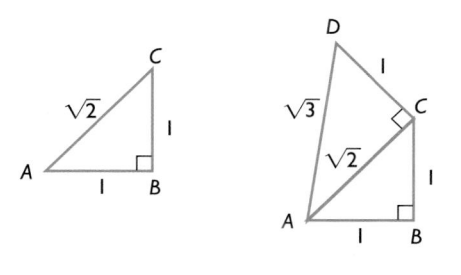

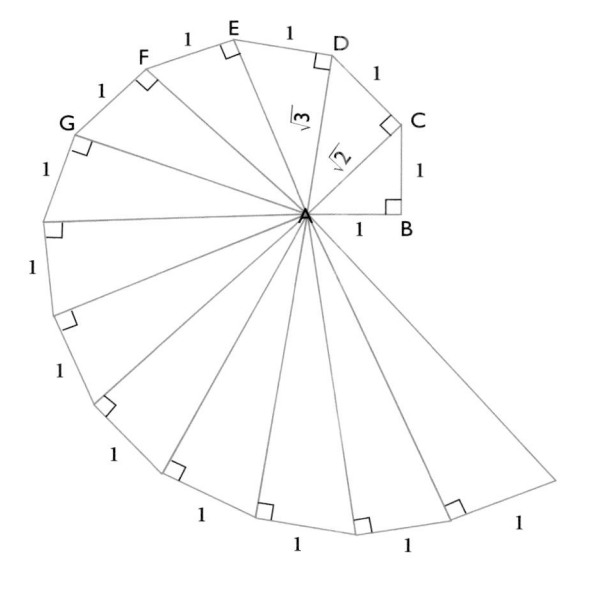

a) Explain why the length of *AC* is $\sqrt{2}$ and *AD* is $\sqrt{3}$.

b) Calculate the lengths of the hypotenuses *AE*, *AF*, and *AG*.

c) Predict the hypotenuse for the 10th triangle in the spiral.

8. Use the spiral in Problem 7.
   a) What is the measure of $\angle CAB$ in $\triangle ABC$?
   b) Calculate the measure of these inside angles to the nearest degree, using trigonometry.
   • $\angle DAC$
   • $\angle EAD$
   • $\angle FAE$
   • $\angle GAF$
   c) Describe the pattern of the inside angles as the spiral grows.

9. The mass of a snowflake is about 10^{-6} g. A litre of water has a mass of 1 kg. How many snowflakes can be made from 1 L of water?

10. It has been estimated that 10^{35} snowflakes have fallen to Earth to date. Estimate the total mass of snowflakes in tonnes.

DID YOU HNOW

The largest concentration of animals was a swarm of 12 500 000 000 000 locusts that appeared in Nebraska in 1875. If a locust has a mass of 2 g, what was the mass of the swarm in scientific notation in grams? kilograms? tonnes?

Making Sense of DATA

Making Data Meaningful

It's sometimes difficult to get a sense of just how unusual things are unless the data is related to something familiar.

Jean-Pierre Bernard ran to victory during the Hong Kong Waiters' Race. The 36-year-old waiter was challenged by South Korea's Kim Young Sik, who was later disqualified for spilling too much water. Bernard ran the 400-m race in just over 11 s.

Karen knows that she walks at a speed of about 4 km/h. She thought the waiter's speed was incorrect. She decided to express *400 m in 11 s* as kilometres per hour.

> I divide 400 by 11 to get the waiter's speed in metres per second, 36 m/s. Then I multiply by 60 twice to get it in metres per hour, 130 909 m/h. Finally I divide by 1000 to get it in kilometres per hour, 131 km/h.

1. a) Why did Karen find the speed in kilometres per hour?
   b) Do you think the waiter's speed was remarkable? Explain.
   c) What do you think the waiter's speed actually was?

2. Brent is a 100-m sprinter. He changed 400 m in 11 s to 100 m in 2.75 s.
   a) Explain what he did.
   b) Why might Brent find it more meaningful to express the speed as 2.75 s to run 100 m to determine if the waiter's speed was reasonable?

Applications

3. The West Edmonton Mall, including its parking lot, covers 49 hectares. (1 ha = 10 000 m^2)
   a) What is its area in square metres?
   b) What would be the perimeter, in kilometres, of a square with the same area?
   c) About how long would it take to walk the perimeter of the square at 4 km/h?

4. The blood system is about 1.6×10^{11} mm long. The distance around Earth is about 40 000 km. Which is greater? How many times as great?

5. A period in this book has a mass of 6×10^{-9} kg. How many periods have the same mass as 500 g of butter?

6. The width of a hair is about 50 μm (micrometres) or 0.05 mm. How many hairs are there in 1 mm? 1 cm? 1 m?

7. Would you have done anything different to the data in any of the problems to make it more meaningful to you? Explain.

8. Which of the pieces of information above did you find the most remarkable? Explain.

WHAT Unusual Facts Can We Learn About Places on Earth?

Mount Everest, named after its first surveyor, Sir George Everest, is the world's tallest mountain. Its height above sea level has been measured several times using different methods. The most recent survey measured the height at 8872 m ± 20 m.

Concept Development

1. a) The expression ± 20 m is called the *margin of error*. What does ± 20 m mean?
b) What is 20 m as a percent of 8872 m rounded to 2 decimal places?
c) What does 8872 m ± 0.23% mean?

2. K2, a mountain in the same range as Mt. Everest, is 8616 m ± 7 m tall.
a) Express K2's height using percent rounded to 2 decimal places, 8616 ± ■%.
b) K2 was measured more accurately than Mt. Everest. Explain how you know.

3. Which height was measured more accurately? Explain.

     A   B
1000 m ± 20 m   100 000 ± 200 m

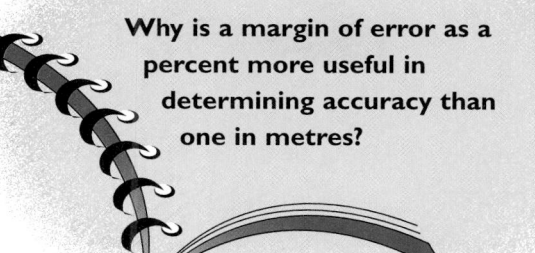

In Your Journal

Why is a margin of error as a percent more useful in determining accuracy than one in metres?

293

Round all answers to 1 decimal place.

1. What percent of Mt. Everest's height is the height of each of the 3 tallest mountains in Canada?

Mountain	Height (m)	Province/ Territory
a) Mt. Logan	5959	Yukon
b) Fairweather Mtn.	4663	British Columbia
c) Mt. Columbia	3747	Alberta

2. Most people imagine Earth as having a very rough surface. To get a sense of what the Earth's surface is like, imagine Earth as a ball, 1 m in diameter.

Let h be the height of Mt. Everest on the scale model in metres.
$$\frac{h}{8872} = \frac{1}{12\ 756\ 000}$$

Scale: 1 m represents 12 756 km

a) Explain why the scale factor can be expressed as $\frac{1}{12\ 756\ 000}$.

b) Find the height of Mt. Everest on the scale model in millimetres.

c) The deepest point on Earth is the Mariana Trench in the Pacific Ocean. Its depth is 10 924 m. Find its depth on the scale model in millimetres.

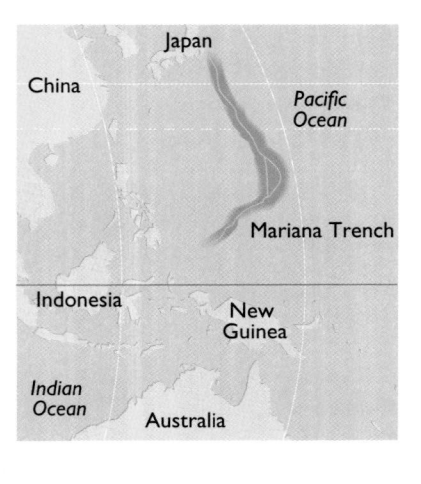

d) Would you describe Earth's surface as relatively smooth or rough? Explain.

3. Earth is not a true sphere. The diameter at the equator is about 12 756 km while the polar diameter is about 12 714 km. What is the polar diameter as a percent of the equatorial diameter?

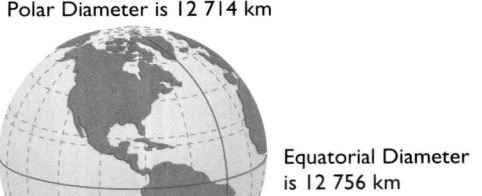

Polar Diameter is 12 714 km

Equatorial Diameter is 12 756 km

4. To investigate the difference between the diameters, you can use the scale model of Earth again.
a) If the equatorial diameter of the scale model is 1 m, find the polar diameter.
b) Would you describe Earth as more ball-shaped or egg-shaped? Explain.

This table displays 1991 data for the provinces and territories in Canada.

Province/Territory	Land Area (km²)	Population (1991)
Canada	9 215 430	27 297 000
Newfoundland	371 690	568 000
Prince Edward Island	5 660	130 000
Nova Scotia	52 840	900 000
New Brunswick	72 090	724 000
Quebec	1 356 790	6 896 000
Ontario	891 190	10 085 000
Manitoba	548 360	1 092 000
Saskatchewan	570 700	989 000
Alberta	644 390	2 546 000
British Columbia	929 730	3 282 000
Yukon	478 970	28 000
North West Territories	3 293 020	58 000

5. To get a sense of how the populations of the provinces and territories compare, imagine Canada as a community of 1000 people.
a) Solve a proportion to find the number of Albertans.
b) Solve proportions for 3 other provinces or territories.

6. This circle graph shows how the area of Alberta compares to the area of Canada. The sector for Alberta has an angle of 25.2°.

Alberta as Part of Canada by Area

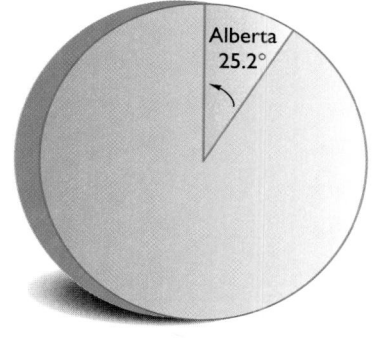

Alberta
25.2°

a) Explain how you could use a proportion to find the sector angle for Alberta's area.
b) Find the angle of each sector for 3 other provinces' or territories' areas.

7. To investigate the relationship between area and population of the provinces and territories, a scatter plot can be used.
a) Explain why area is the independent variable and population is the dependent variable.
b) What are some possible control variables which might affect the relationship between area and population?
c) Create a scatter plot. Find the line of best fit if possible.

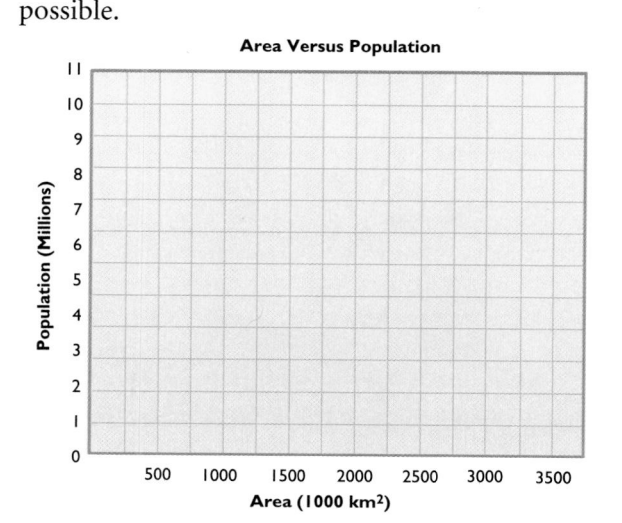

Area Versus Population

d) What conclusions can you make from your scatter plot?

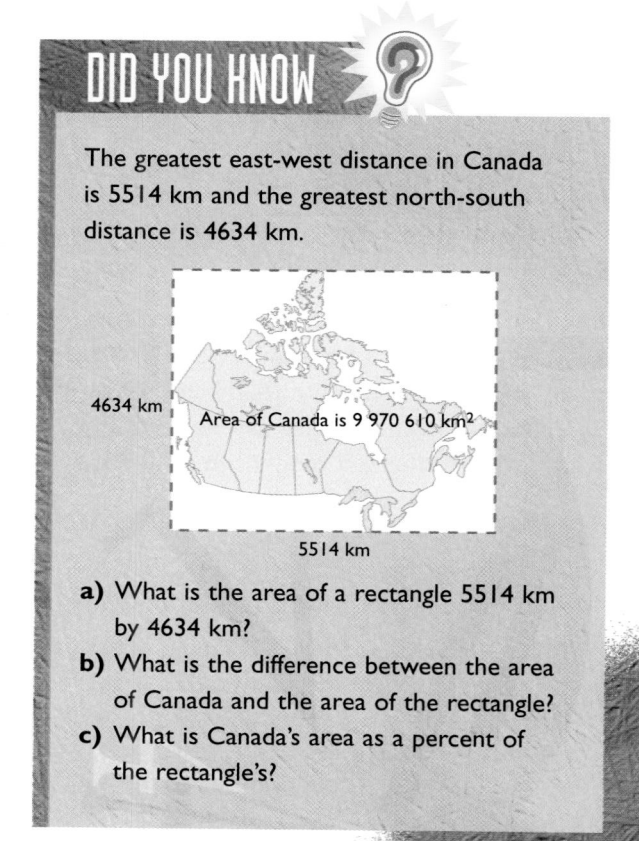

DID YOU KNOW ?

The greatest east-west distance in Canada is 5514 km and the greatest north-south distance is 4634 km.

4634 km

Area of Canada is 9 970 610 km²

5514 km

a) What is the area of a rectangle 5514 km by 4634 km?
b) What is the difference between the area of Canada and the area of the rectangle?
c) What is Canada's area as a percent of the rectangle's?

 Numbers Are Used to Describe Extra-Terrestrial Places?

One astronomical unit,
AU, is the mean distance
from the Sun to Earth, a
distance of 1.496×10^8 km.

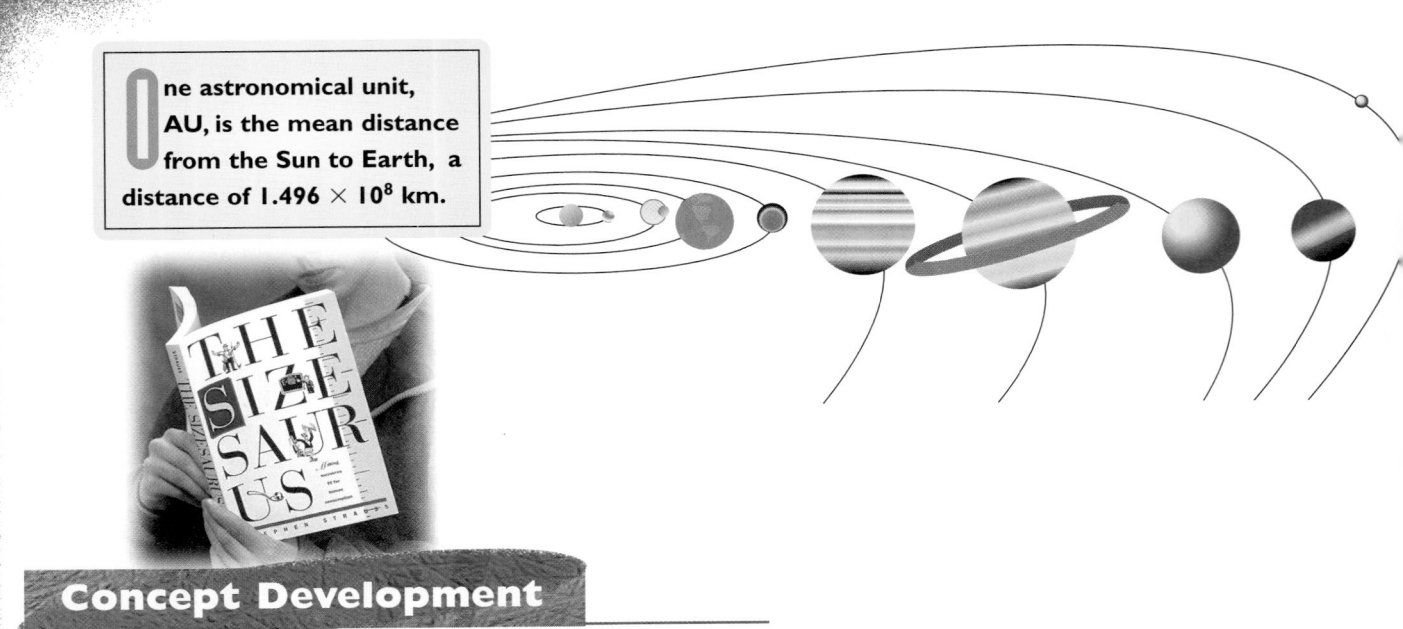

Concept Development

1. Describe the shape of the orbit of a planet around the sun.
Why is the *mean* distance used? What other distances
might be used?

2. **a)** Explain why this calculation gives the AU for Mercury.

$$\frac{5.790 \times 10^7}{1.496 \times 10^8}$$

5.79 [EXP] 7 [÷] 1.496 [EXP] 8 [=] | 0.387032085

$\cong 0.387$

b) Calculate the AU to 3 decimal places for each of the
other planets. Record your data in a table.

3. Use your table to determine which planet is
   a) about twice as far from the Sun as Saturn
   b) farther from the Sun than Neptune by about 33%
   c) farther from the Sun than Earth by about 50%
   d) closer to the Sun than Pluto by about half

Planet	Mean Distance from Sun (km)	Mean Distance from Sun (AU)
Mercury	5.7900×10^7	0.387
Venus	1.0820×10^8	
Earth	1.4960×10^8	1.000
Mars	2.2790×10^8	
Jupiter	7.7840×10^8	
Saturn	1.4238×10^9	
Uranus	2.8687×10^9	
Neptune	4.4921×10^9	
Pluto	5.9265×10^9	

4. **a)** Plot the planets on an AU number line. Earth is done for you.

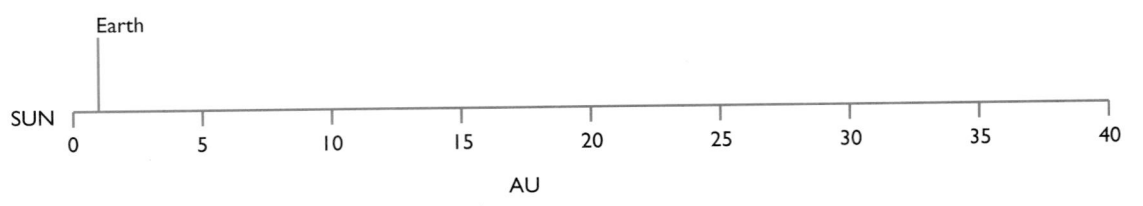

b) Describe the distribution of the planets along the number line.

Applications

Round all answers to 1 decimal place.

1. The largest scale model of the Solar System is at the Lakeview Museum of Arts and Sciences in Peoria, Illinois. The model distance from the Sun to Earth is 1.2 km.
a) Estimate the model distance from the Sun to Uranus.

Let x be the model distance from the Sun to Uranus in kilometres.
$$\frac{1.2}{x} = \frac{1}{19.176}$$

b) Estimate the model distance from the Sun to Mercury and to Pluto.

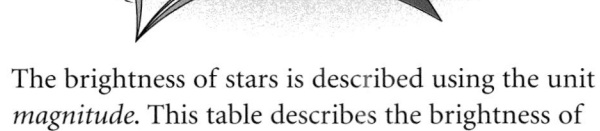

In Your Journal

The Lakeview Museum's model distance from the Sun to Pluto is 64 km. How does this compare to your estimate in Problem 1b)?

Do you think the mean distances or the greatest distances were used to build the model? Explain.

The brightness of stars is described using the unit *magnitude*. This table describes the brightness of selected magnitudes.

magnitude	comments	decreasing brightness
+1	very bright	
+6	faint but can be seen by unaided human eye	
+7	cannot be seen by unaided human eye	
+9	can be seen through binoculars	
+13	can be seen through an amateur telescope	
+20	can be seen through the Mt. Palomar telescope	
+30	can be seen through the Hubble space telescope	

2. A +1 star is brighter than a
+2 star by a factor of 2.512
+3 star by a factor of 2.512^2 or 6.3
+4 star by a factor of 2.512^3 or 15.9

How many times as bright is a +1 star as a
a) + 5 star?
b) + 6 star?

3. This expression can be used to compare the brightness of two stars.

2.512^n, where n is the difference between the magnitudes of the stars.

Which is brighter? How many times as bright is it?
a) Pluto +14 and Neptune +8
b) Uranus +6 and Pluto +14
c) +6 star and +9 star
d) +6 star and +13 star
e) +6 star and +20 star
f) +6 star and +30 star

4. Negative integers are used to describe the brightness of some stars and planets. Venus has a magnitude of about −5.
a) How would you describe Venus's brightness? Explain.
b) What is the difference between the magnitudes of Venus and Pluto? Venus and Neptune? Venus and Uranus?
c) How many times brighter is Venus as Pluto? Neptune? Uranus?

DID YOU KNOW

The brightest object in the daylight sky is the Sun. It is a −26 star.
How many times as bright is the Sun as a +1 star? +6 star? +30 star?

Are Some Unusual Ways to Measure Unusual Events?

A major league baseball fan gets hit by a baseball during a game. Probability is 1 in 300 000.

Two people picked at random have identical fingerprints. Probability is 1 in 64 million.

A professional golfer gets a hole-in-one on a par 3 hole in a PGA tournament. Probability is 1 in 3708.

Concept Development

1. **a)** What does a probability of 1 in 3708 mean?
   b) What is the probability of a baseball fan *not* getting hit by a ball during a game?
   c) What are the odds of a professional golfer getting a hole-in-one on a par 3 hole in a PGA tournament?

2. Which of the three events above is least likely? Explain.

3. What is the theoretical probability of tossing 1 coin and getting tails? 2 coins and getting 2 tails? 3 coins and getting 3 tails?

4. The formula $P(\text{all tails}) = \frac{1}{2^n}$ can be used to find the probability of all the coins in a toss landing tails, where n is the number of coins tossed.
   a) Describe what happens to the probability as the number of coins increases.
   b) Is a probability of 1 possible? Explain.

5. Suppose every student in your class tossed a coin and all the coins came up heads.
   a) Predict whether this is more or less likely than two people having the same fingerprints.
   b) Calculate the probability. Was your prediction correct?

Round answers to 1 decimal place when appropriate.

1. This graph shows the probability of at least two people in a group having the same birthday.

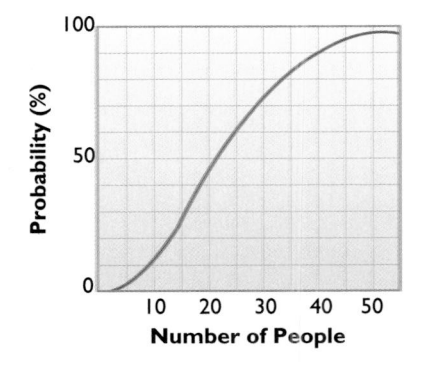

a) What happens to the probability as the group size increases? Explain why.
b) Use the graph to estimate the theoretical probability of at least two people in your class sharing a birthday.
c) About how many people must be in a group for the theoretical probability to be 25%? 50%? 75%?

2. a) Explain why it's possible that, in a group as large as 365, there could still be no birthday matches.

b) How many people must there be in a group to be absolutely certain of a birthday match?
c) Is it possible for there to be a birthday match in a group of 2? Explain.

3. According to the 1991 Census, 3500 people out of the 27 297 000 people living in Canada were aged 100 years or older.
What is the probability of living to be 100 years or older if you live in Canada?

4. The probability of a person reaching the age of 115 is about 1 in 2.1 billion.
a) The world population in 1991 was about 5 423 000 000. How many people aged 115 years or over were there in the world?
b) About 7.0×10^{10} people have existed in the world. About how many of those lived to 115 years?

5. Suppose you were investigating the relationship between a country's wealth (per capita GDP, Gross Domestic Product — see page 2 in Unit 1) and the average life expectancy of its population.
a) Create a question for this investigation, and then make a prediction.
b) What is the independent variable? the dependent variable?
c) War might affect how the two variables relate. List some other possible control variables.

In Your Journal

Explain why people might be expected to live longer in a country with a high per capita GDP compared to a country with a low per capita GDP.

6. This table displays data on the ages of various things, living and non-living.

Age (years)	
the universe	1.2×10^9
Earth	4.5×10^8
oldest Egyptian pyramid	4600
oldest human	120

a) This set of keystrokes compares the ages of two things in the table. What are they? How many times as old is the older one as the other?

$$1.2 \boxed{\text{EXP}} \ 9 \ \div \ 4.5 \ \boxed{\text{EXP}} \ 8 \ \boxed{=}$$

b) How many times as old is Earth as the oldest living human?

c) What fraction of the age of the universe is the age of the oldest human?

In Your Journal

It has been said that the life span of a human is merely an *eyeblink* compared to the age of the universe. Explain what this means.

7. This table displays data on the speed of various things.

Speed	
light	3.0×10^8 km/s
lightning	5.0×10^6 km/s
Earth travelling around the Sun	1.1×10^5 km/h
Apollo 10's trip to the moon	40 000 km/h
Concorde jetliner	2 333 km/h

a) Which speeds do you find difficult to compare by examining the table? Explain.

b) Explain what you would do to find how many times as fast as the speed of the Concorde the speed of lightning is.

8. How many times as fast is the first item in each pair as the second?
  a) light and lightning
  b) Apollo 10 and the Concorde
  c) Earth and the Concorde
  d) lightning and Earth
  e) light and Apollo 10

9. A year is the time it takes for Earth to orbit the Sun. A year is 365.2422 days or 365 d 5 h 48 min 45 s.
  a) How many seconds are in 5 h 48 min 45 s?
  b) Explain how the 0.2422 of a day was calculated.

10. Without a leap year every four years, in about 730 years, summer would start in December and winter in June. Explain how a leap year compensates for the extra 0.2422 d each year.

DID YOU KNOW

Earth's rotation is slowing down. In 3000 years, relative time will be pushed back 12 h. That means that if nothing is done to compensate, in 3000 years it will be dark at noon and light at midnight all year long.

a) About what fraction of a second is Earth's rotation slowing down per year? per day? Explain.

b) Periodically, as at midnight on December 31, 1995, one second — a leap second — is added to the world's timekeeping clocks. How many leap seconds will have to be added over the next 3000 years? How many leap seconds is that per year?

300

Communicate Your Knowledge

 **1.** The British publication *Fortean Times* specializes in the recording of unusual events such as frog showers, spontaneous human combustion, and flying goats. It reported that world weirdness was down 2% from last year. Does this figure have any real meaning? Explain.

6. The community of Gary, Indiana, had the greatest decline in population in North America. Over a 10-year period the population dropped by about 35 000. Explain why knowing the population before the decline (151 968) is necessary to determine whether or not the decline is remarkable.

 **2.** Create a list of the types of publications, on-line sites, and other data sources which would provide information about unusual places, people, things, and events.

5. Shaq O'Neil's shoe size is 22. Do you think this is as unusual among pro basketball players as it is among the general population? What should you consider before determining if something is unusual?

3. Explain the difference between unusual facts about regular things and regular facts about unusual things. Use examples from the unit to help you.

4. Write a definition for the word "unusual" based on what you learned in this unit. Include a list of synonyms.

What unusual facts have you learned in this unit that you will tell others about?

Worked Examples

UNIT 1 Data Analysis

1.1 Example 1, page 3
Assess whether or not the following has the features of a good question. Defend your decision.
Which make of van has the most headroom?

Solution
I ask myself:
- Does the question compare things?
  – yes, different makes of vans
- Is it clear what's being investigated?
  – yes, headroom
- Is an experiment suggested?
  – yes, you'd have to measure headroom in each van
For these reasons, it is a good question.

1.1 Example 2, page 3
Identify the independent variable, dependent variable, and 2 control variables for an investigation on van headroom.

Solution
The independent variable is the one you change: different makes of vans from different companies over the past, say 2, years.
The dependent variable may change as the make of van changes: the headroom, measured in centimetres. The control variables are kept constant: headroom measured from the same point each time – from surface of driver's seat in its most forward position; headroom measured the same way each time – perpendicular from seat to ceiling.

1.2 Example 1, page 5
How might the following sample be biased? Who would you sample to obtain unbiased results? Explain.
A group of city politicians are asked about cutting back the number of civil servants that work at city hall.

Solution
I think city politicians wouldn't want to cut back on the number of civil servants working because they might know many of them personally, and they probably would have less help and more work to do. I'd survey people in the city randomly using names from the phone book.

1.2 Example 2, page 5
What method of collecting and organizing data would you use if you investigated this question?
Is the home team more likely to win in our school sports?

Solution
I would collect data from the physical education department for each of the competitive sports played at our school for as many years as possible. I'd record the ratio of wins at home to games played at home in a table like the following:

	Team	
	Boys' Junior Basketball	**Girls' Senior Basketball**
1993	$\frac{7}{12}$	
1994	$\frac{6}{14}$	
1995	$\frac{8}{13}$	

1.3 Example 1, page 9
What does the clustering of the points mean in this scatter plot?

Measurements for Our Class

Solution
The measurements for foot length and length from wrist to elbow vary a little bit for the students. The relationship between the lengths is fairly

strong–for any student the two lengths appear to be about the same.

1.3 Example 2, page 9
Some employees at a company kept a record of the distance driven and of their vehicle expenses for 1 month. The results, rounded to the nearest 100 km and to the nearest dollar, were as follows:

Distance driven (km)	Expenses ($)
900	211
1100	258
1200	258
1200	264
1500	297
1600	364
1600	376
1800	385
2100	438
2200	459

a) What prediction would you make for this question?
How does the distance driven affect vehicle expenses?
b) Make a scatter plot.
c) Does your scatter plot show a strong or weak relationship? Explain.

Solution
a) I predict that the greater the distance driven, the greater the vehicle expenses, because there is more gasoline and vehicle maintenance to pay for.
b)

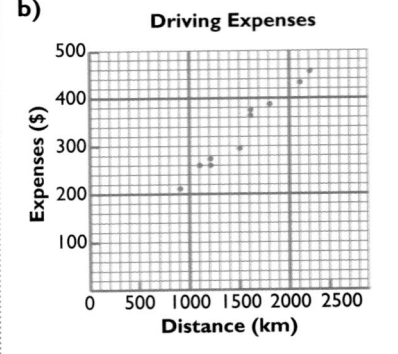

Driving Expenses

302

c) The relationship is strong because I can confidently predict the expenses for the distance driven.

1.4 Example 1, page 11
a) Find the line of best fit for the scatter plot in Example 2b) from 1.3.
b) What is the estimated expense of driving 700 km? 1000 km? 2500 km?

Solution

a)

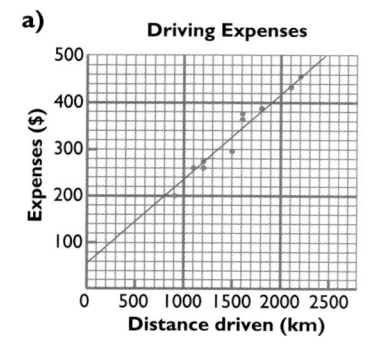

b) Go across the horizontal axis to 700 km, and then up until you reach the line of best fit. Read the other coordinate of that point from the vertical axis. The estimated expense for driving 700 km is about $180. For 1000 km, the estimated expense is about $225; for 2500 km, about $500.

1.4 Example 2, page 12
The heights and masses of the 22 players on a soccer field were graphed. Is it possible to find a line of best fit for this scatter plot? Justify your decision.

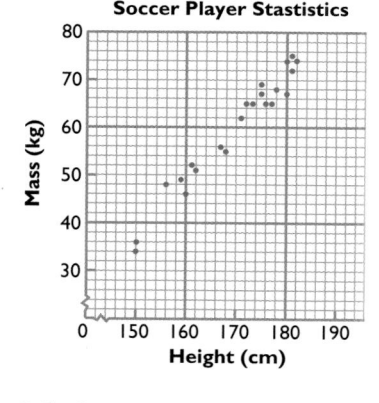

Solution

The points fall into an almost straight line, so the data shows a

---

linear relationship and a line of best fit can be found.

1.5 Example 1, page 16
a) Find the line of best fit of the scatter plot in 1.4, Example 2.
b) What relationship does the line represent?
c) Explain the meaning of the points above your line, and below your line.
d) How well can you predict with your line?
e) Predict the mass of a soccer player whose height is 170 cm.
f) Predict the height of a soccer player whose mass is 50 kg.

Solution

a)

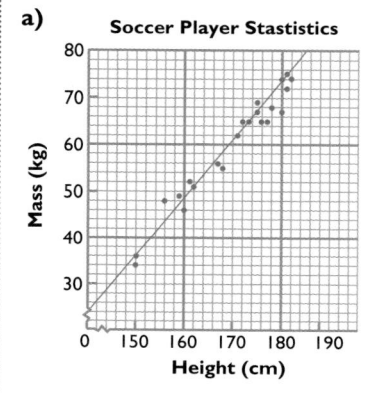

b) The line slants upwards. As the heights of soccer players increase, their masses also increase.
c) The points above the line represent players who have greater mass than the average player at that height. The points below the line represent players who have lesser mass than the average player at that height.
d) I can predict quite reliably because most of the points are on the line of best fit or are very close to it. My predictions would only be reliable for similar soccer players— that is, the same gender and about the same age.
e) The point on the line up from 170 cm shows a mass of about 61 kg.
f) The point on the line across from 50 kg shows a height of about 161 cm.

1.5 Example 2, page 16
Use the scatter plot below.
a) What conclusions can you make from the data?
b) From this data, does it appear that a student's Math mark is a good indication of his or her English mark? Explain.

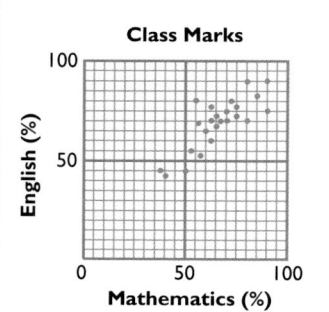

Solution
a) There appears to be 24 points plotted, so there would be 24 students in the class. The points form a line that slants upwards. In this class, as the Math marks increase, the English marks also increase.
b) There appears to be a fairly strong relationship, but one subject doesn't really affect the other. Perhaps the scatter plot indicates the measure of a student's attitude, effort, and ability.

1.6 Example 1, page 18
If you read that 57% of Canadian voters voted yes in a referendum, should you assume that the majority of Canadians support the issue? Explain.

Solution
You can't assume that the majority of Canadians agree with the issue because not everyone in Canada is eligible to vote. You have to be a Canadian citizen 18 years or older. Also, not everyone that is eligible votes.

1.6 Example 2, page 19
In 1989, the *Globe and Mail* reported that the incidence of leukemia within 25 km of the Bruce Nuclear Power

Station in Ontario was three times the national average.

Before deciding whether the power plant might be related to the higher rate of leukemia, why might you need to know each of these facts?

a) the incidence of leukemia in the area before the power station was built

b) the incidence of leukemia within 25 km of another nuclear power station

c) the ages of people most susceptible to leukemia and the ages of people in the area

Solution

a) The incidence of leukemia in the area might have been high before the plant was in operation.

b) If the incidence of leukemia near another nuclear power station was also high, it might indicate that the plant was related.

c) A certain age range might be more susceptible and the area might have a significantly higher percent of that age range.

UNIT 2 Powers and Roots

2.1 *Example 1, page 29*

Find the missing exponents.

a) $10^{\blacksquare} \times 10^3 = 10^9$

b) $10^{\blacksquare} \times 10^5 = 10^{\blacksquare}$

Solution

a) Since the bases are the same,
$\blacksquare + 3 = 9$.
What do I add to 3 to get 9? 6
$10^6 \times 10^3 = 10^9$

b) Since the bases are the same,
$\blacksquare + 5 = \blacksquare$.
The second unknown can be any number 5 greater than the first one.
Since $6 + 5 = 11$, I'll use 6 and 11.
$10^6 \times 10^5 = 10^{11}$

2.1 *Example 2, page 30*

Which pair of exponents makes this equation true?

$3^{\blacksquare} \times 3^{\blacksquare} = 3^8$

−4 and −2   or   −3 and 11

Solution

Since the bases are the same,
$\blacksquare + \blacksquare = 8$.
$-4 + (-2) = -6$ so −4 and −2 do not make the equation true.
$-3 + 11 = 8$ so −3 and 11 do make the equation true.

2.2 *Example 1, page 32*

How many years would it take to spend Bill Gates' fortune at each annual rate?

a) $100 000   b) $10 000

Solution

a) $\frac{12.9 \text{ billion}}{100\ 000} = \frac{12.9 \times 10^9}{10^5}$
$= 12.9 \times 10^4$
$= 129\ 000$

It would take 129 000 years.

b) Since 10 000 is $\frac{1}{10}$ of 100 000, it should take 10 times as long as in part (a) or 1 290 000 years.
Check.

$\frac{12.9 \text{ billion}}{10\ 000} = \frac{12.9 \times 10^9}{10^4}$
$= 12.9 \times 10^5$
$= 1\ 290\ 000$

2.2 *Example 2, page 32*

Find the missing exponents.

a) $(-3)^{\blacksquare} \div (-3)^5 = (-3)^2$

b) $4^3 \div 4^{-8} = 4^{\blacksquare}$

Solution

a) Since the bases are the same,
$\blacksquare - 5 = 2$.
I can subtract 5 from 7 to get 2.
$(-3)^7 \div (-3)^5 = (-3)^2$

b) Since the bases are the same,
$3 - (-8) = \blacksquare$
$3 + 8 = \blacksquare$
$11 = \blacksquare$
$4^3 \div 4^{-8} = 4^{11}$

2.3 *Example 1, page 34*

Find the missing exponents.

a) $(-8)^6 = [(-8)^{\blacksquare}]^2$

b) $11^{-24} = (11^4)^{\blacksquare}$

Solution

a) Since the bases are the same,
$6 = \blacksquare \times 2$.
What do I multiply 2 by to get 6? 3
$(-8)^6 = [(-8)^3]^2$

b) Since the bases are the same,
$-24 = 4 \times \blacksquare$.
What do I multiply 4 by to get −24?
−6
$11^{-24} = (11^4)^{-6}$

2.3 *Example 2, page 34*

Use $(4^5)^2 = 1\ 048\ 576$ to help you write each number as a fraction or in standard form.

a) $(4^{-5})^2$ b) $(4^{-5})^{-2}$

Solution

a) $(4^{-5})^2 = (\frac{1}{4^5})^2$
$= \frac{1}{1\ 048\ 576}$

b) $(4^{-5})^{-2} = 4^{10}$
$= (4^5)^2$
$= 1\ 048\ 576$

2.4 *Example 1, page 36*

Express as a single power so the product can be found mentally.

$2^{-6} \times 5^{-6}$

Solution

Since the exponents are the same,
$2^{-6} \times 5^{-6} = (2 \times 5)^{-6}$
$= 10^{-6}$
$= 0.000\ 001$

2.4 *Example 2, page 36*

Express as a power of 10.

$25^{-3} \times 4^{-3}$

Solution

Since the exponents are the same,
$25^{-3} \times 4^{-3} = (25 \times 4)^{-3}$
$= 100^{-3}$
$= (10^2)^{-3}$
$= 10^{-6}$

2.5 *Example 1, page 39*

Use a calculator and an exponent rule to find the product in scientific notation.

$(3.6 \times 10^{-1}) \times (2.8 \times 10^4)$

Solution

$(3.6 \times 10^{-1}) \times (2.8 \times 10^4)$
$= 3.6 \times 2.8 \times 10^{-1} \times 10^4$
$= 10.08 \times 10^3$
$= 1.008 \times 10^1 \times 10^3$
$= 1.008 \times 10^4$

3.6 ⊗ 2.8 ⊜   `10.08`

2.5 Example 2, page 39

Predict the exponent in the quotient when the quotient is in scientific notation.
$(3.2 \times 10^6) \div (5 \times 10^3)$

Solution

I'll estimate the quotient of 3.2 and 5, and calculate the quotient of 10^6 and 10^3.

$\quad (3.2 \times 10^6) \div (5 \times 10^3)$
$\approx (3 \div 5) \times (10^6 \div 10^3)$
$= 0.6 \times 10^3$
$= 6 \times 10^{-1} \times 10^3$
$= 6 \times 10^2$

The exponent will be 2.

2.6 Example 1, page 42

Calculate and express the answer in scientific notation.
$(8.2 \times 10^7) \div (2.4 \times 10^{-5})$

Solution

$\quad (8.2 \times 10^7) \div (2.4 \times 10^{-5})$
$= 3.4 \times 10^{12}$ rounded to 1 decimal place

8.2 [Exp] 7 [÷] 2.4 [Exp] 5 [+/−] [=]

| 3.4166666 12 |

2.6 Example 2, page 42

Write the keystrokes and evaluate $3^{-5} \times 4^7$.

Solution

3 [yˣ] 5 [+/−] [×] 4 [yˣ] 7 [=]

| 67.43238631 |

$3^{-5} \times 4^7 = 67.4$ to 1 decimal place

2.7 Example 1, page 43

Use the exponent rules to find the square root of each number and express it as a power.
a) 1 000 000   **b)** 10^{-10} **c)** 3^8

Solution

a) $1\,000\,000 = 10^6 = (10^3)^2$
So $\sqrt{1\,000\,000} = \sqrt{(10^3)^2}$
b) $10^{-10} = (10^{-5})^2$
So $\sqrt{10^{-10}} = \sqrt{(10^{-5})^2}$
c) $3^8 = (3^4)^2$
So $\sqrt{3^8} = \sqrt{(3^4)^2} = 3^4$

2.7 Example 2, page 43

Can you find the whole-number square root of 10^5 using the method of Example 1? Explain.

Solution

$10^5 = (10^■)^2$ $■ \times 2 = 5$
No, there is no whole-number value for $■$.

UNIT 3   Transformations

3.1 Example 1, page 57

Copy the diagram onto grid paper. Locate and label the reflection image.

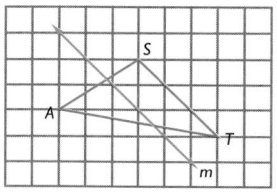

Solution

The ways I know to find the reflection image are
• fold in the reflection line
• use a Mira
• count grid spaces
I can't count grid spaces here because the reflection line is not a grid line, so I could measure perpendicular distances.
I think I will use folding.

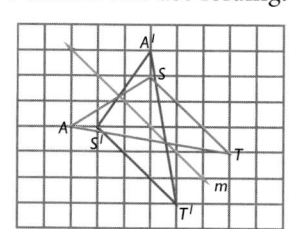

3.1 Example 2, page 59

Find the reflection image of quadrilateral *TAKE* when reflected in the *x*-axis.

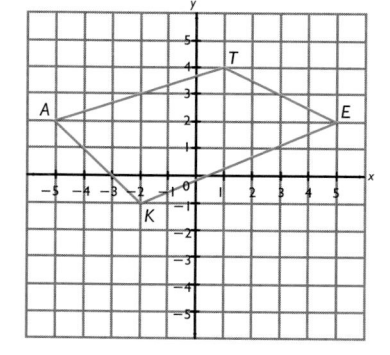

Solution

I can count grid spaces from each vertex to the *x*-axis, and then go as far on the other side because the reflection line, the *x*-axis, is a grid line.

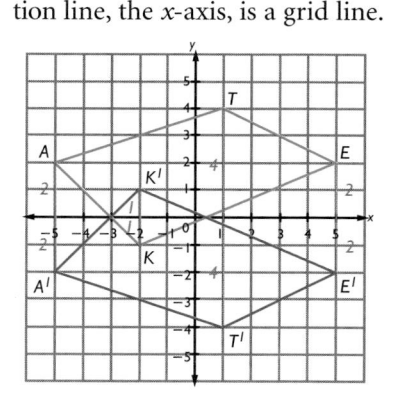

3.2 Example 1, page 61

Copy the diagram onto grid paper. Locate and label the translation image.

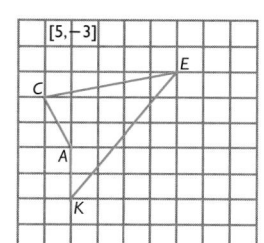

Solution

$[5, -3]$ means each vertex moves 5 places to the right and 3 places down.

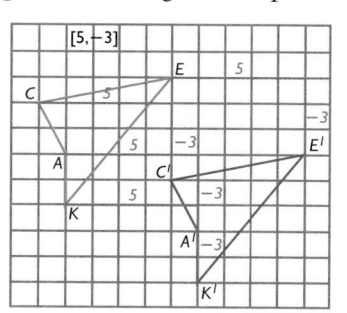

3.2 Example 2, page 62

What is the translation rule for $F(7, -2) \to F'(1, 3)$?

Solution

How do I get from 7 to 1? subtract 6
How do I get from -2 to 3? add 5
So the translation rule is $[-6, 5]$.
Check. $7 + (-6) = 1$
$\qquad\quad -2 + 5 = 3$

3.3 Example 1, page 64

Copy the diagram onto grid paper. Locate and label the rotation image.

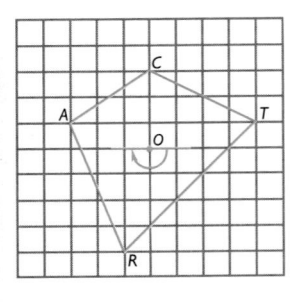

Solution

Even though the turn centre is inside the quadrilateral, I still trace the diagram onto tracing paper, and while holding it down at centre O, turn it 180° cw to locate the image points.

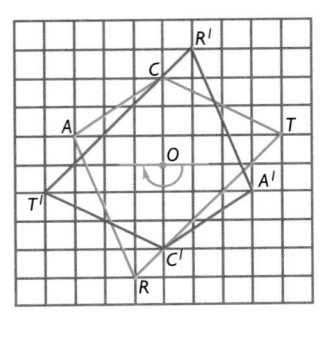

3.3 Example 2, page 66

What is the angle of rotation about the origin for $W(5, -1) \rightarrow W'(1, 5)$?

Solution

To find the angle of rotation about the origin, I need to find the number of degrees and the direction, and I can use the summary from my journal.

The x-coordinate became 1 which is the opposite of the original y-coordinate.

The y-coordinate became 5 which is the original x-coordinate.

I know for 90° ccw, x becomes $-y$ of the original and y becomes x of the original.

So the angle of rotation is 90° ccw.

Check.

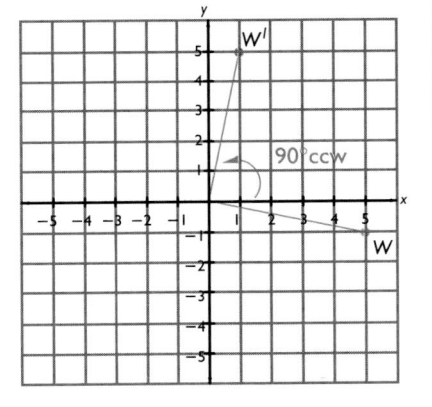

3.4 Example 1, page 69

Round the Imax scale factor to the nearest 50. Use it to estimate the height on the screen of a dog 20 mm high on a frame.

Solution

342 rounds to 350

   height on screen

= scale factor × height on frame

= 350 × 20

= 70 × 5 × 20

= 70 × 100

= 7000

The height of the dog on the screen would be about 7000 mm or 7 m.

3.4 Example 2, page 71

What is the scale factor for a dilatation about the origin where $T(6, 9) \rightarrow T'(2, 3)$?

Solution

The scale factor is the number that both of the original coordinates are multiplied by to get the image coordinates.

What do I multiply 6 by to get 2? $\frac{1}{3}$

What do I multiply 9 by to get 3? $\frac{1}{3}$

So the scale factor is $\frac{1}{3}$.

UNIT 4 Rational Numbers

4.1 Example 1, page 82

Give two examples of an integer that is not a natural number.

Solution

Since natural numbers are 1, 2, 3, ..., any of their opposites or 0 are possible.

My examples are 0 and −100.

4.2 Example 1, page 83

Which of the following are rational numbers?

a) −3.828 282 ...

b) $6.\overline{45}$

c) 3.151 551 555 155 ...

d) −4.6125

Solution

Since rational numbers are either terminating or repeating when they are in decimal form,

a) is rational because 82 repeats

b) is rational because 45 repeats

c) is not rational because it goes on without particular digits repeating

d) is rational because it terminates

4.3 Example 1, pages 84, 85

Estimate and calculate $\sqrt{75}$.

Solution

75 is between perfect squares, 64 and 81.

It is 6 less than 81 and 11 more than 64. $\sqrt{64} = 8$ and $\sqrt{81} = 9$, so $\sqrt{75}$ is about 8.66.

$\sqrt{75} = 8.660\ 254\ 038$

$\sqrt{}$ 75 $=$ `8.660254038`

4.3 Example 2, page 85

What are two values that satisfy $g^2 = 12.25$?

Solution

$g^2 = 12.25$

$g = \sqrt{12.25}$ or $-\sqrt{12.25}$

$g = 3.5$ or -3.5

$\sqrt{}$ 12.25 $=$ `3.5`

4.4 Example 1, page 87

Estimate the perimeter of this shape.

1.6 m   1.2 m   6.9 m   2.8 m   5.1 m   12.7 m

Solution

  Perimeter

= sum of sides

= 2.8 + 12.7 + 5.1 + 6.9 + 1.2 + 1.6

≈ 3 + 13 + 5 + 7 + 1 + 2

= 31

The perimeter is about 31 m.

4.4 *Example 2, page 88*

Estimate the volume of this cylinder.

$V = \pi r^2 h$

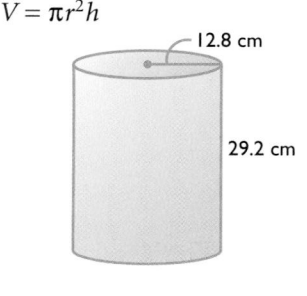
12.8 cm

29.2 cm

Solution

$V = \pi r^2 h$
$V = \pi (12.8)^2 (29.2)$
$V \approx 3(13)^2(30)$
$V = 3(169)(30)$
$V \approx 90(170)$
$V = 15\ 300$

The volume is about 15 300 cm^3.

4.5 *Example 1, page 90*

Estimate and then calculate the height of this cylinder using the reciprocal key.

$h = \dfrac{V}{\pi r^2}$

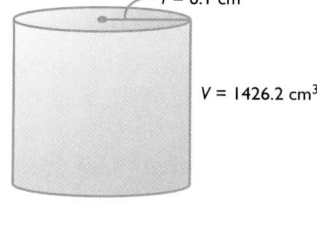
r = 6.1 cm

V = 1426.2 cm^3

Solution

Estimate.
$h = \dfrac{V}{\pi r^2}$
$h = \dfrac{1426.2}{\pi (6.1)^2}$
$h \approx \dfrac{1400}{3(36)}$
$h \approx \dfrac{1400}{100}$
$h = 14$

Calculate.
$h = \dfrac{V}{\pi r^2}$
$h = \dfrac{1426.2}{\pi (6.1)^2}$

π ☒ 6.1 x² ☐ x⁻¹ ☒
1426.2 ☐ | 12.20031066 |

The height is 12.2 cm^3 rounded to 1 decimal place.

4.5 *Example 2, page 90*

Estimate, and then calculate using an efficient set of keystrokes.
$-7.2 \times (43.4 - 17.9)$

Solution

Estimate.
$-7.2 \times (43.4 - 17.9)$
$\approx -7 \times (43 - 18)$
$= -7 \times 25$
$= -175$

Calculate.
Using brackets will be efficient here. I just have to enter the expression as it is written except -7.2 will be 7.2 +/− .
$-7.2 \times (43.4 - 17.9)$
$= -183.6$

7.2 +/− ☒ (43.4 − 17.9
) ☐ | -183.6 |

4.6 *Example 1, pages 91, 92*

Use the Exchange Rates table. How much would you receive in Iraq dinars for $200 Canadian?

Solution

1 Iraq dinar = $2.3553
I'll solve a proportion.
Let x be the number of Iraq dinars.
$\dfrac{x}{200} = \dfrac{1}{2.3553}$
$x = 200 \times \dfrac{1}{2.3553}$
$x = 84.9$ rounded to the nearest tenth of a dinar

200 ÷ 2.3553 ☐ | 84.91487284 |

You would receive 84.9 Iraq dinars for $200 Canadian.

4.6 *Example 2, page 92*

Use the Exchange Rates table. If you had 3000 UK pounds, how many Canadian dollars would you receive?

Solution

1 UK pound = $2.2257
3000 UK pounds = $2.2257 × 3000
= $6677.1

2.2257 ☒ 3000 ☐ | 6677.1 |

You would receive $6677.10 Canadian.

UNIT 5 Polynomials (I)

5.1 *Example 1, page 105*

Identify the terms, variables, constants, and numerical coefficients in the expression $4 - r^2 + 2rt + t - \dfrac{5rt}{3}$.

Solution

- A term doesn't have to contain a variable. There are 5 terms because there are 5 signs. The sign goes with the term following it, but you don't have to write the + sign because it's understood. The terms are 4, $-r^2$, $2rt$, t, and $\dfrac{-5rt}{3}$.
- There are 2 variables, r and t. In r^2, the exponent tells what operation to do with the variable r.
- There is 1 constant, the number 4. It has no variable.
- The numerical coefficients are usually written in front of the variable(s) unless it's understood to be 1 or a fraction with numerator 1. The numerical coefficients are -1, 2, 1, and $\dfrac{-5}{3}$.

5.1 *Example 2, page 105*

Create an expression with no constants, two variables and four terms.

Solution

The variables are two different letters, such as a and b.
Since there are no constants, all four terms must have at least one variable. I can use exponents if I want to. My expression is $b^3 + b^2 - 4ab + 12a$.

5.2 *Example 1, page 107*

Create an expression that has the following property: doubling the value of the variable quadruples the value of the expression.

Solution

I'll guess and test using the variable x. If the expression is $x + 2$ and I let $x = 3$, the value of the expression is 5. If I double the value of x, $x = 6$ and the expression has the value 8, which isn't double 5. This time I won't include a constant, but use an expression like $2x$. If $x = 3$, the expression has the value 6. If $x = 6$, the expression has the value 12, which isn't quadruple 3, only double 3.

This time I'll try squaring the expression to make the value increase faster. I'll try the expression x^2. If $x = 3$, the expression has the value 9. If $x = 6$, the expression has the value 36, which is 4 times 9.

5.2 Example 2, page 107
Find one value for m and one value for n which make $2m^3 - 4mn$
a) negative   b) positive

Solution

a) If m is negative, the cubed term will stay negative. If n is also negative, the second term will be negative.
Try $m = -1$ and $n = -2$.
$$2m^3 - 4mn$$
$$= 2(-1)^3 - 4(-1)(-2)$$
$$= -2 - 8$$
$$= -10$$

b) Try $m = 2$ and $n = 3$.
$$2m^3 - 4mn$$
$$= 2(2)^3 - 4(2)(3)$$
$$= 2(8) - 24$$
$$= 16 - 24$$
$$= -8 \text{ which isn't positive.}$$

Try a negative value for n to make the second term positive. Try $m = 2$ and $n = -1$.
$$2m^3 - 4mn$$
$$= 2(2)^3 - 4(2)(-1)$$
$$= 16 + 8$$
$$= 24$$

5.3 Example 1, page 111
Identify the like terms: $2n, 2m, -2n,$ $n^2, -2, 13n, 2mn, m^2, \frac{n}{2}, \frac{3n}{7}, 3nm$

Solution

Like terms have the same variable and same exponent. The numerical coefficients are the only parts that are different.

The like terms are $2n, -2n, 13n,$ $\frac{1}{2}n$ or $\frac{n}{2}$, and $\frac{3}{7}n$ or $\frac{3n}{7}$. Another group of like terms is $2mn$ and $3nm$. The order in which the variables are written doesn't matter.

5.3 Example 2, page 111
Use algebra tiles to model. Then simplify the expression by combining like terms. $-2 + x^2 + 2x + 3y^2$ $- 4y + 5 - 3x + 6y - 4$

Solution

A flipped tile (white) is the opposite of the same shape of tile (colored). When you group the same number of tiles and their opposites, you get zero.

• I'll model each of the 9 terms.
2 flipped red squares
l green square
2 green rods
3 orange squares
4 flipped orange rods
5 red squares
3 flipped green rods
6 orange rods
4 flipped red squares

• Then I'll group them.

2 green rods
3 flipped green rods
───────────────
1 flipped green rod

4 flipped orange rods
6 orange rods
───────────────
2 orange rods

2 flipped red squares
5 red squares
4 flipped red squares
───────────────
1 flipped red square

The simplified expression is $x^2 + 3y^2 - x + 2y - 1$.

5.4 Example 1, page 112
Use algebra tiles to model. Then find the sum of these two expressions.
$(-2x^2 + 5x + 4) + (-3x + 5x^2 - 7)$

Solution

$$\left(\begin{array}{l} 2 \text{ flipped green squares} \\ 5 \text{ green rods} \\ 4 \text{ red squares} \end{array} \right)$$
$$+ \left(\begin{array}{l} 5 \text{ green squares} \\ 3 \text{ flipped green rods} \\ 7 \text{ flipped red squares} \end{array} \right)$$
$$= \left(\begin{array}{l} 3 \text{ green squares} \\ 2 \text{ green rods} \\ 3 \text{ flipped red squares} \end{array} \right)$$

The expression for the sum is $3x^2 + 2x - 3$.

5.4 Example 2, page 113
Write the related addition to subtract these two expressions. Use algebra tiles to find the difference. $(-2x^2 + 3x + 1) - (5x^2 + 2x - 7)$

Solution

I can think of a simpler subtraction to recall what a related addition sentence should look like.
$12 - 7 = \blacksquare$ and $12 = \blacksquare + 7$.
Using this as a guide,
$(-2x^2 + 3x + 1) - (5x^2 + 2x - 7) = \blacksquare$
and
$(-2x^2 + 3x + 1) = \blacksquare + (5x^2 + 2x - 7)$
What must I add to 5 green squares to get 2 flipped green squares?
7 flipped green squares
What must I add to 2 green rods to get 3 green rods?
1 green rod
What must I add to 7 flipped red squares to get 1 red square?
8 red squares
The expression for the difference is $-7x^2 + x + 8$.

5.5 Example 1, page 116
Write and simplify an expression for the perimeter of this shape.

Solution

Perimeter means total distance around. The right-angle symbols mean that the sides are perpendicular to one another.

I'll draw the shape and label the lengths of all the sides.

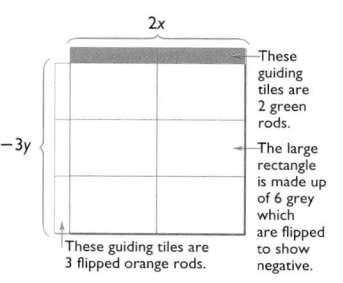

I could subtract to find the 2 unknown sides, but it's not necessary because those sides can be moved to make 1 large rectangle with dimensions $a + 4$ by $3a - 1$.
$(3a - 1) + (a + 4) + (3a - 1) + (a + 4)$
$= 8a + 6.$

5.5 Example 2, page 116
Write a related addition sentence for the subtraction. Then, use a number line to find the difference.
$(-4c^3 - 5c^2) - (-2c^2 + 8 - 6c^3)$

Solution
The related addition is $(-4c^3 - 5c^2)$
$= \blacksquare + (-2c^2 + 8 - 6c^3)$.
For the c^3 terms, what number added to -6 gives -4?

```
        2
 ←—•——————→—————————————→
  -8 -7 -6 -5 -4 -3 -2 -1  0
```

So the c^3 term is $2c^{3.}$
For the c^2 terms, what number added to -2 gives -5?

```
          -3
 ←———————←—————•———————————→
  -8 -7 -6 -5 -4 -3 -2 -1  0
```

So the c^2 term is $-3c^2$.
For the constants, what number added to 8 gives 0?

```
          -8
 ←———————————————————————•→
   0  1  2  3  4  5  6  7  8
```

The constant term is -8.
$\blacksquare = 2c^3 - 3c^2 - 8.$
So, $(-4c^3 - 5c^2) - (-2c^2 + 8 - 6c^3)$
$= 2c^3 - 3c^2 - 8.$

5.6 Example 1, page 120
Find the product of $(-3y)(2x)$.

Solution
First I multiply the numerical coefficients together, $-3 \times 2 = -6$.
Then I multiply the variables together, $y \times x = yx$ or xy. The product is $-6xy$.
To check, I can use algebra tiles to model a rectangle with these dimensions and find the area.

```
                2x
         ┌──────────────┐  ──These
         │              │    guiding
         │              │    tiles are
  -3y    │              │    2 green
         │              │    rods.
         │              │  ──The large
         │              │    rectangle
         │              │    is made up
         │              │    of 6 grey
  These guiding tiles are    which
  3 flipped orange rods.     are flipped
                             to show
                             negative.
```

5.6 Example 2, page 120
Find the product of $(-r^2t^3)(4r^3t)$.

Solution
First I multiply the numerical coefficients together, $-1 \times 4 = -4$.
Then I multiply each of the variables.
For $r^2 \times r^3$, add the exponents to get r^5. For $t^3 \times t$, add the exponents to get t^4. The product is $-4r^5t^4$.

5.7 Example 1, page 122
Find the quotient of $(12xy) \div (-4y)$.

Solution
First I divide the numerical coefficients, $\frac{12}{-4} = -3$. Then I divide the variables, $\frac{xy}{y} = x$ (since $\frac{y}{y} = 1$).
So the quotient is $-3x$. To check, I can use algebra tiles to model a rectangle using 12 grey tiles so that one of its dimensions is $-4y$. The other dimension must be negative since 2 negatives give a positive area.

```
              -4y
         ┌──────────┐  ──These
         │          │    guiding
         │          │    tiles are
         │          │    4 flipped
    ?    │          │    orange
         │          │    rods.
         │          │  ──The area
         │          │    is 12xy,
         │          │    which is
         │          │    12 grey
         │          │    tiles.
         └──────────┘
  These guiding tiles must be negative since
  (-dimension) × (-dimension) = (+area)
```

5.7 Example 2, page 123
Find the quotient of $\frac{-9xy + 12x^2}{-3x}$.

Solution
I can rewrite the division as $\frac{-9xy}{-3x} + \frac{12x^2}{-3x}$.
I find the quotient of each part. Then combine the quotients into 1 answer.
For $\frac{-9xy}{-3x}$, first I divide the numerical coefficients, $\frac{-9}{-3} = 3$.
Then I divide the variables, $\frac{xy}{x} = y$ (since $\frac{x}{x} = 1$). That quotient is $3y$.
For $\frac{12x^2}{-3x}$, $\frac{12}{-3} = -4$ and $\frac{x^2}{x} = x$, so this quotient is $-4x$.
Combining the quotients gives $3y - 4x$.
I can check by modelling with algebra tiles.

```
              -3x
         ┌──────────┐  ──These
         │░░│       │    guiding
         │░░│       │    tiles are
    ?    │░░│       │    3 flipped
         │░░│       │    green
         └──────────┘    rods.
                       ──Area is
                         -9xy,
                         which is
                         9 flipped
                         grey
                         rectangles.
  These guiding tiles must be positive since
  (+dimension) × (-dimension) = (+area)
```

```
              -3x
         ┌──────────┐  ──These
         │██████████│    guiding
         │██████████│    tiles are
         │██████████│    3 flipped
         │██████████│    green
    ?    │██████████│    rods.
         │██████████│
         │██████████│  ──Area is
         │██████████│    12x²,
         │██████████│    which is
         └──────────┘    12 green
                         squares.
  These guiding tiles must be negative since
  (-dimension) × (-dimension) = (+area)
```

UNIT 7 Polynomials (II)

7.1 Example 1, page 151
Use algebra tiles to find the area of a rectangle with the dimensions $3x$ and $(2x + y + 1)$.

Solution
Place guiding tiles for the two dimensions, and then fill in the rectangle.

Area is 6 green tiles, 3 grey rectangles, and 3 green rods.

Algebraically, I can write
$3x(2x + y + 1) = 6x^2 + 3xy + 3x$.

7.1 Example 2, page 152
Find the perimeter and the area.

Solution
The perimeter or distance around the triangle is
$15a + 8a + 17a$
$= 40a$.
The formula for area of a triangle is $\frac{1}{2}$ base × height.
If the base of the triangle is $8a$, the height is $15a$.
$\frac{1}{2}(8a)(15a)$
$= (4a)(15a)$
$= 60a^2$

7.2 Example 1, page 155
Use algebra tiles to find the missing factors.
$6y + 15x + 9 = 3(\blacksquare + \bullet + \blacktriangle)$.

Solution
I could divide the 6 orange rods, 15 green rods, and 9 red squares into 3 equal groups. There are 2 orange rods, 5 green rods, and 3 red squares in each group, so the missing factor is $2y + 5x + 3$.
Or, I could place 3 red squares as the guiding tiles for the width; arrange the 6 orange rods, 15 green rods, and 9 red squares to form the rectangle; and then find the dimension for length.

7.2 Example 2, page 155
Find the factors of $4x^2 - 10y$. Check by multiplying.

Solution
The numerical coefficients are both multiples of 2, so 2 is a factor.
To find the other factor, I can
• divide 4 green squares and 10 flipped orange rods into 2 equal groups, or
• model a rectangle with the given area, and find the dimensions, or
• divide each term by 2 and then write the quotients as one answer.
I'll try this.
$\frac{4x^2}{2} = 2x^2$ and $\frac{-10y}{2} = -5y$.
The other factor is $2x^2 - 5y$.
Check by multiplying.

$2(2x^2 - 5y) = 4x^2 - 10y$

7.3 Example 1, page 157
Find the factors of $12y + 8y^2$. Check by multiplying.

Solution
I can model a rectangle with the given area, and find both dimensions.

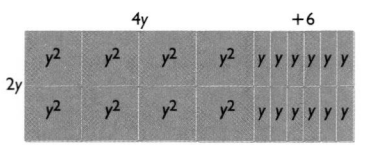

Can I rearrange the tiles to form a rectangle closer to a square?

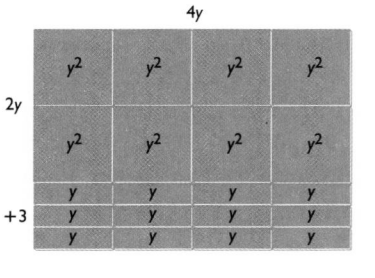

The dimensions are $(2y + 3)$ and $(4y)$. Check by multiplying. I can write the monomial factor first to make it easier to use my pattern.

$(4y)(2y + 3) = 8y^2 + 12y$

7.3 Example 2, page 157
The area of a rectangle is $21mn^2 - 15m^2n$. Find the dimensions, and then the perimeter.

Solution
I need to factor the expression for area. Both terms contain the variables m and n, so mn is a factor. Also, both numerical coefficients have 3 as a factor, so $3mn$ is a factor. To find the other factor I can divide each term by $3mn$ and then write the quotients.
For $\frac{21mn^2}{3mn}$, divide the numerical coefficients, $\frac{21}{3} = 7$; then the variables, $\frac{m}{m} = 1$ and $\frac{n^2}{n} = n$; so that quotient is $7n$.
For $\frac{-15m^2n}{3mn}$, $\frac{-15}{3} = -5$ and $\frac{m^2}{m} = m$ and $\frac{n}{n} = 1$; so that quotient is $-5m$.
The other factor is $7n - 5m$.
Check by multiplying.

$(3mn)(7n - 5m) = 21mn^2 - 15m^2n$

To find the perimeter, I'll sketch the rectangle and label the dimensions.

$7n - 5m$

$3mn$

Perimeter is 2(length + width), so I can substitute my expressions for length and width, and then multiply.

$2[(3mn) + (7n - 5m)] = 6mn + 14n - 10m$

7.4 Example 1, page 160
Use algebra tiles to find the product of $(2x + 3y)(x + 2y)$. What pattern do you notice?

Solution
I'll use guiding tiles to model the dimensions, and then find the area of the rectangle.

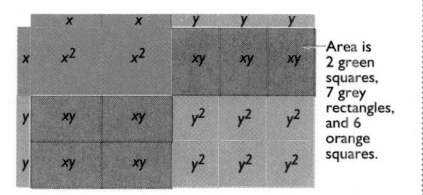

Area is 2 green squares, 7 grey rectangles, and 6 orange squares.

$(2x + 3y)(x + 2y) = 2x^2 + 7xy + 6y^2$
The pattern is:
- multiply the first terms in the binomials to get the first term in the trinomial
- multiply the last terms in the binomials to get the last term in the trinomial
- to get the middle term in the trinomial, multiply the two inner terms and multiply the two outer terms then add these products

$$3xy$$
$$(2x + 3y)(x + 2y) = 3xy + 4xy$$
$$= 7xy$$
$$4xy$$

7.4 Example 2, page 160

Use the pattern to find the product of $(-2 + 3x)(4 - x)$. Check by using algebra tiles.

Solution

- The first term in the trinomial is $(-2)(4) = -8$.
- The last term in the trinomial is $(3x)(-x) = -3x^2$.
- The middle term is
$(3x)(4) + (-2)(-x) =$
$12x + 2x = 14x$.
So $(-2 + 3x)(4 - x) =$
$-8 + 14x - 3x^2$
I can check by using guiding tiles for the dimensions, then finding the area of the rectangle.

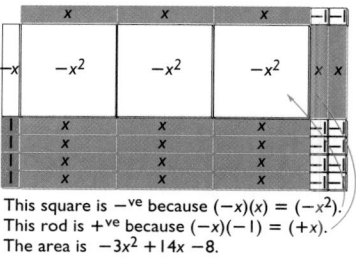

This square is $^{-ve}$ because $(-x)(x) = (-x^2)$.
This rod is $^{+ve}$ because $(-x)(-1) = (+x)$.
The area is $-3x^2 + 14x - 8$.

7.5 Example 1, page 162

Use algebra tiles to find the dimensions of a rectangle with area $y^2 + 3xy + 2x^2$. Write the area as a product of the length and the width.

Solution

Arrange the tiles to form a rectangle, and find the dimensions.

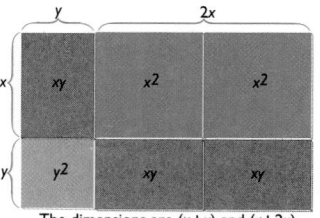

The dimensions are $(x+y)$ and $(y+2x)$.

$y^2 + 3xy + 2x^2 = (x + y)(y + 2x)$
I can check by multiplying the factors.

$$(x + y)(y + 2x) = xy + y^2 + 2x^2 + 2xy$$
$$= 3xy + y^2 + 2x^2$$

I could rearrange the terms.
$y^2 + 3xy + 2x^2 = (y + x)(y + 2x)$

7.5 Example 2, page 163

Use different methods to factor $x^2 - 9x + 14$.

Solution

I can use logical thinking and work backwards.
- The first term in each binomial must be x to give x^2.
- For the last terms, what two numbers multiply to give 14?
  2 and 7, 1 and 14
  -7 and -2, or -14 and -1
- Of these possible pairs, which two numbers add to -9?
  -2 and -7.
So, $x^2 - 9x + 14 = (x - 2)(x - 7)$
I can check by multiplying.

$$(x - 2)(x - 7) = x^2 - 2x - 7x + 14$$
$$= x^2 - 9x + 14$$

I can use algebra tiles to model a rectangle, and find its dimensions.
- First I place the green square.
- Then I place the 14 red squares in 2 rows of 7 since that's more likely than 1 row of 14.

- Then I fill in the rectangle by placing the 9 rods which are flipped to show negative.

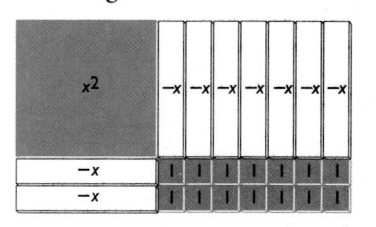

I can check by multiplying this way:

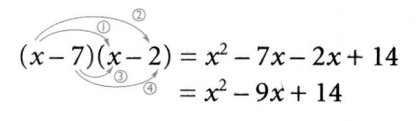

$$(x - 7)(x - 2) = x^2 - 7x - 2x + 14$$
$$= x^2 - 9x + 14$$

7.6 Example 1, page 165

Factor $6x^2 - 20x - 16$ completely.

Solution

Each term contains a number that is a multiple of 2, so 2 is a factor. When I divide each term by 2, I get $2(3x^2 - 10x - 8)$. I can check by multiplying.

$$2(3x^2 - 10x - 8) = 6x^2 - 20x - 16$$

Maybe the trinomial can be factored into two binomials.
- Both the first terms in the binomials should contain x to give x^2. To find their numerical coefficients, what two terms multiply to give $3x^2$? x and $3x$
- For the last terms, what two numbers multiply to give -8? One term has to be positive and the other negative. $(3x + \blacksquare)(x - \blacksquare)$
Try 4 and -2. $(3x + 4)(x - 2)$
The middle term is $4x - 6x = -2x$.
Try 1 and -8. $(3x + 1)(x - 8)$
The middle term is $x - 24x = -23x$.
Try 2 and -4. $(3x + 2)(x - 4)$
The middle term is $2x - 12x = -10x$.
So, $6x^2 - 20x - 16 = 2(3x + 2)(x - 4)$
I can check by multiplying this way:

$$2(3x + 2)(x - 4)$$
$$= (6x + 4)(x - 4)$$
$$= 6x^2 + 4x - 24x - 16$$
$$= 6x^2 - 20x - 16$$

7.6 Example 2, page 165

Simplify $(9x^3 - 27x^2 + 18x) \div 3x$.

Solution

First I can divide each term by $3x$.

$\frac{9x^3}{3x} = 3x^2$, and $\frac{-27x^2}{3x} = -9x$, and

$\frac{18x}{3x} = 6$; so the result is

$3x^2 - 9x + 6$.

Each term still contains a multiple of 3, so 3 is a common factor.

$3(x^2 - 3x + 2)$

I'll try to factor the trinomial.

$x^2 - 3x + 2 = (x - 2)(x - 1)$

Check by multiplying.

$(x - 2)(x - 1) = x^2 - 2x - x + 2$
$\qquad\qquad\quad = x^2 - 3x + 2$

So the final answer is $3(x - 2)(x - 1)$.
I could have factored the trinomial first, and then divided.

$\quad (9x^3 - 27x^2 + 18x) \div 3x$

$= 9x(x^2 - 3x + 2) \div 3x$

$= 9x(x - 2)(x - 1) \div 3x$

$= 3(x - 2)(x - 1)$

UNIT 8   Probability

8.1 Example 1, page 175

Suppose two dice are tossed with different outcomes.

a) What outcomes could die A have?
b) How many outcomes are left for die B?
c) Complete this calculation for the probability of two dice being tossed with different outcomes.

$P(\text{different numbers}) = P(A) \times P(B)$

d) Check using a tree diagram.

Solution

a) Die A could be any of the six possible outcomes, 1, 2, 3, 4, 5, or 6.
b) There are five of the six possible outcomes left for die B.
c) $P(A) = 1$ because, for the first die, there are 6 favorable outcomes out of the 6 possible.
$P(B) = \frac{5}{6}$ because, for the second die, there are 5 favorable outcomes out of the 6 possible.

$P(\text{different outcomes})$
$= P(A) \times P(B)$
$= 1 \times \frac{5}{6}$
$= \frac{5}{6}$

d)

First Die	Second Die	Outcome	Same/ Different
1	1	1, 1	same
	2	1, 2	different ✓
	3	1, 3	different ✓
	4	1, 4	different ✓
	5	1, 5	different ✓
	6	1, 6	different ✓
2	1	2, 1	different ✓
	2	2, 2	same
	3	2, 3	different ✓
	4	2, 4	different ✓
	5	2, 5	different ✓
	6	2, 6	different ✓
3	1	3, 1	different ✓
	2	3, 2	different ✓
	3	3, 3	same
	4	3, 4	different ✓
	5	3, 5	different ✓
	6	3, 6	different ✓
4	1	4, 1	different ✓
	2	4, 2	different ✓
	3	4, 3	different ✓
	4	4, 4	same
	5	4, 5	different ✓
	6	4, 6	different ✓
5	1	5, 1	different ✓
	2	5, 2	different ✓
	3	5, 3	different ✓
	4	5, 4	different ✓
	5	5, 5	same
	6	5, 6	different ✓
6	1	6, 1	different ✓
	2	6, 2	different ✓
	3	6, 3	different ✓
	4	6, 4	different ✓
	5	6, 5	different ✓
	6	6, 6	same

30 out of the 36 possible outcomes are different. So the probability is $\frac{5}{6}$.

8.1 Example 2, page 176

Find the probability of two spins of this spinner both landing on red by
a) using a tree diagram
b) calculating $P(\text{red/red})$
$= P(A) \times P(B)$

Solution

First Spin	Second Spin	Outcome	Both Red
red	red	red, red	✓
	yellow	red, yellow	
	blue	red, blue	
yellow	red	yellow, red	
	yellow	yellow, yellow	
	blue	yellow, blue	
blue	red	blue, red	
	yellow	blue, yellow	
	blue	blue, blue	

1 out of 9 possible outcomes are both red. So the probability is $\frac{1}{9}$.
b) $P(A)$ is $\frac{1}{3}$ because, for the first spin, there is one favorable outcome out of the three possible.
$P(B)$ is $\frac{1}{3}$ because, for the second spin, there is also one favorable outcome out of the three possible.

$P(\text{red/red}) = P(A) \times P(B)$
$\qquad\qquad\quad = \frac{1}{3} \times \frac{1}{3}$
$\qquad\qquad\quad = \frac{1}{9}$

8.2 Example 1, page 178

Draw a diagram to show the probability of choosing a grade 10 girl if there were 900 boys and 300 girls at Jenkins, and equal numbers in each grade.

Solution

Divide a square in fourths horizontally (or vertically) because there are four grades with equal numbers in each.

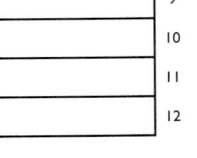

Divide the square in fourths vertically because 900 of 1200 or $\frac{3}{4}$ are boys and 300 of 1200 or $\frac{1}{4}$ are girls.

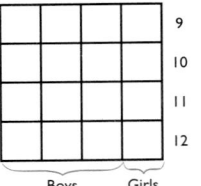

312

Shade the sections that are girls in grade 10.

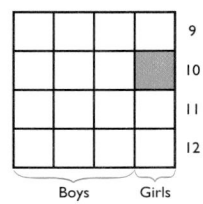

Boys | Girls

$P(\text{Grade 10/girl}) = \frac{1}{4} \times \frac{1}{4}$

$= \frac{1}{16}$

There is only one of 16 sections. So the probability is $\frac{1}{16}$.

8.2 Example 2, page 179

In a class of 29 students, 14 are girls, 20 are taking history, and 10 are going on the school trip. Estimate the probability of choosing a student from the class that is a girl, taking history, and going on the school trip.

Solution

Divide a square in half vertically (or horizontally) because 14 girls of 29 students is about $\frac{1}{2}$.

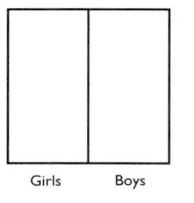

Girls | Boys

Divide the square in thirds horizontally because 20 taking history out of 29 is about $\frac{2}{3}$.

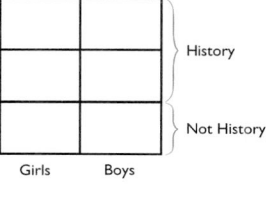

History | Not History

Girls | Boys

Divide both the boys' half and the girls' half in thirds because 10 going on the trip out of 29 is about $\frac{1}{3}$.

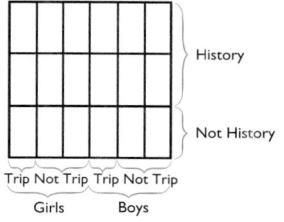

History | Not History

Trip Not Trip Trip Not Trip
Girls | Boys

Shade the sections that are girls, taking history, and going on the trip.

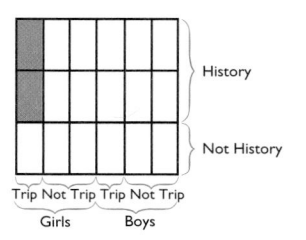

History | Not History

Trip Not Trip Trip Not Trip
Girls | Boys

There are 2 of 18 sections. So the estimated probability is about $\frac{1}{9}$.

8.3 Example 1, page 183

One of 10 000 raffle tickets is the winning ticket. You have one ticket. What is the probability that you will win?

Solution

You have one ticket so there is one favorable outcome out of a possible 10 000 outcomes. So the probability is $\frac{1}{10\ 000}$.

8.3 Example 2, page 183

Your probability of winning a lottery is $\frac{1}{150\ 000}$. Which is more likely—you winning the raffle in Example 1 or this lottery? How many times as likely is it?

Solution

$\frac{1}{10\ 000} > \frac{1}{150\ 000}$, so winning the raffle is more likely.

150 000 divided by 10 000 is 15. So it is 15 times as likely.

8.4 Example 1, page 185

If you consider only the 96 times Olerud has hit this season, the probability of Olerud hitting a home run is $\frac{6}{96}$ or $\frac{1}{16}$ and the odds are 1:15.

Express the probability as a fraction and as an odds ratio for Olerud hitting
a triple   a double   a single

Solution (see table on page 185)

Olerud had 0 triples (3B). So the probability of a hit being a triple is $\frac{0}{96}$ or 0, and as an odds ratio, 0:96.

Olerud has 22 doubles (2B). So the probability of a hit being a double is $\frac{22}{96}$ or $\frac{11}{48}$, and as an odds ratio, $48 - 11 = 37$, so 11:37.

Olerud had $96 - (22 + 0 + 6) = 68$ singles. So the probability of a hit being a single is $\frac{68}{96}$ or $\frac{17}{24}$, and as an odds ratio, $24 - 17 = 7$, so 17:7.

8.4 Example 2, page 185

Why is the probability of Olerud hitting a home run each time he hits greater than the probability of hitting a home run each time he is at bat?

Solution

The probability of Olerud hitting a home run each time he hits is $\frac{6}{96}$ or $\frac{1}{16}$.

The probability of Olerud hitting a home run each time he is at bat is $\frac{6}{350}$ or $\frac{3}{175}$.

$\frac{1}{6} > \frac{3}{175}$

UNIT 9   Measurement and Geometry

9.1 Example 1, page 197

Find the volume of a square-based pyramid with a height of 75 cm and side length of 1.5 m.

Solution

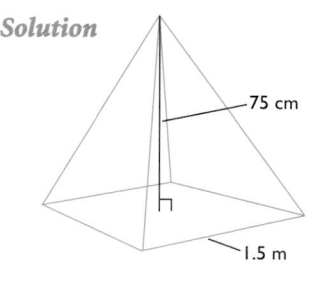

75 cm

1.5 m

$h = 75$ cm and $s = 1.5$ m
Both should be in the same units.
I'll use $h = 75$ cm and $s = 150$ cm.
$V = \frac{1}{3}A_{\text{base}} \times h$
$V = \frac{1}{3}s^2 \times h$
$V = \frac{1}{3}(150)^2(75)$
$V = 562\ 500$

1 $\div$ 3 $\times$ 150 x^2 $\times$ 75 $=$

562500.

The volume of the pyramid is 562 500 cm³.

9.1 Example 2, page 197

Find the height of a pyramid with a volume of 50 cm^3 and a triangular base. The triangular base has a base of 7 cm and a height of 5 cm.

Solution

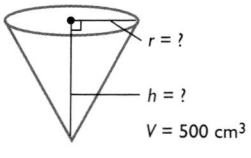

$$A_{\text{triangle}} = \tfrac{1}{2}bh$$
$$A = \tfrac{1}{2}(7)(5) \text{ or } 17.5$$
$$V_{\text{pyramid}} = \tfrac{1}{2}(\text{base})(h)$$
$$50 = \tfrac{1}{3}(17.5)h$$
$$h = \tfrac{3(50)}{17.5}$$
$$h = 8.6 \text{ rounded to 1 decimal place}$$

3 ☒ 50 ☒ 17.5 ☐

    8.571428571

The height of the pyramid is 8.6 cm.

9.2 Example 1, page 199

Find the volume of a cone with a base circumference of 50 cm and height of 30 cm.

Solution

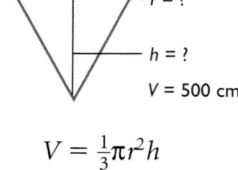

$$C = 2\pi r$$
$$50 = 2(3.14) \times r$$
$$50 = 6.28\,r$$
$$r = 7.96$$
$$V = \tfrac{1}{3}\pi r^2 h$$
$$V = \tfrac{1}{3}\pi (7.96)^2 (30)$$
$$V = 1989.6 \text{ rounded to 1 decimal place}$$

1 ☒ 3 ☒ π ☒ 7.96 x^2

☒ 30 ☐   1989.55424

The volume of the cone is 1989.6 cm^3.

9.2 Example 2, page 200

If the volume of a cone is 500 cm^3, what are two possible sets of dimensions?

Solution

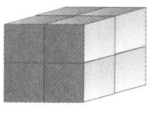

$$V = \tfrac{1}{3}\pi r^2 h$$
$$500 = \tfrac{1}{3}\pi r^2 h$$
$$\tfrac{500 \times 3}{\pi} = r^2 h$$
$$477.5 = r^2 h \text{ rounded to 1 decimal}$$
place

500 ☒ 3 ☒ π ☐

    477.46488293

First set
Let $h = 10$.
$$\tfrac{477.5}{10} = r^2$$
$$47.75 = r^2$$
$$6.9 = r \text{ rounded to 1 decimal}$$
place

√ 47.75 ☐   6.910137481

Second set
Let $h = 20$.
$$\tfrac{477.5}{20} = r^2$$
477.5 ☒ 20 ☐   23.875
$$23.875 = r^2$$
$$4.9 = r \quad \text{rounded to 1}$$
decimal place

√ 23.875 ☐   4.886205071

Two possible sets of dimensions are height 10 cm and radius 6.9 cm, and height 20 cm and radius 4.9 cm.

9.3 Example 1, page 201

Use 8 connecting cubes. Design three different rectangular prism boxes that would just hold the cubes. Find the surface area of each box.

Solution

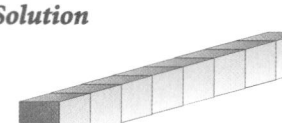

$$SA = \text{sum of Areas of the six faces}$$
$$SA = 2 \text{ faces} \times 1 \times 1 + 4 \text{ faces} \times 1 \times 8$$
$$SA = 2 + 32$$
$$SA = 34$$
Its surface area is 34 square units.

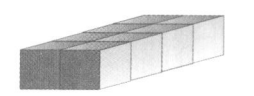

$$SA = 2 \text{ faces} \times 2 \times 1 + 2 \text{ faces} \times 2$$
$$\times 4 + 2 \text{ faces} \times 1 \times 4$$
$$SA = 4 + 16 + 8$$
$$SA = 28$$
Its surface area is 28 square units.

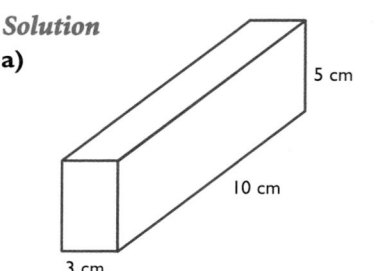

$$SA = 6 \text{ faces} \times 2 \times 2$$
$$SA = 24$$
Its surface area is 24 square units.

9.3 Example 2, page 202

a) Find the volume and surface area for a rectangular prism that is 10 cm long, 3 cm wide, and 5 cm high.
b) If the height is doubled, what are the new volume and surface area?
c) Which has the greater percent increase, the volume or surface area?

Solution
a)

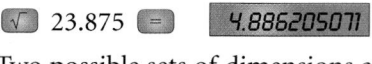

$$V = A_{\text{base}} \times h$$
$$V = 10 \times 3 \times 5$$
$$V = 150$$
The volume is 150 cm^3.
$$SA = \text{sum of Areas of the six faces}$$
$$SA = 2 \text{ faces} \times 3 \times 5 + 2 \text{ faces} \times 5 \times$$
$$10 + 2 \text{ faces} \times 3 \times 10$$
$$SA = 30 + 100 + 60$$
$$SA = 190$$
The surface area is 190 cm^2.

b)

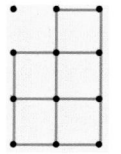

now $h = 10$
$V = 10 \times 3 \times 10$
$V = 300$
The new volume is 300 cm³.
$SA = 4 \text{ faces} \times 3 \times 10 + 2 \text{ faces}$
$\qquad \times 10 \times 10$
$SA = 120 + 200$
$SA = 320$
The new surface area is 320 cm².
c) The volume has doubled from
150 cm³ to 300 cm³. The surface
area has less than doubled from
190 cm² to 320 cm². I do not need
to calculate percent increases to
know the volume has the greater
percent increase.

9.4 Example 1, page 203
Use 16 square tiles. Design all the
different rectangles possible. What
is the perimeter of each rectangle?

Solution

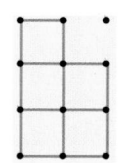

$P = 2(l + w)$
$P = 2(16 + 1)$
$P = 2(17)$
$P = 34$

Its perimeter is 34 units.

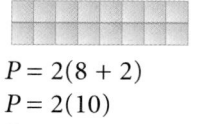

$P = 2(8 + 2)$
$P = 2(10)$
$P = 20$

Its perimeter is 20 units.

$P = 2(4 + 4)$
$P = 2(8)$
$P = 16$

Its perimeter is 16 units.

9.4 Example 2, page 204
What are the dimensions and the
area for the largest rectangular field
that can be fenced on all four sides
by 96 m of fencing?

Solution
The largest rectangle is one with the
greatest area. For a given perimeter,
the rectangle with the greatest area
is a square.
 $P = 96$ and $P = 4s$, so
$4s = 96$
 $s = 24$
$A = s^2$
$A = (24)^2 \quad$ 24 $\boxed{x^2}$ $\quad$ `576.`
$A = 576$
The dimensions are 24 m by 24 m,
and the area is 576 m².

9.5 Example 1, page 209
Draw and label the base plan, front
elevation, left elevation, and right
elevation. Make a model with cubes
first if you wish.

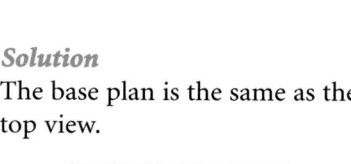

Solution
The base plan is the same as the
top view.

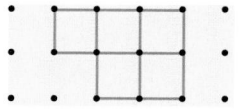

The front elevation is what you see
looking directly at its front.

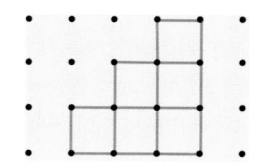

The left elevation is what you see
looking directly at its left side.

The right elevation is what **you** see
looking directly at its right side.

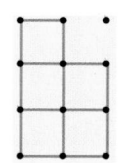

9.5 Example 2, page 209
Draw and label the base plan, front
elevation, left elevation, and right
elevation.

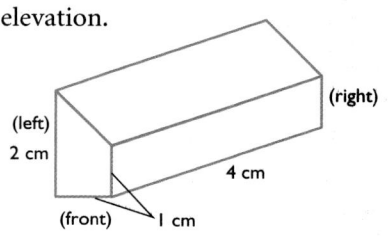

Solution
The base plan is the same as the
top view.

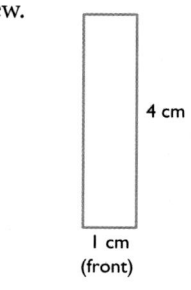

The front elevation is what you
see looking directly at its front.

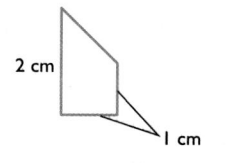

The left elevation is what you see
looking directly at its left side.

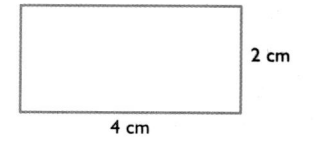

The right elevation is what you see looking directly at its right side.

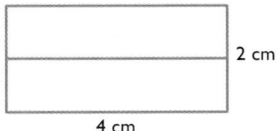

2 cm

4 cm

9.6 Example 1, page 211
Build a model.

Base Plan

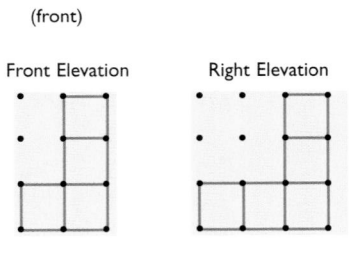

(front)

Front Elevation   Right Elevation

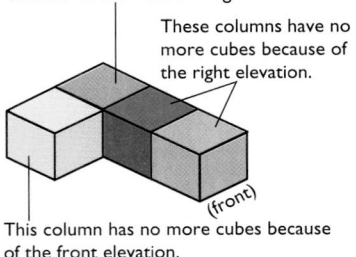

Solution

This column has two more cubes because of the front and right elevations.

These columns have no more cubes because of the right elevation.

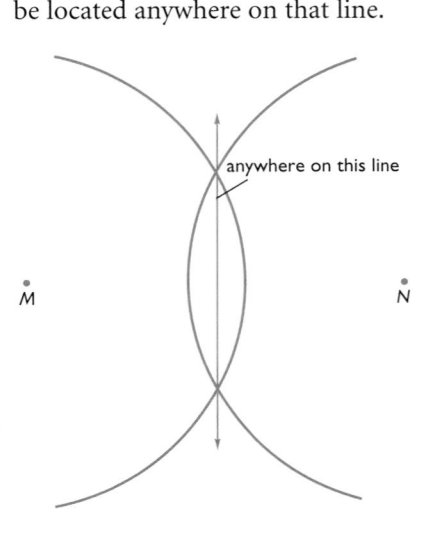

(front)

This column has no more cubes because of the front elevation.

(front)

9.6 Example 2, page 212
Base plans can be drawn with numbers to tell how many cubes there are in each column.

Base Plan

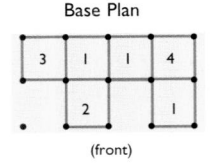

| 3 | 1 | 1 | 4 |
| | 2 | | 1 |

(front)

Draw the front and right elevations.

Solution
Elevations always show the tallest columns.

Front Elevation   Right Elevation

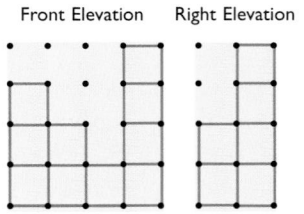

9.7 Example 1, page 214
Radio transmitter X can transmit a distance of 100 km. Located 200 km due west of it is transmitter Y that can transmit a distance of 150 km. Show the area that receives from
a) just transmitter X
b) just transmitter Y
c) both transmitters

Solution
A radio transmitter would be a point. So its transmission area will be a circle.
Let 1 cm represent 100 km.
A distance of 100 km from X will be a circle with a radius of 1 cm about X.
A distance of 200 km due west of X will be 2 cm left.
A distance of 150 km from Y will be a circle with a radius of 1.5 cm about Y.

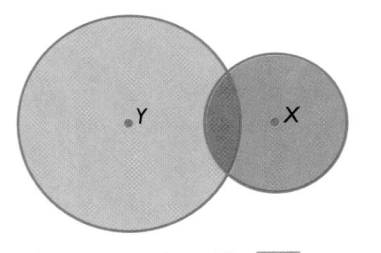

a) just transmitter X
b) just transmitter Y
c) both transmitters

9.7 Example 2, page 214
A street light is to be located the same distance from two signs, M and N, which are 50 m apart. Show where the street light could be located.

Solution
Let 1 cm represent 10 m.
The point midway between M and

N, 2.5 cm from each, is one location. However, there are many points the same distance from M and N. For example, 3 cm from both, 5 cm from both, and so on.
I will set the radius greater than 2.5 cm and draw an arc from each point, and then draw the line through the two points where the arcs intersect. The street light could be located anywhere on that line.

anywhere on this line

•
M

•
N

UNIT 10   Equations

10.1 Example 1, page 225
What are the next 3 numbers in the pattern? $\frac{3}{2}, \frac{5}{2}, \frac{7}{2}, \frac{9}{2}, ...$
Write an expression for the pattern.

Solution
The numerators increase by 2. They're odd numbers. The denominators are all 2.
$\frac{11}{2}, \frac{13}{2}, \frac{15}{2}$
An expression for odd numbers is $2n - 1$ or $2n + 1$. Use $2n + 1$ because the first number has $n = 1$, and $2(1) + 1 = 3$, which is the first numerator.
The expression is $\frac{2n + 1}{2}$.
Check.
The second number has $n = 2$, and $\frac{2(2) + 1}{2} = \frac{5}{2}$. ✓
The fourth number has $n = 4$, and $\frac{2(4) + 1}{2} = \frac{9}{2}$. ✓

10.1 Example 2, page 225

Write an equation that represents the situation.

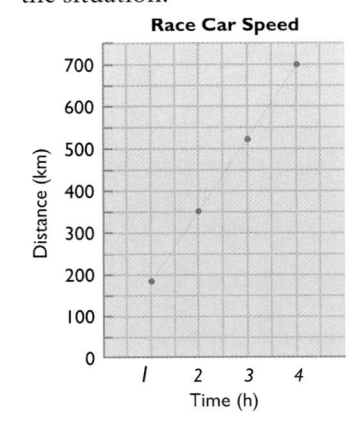

Race Car Speed

Solution

I can write the coordinates of the points in a table.

Time (h)	I	2	3	4
Distance (km)	I75	350	525	700

Every hour the race car travels 175 km. Its speed is 175 km/h and is constant because the points are connected by a straight line.
The relationship is $d = 175t$, where t is time in hours and d is distance in kilometres.
I know this is correct because when I substitute $t = 1, 2, 3, 4$ into the equation, I get the values for d as shown in the table and line graph.

10.2 Example 1, page 226

Complete each equation so that it is equivalent to $\frac{x}{6} = 4$.
a) $2x = \blacksquare$
b) $x - 1 = \blacksquare$
c) $\frac{x}{2} + 1 = \blacksquare$

Solution

a) If I multiply $\frac{x}{6}$ by 6, I get x. If I multiply $\frac{x}{6}$ by 12, I get $2x$. So I have to multiply the right side of the equation by 12 to keep the equation balanced.
$2x = 48$
b) I need to multiply each side of the equation by 6 and then subtract 1.
$x - 1 = 23$
c) If I multiply $\frac{x}{6}$ by 3 (which is half of 6), I get half of x or $\frac{x}{2}$. I need to

multiply each side of the equation by 3 and then add 1.
$\frac{x}{2} + 1 = 13$

10.2 Example 2, page 227

Explain how $x - \frac{1}{2} = 10$, $2x - 1 = 20$, $\frac{x}{2} - \frac{1}{4} = 5$, and $5x - \frac{5}{2} = 50$ are related.

Solution

If you divide each term in the second equation by 2, you get the first equation.
If you divide each term in the second equation by 4, you get the third equation.
If you multiply each term in the first equation by 5, you get the fourth equation.

10.3 Example 1, page 231

Solve the equation $-7 = 2x + 1$. Then check by substitution.

Solution

• To isolate the variable x, first I'll do the inverse operation of $+ 1$ to both sides of the equation.
$$-7 - 1 = 2x + 1 - 1$$
$$-8 = 2x$$
• Then I'll do the inverse operation of $\times 2$ to both sides of the equation.
$$\frac{-8}{2} = \frac{2x}{2}$$
$$-4 = x$$
• Check
$LS = -7 \quad RS = 2x + 1$
$\qquad\qquad\quad = 2(-4) + 1$
$\qquad\qquad\quad = -8 + 1$
$\qquad\qquad\quad = -7$
$\qquad\qquad LS = RS ✓$

10.3 Example 2, page 231

Are the following equations equivalent? Explain.
$c^2 = a^2 + b^2$, $a^2 = c^2 - b^2$, and $-a^2 + c^2 = b^2$

Solution

The first equation happens to describe the Pythagorean relationship.
• If you subtract b^2 from both sides of the first equation, you get $c^2 - b^2 = a^2$. (It doesn't matter if

you switch the left side and the right side of the equation.)
• If you subtract a^2 from both sides of the first equation, you get $c^2 - a^2 = b^2$. (It doesn't matter if you switch the order of the terms on one side of the equation.)
The three equations are equivalent.

10.4 Example 1, page 234

Solve $3x - 2 = -x + 6$ using algebra tiles. Then check.

Solution

• Model each side of the equation.
• Then add 1 x tile to each side.

add x add x

• Then add 2 red squares to each side.

add 2   add 2

• Then divide the tiles on each side into 4 equal groups.

1 x tile equals 2 red squares.
• Check.
$LS = 3x - 2 \qquad RS = -x + 6$
$\quad = 3(2) - 2 \qquad\quad = (-2) + 6$
$\quad = 6 - 2 \qquad\qquad\;\; = 4$
$\quad = 4$
$\qquad\qquad LS = RS ✓$

10.4 Example 2, page 234

Use inverse operations to solve $-5x - 3 = 3x + 5$.

Solution

• I'll add $5x$ to each side to avoid working with $-5x$.
$$-5x + 5x - 3 = 3x + 5x + 5$$
$$-3 = 8x + 5$$
• I'll subtract 5 from each side.
$$-3 - 5 = 8x + 5 - 5$$
$$-8 = 8x$$

- I'll divide each side by 8 to isolate the variable.

$$\frac{-8}{8} = \frac{8x}{8}$$
$$-1 = x$$

- Check.

$$LS = -5x - 3 \qquad RS = 3x + 5$$
$$= -5(-1)-3 \qquad = 3(-1) + 5$$
$$= 5 - 3 \qquad = -3 + 5$$
$$= 2 \qquad = 2$$
$$LS = RS \checkmark$$

10.5 Example 1, page 237

Solve $\frac{2n + 1}{3} - \frac{1}{4} = \frac{5n}{2}$, and then check.

Solution

- To clear the denominators, I'll multiply by the GCF of 2, 3, 4.

$$12\left(\frac{2n + 1}{3}\right) - \frac{1}{4}(12) = 12\left(\frac{5n}{2}\right)$$

- Then I'll simplify the equation as much as I can.

$$4(2n + 1) - 3 = 6(5n)$$
$$8n + 4 - 3 = 30n$$
$$8n + 1 = 30n$$

- Then I'll subtract $8n$ to place the variable on one side.

$$8n - 8n + 1 = 30n - 8n$$
$$1 = 22n$$

- Then I'll divide both sides by 22.

$$\frac{1}{22} = n$$

- Check.

$$LS = \frac{2n + 1}{3} - \frac{1}{4} \qquad RS = \frac{5n}{2}$$

$$= \frac{4(2n + 1) - 3}{12} \qquad = \frac{5\left(\frac{1}{22}\right)}{2}$$

$$= \frac{4(2(\frac{1}{22}) + 1) - 3}{12} \qquad = \frac{5}{22} \times \frac{1}{2}$$

$$= \frac{4(\frac{12}{11}) - \frac{33}{11}}{12} \qquad = \frac{5}{44}$$

$$= \frac{\frac{48 - 33}{11}}{12}$$

$$= \frac{15}{132}$$

$$= \frac{5}{44}$$
$$LS = RS \checkmark$$

10.5 Example 2, page 237

Solve $\frac{-9}{x} = 18$.

Solution

- I'll multiply both sides by x to clear the denominator.

$$-\frac{9}{x}(x) = 18x$$
$$-9 = 18x$$

- I'll divide both sides by 18 to isolate the variable.

$$\frac{-9}{18} = \frac{18x}{18}$$

$$\frac{-1}{2} = x$$

- Check.

$$LS = \frac{-9}{x} \qquad\qquad RS = 18$$

$$= \frac{-9}{(\frac{-1}{2})}$$

$$= -9(-\frac{2}{1})$$

$$= 18$$
$$LS = RS \checkmark$$

10.6 Example 1, page 239

It is recommended that no more than 30% of a family's income be spent on housing. The rent for a house is $1020 per month. What is the minimum monthly income a family should have to rent this house?

Solution

Let the minimum monthly income be x dollars.
30% means $\frac{30}{100}$.
I can organize the information in a proportion and solve for x.

$$\frac{30}{100} = \frac{1020}{x}$$

$$x\left(\frac{30}{100}\right) = x\left(\frac{1020}{x}\right)$$

$$\frac{30x}{100} = 1020$$

$$100\left(\frac{30x}{100}\right) = 100(1020)$$

$$30x = 102\,000$$

$$\frac{30x}{30} = \frac{102\,000}{30}$$

$$x = 3400$$

Check.
30% of $3400 should be $1020.

3400 ⊠ 30 ⊠%   *1020*

The family's monthly income should be at least $3400.

10.6 Example 2, page 239

Two consecutive even numbers have a sum of 1490. What are the numbers?

Solution

Let the first even number be n.
Then the second number will be 2 greater or $n + 2$.

The equation is:

$$n + n + 2 = 1490$$
$$2n + 2 = 1490$$
$$2n + 2 - 2 = 1490 - 2$$
$$2n = 1488$$
$$\frac{2n}{2} = \frac{1488}{2}$$
$$n = 744$$

744 is even; $n + 2 = 746$
Check.
$744 + 746 = 1490$ ✓
The numbers are 744 and 746.

10.7 Example 1, page 243

Are 3, -3, 6, and 2 all solutions to $\frac{y}{3} - 2 < -1$? Explain.

Solution

For $y = 3$, $\quad LS = \frac{y}{3} - 2 \quad RS = -1$
$$= \frac{(3)}{3} - 2$$
$$= 1 - 2$$
$$= -1$$

LS is not less than RS, so $y \neq 3$.

For $y = -3$,
$$LS = \frac{-3}{3} - 2 \qquad RS = -1$$
$$= -1 - 2$$
$$= -3$$

LS is less than RS, so $y = -3$.

For $y = 6$, $\quad LS = \frac{(6)}{3} - 2 \quad RS = -1$
$$= 2 - 2$$
$$= 0$$

LS is not less than RS, so $y \neq 6$.

For $y = 2$, $\quad LS = \frac{(2)}{3} - 2 \quad RS = -1$
$$= \frac{2}{3} - 2$$
$$= -1\frac{1}{3}$$

LS is less than RS, so $y = 2$.

Only -3 and 2 are solutions.

10.7 Example 2, page 243

Solve $-2(y + 1) \leq -(y + 1)$, and then check.

Solution

- First I'll simplify.

$$-2(y + 1) \leq -(y + 1)$$
$$-2y - 2 \leq -y - 1$$

- Then I'll put the variables all on the left side.

$$-2y + y - 2 \leq -y + y - 1$$
$$-y - 2 \leq -1$$

- I'll put all the numbers on the right side.

$$-y - 2 + 2 \leq -1 + 2$$
$$-y \leq 1$$

- Now I have to multiply both sides by -1, so I have to change the direction of the sign.

$$y \geq -1$$

- Check by substituting into the original inequation.

$$LS = -2(y + 1) \quad RS = 1(y + 1)$$
$$= -2[(-1) + 1] \quad = -[(-1) + 1]$$
$$= -2(0) \quad\quad = -(0)$$
$$= 0 \quad\quad\quad = 0$$
$$LS = RS \checkmark$$

So, -1 is a solution when I consider the $=$ sign part of the inequation. Now I need to pick a value for y that is greater than -1 and see if it makes the left side less than the right side.

For $y = 0$,
$$LS = -2(y + 1) \quad RS = (y + 1)$$
$$= -2[(0) + 1] \quad = -[(0) + 1]$$
$$= -2(1) \quad\quad = -1$$
$$= -2$$
$$LS < RS \checkmark$$

10.8 Example 1, page 244

Write an inequality for the graph.

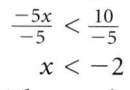

Solution

The graph shows all the numbers less than 2. If the variable is x, an inequality is $x < 2$ when $x \in$ R.
Another inequality is $x + 3 < 5$ (I added 3 to both sides), or $4x < 8$ (I multiplied both sides by 4).

10.8 Example 2, page 245

Solve $-2(x + 5) > 3x$ and graph when $x \in$ I.

Solution

- First I'll simplify.
$$-2(x + 5) > 3x$$
$$-2x - 10 > 3x$$

- Then I'll put the variables on one side.
$$-2x + 2x - 10 > 3x + 2x$$
$$-10 > 5x$$

- I'll isolate the variable.
$$\frac{-10}{5} > \frac{5x}{5}$$
$$-2 > x$$

-2 is greater than x, so x must be less than -2.

- I could solve it another way to check.
$$-2(x + 5) > 3x$$
$$-2x - 10 > 3x$$
$$-2x - 3x - 10 > 3x - 3x$$
$$-5x - 10 + 10 > 0 + 10$$
$$-5x > 10$$

I need to change the sign when dividing by a negative number.
$$\frac{-5x}{-5} < \frac{10}{-5}$$
$$x < -2$$

The graph of the inequality should show only integers because $x \in$ I.

UNIT 11 Similarity and Trigonometry

11.1 Example 1, page 255

Make a sketch and then draw $\triangle XYZ$ where $XY = 2$ cm and $YZ = 3$ cm.

Solution

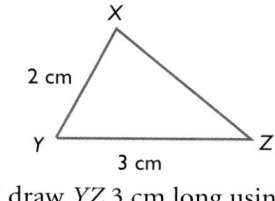

I'll draw YZ 3 cm long using a ruler and compasses.

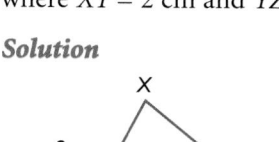

Then with centre Y, I'll cut an arc 2 cm to locate X.

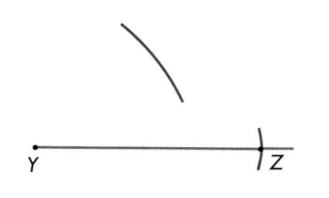

X can be anywhere on that arc.

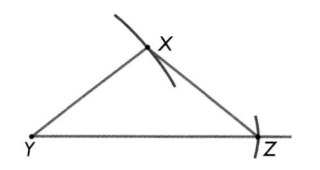

11.1 Example 2, page 255

Make a sketch and then draw $\triangle ABC$ where $\angle B = 30°$, $BC = 4$ cm, and $\angle C = 50°$.

Solution

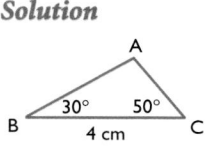

I'll draw BC 4 cm long using a ruler and compasses.

Then I'll use a protractor to draw $\angle B$ 30° with centre B and side BC as one arm.

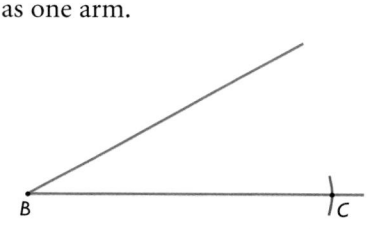

Then I'll use a protractor to draw $\angle C$ 50° with centre C and side BC as one arm.
Where the two arms from $\angle B$ and $\angle C$ intersect will be $\angle A$.

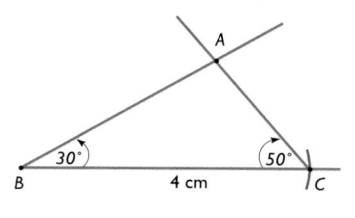

11.2 Example 1, page 257

Which set of conditions for congruence, AAS, ASA, SAS, or SSS, tells if this pair of triangles is congruent?

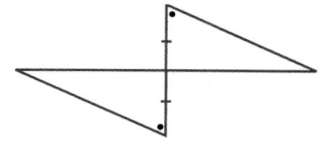

Solution
One pair of angles is equal, and one pair of sides is equal. I need a second pair of angles, or a second pair of sides so that the angle will be contained.

These angles are equal because they are vertically opposite. The set of conditions for congruence is ASA.

11.2 Example 2, page 257

Measure and use a set of conditions for congruence to determine if the triangles are congruent.

Solution
I can use any of AAS, ASA, SAS, or SSS. I will use SSS and measure all the sides.
The sides in the top triangle are 4 cm, 5 cm, and 6 cm, and the sides in the other triangle are the same. So the triangles are congruent by SSS.

11.3 Example 1, page 259

Measure the unknown angles and sides to see if all pairs of corresponding angles are equal and all pairs of corresponding sides are in the same ratio. Then the triangles are said to be similar.

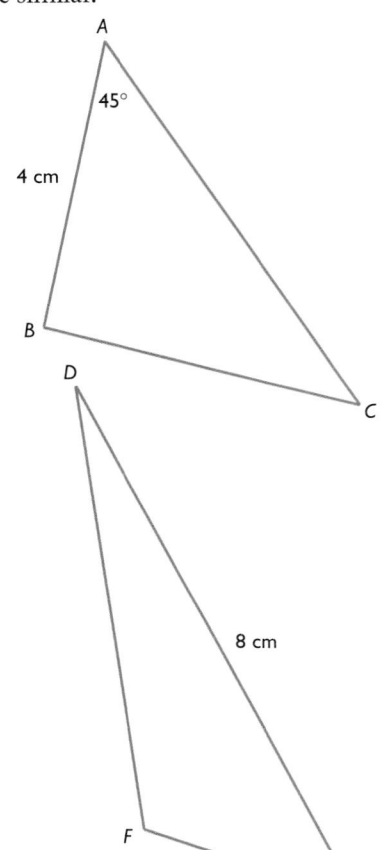

Solution

$\angle A = 45°$	$\angle E = 45°$
$AB = 4$ cm	$DE = 8$ cm
$\angle B = 95°$	$\angle F = 115°$
$\angle C = 40°$	$\angle D = 20°$
$AC = 6$ cm	$DF = 6.2$ cm
$BC = 4.3$ cm	$EF = 3$ cm

$\angle B \neq \angle F$ and $\angle C \neq \angle D$

$\frac{AB}{DE} = \frac{4}{8} \neq \frac{AC}{DF} = \frac{6.0}{6.2} \neq \frac{BC}{EF} = \frac{4.3}{3.0}$

The triangles are not similar.

11.3 Example 2, page 260

Measure the unknown angles and sides to see if all pairs of corresponding angles are equal and all pairs of corresponding sides are in the same ratio. Then the triangles are similar.

Solution

$ST = 3$ cm	$XV = 6$ cm
$SU = 4$ cm	$XW = 8$ cm
$\angle T = 40°$	$\angle W = 40°$
$\angle S = 110°$	$\angle X = 75°$
$\angle U = 30°$	$\angle V = 65°$
$TU = 5.7$ cm	$VW = 8.7$ cm

$\angle S \neq \angle X$ and $\angle U \neq \angle V$

$\frac{ST}{XV} = \frac{3}{6} = \frac{SU}{XW} = \frac{4}{8} \neq \frac{TU}{VW} = \frac{5.7}{8.7}$

The triangles are not similar.

11.4 Example 1, page 262

Identify corresponding sides in the similar triangles. Then find the height of the flagpole.

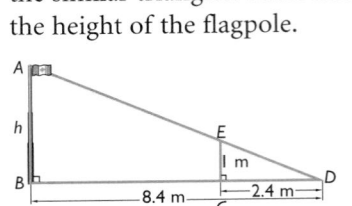

Solution

$\triangle ABD \sim \triangle ECD$

AB corresponds to EC.

BD corresponds to CD.

$\frac{AB}{BD} = \frac{EC}{CD}$

$\frac{h}{8.4} = \frac{1}{2.4}$

$h = \frac{1}{2.4} \times 8.4$

$h = 3.5$

The flagpole is 3.5 m tall.

11.4 Example 2, page 262

Identify corresponding sides in the similar triangles. Then find the height of the tree.

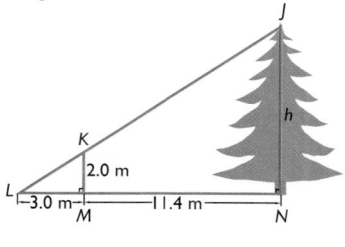

Solution

$\triangle KLM \sim \triangle JLN$

KM corresponds to JN.

LM corresponds to LN.

$\frac{KM}{LM} = \frac{JN}{LN}$

$\frac{2.0}{3.0} = \frac{h}{3.0 + 11.4}$

$\frac{2.0}{3.0} = \frac{h}{14.4}$

$\frac{2.0}{3.0} \times 14.4 = h$

$9.6 = h$

The tree is 9.6 m tall.

11.5 Example 1, page 265

Predict whether the tangent of the given angle is greater than, less than, or equal to 1. Calculate it using the measurements. Then calculate it using the [tan] key.

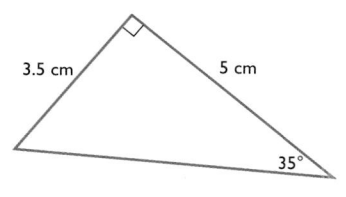

Solution

tangent $= \frac{\text{opposite side}}{\text{adjacent side}}$

3.5 cm is opposite 35° and 5.0 cm is adjacent to 35°.

3.5 cm < 5.0 cm

So tan 35° will be less than 1.

$\tan 35° = \frac{3.5}{5.0}$

$\tan 35° = 0.7$

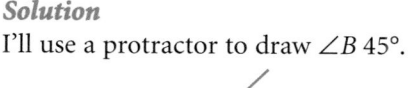

tan 35° = 0.7 rounded to 1 decimal place

11.5 Example 2, page 265

Draw a right triangle with an angle of 45°. Measure the appropriate sides to the nearest millimetre to calculate the tangent of 45°. Then calculate the tangent using the [tan] key.

Solution

I'll use a protractor to draw $\angle B$ 45°.

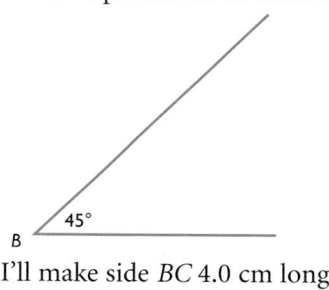

I'll make side BC 4.0 cm long.

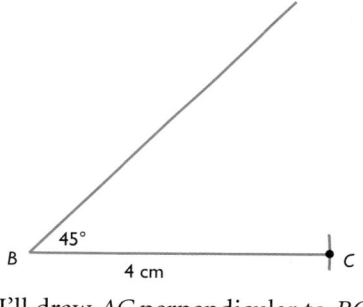

I'll draw AC perpendicular to BC at C using a protractor and measure it.

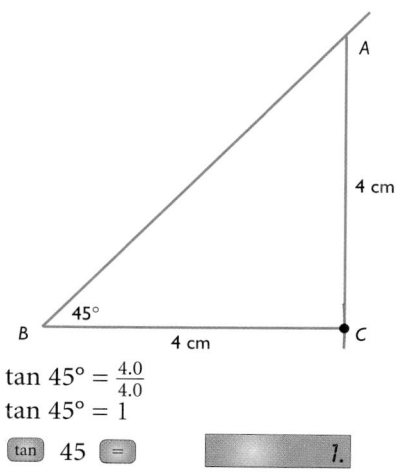

$\tan 45° = \frac{4.0}{4.0}$

$\tan 45° = 1$

tan 45 = 1.

$\tan 45° = 1$

11.6 Example 1, page 267

The angle of depression from the top of a lighthouse 240 m above sea level to a ship is 15°. What is the horizontal distance from the lighthouse to the ship?

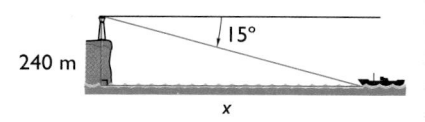

Solution

Let x be the horizontal distance from the lighthouse to the ship.

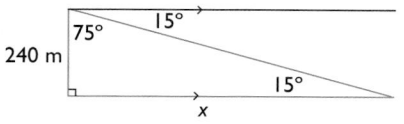

I can use tan 75° or tan 15°, but for tan 75°, side x is the opposite side and in the numerator.

$\tan 75° = \frac{x}{240}$

$\tan 75° \times 240 = x$

$895.7 = x$ rounded to 1 decimal place

tan 75 × 240 = 895.6921938

The horizontal distance is 895.7 m.

11.6 Example 2, page 267

The angle a kite string makes with the ground is 30°. The horizontal distance is 80 m. What is
a) the height of the kite?
b) the length of the kite string?

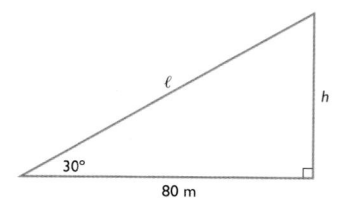

Solution

Let h be the height of the kite and ℓ be the length of the kite string.

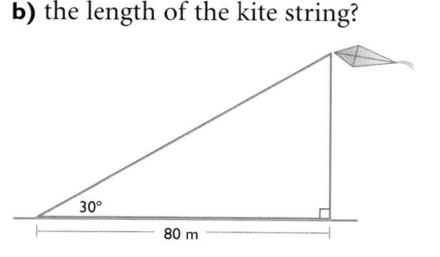

a)
$$\tan 30° = \frac{h}{80}$$
$$\tan 30° \times 80 = h$$
$$46.2 = h \text{ rounded to 1}$$
$$\text{decimal place}$$

[tan] 30 [×] 80 [=] `46.18802154`

The height of the kite is 46.2 m.
b) Since side ℓ is the hypotenuse, I'll use the Pythagorean relationship.
$$\ell^2 = 46.2^2 + 80^2$$
$$\ell = \sqrt{46.2^2 + 80^2}$$
$$\ell = 92.4 \text{ rounded to 1 decimal place}$$

[√] [(] 46.2 [x²] [+] 80 [x²]

[)] [=] `92.38203289`

The length of the kite string is 92.4 m.

11.7 Example 1, page 269
Find the sine and cosine rounded to the nearest hundredth for both acute angles by doing only two calculations.

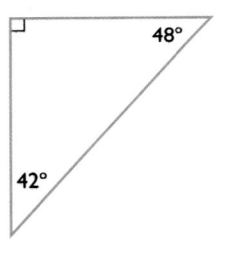

Solution
$$\sin 42° = \cos 48°$$
$$\sin 48° = \cos 42°$$
So I'll find both sines.
$$\sin 42° = 0.67$$

[sin] 42 [=] `0.669130606`

So cos 48° = 0.67
$$\sin 48° = 0.74$$

[sin] 48 [=] `0.743144825`

So cos 42° = 0.74

11.7 Example 2, page 269
Complete this statement.
Since sin 60° ≈ 0.866, cos ■ ≈ 0.866.

Solution
Since sine of one acute angle equals cosine of its complement, ■ = 30°.
Since sin 60° ≈ 0.866, cos 30° ≈ 0.866.

322

11.8 Example 1, page 271
The angle of depression from a hot air balloon to a car on the ground is 30°. The height of the balloon is 450 m. What is the horizontal distance from the balloon to the car?

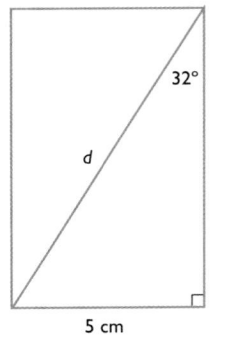

Solution
Let x be the horizontal distance from the balloon to the car.

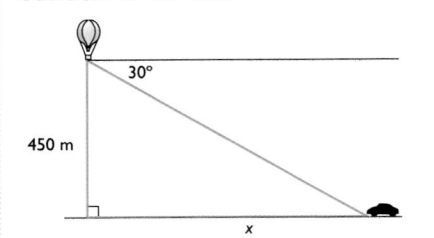

I can use tan 60° or tan 30°, but for tan 60°, side x is the opposite side and in the numerator.
$$\tan 60° = \frac{x}{450}$$
$$\tan 60° \times 450 = x$$
$$779.4 = x \text{ rounded to 1 decimal place}$$

[tan] 60 [×] 450 [=] `779.4228634`

The horizontal distance between the balloon and the car is 779.4 m.

11.8 Example 2, page 271
What is the length of a diagonal in a rectangle that meets the longer side at 32° if the shorter side is 5 cm long?

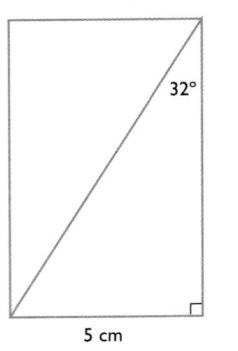

Solution
Let d be the length of the diagonal.

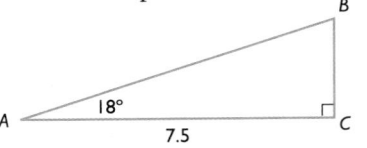

$$\sin 32° = \frac{5}{d}$$
$$d \times \sin 32° = 5$$
$$d = \frac{5}{\sin 32°}$$
$$d = 9.4 \text{ rounded to 1 decimal place}$$

5 [÷] [sin] 32 [=] `9.43539957`

The diagonal is 9.4 cm long.

11.9 Example 1, page 274
Solve △ABC rounding all answers to 1 decimal place.

Solution
$$\angle A = 18°$$
$$\angle C = 90°$$
$$AC = 7.5$$
$$\angle B = 90 - 18$$
$$= 72°$$
I can find BC using tan 18° or tan 72°.
$$\tan 18° = \frac{BC}{7.5}$$
$$\tan 18° \times 7.5 = BC$$
$$2.4 = BC$$

[tan] 18 [×] 7.5 [=] `2.43689772`

I can find AB using the Pythagorean relationship, cos 18°, or sin 72°.
I'll use the Pythagorean relationship.
$$AB^2 = 7.5^2 + 2.3^2$$
$$AB = \sqrt{7.5^2 + 2.3^2}$$
$$AB = \sqrt{61.54}$$
$$AB = 7.8$$

[√] [(] 7.5 [x²] [−] 2.3 [x²] [)]

[=] `7.844743463`

11.9 Example 2, page 275

The base of a ladder 4.0 m long is 1.4 m from a wall.

a) At what angle does it meet the ground?

b) What height does it reach on the wall?

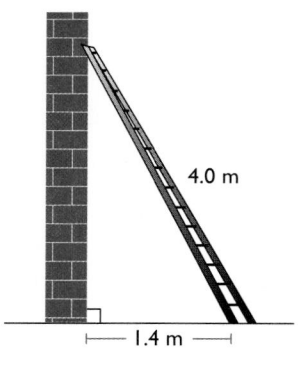

Solution

Let x be the angle the ladder makes with the ground and h be the height it reaches on the wall.

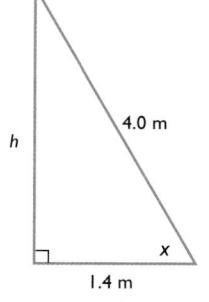

a) Since 1.4 m is adjacent to $\angle x$ and 4.0 m is the hypotenuse, I'll use cosine.

$\cos x = \frac{1.4}{4.0}$

$\cos x = 0.35$

$x = 69.5$ rounded to 1 decimal place

The angle it makes with the ground is about 69.5°.

b) Since side h is the only unknown side, I'll use the Pythagorean relationship.

$h^2 = 4.0^2 - 1.4^2$

$h = \sqrt{4.0^2 - 1.4^2}$

$h = 3.7$ rounded to 1 decimal place

√ (4 x^2 + 1.4 x^2)

= 3.746998799

The height the ladder reaches on the wall is about 3.7 m.

Glossary

A

AAS: (See **conditions for congruency**.)

abundant number: one in which the sum of all its factors, other than the number itself, is greater than the number. For example, 24 because the sum of the other factors of 24, 1+2+3+4+6+8+12 is 36.

acute angle: one that has a measure less than 90°.

acute triangle: one in which all angles have measures less the 90°.

algebra tiles: used to represent algebraic situations.

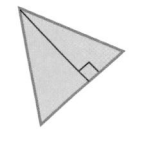

algebraic expression: one or more variables and possibly numbers and operation symbols. $3x + 6$, x, and $5x$ are algebraic expressions.

alternate angles: ones on opposite sides of a transversal when it crosses lines. The angles are equal when the lines are parallel. They form one of these Z patterns: Z, Ƨ, ⋈ , ⋈

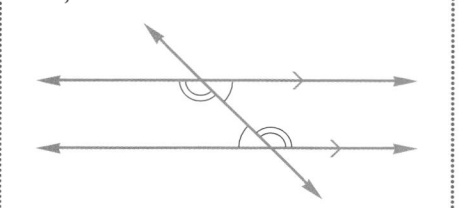

altitude of a triangle: a perpendicular line segment from a vertex to the opposite side.

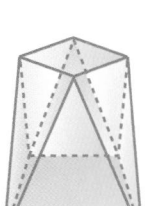

angle: two rays with a common end point.

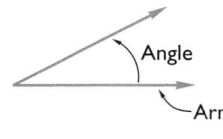

angle bisector: a ray dividing an angle into two equal parts.

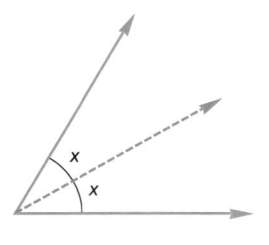

angle of depression: one between the horizontal and a line of sight to something below.

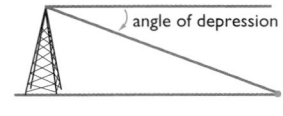

angle of elevation: one between the horizontal and a line of sight to something above.

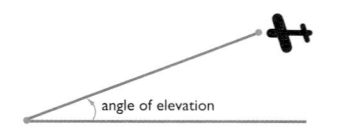

angle of rotation: the number of degrees, direction, and centre for the rotation of a figure. For this rotation, it is 90° clockwise about *C*.

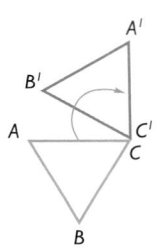

anti-prism: one formed by rotating one base.

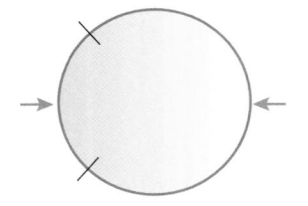

arc: a part of the circumference of a circle.

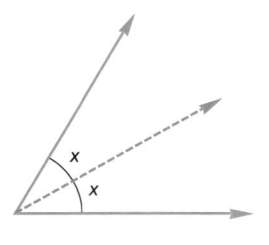

area: the amount of surface inside a region, measured in square units such as square centimetres.

ASA: (See **conditions for congruency**.)

average: the mean or the sum of a set of numbers divided by the number of numbers. The average of 10, 20, and 30 is $60 \div 3 = 20$.

axis (plural axes): either of the number lines of a graph. They meet at 90° at the origin.

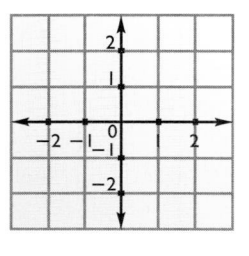

B

bar graph: a diagram consisting of bars that represent data.

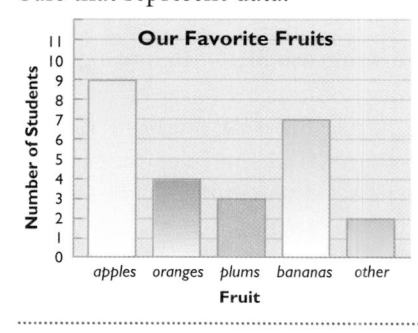

base of a power: the number used as the factor for repeated multiplication.

3^4

base plan: the 2-D outline of the bottom of a structure, what it looks like from the top.

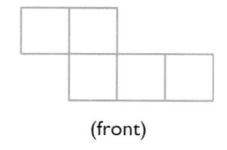

(front)

bias: an emphasis on characteristics that are not typical of the entire population. For example, an opinion survey on a national issue based on the views of callers to a radio show could be biased because the callers might over-represent those with extreme views.

binomial: an algebraic expression with two terms. For example, $2x + 4y$, $5k - 3n$, and $2x^2 + 5$

bisector: a line that divides a line segment or a figure into two equal halves.

box-and-whisker plot: an organization of data that shows the distribution of data in each quartile, that is, in each 25% of the data.

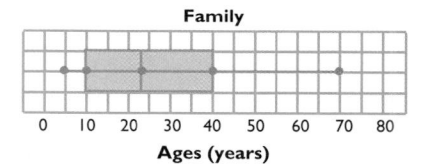

broken-line graph: a display of data on a coordinate grid formed by line segments that join points representing data.

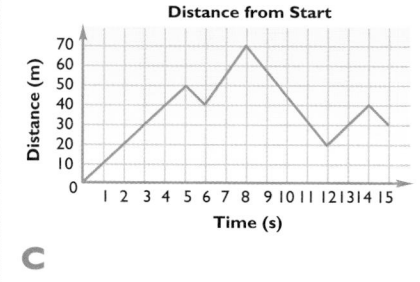

C

capacity: the amount of space a 3-D object contains, usually measured in millilitres or litres.

chord: a line segment that connects two points on a circle.

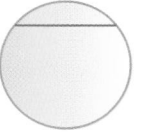

centre of dilatation: the point about which a figure is dilatated. For this enlargement, it is O.

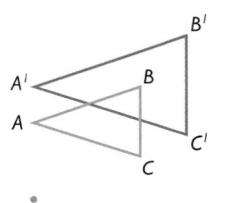

circle: a closed curve all of whose points are the same distance from its centre.

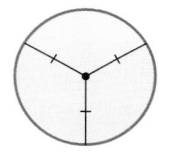

circle graph: a diagram in which a circle represents a whole and is divided into parts that represent parts of the whole.

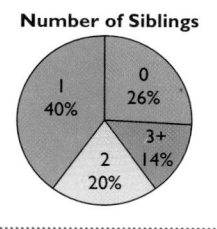

circumference: the distance around a circle, its perimeter.

coefficient: part of a term. The numerical factor is a numerical coefficient, and the variable factor is a variable coefficient. For example, in $5y$, 5 is the numerical coefficient and y is the variable coefficient.

co-interior angles: ones between the lines and on the same side of the transversal. When the lines are parallel, the angles add to 180°. They form a [,] , ⌐, or ⌐ pattern.

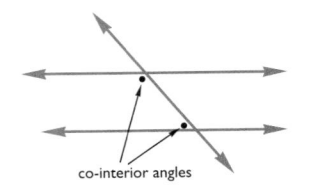

co-interior angles

common denominator: a number that is a common multiple of the denominators of a set of fractions. A common denominator of $\frac{1}{3}$ and $\frac{1}{2}$ is 6.

common factor: a number that is a factor of two or more numbers. A common factor of 6 and 18 is 3.

common multiple: a number that is a multiple of two or more numbers. A common multiple of 2 and 3 is 18.

complementary angles: ones whose sum is 90°.

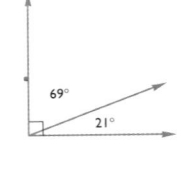

composite number: one that has factors other than itself and 1. For example, 4 because it has 1, 2, and 4 as factors.

computer spreadsheet: software to help you organize and use information using rows and columns.

	A	B	C	D	E	F	G
1							
2							
3							
4							
5							
6							
7							
8							
9							

conditions for congruency: two figures are congruent if all three pairs of corresponding sides are equal (SSS), or two pairs of corresponding sides and a pair of contained angles are equal (SAS), or two pairs of corresponding angles and a pair of contained sides are equal (ASA), or if two pairs of corresponding angles and a pair of non-contained sides are equal (AAS).

cone: a three-dimensional figure with one circular base and one vertex.

congruent figures: those that have the same size and shape.

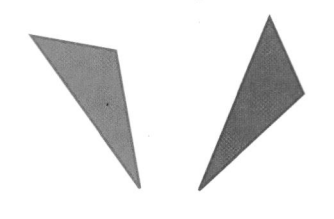

constant function/feature: on a calculator, the function that allows repetitive calculation. For example, $3 + 4 + 4 + 4 + 4 + 4$ can be found on some calculators using the keystrokes 3 ⊕ 4 ⊜ ⊜ ⊜ ⊜ ⊜ .

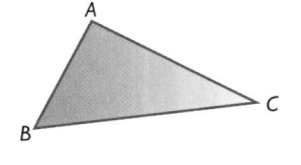

constant term: one that is a number. For example, in the expression $3x + 5$, 5 is the constant term.

contained side angle: one that is contained between two angles or two sides. For example, $<A$ is contained between sides AB and AC. Side BC is contained between $<B$ and $<C$.

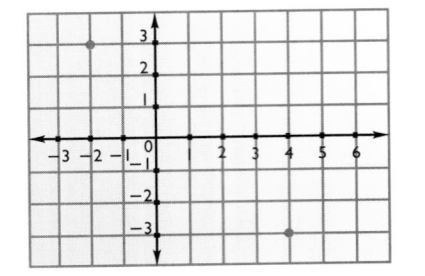

control variable: in an investigation, what controls the fairness. For example, in an investigation of the sweetness of apple juice, the same serving temperature would be a control variable.

coordinate plane: what results when two perpendicular number lines intersect at their zero points.

coordinates: an ordered pair of numbers that locates a point on a grid.

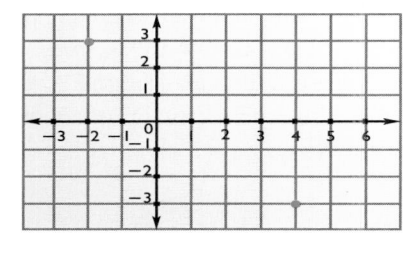

corresponding angles: ones on the same side of a transversal and either above or below, or to the right or the left of the lines the transversal intersects. When the lines are parallel, corresponding angles are equal. They form one of these F patterns: ⊏ , ⊐ , ⊢ , ⊣ , ⊓ , ⊔ , ⊏ , or ⊔ .

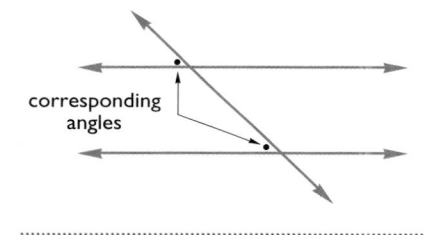

corresponding
angles

corresponding angles/sides: matching angles/sides of figures.

A and A′
B and B′
C and C′
AB and A′B′
BC and B′C′
AC and A′C′

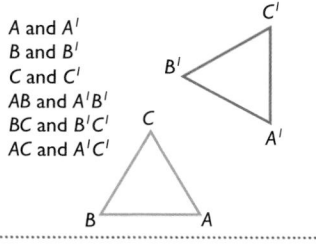

cosine: for an acute angle in a right triangle, the ratio of the length of its adjacent side to the length of the hypotenuse.

cube: a polyhedron with each of its six faces a square.

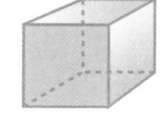

---

cube root: one of three equal factors of a given number. 3 is a cube root of 27 because $27 = 3 \times 3 \times 3$.

cylinder: a 3-D object with two parallel, congruent, circular faces.

D

dart (chevron): a quadrilateral in the shape of an arrowhead.

data: facts or information.

database: an organized and sorted list of facts or information, usually generated by a computer.

decagon: a polygon with ten sides.

deficient number: one in which the sum of all its factors, other than the number itself, is less than the number. For example, 8, because the sum of the other factors of 8, $1 + 2 + 4$ is 7.

degree (measure of an angle): a unit for measuring angles, $\frac{1}{360}$ of a full turn.

---

denominator: the number of equal parts in a whole or a group, or the bottom number in a fraction.

$$\frac{3}{4} \leftarrow$$

dependent variable: in an investigation, what changes as the independent variable changes. For example, in an investigation of the sweetness of apple juice, the brand of juice is the independent variable and the sweetness is the dependent variable.

diagonal (of a polygon): a line segment that joins vertices of a polygon, but is not a side.

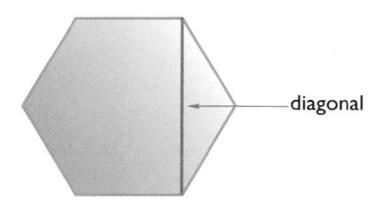
diagonal

diameter: a line segment connecting two points on a circle that passes through the centre.

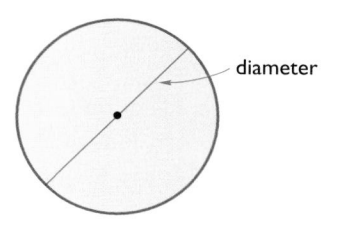
diameter

dilatation: a transformation where the image is the same shape as the original. It can be an enlargement or a reduction.

discount: an amount by which a price is reduced. It is often stated as a fraction or a percent of the price.

divisible: can be divided with no remainder. For example, 10 is divisible by 2.

dodecahedron: a polygon with twelve sides.

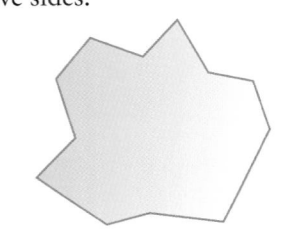

E

edge: the line segment where two faces of a 3-D object meet.

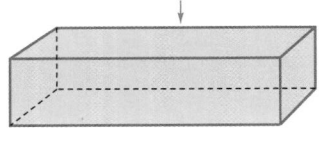

elevation: in architecture, a 2-D representation of an outline of what you see when looking at one side of a structure.

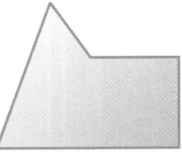

enlargement: a dilatation in which all the linear dimensions of the original are multiplied by the same amount greater than 1.

equation: a number sentence with the same amount on each side of an equals sign.

equivalent expressions/equations: ones that have the same value. For example, $3y(y + 2y)$ and $3y^2 + 6y^2$ are equivalent expressions, and

$2x = 8$ and $3x = 12$ are equivalent equations.

equilateral triangle: one that has three sides of equal length.

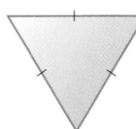

equivalent fractions: ones that name the same part of a whole or set. $\frac{1}{2}, \frac{2}{4}, \frac{3}{6}$ are equivalent fractions.

equivalent ratios: ones that have the same lowest terms. 1:3, 2:6, and 3:9 are equivalent ratios.

evaluate: substitute values for the variables and then perform the operations according to the order of operations. For example, if $x = 2$,
$$x^2 + 5x$$
$$= (2)^2 + 5(2)$$
$$= 4 + 10$$
$$= 14$$

expanded form: a way in which numbers are written to show the value of each digit.
$$432 = 4 \times 100 + 3 \times 10 + 2 \times 1$$

expected probability: the chance of an event occurring based on possibilities. For example, the expected probability of spinning red on this spinner is $\frac{1}{3}$ because there is 1 favorable outcome (red) out of 3 possible outcomes (red, green, and blue).

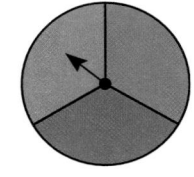

experimental probability: the chance of an event occurring based on the results of an experiment. For example, if you spun this spinner 10 times and it landed on red 7 times, the experimental probability would be $\frac{7}{10}$.

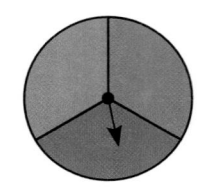

exponent: a raised number that tells how many times the base is multiplied by itself.

exponential form: a shorthand method for writing repeated multiplication. In 5^3, 3 is the exponent and indicates 5 is to be multiplied by itself three times. 5^3 is in exponential form.

expression: (See **algebraic expressions**.)

F

face: a surface of a 3-D object.

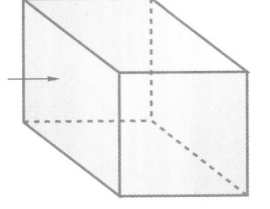

factoring: writing a polynomial as a product of its factors. For example, $x^2 - 7x + 10 = (x - 2)(x - 5)$, $x^2 + 2x - 8 = (x - 2)(x + 4)$, and $x^2 + 5x = x(x + 5)$.

factors: numbers or expressions that are multiplied. For example, 3 and 4 are factors of 12, and x and $x + 1$ are factors of $x^2 + x$.

factor tree: a diagram used to find the prime factors of a number.

Fibonacci sequence: numbers in order, each of which is the sum of the two previous numbers.
1, 1, 2, 3, 5, 8, 13, 21, ...

formula: an equation that shows a relationship. For example, the formula for volume of a cone is $V = \frac{1}{3}\pi r^2 h$.

fraction: a part of a whole or a group. $\frac{2}{3}$, $\frac{2}{2}$, and $\frac{6}{4}$ are fractions.

frequency: the number of times an event or item occurs.

G

generator: a number that generates another from the sum of its digits and itself. For example, 23 is a generator of 28 because $2 + 3 + 23 = 28$.

golden rectangle: one in which the ratio of length to width is about 1.6180.

graph: a representation of data in pictorial form.

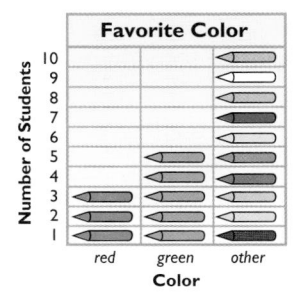

greatest common factor, GCF: the largest of the factors common to two or more numbers. The greatest common factor of 8, 12, and 24 is 4.

grid: a pattern of lines or dots.

H

hectare (ha): a unit for measuring area which is equal to 10 000 m².

height of a triangle: (See **altitude**.)

heptagon: a polygon with seven sides.

hexagon: a polygon with six sides.

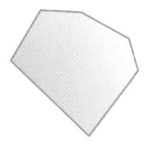

histogram: a graph that uses bars to display continuous data.

hypotenuse: the side of a right triangle opposite the right angle.

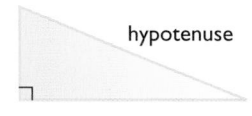

I

image: the figure produced by a transformation of a figure.

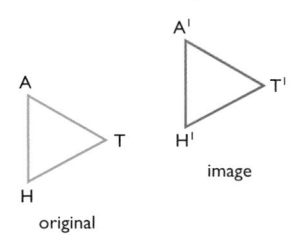

improper fraction: one whose numerator is greater than its denominator. $\frac{13}{7}$ is an improper fraction.

independent variable: (See **dependent variable**.)

inequality/inequation: a sentence that contains $<$, $>$, $\leq$, or $\geq$ or $\neq$. For example, $x + 4 \geq 5$, $8 + x \neq 8$, and $3x^2 + 5x < 60$.

integers: the numbers $..., -4, -3, -2, -1, 0, 1, 2, 3, 4, ...$

intersecting lines: ones with a point in common, the point of intersection.

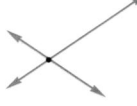

inverse of tangent/cosine/sine: used to find the measure of an angle if the ratio of the lengths of the sides is known. For example, if $\tan x = 0.5$, then $x = 26.6°$ using the $\boxed{\text{TAN}^{-1}}$ key on a scientific calculator.

inverse operations: ones that undo each other. For example, subtraction is the inverse of addition, and division is the inverse of multiplication.

irrational numbers: ones that cannot be written in the form $\frac{a}{b}$, where a and b are integers and $b \neq 0$. For example, $2 = 0.313\ 113\ 111\ 311\ 11...$

isometric dot paper: triangular dot paper, often used to draw representations of 3-D shapes.

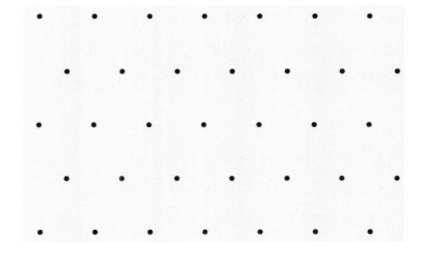

isosceles triangle: one that has two sides of equal length.

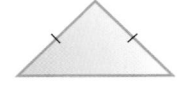

K

keystrokes: keys to be pressed to find the value of an expression. For example, the keystrokes for $5^2 \times 7(3 - 42)$ could be $5\ \boxed{x^2}\ \boxed{\times}\ 7\ \boxed{(}\ 3\ \boxed{-}\ 42\ \boxed{)}\ \boxed{=}$.

kite: a quadrilateral with one line of symmetry.

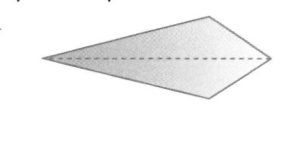

L

like terms: ones with identical variable coefficients. For example, in $3y + 2y^2 - 2y + x$, $3y$ and $-2y$ are like terms.

linear relationship: one that has a straight-line graph.

line: a set of points that has no end points.

line symmetry: if a figure has at least one line of symmetry, it is said to have line symmetry. For example, trapezoid *ABCD* has line symmetry.

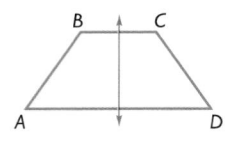

line of symmetry: one that divides a shape into two parts that can be matched by folding the shape in half.

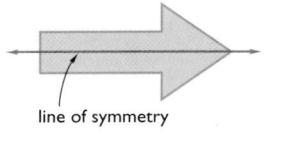

line of symmetry

line of best fit: one that can sometimes be determined on a scatter plot. If a line of best fit can be found, a relationship exists between the independent and dependent variables.

line segment: a set of points that has end points.

lonely number: one that cannot be generated by adding another number with its digits. For example, 31 and 64.

lowest common denominator, LCD: the least common multiple of the denominators. The LCD of $\frac{3}{4}$ and $\frac{5}{6}$ is 12.

lowest common multiple, LCM: the least of the multiples common to two or more numbers. The LCM of 4 and 6 is 12.

lowest terms: when the GCF of the numerator and denominator of a fraction (or of all the terms of a ratio) is 1. For example, $\frac{2}{3}$ and $\frac{1}{2}$ are both in lowest terms.

M

mass: the amount of matter in an object usually measured in grams, kilograms, or tonnes.

mean: the sum of a set of numbers divided by the number of numbers in the set. For example, the mean of 56, 68, and 74 is $(56 + 68 + 74) \div 3$ or 66.

median: the number such that half the numbers in a set are less than it and half are greater than it. For example, 14 is the median of 7, 9, 14, 21, and 39. If there is an even number of numbers, the median is the mean of the two middle numbers. For example, 11 is the median of 5, 10, 12, and 28.

mean deviation: the difference between one piece of data and the mean of the data. For example, for 27°C, 32°C, 26°C, 31°C, and 34°C, the mean is 30°C. 32°C has a deviation of +2°C and 27°C has a deviation of −3°C.

midpoint: the centre point of a line segment.

Mira: a tool used in geometry to locate reflection lines, reflection images, and lines of symmetry, and to determine congruency and line symmetry.

mixed number: one that is the sum of a whole number and a fraction. For example, $7\frac{1}{2}$ or 7.5.

mode: the number that occurs most often in a set of data.

monomial: an algebraic expression with one term. For example, $2x$ and $5xy^2$.

multiples: all numbers that have a factor in common. For example, 5, 10, 15, 20, ... are all multiples of 5.

multiple bar graph: one that uses sets of bars to show relationships between data.

N

natural numbers: the counting numbers. 1, 2, 3, 4, ...

negative square root: the negative number that multiplies by itself to give the number whose square root is being found. For example, $(-3)^2 = 9$, so $-\sqrt{9} = -3$.

net: a pattern that you can fold to make a 3-D object.

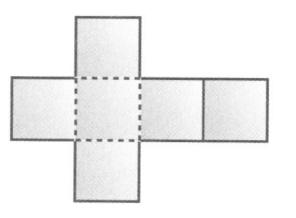

network: a set of vertices joined by paths.

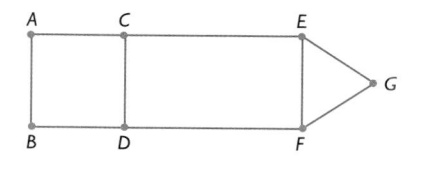

nonagon: a polygon with nine sides.

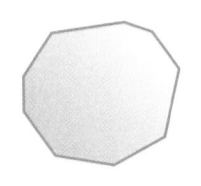

non-contained side/angle: (See **contained side/angle.**)

non-terminating, non-repeating decimal: one that continues without end and shows no repeating pattern. For example, 0.212 112 111...

number line: one that matches a set of numbers and a set of points, one to one.

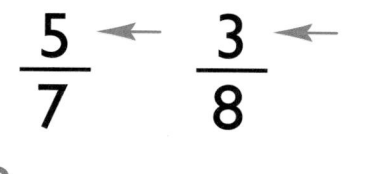

numerator: the number of equal parts of a whole or of a set that are being considered, or the top number in a fraction.

$$\frac{5}{7} \leftarrow \qquad \frac{3}{8} \leftarrow$$

O

obtuse angle: one whose measure is greater than 90° but less than 180°.

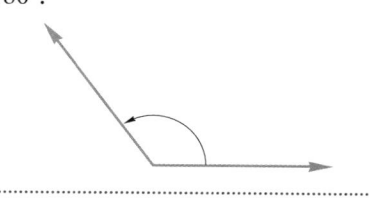

obtuse triangle: that has one obtuse angle.

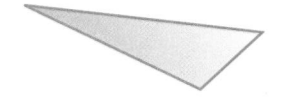

octagon: a polygon with eight sides.

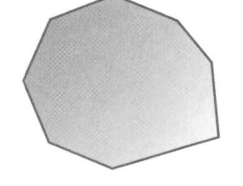

odds: a ratio of the probability that an event will happen to the probability that it will not happen.

opposite angles: the equal angles formed by two intersecting lines.

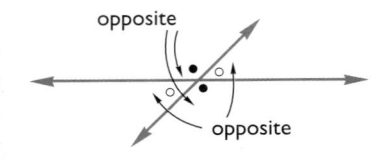

order of operations: the rules used to simplify expressions.
1. brackets
2. exponents
3. multiplication and division
4. addition and subtraction

ordered pair: two numbers in order such as (2, 6). The first number is the horizontal coordinate of the point. The second is the vertical coordinate of the point.

origin: the point on a graph where the horizontal and vertical axes meet. The origin has coordinates (0, 0).

outcome: the results of an experiment.

P

parallel lines: ones in the same plane that do not intersect.

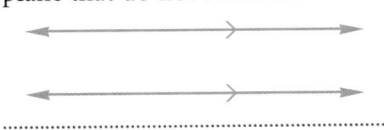

parallelogram: a quadrilateral with opposite sides parallel and equal.

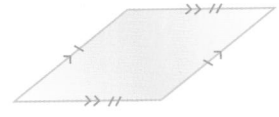

pentagon: a polygon with five sides.

percent: a ratio with a second term of 100.

percent change: the difference from a given amount expressed as a percent. For example, the percent change from $20 to $30 is a percent increase of 50% but an actual increase of $10. The percent change from $50 to $40 is a percent decrease of 20% but an actual decrease of $10.

percent decrease: (See **percent change.**)

percent increase: (See **percent change.**)

perfect number: one whose factors, other than the number itself, add up to the number:
6 because 6 = 1 + 2 + 3.

perfect square number: the product of an integer multiplied by itself. For example,
9 = 3 × 3, so 9 is a perfect square.

perimeter: the distance around a closed figure.

perpendicular lines: ones that intersect at a 90° angle.

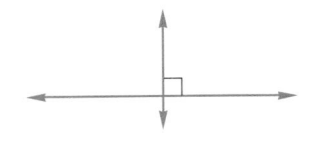

pi (π): the ratio of circumference of a circle to its diameter. 3.14…

pictograph: an illustration of data using pictures or symbols.

Number of Pumpkins Sold	
Fri.	🎃🎃🎃
Sat.	🎃🎃🎃🎃◗
Sun.	🎃🎃🎃🎃🎃🎃
Mon.	🎃◗

🎃 represents 10 pumpkins.

polygon: a closed figure formed by three or more line segments. Some examples are triangles, squares, quadrilaterals, pentagons, and octagons.

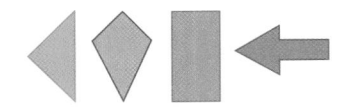

polyhedron: a 3-D object that has polygons as faces. Some examples are prisms and pyramids.

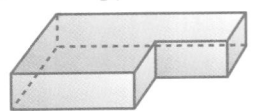

polynomial: an algebra expression. For example, $6x$, $3x - 2$ and $4x^2 + 5x - 4$.

polyomino: a shape made of squares joined along whole edges.

population: the set of all things or people being considered. For example, in an opinion survey for a school election, all students in the school would be the population.

power: a number written in exponential form, a shorter way of writing repeated multiplication. 10^2 and 2^6 are powers.

primary-source data: information that is collected directly or first hand. Data from a person-on-the-street survey is primary-source data.

prime factorization: an expression showing a composite number as a product of its prime factors. The prime factorization for 42 is $2 \times 3 \times 7$.

prime number: a whole number, greater than 1, that has only two factors, itself and 1. For example, 7 because its factors are only 1 and 7.

principal square root: the positive square root of a number. For example, $2^2 = 4$, $(-2)^2 = 4$, but $\sqrt{4} = 2$.

prism: a polyhedron with two parallel bases that are congruent polygons and other faces that are parallelograms.

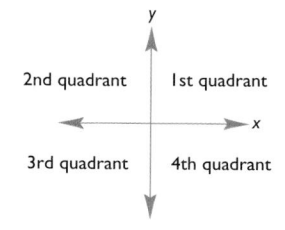

probability: (See **expected probability**, **experimental probability**, and **theoretical probability**.)

proper fraction: one whose numerator is less than its denominator. $\frac{4}{5}$ is a proper fraction.

proportion: a number sentence showing that two ratios are equal: $\frac{2}{3} = \frac{6}{9}$ is a proportion.

pyramid: a polyhedron with a base that is any polygon and other faces that are triangular and meet at a vertex.

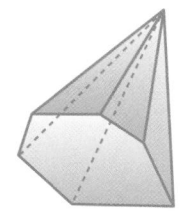

Pythagorean relationship: the square of the length of the hypotenuse is equal to the sum of the squares of the other two sides in a right triangle.

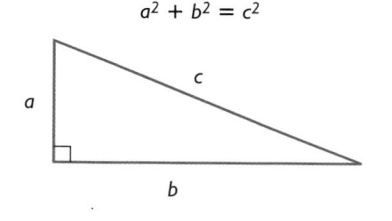

$$a^2 + b^2 = c^2$$

Pythagorean triple: three numbers that satisfy the Pythagorean relationship. For example, 5, 12, and 13 because $5^2 + 12^2 = 13^2$.

Q

quadrant: one of the four parts that the y-axis and x-axis separate a coordinate grid into. The axes are not part of the quadrants.

| 2nd quadrant | 1st quadrant |
| 3rd quadrant | 4th quadrant |

quadrilateral: a polygon with four sides.

quartile: 25% of a group of data.

quotient: the result when one number is divided by another.

R

radius: a line segment whose end points are the centre of the circle and a point on the circle.

radius

random number: one selected by chance such as spinning a spinner, rolling a die, using the random function of a calculator or computer.

random number table: a list of digits with no predictable pattern.

range: the difference between the greatest and lowest numbers in a group of numbers. For 8, 9, 12, 13, 17, 20, and 21, the range is $21 - 8$ or 13.

rate: a comparison of quantities with units that are different, such as kilometres and hours. 100 km/h is a rate.

ratio: a comparison of like quantities. 3: 4, 5: 7 : 3, and 1: 2: 1 are ratios.

rational numbers: ones that can be expressed as the quotient of two integers where the divisor is not 0.

reciprocals: two numbers whose product is 1. 4 and $\frac{1}{4}$ are reciprocals. $\frac{3}{2}$ and $\frac{2}{3}$ are also reciprocals.

real numbers: rational and irrational numbers.

rectangle: a quadrilateral with four right angles and parallel and opposite sides equal.

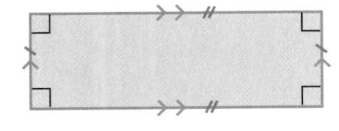

rectangular prism: one whose bases are congruent rectangles.

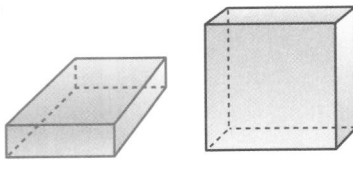

reduction: a dilatation in which all the linear dimensions of the original are multiplied by the same amount between 0 and 1.

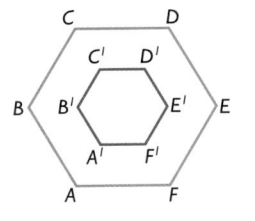

reflection: a flip transformation in a mirror or reflection line.

reflection line: one in which a figure is reflected to produce a reflection image.

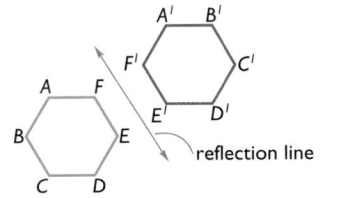

reflex angle: one whose measure is greater than 180° but less than 360°.

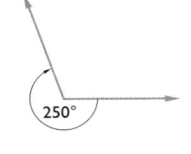

250°

regular polygon: one that has all sides of equal length and all angles of equal measure.

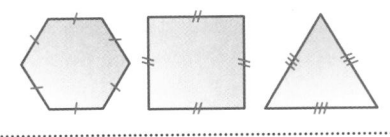

regular polyhedron: one whose faces are regular congruent polygons.

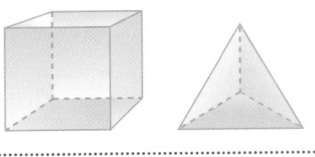

repeating decimal: one in which one or more digits repeat. For example, 0.333… or 0.$\overline{3}$, 7.454 545… or 7.$\overline{45}$.

rhombus: a parallelogram with four sides of equal length.

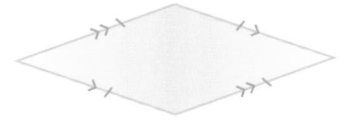

right angle: one whose measure is 90°.

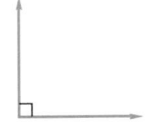

right bisector: a line that divides a line segment into 2 equal line segments at a 90° angle.

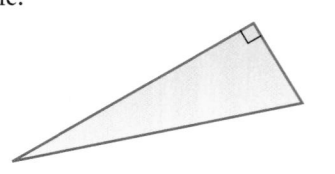

right triangle: one with one right angle.

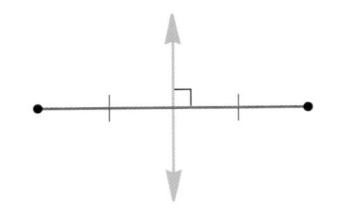

rotation: a turn of a figure about a fixed point.

rounding: changing a number to the nearest hundredth, tenth, whole, ten, hundred, thousand, and so on. 348 rounded to the nearest ten is 350. 9.8463 rounded to the nearest hundredth is 9.85.

S

sample: a small, representative group, chosen from the population, that is examined in order to make predictions about the population.

sample size: the number of items selected from a whole group or population.

SAS: (See **conditions for congruency**.)

scale drawing: one in which the lengths are reductions or enlargements of actual lengths.

scale factor: the ratio of lengths in an enlargement or reduction to actual lengths.

scatter plot: a graph with points plotted on a coordinate grid that attempts to show a relationship between two variables.

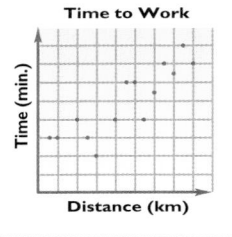

scientific notation: a way of writing a number as the product of a number between 1 and 10 and a power of 10.
58 000 000 is 5.8×10^7 written in scientific notation.

secondary-source data: information that is not collected first hand. For example, data from a government document.

set: a collection of data or numbers.

shell: a 3-D object whose interior is completely empty.

similar figures: ones that have the same shape but not always the same size.

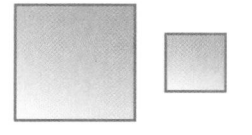

simplify: remove brackets and combine like terms. For example,
$$7x + (3x + 3) - 1$$
$$= 7x + 3x - 3 - 1$$
$$= 10x - 4$$

simulation: a probability experiment to test the likelihood of an event. For example, tossing a coin is a simulation of whether the next person you meet is male or female.

sine: for an acute angle in a right triangle, the ratio of the length of its opposite side to the length of the hypotenuse.

skeleton: a 3-D object showing only the edges and vertices.

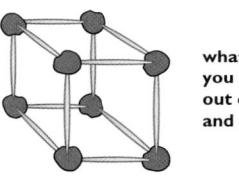

what you get when you make an object out of toothpicks and plasticine

slope: the ratio of vertical distance to horizontal distance or rise to run.
slope $= \frac{\text{rise}}{\text{run}}$

social number: one that can be generated from the sum of another number and its digits. For example, 85 because $74 + 4 + 7 = 85$.

solid: a 3-D object whose interior is completely filled.

solve: to find the value for the variable in an equation. For example, if $y - 5 = 7$
$$y - 5 + 5 = 7 + 5$$
$$y = 12$$

sphere: a 3-D object in the shape of a ball with a fixed point called the centre and all points on the surface exactly the same distance, the radius, from the centre.

spreadsheet: (See **computer spreadsheet**.)

square: a rectangle with four sides of equal length.

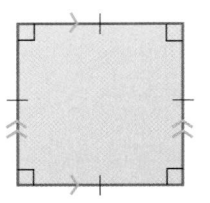

square root: (See **principal square root**, and **negative square root**.)

SSS: (See **conditions for congruency**.)

standard form: a way of writing a number with each digit having a place value according to its position in relation to the other digits.
7856 is in standard from.

stem-and-leaf plot: an organization of data into categories based on place values.

Times (min.)

2	2				
3	0	2	5	8	9
4	2	3	5	7	7	8
5	5	5	9		
6	2				
7	9	9	9		

straight angle: one whose measure is 180°.

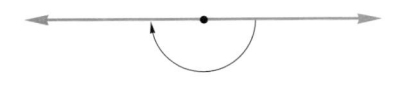

surface area: the sum of the areas of the faces of a 3-D object.

supplementary angles: ones whose sum is 180°.

survey: a sampling of information.

T

tally chart: the use of tally marks to count data and record frequencies.

tangent: for an acute angle in a right triangle, the ratio of the length of its opposite side to the length of its adjacent side.

tangram: an ancient Chinese puzzle made from a square cut into seven pieces resulting in two large triangles, one medium-sized triangle, two small triangles, one square, and one parallelogram.

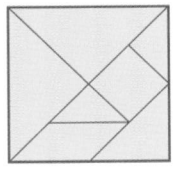

term: part of an expression separated from others by the operations $-$ and $+$. For example, in $3x + y - 4$, the three terms are $3x$, y, and -4.

terminating decimal: one that comes to an end, with a countable number of digits. For example, 3.894, 9.44, 3.8.

tessellation: a tiling pattern made with shapes fitted together with no gaps or overlaps.

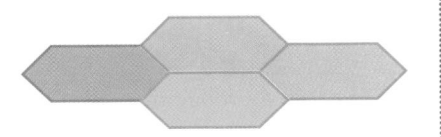

tetrahedron: a polyhedron with four trianglar faces, a triangular pyramid.

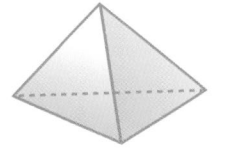

theoretical probability: the number of favorable outcomes divided by the number of possible outcomes.

transformation: a change in a figure which results in a different position, shape, size, and/or orientation. For example, translations, rotations, reflections, and dilatations.

translation: a slide transformation.

translation rule: the direction and distance a figure is moved to create a translation image. For example, the rule $[-5, 2]$ means each vertex is moved 5 units to the left and 2 units up.

transversal: a line that intersects two or more lines.

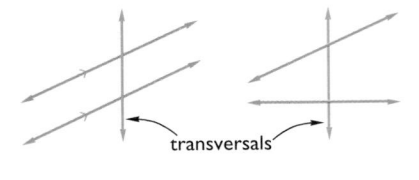
transversals

trapezoid: a quadrilateral with exactly one pair of parallel sides.

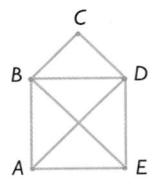

traversable network: one that you can travel completely, without retracing any part of your route. For example, this network is traversable with route A, B, C, D, B, E, D, A, E.

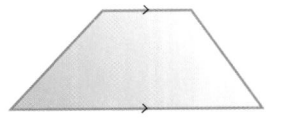

tree diagram: a branching diagram which shows all possible combinations or outcomes.

triangle: a polygon with three sides.

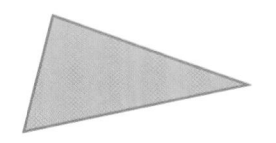

triangle sum property: the sum of the interior angles in a triangle is 180°.

triangular number: one that can be represented by a triangular array. 1, 3, 6, 10, 15 are triangular numbers.

trigonometry: a branch of mathematics combining arithmetic, algebra, and geometry, based on relationships and patterns in right triangles. It is used in surveying, navigation, and sciences such as physics.

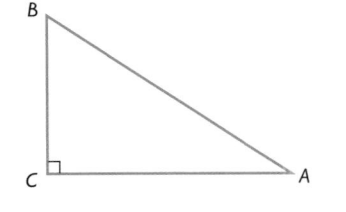

$$\tan < A = \frac{\text{opposite side}}{\text{adjacent side}} = \frac{BC}{AC}$$

$$\sin < A = \frac{\text{opposite side}}{\text{hypotenuse}} = \frac{BC}{AB}$$

$$\cos < A = \frac{\text{adjacent side}}{\text{hypotenuse}} = \frac{AC}{AB}$$

trinomial : an algebraic expression with three terms. For example, $6ab^3 - 3\,ab + 7$.

U

unit fraction: one with 1 as the numerator. For example, $\frac{1}{2}$ or $\frac{1}{5}$.

unit price: the cost of one item or of one unit (of mass or volume). The unit price is used for comparison shopping. For example, \$4.50/kg, 85¢/cookie.

unit rate: a comparison of unlike quantities where the final quantity is 1. For example, 1.5m²/m.

unlike terms: ones with different variable coefficients. For example, $3x^2 + 5y - 6y + 3xy + 5$ contains two like terms, $5y$ and $-6y$, and three unlike terms, $3x^2$, $3xy$ and 5.

V

variable: a letter or symbol used to represent a number.

vertex: the common end point of the two line segments or rays.

visible factor number: one that is divisible by each of its non-zero digits. For example, 24 because it is divisible by 2 and 4.

volume: the amount of space occupied by a 3-D object, measured in cubic units such as cubic centimetres.

W

whole numbers: the natural numbers and 0.
0, 1, 2, 3, 4, 5, ...

Z

zero model: adding one or more positive tiles and the same number of negative tiles to a model. It doesn't change the value because these tiles are opposites and add to zero.

For example, factor $x^2 + 2x - 8$:

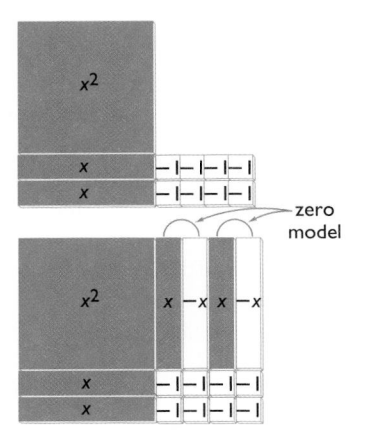

The factors $x + 4$ and $x - 2$.

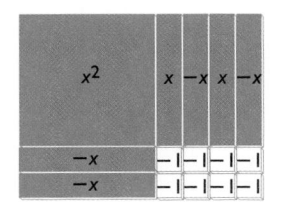

GLOSSARY

337

UNIT 1 Data Analysis

1.1, pages 2-3

1. a) can be measured, has a time frame, can be used to make reasonable predictions
b) *example*: simple and compares one thing to another and would be easy to do alone, but there are many other factors such as location, climate, natural resources, so it's difficult to make a reasonable prediction; not a good question

2. a) not a good question; best is too vague – should focus on a specific characteristic of the juice
b) good question; thickness can be measured, it's a simple comparison between restaurant chains and milkshake thickness
c) not a good question; doesn't compare one situation with another
d) good question; saltiness can be measured by tasting, it's a simple comparison between restaurant chains and saltiness of french fries
e) good question; extension can be measured, it's easy to make a reasonable prediction
f) good question; compares two things, can find data for each
g) not a good question; no experiment is suggested

3. *examples*: a) If a country has a large area, it will probably have a high GDP since there is more space and natural resources.
b) the higher the price, the thicker the milkshake, since it uses more costly ingredients; the fast food restaurant with the highest milkshake price will have the thickest shake

4. a) *examples*: serving temperature, same type of ingredients, amount of time stirring
b) for 2 e): independent variable: mass; dependent variable: extension of spring; control variables: *examples*: position of spring (hangs freely suspended), calibration of spring (not overstretched, starts at zero mark)

5. *example*: Do people with big hands have big feet? prediction: the larger the handspan, the greater the shoe size: independent variable: measure of handspan; dependent variable: shoe size; control variables: *examples*: same measurement made on each person; person wears adult-sized shoes, not infants' or children's; gender data is not mixed together since shoe size is not equivalent between men's and women's sizes

1.2, page 5

1. no; different governments, standards of living, and approach to health care

2. a) *example*: the greater the number of patients/doctor, the poorer the health care so the shorter the life expectancy
b) independent variable: number of patients/doctor; dependent variable: life expectancy
c) *examples*: all doctors have minimum medical licence, all doctors included – specialists as well

3. *example*: a) Does the GDP affect the number of patients/doctor?

b)

Country	GDP (U.S.$)	Patients/Doctor
Canada	521.5 B	538
Columbia	45 B	1277
El Salvador	5.5 B	3244
Guyana	250 M	3367
Honduras	5.2 B	2238
Mexico	289 B	1592
Panama	5 B	900
Peru	20.6 B	1102

c) the greater the GDP, the fewer patients/ doctor because there would be more facilities to train doctors and more money to pay doctors
d) independent variable: GDP; dependent variable: number of patients/doctor

e) data for patients/doctor would have to be collected in a similar way, whether or not health care is socialized

4. a) doctors likely won't criticize their profession
b) parents likely can't give accurate information
c) members would focus on negative effects
d) students there all like pizza

5. *examples*: a) send questionnaires to a random sample of people from a phone book
b) give a reading test to a random sample of students
c) select a random sample of people from the phone books of affected communities
d) survey people randomly by phone or in a mall

6. a) the same number, say 50, from each grade
b) random selection; likely will have a range of computer knowledge
c) *example*: may not be equal representation by gender or course type

7. a) experiment and observe
b) use school athletes' records from track meets
c) experiment or contact paper airplane club for records
d) measure
e) access a database
f) telephone interviews

8. *examples*: a) local restaurant owners; to save money
b) track and field coaches; to help select athletes
c) paper airplane contestants; to win a flying contest
d) clothing manufacturers and pattern makers; to design clothes that have marketable proportions
e) health minister; to plan more realistic budgets

f) pizza restaurant owners; to improve delivery service if necessary to be competitive

More Than One Strategy, page 6

2. *examples*: tally chart: can compare the number of active volcanoes in the 6 countries, but can't tell how big they are or what they're called; table: tells the number of volcanoes in each country, their names and heights, but difficult to compare all the volcanoes by height (can only compare volcanoes in each country by height); computer, alphabetically: easier to find a specific volcano by name but difficult to compare by height; computer, by height: easily compare all the volanoes by height but difficult to locate a specific volcano if there were a lot in the list

Problems to Investigate, page 7

The Great Predictor: *example*: of the 65 pages in Maclean's, there were:

1	2-page ad
15	1-page ads (full page)
2	$\frac{1}{2}$-page ads
2	$\frac{1}{4}$-page ads
2	$< \frac{1}{4}$-page ads

most common full-page ad; least common 2-page ad

The Flip Test: *example*: of the 4 ads which were $\frac{1}{4}$-page or smaller, 2 were on the left-page edge and 2 were on the right-page edge; edges most common, either left or right; results were similar in 2 other magazines – almost all small ads were on the edge of the page

What's The Question?: *examples:* How does the rate of stirring affect the temperature of the liquid?; How does the number of stirs affect the temperature of the liquid?; How does the size of the container affect the temperature of the liquid?

Searching For Dependents:
examples: **a)** price, sweetness, number of calories, quantity sold, dollars spent on advertising, what shelf it's located on in stores
b) price, size, saltiness, number of stores available in
c) price size

Collection Methods:
examples: **a)** opinions about current political leaders
b) details about whether people drive and how much, how often
c) population
d) number of people per vehicle driving on major highways
e) number of Olympic medals won by country

1.3, pages 9-10

1. a) around (37, 75), around (56, 85), around (72, 90)
b) around (56, 90)
c) similar relative values for different countries

2. a) up to the right
b) Paraguay and Costa Rica: *example*: most have elementary education but stop before age 15; Nicaragua and Guatemala: *example*: have had wars: perhaps too dangerous to attend school, or students may have been forced to join army
c) as one increases, the other increases
d) strong, because points are fairly close together; can confidently predict value of one variable from other variable

3. a) 56
b) Colombia, Ecuador, Guyana
c) no; *example*: Costa Rica (42, 93) and Nicaragua (42, 57)
d) *examples*: perhaps literacy measured differently; some countries may spend more money on literacy than others

4. *examples*: **a)** range of population in Central and South America that reached secondary school is 20%–74%

b) In what range does 50% of the data lie? What is the median? mode? Can you find the mean?

5. *example*: depends on the question; to find mode of percent of population reaching secondary school, you could check the graph, but to be exact, check the table

6. a) *example*: as number of fouls increases, number of points increases
b)

Personal Fouls vs Points Scored

c) weak; quite a bit of spread in data, would be difficult to confidently predict number of points scored from number of fouls
d) not reliable, range is wide, 62, 122, and 164 are possibilities

7.

Relation Between Literacy Rate and Population Density

examples: **a)** predict as population density increases, literacy rate decreases, since less government money to spend on education

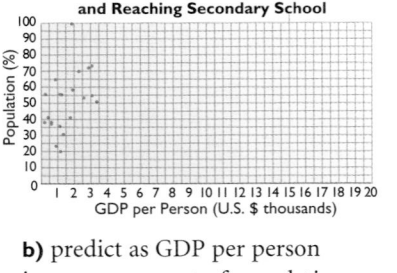

Relation Between GDP and Reaching Secondary School

b) predict as GDP per person increases, percent of population reaching secondary school increases, since more money available to educate each person

8. *example:* **a)** predict number of cars in school parking lot at 9:00 a.m. is not related to the day of the week **b)** independent variable: day of week; dependent variable; number of cars; control variables: *examples:* count cars only each day, not vans, trucks, motorcycles, bicycles, etc., count cars in all areas of parking lot each day including staff, student, and visitor areas
c)

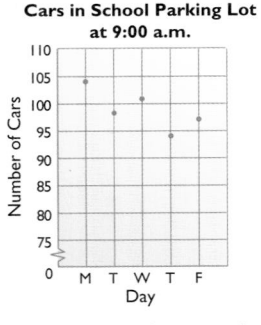

Cars in School Parking Lot at 9:00 a.m.

d) The number of cars in the parking lot varied very slightly from day to day. Variation could be due to some senior students having first period free and arriving later some days, some students or staff driving some days and not others, and visitors to the school.

1.4, pages 11–12

1. **a)**

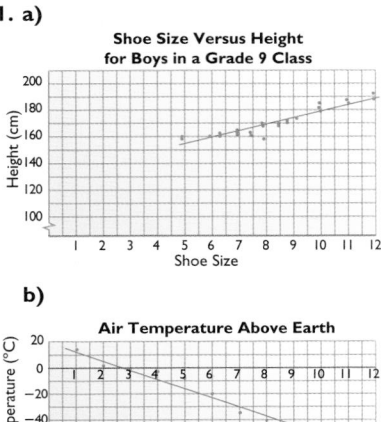

Shoe Size Versus Height for Boys in a Grade 9 Class

b)

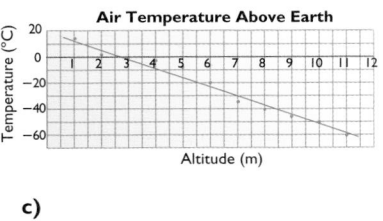

Air Temperature Above Earth

c)

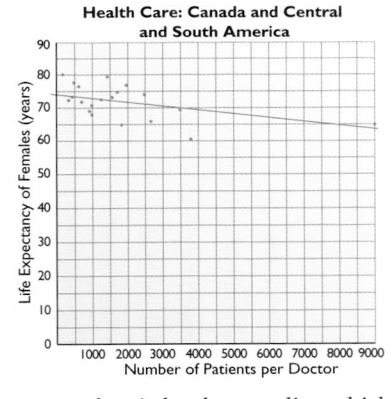

Health Care: Canada and Central and South America

example: tried to locate a line which went through as many of the points as possible, with the remaining points evenly spaced above and below the line

3. part c) is most difficult line to find; most points show a slant down to the right but 6 or 7 don't fit pattern; wide gap before last point makes slant difficult to determine

4. **a)** upward slant means that an increase in 1 variable also creates an increase in the other; downward slant means that an increase in 1 variable creates a decrease in the other; almost horizontal slant means that as 1 variable increases, the other remains constant

b) *examples:* make sure shoe sizing is uniform; use same thermometer; ensure wind speed is constant at each measurement; make all measurements with same device and by same person; ensure life expectancy is calculated the same way and determined on same date in calendar; ensure number of patients/ doctor is calculated the same way
c) *example:* for scatter plot 1 a): taller than expected for given shoe size; shorter than expected from given shoe size; expected height for shoe size

5. no, points don't show a linear pattern; as GDP growth increases, population growth doesn't follow a consistent increasing or decreasing pattern

6. **a)**

Times for the Women's 100–m

b) can't really predict
c) *examples:* there's a limit to human achievement both in time and distance; trying to use a line of best fit to predict the year that a woman will run 100 m in 5 s isn't realistic
d) *examples:* speed reading, typing

Making Sense of Data, page 13

4. scatter plots, stem-and-leaf plots, box-and-whisker plots, line graphs, broken-line graphs, rectangular or circle graphs, pictographs

5. **a)** stacked bar graph
b) rectangular graph
c) circle graph
d) multiple bar graph
e) broken-line graph
f) multiple bar graph

A Nameless Plot: *example:* number of hours spent on project vs. marks received out of 70; points represent situations for 9 pairs of students

Decisions-Decisions: it's possible if both lines slant 45° up to the right; both at a 45° angle slanting up to the right

A Different Slant: *example:* might have been points above and below the line but they would be equal and there might have been points along the line, points were probably spread out linearly along the line; would still slant upwards but steeper

The Final Check: count the number on the line and then subtract from 129; result should equal the number below (or above) the line multiplied by 2

A Swisher: *example:* It looks like Colleen's had lots of practice shooting from various distances and can usually score baskets about half the time from 7 m or less.

1.5, page 16

1. a) Guyana and Colombia unusually low; *example:* might be poor health care for expectant mothers or high level of birth control; Honduras unusually high; *example:* might be culture where women start having children at an early age
   b) no; weak; much variation in vertical spread of points

2. a) no; Chile and Brazil
   b) *example:* Chile may educate and provide inexpensive/free birth control

3. a) no; Guatemala and Nicaragua; Guyana and Uruguay; Venezuela, Peru, and Mexico
   b) *example:* Nicaragua recently involved in war so low GDP

4. b) points above line show higher than expected birth rate for the

GDP; points below line show lower than expected
   c) about 2.9; predicted value could vary between 2.5 and 3.3
   d) harder to predict when GDP less than $300 per person

5. a) census taken every 5 years 1955 to 1990; *example:* 1995 to 2025 might be based on previous birth rates, 1980 to 1990, and then extrapolated
   b)

Population of Brazilian Youth Under the Age of 15

   c) rapid increase til 1990; gradual decrease after 1990 and levelling off
   d) *example:* government; projecting future work force; youth-oriented companies; projecting sales for products

6. a) as number of fouls increases, number of points scored increases
   b) *example:* tell players to take chances to make plays; that's the way to score points

7. a) higher attendance, more likely to win; seems to be a home advantage
   b) increase home attendance
   c) no, points would be in 2 rows
   d) hard to predict; might depend if it's a weekend/weekday game or in the afternoon/evening

8. *example:* predict as age increases, reaction time increases; reaction time quicker during day than in evening

1.6, pages 18-19

1. a) doesn't tell total number of lakes, so can't determine percent
   b) *example:* perhaps based estimate on number in sample area
   c) *example:* probably refers only to sport fish; perhaps assumed every lake

should support sport fish, or maybe interviewed some local residents
   d) tests done over a period of time; pollutants, algae bloom, change in water flow in area
   e) boundaries and size not given; don't know number of lakes

2. a) $124 million; $310 million
   b) $8.68 million
   c) estimate amount lost in 8 years (to 1996) to be about $70 million

3. *examples:* In what areas of Europe are the 4 million hectares? In what other parts of Canada is the maple syrup industry? How was the cost of respiratory ailments estimated?

4. for every 3 dentists asked, 2 chose brand X; could have created any ratio desired by selecting biased dentists to include in sample

5. a) time spent watching TV by all Canadians
   b) based on survey
   c) sample; if random, the results should reflect the general population and is more efficient
   d) no; doesn't say what the viewing time was in the '80s
   e) children and youth watch less TV than 10 years ago; amount of TV watched increases with age; Canadians watch less TV than Americans, but more TV than non-North Americans; not all conclusions have data given to support them
   f) programs aren't relevant; spending more time with interactive systems; *example:* could be spending more time in fitness activities
   g) *example:* the average number of hours watching TV for our class was 10 h; a lot less than the 17.1 h in the report; we live in an area where there's no cable TV
   h) *examples:* How many hours of TV did teens watch in the '80s? How many hours of TV do non-North Americans watch?

6. a) seasonally adjusted rate allows for variations in employment rates at times such as Christmas or during winter and summer when some businesses shut down
b) sample (interview selected households across Canada); would be too costly and time consuming to survey the entire population
c) 9.9% to 10.1%
d) based on past data for various economic situations
e) *example*: probably a decrease in number of jobs since technology eliminating many jobs and economic growth will likely be slow

Problems to Investigate, page 20

Tall Tales: a) as height increases, score increases
b) age, math experience
c) *examples*: amount of money earned vs. amount of money spent, or time spent studying vs. marks

Elliptical Plot:

Elliptical Plot

linear relationship decreasing left to right; line gets shorter and farther from origin, but slope stays same; as tack holes move closer together, distances from W and Z are getting closer; when distances are the same, get a circle

Read the Clues:

Seven Friends Play a Video Game

assume Hafsa had 2nd lowest score; assume Gina played greatest number of games

Brand X or Y?: if 100 people expressed an opinion, 90 said no difference between Brand X and Y, and 10 said Brand Y better than Brand X; it's possible that 100% of people thought Brand Y better than or no different from Brand X

Solve Problems by Thinking Logically, page 21

Just a Snack: Tammy, Raffi, and Jenny ordered submarines; Rifka and Grant ordered pizza

The Rafters: 11

Who Broke It?: Kim

Review and Practise, page 22

1. a) good question; compares two things – brands of tennis balls with how long they last, simple, suggests an experiment
b) not a good question; no experiment is suggested
c) good question: both variables can be measured, suggests collecting and organizing data
d) good question: relates one variable to another, both variables can be measured, suggests a survey

2. a) *example*: predict deeper the plant is planted, stronger the plant so produces larger tomatoes
b) independent variable: depth of plant; dependent variable: size of tomatoes produced; control

variables: type of plant, type of soil, amount of water, light, and nutrients

3. *examples*: **a)** How does the length of the string affect the distance a pendulum swings? suggests an experiment, can be measured, clear and simple
b) predict longer the string, further the pendulum swings; independent variable: length of string; dependent variable: distance pendulum swings; control variables: start position of swing, mass on string

4. *examples*: **a)** survey, interview, questionnaire; questionnaire at repair shops would be easiest but takes time; telephone interview would be quickest
b) vehicle repair shops, to advertise statistics and get customers to come in more often
c) might list in numerical order of oil changes per year
d) yes; more oil changes per year, less the repair costs will likely be

5. *examples*: **a)** about a quarter of the town's population
b) send to all ages so everyone has chance to voice opinion
c) if only sent to families with school-age children, would likely get pro-helmet opinions; if only sent to people age 16 to 25, would likely say they're unnecessary

6. *example*: more fit a person is, fewer number of times needed to see a doctor

7. *example*: more people invited to a party, more it costs to have the party

8. a) 1 million hectares is taken up by roads in Ontario, $\frac{1}{3}$ of the land in cities is taken up by roads; logical to conclude that 6.5 hectares/km $\times$ 155 000 km > 1 million hectares; don't know what type of road was used to estimate, don't know how $\frac{1}{3}$ the area of a city was determined

b) could have been anything from 2-lane roads to 16-lane highways
c) sample; different cities have different transportation systems and designs
d) city streets which have no shoulders; *examples*: arenas, parking lots, shopping malls

Test Your Knowledge, page 24

1. *example*: need to suggest an experiment that compares one situation with another; should be simple and measurable

2. *examples*: **a)** same wattage, same frequency of being switched off and on
b) same temperature, same weather conditions, same type of surface
c) same amount of water and sun, same type of seed and soil
d) same measuring equipment, same technique, same temperature

3. *examples*: **a)** more tubelike the flower, greater the likelihood of attracting insects, hummingbirds
b) deeper the lake, more the water temperature decreases from top to bottom
c) temperature will be greater during the day especially if it's sunny, and maximum temperature will probably be reached by early afternoon

4. *examples*: **a)** observation by video camera, use reference books for research, interview a botanist
b) interview a scientist, use science journals for research, record temperatures by sinking a minimum-temperature thermometer tied to a length of rope at different depths
c) measure, phone the weather office

5. **a)** data almost the same for different trials
b) strong if little variation and easy to make predictions; weak if points scattered and show no pattern

c) as independent variable (on horizontal axis) increases, dependent variable (on vertical axis) decreases
d) as independent variable increases, dependent variable increases

6. **a)** rapid decline in jumping height with increasing mass within a narrow range of 8 kg to 11 kg
b) strong relationship; points close together and form a straight line
c) about 26 cm
d)

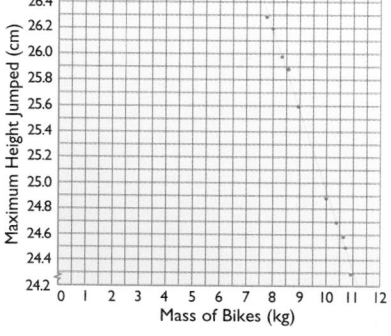

Mass of Bikes and Jumping Height

e) lighter the bike, the greater the jumping height

7. no predictable values for given points

8. *example*: try to fit as many points on the line as possible and have the same number above the line as below it

9. *examples*: number of people who participated in an annual fund-raising walkathon and the amount of money raised; depends on weather, what else is going on that day, publicity, and success of participants to find pledges; amount of advertising dollars spent versus money received from sales; depends on how well public likes product, needs product, competition from other companies, ...

10. *examples*: **a)** illogical; depends on where police are dispatched and types of crime – more general street officers wouldn't help decrease high level technology-related crimes, or more traffic

police wouldn't help decrease family-dispute crimes
b) increase in city population, unemployment, taxes and cost of living; changes in laws and/or punishment of criminals

UNIT 2   Powers and Roots

2.1, pages 29-30

1. **a)** 10^{10} **b)** 10^{23} **c)** 10^6

2. **a)** 8   **b)** 12
c) any pair of exponents that add to 10, *example*: 7 and 3

3. **a)** $7 \times 7 \times 7 \times 7 \times 7$ and 7×7
b) $(7 \times 7 \times 7 \times 7 \times 7) \times (7 \times 7) = 7^7$

4. **a)** 3^{13} **b)** $(-5)^{11}$
c) 6^{14} **d)** 2^{15}

5. **b)** 10 and 2   **d)** 6 and 6
e) 9 and 3

6. $a^m \times a^n = a^{m+n}$; The rule only applies if the bases of the factors are the same.

7. **a)** 3^{13} **b)** 5^{18} **c)** 6^{11}
d) $(-9)^{15}$ **e)** 10^{12} **f)** 10^{11}
g) $(-10)^9$ **h)** 7^9 **i)** 5^5
j) 4^5 or 2^{10} **k)** 3^8 **l)** 10^9

8. Row 2: $\frac{1}{10^2}, \frac{1}{10^3}, \frac{1}{10^4}$; Row 3: 10 000, 1000, 100, 10, 1, $\frac{1}{100}, \frac{1}{1000}, \frac{1}{10\,000}$; Row 4: 0.01, 0.001, 0.0001, 0.000 01

9. **a)** Row 1: $\frac{1}{2^2}, \frac{1}{2^3}, \frac{1}{2^4}$; Row 2: 16, 8, 4, 2, 1, $\frac{1}{4}, \frac{1}{8}, \frac{1}{16}$; Row 3: 0.25, 0.125, 0.0625, 0.031 25
b) 1 is divided by the power with the corresponding positive exponent, *for example*, $2^{-2} = \frac{1}{2^2}$.
c) dividing by the standard form of the denominator OR dividing by 2 repeatedly, *for example*, $0.5 \div 2 = 0.25$ and $0.25 \div 2$ is 0.125 and so on
d) $\frac{2^3}{2^{-3}}$ or $8 \div \frac{1}{8}$ is 64; $4^3 = 64$ and $4^{-3} = \frac{1}{64}$ so $\frac{4^3}{4^{-3}} = 64 \div \frac{1}{64} = 4096$ so 4^3 is 4096 times as great as 4^{-3}

10. $a^{-n} = \frac{1}{a^n}$; the meaning of a^{-n} places a in the denominator, and division by 0 is undefined

11. a) For every decrease of 1 in the exponent, the value of the power is one-half so since $2^1 = 2$, then 2^0 must be 1.
b) Powers of 0 don't follow the same pattern as other powers, $0^5 = 0$, $0^4 = 0$, $0^3 = 0$, $0^2 = 0$, $0^1 = 0$ so it doesn't follow that 0^0 would be 1.

12. a) $\frac{2 \times 2 \times \cancel{2} \times \cancel{2} \times \cancel{2}}{\cancel{2} \times \cancel{2} \times \cancel{2}} = 2^2$
b) $2^3 \times 2^{-5} = \frac{\cancel{2} \times \cancel{2} \times \cancel{2}}{\cancel{2} \times \cancel{2} \times \cancel{2} \times 2 \times 2} = \frac{1}{2^2}$
$2^{-3} \times 2^{-5} = \frac{1}{2 \times 2 \times 2} \times$
$\frac{1}{2 \times 2 \times 2 \times 2 \times 2}$
$= \frac{1}{2 \times 2 \times 2 \times 2 \times 2 \times 2 \times 2 \times 2} = \frac{1}{2^8}$
c) yes

13. a) $(-3)^{-12}$ **b)** 4^3 **c)** 10^{-9}

14. c) -3 and 8 **e)** 10 and -5 **f)** 5 and 0

15. greater than 1: parts b), f), i)
equal to 1: parts c), e), g), k), l)
less than 1: parts a), d), h), j), m), n), o)

16. a) 2 or -2 **b)** 3 **c)** 5
d) 4 **e)** 2
f) n can have any value but 0

2.2, page 32

1. a) 6500 years
b) 65 000 years
c) 650 000 years

2. $a^m \div a^n = a^{m-n}$ or $\frac{a^m}{a^n} = a^{m-n}$; The bases of the dividend and divisor or numerator and denominator must be the same.

3. a) 2 **b)** 9 **c)** 5
d) 7 **e)** 11 **f)** -9
g) 2 **h)** 9 **i)** 8
j) any two numbers with a difference of -3, *example:* -6 and -3
k) -4 **l)** 9

4. parts b), d), and e)

5. a) $10^3 \times \frac{1}{10^3} = 1$; yes; $\frac{1}{10^3} = 10^{-3}$ and $10^3 \times \frac{1}{10^3} = 1$

b) $\frac{1}{10^{-3}} \times 10^{-3} = 1$; $\frac{1}{10^{-3}} = 10^3$
c) $\frac{1}{2^{-5}} \times 2^{-5} = 1$

6. a) 5 **b)** 3 **c)** -4

7. a) 10^{-3} means $\frac{1}{10^3}$.
b) 10^{-3} is $\frac{1}{10^3}$ and when you divide by a fraction, you invert and multiply.

8. a) 5, -2 **b)** 3, 6
c) 8, -5 **d)** 7, 4

9. Change the sign of the exponent in the divisor/denominator, and then multiply. $5^{15} \div 5^8 = 5^{15} \times 5^{-8}$ and $\frac{3^5}{3^{-8}} = 3^5 \times 3^8$

10. *example:* No, if it takes 12 900 years at \$1 million a year, then it would take $\frac{12\,900}{12}$ or about 1000 years at \$12 million a year which is still more than a lifetime; part b), to divide by 10^6 you must multiply by 10^{-6}.

11. a) 1075 years
b) *example:* part d), because $10^{-6} \times 10^6 = 1$ so you just have to divide 12 900 by 12.

12. a) Buffet: about 892 years; Rausing and Tsutsumi: about 750 years; Sacher: about 717 years; Wan-lin: about 708 years; Shau Kee and Thomson: about 542 years; Ju-yung: about 517 years; Ka-shing: about 492 years
b) Gates: about 248 years; Buffet: about 206 years; Rausing and Tsutsumi: about 173 years; Sacher: about 165 years; Wan-lin: about 163 years; Shau Kee and Thomson: 125 years; Ju-yung: about 119 years; Ka-shing: about 113 years
c) Gates: about 35 years; Buffet: about 29 years; Rausing and Tsutsumi: about 25 years; Sacher: about 24 years; Wan-lin: about 23 years; Shau Kee and Thomson: about 18 years; Ju-yung: about 17 years; Ka-shing: about 16 years

13. a) 5 or -5 **b)** any value but 0
c) 3 **d)** 6 **e)** 2 **f)** 6 or -6

14. a) 50 **b)** 6 **c)** 4 **d)** 108

2.3, page 34

1. a) $(10^4)^5$ **b)** $[(-5)^5]^3$ **c)** 10^{21}
d) any pair of exponents with a product of 24

2. $(a^m)^n = a^{mn}$

3. a) 10^{15}, 1 quadrillion
b) 10^{18}, 1 quintillion
c) 10^{21}, 1 sextillion

4. *examples:* $5^6 \times 5^6 \times 5^6 = 5^{18}$ and $5^3 \times 5^3 \times 5^3 \times 5^3 \times 5^3 \times 5^3 = 5^{18}$

5. $2^{10} = (2^5)^2$ so the square root of 2^{10} is $2^5 = 32$

6. a) exa, $(10^6)^3 = 10^{18}$
b) exa, $(10^9)^2 = 10^{18}$
c) yotta, $(10^{12})^2 = 10^{24}$

7. a) $(2^{-3})^2 = 2^{-6} = \frac{1}{2^6}$ or $\frac{1}{64}$ and $(-2)^6$
$= -2 \times (-2) \times (-2) \times (-2) \times (-2) \times (-2) = 64$
b) -2^6 means $-(2 \times 2 \times 2 \times 2 \times 2 \times 2)$ so it would be -64; $(-2)^6$ means $-2 \times (-2) \times (-2) \times (-2) \times (-2) \times (-2) = 64$

8. a) $\frac{1}{6561}$ **b)** $\frac{1}{6561}$ **c)** 6561

9. $(3^2)^1$ or $(3^1)^2$; $(1^2)^3$ or $(1^3)^2$

10. a) 3 or -3 **b)** 2 or -2 **c)** any base but 0
d) 1 or -1 **e)** 2 or -2 **f)** 2 or -2

11. a) 5 **b)** 85 **c)** 6 **d)** 97

12. a) 5, 4, 3, 2; $3^{400}, 4^{300}, 2^{500}, 5^{200}$; $(3^4)^{100} = 81^{100}$, $(4^3)^{100} = 64^{100}$, $(2^5)^{100} = 32^{100}$, and $(5^2)^{100} = 25^{100}$ and a greater number to the same power as a lesser number has a greater value.
b) $4^{555}, 3^{666}, 5^{444}, 6^{333}$
c) *example:* Order these powers. $2^{300}, 3^{400}, 4^{500}, 6^{600}$

2.4, pages 35–36

1. a) 5, 5 **b)** 6, 6, 6 **c)** 3, 5, 15^{-4}
d) 5, 4, 6 **e)** 6, 70^6 **f)** 3, 6, 6

2. $a^m \times b^m = (a \times b)^m$

3. a) 10^5; yes; $10^5 = 100\,000$ **b)** 15^5
  c) 10^{14}; yes; $10^{14} = 100\,000\,000\,000\,000$
  d) $(-24)^6$ **e)** 54^3
  f) 10^{-7}; yes; $10^{-7} = \frac{1}{10\,000\,000}$
  or $0.000\,000\,1$
  g) 15^6 **h)** 56^7

4. a) 10^6 **b)** 10^{10} **c)** 10^{24} **d)** 10^6

5. a) 10^4 **b)** 10^{14} **c)** 10^{-10}
  d) 10^{12} **e)** 10^6 **f)** 10^{12}

6. 1 million $= (2 \times 5)^6 = 2^6 \times 5^6$
  $= 64 \times 15\,625$

7. a) 900 **b)** $160\,000$
  c) $27\,000$ **d)** $40\,000$

8. $(3^4 \times 2^3)^2 = (3^4 \times 2^3) \times (3^4 \times 2^3)$
  $= (3^4 \times 3^4) \times (2^3 \times 2^3) = 3^8 \times 2^6$

9. a) $5^{24} \times 3^{12}$ **b)** $3^{28} \times 4^{20}$
  c) $10^6 \times 4^{21}$

10. a) $\frac{7^4}{8^4} = \frac{7 \times 7 \times 7 \times 7}{8 \times 8 \times 8 \times 8} = \frac{7}{8} \times \frac{7}{8} \times \frac{7}{8} \times \frac{7}{8}$
  $= \left(\frac{7}{8}\right)^4$
  b) $\frac{a^m}{b^m} = \left(\frac{a}{b}\right)^m$ and $a^m \div b^m$
  $= (a \div b)^m,\ b \neq 0$

11. $7^4 \div 8^4 = 7^4 \times \frac{1}{8^4}$ and $\frac{1}{8^4} = 8^{-4}$

12. a) $\frac{2^4}{3^4}$ **b)** $\frac{5^{-7}}{6^{-7}}$
  c) $\left(\frac{10}{11}\right)^5 = \frac{10^5}{11^5}$ **d)** $\frac{(-5)^4}{7^4}$
  e) $(3 \div 4)^3$ **f)** $\left(\frac{4}{5}\right)^6$
  g) $2^4 \times 3^{-4}$ **h)** $5^{-7} \times (-6)^7$
  i) $(-3)^4 \times 7^{-4}$

13. a) Step 1: 10^7 was changed into
  $10^2 \times 10^5$. Step 2: 10^5 was changed
  into $(5 \times 2)^5$. Step 3: $(5 \times 2)^5$ was
  changed to $5^5 \times 2^5$ so that dividing
  2^5 in the numerator by 2^5 in the
  denominator leaves you with $10^2 \times$
  5^5 which is $100 \times 3125 = 312\,500$.
  b) $\frac{10^8}{2^3} = \frac{10^5 \times 10^3}{2^3} = \frac{10^5 \times (2 \times 5)^3}{2^3}$
  $= \frac{10^5 \times 2^3 \times 5^3}{2^3} = 10^5 \times 5^3$
  $= 10^5 \times 125 = 12\,500\,000$

14. a) 1 **b)** 810

Problems to Investigate, page 37

What Watt?: 20×10^7 or 2.0×10^8

Tricky Substitution: *example*: 5 to any
power; 25 to any power

Approaching One: $\frac{1}{2}, \frac{3}{4}, \frac{7}{8}, \frac{15}{16}$;
No, the fraction will increase in value
but it will never reach 1 because the
numerator will always be one less
than the denominator.

Broken Keys: *example*: $81^3 = (9^2)^3 = 9^6$
$= 531\,441$

As Great As: 3^8 or 6561 times as great

Reducing Exponentially: about 9 cm;
$20 \div \left(\frac{2}{3}\right)^{10}$ because you need to multiply
not divide by $\frac{2}{3}$ ten times, $[\times \left(\frac{2}{3}\right)^{10}]$;
about 0.3468 cm or about 3.5 mm

2.5, pages 39-40

1. a) 5.2029×10^{17}
  b) 3.41×10^{16}
  c) 9.9198×10^{23}
  d) 9.8968×10^{17}

2. The product is actually 30×10^{17}
  and to express it in scientific
  notation, you change it to 3.0×10^{18}.

3. a) 16 **b)** 20 **c)** 17 **d)** 15

4. ( ) optional when multiplying
  a) $(2.17 \times 10^9) \times (7.12 \times 10^6)$
  $= 1.545\,04 \times 10^{16}$
  b) $(5.42 \times 10^8) \times (4.87 \times 10^{11})$
  $= 2.639\,54 \times 10^{20}$
  c) $(3.47 \times 10^{12}) \times (5.02 \times 10^7)$
  $= 1.741\,94 \times 10^{20}$
  d) $(9.9 \times 10^6) \times (9.8 \times 10^7)$
  $= 9.702 \times 10^{14}$

5. 1.5×10^2

6. a) $0.75 \times 10^4 = 7.5 \times 10^3$
  b) $0.75 \times 10^{-4} = 7.5 \times 10^{-5}$

7. a) -3 **b)** 3 **c)** -7 **d)** -5

8. a) $(1.35 \times 10^9) \div (2.4 \times 10^6)$
  $= 5.625 \times 10^2$
  b) $(2.4 \times 10^6) \times (1.2 \times 10^3)$
  $= 2.88 \times 10^9$
  c) $\frac{6.3 \times 10^8}{3.0 \times 10^{10}} = 2.1 \times 10^{-2}$
  d) $(4.98 \times 10^9) \div (6.573 \times 10^9)$
  $= 7.576\,449 \times 10^{-1}$

9. a) 5.625×10^0 **b)** 2.0×10^3
  c) $2.032\,258 \times 10^{-2}$
  d) $6.532\,11 \times 10^{-2}$

10. The product takes up too much
  space for the display, that is, it is
  less than $0.000\,000\,1$.

11. a) 5.44×10^{-10} **b)** 12

12. a) $6.7 \times 10^{-5} \times 4.51 \times 10^{-3}$
  $= 3.0217 \times 10^{-7}$; $0.000\,000\,302\,17$
  b) $7.6 \times 10^{-5} \times 5.689 \times 10^6$
  $= 4.323\,64 \times 10^2$; 432.364
  c) $5.39 \times 10^{-4} \times 9.8 \times 10^{-3} \times 12 \times$
  $10^7 = 5.2822 \times 10^{-6}$; $0.000\,005\,282\,2$
  d) $4.5 \times 10^{-7} \div (3.6 \times 10^{-4})$
  $= 1.25 \times 10^{-3}$; $0.001\,25$
  e) $4 \times 10^{-6} \div (2 \times 10^{-7})$
  $= 2.0 \times 10^1$; 20
  f) $6 \times 10^9 \times 1.2 \times 10^{-7} = 7.2 \times 10^2$; 720

13. $(5 \times 10^{10}) \times (1 \times 10^{-9}) = 5 \times 10 = 50$

14. a) about $10\,000$ **b)** about 2000
  c) about $500\,000$

15. about two times the surface area;
  about two times the volume

16. about 10 times as far

17. *example*: for a 40-kg student,
  4×10^{10} or about $40\,000\,000\,000$
  organisms

2.6, page 42

1. *examples*: **a)** 8.362 [Exp] 6 [×]
  5.497 [Exp] 5 [=] ; 12;
  $4.596\,591\,4 \times 10^{12}$
  b) 4.12 [Exp] 7 [÷] 2.21 [Exp] 5 [=] ;
  2; $1.864\,253\,394 \times 10^2$

2. a) It tells the calculator that the
  number preceding it is the base of a
  power and that the next number
  indicates its power.
  b) 8.362 [×] 10 [y^x] 6 [×] 5.497
  [×] 10 [y^x] 5 [=]
  c) yes
  d) With the [Exp] key, you don't have
  to use the multiplication key or
  enter the digits 1 and 0 for numbers
  in scientific notation. It's more
  efficient. But with the [y^x] key, you
  can multiply by a power with a base
  other than 10.

3. *examples*: **a)** 5.3 $\boxed{\times}$ 10 $\boxed{y^x}$ 6
$\boxed{\times}$ 3.3 $\boxed{\times}$ 10 $\boxed{y^x}$ 12 $\boxed{=}$

b) 2.13 $\boxed{\times}$ 10 $\boxed{y^x}$ 5 $\boxed{\div}$ $\boxed{(}$ 1.2
$\boxed{\times}$ 10 $\boxed{y^x}$ 4 $\boxed{)}$ $\boxed{=}$; calculator
follows order of operations

4. a) It tells the calculator that the
number entered just before it is
negative.
b) 32; 1.6×10^{32}
c) $2.76 \times 10^{-2} \times 3.08 \times 10^4$

5. *examples*: 5.1 $\boxed{Exp}$ 6 $\boxed{\times}$ 2.34 $\boxed{Exp}$
2 $\boxed{+/-}$ $\boxed{=}$;
5.1 $\boxed{\times}$ 10 $\boxed{y^x}$ 6 $\boxed{\times}$ 2.34 $\boxed{\times}$
10 $\boxed{y^x}$ 2 $\boxed{+/-}$ $\boxed{=}$

6. a) 1.854×10^3 **b)** 1.7992×10^{16}
   c) 2.6×10^{12} **d)** 5.014×10^2
   e) 2.5×10^6 **f)** 1.755×10^{-7}
   g) 1.23×10^1 **h)** 5.65×10^5

7. *examples*: 10^4: $\boxed{Exp}$ 4 $\boxed{=}$ or
10 $\boxed{y^x}$ 4 $\boxed{=}$; 2^3: 2 $\boxed{y^x}$ 3 $\boxed{=}$

8. *examples*: **a)** $\boxed{Exp}$ 5 $\boxed{+/-}$ $\boxed{=}$ or
10 $\boxed{y^x}$ 5 $\boxed{+/-}$ $\boxed{=}$ 0.000 01
b) 21 $\boxed{y^x}$ 8 $\boxed{=}$ 3.782 285 935 $\times$
10^{10}
c) 4 $\boxed{y^x}$ 8 $\boxed{\div}$ 3 $\boxed{y^x}$ 9 $\boxed{=}$
3.329 573 744
d) 12 $\boxed{y^x}$ 5 $\boxed{+/-}$ $\boxed{\times}$ 2 $\boxed{y^x}$ 99
$\boxed{=}$ 2.547 201 727 $\times 10^{24}$

9. With the first one, the display showed
the entire product, but the second
display was in scientific notation.
The product of the first one must be
small enough to fit on the display.
The second product was too large
for the display so the calculator
converted it to scientific notation.
The third calculation was entered in
standard form but the answer was
in scientific notation because the
product was too large for the display.

2.7, pages 43–44

1. a) 10^5 **b)** 10^6 **c)** 10^{-2}
   d) 10^{-7} **e)** 10^4 **f)** 10^2
   g) 2^5 **h)** 5^{-2} **i)** 3^3

---

2. No, the exponent must be divisible
by 2.

3. $\sqrt{a^m} = a^{m \div 2}$ when m is even

4. a) $\sqrt{100} \times \sqrt{25} = 10 \times 5$ because
$\sqrt{100} = 10$ and $\sqrt{25} = 5$,
$\sqrt{100 \times 25} = 10 \times 5$ because
$\sqrt{100 \times 25} = \sqrt{(10 \times 10) \times (5 \times 5)}$
$= \sqrt{(10 \times 5) \times (10 \times 5)} = 10 \times 5$
b) $\sqrt{a} \times \sqrt{b} = \sqrt{a \times b}$

5. a) $\sqrt{36} = 6$
b) $\sqrt{20 \times 5} = \sqrt{100} = 10$
c) $\sqrt{32} \times \sqrt{2} = \sqrt{64} = 8$
d) $\sqrt{2 \times 8} = \sqrt{16} = 4$
e) $\sqrt{10^{12}} = 10^6 = 1\,000\,000$

6. You'd have to use a calculator to
find $\sqrt{2}$ and $\sqrt{8}$ but 16 is a
perfect square and most people
know its square root is 4.

7. a) $\sqrt{\dfrac{9}{16}} = \sqrt{\dfrac{4}{9}}$ because $\sqrt{\dfrac{4}{9}} = \sqrt{\dfrac{2 \times 2}{3 \times 3}}$
$= \sqrt{\dfrac{2}{3} \times \dfrac{2}{3}} = \dfrac{2}{3}$ and $\dfrac{\sqrt{4}}{\sqrt{9}} = \dfrac{2}{3}$ because
$\sqrt{4} = 2$ and $\sqrt{9} = 3$
b) $\sqrt{\dfrac{a}{b}} = \dfrac{\sqrt{a}}{\sqrt{b}}$; $\sqrt{a \div b} = \sqrt{a} \div \sqrt{b}$

8. a) $\dfrac{2}{5}$
b) $\dfrac{\sqrt{36}}{\sqrt{81}} = \dfrac{6}{9}$ or $\dfrac{2}{3}$
c) $\sqrt{\dfrac{72}{8}} = \sqrt{9} = 3$
d) $\dfrac{10}{12}$ or $\dfrac{5}{6}$
e) $\dfrac{5}{10}$ or $\dfrac{1}{2}$

9. a) 7   **b)** 110   **c)** 11   **d)** 6

10. a) 10^8 **b)** $\sqrt{10^{-8}}$

11. $10^{-6} = \dfrac{1}{10^6}$ and because 10^6 is the
denominator and its square root,
10^3, has a lesser value, then value of
the fraction increases, $\sqrt{\dfrac{1}{10^6}} > \dfrac{1}{10^6}$ so
$\dfrac{1}{10^3} > \dfrac{1}{10^6}$

12. $6.5 \times \sqrt{10^{16}} = 6.5 \times 10^8$
$= 650\,000\,000$

13. a) about 40 000
b) about 20 000
c) about 0.06   **d)** about 0.000 001

More Than One Strategy, page 45

1. about 8; 8.25

2. about 4×10^{14}

3. about $10^{-1} = 0.1$

4. about $0.127 \times 10^{13} =$
1 270 000 000 000

Problems to Investigate, page 46

Mighty Small: *example*: for a 60-cm
wide desk, $\dfrac{6 \times 10^{-1}}{1.7 \times 10^{-10}} = 3.529 \times 10^9$ or
about 3 529 000 000

Mental Squares: $87^{16} = (87)^{2 \times 2 \times 2 \times 2}$
$= ((((87)^2)^2)^2)^2$; four times

Crowded Square: *example*: for 6
people in $1\,m^2$, $1 \times 10^9\,m^2$, sides about
3.0×10^4 or a 30 km $\times$ 30 km square

Just Checking: $999\,999^2 =$
$(27 \times 37\,037)^2 = 27^2 \times 37\,037^2 =$
999 998 000 001.
$\sqrt{999\,998\,000\,000}$ is about
$\sqrt{1.0 \times 10^{12}}$ or 1 000 000

How Far Can You See?: about 68 km;
$\sqrt{12.96} = 3.6$

The Perfect Display: 99 980 001

Making Sense of Data, page 47

4. a) 9, 4, 1, 0, 1, 4, 9, 16, 25; −64, −27,
−8, −1, 0, 1, 8, 27, 64, 125

b)

c) *examples*: The points on the
(b, b^2) graph are all above the

horizontal axis while (b, b^3) has points above and below. The (b, b^3) curve rises more rapidly. They intersect at $(0, 0)$ and nowhere else.

5. a) 4, 9, 16, 25, 36, 49, 64, 81, 100; 1.4, 1.7, 2, 2.2, 2.4, 2.6, 2.8, 3, 3.2

b)

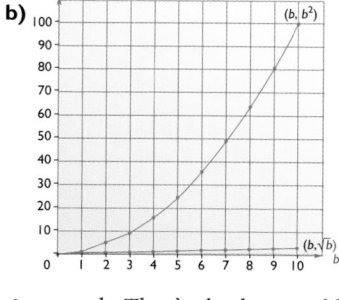

c) *example*: They're both curved but the $(b, \sqrt{b})$ curve is much flatter. They intersect at the origin and nowhere else.

d) for $2\sqrt{b}$: 0, 2, 2.8, 3.4, 4, 4.4, 4.8, 5.2, 5.6, 6, 6.4; for $\sqrt{4b}$: 0, 2, 2.8, 3.4, 4, 4.4, 4.8, 5.2, 5.6, 6, 6.4

e)

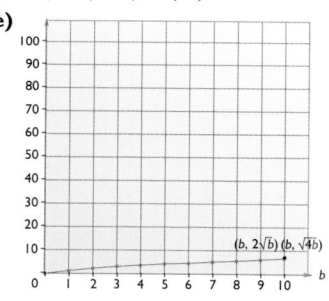

The $(b, 2\sqrt{b})$ and $(b, \sqrt{4b})$ graphs are the same. The $(b, \sqrt{b})$ curve is flatter than $(b, 2\sqrt{b})$ and the height of each point in $(b, \sqrt{b})$ is half the height of $(b, 2\sqrt{b})$. They all intersect at the origin and nowhere else.

Solve Problems By Making Tables, page 48

Closer and Closer: Each square root remains less than 1 but is closer to 1 than the previous square root.

Last Digit: 1

Consecutive Squares: You always get positive whole numbers, 1 to 11, the value is $x + 1$; 101

Review and Practise, page 49

1. a) *example*:

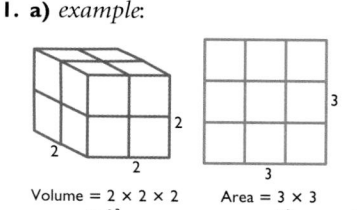

Volume = $2 \times 2 \times 2$ = 2^3 Area = 3×3 = 3^2

b) 3^2; 2^{-3}; Negative exponents reverse the order.

2. a) 10^{10} g   **b)** 10^7 kg   **c)** 10^4 t

3. I know that $9^3 = 729$ so its dimensions are 9 cm $\times$ 9 cm $\times$ 9 cm. The surface area would be $6 \times 81 = 486$ cm^2.

4. $\frac{4^4}{3^4} = \frac{256}{81} = 3.1605$

5. a) 1   **b)** 5   **c)** 5   **d)** 10   **e)** 5   **f)** 3

6. *examples*: $20^3 = 8000$; $5^3 \times 4^3$ = 125×64 or 8000; $5^3 \times 2^3 \times 2^3$ = $(5 \times 2)^3 \times 2^3 = 1000 \times 8$

7. $(2^3)^2 = 2^3 \times 2^3 = 2 \times 2 \times 2 \times 2 \times 2 \times 2 = 2^6$

8. $(25 \times 4)^7 = 100^7 = (10^2)^7 = 10^{14} =$ 100 000 000 000 000

9. a) 10   **b)** 1   **c)** 3

10. *example*: $\frac{7^3 \times 8^5 \times 7^{-3}}{2^5 \times 4^5}$

11. 9.99×10^{12} is about 10×10^{12} or 10^{13} and 1.99×10^{-10} is about 2×10^{-10} so $10^{13} \times 2 \times 10^{-10}$ = $2 \times 10^3 = 2000$

12. a)

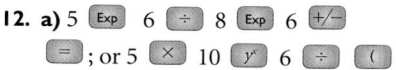

; or 5 ⨯ 10 y^x 6 ÷ (
8 ⨯ 10 y^x 6 +/−) = ; 11
b) with a power with a base of 10

13. a) $123^{45} = 1.111\,040\,818 \times 10^{94}$
b) $123^{-45} = 9.000\,569\,408 \times 10^{-95}$

14. rounded to 2 decimal places
a) 9.55×10^{11} **b)** 2.0×10^{-7}
c) 8.0×10^{12} **d)** 5.0×10^0
e) 1×10^4 **f)** 8.0×10^2
g) 1.88×10^6 **h)** 1.03×10^{18}
i) 3.15×10^{11}

Problems to Investigate, page 51

Doubling Prices: *example*: for a $1.75 hamburger, about $1750.

Sum of Cubes: $1^3 + 2^3 = 3^2$, $1^3 + 2^3 + 3^3 = 6^2$, $1^3 + 2^3 + 3^3 + 4^3 = 10^2$, $1^3 + 2^3 + 3^3 + 4^3 + 5^3 = 15^2$

How Many Blinks?: 0.864 s; for a 6-h school day, 25 000 blinks; for a 14-year old, about 500 000 000 blinks

Mental Multiplication Trick: The square of the number between the two factors is 1 more than the product of the two factors. 2499

Same Number: *examples*: 6 mm $\times$ 6 mm $\times$ 6 mm, 6 cm $\times$ 6 cm $\times$ 6 cm

Digital Roots: A perfect square has a digital root of either 1, 4, 7, or 9. 2 987 654 321 has a digital root of 2 so it's not a perfect square.

Test Your Knowledge, page 52

1. *example*: $(-2)^6$ is $[-2 \times (-2)] \times [-2 \times (-2)] \times [-2 \times (-2)]$ which is positive because each pair of -2 factors has a positive product; $(-2)^7$ has an extra factor of -2 so it's negative, $[-2 \times (-2)] \times [-2 \times (-2)] \times [-2 \times (-2)] \times (-2)$

2. All squares are positive so even if n is negative, its square is positive; n^2 can be even or odd, but multiplying it by 2 makes its value even, so when you add 1, it would make it odd.

3. a) $2^2 \times 2^3 = (2 \times 2) \times (2 \times 2 \times 2)$ = 2^5
b) $2^6 \div 2^3 = \frac{2 \times 2 \times 2 \times 2 \times 2 \times 2}{2 \times 2 \times 2} = 2^3$
c) $2^{-5} = \frac{1}{2^5}$ so $2^8 \times \frac{1}{2^5} = 2^8 \times 2^{-5}$

4. a) 3.7×10^{10}
b) about 101 years; about 37 000 years

5. $(2^3)^4 = 2^{12}$ and $2^{12} = (2^6)^2$ or $64^2 = 4096$

6. $4^{50} = (2 \times 2)^{50} = 2^{50} \times 2^{50} = 2^{100}$

7. $(2^1 \times 2^5) \times 5^5 = 2 \times (2 \times 5)^5$ = $2 \times 10^5 = 200\,000$

8. a) 12　　**b)** 1001　　**c)** 6

9. *example*: $6^{20} = (2 \times 3)^{20}$ so 2, 3, and 6 are divisors, and $(2 \times 3)^{20} = 2^{20} \times 3^{20} = 2^2 \times 2^{18} \times 3^1 \times 3^{19} = (2^2 \times 3) \times (2^{18} \times 3^{19}) = 12 \times (2^{18} \times 3^{19})$ so 12 is also a divisor.

10. a) about 4×10^2
b) about 5×10^{-11}
c) about 4×10^{14}

11. 0.000 000 001 is 10^{-9}, and when you divide it by 10, it becomes 0.000 000 000 1 or 10^{-10}. But 0.000 000 000 1 won't fit on the display so it's shown in scientific notation, 1×10^{-10}.

12. *examples*: **a)** 7 [Exp] 3 [+/−] [×] 3 [Exp] 8 [+/−] [=] ; 2.1×10^{-10}; $21 \times 10^{-11} = 2.1 \times 10^{-10}$
b) 4 [Exp] 7 [+/−] [÷] 8 [Exp] 23 [+/−] [=] ; 5×10^{15}; $0.5 \times 10^{16} = 5 \times 10^{15}$

13. a) 5.0158×10^{26}
b) $1.477\ 140\ 002 \times 10^{11}$

14. a) $6 \times 10^{-7} \div (3.01 \times 10^9) = 1.993\ 355\ 482 \times 10^{-16}$
b) $3^8 \times 4^{-6} = 1.601\ 806\ 641$
c) $5 \times 10^3 \div (3 \times 10^4) = 0.16$

15. a) 1000　　**b)** 0.04　　**c)** 0.001

16. 3^{36}; 3^9

17. $\sqrt{32} \times \sqrt{2} = \sqrt{64} = +8\ or\ -8$

18. a) about 5000　　**b)** 0.001

UNIT 3　Transformations

3.1, pages 57–59

1. a)

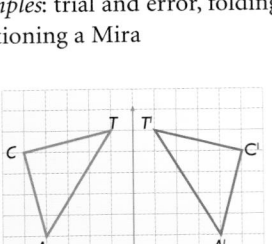

b) same; same; opposite or backwards
c) 90°; yes

d) equal, both 4; yes, Y and Y' both 2, C and C' both 2, U and U' both 6

2. a)

b)

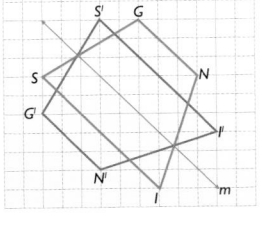

d)

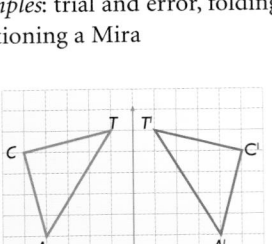

3. *examples*: use a Mira, copy onto a grid and fold, trace and flip; parts b) and d); part a) image farther from reflection line, part c) triangles different sizes

4. *examples*: trial and error, folding, positioning a Mira

a)

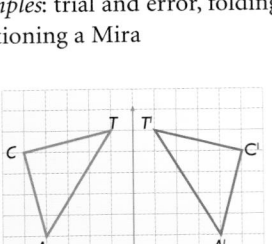

b)

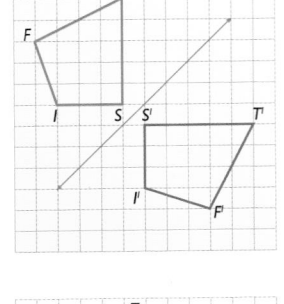

c)

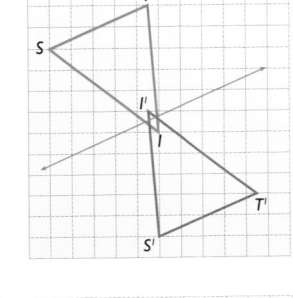

d)

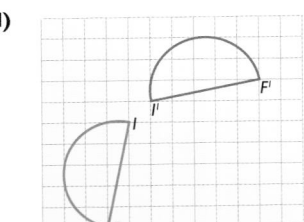

5. a) Move a tracing of one on top of the other. Measure the sides and angles; yes
b) no; *example*: If I trace them, I can't find a fold line where I can get one figure to match the other.

6. Corresponding vertices are same distance from the reflection line so you can just measure or count spaces.
a)

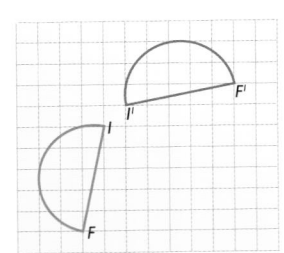

b)

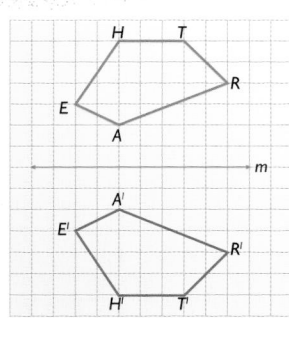

c)

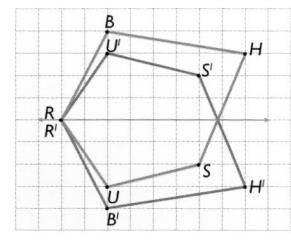

7. a)

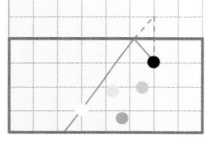

b)

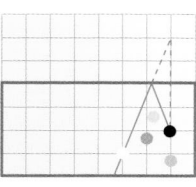

c)

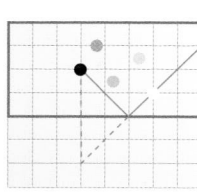

8. a) b)

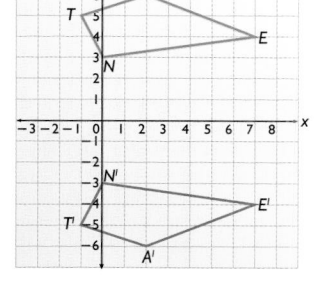

c) $N'(0, -3)$, $E'(7, -4)$, $A'(2, -6)$, $T'(-1, -5)$

d) x-coordinates don't change. y-coordinates become the opposite.

9. a) b)

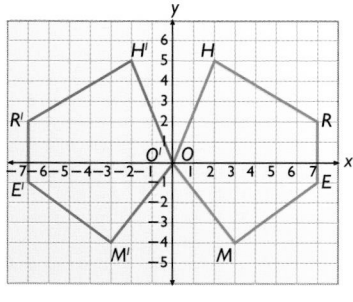

c) $H'(-2, 5)$, $O'(0, 0)$, $M'(-3, -4)$, $E'(-7, -1)$, $R'(-7, 2)$

d) x-coordinates become the opposite. y-coordinates stay the same.

10. a) y **b)** y **c)** x
d) y **e)** x **f)** both

11. *examples:* **a) b)**

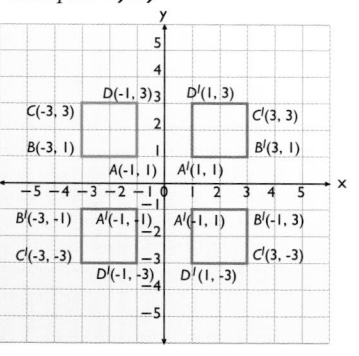

c) to 1st quadrant: y-axis, x-coordinates became positive; to 3rd quadrant, x-axis, y-coordinates became negative; to 4th quadrant, both axes, x-coordinates became positive and y-coordinates became negative

12. a) $B'(-2, -4)$, $A'(-3, 1)$, $T'(2, -2)$
b) $F'(2, 3)$, $L'(4, -2)$, $I'(-4, -2)$, $P'(-5, 3)$

3.2, pages 60-62

1. a) $(R\ 11, D\ 2)$
b)

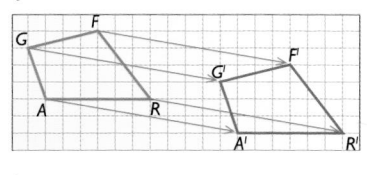

c) same; same; same
d) Answer will depend on size of grid. *example*: for 0.5-cm grid, 5.7 cm
e) same length and going in the same direction so appears to be parallel

2. a) $[-2, -4]$ **b)** $[0, 5]$
c) $[6, 1]$ **d)** $[4, -4]$
e) $[6, -1]$ **f)** $[0, 3]$
g) $[-3, -2]$ **h)** $[-5, 7]$

3.

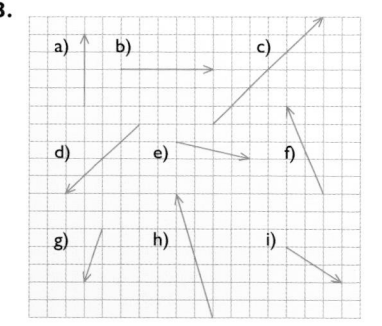

4. a)

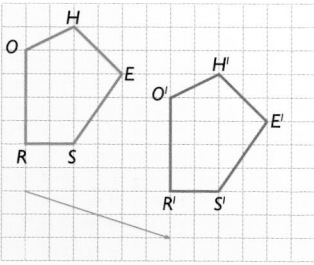

b)

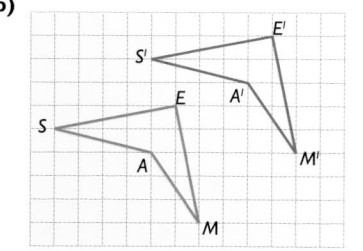

c)

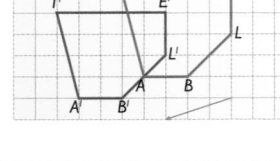

d)

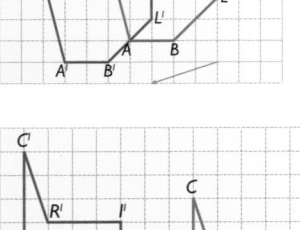

[-7, 2]

5. *example*: apply the translation arrow or rule to each vertex by counting grid spaces or sliding a tracing; parts a) and c); part b) not the same size and shape, part d) not the same orientation and only one vertex follows the translation arrow

6. Count from each vertex to the vertex of the image that appears to correspond.

a) [3, −3]

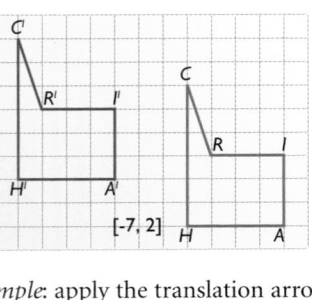

b) [−1, 2]

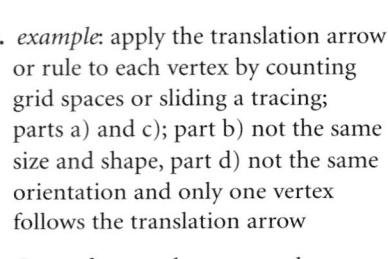

c) [6, −4]

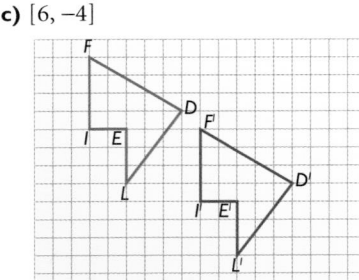

7. a) [−3, 3] **b)** [1, −2] **c)** [−6, 4]

8. a) b)

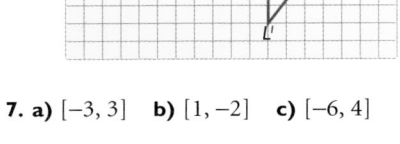

c) $H'(7, 8)$, $A'(5, 4)$, $T'(8, 3)$
d) *x*-coordinates increased by 4

9. a) $T'(−5, 5)$, $I'(−7, 3)$, $G'(−7, 1)$, $E'(−2, 1)$, $R'(−2, 3)$; *y*-coordinates increased by 6

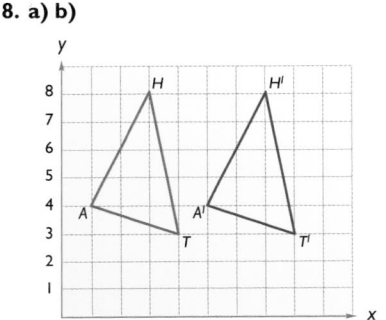

b) $S'(−5, 11)$, $T'(−8, 9)$, $O'(−7, 5)$, $P'(−2, 6)$; *x*-coordinates increased by 7, *y*-coordinates increased by 5

10. a) [3, 0] **b)** [0, −10]
c) [−3, 1] **d)** [1, −6]

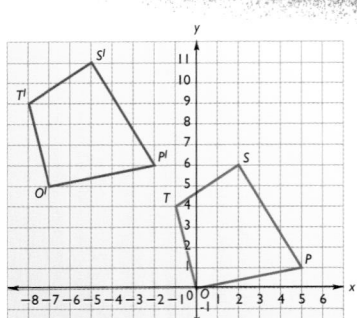

11. *examples*: **a) b)**

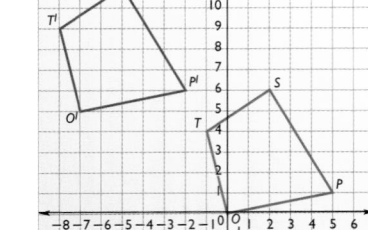

c) to 2nd quadrant: [0,6], *y*-coordinates increase by 6; to 1st quadrant: [8, 6], *x*-coordinates increase by 8, and *y*-coordinates increase by 6; to 3rd quadrant: [8, 0], *x*-coordinates increase by 8

12. a) $A'(−2, 12)$
b) $B'(−3, 3)$
c) $C'(9, −7)$, $D'(5, −1)$
d) $T'(1, −1)$, $U'(−1, −5)$, $N'(5, −5)$, $A'(7, −1)$

14. a) [−4, 0]
b)

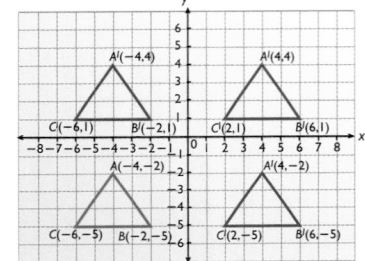

3.3, pages 64-66

1. a)

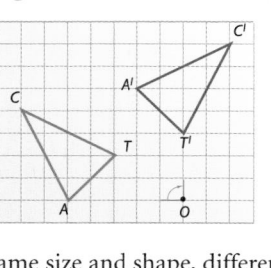

b) same size and shape, different orientation

c) 90°, $OT = OT'$

d) all angles 90°; $OA = OA'$, $OC = OC'$

2. a)

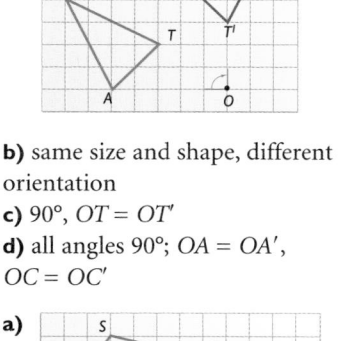

b)

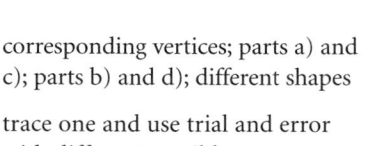

c)

3. same as for 180° cw

4. *example*: trace and turn, or measure distances from corresponding vertices to centre of rotation and measure angles formed at centre of rotation when it is joined to each pair of corresponding vertices; parts a) and c); parts b) and d); different shapes

5. trace one and use trial and error with different possible centres;

a)

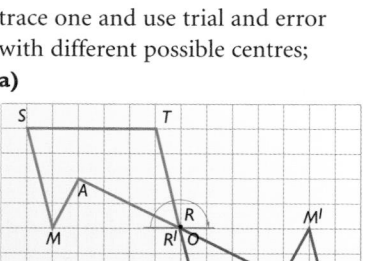

b)

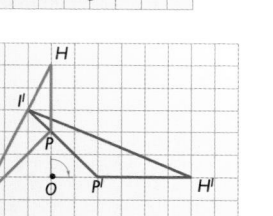

c)

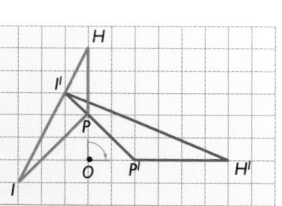

6. a) 180° cw or ccw about same point
b) 90° cw about same point
c) 90° ccw about same point

7. a) b)

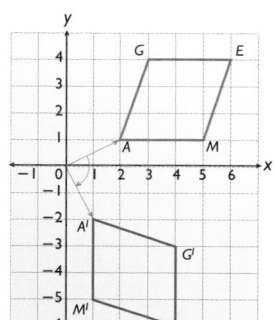

c) $H'(-5, -7)$, $I'(-2, -2)$, $T'(-6, -1)$
d) same numbers but opposite

e)

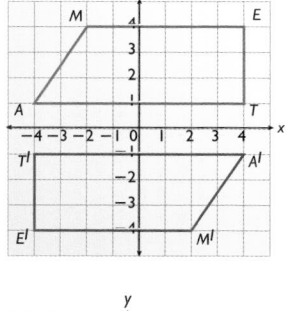

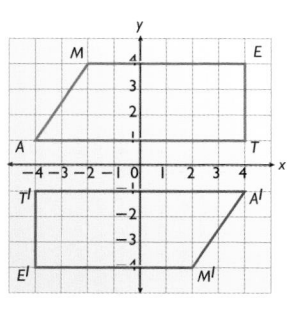

$M'(2, -4)$, $A'(4, -1)$, $T'(-4, -1)$, $E'(-4, -4)$; $B'(-1, -5)$, $I'(4, -1)$, $T'(-1, 2)$

8. a) b)

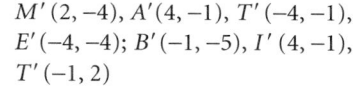

c) $G'(4, -3)$, $A'(1, -2)$, $M'(1, -5)$, $E'(4, -6)$

d) x- and y-coordinates switch places and y-coordinate gets opposite sign

e)

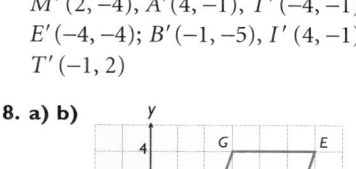

351

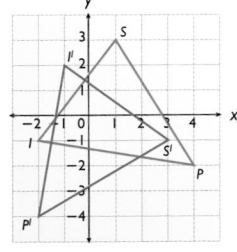

$F'(4, 2), A'(1, 2), R'(2, -2);$
$S'(3, -1), I'(-1, 2), P'(-2, -4)$

9. a) b)

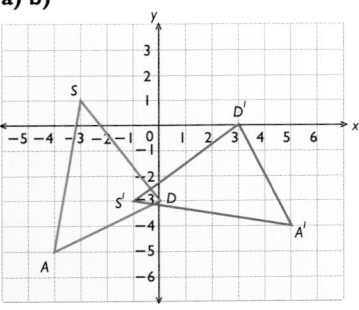

c) $S'(-1, -3), A'(5, -4), D'(3, 0)$
d) *x*-coordinate becomes
$-y$-coordinate of original;
y-coordinate becomes *x*-coordinate
of original

e)

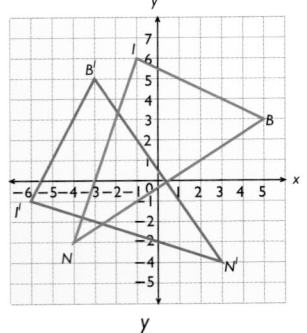

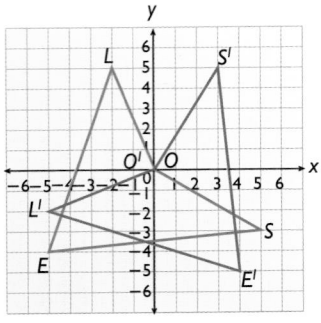

$B'(-3, 5), I'(-6, -1), N'(3, -4);$
$S'(3, 5), O'(0, 0), L'(-5, -2),$
$E'(4, -5)$

10. a) 90° ccw about *O*
  b) 180° about *O*
  c) 90° cw about *O*

11. 360°; 180°

12. a) $A'(4, 3)$
  b) $B'(-4, 5)$
  c) $C'(-3, 5), D'(1, -1)$
  d) $E'(6, 1), F'(-2, 3)$
  e) $P'(4, 5), A'(-3, 1), L'(3, -4)$

13. a) b) c)

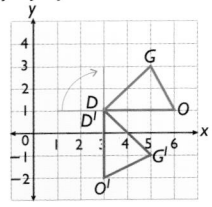

d) congruent; different orientations
e)

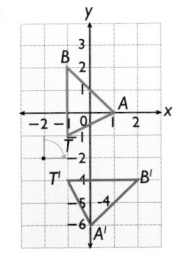

congruent; different orientations

More Than One Strategy, page 67

1. a) *example:*

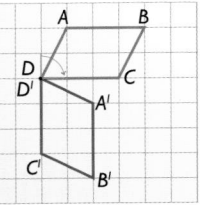

b) *example:*

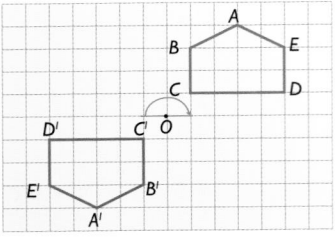

c) *example:*

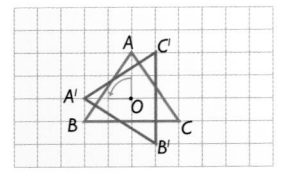

Problems to Investigate, page 68

Overlapping: *example:*

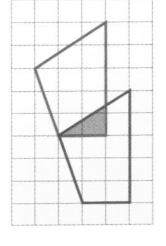

no

Rotating Rectangle:

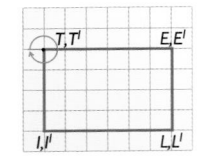

360° cw or ccw

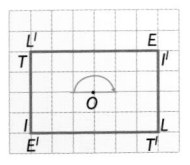

180° cw or ccw

Reflecting in Y = X: use a Mira, flip a
tracing, fold, or measure using equal
perpendicular distance property;

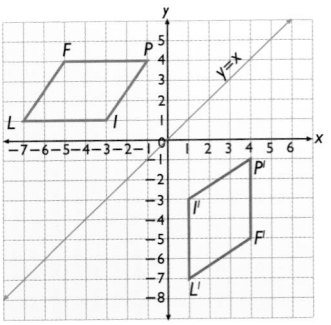

$F'(4, -5), L'(1, -7), I'(1, -3), P'(4, -1);$
x- and *y*-coordinates interchanged

Congruency Transformations: For each of these transformations, the size and shape do not change so the image is always congruent to the original.

3.4, pages 69-71

1. 350; **a)** about 14 m
   b) about 10.5 m
   c) about 21 m
   d) about 17.5 m

2. **a) b) d)**

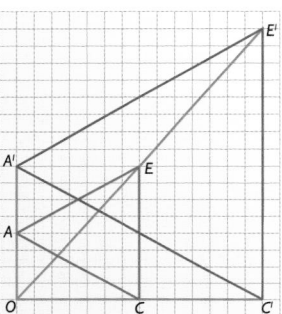

   c) on 0.5-cm grid paper, 20 mm
   e) *OC* 35 mm, *OE* 53 mm
   f) same shape and orientation but image larger so different sizes
   g) sides of image twice as long as corresponding sides of original; corresponding angles equal

3. **a) b) d)**

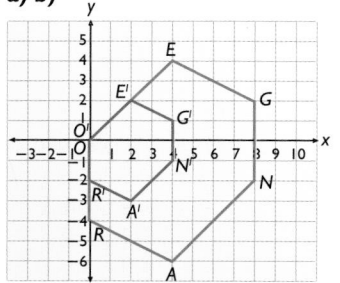

   c) on 0.5-cm grid paper, 16 mm
   e) *OH* 30 mm, *OR* 16 mm, *OD* 30 mm
   f) same shape and orientation but image larger so different sizes
   g) sides of image three times as long as corresponding sides of original; corresponding angles equal

4. **a) b) d) e)**

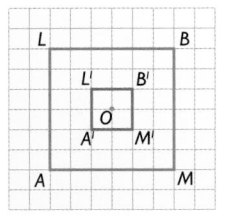

   c) 11 mm
   e) *OA* 20 mm, *OP* 34 mm
   f) same shape and orientation but image smaller so different sizes; sides of image half as long as corresponding sides of original and corresponding angles equal

5. **a)** *examples*: measure corresponding angles to see if they're equal, measure corresponding sides to see if they're in the same ratio
   b) triangles and squares; rectangles: larger figure twice as tall but three times the width
   c) only triangles

6. *examples*: join corresponding vertices and then extend lines, where all lines intersect is the centre; find ratio of image side length to corresponding original side length
   a) centre *O*; $\frac{1}{2}$

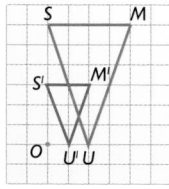

   b) centre *O*; 2;

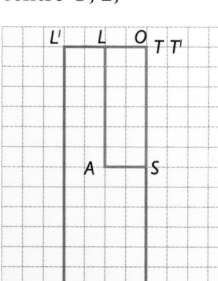

c) centre *O*; $\frac{1}{3}$;

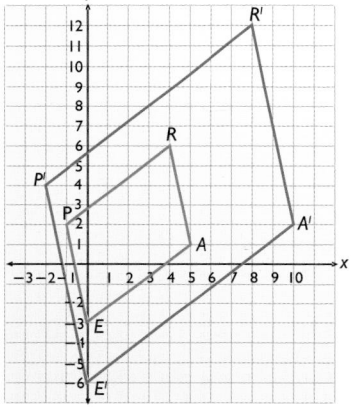

7. **a)** 2 about same centre
   b) $\frac{1}{2}$ about same centre
   c) 3 about same centre

8. **a)** 3 **b)** $\frac{1}{10}$ **c)** 30 **d)** $\frac{1}{50}$

9. **a) b)**

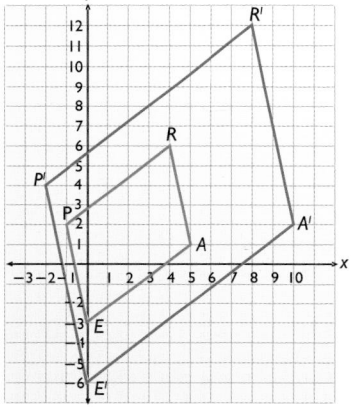

   c) *P'*(−2, 4), *E'*(0, −6), *A'*(10, 2), *R'*(8, 12)
   d) each twice original
   e) corresponding angles equal, corresponding sides proportional

10. **a) b)**

   c) *O'*(0, 0), *R'*(0, −2), *A'*(2, −3), *N'*(4, −1), *G'*(4, 1), *E'*(2, 2)
   d) each half original
   e) corresponding angles equal, corresponding sides proportional

11. a) b)

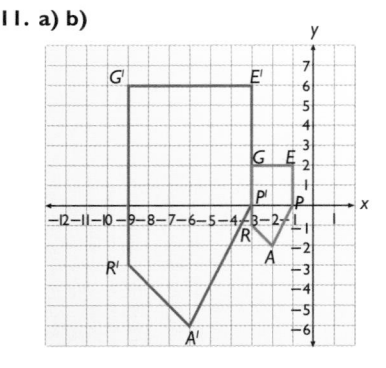

c) G'(−9, 6), R'(−9, −3), A'(−6, −6), P'(−3, 0), E'(−3, 6)

d) each three times original

e) corresponding angles equal, corresponding sides proportional

12. a) 2   **b)** $\frac{1}{4}$ **c)** 3

13. a) P'(0, 2), E'(−1, −1), A'(1, −2)

b) B'(−4, 8), E'(−4, −4), A'(16, −4), N'(16, 8)

c) R'(−1, 2), A'(−3, 0), D'(−2, −1), I'(1, −2), S'(2, 0), H'(1, 2)

d) C'(4, 6), A'(8, 12), T'(10, 8)

Making Sense of Data, page 72

4. a) misleading; slice representing up to 12 is more than twice the height and width of the other; *example*: could make it same height as now but no wider than first slice

b) accurate; second carrot twice the height but same width as first

c) misleading; second chicken leg is about $1\frac{1}{2}$ times the height and width of the first one; *example*: could make it same height as now but no wider than first leg

5. a) *example*: to create a false impression

b) *example*: Each one shows a dilatation with a scale factor equal to how many times as great one set of data is compared to the other.

6. a) *example*: show accurately; actual data impressive enough

b) *example*: show 7 small slices of bread and one big piece of meat; to minimize the difference

Problems to Investigate, page 73

Similar Coins:

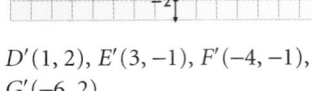

moves away; moves closer; moves much closer

Moving the Centre:
for centre (1, 1): B'(3, 5), I'(−7, −1), G'(−3, −9); for centre (2, 2): B'(2, 4), I'(−8, −2), G'(−4, −10); for centre (1, 2): B'(3, 4), I'(−7, −2), G'(−3, −10); x-coordinates are double less the x-coordinate of the centre; similarly for y-coordinates

Negative Scale Factor: H'(−2, −2), A'(−8, 4), T'(−8, −4);

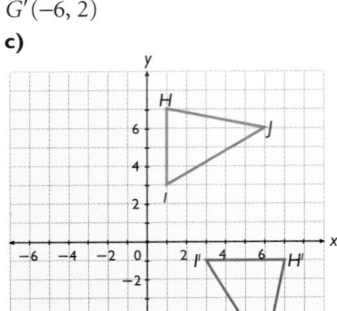

like rotating 180° and using a dilatation with scale factor 2

Area Doubled: about 1.4

Solve Problems By Working Backwards, page 74

The Cookies: 60

Rotating Box: B(0, 2), O(0, 0), X(3, 2)

Daily Servings: 6 and 7, 5 and 8, or 4 and 9, etc.

Growing Bacteria: 16

Review and Practise, page 75

1. a)

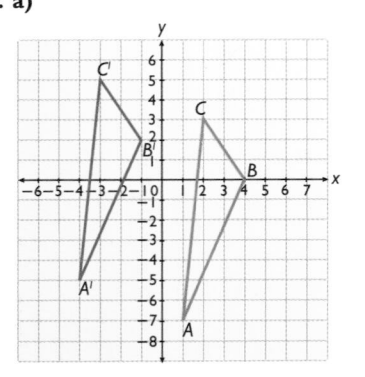

A'(−4, −5), B'(−1, 2), C'(−3, 5)

b)

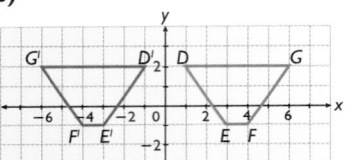

D'(1, 2), E'(3, −1), F'(−4, −1), G'(−6, 2)

c)

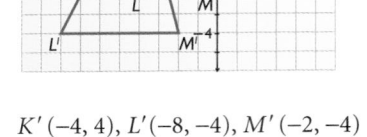

H'(7, −1), I'(3, −1), J'(6, −6)

d)

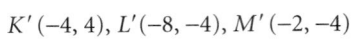

K'(−4, 4), L'(−8, −4), M'(−2, −4)

e)

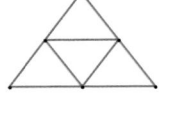

$N'(2, -3)$, $P'(3, 1)$,
$Q'(-1, 3)$, $R'(-3, -4)$

f)

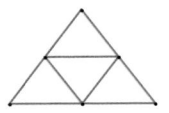

$S''(5, -7)$, $T''(2, 0)$, $U''(7, -2)$

2. a) $A'(-6, -7)$, $B'(2, -3)$
  b) $C'(-2, 2)$, $D'(7, 1)$
  c) $E'(0, -3)$, $F'(-6, 2)$
  d) $G'(-4, 0)$, $H'(1, -2)$
  e) $I'(1, 3)$, $J'(4, -1)$
  f) $K''(3, 12)$, $L''(-6, 3)$
  g) $M'(-2, -3)$, $N'(-1, 5)$

3. a) reflection; *example*: When I place a Mira diagonally half way between the figures, one figure is reflected onto the other.

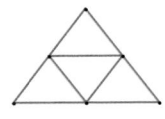

  b) translation; *example*: When I move a tracing of one onto the other, they match.

---

4. parts a), b), and c); all corresponding angles equal and all corresponding sides in same ratio; parts a) and c); in part b), corresponding image and original vertices not in line from O; no; scale factor or centre must change for similar triangles in b) to become a dilatation

5. a) $-y$ **b)** y **c)** $y + b$
  d) $-y$ **e)** $(y, -x)$ **f)** $(-y, x)$
  g) (kx, ky)

Problems to Investigate, page 77

Final Images: reflection, then translation: $C''(0, -4)$, $A''(6, 0)$, $N''(4, -6)$; translation, then reflection: $C''(0, -2)$, $A''(6, 2)$, $N''(4, -4)$; x-coordinates are the same and there is a difference of 2 in the y-coordinates

Estimating Wall Length: The eye is the dilatation centre so you need to know the horizontal distance from eye to ruler and from ruler to wall.

Joining Midpoints:

sides half as long as original; yes

Creating Rotational Symmetry:

---

1. a) dilatation **b)** rotation
  c) rotation **d)** translation
  e) rotation

2. a) if translation rule is $[a, b]$, then (x, y) becomes $(x + a, y + b)$
  b) x-coordinate stays the same, y-coordinate becomes opposite
  c) y-coordinate stays the same, x-coordinate becomes opposite
  d) both x-coordinate and y-coordinate become opposite
  e) x-coordinate becomes the y-coordinate of the original, y-coordinate becomes the opposite of the original x-coordinate
  f) x-coordinate becomes the opposite of the original y-coordinate, y-coordinate becomes the x-coordinate of the original
  g) if scale factor is k, then (x, y) becomes (kx, ky)

3. a) dilatation about origin with scale factor 4 **b)** rotation 90° cw about origin **c)** translation $[9, -1]$
  d) reflection in x-axis **e)** dilatation about origin with scale factor $\frac{1}{3}$
  f) reflection in y-axis **g)** rotation 180° about origin **h)** rotation 90° ccw about origin

4. a) translations, reflections, and rotations; all create a congruent image
  b) dilatation, translations, reflections, and rotations; all create similar images

5. reflection in y-axis

6. reflection in vertical line $x = 3$

7. $M(-2, 3)$, $A(-8, 5)$, $P(-6, -1)$

8. *examples*:

355

a) translate [5, 4]; rotate 180° about origin

b) translate [6, 1]; reflect in *y*-axis

c) translate [−1, −2]; dilatation with scale factor 2 about origin

d) rotate 90° ccw about origin; reflection in *x*-axis

9. middle of bottom side; 5 or $\frac{1}{5}$ depending on which is the original

10. $\frac{1}{3}$ **11.** 1

12. No, dilatation images are always similar.

UNIT 4   Rational Numbers

4.1, page 82

1. a) *example*: 1, 100, 5000
   b) *example*: 0, 15, 300
   c) *example*: −25, −6, 24
   d) *example*: $\frac{3}{4}$, $-\frac{1}{2}$, 7

2. a) *example*: 75, 80
   b) *example*: 0, 16
   c) *example*: −7, 50
   d) *example*: 13, 200

3. a) 0   **b)** *example*: −31
   c) *example*: $-\frac{5}{2}$ **d)** not possible

4. a) 7 is a counting number, so it is a natural number, a whole number, and an integer; 7 can be expressed as $\frac{7}{1}$ so it is rational
   b) −7 is negative so it is not a whole number but it can be expressed as $\frac{-7}{1}$ so it is rational

5. a) all four
   b) integers and rationals
   c) all except natural numbers
   d) only rationals
   e) only rationals
   f) only rationals

4.2, page 83

1. a) no **b)** yes **c)** yes **d)** no
   e) yes **f)** yes **g)** no

2. a) 1.414 213 6

b) $\sqrt{3}$, $\sqrt{5}$, $\sqrt{6}$, $\sqrt{7}$, $\sqrt{8}$, $\sqrt{10}$, $\sqrt{11}$, $\sqrt{12}$, $\sqrt{13}$, $\sqrt{14}$, $\sqrt{15}$, $\sqrt{17}$, $\sqrt{18}$, $\sqrt{19}$, $\sqrt{20}$, $\sqrt{21}$, $\sqrt{22}$, $\sqrt{23}$, $\sqrt{24}$

3. π is irrational because it is non-terminating, non-repeating.

4.3, pages 85

1. a) 9   **b)** 5.5   **c)** 11
   d) 2.6   **e)** −2   **f)** −8.4
   g) −2.1   **h)** 60   **i)** −70

2. a) positive square root of 64, 8
   b) negative square root of 64, −8
   c) square root of −64, not possible

3. a) *example*: 3.2, 3.162 277 766
   b) *example*: −6.7, −6.708 203 932
   c) *example*: −4.9, −4.898 979 486
   d) *example*: −5.7, −5.656 854 249
   e) *example*: 4.24, 4.242 640 687
   f) *example*: −7.75, −7.745 966 692

4. None are rational.

5. a) 4, −4   **b)** 2.5, −2.5
   c) 13, −13   **d)** 5.4, −5.4
   e) 6.3, −6.3   **f)** 1.8, −1.8

6. only one; length must be positive

7. only one; about 8.4 cm, *example*: used $r = \sqrt{\frac{A}{\pi}}$ and calculator

8. only one; about 6.5 cm; *example*: used $r = \sqrt{\frac{A}{\pi h}}$ and calculator

9. a) Pythagorean, $a^2 + b^2 = c^2$
   b) Length must be positive.

10. (0, 4) (4, 4), (4,0) or (0, 4) (−4, 4), (−4, 0) or (0, −4), (−4, −4), (−4, 0), or (0, −4), (4, −4), (4, 0)

Problems to Investigate, page 86

Between: *examples*: $0.63\overline{5}$, $0.635\overline{8}$ are rationals, 0.636 636 663... and $\sqrt{0.4}$ are irrational

Greater or Less: When you are finding the positive square root of a number greater than 1 or the negative square root of any number, the square root is always less than the number. When you are finding the positive square root of a number between 0 and 1, the square root is greater than the number.

True or False: The first is true because you just divide *a* of $\frac{a}{b}$ by *b*. The second is false because non-repeating, non-terminating decimals cannot be expressed as $\frac{a}{b}$.

How Many?: 18; −2.34, −2.43, −3.24, −3.42, −4.23, −4.32, −23.4, −24.3, −32.4, −34.2, −42.3, −43.2, −234, −243, −324, −342, −423, −432

Root of a Root of a Root: The answer eventually becomes 1 as you keep finding the square root of successively smaller numbers that are greater than 1.

The Vertices Are...: (2, 2), (0, 4) (−2, 2) or (−2, 2), (−4, 0), (−2, −2) or (2, 2), (4, 0), (2, −2) or (2, 2), (0, 4), (−2, −2)

4.4, pages 87-88

All estimates are examples.

1. a) about 35 m   **b)** about 103 m

2. a) about 290 m^2
   b) about 450 cm^2
   c) about 2250 cm^3
   d) about 1200 cm^3
   e) about 2150 cm^2
   f) about 195 cm^2

3. a) about $51   **b)** about $95
   c) about $11   **d)** about $0.80
   e) about $5.70   **f)** about $6.50

4. a) no   **b)** no   **c)** yes   **d)** no
   e) no   **f)** no   **g)** yes

5. a) about −22   **b)** about 410
   c) about 20   **d)** about 11
   e) about 40   **f)** about −5
   g) about −120   **h)** about 0

4.5, page 90

Keystrokes are examples as calculators vary.

1. *example*: about −13

2. Part a) subtracts 2 from the product instead of the product from 2; part b) subtracts before multiplying.

3. Part c) uses memory keys which are not needed because the calculator will follow the order of operations; part e) uses the [+/−] key which is unnecessary since the calculator will following the order of operations.

4. *example*: about 12.5

a) [π] [×] 4.2 [x^2] [=] [1/x] [×] 581.9 [=] 10.500 256 39

b) 581.9 [÷] [(] [π] [×] 4.2 [x^2] [)] [=]

c) [π] [×] 4.2 [x^2] [STO] 581.9 [÷] [RCL] [=]

5. Answers will vary.

6. a) *examples*: [(] 11.5 [+] 10.5 [+] 12.2 [)] [÷] 3 [=] 11.4; 11.5 [+] 10.5 [+] 12.2 [=] [÷] 3 [=]

b) Answers will vary.

7. *examples*: [(] 23.1 [−] 17.3 [)] [×] [(] 18.2 [+] 4.6 [)] [=] 132.24; 23.1 [−] 17.3 [=] [×] [(] 18.2 [+] 4.6 [)] [=]; 18.2 [+] 4.6 [=] [STO] 23.1 [−] 17.3 [=] [×] [RCL] [=];

8. *example*: about 0.5 **a)** *examples*: 17.4 [−] 7.8 [=] [×] 12.6 [=] [1/x] [×] 61.2 [=] 0.505 952 381; 17.4 [−] 7.8 [=] [×] 12.6 [STO] 61.2 [÷] [RCL] [=]; 12.6 [STO] [(] 17.4 − 7.8 [)] [×] [RCL] [=] [1/x] [×] 61.2 [=]; 61.2 [÷] [(] 12.6 [×] [(] 17.4 [−] 7.8 [)] [)] [=]

b) *examples*: The first one multiplies the reciprocal of the denominator by the numerator; the second one finds the denominator, places it in

memory, and then the numerator is divided by it; the third one uses the memory and reciprocal keys to find the denominator first; the last one uses brackets keys to follow the order in which the expression is written. **c)** Answers will vary.

9. a) *example*: 150; 155.825

b) −45; −42.75

c) *example*: $2\frac{1}{2}$; $2.\overline{56}$

d) *example*: $\frac{1}{2}$; $0.\overline{5}$

e) *example*: $\frac{1}{2}$; 0.550 458 715

f) *example*: −10, −9.995 505 618

g) *example*: −28, −27.3

h) *example*: −3, −2.914 285 714

10. a) *examples*: [√] [(] 706.8 [÷] [(] 4 [×] [π] [)] [)] [=] 7.499 690 453; [√] [(] 706.8 [÷] 4 [÷] [π] [)] [=]

b) Answers will vary.

4.6, pages 92

1. a) 72.55 Austria shillings, 168.35 Finland marks, 91.1 Hong Kong dollars, 454.45 Netherlands guilders
b) Singapore; Its amount for $500 was closest to $500.
c) $3184.31 **d)** $14850.02

2. a) hits ÷ at bats, rounded to 3 decimal places
b) Alomar 0.326, Molitar 0.332, Olerud 0.363, White 0.273
c) Olerud, Molitar, Alomar, White, Carter **d)** 0.310
e) decrease; The denominator increased, so it divides into the numerator fewer times.

3. $1\frac{3}{7}$ h **4.** $52.80

5. a) net pay = earnings − (total deductions)
b) 16.2% **c)** $10.74, $9.00

6. a) unit price = cost ÷ number of units
b) Super Brand: 1.029 47¢/L; Value Brand: 1.1¢/L Star Brand: 1.050 19¢/L
c) Super Brand

7. AB = 6 units, CD = 7.2 units, EF = 8.2 units

8. a) 100°C **b)** 0° **c)** $37.\overline{6}$°C
d) 20°C **e)** $-17.\overline{7}$°C **f)** −40°C

9. 4 h

More Than One Strategy, page 93

1. −185.95 **2.** −5.2 **3.** −12.1 **4.** 11.3

Problems to Investigate, page 94

Estimate: *example*: in brackets 4 + 6 = 10, in numerator 5 × 10 = 50, in denominator 14 ÷ 2 = 7, divide 50 ÷ 7 is about 7

Continuous Rationals: 0.414 285 714

Greatest Volume: cylinder

Diaphantus: 84 years

Efficient Keystrokes: *example*: 1; 1; Justification answers will vary.

Calculating π: $\frac{4}{11}$, $\frac{4}{13}$; 3.283 738 484

Making Sense of Data, page 95

2. a) N.W.T. **b)** Ontario
c) Québec **d)** Nova Scotia

3. a) women **b)** women

4. a) men with degrees; women without degrees **b)** 54 to 64; about the same for 45 to 54 and 55 to 64

5. a) 1970 and 1975 **b)** 1980 and 1985

Solve Problems by Looking for Patterns, page 96

Play Ball: 56

Take a Number: 9 zeros, 20 of each of 1 to 9

Repeating Decimals: $\frac{2}{9}$, $-\frac{3}{9}$, or $-\frac{1}{3}$, $-\frac{8}{9}$, $1\frac{5}{9}$ or $\frac{14}{9}$; $\frac{31}{99}$, $-\frac{57}{99}$, $1\frac{83}{99}$ or $\frac{182}{99}$, $\frac{123}{999}$ or $\frac{41}{333}$, $-\frac{457}{999}$, $-\frac{2546}{9999}$, $\frac{4007}{9999}$

Review and Practise, page 97

1. a) *example*: −25, −99
b) *example*: $-\frac{7}{2}$, 1.6
c) *example*: 1.121 221 222…

2. a) repeating and terminating
   b) *example*: $1.\overline{6}$, $9.\overline{4}$, 6.125, 0.4

3. a) 19, -19 **b)** 6.1, -6.1
   c) 62, -62 **d)** 9.8, -9.8

4. 1.2 m   **5.** 8.9 cm

6. *examples*: **a)** about 29   **b)** about 64
   c) about 5

7. *examples*: perimeter about 110 m;
   area about 580 m^2

8. *examples*: **a)** about 35; 34.45
   b) about 1.5; 1.5

9. $170.78

10. a) $60   **b)** mean $100.92; median
   $98.50 mode $83

Problems to Investigate, page 99

Rational? Integer? Whole?: -4 is
rational because it can be expressed
in the form $\frac{a}{b}$ where $b \neq 0$, $\frac{-4}{1}$; and it
is an integer because it is the opposite
of the whole number, 4. It is not a
whole number because it is negative
and whole numbers are 0 and the
counting numbers.

Squares: 12 cm, 8.49 cm, 6 cm, 4.24 cm

Magic Squares: 445;

117.8		2.6		
	37.6		140.4	
		132.2		17.0
74.6		175.4	8.8	60.2

Areas of Circles: doubled

Calculator Order: *example*: The last
one is the most efficient because it and
the first one have the fewest keystrokes.
But in the first one, there is no need to
reorder because scientific calculators do
the operations in the right order. The

other three are equally inefficient
because there is no need to use memory
keys, brackets keys, or equals keys to
complete a subpart, but from fourth to
third to second, they involve increasing
numbers of keystrokes.

Handshakes: 210

Test Your Knowledge, page 100

1. a) natural numbers, whole
   numbers, integers, rationals
   b) *example*: All natural numbers
   are whole numbers, all whole
   numbers are integers, and all
   integers are rationals.

2. a) terminating; repeating; non-
   terminating, non-repeating
   b) 3.6, $3.\overline{6}$, 3.616 116 111…
   c) terminating and repeating
   because both types can be written
   as $\frac{a}{b}$ where $b \neq 0$

3. $\sqrt{5}$ is a non-terminating, non-
   repeating decimal which cannot be
   expressed in fractional form.

4. a) 13   **b)** -15
   c) not possible

5. 8.8, -8.8 because $8.8^2 = 77.44$ and
   $(-8.8)^2 = 77.44$

6. one; 6.8 cm rounded to one
   decimal place

7. *example*: about $7.90

8. a) no   **b)** no   **c)** yes

9. *example*: 3.2 ×̄ 4.6 −̄ 1.5
   ×̄ 2.7 =̄ 10.67; just enter, no
   need for memory keys or bracket
   keys or completing subparts with
   equals key because the calculator
   uses the order of operations

10. about -4;
   examples: (̄ 10.9 +̄ 8.6)̄
   ÷̄ (̄ 15.2 −̄ 9.5 ×̄ 2.1
)̄ =̄ $-4.315\ 789\ 474$; using
   brackets around the numerator and
   denominator lets you use the

calculator to follow the order of
operations

11. 127.16 cm^2

12. a) 2 m; 0.5 m; between 1 m and
   1.25 m; between 3 m and 3.25 m
   b) 6 s
   c) 2; 0.5 m; 1.125 m; 3.125 m; 6 s
   d) same but calculation more
   precise for some

UNIT 5   Polynomials (I)

5.1, page 105

1. a) 3   **b)** 2   **c)** 4   **d)** 1

2. not necessary to write + sign for the
   first term in an expression because
   the positive sign is always assumed
   if there is no sign

3.

	variables	constants	numerical coefficients
a)	h, t, m	19	$2, 4, -18$
b)	a, b	none	-6
c)	a, b	-1	$3, -12$
d)	b, c, r	-11	$-5, -4, 1$
e)	x	none	-1
f)	b, d, h	none	$-1, 1$
g)	x	none	$\frac{1}{5}$
h)	A, b, h	none	$\frac{1}{\pi}$
i)	x, y	-3	$4, 2$
j)	C, r	none	2π

4. a) *examples*: i. $-5ab + 8c^2 + m^3 - 7$
   ii. $-5 + ac^2 + 8m^3 - 7b$
   iii. $-5m^3 - 7c^2 + \frac{ab}{8}$
   iv. $-5m^3 + 8c^2 + a - \frac{b}{7}$

   b)

	number of terms	numerical coefficients	constants
i.	4	$-5, 8, 1$	-7
ii.	4	$1, 8, -7$	-5
iii.	3	$-5, -7, \frac{1}{8}$	none
iv.	4	$-5, 8, 1, -\frac{1}{7}$	none

   c) 2 terms, 7 terms

5. *examples*: **a)** $\frac{x^2}{4}$
   b) $2y - 1$ **c)** $a^2 + b + c$
   d) $ab + cd + e + f + ghi$

6. *example*: $7 + 6$; no variables and no
   equals sign

7. An equation is a mathematical sentence with an equals sign, and an expression doesn't have an equals sign. With an equation, the left side has the same value as the right side when you substitute for n.

8. *examples:* **a)** $2x = 3y$ **b)** $d = \frac{s}{t}$

9. *examples:* **a)** $xy = 3$ **b)** $a^2 + 3b = 9$

10. *examples:* **a)** $-p + q + 1$
b) $-4nm^3 - 7$ **c)** $4ad + 5 - 2$
d) $2a^2 - 5a^3$

11. a) *examples:*
i. $9n^2m - 4$
ii. $-4 + 9mn^2$
iii. $-4n^2m + 9$
iv. $-4n^2 + 9m$
v. $9n^2 - 4m$
vi. $-4n^2 + 9 + m$
vii. $9n^2 - 4 + m$
viii. $n^2 + 9m - 4$
ix. $n^2 - 4m + 9$
x. $m - 4n^2 + 9$
xi. $n^2 + 9 + m - 4$
xii. $9m - 4 + n^2$
b) 4 terms, 2 terms; 2 constants, 0 constants **c)** *examples:* i. and ii., vi. and x., and viii. and xii.; same terms in different order
d) *examples:* all but ii., x., and xii.; different terms

12. *examples:* variables: number of people attending, finish time, number of songs played, amount of money taken in; constants: number of people in band, start time, price of ticket

13. *example:* at school, variables: number of students present, amount of homework assigned; constants: start time, finish time, lunch time, length of each class

5.2, page 107

1. a) 5, 10, 15, 20, 30, 40, 45
b) 6, 7, 8, 9, 11, 13, 14
c) $-4, -3, -2, -1, 1, 3, 4$
d) 4, 3, 2, 1, $-1, -3, -4$
e) $\frac{1}{5}, \frac{2}{5}, \frac{3}{5}, \frac{4}{5}, \frac{6}{5}, \frac{8}{5}, \frac{9}{5}$

f) $5, \frac{5}{2}, \frac{5}{3}, \frac{5}{4}, \frac{5}{6}, \frac{5}{8}, \frac{5}{9}$

2. a) parts a), b), c), and e)
b) part a) multiply m by 5; part e) multiply m by $\frac{1}{5}$
c) part a) doubles; triples; quadruples; part b) doubles minus 5; triples, minus 10; quadruples, minus 15; part c) doubles, plus 5; triples, plus 10; quadruples, plus 15; part d) doubles minus 5; triples minus 10; quadruples, minus 15; part e) doubles; triples; quadruples; part f) halved; third; fourth

3. a) 5, 20, 45, 80, 180, 320, 405
b) 6, 9, 14, 21, 41, 69, 86
c) $-4, -1, 4, 11, 31, 59, 76$
d) 4, 1, $-4, -11, -31, -59, -76$
e) $\frac{1}{5}, \frac{4}{5}, \frac{9}{5}, \frac{16}{5}, \frac{36}{5}, \frac{64}{5}, \frac{81}{5}$
f) $5, \frac{5}{4}, \frac{5}{9}, \frac{5}{16}, \frac{5}{36}, \frac{5}{64}, \frac{5}{81}$

4. a) parts a), b), c), and e)
b) part a) multiply n^2 by 5; part e) multiply n^2 by $\frac{1}{5}$

5. a) 5, 40, 135, 320, 1080, 2560, 3645
b) 6, 13, 32, 69, 221, 517, 734
c) $-4, 3, 22, 59, 211, 507, 724$
d) 4, $-3, -22, -59, -211, -507, -724$
e) $\frac{1}{5}, \frac{8}{5}, \frac{27}{5}, \frac{64}{5}, \frac{216}{5}, \frac{512}{5}, \frac{729}{5}$
f) $5, \frac{5}{8}, \frac{5}{27}, \frac{5}{64}, \frac{5}{216}, \frac{5}{512}, \frac{5}{729}$

6. a) parts a), b), c), and e)
b) part a) multiply b^3 by 5;
e) multiply b^3 by $\frac{1}{5}$

7. Problems 1, 3, 5 parts a), e), and f); addition or subtraction is not involved

8. *examples:* **a)** $3x$ **b)** $x + 3$
c) $3 - x$ **d)** $4x$

9. a) 43, 53, 83, 131, 421, 641, 971
b) all odd numbers; all prime numbers
c) 1681; odd but not prime; $41^2 - 41 + 41 = 41^2$, and square numbers cannot be prime

10. a) $-1, -4, -5, -4, -1, 4, 11$
b) 1, $-2, -3, -2, 1, 6, 13$

c) 3, 0, -1, 0, 3, 8, 15
d) 5, 2, 1, 2, 5, 10, 17

11. value of expressions increases by 2

12. 5; as ℓ increases to 5, the value increases to 50, and as ℓ increases greater than 5, the value decreases

13. a) \$399.00 **b)** \$841.00 **c)** \$221.20

14. *examples:* $x = 0, y = -1$; $x = 0,$ $y = -2$; $x = 1, y = -3$

15. *examples:* $a = 0, b = -1$; $a = 1,$ $b = -2$; $a = -1, b = -3$

Making Sense of Data, page 108

5. a) cell C1 shows Time(months), cell D2 shows $= \frac{A2*B2*C2}{12}$
b) cell C1 shows Time(days), cell D2 shows $= \frac{A2*B2*C2}{365.25}$

6. a) \$5.33, \$6.67, \$12.00
b) \$5.26, \$13.15, \$3.95

7. cell E1 shows Total(\$), cell E2 shows $=$ D2+A2

Problems to Investigate, page 109

Poster Pondering: *example:* Date: first Monday of every month; Time: after school; Location: vacant computer lab A, B or C; Cost: pay what you can

Four in a Row:

a	b	c	d		a	b	c	d
3	1	2	4		3	4	2	1
4	2	3	5		4	5	3	2
5	3	4	6		5	6	4	3
6	4	5	7		6	7	5	4
and so on					and so on			

The sum of the least and greatest numbers equals the difference of the squares of the other two numbers.

A Trying Problem:

x	0	1	3	6	10	15	...
y	1	3	5	7	9	11	...
	-1	-3	-5	-7	-9	-11	...

x values increase by 1, 2, 3 4,... and after 0, they are triangular numbers. y values are the odd numbers and their opposites.

Evaluation Quest: -3; positive when $x = ..., -3, -2, 1, 2, 3, ...$; negative when $x = 0, -1$

Expressions Galore: *examples:*
$4n + 6m - 5p$, $4m + 6n - 5p$,
$4p + 6n - 5m$, $4n - 6m + 5p$,
$4m - 6n + 5p$, $4p - 6n + 5m$,
$4n + 6p - 5m$, $4m + 6p - 5n$,
$-4np + m + 65$, $-m + 4np + 65$,
$4 - 65np + m$, $4 + 65np - m$;
greatest value: $4 - 65np + m = 396$;
least value: $4 + 65np - m = -388$;
value of 0: $4n + 6p - 5m$

5.3, page 111

1. **a)** place 1 green rod; add 5 red squares; add another green rod and 5 more red squares; remove 8 red squares; remove 1 green rod and 1 red square; remove 1 red square; 1 green rod remains
   b) a; $a + 5$; $a + 5 + a + 5 = 2(a + 5)$ $= 2a + 10$; $2a + 10 - 8 = 2a + 2$; $\frac{2a+2}{2} = a + 1$; $a + 1 - 1 = a$
   c) subtract 10 from the results, then divide by 2

2. **a)** *example:* Step 5 Divide by 3. Step 6 Subtract 1.
   b) Step 2 Double it. Step 3 Add 3. Step 4 Add the age.; a, $2a$, $2a + 3$, $3a + 3$, $a + 1$, a

3. **a)** different dimensions, 1 by 1 and x by 1; different colors
   b) not same type of tile
   c) same type of tile, same dimensions, just different color, flip over green rod to get white rod

4. **a)** different dimensions x by 1 and x by x
   b) not same type of tile
   c) same type of tile, same dimensions, just different color, flip over green square to get white square

5. **a)** $2x$, $-3x$ and 2, -3
   b) $7a$, $-7a$, a

---

c) $-4b^2$, $3b^2$ and $-4b$, $3b$
   d) a^3, $2a^3$ and $2a^2$, $-3a^2$ and a, $-4a$

6. **a)** y^2; $-y$, $-y^2$
   b) $y^2 - y^2 = 0y^2$ or 0; combine to give zero

7. **a)** Group I: 2 green squares, 2 green rods, 2 orange squares, 4 orange rods; Group II: 1 green square, 3 green rods, 3 white (flipped orange) squares, 2 white (flipped orange) rods; Group III: 2 white (flipped green) squares, 2 white (flipped green) rods, 2 orange squares, 3 orange rods
   b) Group I: $2x^2 + 2x + 2y^2 + 4y$; Group II: $x^2 + 3x - 3y^2 - 2y$; Group III: $-2x^2 - 2x + 2y^2 + 3y$

8. **a)** $3x^2 + 5x - y^2 + 2y$
   b) $4y^2 + 7y$
   c) $x^2 + 3x + y^2 + 5y$

9. **a)** $2x + 5$ **b)** $3x^2 - 3x$
   c) $x^2 - 3$ **d)** $-y - 6x + 5$
   e) $2x^2 + 2y + x + y^2$

10. For each group of like terms, add the numerical coefficients of the terms and then write the variable after the sum.

11. **a)** $2y + 4y$, $y + 5y$, $7y - y$,...
    b) $6y + 3y - 3y$, $2y + 2y + 2y$, $3y - 5y + 8y$,...

12. **a)** doesn't matter what order the terms are in; sum the same, if terms the same
    b) don't give the same number since terms not identical
    c) *example:* $4x - 1$ and $-4x + 1$

13. *examples:* **a)** $2xy$, $7xy$, $-xy$, $-5x$, ab
    b) $2a^2b^2$, $-2a^2b^2$, a^2b^2 and ab, a^2; $-2xy^2$, $4xy^2$, xy^2 and $-x$, $2y^2$

5.4, pages 112-114

1. **a)** $(4x^2 - 3x + 5) + (4x - 2)$; 4 green squares + 1 green rod + 3 red squares
   b) $(-4x - 3) + (2 - 2x^2)$; 4 flipped green rods + 1 flipped red square + 2 flipped green squares

---

c) $(4 + 5x) + (2x^2 - 3x)$; 4 red squares + 2 green rods + 2 green squares

2. **a)** no; Rearranging tiles doesn't affect their type or size, therefore their value is the same.
   b) part a) $4x^2 + x + 3$, part b) $-4x - 1 - 2x^2$, part c) $4 + 2x + 2x^2$

3. Tiles of same type are grouped together. Only the positions of the groups change. You can write the terms in any order as long as the sign, $+$, $-$, remains with the term.

4. **a)** *examples:* 1 green square, 1 flipped green rod + 2 green squares, 1 flipped green rod, $(x^2 - x) + (2x^2 - x) = 3x^2 - 2x$; 4 green squares, 1 green rod + 1 flipped green square, 3 flipped green rods, $(4x^2 + x) + (-x^2 - 3x) = 3x^2 - 2x$

5. **a)** 3 flipped green squares, 2 green rods, 1 red square; $-3x^2 + 2x + 1$
   b) 1 green square, 3 green rods; $x^2 + 3x$

6. **a)** 1 flipped green square, 3 green rods, 3 red squares
   b) $-x^2 + 3x + 3$

7. **a)** 1 flipped green square, 3 flipped green rods, 3 red squares; $-x^2 - 3x + 3$
   b) 2 green squares, 1 green rod, 1 flipped red square; $2x^2 + x - 1$

8. $-7x^2 + 5x + 1$; added 7 flipped green squares, 5 green rods, and 1 red square to 4 green squares and 3 flipped red squares to get 3 flipped green squares, 5 green rods, and 2 flipped red squares

9. **a)** 8 green squares, 4 flipped green rods, 1 flipped red square; (8 green squares, 4 flipped green rods, 1 flipped red square) combines with (4 flipped green squares, 1 green rod, 3 red squares) to give (4 green squares, 3 flipped green rods, 2 red squares)
   b) $(4x^2 - 3x + 2) - (3 + x - 4x^2)$ $= 8x^2 - 4x - 1$

10. a) (6 green rods, 1 flipped green square) − (1 green square, 3 red squares) = (6 green rods, 2 flipped green squares, 3 flipped red squares); (6 green rods, 2 flipped green squares, 3 flipped red squares) combines with (1 green square, 3 red squares) to give (6 green rods, 1 flipped green square)
b) $6x - 2x^2 - 3$

11. a) missing tiles are 2 flipped red squares, 1 green rod, 2 green squares because (6 flipped red squares, 3 green rods, 1 green square) combines with (4 red squares, 2 flipped green rods, 1 green square) to give (2 flipped red squares, 1 green rod, 2 green squares); $-2 + x + 2x^2$
b) missing tiles are 5 flipped red squares, 3 flipped green rods, 3 flipped green squares because (5 flipped red squares, 3 flipped green rods, 3 flipped green squares) combines with (4 flipped green rods, 3 green squares) to give (5 flipped red squares, 7 flipped green rods): $-5 - 3x - 3x^2$

12. a) $-x^2$ **b)** $7x$; started at -4 and counted to see how much I needed to add to get to 3   **c)** -4
d) $-x^2 + 7x - 4$

13. a) $-2x^2 + 7x + 7$ **b)** $2x^2 - x - 4$

14. a) 1 flipped green square, 1 green rod, 2 red squares; 1 green square, 1 flipped green rod, 2 flipped red squares
b) 4 flipped green squares, 4 green rods, 8 red squares; 6 flipped green squares, 6 green rods, 12 red squares

5.5, pages 115-116

1. Add the numerical coefficients of like terms.
a) $10x^2 + 6x + 13$ **b)** $6x^2 + 9x - 6$
c) $2x - x^2 + 3$ **d)** $3 + 2x + 3x^2$

2. a) $25t + 15c$ **b)** $15t + 10c$
c) $40t + 25c$

3. a) part a) \$11 400, part b) \$6975, part c) \$18 375
b) fewer calculations required

4. parts b) and d); Sum of the numerical coefficients of x^2 terms is 0.

5. a) parts c) and d); Sum of the numerical coefficients of x is 0.
b) Check if the numerical coefficients for each term are opposites.

6. *examples*:
a) $(4x^2 + 2x - 1) + (-6x^2 - x + 3)$
b) $(-x^2 + 4x - 6) + (4x^2 - 4x + 2)$
c) $(7x^2 - 3x + 1) + (-7x^2 + 3x - 1)$

7. a) $(a^2 + 2a) + a + (a + 1) + (a + 1) + (a^2 + 2a + a + 1) + (a + 1 + a)$
$= 2a^2 + 10a + 4$
b) 32 cm
c) *example*: For 4 cm, it will be more but not twice as long because a is squared and then 4 is added to it. For 6 cm, it will be more but not three times as long. For 1 cm, it will be less but not half as long.
d) *example*: For 4 cm (and 6 cm) I was right. The perimeter was longer, 76 cm (and 136 cm), but not twice (three times) as long. But I was wrong for 1 cm because the perimeter turned out to be half as long.

8. a) $4(2x + 3)$ or $8x + 12$; fewer calculations required
b) $3(x^2 + x)$ or $3x^2 + 3x$
c) $6(3x + 5)$ or $18x + 30$

9. *examples*: $(2x + 2), (2x + 2)$ and (x), or $(x + 1), (x + 1)$, and $(3x + 2)$, or $(x + 2), (x + 2)$, and $3x$

10. a) $3x^2 + 5x + 6 = (2x^2 + x + 2) + (x^2 + 4x + 4)$
b) $5x^2 - 7x - 2 = (6x^2 - 5x - 1) + (-x^2 - 2x - 1)$
c) $6x^2 - 4x - 5 = (-2x^2 - x + 4) + (8x^2 - 3x - 9)$
d) $5a - 2a^2 = (-4a^2 + a) + (2a^2 + 4a)$
e) $3 + 4b - 5b^2 = (-3b - 2 + 3b^2) + (7b + 5 - 8b^2)$
f) $-11 - c^2 + 3c = (-6c^2 + 1) + (5c^2 + 3c - 12)$

11. Rewrite the expression being subtracted by changing the sign of each term and then add the like terms. Or add the opposite of the second expression.

12. parts a) and d); Numerical coefficients of x^2 terms are opposites.

13. a) part c); Numerical coefficients of x are opposites.
b) Change the sign of the subtracted term, and then check to see if the sum of their numerical coefficients is 0. Or check to see if the like terms have the same numerical coefficients but opposite signs.

14. *examples*: **a)** $(5x^2 - x + 6) - (-2x + 3)$
b) $(2x^2 - 3x + 2) - (5x^2 - 3x + 6)$
c) $(x^2 + 9) - (x^2 + 9)$

15. *examples*: **a)** $(3x - 2x^2 - 6) - (-x - 11x^2 - 3) = 4x + 9x^2 - 3$
b) $(3x - 2x^2 - 6) - (2x + 3x^2 + 2) = x - 5x^2 - 8$

16. a) shape A: $10x + 8$, shape B: $8x + 5$
b) $2x + 3$
c) 13 cm; 8 cm; 43 cm

Problems to Investigate, page 117

What To Do?: *examples*: Include different exponents other than 1 with either or both variables in either term, delete one or both variables from either term, multiply either term by one or more different variables with or without exponents, divide either term by one or more different variables with or without exponents.

Magic Algebraic Square:

$x^2 + 5x - 4$	$2x^2 - x$	$2x - 5$
$-x - 4$	$x^2 + 2x - 3$	$2x^2 + 5x - 2$
$2x^2 + 2x - 1$	$-6 + 5x$	$x^2 - x - 2$

That Makes Sense: 30; 4; 30; 4; same; can do it in either order; Yes, the actual sum and difference will be different, for

ANSWERS

example, if $x = 3$, sum is 57 and difference is 1, but you will get the same sum and difference by doing it either way.

Class Pizza Party: a) $-0.5p + 0.25t + 0.25d$ or $0.5p - 0.25t - 0.25d$; *example*: for a class of 28, $p = 4$, $t = 12$, $d = 28$, $8.00
b) *example*: Company B could decrease price of a pizza by $0.50, increase price per topping by $0.25, and increase price per drink by $0.25.

Two-Digit Mystery: 11 in both terms; 9 in both terms; sum a multiple of 11 and difference a multiple of 9

Arranging Tiles:
a) a rectangle with dimensions $(x + 1)$ by $(4x + 2)$; $8x + 6$
b) a rectangle with dimensions $(2x + 2)$ by $(2x + 1)$; $10x + 6$; $28x + 20$

5.6, pages 119-120

1. a) $14x$; 6 squares in a row have $2x$ on opposite sides of each tile and $2x$ on both ends of the row, so there are 7 groups of $2x$.
b) $10x$ (2 by 3 array of green squares); $5(2x)$
c) Multiply the numerical factor by the numerical coefficient of the other factor, and then write the variable.

2. $6xy$; $3x(2y)$ must be equal to $6xy$.

3. a) length × width = $(x + x + x)(y + y + y)$ or $(3x)(3y)$
b) $(x + x + x)(y + y + y + y)$ = $(3x)(4y)$
c) $3x(3y) = 9xy$; $3x(4y) = 12xy$
d) Multiply the numerical coefficients, and then multiply the variables.
$\overset{\textcircled{1}}{3x}\overset{\textcircled{2}}{(4y)} = 12xy$

4. 2 by 3 array of grey rectangles; $6xy$

5. a) 2 by 4 array of orange rods; $8y$
b) 5 by 2 array of grey rectangles; $10xy$
c) 1 by 3 array of grey rectangles; $3xy$
d) 5 by 5 array of green rods; $25x$

6. a) $20xy$ **b)** $6xy$
c) $24xy$ **d)** $36xy$
e) $16xy$ **f)** $-15xy$
g) $-125xy$ **h)** 0

7. a) $6x^2$
b) $(3x)(3x)$ or $9x^2$; $(4x)(3x)$ or $12x^2$
c) Multiplied the numerical coefficients, and then multiplied the like variables by adding their exponents and keeping the base the same.

8. a) $3^2 \times 3^3 = 3^{2+3}$ or 3^5, and $(x^2)(x^3) = x^{2+3}$ or x^5; You can use the same rule for multiplying powers with same bases except the numerical base becomes a variable base.
b) For both examples, you have to evaluate each power separately, and then multiply because they have different bases.

9. a) 2 by 4 array of orange squares; $8y^2$
b) 2 by 2 array of orange squares; $4y^2$
c) 1 by 3 array of green squares; $3x^2$
d) 5 by 2 array of green squares; $10x^2$

10. a) $-6y^4$ **b)** $-10x^3y^2$
c) $6x^3y$ **d)** $3x^3y^3$
e) $-8x^4y^3$ **f)** $5a^4b^4$
g) $-24a^3b^4c^2$

11. a) yes; $(2^3)^2 = 8^2$ or 64, which equals 2^6
b) yes; $(5 \times 2 \times 3)^2 = 30^2$ or 900, which equals $5^2 \times 2^2 \times 3^2$
c) first set evaluate left side, and second set evaluate right side; yes; $(2 \times 3^2)^3 = 18^3$ or 5832, which equals $2^3 \times 3^6$

12. a) exponents should be added, not multiplied; a^8
b) exponents should be multiplied, not added; a^{24}
c) can't add exponents because unlike terms; $a^5 + a^2$
d) can't add exponents because variables are different; a^3b^4

5.7, pages 122-123

1. a) Area of each rod is y square units, and there are 12 of them.

b) 6; 1 by $12y$, 2 by $6y$, 3 by $4y$, 4 by $3y$, 6 by $2y$, 12 by y
c) 6 by $2y$; Area, $12y$, divided by width, 6, equals length.
d) 4 by $3y$; Area, $12y$, divided by width, 4, equals length.
e) Divide the numbers, and then write the resulting numerical coefficient next to the variable, so for part c), $2y$, and for part d), $3y$.

2. a) $10xy$ **b)** $5x$

3. a) Area, $15xy$, divided by length, $3y$, equals width, $5x$.
b) Area, $20xy$, divided by width, $5x$, equals length $4y$.
c) Divide the numerical coefficients, and then divide the variables by subtracting exponents or like terms.

4. a) 3 by 3 array of green rods; $3x$
b) 2 by 4 array of orange rods; $2y$
c) 1 by 7 array of green rods; 7
d) 3 by 2 array of grey rectangles; $3y$
e) 2 by 7 array of grey rectangles; $2x$

5. a) 3 **b)** $-6y$
c) $-12y$ **d)** 3
e) $4b$ **f)** $18h$
g) $9mp$ **h)** $\frac{9m}{p}$

6. a) $12x^2$ **b)** $\frac{12x^2}{3x} = 4x$

7. a) $\frac{24x^2}{6x}$ **b)** $\frac{30y^2}{2y}$

8. Divide the numerical coefficients, and then divide the like variables by subtracting their exponents, so $\frac{24x^2}{6x} = 4x$ and $\frac{30y^2}{2y} = 15y$.

9. a) $3^5 \div 3^2 = 3^{5-2}$ or 3^3, and $y^5 \div y^2 = y^{5-2}$ or y^5; Use the same rule for dividing powers with same bases except the numerical base is a variable.
b) $(2^4 \times 3^5) \div (2^3 \times 3^4) = 2^{4-3} \times 3^{5-4}$ or $2 \times 3 = 6$, and $(x^4y^5) \div (x^3y^4) = x^{4-3}y^{5-4}$ or xy; Divide the powers with like bases, and then multiply the results.

10. a) x^3 **b)** m^7 **c)** p^6
d) $6m^2$ **e)** $-5h^5$ **f)** h^2m^3
g) w^5p^5 **h)** $4c^2b^3$ **i)** $-3g^3h^6$

11. a) $x^{3-3} = x^0$, and $\frac{x^3}{x^3} = 1$ since you divide both terms by x^3

b) $y^{5-5} = y^0$, and $\frac{y^5}{y^5} = 1$ since you divide both terms by y^5

c) Any base ($\neq 0$) with an exponent of 0 equals 1. The 0 exponent came from dividing two identical terms. If the base is 0, you must divide by 0 which isn't possible.

12. parts a) and b) because $m^0 = 1$ and $(-m)^0 = 1$; parts c) and d) because $-(m)^0 = -(1)$ and $-m^0 = -1$

13. a) $x^{3-4} = x^{-1}$ and $\frac{x^3}{x^4} = \frac{1}{x}$ since you divide both terms by x^3

b) $y^{4-5} = y^{-1}$ and $\frac{y^4}{y^5} = \frac{1}{y}$ since you divide both terms by y^4

c) Any base ($\neq 0$) with a negative exponent equals the reciprocal of the base. If the base is 0, you must divide by 0 which isn't possible.

14. a) $\frac{1}{m}$ **b)** $\frac{1}{m^2}$

c) $\frac{1}{(mn)^4}$ or $\frac{1}{m^4n^4}$ **d)** $\frac{3}{y}$

e) $\frac{1}{3}y$ **f)** $\frac{-3}{y}$

g) $\frac{1}{-3y}$ **h)** $\frac{1}{(3y)^2}$ or $\frac{1}{9y^2}$

15. a) $2n^{-4}$ **b)** $3a^{-3}b^{-1}$

c) $3x^{-6}y^8$

16. 3 green squares, 6 green rods, 9 flipped red squares

a) divide the tiles into 3 equal groups

b) 1 green square, 2 green rods, 3 flipped red squares; $x^2 + 2x - 3$

17. a) 3 green squares; 1 green square, or x^2 **b)** 6 green rods; 2 green rods, or $2x$ **c)** 9 flipped red squares; 3 flipped red squares, or -3

18. a) Quotient is the sum of the individual quotients.

b) $\frac{3x^2 + 6x - 9}{3} = \frac{3x^2}{3} + \frac{6x}{3} - \frac{9}{3}$

19. a) $y^2 + 2y + 2$; divided each term in the dividend, $5y^2$, $10y$, and 10, by the divisor, 5

b) $2xy + 4y$; divided each term in the dividend, $6xy$ and $12y$, by the divisor, 3

c) $-3x^2 + 3x + 6$; divided each term in the dividend, $6x^2$, $-6x$, and -12, by the divisor, -2

20. a) $2y + 3x$

b) $5y + 2x + 1$

c) $3x^2 - 4x + 2$

d) $3n + 2m + 1$

e) $-2ab^2 - a^2$

f) $b - a + 1$

21. a) $4n + 3.5m + 2$

b) $\frac{2}{n} + \frac{3}{m} + \frac{5}{h}$

c) $2ab^2 + \frac{b^3}{a} + 1$

d) $\frac{4}{y} - 3xy + y$, or $4y^{-1} - 3xy + y$

e) $\frac{1}{wz} - \frac{2}{w} - \frac{2}{z}$, or $w^{-1}z^{-1} - 2w^{-1} - 2z^{-1}$

f) $\frac{2}{p^3q^3} - \frac{4.5}{p^2q^2} - \frac{3.5}{pq}$, or $2p^{-3}q^{-3} - 4.5p^{-2}q^{-2} - 3.5p^{-1}q^{-1}$

More Than One Strategy, page 124

1. *example*: $2(4x^2) + 2(3x) = 8x^2 + 6x$ so the quotient is $4x^2 + 3x$; or $8x^2 = 2 \times 4x^2$ and $6x = 2 \times 3x$, so $\frac{2 \times 4x^2}{2} = 4x^2$ and $\frac{2 \times 3x}{2} = 3x$ so the quotient is $4x^2 + 3x$

2. $-2 - 4x$ **3.** $-4b - 2c$

4. $3 + 5z$ **5.** $4x + x^2 - 2$

6. $3d - c$

Problems to Investigate, page 125

An Arrangement of Tiles: $8x$ by $3y$

Sharing Tiles:

green squares	3	3	3	3	3	6	6	6	6	6
green rods	6	15	9	12	3	18	3	15	6	12	9
red squares	15	6	12	9	18	3	15	3	12	6	9
green squares	9	9	9	9	12	12	12	15	15	18
green rods	3	12	6	9	3	9	6	3	6	3
red squares	12	3	9	6	9	3	6	6	3	3

Evaluation Quest: $-7\frac{7}{8}$ and $7\frac{7}{8}$; same digits; opposite signs

Magic Multiplication Square:

$4y^2$	$3xy$	$2x^3y$
$3x^2y$	$2xy$	$4xy^2$
$2x^2y$	$4x^2y^2$	$3y$

Great Explanations: $\frac{6xy}{3} = \frac{(6)(xy)}{3} = 2xy$ and $\frac{3}{6xy} = \frac{3}{3(2xy)} = \frac{1}{2xy}$; $6xy \div 3$ means how many groups of 3 are there in $6xy$, and $3 \div 6xy$ means how many groups of $6xy$ are there in 3.

Food Stains:

$$\frac{-16\ x^{\boxed{3}}y^4\ \boxed{+}\ 8\ \boxed{x^2}y^3 - \boxed{2}x^2y^2}{-2x^{\boxed{2}}\boxed{y^2}}$$

Solve Problems Using More Than One Way, page 126

Number of ways will vary.

The Shady Area: figure A 13 square units; figure B 15 square units

Tall versus Squatty: wider shorter cylinder

A Shining Sum: $108°$

Review and Practise, page 127

1.

	constant	variable(s)	numerical coefficient(s)
a)	24	x	3
b)	-5	b, c, x	$-3, -12$
c)	-12	a	$1, -1$

2. *examples*: **a)** $a^2 - 2b + ab - 3c^2 + 5$

b) $xyz - 2 + x^2 - y$

c) $2m - n + 3m^2 - 4 + 12n^2 + mn$

3. a) -21 **b)** -3 **c)** -48

4. *example*: $m^2 - 3m + 1$

5. *example*: $-2b^2 - 6b - 2$

6. a) mn and nm; $2m$ and $-5m$

b) $-d^2$ and $3d^2$

c) abc, bac, and $2cba$

d) m^2n^2 and n^2m^2

The order doesn't matter when variables are multiplied.

7. a) $20a + 8$ **b)** $12b + 18a - 6$

8. $7x^2 - x + 2$

9. $-x^2 - 5x$

10. **a)** $3x^2 + 2x + 2$ **b)** $6y^3 - 5y + 1$
    c) $-7p + 2r - 4$ **d)** $xy - 10x$

11. $25m^2n^2$ square units

12. $3b^2$ units

13. **a)** $21abdk$ **b)** $8a^2c^2$
    c) $-6r^2$ **d)** $3ac$
    e) $\frac{2g}{k}$ **f)** $3d^2$
    g) $-3a^2b^2$

14. $2x^2 + 3x - 2$

15. **a)** $3a + c$ **b)** $-3a - 4a^2 + 5$

Test Your Knowledge, page 129

1. *examples:* $3xy + 4x + 2y - 12$;
$4 + x^2 + 3x - 2y$

2. *example:* constants: start time, date, location; variables: cost (Pay what you can: all proceeds donated to a local charity.), music played, prizes given out, finish time (Dance ends between 11:30 and midnight.)

3. 0, 1, 2   **4.** 5, -3

5. *examples:* (2 flipped green squares, 1 green rod) + (3 green rods, 2 red squares); (1 green square, 1 flipped green rod, 1 red square) + (3 flipped green squares, 5 green rods, 1 red square)

6. *example:* $(-2x^2 + x) + (3x + 2) =$
$-2x^2 + 4x + 2$; $(x^2 - x + 1) +$
$(-3x^2 + 5x + 1) = -2x^2 + 4x + 2$

7. *examples:* (6 green squares, 5 flipped green rods, 5 red) $-$
(3 green squares, 2 flipped green rods, 8 red squares); (5 green squares, 3 flipped red squares) $-$
(2 green squares, 3 green rods)

8. *example:* $(6x^2 - 5x + 5) - (3x^2 -$
$2x + 9) = 3x^2 - 3x - 4$; $(5x^2 - 4)$
$- (2x^2 + 3x) = 3x^2 - 3x - 4$

9. **a)** perimeter B   **b)** $\frac{a}{2} - 2$ **c)** 4

10. **a)** $2.99s + 0.5a + 4.55g + 0.75b$
    b) *example:* 50 small, 4 small additional fillings, 20 large, and 10 large additional fillings

11. $9x^2$ by 2, 9 by $2x^2$, $6x^2$ by 3, 6 by $3x^2$, $18x^2$ by 1, x^2 by 18, $9x$ by $2x$, $6x$ by $3x$, $18x^2$ by x; can model $9x$ by $2x$, $6x$ by $3x$, $18x$ by x

12. $12y$ by $2y$

13. **a)** $(x + \frac{10}{4})$ units
    b) 10.5 cm, 18.5 cm, 6.5 cm
    c) no; no; have to add the constant $\frac{10}{4}$ or 2.5

14. *examples:* $\frac{16xy^2}{2}$; $\frac{16x^2y^2}{2x}$; $\frac{16xy^3}{2y}$

UNIT 6   Investigating Earning and Spending

6.1, pages 132-133

1. *Herald* 66 000; *Star Phoenix* 90 200; *Free Press* 180 000

2. *Herald* $8408.40; *Star Phoenix* $10 336.92; *Free Press* $19 170

3. **a)** for 30-day months *Herald* 28%; *Star Phoenix* 31%; *Free Press* 25%
    b) *examples:* cost of newsprint, salaries for reporters

4. **a)** $30 225.65
    b) *examples:* They work part time. They walk rather than drive.

6. **b)** $1633.47 is total income; $1210.08 is total expenses; $423.39 is revenue $-$ total expenses; $211.70 is 50% of net income; $211.69 is net income $-$ profit tax

7. **a)** 57.6%   **b)** 17.9%   **c)** 13.3%

8. **a)** $423.39 $\div$ 20 = $21.17
    b) $10.58   **c)** $5.58   **d)** 112%

9. **a)** sales income; $23.26
    b) commissions; $2.29
    c) 9.8%

6.2 pages 135-137

1. **b)** Multiplying $1000 by 1.1542 is the same as finding 15.42% of $1000 and then adding it to $1000. She repeatedly multiplies by 1.1542

because after each year she must find 15.42% of the new amount.
    c) 20 times
    d) She could find 15.42% of $1000 and add it to $1000 to get $1154.20, and then 15.42% of $1154.20 to get $1132.18, and so on.
    e) $1774.70; $1191.61; $1031.16

2. **a)** $16 604.41, $1402.50; $165.80
    b) about 1600%; about 140%; about 16%

3. *example:* for 9% interest, 8 years to double and 13 years to triple;

1000×1.09 ▭ ▭ ▭ ▭ ▭

▭ ▭ ▭ ▭ `2171.893279`

▭ ▭ ▭ ▭ `3065.804612`

4. The formula in Problem 3 has d factored out of each term in the numerator.

5. **a)** $\frac{(11 + 1) \times d}{24} = \frac{12d}{24} = \frac{1}{2}d$
    b) 5 years

7. **a)** 1000 : 1   **b)** $\frac{1}{1000}$; 0.001
    c) red 5×10^9; white 5×10^6
    d) red (5×10^{10}) to 10^{11}; white (5×10^7) to 10^8
    e) red 2.5×10^{13}; white 2.5×10^{10}
    f) 20

8. $6^2 + 8^2 = 10^2$, Pythagorean relationship

9. **a)** 50 cm   **b)** 15 dm or 1.5 m

11. **a)** 538.4 cm^3 **b)** 538.4 mL
    c) 0.5384 L

12. 4.31 L

6.3 page 139

1. 1950: 3.6%; 1960: 7%; 1970: 5.7%; 1980: 8.9%; 1990: 6.8%

2. 2.9

3. **a)** 122 222   **b)** 64.7%

4. Women made less than men regardless of age or education although the gap was narrower for university graduates.

5. a) $1\frac{1}{2}$ times as much is the same as 50% more.
b) 74% is about $\frac{3}{4}$, so men make $\frac{4}{3}$ or $1\frac{1}{3}$ times as much or 33% more.

6. a) Since a woman earns 74% of a man, or $23 860, then 100% is what a man earns; $32 243.24
b) 35-44, $37 161.76; 45-54, $40 447.76

7. high school $762 300; university $1 243 100; *examples:* University graduates can expect to earn 63.0% more than high school graduates. High school graduates can expect to earn 61.3% of university graduates.

6.4, pages 140-141

1. annual   **2. a)** 41% **b)** 59%

3. 9.4 g; less than 1¢   **4.** $584 598 814.30

5. 47.1%   **6.** about $25 862

7. Canucks $11 812.92; Flames $9214.80; Jets $8121.54; Oilers $7731.36; Maple Leafs $12 247.20; Senators $10 468.92; Canadiens $9513.00

8. Canucks 70.4%; Flames 69.3%; Jets: 67%; Oilers 64.4%; Maple Leafs 70.2%; Senators 70.3%; Canadiens 70.6%

9. a) 1966: 17.8%; 1975: 18%; 1980: 20.2%; 1990: 22.5%; 1993: 24% **b)** 1966: 17.5%; 1975: 14.9%; 1980: 13.5%; 1990: 15.6%; 1993: 10.4%;

10. Rent and fuel increased as a percent of total expenses. Food as a percent of total expenses decreased overall but 1980–1990 showed an increase.

11. a)   **Canadian Expenses**

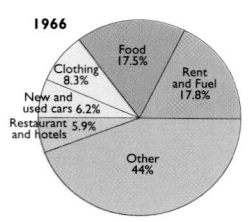

1975

1980

1990

1993

b) Other is about half of total.

6.5, pages 142-143

1. *examples:* VCRs in most provinces are highest percent ownership. Computers are lowest percent ownership. Alberta is highest with computers, CD players, and VCRs, but not with cable TV.

2. a) 2937 is about 2×1463.
b) 52.4% is about $\frac{1}{2}$, and $\frac{1}{2}$ of 1 009 000 is about 500 000.
c) 78.2% is about $\frac{3}{4}$, and $\frac{3}{4}$ of 4 143 000 is 3 000 000.
d) 24.8% is about $\frac{1}{4}$, and $\frac{1}{4}$ of 419 000 is about 100 000.

3.

	Cable	VCR	CD	Computer
Nfld.	159 080	161 990	79 928	38 024
P.E.I.	40 800	48 000	22 800	9 600
N.S.	269 892	289 884	147 084	79 968

	Cable	VCR	CD	Computer
N.B.	197 912	231 946	108 966	56 914
Que.	1 885 554	2 282 099	1 301 091	610 195
Ont.	3 239 826	3 492 549	2 030 070	1 350 618
Man.	279 892	333 943	186 036	103 412
Sask.	227 150	299 915	152 845	90 090
Alta.	713 363	868 749	528 716	345 078
B.C.	1 249 402	1 233 309	772 464	478 401

4. a) Nfld. 81.4%; P.E.I. 86.0%; N.S. 82.6%; N.B. 84.6%; Que. 80.2%; Ont. 83.5%; Man. 85.4%; Sask. 88.1%; Alta. 90.8%; B.C. 86.3%; Canada 83.9% **b)** P.E.I., Man., Sask., Alta., B.C. **c)** Alberta

5. Vehicle Ownership

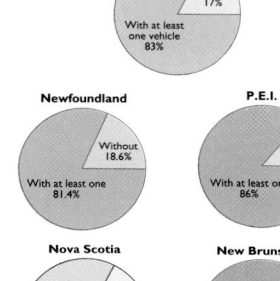

6. 0.47

7. a) motorcycles 39 000, −11.2% mopeds 4000, −13.3%
b) *examples:* cost of motorcycles, safety concerns, mopeds less trendy

6.6 page 145

1. a) not true; a CPI of 138.7 is less than 146.2
b) true; a CPI of 125.5 is a rate of inflation of about 25%
c) true; just less than $\frac{1}{3}$ or 32.7%

2. a) $13.11   **b)** $7.99
c) $92.88   **d)** $5.89
e) $277.70   **f)** $26 346.07

3. $33.91

4. a) $319.14   **b)** $52.70
c) $489.55   **d)** $6.77
e) $6.76

5. a) from 1925 to 1935
b) the Great Depression

6. In 1985, the CPI was about 100, and in 1915, it was 10.

7. a) 1975–1985; steepest slope up
b) about 120%

Making Sense of Data, page 146

4. a) 96 km/h
b) about 136 km/h

5. no; The 72–m skid mark was twice as long, but the speed was only 41.7% times as fast.

6. a) 160 km/h
b) 160 km/h
c) same; Even though in part a) the skid mark was longer, the road conditions were poorer.

7. They are equivalent. $S^2 = 256\ell f$
$\rightarrow S = \sqrt{256\ell f} \rightarrow S = 16\sqrt{\ell f}$

8. a)

Speed (km/h)			
ℓ(m)	f		
	0.5	1.0	1.5
1	11.3	16.0	19.6
2	16.0	22.6	26.7
3	19.6	27.7	33.9
4	22.6	32.0	39.2
5	25.3	35.8	43.8

b) *example*: about 21; 21.2
c) *example*: about 25; 25.3

UNIT 7 Polynomials (II)

7.1, page 152

1. a) $x(x + 1) = x^2 + x$
b) $2x(x + 2) = 2x^2 + 4x$
c) $3(2y + 1) = 6y + 3$
d) $y(x + 1) = xy + y$
e) $y(x + y + 1) = xy + y^2 + y$

2. parts b) and d); all; Sets can't be used for a variable number of set.
a) $3x^2 + x$ **b)** $12y + 4$
c) $2xy + y^2 + y$**d)** $6x + 3y + 9$

3. a) $6x + 9$ **b)** $2x^2 + 3x$
c) $4x + 4$ **d)** $3y^2 + 2y$
e) $2x^2 + 4x$ **f)** $3y^2 + 9y$
g) $2x^2 + 2xy + 3x$
h) $3xy + 3y^2 + 3y$

4. a) $6x^2 + 10x$ **b)** $6y^2 + 9y$
c) $12x + 8y + 4$ **d)** $4y^2 + 8y$
e) $3xy + 6x$ **f)** $4xy + 8y^2 + 12y$

6. The guiding tiles that represent the dimensions of the rectangle are 2 green rods ($2x$) by a green rod and 2 flipped red squares ($x - 2$). $2x(x - 2) = 2x^2 - 4x$ or 2 green squares (x^2) and 4 flipped green rods ($-4x$)

7. a) $6x - 9$
b) Use these guiding tiles to show dimensions: 3 flipped red squares by 2 flipped green rods and 3 red squares. Area is filled in with 6 green rods and 9 red squares.; negative signs

8. a) $10x^2 - 12$ **b)** $x^2 + 3xy + x$
c) $3a^3 + a^2$ **d)** $6p - 9p^2 + 3p^3$
e) $-6t^3 + 3t^2 + 6t$
f) $-8x^3y + 4x^2y^3$

9. a) $14x + 6$; $10x^2 + 6x$
b) $10y$; $\frac{1}{2}(8y^2)$ or $4y^2$

10. $52w + 120$

11. a) $3x + x^2$ **b)** $3x^2 + 4x$
c) $\frac{x^2}{2} + 2x$

12. a) $6x + 4$
b) $2p^2 + 7pq - 7p$
c) $-4d^3 - 2d^2e + 12d^2 - 2d$

13. example: **a)**: $4[2(1) + 3] - 2[(1) + 4] = 10, 6(1) + 4 = 10$

14. a) 315   **b)** 903   **c)** 15

Making Sense of Data, page 153

6. a), c)

Males		Females	
b (cm)	h (cm)	b (cm)	h (cm)
20	128.44	20	126.48
22	134.22	22	131.98
24	140.00	24	137.48
26	145.78	26	142.98
28	151.56	28	148.48
30	157.34	30	153.48
32	163.12	32	159.48
34	168.90	34	164.98

b) *example*: very similar

7. male; When $b = 23$ cm, $h = 137.1$ cm for males and $h = 134.7$ cm for females.

7.2, page 155

1. a) $5(x)$ **b)** $2(y)$
c) $8(x), 4(2x),$ or $2(4x)$
d) $10(y), 2(5y),$ or $5(2y)$

2. a) $3w$ **b)** $4n$
c) $2pq$ **d)** $4mp$
e) $2e$ **f)** $5d$

3. a) 6   **b)** 5
c) $2y + 1$ **d)** $2x + y$
e) 2   **f)** $4y + x + 2$

4. a) $3(x + 2)$ **b)** $3(2y + 3)$
c) $3(2x + 1)$ **d)** $3(x + 2y)$
e) $5(2x + y)$ **f)** $2(3y + 4x)$
g) $2(x + y + 1)$ **h)** $3(x + y - 1)$

5. a) $(2)(2a + b)$ **b)** $3(mn - 2p)$

c) $6(2x + 3z)$ **d)** $4(2a - b + 3c)$
e) $5(m^2 + 2n^2)$ **f)** $5(2ef + 3f - 4e)$

6. a) 4 by $(x^2 + 2)$; $12 + 2x^2$
 b) 3 by $(2y + 1)$; $8 + 4y$
 c) 2 by $(4y + 3x)$; $4 + 8y + 6x$

7. a) 99 **b)** 28 **c)** 9800

8. *example*: $32 \times 18 + 32 \times 12$

9. a) $12r + 9b + 6y$
 b) 3; 4 red; 3 blue; 2 yellow

7.3, page 157

1. a) x **b)** $2y + 1$
 c) x **d)** $2x + 3$
 e) $x + y$ **f)** $3y$
 g) y **h)** $2y + 2 - x$

2. a) $3x(y + 2)$ **b)** $2y(x + 2)$
 c) $2y(3y + 2)$ **d)** $2x(4 + 3x)$
 e) $7y(x + 1)$ **f)** $2x(5 + x)$
 g) $2x(x + 2 + y)$ **h)** $3x(2x + 1 + 2y)$
 i) $2x(2x + 1 + 3y)$

3. a) $4ab(a + 2)$ **b)** $6mn(mn - 2)$
 c) $2d(3e - 4d)$ **d)** $4f(1 - 2f + 3e)$
 e) $2d(3c^2 + 2c - 4d)$
 f) $6gh(1 - 2gh)$

4. a) $6ab$ by $(4a + 3b)$; $12ab + 8a + 6b$
 b) $12m^2n$ by $(4n + 3)$; $24m^2n + 8n + 6$
 c) $5p$ by $(3q - 2 + 4pq)$; $10p + 6q - 4 + 8pq$

5. a) $2(bh + hH + bH)$; 108 cm^2
 b) $b(h + 3H)$; 170 cm^2
 c) $2\pi r(r + H)$; 351.9 cm^2

6. $3p + 6$

Problems to Investigate, page 158

Using Division: GCF $3x$; $\frac{3x^2 - 6x}{3x} =$
$x - 2$; $3x^2 - 6x = 3x(x - 2)$
a) $3a(6 - 7a)$
b) $6m(5m + 2)$
c) $4e(2 + e + 3f)$
d) $7p(2p - 4q + 5q^2)$

Many Possibilities: $6x$ by $(x + 2)$,
$3x$ by $(2x + 4)$, $2x$ by $(3x + 6)$, x by
$(6x + 12)$; $6x(x + 2)$

Complex Figures:
a) x by $(x + 1)$ and y by $(x + 1)$
b) $(x + 1)$ by $(x + y)$; Dimensions of
large rectangle are the sum of
dimensions of 2 smaller connected
rectangles.
$y(y + 1) + x(y + 1)$; $(y + 1)(x + y)$;
$2y(x + 2) + 2x(x + 2)$; $(x + 2)(2y + 2x)$

Negative Tiles: a) $3x^2 + 3xy - 3x$
b) $2x(x - 4)$

Surface Area: a) $8x(4x + 1)$;
$3y(7y + 16)$; $6\pi r(7r + 5)$
b) triangular prism
c) 3280 cm^2; 2580 cm^2; $14\,137$ cm^2

7.4, page 160

1. a) $(x + 1)$ by $(x + 2)$; $x^2 + 3x + 2$
 b) $(2y + 1)$ by $(2y + 1)$; $4y^2 + 4y + 1$
 c) $(y + x)$ by $(x + 1)$; $x^2 + xy + x + y$

2. a) $y^2 + 4y + 3$
 b) $2x^2 + 5x + 3$
 c) $2x^2 + 3xy + y^2$
 d) $3x^2 + 4xy + y^2$
 e) $x^2 + xy + 2x + y + 1$
 f) $3x^2 + 4xy + x + y^2 + y$

3. There are the same number of unit
 tiles in the area as the product of
 unit tiles in the dimensions.

4. a) $y^2 + 8y + 12$
 b) $2y^2 + 7y + 3$
 c) $3x^2 + 4x + 1$
 d) $2x^2 + 3xy + y^2$
 e) $x^2 + 2xy + 2x + 2y + 1$
 f) $x^2 + 3xy + x + 2y^2 + y$

6. a) $2a^2 + 7a + 3$
 b) $6b^2 + 11b + 3$
 c) $4c^2 + 7c + 3$
 d) $3d^2 + 5d - 2$
 e) $8e^2 - 6e - 5$
 f) $2m^2 - 11m + 15$
 g) $10ef + 5f^2 - 4f + 2e - 1$
 h) $4mn + 8n^2 - 18n - 3m + 9$

7. *example:* **a)** $[2(3) + 1][(3) + 3]$
 $= 42, 2(3)^2 + 7(3) + 3 = 42$

8. a) $-6x^2 - 17x - 12$

b) Use these guiding tiles to show
dimensions: 2 flipped green rods and
3 flipped red squares by 3 green rods
and 4 red squares. Area is filled in
with 6 green squares, 17 green rods,
and 12 red squares.; negative signs

9. a) $y^2 + 4y + 4$
 b) $4x^2 + 12x + 9$
 c) $4x^2 - 20x + 25$
 d) $9y^2 + 6y + 1$
 e) $16x^2 + 24x + 9$
 f) $4x^2 + 4xy + y^2$
When two binomials are the same,
you can square the first term,
double the product of the inside
two terms, and square the last term.

10. a) $y^2 - 4$ **b)** $x^2 - 9$
 c) $4x^2 - 1$ **d)** $9y^2 - 16$
 e) $9x^2 - 4$ **f)** $4x^2 - 9y^2$
 g) $y^2 - 4$ **h)** $4 - x^2$
When the second binomial is like
the first binomial except the second
term has the opposite sign, you can
square the first term, and square
the second term. The middle terms
always result in zero.

11. The two squares are subtracted.

12. a) $10x$; $6x^2 + x - 1$
 b) $4x + 11$; $x^2 + 2x + 1$
 c) $12x + 10$; $7x^2 + 11x + 4$
 d) $12x + 15$; $15x^2 + 41x + 28$

13. a) 899 **b)** 8096 **c)** 3591

14. a) $3x^2 + 2x - 5$
 b) $-3x^2 + 4xy - y^2$
 c) $3y^2 - 3y - 2$
 d) $10y^2 + 10y + 5$
 e) $10m^2 - 8m + 12$
 f) $2x^2 + 2xy + 5y^2$
 g) $2d^2 + 9d - 5$

15. a) $(3n + 4)^2 - (n + 2)^2$
 b) $8n^2 + 20n + 12$
 c) 144

More Than One Strategy, page 161

1. a) $x^2 + 7x + 10$ **b)** $x^2 + x - 20$
 c) $x^2 - 9x + 20$ **d)** $x^2 - 16$
 e) $x^2 - xy - 5x + 4y + 4$

3. *example:*

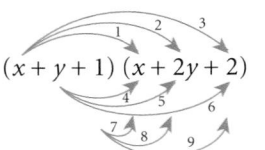

$$= x^2 + 2xy + 2x + xy + 2y^2 + 2y + x$$
$$+ 2y + 22$$
$$= x^2 + 3xy + 3x + 4y + 2y^2 + 2$$

7.5, page 163

1. a) $x + 2$ **b)** $y + 3$ **c)** $x + 5$
d) $(y + 6)(y + 5)$
e) $(x + 1)(x + 1)$
f) $(x + 5)(x + 4)$

2. a) $(x + 4)(x + 1)$
b) $(y + 3)(y + 2)$
c) $(x + 6)(x + 2)$
d) $(y + 4)(y + 4)$
e) $(y + 6)(y + 3)$
f) $(x + 7)(x + 2)$

4. a) $(x - 2)(x + 4)$
b) $(x - 1)(x + 5)$
c) $(y - 2)(y + 5)$
d) $(x - 2)(x + 1)$
e) $(y - 3)(y + 1)$
f) $(x + 1)(x - 6)$
g) $(a + 3)(a + 2)$
h) $(b - 5)(b - 2)$
i) $(c + 1)(c + 10)$
j) $(d - 3)(d - 2)$
k) $(f - 11)(f + 1)$
l) $(z + 8)(z - 2)$

6. b)

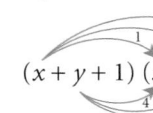

Add 1 (x) rod and 1 ($-x$) rod to fill in the rectangle.

c)

Add 2 (y) rods and 2 ($-y$) rods to fill in the rectangle.

---

d)

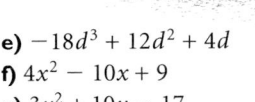

Add 1 (x) rod and 1 ($-x$) rod to fill in the rectangle.

e)

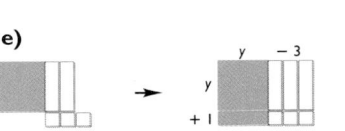

Add 1 (y) rod and 1 ($-y$) rod to fill in the rectangle.

f)

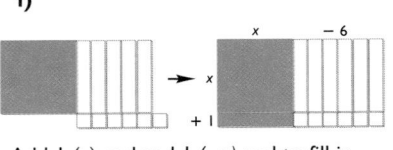

Add 1 (x) rod and 1 ($-x$) rod to fill in the rectangle.

7. a) $(x + 6)$
b) Luxury Pool Co. $(x + 3)$; Popular Pool Co. $(x + 4)$
c) Luxury Pool Co.; Dimensions of yard are $(x + 3)$ by $(x + 7)$. Other pool is too wide.

8. a) $2(a^2 + 4a + 3) = 2(a + 3)(a + 1)$
b) $3(b^2 + 2b + 1) = 3(b + 1)(b + 1)$
c) $5(y^2 - 5y + 4) = 5(y - 1)(y - 4)$
d) $10(y^2 - 3y + 2) = 10(y - 2)(y - 1)$

9. a) $(x - 1)(x + 1)$
b) $(y - 3)(y + 3)$
c) $(x - y)(x + y)$
d) $(x - 2y)(x + 2y)$

10. a) $(x + 5)(x - 5)$
b) $(x - 7)(x + 7)$
c) $(x - 3y)(x + 3y)$

11. a) $(2x + 1)(x + 1)$
b) $(2y + 3)(y + 1)$
c) $(3y + 2)(y + 1)$
d) $(2x + 1)(2x + 1)$

7.6, page 165

1. a) $3y^3 - 3y^2 - 18y$
b) $-8e^3 - 12e^2 + 20e$
c) $-4x^3 + 9x$
d) $-20m^2 + 100m - 125$

---

e) $-18d^3 + 12d^2 + 4d$
f) $4x^2 - 10x + 9$
g) $3y^2 + 10y - 17$

2. a) need to multiply $(4x^2 - 4x)$ by $(x - 4)$;
$(4x^2 - 4x)(x - 4)$
$= 4x^3 - 16x^2 - 4x^2 + 16x$
$= 4x^3 - 20x^2 + 16x$
b) can't collect like terms before multiplying;
$3x - 2x(x^2 - 2x + 1)$
$= 3x - 2x^3 + 4x^2 - 2x$
$= -2x^3 + 4x^2 + x$
c) need to multiply monomial by trinomial;
$4x(2x^2 + 6x - x - 3)$
$= 8x^3 + 20x^2 - 12x$

4. a) might write $-2x - x$ as $-3x$ before multiplying;
$3x - 3 - 2x - x^2 - 3x$
$= -x^2 - 2x - 3$
b) might write $5y + 3y$ as $8y$ before multiplying;
$5y + 3y(y^2 + 3y - 4)$
$= 5y + 3y^3 + 9y^2 - 12y$
$= 3y^3 + 9y^2 - 7y$

5. a) $3(x + 1)(x + 1)$
b) $6y(x - 3)(x + 1)$
c) $-3m(m - 1)(m + 6)$ or $3m(m + 1)(-m + 6)$

6. a) $(x + 5)(x + 2)$ **b)** $3(x + 2)(x + 3)$
c) $7(x^2 - 3x + 1)$ **d)** $8(x - 4)(x - 1)$

7. a) $3x(2x - 1)$
b) $3y(3y + 1)$
c) $(x + 2)(x + 1)$
d) $(y - 3)(y + 5)$
e) $(x + 9)(x + 1)$
f) $y^2 + 2y - 1$
g) $3(x - 2)(x + 1)$
h) $-2x(x + 3)(x - 2)$
i) $-x^2 - 11x + 10$
j) $2x(2x + 1)(x - 1)$

8. a) $3x^2 - 4x + 2$ **b)** same result

9. a) $3x^2 + 2x + 1$ **b)** $2y^3 + 4y - 1$
c) $a(3c + 2)$ **d)** $2 - 4e^2f + e^3$
e) $\dfrac{y - 11}{3}$

Problems to Investigate, page 166

What's Missing?: $19, -19, 11, -11, 9, -9$

Mental Math: $x^2 - 2x + 1$;
$y^2 + 4y + 4$; $4f^2 + 4f + 1$; $9e^2 + 12e + 4$;
Square first term, double product of
the two terms, and square last term.
a) $(40 + 2)^2 = 1600 + 160 + 4 = 1764$
b) $(60 + 5)^2 = 3600 + 600 + 25 = 4225$
c) $(100 - 1)^2 = 10\,000 - 200 + 1 = 9801$
d) $(80 - 2)^2 = 6400 - 320 + 4 = 6084$

Quotient Quandary: a) $x + 2$
b) $x + 10$ **c)** $x + 1$

Versatile Tiles: a) $2x^2 - 6x$
b) $x^2 + x - 2$
Use tiles that add no value in order to
make a rectangle which represents the
area of each polynomial.

Root Magic: a) $(2x + 1)(2x + 1)$
b) $(3x + 1)(3x + 1)$ **c)** $(2y + 3)(2y + 3)$;
yes; Find square root of first term, find
square root of second term, and
multiply to check.

Difference of Squares:
a) $(74 + 26)(74 - 26) = 100(48) = 4800$
b) $(601 + 399)(601 - 399) =$
$1000(202) = 202\,000$

Solve Problems by Guessing and Testing, page 167

Animal Crackers: 5 chickens, 10 cows

Got Any Change?: 4 nickels, 8 dimes

Cents for Sense: 32 quizzes

Just Motoring: 72 km

Review and Practise, page 168

1. a) $2x^2 + 6x$
b) $x^2 + 7x + 12$
c) $4x^2 + 4xy + y^2$
d) $x^2 - 9y^2$

2. a) $10x + 2$; $6x^2 + 3x$
b) $9b + 5$; $2b^2 + 2b$
c) $9y + 2$; $5y^2 + y$

3. a) $9x^2 + 3x$
b) $2y^2 - 10y - 2$
c) $-2y^2 - 3y + 4xy - x - 3$

d) $-4x^2 + 4xy + 11x$
e) $d^2 + 10d + 24$
f) $3f^2 + 5f - 2$
g) $4m^2 + m - 3$
h) $9p^2 + 12p + 4$
i) $25p^2 - 9$
j) $13x^2 - 12x + 8$
k) $5d^2 - 4d - 21$
l) $18e^2 + 33e + 28$

4. a) $5(2x + y)$
b) $2y(2y + 3)$
c) $3x(x + 2y)$
d) $(x + 3)(x + 1)$
e) $(x + 6)(x + 3)$
f) $(x + 10)(x + 2)$
g) $(x + 2y)(x + 3y)$
h) $(x + 2y)(x + 2y)$
i) $(2x + y)(2x + y)$
j) $(y - 4)(y + 4)$
k) $(2x - 3)(2x + 3)$
l) $x(x + y + 1)$

5. a) $4(2y - 3)$
b) $6x(2y - 3)$
c) $6pq(7p - 8)$
d) $7n(2m + 7)$
e) $8ef(4f + 2e - 3)$

6. a) $(x + 5)(x + 6)$
b) not possible
c) $(x - 12)(x + 2)$
d) $(x - 8)(x - 2)$
e) $(x + 12)(x - 2)$
f) $(y - 3)(y + 8)$
g) $(c - 6)(c + 3)$
h) not possible
i) $(m - 4)(m + 3)$

7. a) $(x - 4)(x + 4)$
b) $(2y - 2)(2y + 2)$
c) $(d - 3)(d + 3)$
d) $(4f - 5)(4f + 5)$

8. a) $3(x + 2)(x + 1)$
b) $4(y + 5)(y + 1)$
c) $2(m - 4)(m + 1)$
d) $5e(f + 3)(f - 2)$

9. a) $8x^3 + 12x^2 + 6x + 1$
b) $24x^3 + 38x^2 + 10x$

10. a) $8x^3 + 20x^2 - 12x$
b) $11y^2 - 7y - 2$
c) $80m^3 - 200m^2 + 125$

d) $-2e^3 - 4e^2 + 9e$
e) $12p^2 - 16p + 13$
f) $-6x^2 + 22x - 3xy$

11. a) $(a - 2)(a + 6)$
b) $3d(d + e)$
c) $(2m - 3)(2m - 3)$
d) $(e - 2)(e + 2)$

Test Your Knowledge, page 170

1. a) $2(4xy - 3z)$
b) $3y(y + 3)$ **c)** $5(3x^2 + y^2)$
d) $4x(-x + 5 - 3y)$ or $-4x(x - 5 + 3y)$

2. a) $45y^3 - 12y^2 - 13y + 2$
b) $12x^3 - 11x^2 - 5x$
c) $2\pi x^3 + \pi x^2 - 4\pi x - 3\pi$

3. a) $78y^2 - 8y - 6$
b) $38x^2 + 17x - 72$
c) $6\pi x^2 + 2\pi x - 4\pi$

4. a) $3x^2 - 3x$ **b)** $x^2 - x - 2$
c) $x^2 + 2xy - x + y^2 - y$

5. a) $23, 10, 5, 2, -2, -5, -10, -23$
b) $-8, 0$; in second binomial factor,
the second term is opposite of that
in first binomial factor

6. a) $\pi(x^2 + 16x + 64)$
b) $\pi(64 - 16x + x^2)$
c) $\pi(r^2 + 20r + 100)$

7. $5(-5) = -25$ and $5 + (-5) = 0$,
but no two numbers multiply to
give 25 and combine to give 0.

8. a) $(x + 2)(x - 2)$ **b)** $(x + 6)(x - 6)$
c) $(2x - y)(2x + y)$
They completed the area but were
the zero model, thus adding
nothing to the original expression.

9. $4y^2 - 16$
$= 4(y^2 - 4)$
$= 4(y + 2)(y - 2)$
$4y^2 - 16$
$= (2y + 4)(2y - 4)$
$= 2(y + 2)(2)(y - 2)$
$= 4(y + 2)(y - 2)$

10. a) 600   **b)** 99   **c)** 285

11. a) $4x^2 - 5x - 3$
b) $\dfrac{2xy + 1}{y}$ **c)** $\dfrac{x + 2}{2x}$

12. a) $(3x + 27)$ km/h
b) x might be 0 or -1 or -2

UNIT 8 Probability

8.1, pages 175-176

1. Yes, there are no other possibilities. Two people either share a birth season or have different birth seasons, and the probabilities add to 1.

2. a) There are 12 different season combinations out of 16 possible so the probability is $\frac{12}{16}$ or $\frac{3}{4}$.
b) P(Different Seasons) $= 1 \times \frac{3}{4} = \frac{3}{4}$

3. a) any of the 12   **b)** 11
c) $1 \times \frac{11}{12} = \frac{11}{12}$

4. a) $\frac{1}{16}$ **b)** $\frac{1}{16}$

5. $\frac{1}{4} \times \frac{1}{4} = \frac{1}{16}$ for each

6. $\frac{1}{144}$; $\frac{1}{12} \times \frac{1}{12}$

7. a) Person A has 4 seasons to choose from. For each of those 4, Person B has 4 seasons. That's 16. For each of those 16, Person C has 4 seasons. That's $(4 \times 4) \times 4 = 64$.
b) The first combination at the top is the only time you can get Spring-Spring-Spring.
c) $\frac{1}{64}$
d) $\frac{1}{4} \times \frac{1}{4} \times \frac{1}{4} = \frac{1}{64}$

8. a) $\frac{55}{72}$ **b)** $\frac{1}{1728}$ **c)** $\frac{1}{1728}$ **d)** $\frac{1}{1728}$

9. a) $\frac{1}{365}$ **b)** $\frac{364}{365}$ **c)** $\frac{1}{133\,225}$

10. *example*: What's the probability of three people having birthdays on New Year's Day?
$\left(\frac{1}{365} \times \frac{1}{365} \times \frac{1}{365} = \frac{1}{48\,627\,125}\right)$

8.2, pages 178-179

1. a) greater; Probability of a girl is $\frac{2}{3}$ now instead of $\frac{1}{2}$, and probability of grade 9 is the same, $\frac{1}{4}$.
b) The diagram has to be divided into $\frac{2}{3}$ for girls and $\frac{1}{3}$ for boys because $\frac{800}{1200}$ or $\frac{2}{3}$ of the students are

girls and $\frac{400}{1200}$ or $\frac{1}{3}$ are boys. The divisions for the four grades stay the same at $\frac{1}{4}$ each. The shaded section is the fraction that is both girls and grade 9.
c) $\frac{1}{6}$; $\frac{1}{12}$

2. $\frac{3}{16}$
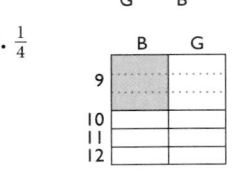

3. $\frac{1}{4}$

4. a) $\frac{1}{4}$ **b)** 1:1
c) The first diagram is in fourths because each grade has a $\frac{1}{4}$ chance. The second diagram is in halves because girls and boys each have a $\frac{1}{2}$ chance. So, in each grade, both boys and girls each have $\frac{1}{2}$ of $\frac{1}{4}$ or $\frac{1}{8}$ chance. In the third diagram, each $\frac{1}{8}$ is divided into halves because half the students are taking English. So, in each grade, boys and girls each have a $\frac{1}{2}$ of $\frac{1}{8}$ or $\frac{1}{16}$ chance.

5. $\frac{1}{24}$
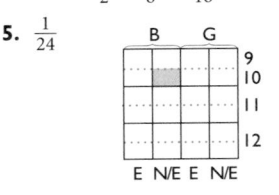

6. a) about $\frac{1}{12}$
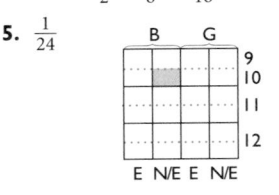

b) *examples*: probability of student not taking the bus, not on a school team, and taking Physics; probability of a student taking the bus, on a school team, and not taking Physics

7. a) 1 : 2   **b)** 6   **d)** $\frac{1}{4}$

8. a) *example*: In a school of 1000 students, 250 are girls and 250 speak English as a second language. What's the probability of choosing a student that is a boy who speaks English as a second language? $\left(\frac{3}{16}\right)$

9. *example*: There are 29 students in my class. 20 sit at desks and 10 sit at tables. Five wear glasses and 15 ride the bus. Estimate the probability of choosing a student that sits at a desk, wears glasses, and is in my class. (about $\frac{1}{18}$)

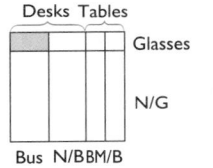

More Than One Strategy, page 180

1. $\frac{11}{18}$ **2.** $\frac{1}{16}$ **3.** $\frac{1}{27}$ **4.** $\frac{1}{90}$

Problems to Investigate, page 181

Calculating Combinations: $\frac{1}{2500}$; 50 times; Yes, it's possible but not likely. Since there are 2500 possible combinations, she might get the right one in ten tries or she might get it after a 1000 tries or after 2000 tries or...

Lefties: $\frac{729}{1000}$; $\frac{1}{1000}$; Label $\frac{1}{10}$ of a spinner left and $\frac{9}{10}$ right. Spin it three times, and then repeat 99 more times. Find the fraction of the time RRR was spun, and then find the fraction of the time LLL was spun.

Different Dice: red and green; Probability of rolling a 4 is $\frac{3}{4}$ with the red die and $\frac{2}{4}$ with the green die. So the $P(4 + 4 \text{ or a sum of } 8) = \frac{6}{16}$ or $\frac{3}{8}$. Any combination of two dice which includes the blue die will have a lesser likelihood of rolling 8 because the probability of rolling a 4 with the blue die is $\frac{1}{4}$; $\frac{3}{32}$

Working Backwards: $\frac{1}{4}$; $\frac{1}{2}$;

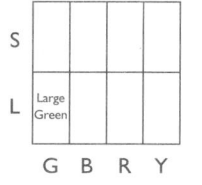

Guess and Test: Answers will vary.

8.3, pages 182-183

1. $\frac{1}{13\,983\,816}$

2. injured by lightning; about 20 times as likely

3. randomly

4. a) 1; You would have every possible number combination.
   b) He does need to buy 6 991 908 tickets but they all have to be different number combinations. If he buys 6 991 908 tickets, all with the same combination, his chances are still $\frac{1}{13\,983\,816}$.
   c) Even if 28 000 000 tickets were sold, it's likely that many of them will be the same number combination.

5. left to right: *examples*: Choosing numbers randomly is better.; A pattern is less likely to win because it's predictable.; If the numbers are evenly spread, the chances are greater.; If a number doesn't win one time, it's not lucky.; Results of one lottery is related to another.

6. *example*: Each person in a group of 10 choosing 10 different number combinations pays for $\frac{1}{10}$ of 10 tickets, but has a chance of winning 10 times as great as having bought one ticket. If they win, each gets $\frac{1}{10}$ of the prize money.

8. *examples*: enjoyment; ticket cost is low and there's always a chance of winning; don't expect to win the jackpot, satisfied with the lesser prizes; to support hospitals and sports groups partially funded by lottery corporations

9. a) The ad suggests that the greater the number of number combinations, the more ways to win. In reality, it's the opposite.

8.4, page 185

1. *examples*: Alomar .305, $\frac{113}{370}$, 113 : 257; White .291, $\frac{106}{364}$, 106 : 258; Olerud .274, $\frac{96}{350}$, 96 : 254; Sprague .265, $\frac{94}{355}$, 94 : 261; Carter .262, $\frac{101}{386}$, 101 : 285; Parrish .195, $\frac{30}{154}$, 30 : 124

2. a) home run $\frac{1}{26}$, .038, 1 : 25; triple 0, 0, 0 : 26; double $\frac{2}{26}$, .077, 2 : 24; single $\frac{5}{26}$, .192, 5 : 21
   b) triple 0, 0 : 8; double $\frac{2}{8}$, 2 : 6; single $\frac{5}{8}$, 5 : 3

3. $\frac{1}{8} > \frac{1}{26}$

4. a) $\frac{11}{113}$ and $\frac{9}{106}$ are too close to estimate.
   b) express each as a decimal, $\frac{11}{113} = .097$ and $\frac{9}{106} = .085$

5. Sprague, 16 : 78

6. Alomar, 37 : 333

7. His batting performance has improved.

8. It would depend on how long the player has played and how well he's doing in the season. A player that has played a long time and is having a good season, will likely have lower lifetime odds than season odds. If he's a long-time star player that is in a slump, it might be the opposite. If it's the first season for a player, the odds will be the same.

9. *examples*: coaches choosing positions for players, owners making decisions for trading players, players negotiating for salaries, sports enthusiasts trading sports cards and playing sports pools

Making Sense of Data, page 186

4. $\frac{2}{53}$; $\frac{1}{3}$; $\frac{1}{19}$

5. a) $\frac{1}{2}$; 2 : 1
   b) *Four Weddings* 10 : 1; *Pulp Fiction* 5 : 1; *Quiz Show* 20 : 1; *Shawshank* 10 : 1; others 20 : 1
   c) same order except *Shawshank* and *Four Weddings* tied, *Four Weddings'*, *Quiz Show's*, and *Shawshank's* chances of winning higher than the actual odds, *Pulp Fiction's* chances lower than the actual odds

6. for betting, for pricing/trading horses

7. alike: Both are ratios and reflect the chances of something happening.; different: for the Oscarnet and horse racing odds, the higher the first number compared to the second, the lower the chances. For the other odds, the higher the first number compared to the second, the better the chances.

Problems to Investigate, page 187

Reported Results: Odds of 3 : 2 could mean $\frac{2}{3}$ or about 66% of those surveyed supported Keri, or it could mean $\frac{3}{5}$ or 60%. Many of those surveyed who showed support for Keri might not be eligible to vote or may not actually turn out for the election.

Whether Weather: *example*: A 70% chance of rain is not a certainty. Even a 100% is not absolutely certain because it is a prediction based on weather patterns. John may have felt that the likelihood of it not raining was still high enough. He may have rain gear and like to ride in the rain. Even though the chance of rain dropped, he may have been tired or he may have had other priorities.

Dicey Decisions: *examples*: sum from 4 to 6, sum from 8 to 10, sum from 2 to 4 or 10 to 12

Eyes and Odds: *example*: Select 100 people randomly and count the number with blue eyes. If 30 had blue eyes, the odds would be 30 : 70 or 3 : 7.

Better Bet: 4/19; fewer possible number combinations so the chances of winning higher, prize greater

Solve Problems By Conducting Experiments, page 188

Answers will vary because of experimental results.

Review and Practise, page 189

1. **a)** $\frac{1}{2}$ **b)** $\frac{3}{4}$ **c)** $\frac{1}{2}$

2. **a)** $\frac{1}{8}$ **b)** $\frac{1}{1000}$

3. part a)

4. *example*: Choose 100 groups of 3 students randomly. Find the fraction of the time all 3 students in a group had blue eyes.

5. $\frac{1}{6}$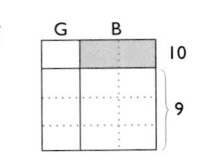

6. **a)** $\frac{1}{8}$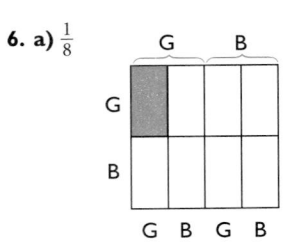

   b) $\frac{1}{8}$

7. Lottery 5/10; When you choose different numbers, there are less possible number combinations than if you repeat numbers.

8. Lottery 6/10; When the order doesn't matter, there are fewer possible number combinations.

9. **a)** 3 : 5 **b)** 5 : 4 **c)** 1 : 99

---

10. **a)** $\frac{3}{11}$ **b)** $\frac{4}{9}$ **c)** $\frac{34}{47}$

11. d), c), b), a)

12. If it is an odds for and against ratio, then it would mean the chances are $\frac{2}{3}$ and a yes vote would be likely. Although it will depend on voter turn out and events between the survey and the vote. If it is the other type of odds, where 2 : 1 means $\frac{1}{2}$ of those surveyed would vote yes, it's too close to call.

Problems to Investigate, page 191

Canadian Content: about $\frac{1}{27}$; $\frac{1}{1000}$; $\frac{1}{27\,000}$

Multiplying to Ad: 9 999 999 999 : 1; *example*: Your odds of losing may be high, but you'll be a winner to children in need.

Less Than Ten: expected probability $\frac{220}{1000}$

Slim Pickings: Each shaded sixteenth shows the probability of two cards the same suit, so $\frac{4}{16}$ or $\frac{1}{4}$;

$\frac{1}{2}$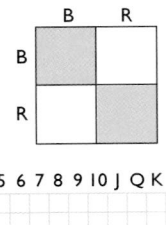

$\frac{1}{13}$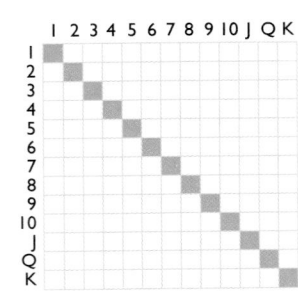

Drawing Marbles: 1:8; 1:26; 1:26; You could draw indefinitely.; *example*: Use a spinner in thirds labelled red, blue, and black. Spin it until red is spun, and record the numbers of times it took. Repeat 10 more times, and find the average number of times it took to spin red.

Test Your Knowledge, page 192

1. 12 or 24

2. $\frac{27}{64}$

3. **a)** $\frac{1}{216}$ **b)** $\frac{1}{36}$

   c) For Brenda, the probability for rolling the first five was 1, not $\frac{1}{6}$, because it was certain as she had already rolled it.

4. **a)** A, B
   b) A, A; it's $\frac{1}{4}$; BB, BC, CB, or CC they're each $\frac{1}{16}$
   c) $\frac{1}{8}$; $\frac{1}{64}$
   d) $\frac{1}{32}$

5. **a)** *example*: the first die represents gender. If the numbers 1, 2, 3, or 4 are rolled, it means a girl, and 5 or 6 means a boy. The other die represents the grade. Rolling 1 or 2 means grade 9, 3 means grade 10, 4 means grade 11, and 5 or 6 means grade 12. Roll both dice 50 times, and find the fraction of the time girl–grade 9 was rolled.
   b) $\frac{2}{9}$

6. **a)** $\frac{1}{3\,838\,380}$; $\frac{3\,838\,379}{3\,838\,380}$
   b) 12 794 60; Each different combination has a $\frac{1}{3\,838\,380}$ chance of winning.

7. $a < b$

8. **a)** $\frac{23}{79}$ **b)** $\frac{7}{10}$ **c)** $\frac{349}{1214}$
   d) $\frac{10}{19}$ **e)** $\frac{5}{11}$ **f)** $\frac{7}{8}$

9. c), a), e), d), b), f)

10. Player A 15:21, Player B 21:15; no, *example*: Assign even sums to Player A and odd sums to Player B.

UNIT 9 Measurement and Geometry

9.1, pages 197-198

1. a) 3000 cm^3
b) 0.7 m^3 or 66 666.7 cm^3
c) 333.3 cm^3
d) 166.7 m^3

2. a) $h = \frac{3V}{A \text{ of base}}$
b) $A \text{ of base} = \frac{3V}{h}$

3. a) 18 cm **b)** 4.5 m
c) 120 m **d)** 9 m

4. a) 18 333.3 m^2 **b)** 428.2 m

5. 79.9 m

6. smaller 38/m^2, larger 660 m^2

7. *examples:* side length 30 m and height 100 m, side length 42.4 m and height 50 m

8. a) 30 cm **b)** 18 cm

9. a) 3 cm **b)** 5 cm

10. part b) **11.** part a) **12.** part a)

13. For two square-based pyramids, where the height of one is the side length of the other's base (and vice versa), the one with the greater side length has the greater volume.

14. a) 2500 **b)** 3300 **c)** 63.84

15. *examples:* for a 600–m^3 classroom,
a) 4167 **b)** 5500 **c)** 106.4

16. 3 times as high as it is now

9.2, pages 199-200

1. a) 8377.6 cm^3
b) 0.4 m^3
c) 0.5 m^3 or 523 598.8 cm^3
d) 954.9 cm^3

2. a) $h = \frac{3V}{\pi r^2}$ **b)** $r = \sqrt{\frac{3V}{\pi h}}$

3. a) 11.5 m **b)** 18.7 m
c) 24 cm **d)** 50 cm

4. a) 5.5 cm **b)** 7.8 cm
c) 6.9 cm **d)** 6 cm

5. *examples:* height 10 m and radius 3.8 m, height 6 m and radius 4.9 m

6. *examples:* height 10 cm and diameter 8.7 cm

7. a) 22.5 cm **b)** 6 m

8. a) 6 cm **b)** 0.6 m

9. a) doubled **b)** quadrupled
c) doubled

10. *examples:* height 8 m and radius 3.1 m, height 4.0 m and radius 4.4 m

9.3, pages 201-202

1. $1 \times 1 \times 12$, $1 \times 2 \times 6$, $2 \times 2 \times 3$
b) $2 \times 2 \times 3$; Counted exterior faces of each connecting cube as 1 unit. Calculated the areas of each prism's faces and added.

2. b) 24 cubic units, 98 square units; 24 cubic units, 76 square units; 24 cubic units, 56 square units; 24 cubic units, 52 square units
c) As the shape gets closer to a cube, the surface area decreases.

3. a) $1 \times 1 \times 27$, $1 \times 3 \times 9$, $3 \times 3 \times 3$
b) $3 \times 3 \times 3$; It's a cube.

4. a) 54 square units
c) 54 square units, 18 cubic units
d) same surface area, prism's volume less than cube's volume
e) No, to have a volume greater than the cube's, you need to use 28 or more cubes, and any arrangement of 28 cubes has a surface area greater than the cube's 54 square units.

5. 10 cm × 10 cm × 10 cm; A cube has the least surface for a given volume.

6. a) 96 cm^3, 136 cm^2
b) 192 cm^3, 224 cm^2 **c)** volume

7. a) 1570.8 cm^3, 785.4 cm^2
b) 14 137.2 cm^3, 3298.7 cm^2
c) volume

8. a)

h (cm)	SA (cm^2)	h (cm)	V (cm^3)
4	131.9	4	113.1
5	150.8	5	141.4
6	169.6	6	169.6
7	188.5	7	197.9
8	207.3	8	226.2
9	226.2	9	254.5
10	245.0	10	282.7

b)

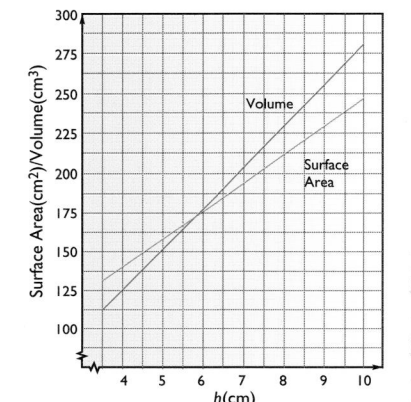

c) volume

9. d) outside surface made from identical sized rectangles
e) for 6 cm height, $r = 1.9$ cm, $V = 68.0$ cm^3; for 12 cm height, $r = 1.0$ cm, $V = 34$ m^3

10. b) for 6 cm height, $r = 1.9$ cm, $SA = 94.7$ cm^2; for 12 cm height, $r = 1.0$ cm, $SA = 78.3$ cm^2
c) The cylinder with the 6 cm height has the greater volume and the greater surface area, but its volume compared to its surface area is greater than the other cylinder. So the cylinder with the 6 cm height is the more cost effective to make.

11. a) Consider 24 cm by 8 cm the base of the carton. Place 16 boxes (4×4 array) in each of three layers with 6 cm side along 24 cm side and 2 cm side along 8 cm. There is no waste in each layer but 2 cm waste above top layer. There are 48 boxes in carton. **b)** 448

9.4, pages 203-204

1. **a)** 1×36, 2×18, 2×12, 4×9, 6×6
   b) 6×6

2. **a)** 1×16, 2×8, 4×4 **b)** 4×4

3. **a)** 24 cm, 11 cm² **b)** 24 cm, 20 cm²
   c) 24 cm, 27 cm² **d)** 24 cm, 32 cm²
   e) 24 cm, 35 cm² **f)** 24 cm, 36 cm²

4. **a)** 16 cm, 7 cm² **b)** 16 cm, 12 cm²
   c) 16 cm, 15 cm² **d)** 16 cm, 16 cm²

5. **a)** *examples:* 100 km × 453.5 km;
   45 350 km²
   b) 276.8 km; 76 618.2 km²
   c) 176.2 km; 97 535.3 km²
   d) circle
   e) Its perimeter is its coastline
   which has a lot of ins and outs
   which greatly increases the distance
   around it.

6. **a)** *examples:* rectangles 14 cm ×
   1 cm, 13 cm × 2 cm, 12 cm × 3 cm,
   11 cm × 4 cm, 10 cm × 5 cm,
   9 cm × 6 cm, 8 cm × 7 cm; square
   7.5 cm × 7.5 cm; circle r = 4.8 cm
   b) *examples:* rectangles 14 cm²,
   26 cm², 36 cm², 44 cm², 50 cm²,
   54 cm², 56 cm²; square 56.3 cm²;
   circle 72.4 cm²
   c) circle

7. 3 m × 3 m; 9 m²

8. 3 m × 4 m; 12 m²

9. 5 m × 5 m; 25 m²

10. circle; 27.2 m²

11. **a)** 22.6 m²; square
    b) 20.1 m²; circle

Making Sense of Data, page 205

All answers are examples only.

2. **a)** for fencing or a garden border
   b) for fertilizing, seeding, cutting,
   weed killing

3. **a)** how easy it is to carry
   b) to determine how much is needed

4. **a)** to determine time to travel its length
   b) for navigating large, deep boats
   or for fishing

c) to determine evaporation rates
d) to determine how much water
front property

5. **a)** to determine if it will fit
   in/through; to find its volume,
   capacity and surface area
   b) how easy it is to carry
   c) how much can be put in it
   d) how much space it will take up
   e) how much material is required to
   cover or wrap it

6. **a)** to determine ability (speed) to
   process to software
   b) to determine ability (speed) to
   process to software
   c) to determine if it will fit
   d) to determine how easy it is to carry

7. *l*, *w*, *h* for ease of parking, fit in
   garage; headroom and legroom for
   tall people comfort; cargo capacity
   for meeting needs for things you
   transport; fuel consumption to
   determine cost of operating the car;
   mass to determine ability to
   withstand wind

More Than One Strategy, page 206

1. 4.1 cm   2. 7.1 cm   3. 4.0 cm²

Problems to Investigate, page 207

20 Cubes: greatest 82 square units; least
48 square units

Circles to Cones: When the 2nd eighth
is removed, the volume starts to
decrease. So the greatest volume is with
3 eighths removed.

Bumping Out: 1st 36 cm, 81 cm²; 2nd
60 cm, 117 cm²; 3rd 100 cm, 137 cm²;
The perimeter is increasing more
rapidly than the area.

Pancakes: The 120 cm would only
occur if the 10 pancakes were sitting
beside each other in a row. The larger
pancake would not be like that. 34.6 cm

Rectangles: Yes, any rectangle closer to
a square than 4 cm by 6 cm has a

greater area since we are not limited to
whole number measurements. A
4.9 cm by 4.9 cm has the same area, 24
cm², with a perimeter of 19.6 cm.

Truncated Cone: Find the volume of
the cone with $r = \frac{7.5}{2}$ cm and
$h = 22.4$ cm, and the volume of the
cone with $r = \frac{5.6}{2}$ cm
and $h = (22.4 - 6.9)$ cm. Then find
the difference (subtract the part of the
cone that is missing); 202.6 cm³

9.5, page 209

1.
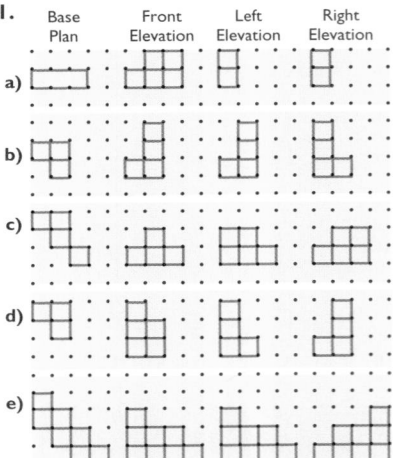

2.
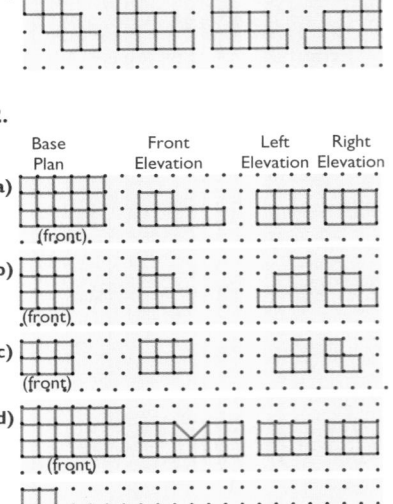

9.6, pages 211-212

1. a)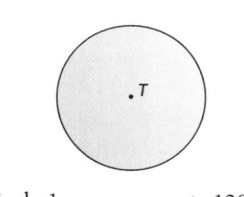

b) (*both places 2nd layer is possible but not necessary)

(*2nd layer is possible but not necessary)

c) (front)

d) (front)

2. a) (front)

b) (front)

c) (front)

d) (front)

3. a) Front Elevation   Right Elevation

c) (front)

5. No, the bottom layer would be rectangular, but it's the tallest columns that are now in elevations. There can be shorter ones. For example, a non-rectangular prism with Base Plan

3	2
1	3
(front)

has all elevations rectangular.

6.

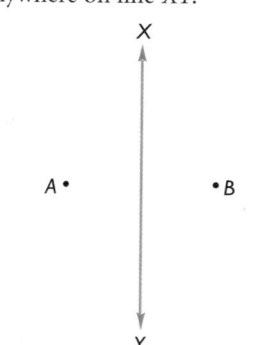

9.7, page 214

1. Scale 1 cm represents 120 km.

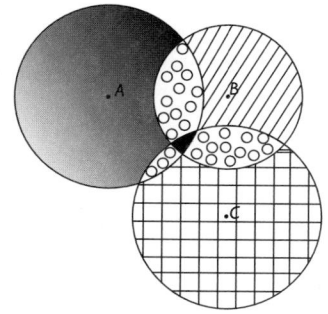

2. Scale 1 cm represents 120 km.

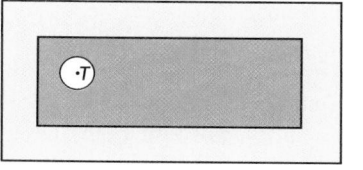

3. Scale 1 cm represents 4 m.

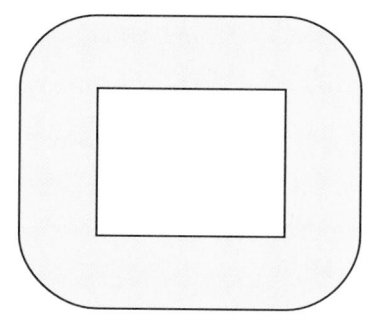

4. Scale 1 cm represents 60 cm.

5. a) Scale 1 cm represents 20 m anywhere on line *XY*.

X

A •   • B

Y

---

b) Found two points a set distance from both *A* and *B* by finding the intersections of arcs with centres A and B and the same radius. Drew line through them because the first part could be repeated and the pairs of points would always be along the line.

6. a) at point D

A •

•C

B •

•D

b) Found the line it could be on if just between A and B, then A and C, and then B and C. Where the three lines intersect is the only spot for it. (Actually only have to find the intersection of two lines.)

7. anywhere in shaded areas

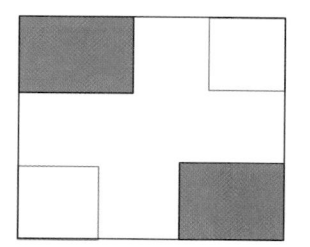

8.

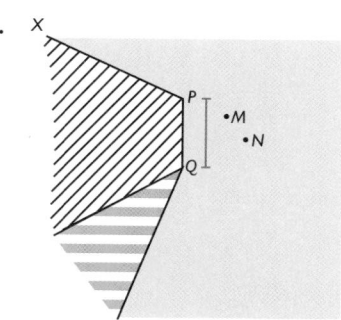

a)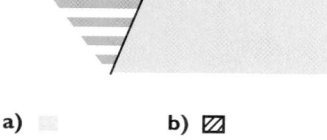

b)

c) on line XP   **d)**

375

Problems to Investigate, page 215

Rolling Circle:

a)   b)

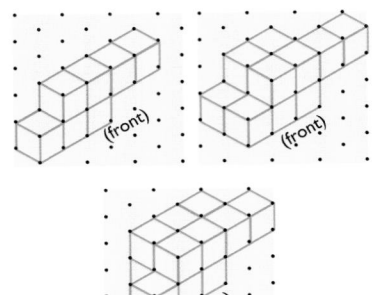

Same Volume: *examples:*

4	3	3
4	3	3
(front)

8	1	1
8	1	1
(front)

5	3	5
2	3	2
(front)

Two Tacks:

egg shape, oval, ellipse

Squares:

2.8 cm
2 cm

Up Front:

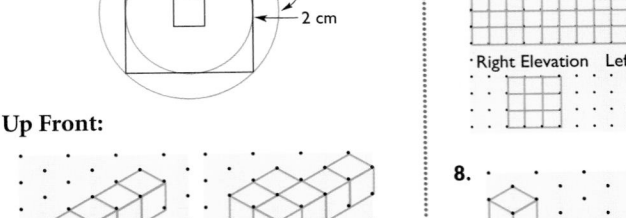

A base plan with numbers shows the bottom layer and the number of cubes in each column, and with this front elevation, there is nothing in the bottom layer of two columns of cubes.

Solve Problems by Using Models, page 216

Cylinder Versus Sphere Surface Area: No, cylinder has more.

Half Cone?: less than half

Volume of a Sphere: cylinder

Wrapping Packages: less than double

Review and Practise, page 217

1. **a)** 50 cm   **b)** 16.7 cm

2. **a)** 270 cm^2 **b)** 16.4 cm   **c)** 90 cm^2

3. **a)** 17.9 cm   **b)** 8.9 cm

4. **a)** *example:* radius 9 cm, height 120 cm
   b) *example:* radius 5 cm, height 156 cm

5. yes, any box more cube shaped;
   example: 8.5 cm × 8.5 cm × 8.5 cm

6. **a)** 12.5 m × 12.5 m; 156.3 m^2
   b) 12 m × 13 m; 156 m^2

7. **a)**

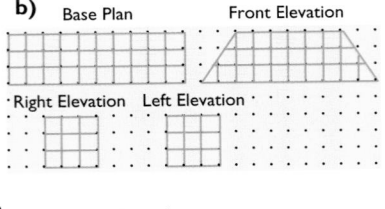

   b)

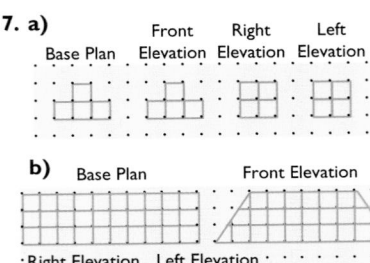

8.

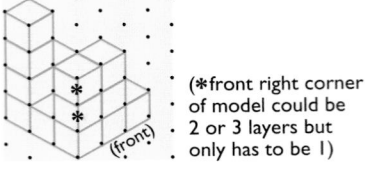

(*front right corner of model could be 2 or 3 layers but only has to be 1)

9.

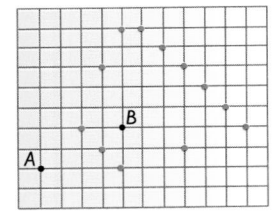

a) ○   b) ◑   c) ●

Problems to Investigate, page 219

Melting Ice: 500 mL is a volume of 500 cm^3. While ice cubes don't fit perfectly, they are close to 500 cm^3 too.; ice cubes; ice cubes; greater the surface area, the faster ice melts

Stellated Cubes: 3000 cm^3

Greatest Surface Area: 62 square units, a 1 × 1 × 15 rectangular prism

8 Cubes: 47

Follow the Grid:

Pentominoes: ▢ has 11 units. All others have 12 units. It's closest to being a square and has greatest number of hidden sides.

Test Your Knowledge, page 220

1. *example:* 25 cm × 25 cm base, 11.2 cm height

2. *example:* base of triangular base 20 cm, height of triangular base 10 cm, height of pyramid 10 cm

3. **a)** *example:* height 20 cm, radius 6.2 cm
   b) *example:* height 20 cm, radius 3.6 cm

4. **a)** 1 × 1 × 18, 1 × 2 × 9, 2 × 3 × 3
   b) 2 × 3 × 3

5. 30 cm long, 20 cm wide, 20 cm high; 3200 cm^2

6. No, since the heights are the same, only concern is perimeters, and a circle with an area of 400 cm^2 has less perimeter than a square with the same area.

ANSWERS

7. a)

Base Plan	Front Elevation	Right and Left Elevations

(front)

Base Plan	Front Elevation	Right and Left Elevations

(front)

8.

(front)

9. The corners of the frame are more than 6 cm out from the corners of the picture. This is what 6 cm out from a rectangle looks like.

UNIT 10   Equations

10.1, page 225

1. a) $25 + 10d$; \$65; \$125
  b) $3.75 + 3.25(m - 1)$; \$10.25; \$33.00

2. a) $20 + 4.5g$, where g represents number of games
  b) $5000 + 229m$, where m represents number of months
  c) $1.5 + 0.9d$, where d represents distance in kilometres
  d) $2.5n$, where n represents number of fruit

3. a) $2n$, where n represents natural numbers
  b) $2n + 1$, where n represents whole numbers

c) $3n + 4$, where n represents natural numbers
  d) $5n - 3$, where n represents natural numbers

4. *examples:*
  a) a number decreased by 4
  b) twice a number, increased by 10
  c) \$3.50 per bouquet of flowers plus \$0.25 wrapping fee
  d) fifty times the number of dots per row
  e) \$0.25 for each quarter, added to a \$5 bill
  f) \$55 service charge and \$10 per phone installed

5. a) $x + 20 + 3x = 180$ or $4x + 20 = 180$
  b) $(3x + 10) + (x - 10) = 180$ or $4x = 180$
  c) $C = \$4.60n$ **d)** $d = 2s$
  e) $V = 3n$ **f)** $L = 0.05n$
  g) $5 + 4n = 24$
  h) $n + n + 1 + n + 2 = 21$, $3n + 3 = 21$, or $3(n + 1) = 21$

6. *examples:*
  a) $n - 4 = 20$, $n = 16$
  b) $2n + 10 = 12$, $n = 1$
  c) $3.5f + 0.25 = 35.25$, $f = 10$
  d) $50d = 100$, $d = 2$
  e) $0.25q + 5 = 30$, $q = 100$
  f) $55 + 10p = 65$, $p = 1$

7. a) 1, 3, 5, 7, 9, 11, 13, 15, 17, 19
  b) X = 3N + 1

8. $n^4 \times n^2 = 64$ **b)** $n = 2$ or -2

10.2, page 227

1. a) second and first; multiply by 2
  b) first and third; divide by 2
  c) all 3; divide third equation by 3
  d) all 3; multiply first equation by 3
  e) all 3; multiply second equation by -1, multiply third equation by 4
  f) first and second; divide by 2
  g) third and first; multiply by 2
  h) all 3; multiply first equation by 2, subtract 2 from second equation

2. If you multiply each term in first equation by 3, you get the second

equation, and if you multiply each term in first equation by 10, you get third equation.

4. a) 1.0, 1.5, 2.0; $s = 10r$
  b) $r = \frac{s}{10}$, $r = 0.1s$

5. a) 200, 240; $c = \frac{a}{8}$
  b) $a = 8c$, $c = 0.125a$

6. a) no
  b) *examples:* $10C = 78.5 + 7t$, $2C = 15.7 + 1.4t$; $10C = 69.5 + 8.8t$, $2C = 13.9 + 1.76t$
  c) 5

Making Sense of Data, page 228

4. a) $n = m + 2$ **b)** $y = 3x - 4$
  c) $y = -2x - 3$
  all linear

5.

r	H
0	-1
1	2
2	5
3	8
4	11
5	14

$H = 3r - 1$

Problems to Investigate, page 229

Three in a Row: $n + n + 1 + n + 2$ or $3n + 3$; Yes, both terms in $3n + 3$ are divisible by 3.

Changing Appearances: a) $2m + m + m + 10$; $4m + 10$; *example:* When m is 72, total number of people is 298.
b) $e + 3 + e + 3e$; $5e + 3$; example: When e is 2 h, total driving time is 13 h.

Graphing Equivalence:
a) for A, $C = \$22 + \$0.90d$, for B, $C = \$20 + \$1.00d$
b) *example:* for A,

d(km)	10	50	100	200
C(\$)	31	65	112	202

for B,

d(km)	10	50	100	200
C(\$)	30	70	120	220

c)

Rental Rates

d) 20 km

Invariant Rates:
a) 12, 30, 60; $n = 12m$
b) 15, 45, 90; $m = 15n$

How Can You Tell?:
a) =; Addition is commutative.
b) ≠; Subtraction is not commutative.
c) =; Substitution always works.
d) =; same order of operations
e) ≠; Substitution doesn't always work.
f) =; same order of operations
g) ≠; different order of operations
h) ≠; Substitution doesn't always work.

10.3, page 231

1. a) -5 **b)** $+5$
   c) $\div 5$ **d)** $\times 5$
   e) $\div (-5)$ **f)** $\times \frac{1}{5}$

2. a) $+4; -4$ **b)** $-1; +1$
   c) $\times 2; \div 2$ **d)** $\times (-3); \div (-3)$
   e) $\div 4; \times 4$ **f)** $\times 2, + 3; -3, \div 2$
   g) $\times 3, -1; +1, \div 3$
   h) $\times 3, \div 2; \times 2, \div 3$

3. a) $x = 6$ **b)** $x = 4$
   c) $x = 3$ **d)** $x = -3$
   e) $x = 8$ **f)** $x = 1$
   g) $x = -2$ **h)** $x = \frac{8}{3}$

4. a) $x = 2; \times x$ **b)** $x = 3; \times x, \div 2$
   c) $x = \frac{4}{5}; \times x, \div 5$

5. a) $\frac{F}{a} = m$ **b)** $\frac{I}{PT} = R$
   c) $P - \frac{2\ell}{2} = w$
   d) $\frac{A - p}{pr} = t$

6. a) yes; $\times$ both sides of first equation by V, then $\div$ by D
b) yes; $\times$ both sides of second equation by 2π
c) yes; $- u$ from both sides of first equation, then $\div$ by t

7. a) $h = \frac{2A}{a + b}$ **b)** $a = \frac{2A}{h} - b$
   c) $b = \frac{2A}{h} - a$

8. $h = 19$ cm, $b = 2.5$ cm, $a = 2$ cm

10.4, page 234

1. $x = -1$

2. Take 3 green rods $(3x)$ from each side. This leaves 2 green rods = 4 red squares. $(2x = 4)$ Then divide both sides by 2. $(x = 2)$

3. a) $x = -1$ **b)** $3 = x$
   c) $x = -4$ **d)** $x = 3$
   e) $x = -3$ **f)** $x = 1$
   g) $-2 = x$ **h)** $x = 3$
   i) $2 = x$ **j)** $x = 4$

4. a) $x = \frac{3}{2}$ **b)** $x = -4$
   c) $x = 1$ **d)** $x = -2$
   e) $x = \frac{5}{3}$

5. a) 4 cm, 7 cm, 10 cm   **b)** 2 cm, 1 cm

10.5, page 237

1. a) $x = -4$ **b)** $x = 1$
   c) $x = 2$

2. a) $x = 2$ **b)** $x = 32$
   c) $y = -1$ **d)** $x = -6$
   e) $x = 5$ **f)** $y = 1$

3. a) 4   **b)** 12
   c) 12   **d)** 6

4. a) $2 = m$ **b)** $y = \frac{5}{8}$
   c) $\frac{4}{9} = d$ **d)** $n = \frac{13}{6}$
   e) $\frac{-19}{6} = x$ **f)** $x = \frac{5}{7}$

5. a) $\frac{4}{3} = m$ **b)** $\frac{4}{3} = m$

6. a) 4 m, 2 m, 1 m
   b) 7 m, 3 m, 3 m

7. $2x - 2 = 2x + 5$, so $0x = 7$ which is not possible

8. a) $n = 10$ **b)** $n = 19$
   c) 5°C; When $n = 1$, $C = 5$ and the number of chirps cannot be fewer than 1.

9. a) $\times x, \div 6; x = 2$
   b) $\times x, \div 3; x = -4$
   c) $\times x, \div (-8); x = \frac{1}{2}$

10. a) $a = 4$ **b)** $x = 5$ or -5

10.6, page 239

1. 4.5 h

2. 28

3. Rebecca

4. French 82%, Math 94%

5. 56

6. a) $y + 2$ **b)** $y - 2$
   c) $y + 3$ **d)** $y - 5$

7. 51 years

8. 18 years, 19 years, 20 years

9. 20 cm, 10 cm, 20 cm

10. 8 m by 20 m

11. a) $\$0.10d$ **b)** $\$0.05(y + 1)$
   c) $\$0.25(3w)$ **d)** $\$1.00(2w + 1)$

12. 10 nickels, 40 quarters, 15 dimes

13. no; area increased 4 times

14. a) $70t$ and $80t$
   b) $70t + 80t = 480$
   c) 3.2 min
   d) 224 m, 256 m

15. 5 s

16. *example:* Mr. Jones is 4 times as old as his son Rick. In 18 years, he will be only twice as old as Rick. How old is Rick now?

17. *example:* Paula bought some CDs one week and the same number the next week. The third week she bought twice the number she bought the week before. If she had 4 CDs to begin with and now has 56, how many did she buy each week?

More Than One Strategy, page 240

1. $x = -6$ **2.** $x = -8$

3. $x = -2$ **4.** $x = 12$

Problems to Investigate, page 241

Versatile Tiles: b) $x = 5$

What's in the Bag?: $x = 6$

Problem Generator: *examples:*
a) The number of parents is the product of the number of children less 1 and 2. How many parents and children are there?
b) The average of maximum temperatures on two consecutive days is 5°C. If the maximum temperature on the first day is -1°C, what is the maximum temperature on the second day?

Sectioning Off: 45 cm, 90 cm, 65 cm

Equating Perimeter and Area:
a) For perimeter, $2(2w - 4 + w)$ or $6w - 8$; for area, $(2w - 4)(w)$ or $2w^2 - 4w$
b) $w = 1$

Consecutive Numbers: a) $n + 4$
b) $2n + 2$ **c)** $n - 4$

10.7, page 243

1. a) yes   **b)** no   **c)** no   **d)** yes
   e) no   **f)** no

2. No, only 7 is because $11 > 5$. The rest aren't true because $-9 < 5$, $5 = 5$, and $-17 < 5$.

3. a) no; $\div 3$ **b)** no; $+ 1, \div 3$
   c) yes; $\times (-2)$ **d)** yes; $\div (-4)$
   e) yes; $+ 1, \div (-5)$
   f) yes; $- 1, \times (-3)$

4. a) $- 1, \div 2$
   b) $+ 6, \div (-3)$; reverse sign
   c) $+ 3, \times 2$
   d) $- 1, \times (-5)$; reverse sign

5. a) $x \leqslant 2$ **b)** $y > 2$
   c) $x < 2$ **d)** $y \geqslant 1$
   e) $x \leqslant \frac{14}{3}$ **f)** $x < -12$
   g) $x \geqslant -6$ **h)** $x \geqslant -7$

6. $\geqslant 219$ **7.** > 8 years

8. 9 years   **9.** $\geqslant 90\%$

10. $\leqslant \$65.21$

10.8, page 245

1. a) ;

b) ;

c) ;

d) ;

e) ;

f) ;

2. a) $x \geqslant -3$ **b)** $x < 6$
   c) $x \leqslant 1$ **d)** $x \leqslant -2$
   e) $x \geqslant 8$ **f)** $x > -9$
   g) $x < -\frac{7}{2}$ **h)** $x < \frac{4}{7}$

3. a) $y < 3$ **b)** $y \leqslant 5$
   c) $y \leqslant 1$ **d)** $y < -8$
   e) $-3 < y$ or $y > -3$
   f) $\frac{4}{7} < y$ or $y > \frac{4}{7}$
   g) $y \leqslant 7$ **h)** $-5 > y$ or $y < -5$

4. a) $x \geqslant -4$ **b)** $x > -2$
   c) $x < 3$ **d)** $x \geqslant 0$
   e) $x \geqslant 0.5$ **f)** $x > -1.5$

5. a) $x \in R$ **b)** $x \in I$
   c) $x \in R$ **d)** $x \in N_0$
   e) $x \in R$ **f)** $x \in R$

6. a) $s \geqslant 40$ and $s \leqslant 90$, or $40 \leqslant s \leqslant 90$
   b) $p \leqslant 250$
   c) $m \leqslant 15$

7. $b \leqslant 200, b \in N_0$

Problems to Investigate, page 246

Two Variable Inequations: Top of plot forms a dot pattern of steps ... ($x = -2$, $y = 5$ and $x = -1$, $y = 5$), ($x = 0$, $y = 4$ and $x = 1$, $y = 4$), ($x = 2$, $y = 3$ and $x = 3$, $y = 3$), ...; All grid intersections below top of steps have dots.

Toothpick Triangles:
3 toothpicks, equilateral, 1 toothpick per side;
4 toothpicks, isosceles, 1 toothpick on equal sides;
5 toothpicks, isosceles, 2 toothpicks on equal sides;
6 toothpicks, equilateral, 2 toothpicks per side; scalene
7 toothpicks, isosceles, 2 toothpicks on equal sides; isosceles, 3 toothpicks on equal sides
8 toothpicks, isosceles, 3 toothpicks on equal sides; scalene
9 toothpicks, equilateral, 3 toothpicks per side; isosceles, 4 toothpicks on equal sides; scalene;
length of longest side < sum of lengths of other 2 sides;
3 equal sides means 3 equal angles;
2 equal sides means 2 equal angles;
largest angle opposite longest side in scalene triangle

Different Graphs: $x \geqslant -8$ and $x \leqslant 3$; Both graphs have same endpoints, but real number line includes integers and all other numbers in between.

Maximum Perimeter: $x < 7$; *examples:*
1 cm, 2 cm, 3 cm, 4 cm, 5 cm, 5.5 cm, 6 cm, 6.5 cm

Solve Problems by Using Algebra, page 247

Passing the Leader: 100 km/h

Home Improvement: 30 cm by 30 cm

Population Control: about 500

Review and Practise, page 248

1. *example:* **a)** $-2x - 3 = -5$
   b) $6x - 4 = 24$
   c) $x - 1 = x + 3$

2. Divide first equation by π, divide first equation by d.

3. a) $\frac{E}{c^2} = m$ **b)** $\frac{y - b}{x} = m$
   c) $E = I(R + r)$ **d)** $h = \frac{3V}{2\pi r^2}$

4. a) $x = 4$ **b)** $y = 12$
c) $y = \frac{1}{3}$ **d)** $10 = x$
e) $3 = x$ **f)** $x = \frac{9}{2}$
g) $-3 = x$

5. a) $x = 3$ **b)** $-5 = y$
c) $x = 6$ **d)** $1 = y$
e) $x = -7$

6. a) $d = 3.1t$ **b)** $70 = 10 + 15t$
c) $s = 1100t$

7. 8 m by 26 m, 8 m by 20 m

8. 24

9. 3 h, 720 km, 960 km

10. 21

11. *example:* If you count 3 s between when you see a flash of lightning and when you hear the thunder, about how far away is the centre of the storm? ($d = 0.96$ km or almost 1 km)

12. a) $x > 7$ **b)** $-1 < y$ or $y > -1$
c) $e \geqslant -14$ **d)** $-7 < h$ or $h > -7$
e) $x > -12$ **f)** $x \leqslant -8$

Test Your Knowledge, page 250

1. $n = s^2 - (s - 2)^2$, where n is number of patio stones, and s is length in whole number of units

2. a) $F = \$3.00 + \$1.10d$
b) $\frac{F - \$3.00}{\$1.10} = d$

3. a) $x = 5$ **b)** $-3 = y$

4. a) $x = -4$ **b)** $1 = y$
c) $y = -5$ **d)** $x = 4$

5. a) All are solutions.
b) yes
c) $5x - 3 = 5x - 3$; Both sides are the same.
d) *example:* $x - 1 + x = 2x - 1 - x - 1$

6. *example:* $2n - 7 = -n - 6 + 3n$

7. $0.35x = \$192.50$; $550

8. a) $D = \frac{m}{V}$
b) gold: $V = 525$, $m = 10\ 143$, $V = 750$, $m = 14\ 490$;
water: $V = 500$, $m = 500$, $V = 25$, $m = 25$;
iron: $V = 200$, $m = 1574$, $V = 300$, $m = 2361$;
quartz: $V = 100$, $m = 266$, $V = 500$, $m = 1330$;
parraffin wax: $V = 100$, $m = 87$, $V = 1000$, $m = 870$
c) about 28 cm^3

9. 34°, 44°, 102°

10. *example:* $C = \$0.596q$, where q represents the quantity of gas in litres

11. a) > **b)** > **c)** > **d)** <

12. a) $18 + 2t < 60$
b) < 21 min

UNIT 11 Similarity and Trigonometry

11.1, page 255

1. a) *example:* 1 cm represents 2 cm.

A

5 cm

C

8 cm

B

b) no

2. a) *example:* 1 cm represents 2 cm.

D

60°

6 cm

F

E

b) no

3. a) *example:*

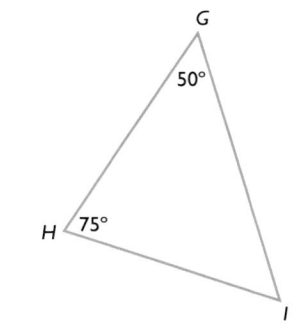

G

50°

H 75°

I

b) no

4. a) *example:*

J

40°

80°

K

60°

L

b) same shape, corresponding angles equal; different sizes, corresponding sides different lengths; no

5. a) 1 cm represents 3 cm.

M

40°

50°

N 6 cm O

b) same in all ways, except orientation; yes

6. a) 1 cm represents 2 cm.

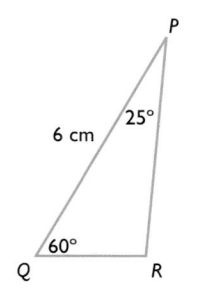

b) same in all ways, except orientation; yes

7. a) 1 cm represents 2 cm.

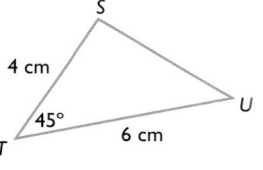

b) same in all ways, except orientation; yes

8. a) *example:* 1 cm represents 2 cm.

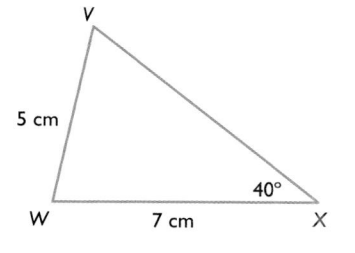

b) two pair of corresponding sides equal, one pair of corresponding angles equal; not same shape, size, or orientation, but only two different triangles resulted; no

9. a) 1 cm represents 2 cm.

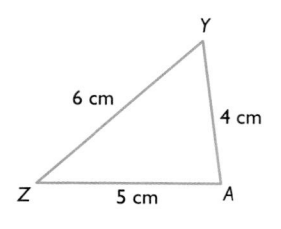

b) same in all ways, except orientation; yes

10. The following are sufficient AAS, ASA, SAS, SSS; *example:* Cut out one and try to fit it on other. Trace one and try to fit tracing on other. Fold if it looks like reflection. Use a Mira. Measure two angles and a side in both, or two sides and the contained angle in both, or three sides in both.

11.2, page 257

1. a) ASA   **b)** SAS   **c)** AAS
    d) SSS   **e)** AAS   **f)** SAS

2. Both parts a) and b) are congruent pairs.

3. a) ASA
    b) 38.5 m, $PQ = ST$ and $ST = 38.5$ m

4. a) Find DE using Pythagorean relationship and then AB, the length of the swamp, equals DE because the triangles are congruent by ASA.
    b) 72 m

11.3, pages 259-260

1. a) pairs of angles not equal, other pair of sides not in same ratio; not similar
    b) other pair of angles equal, corresponding sides are in same ratio; are similar
    c) other pairs of angles not equal, other sides not in same ratio; not similar

2. a) If knowing two pair of angles is sufficient, then finding the third is redundant.
    b) If knowing two pair of angles is sufficient, then finding a pair of sides is redundant.

3. a) all pairs of angles equal, all pairs of corresponding sides in same ratio, similar
    b) other pairs of angles not equal, other pair of sides not in same ratio, not similar
    c) other pairs of angles equal, other pair of sides in same ratio, similar

4. The angles that are given as equal are contained between the sides that are in the same ratio in part c), while in part b), the angles that are given as equal, one is contained, in $\triangle GHI$ and the other is not, in $\triangle JKL$, so they are not corresponding parts.

11.4, page 262

1. a) $f = 5$ **b)** $i = 10.5$

2. a) VW and VZ, VX and VY, WX and ZY; $h = 5$ m
    b) NM and PQ, NO and PO, OM and OQ; $w = 12$ m
    c) AB and DE, BC and EF, AC and DF; $h = 5.25$ m
    d) SR and VU, ST and UT, RT and VT; $h = 4.16$ m
    e) SU and SW, ST and SV, TU and VW; $w = 14.7$ m to 1 decimal place

3. 12.375 m   **4.** 14.6 m

5. 75 m   **6.** 6 m

Problems to Investigate, page 263

Areas of Similar Triangles: Area of enlargement is 9 times the area of original. Area of enlargement is 16 times the area of original.

Paper Sizes:

	A_0	A_1	A_2	A_3
$\frac{l}{w} =$	$\frac{\sqrt{2}}{1}$	$= \frac{1}{\frac{\sqrt{2}}{2}}$	$= \frac{\frac{\sqrt{2}}{2}}{\frac{1}{2}}$	$= \frac{\frac{1}{2}}{\frac{\sqrt{2}}{4}}$

$$A_1: \quad \frac{1}{\frac{\sqrt{2}}{2}} = 1 \div \frac{\sqrt{2}}{2}$$
$$= 1 \times \frac{2}{\sqrt{2}}$$
$$= \frac{2}{\sqrt{2}}$$
$$= \frac{2 \times \sqrt{2}}{\sqrt{2} \times \sqrt{2}}$$
$$= \frac{\sqrt{2}}{1} = \frac{2 \times \sqrt{2}}{2}$$

A_2: $\dfrac{\frac{\sqrt{2}}{2}}{\frac{1}{2}}$ $= \dfrac{\sqrt{2}}{2} \div \dfrac{1}{2}$

$= \dfrac{\sqrt{2}}{2} \times \dfrac{2}{1}$

$= \dfrac{\sqrt{2}}{1}$

A_3: $\dfrac{\frac{1}{2}}{\frac{\sqrt{2}}{4}}$ $= \dfrac{1}{2} \div \dfrac{\sqrt{2}}{4}$

$= \dfrac{1}{2} \times \dfrac{4}{\sqrt{2}}$

$= \dfrac{2}{\sqrt{2}}$ (same as A_1)

$= \dfrac{\sqrt{2}}{1}$ ↓

Shadow Lengths: noon

Conditions for Congruence: AAS and ASA are actually the same because when you know any two angles in a triangle, you know the third because the sum of angles in a triangle is 180°.

How Tall?: 10.8 m

11.5, page 265

1. **a)** less than 1; 0.58, 0.58
   b) greater than 1; 5.67, 5.67
   c) equal to 1; 1, 1

2. **b)** 70°, 2.75; 20°, 0.37
   c) 70°, 2.75; 20°, 0.37
   d) 25°, 0.47, 0.47; 65°, 2.14, 2.14

3. | 10° | 0.18 | 50° | 1.19 |
20°	0.36	60°	1.73
30°	0.58	70°	2.75
40°	0.84	80°	5.67

   As the angle size increases, so does its tangent.

4. **a)** *example:* You could calculate the tangents of angles like 85°, 89°, 89.5°, 89.9°, 89.99° 89.999 999 99° using tan key and see that the tangents are increasing rapidly with tan 89.999 999 99° = 57 295 777 95, and calculate the tangents of angles like 5°, 1°, 0.5°, 0.1°, 0.001, 0.000 000 000 1° and see that the tangents are decreasing rapidly with tan 0.000 000 001° = $1.745\ 329\ 252 \times 10^{-9}$ getting close to 0.

b) shows an error has occurred; 90° has two adjacent sides and the opposite side is the hypotenuse.

5. Trigonometry means three angle measurement, and is the study and application of properties of right triangles.

11.6, page 267

1. 81.1 m
2. 33.3 m
3. 5.1 m
4. 13.0 m
5. 3946.6 m
6. 541.2 m
7. **a)** 5.2 m   **b)** 5.3 m
8. 981.3 m
9. 44 157.1 km

11.7, page 269

1. **a)** △ABC cosine; △DEF sine
   b) △ABC 0.37, 0.93; △DEF 0.74, 0.67
   c) △ABC 0.37, 0.93; △DEF 0.74, 0.67

2. **a)** sin 18° = cos 72° = 0.31;
   cos 18° = sin 72° = 0.95
   b) sin 50° = cos 40° = 0.77;
   cos 50° = sin 40° = 0.64

3. **a)** 60°   **b)** 45°   **c)** $\dfrac{11}{32}$

4. **a)** 13 cm; sin P = cos G = 0.38;
   cos P = sin G = 0.92;
   tan P = 0.42; tan G = 2.4
   b) 24 cm; sin C = cos W = 0.96;
   cos C = W = 0.96; cos C = sin W = 0.28; tan C = 3.43; tan W = 0.29

5. 0.62; **a)** 1; $\dfrac{AC}{AB} = 0.62$ and AC = 0.62,
   $\dfrac{0.62}{1} = 0.62$
   b) 100; $\dfrac{AC}{AB} = 0.62$ and AC = 62,
   $\dfrac{62}{100} = 0.62$
   c) $\dfrac{AC}{AB} = 0.62$ same as AC = 0.62 of AB
   d) AC; $\dfrac{AC}{AB} = 0.62 \rightarrow AC = 0.62 \times AB$
   $\dfrac{AC}{0.62} = AB$
   $AC \times \dfrac{1}{0.62} = AB$
   $AC \times 1.61 = AB$

11.8, pages 271-272

1. **a)** shorter; 5.2 m
   b) shorter; 23.7 m
   c) longer; 8.6 m
   d) longer; 12.4 m

2. 1.1 m
3. 3538.4 m
4. 4.3 m
5. 14.3 cm
6. 52. 0 m
7. 3.8 m
8. 7.5 m
9. 259. 3 m
10. 4.2 m
11. 60.4 m
12. 773.2 m
13. **a)** 5.1 m   **b)** 3.3 m
14. 16.7 m
15. **a)** 2.2 km   **b)** 1.8 km   **c)** 2.6 km
16. 3.9 m
17. 26.4 m

11.9, pages 274-275

1. **a)** ∠G = 55°, IH = 13.5, IG = 9.5
   b) ∠K = 47°, LK = 2.6 , JK = 3.8
   c) ∠M = 56.4°, ∠N = 33.6°, ON = 7.1
   d) PQ = 8.4, ∠P = 63.1°, ∠Q = 26.9°
   e) SU = 2.5, ST = 9.5, ∠S = 75°
   f) V = 48.4°, W = 41.6°, VX = 7.6

2. 44.8°

3. **a)** 8.8°   **b)** 1.3 m

4. 34. 4°

5. **a)** 3.5°   **b)** 0.3 km

6. **a)** 48.1°   **b)** 41.9°

7. 3.0°
8. 31.0°

9. 54.3°
10. 75°

11. longer 25°, shorter 65°

Problems to Investigate, page 276

Using Coordinates: a = 31.0°; m = 45°; w = 71.6°; Use the coordinates to find the tangent, $\dfrac{y}{x}$ = tan, and then using the values of tangent, find an angle with that tangent.

Relating Sides: sin 55° = 0.82; sin 35° = 0.57; 0.82, 0.57; *example:* XY = 82, YZ = 57, XZ = 100

Solving Triangles: ∠T = 22°, OT = 3.7, HT = 4.0, AD = 32.69, ∠D = 35.0°, ∠A = 55.0°

Cotangent: 0.45; reciprocals; ∠A = 65.7°, ∠B = 24.3°

Making Sense of Data, page 278

2. a) 2, *example:* At 15 s it is back at the same level as the loading platform but at the back of the ride, so at 30 s it's back at the loading platform. **b)** 30 s **c)** 18 m

3. a) 90°, 450°; 270°, 630°
b) 225°, 315°, 585°, 675° **c)** 0.7

4. a) 270°, 450°, 630°
b) 0°, 180°, 360°, 540°, 720°

5. a) sine; The sine of one acute angle in a right triangle is the cosine of the other.
b)

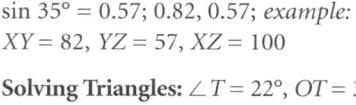

Solve Problems by Drawing Diagrams, page 279

Largest Square: 11.3 cm by 11.3 cm

Flight Altitude: 445.1 m

Distance from Camp: 23.5°; 2.5 km

Back Sliding: 67

Review and Practise, page 280

1. 1 cm represents 2 cm.

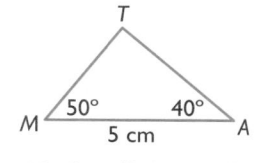

No, ASA is sufficient to show congruence.

2. yes; ∠M = ∠K (given), ME = KE (isosceles triangle), AE = AE (common side), ∠MEA = ∠KEA (other pairs equal and angle sum = 180°), so SAS and ASA congruency conditions met

3. No, other sides are not in same ratio and other pairs of angles not equal.

4. a) 45 m **b)** 120 m

5. a) less than 1 **b)** cos ∠A

6. 10.6 m

7. 4.7 m

8. 24.9°

Problems to Investigate, page 282

Tan 0° and Tan 90°: *y*-coordinate; tan 0° = 0, tan 90° not possible

Equilateral Triangle
△XYP ≅ △XZP; ∠XPY, = ∠XPZ = 90° (given), XP = XP (common side), XY = XZ (given), ∠Y = ∠Z (isosceles triangle), ∠YXP = ∠ZXP (other pairs equal and angle sum = 180°), so SAS and ASA congruency conditions met
YP = ZP = 1; YZ = 2 and △s ≅
$\cos 60° = \frac{1}{2}$ $\sin 60° = \frac{\sqrt{3}}{2}$
        = 0.5   = 0.87
$XP^2 = 2^2 - 1^2$ $\tan 60° = \frac{\sqrt{3}}{1}$
$XP = \sqrt{3}$ = 1.73

same as using keys

Height???: Yes, find *x* using tan 8° and *y* using tan 12° and add *x* and *y*.

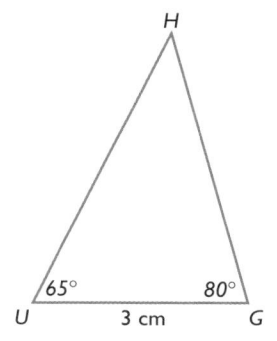

Scale Model: window height 1.4 m; window width 1.68 m; door width 0.84 m; scale factor $\frac{1}{280}$

Congruent Right Triangles:
SSS; the third side must be $\sqrt{\text{hypotenuse}^2 - \text{other side}^2}$

1.

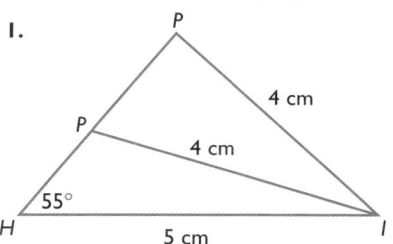

Yes, ASS is not a condition sufficient for congruence.

2. *example:* using ∠P = 65°, PA = 3 cm, ∠A = 80°, ASA

3. Measure two pairs of corresponding angles and if each pair is equal, the triangles are similar.

4. 9 m

5. Similar triangles allow for shorter measurements to be made, thus less difficult and less work.

6. a) 1
b) $\sin ∠O = \frac{1}{\sqrt{2}}$, $\cos ∠O = \frac{1}{\sqrt{2}}$

7. a) ∠S = 75°, SU = 1.4, SN = 5.2
b) ∠F = 24.2°, ∠R = 65.8°, FR = 4.2
c) ∠I = 54.5°, ∠H = 35.5°, HT = 5.0

8. 4.9 m

9. 10.72. 6 m

10. a) 52.6° **b)** 37.4°

11. shorter 47.7 m, taller 70.8 m

ANSWERS

UNIT 12 Investigating the Unusual

12.1, pages 286-288

1. a) 627.2 m²; 918.4 m
   b) 0.7 m²/m
   c) *example:* for a 70 m² classroom, 9.0 times as great
   d) 25.0 m by 25.0 m; 100.0 m
   e) 6.3 m²/m
   f) The unit rate for the square is much greater.

2. a) 7.9 m²; 10.0 m
   b) 0.8 m²/m
   c) *example:* for a 70 m² classroom, 0.1 times as great; it's smaller
   d) 2.8 m by 2.8 m; 11.2 m
   e) 0.7 m²/m
   f) The unit rate for the circle is slightly greater.

3. a) 7000 m²; 340 m
   b) 20.6 m²/m
   c) *example:* for a 70 m² classroom, 100 times as great
   d) 83.7 m by 83.7 m; 334.8 m
   e) 20.9 m²/m
   f) The unit rate for the square is slightly greater.

4. a) 187.5 m³; 243.9 m²
   b) 0.8 m³/m²
   c) *example:* for a 250 m³ classroom, 0.8 times as great, a bit smaller
   d) The length of each edge is the cube root of the volume.
   $\sqrt[3]{187.5} = 5.7$
   e) 1.0 m³/m²
   f) The unit rate for the cube is greater.

5. 9375 L

6. a) 35.2 m   b) 5.8 m
   c) 17.5 m

7. a) ASA; 54°
   b) base; 281 m
   c) tan ∠ x; 193.4 m
   d) 135 863.5 m²

8. *example:* 543 454 m²; 543 454 m²; yes; When side length is doubled, so is height of triangle, so area is quadrupled.

9. a) $13 800; *example:* Changed total cost to scientific notation and divided by volume.
   b) 113 m for each edge

12.2 pages 289-291

1. a) 32 times
   b) 76 years; 76 years

2. a) *example:* 75 beats/min
   b) *example:* 25.368 years; doesn't seem reasonable as most people live for 70 to 80 years

3. a) *example:* using 75 beats/min, 18.75 breaths/min
   b) *example:* 10 breaths/min
   c) same; $h = 4b$
   d) *example:* using 10 breaths/min, 47.56 years
   e) $b = \frac{1902.6}{4a}$; multiplied each side by b and divided each side by a.

4. 301 000 kg

5. a) 60 000 flaps/min; 3 600 000 flaps/h
   b) *example:* 108 flaps/min; 6480 flaps/h

6. a) His hand moves through half a circle in half a flap, so it moves through a full circle in a full flap.
   b) *example:* using 6480 flaps/h and 0.65 m arm length, 26.5 km/h
   c) *example:* using 0.65 m arm length, about 15 000 km/h

7. a) AC is the hypotenuse and its square is the sum of the square of the other two sides, $AC = \sqrt{1^2 + 1^2}$ or $\sqrt{2}$; similarly AD is hypotenuse when sides are $\sqrt{2}$ and 1, so
   $AD = \sqrt{\sqrt{2}^2 + 1}$ or $\sqrt{3}$
   b) $AE = 2$, $AF = \sqrt{5}$, $AG = \sqrt{6}$
   c) $\sqrt{11}$

8. a) 45°
   b) 35°, 30°, 27°, 24°
   c) decreasing in size but each decrease is less than the previous one

9. 10^9 10. 10^{23} t

Making Sense of Data, page 292

3. a) 490 000 m²   b) 2.8 km
   c) 42 min

4. b) blood system; 4 times

5. 8.3×10^7

6. 20; 200; 20 000

7. *example:* I might have compared the area of the West Edmonton Mall to the area of our hockey arena.

8. *example:* I was amazed that the length of the blood system was so long. It's hard to image a length 4 times the circumference of Earth inside a body.

12.3, pages 294-295

1. a) 67.2%   b) 52.6%   c) 42.2%

2. a) 12 756 km = 12 756 000 m
   b) 0.7 mm
   c) 0.9 m
   d) relatively smooth; You would hardly notice less than a millimetre indent or rise on a sphere with a diameter of 1 m.

3. 99.7%

4. a) 0.997 m or 997 mm
   b) ball-shaped; You would hardly notice that the polar diameter was 3 mm less than the equatorial.

5. a) about 93
   b) Nfld.: about 21, P.E.I.: about 5, N.S.: about 33, N.B.: about 27, Que.: about 253, Ont.: about 370, Man.: about 40, Sask.: about 36, B.C.: about 120, YT: about 1, N.W.T.: about 2

6. a) Solve $\frac{x}{360} = \frac{644\ 390}{9\ 215\ 430}$.
   b) Nfld.: 14.5°, P.E.I.: 0.2°, N.S.: 2.1°, N.B.: 2.8°, Que.: 53°, Ont.: 34.8°, Man.: 21.4°, Sask.: 22.3°, B.C.: 36.3°, YT: 18.7°, N.W.T.: 128.6°

7. a) Area is fixed, while population varies and depends on a number of factors.

b) *examples:* climate, proximity to water, terrain, what people do to earn a living

c)

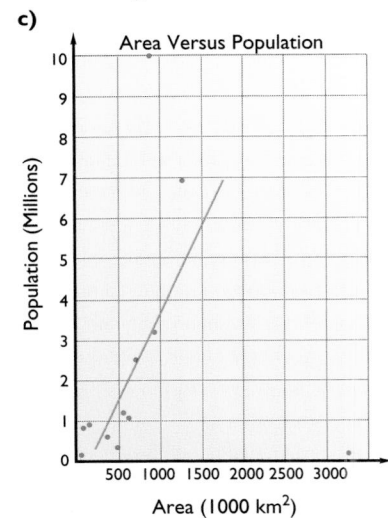

Area Versus Population

d) There is not a definitive relationship between area and population. However, except for a couple, larger areas have greater populations.

12.4, pages 297

1. a) 23.0 km   **b)** 0.5 km; 47.5 km

2. a) 39.8   **b)** 100

3. a) Neptune; 251.3
    b) Uranus; 1585.5

c) +6 star; 15.9
d) +6 star; 631.2
e) +6 star; 398 359.2
f) +6 star; 3 985 393 806

4. a) *example:* If a +1 star is brighter than a +2 star, and so on, then a star with a magnitude of −5, such as Venus, must be extremely bright.
    b) 19; 13; 11
    c) 39 844 929.8; 158 582.5; 25 131.4

12.5, pages 299-300

1. a) increases; *example:* The number of people increases but the number of possible birthdays remains constant.
    b) *examples:* for 25 people, 57% to 60%; for 32 people, 73% to 75%
    c) 14 to 16; 22 to 24; 32 to 34

2. a) *example:* 365 people could all have different birthdays since there are 366 different days possible.
    b) 367
    c) yes, but not probable

3. about 1 in 10 000

4. a) about 2   **b)** 33.3

5. a) *examples:* Is there a relationship between a country's wealth (per capita GDP) and the average life expectancy of its population?; the greater the wealth, the longer the life expectancy

b) wealth; life expectancy
c) examples: number of doctors per person, population density, diet, climate

6. a) the universe and Earth; about 27 times
    b) 3 750 000
    c) $\frac{1}{100\,000\,000}$

7. a) *example:* speeds in kilometres per second with speeds in kilometres per hour, and speeds in scientific notation with speeds in standard notation
    b) *example:* Multiply the speed of lightning by 60×60 and then divide by the speed of the Concorde, using a scientific calculator. (about 8 000 000 times as fast)

8. a) 60   **b)** 17.1   **c)** 47.1
    d) 163 636.4   **e)** 27 000 000

9. a) 20 925 s
    b) 20 925 ÷ 86 400 (the number of seconds in a day)

10. 0.2422 is almost 0.25 or $\frac{1}{4}$ of a day, so every 4 years, four $\frac{1}{4}$ days are needed.

Index

INDEX

Acknowledgments

Acknowledgment is hereby made for kind permission to reprint the following material: Bar Graph: "Population…" Statistics Canada, 1991 Census of Canada, catalogue no. 96-320E; Pie Graph(s): "Percent/Composition…" Statistics Canada, 1991 Census of Canada, catalogue no. 96-317E; Chart: "Average Earnings…" Statistics Canada, 1991 Census of Canada, catalogue no. 96-317E; Graph: taken from Canadian Social Trends, Spring 1995, p. 32; Chart: "Women account…" Statistics Canada, Women in the Labor Force, catalogue no. 75-507E; Chart: "Average earnings of women working…" Statistics Canada, Earnings of Women and Men, catalogue no. 13-217; Chart: "Earnings…" Statistics Canada, Canadian Social Trends, Spring 1995, p. 32; Chart: "More than half of young people…" Statistics Canada, Health and Activity Limitation Survey, catalogue no. 11-008E; Graph: "Most people with severe…" Statistics Canada, 1991 Health and Activity Limitation Survey, catalogue no. 11-008E; Graphs: "Water: The Thirst Grows" and "Fossil Fuels — Who's Doing What With Oil?" reprinted with permission of International Wildlife Federation; Artwork reprinted with permission of Richard Gage; Article: "Teen TV Viewing…", Eric Beauchesne, Southam News, Toronto Star, August 24, 1995; Expert: "…the unemployment rate will rise…" Southam News, Toronto Star, September 6, 1995.

Every reasonable precaution has been taken to trace the owners of copyrighted material and to make due acknowledgment. Any omission will be gladly rectified in future editions.

Photographs

page 4: Image Bank/Alvis Upitis, page 31: Canapress; page 56: Ray Boudreau; page 58: Ray Boudreau; page 63: Ray Boudreau; page 64: Ray Boudreau; page 68: Ray Boudreau; page 69 (top and bottom): Imax Corporation, (centre): Ray Boudreau; page 73: Ray Boudreau; page 74: Ray Boudreau; page 77: Ray Boudreau; page 79: Ray Boudreau; page 80–81: Canapress; page 137: Image Bank/Michael Melford; page 143: Image Bank/David Carol; page 146: Masterfile/Ted Grant; page 179: Brigitte Nielson; page 184: Canapress; page 187: Corel; page 205: Image Bank/David J. Carol; page 213 (top): Philip Gebhardt; (bottom): Image Bank/Michael Melford; page 230: Dave Starrett; page 238: Corel; page 288 (top left): The Bettman Archives; (right centre): Canapress; (bottom right): Norma Kennedy; page 289 (top right): First Light/Stephen Homer; (lower right): The Stock Shop/ H. G. Ross; page 291 (right centre): Masterfile/Imtek Imagineering; (lower right): Masterfile/Ken Lucus; page 293: Masterfile/J.A. Kraulis; page 298: Masterfile; page 299 (left): Image Bank/Anselm Spring; (right): Canadian Forces Photographic Unit; page 300: Canapress/Uniphoto;

Photographs by Trent Photographics on pages: 1, 3, 9, 10, 11, 14, 15, 17, 19, 21, 26, 27, 28, 33, 35, 38, 39, 40, 41, 42, 43, 48, 53, 55, 60, 66, 82, 83, 84, 87, 89, 91, 93, 102–103, 104, 106, 108, 110, 113, 115, 118, 120, 121, 126, 131, 134, 135, 136, 140, 145, 147, 148–149, 150, 153, 154, 156, 159, 162, 164, 171, 172, 173, 174, 175, 177, 182, 183, 185, 188, 193, 194, 195, 196, 197 (top), 201, 208, 209, 210, 216, 217, 218, 220, 221, 222, 223, 224, 232, 242, 252, 253, 254, 255, 256, 258, 261, 265, 266, 273, 278, 285, 288 (bottom left), 289 (top), 290, 292, 296, 297, 301

CREDITS